Linking the Hist

Published in cooperation with the William P. Clements Center for Southwest Studies, Southern Methodist University.

**School for Advanced Research
Advanced Seminar Series**

Linking the Histories of Slavery

Contributors

Eric E. Bowne
Department of Sociology, University of Central Arkansas

James F. Brooks
Departments of History and Anthropology, University of California, Santa Barbara

Catherine M. Cameron
Department of Anthropology, University of Colorado

Paul Conrad
Department of History, Colorado State University, Pueblo

Boyd Cothran
Department of History, York University

Sarah Deer
William Mitchell College of Law

Melissa Farley
Prostitution Research & Education

Mark Allan Goldberg
Department of History, University of Houston

Enrique R. Lamadrid
Department of Spanish and Portuguese, University of New Mexico

Bonnie Martin
Independent Scholar

Calvin Schermerhorn
School of Historical, Philosophical and Religious Studies, Arizona State University

Andrew J. Torget
Department of History, University of North Texas

Natale Zappia
Department of History, Whittier College

Linking the Histories of Slavery
North America and Its Borderlands

Edited by Bonnie Martin and James F. Brooks

School for Advanced Research Press
Santa Fe

School for Advanced Research Press
Post Office Box 2188
Santa Fe, New Mexico 87504-2188
www.sarpress.org

Managing Editor: Sarah Soliz
Editorial Assistant: Ellen Goldberg
Designer and Production Manager: Cynthia Dyer
Manuscript Editor: Diana Rico
Proofreader: Kate Whelan
Indexer: Margaret Moore Booker
Printer: Versa Press, Inc.

Library of Congress Cataloging-in-Publication Data
Linking the histories of slavery : North America and its borderlands / edited by Bonnie Martin and James F. Brooks. — First edition.
    pages cm. — (Advanced seminar series)
  Includes bibliographical references and index.
  ISBN 978-1-938645-60-0 (alk. paper)
  1. Slavery—North America—History. 2. Slavery—United States—History. 3. North America—Race relations. 4. United States—Race relations. I. Martin, Bonnie, editor. II. Brooks, James, 1955- editor.
  E441.L56 2015
  306.3'620973—dc23
                    2015015231

© 2015 by the School for Advanced Research. All rights reserved.
Manufactured in the United States of America
Library of Congress Catalog Card Number 2015015231
International Standard Book Number 978-1-938645-60-0
First edition 2015

© Chapter 7 by Andrew J. Torget from his book *Seeds of Empire: Cotton, Slavery, and the Transformation of the Texas Borderlands, 1800–1850* (Chapel Hill: University of North Carolina Press, 2015).

Cover illustration: Montage created using Alexander DeBatz watercolor painting of Southeastern Indians, seventeenth-century map of middle America, and photograph of slave in chains.

The School for Advanced Research (SAR) promotes the furthering of scholarship on—and public understanding of—human culture, behavior, and evolution. SAR Press publishes cutting-edge scholarly and general-interest books that encourage critical thinking and present new perspectives on topics of interest to all humans. Contributions by authors reflect their own opinions and viewpoints and do not necessarily express the opinions of SAR Press.

To our mentor and friend, David J. Weber

Contents

List of Figures	xi
Acknowledgments	xiii
Introduction	xv
Bonnie Martin and James F. Brooks	
PART I. Links to Early Slavery	3
1. Captives and Slaves in Indigenous North America *Catherine M. Cameron*	9
2. From Westo to Comanche: The Role of Commercial Indian Slaving in the Development of Colonial North America *Eric E. Bowne*	35
PART II. Links to Expanding Slave Networks	63
3. Indians, Convicts, and Slaves: An Apache Diaspora to Cuba at the Start of the Nineteenth Century *Paul Conrad*	67
4. *Lúgsh* and *Laláki:* Slaves, Chiefs, Medicine Men, and the Indigenous Political Landscape of the Upper Klamath Basin, 1820s–1860s *Boyd Cothran*	97
5. Captivity and Economic Landscapes in California and the Far West, 1769–1850 *Natale Zappia*	125
6. "The Time Is Now Just Arriving When Many Capitalists Will Make Fortunes": Indian Removal, Finance, and Slavery in the Making of the American Cotton South *Calvin Schermerhorn*	151

CONTENTS

7. The Saltillo Slavery Debates: Mexicans, Anglo-Americans, and Slavery's Future in Nineteenth-Century North America   171
   Andrew J. Torget

8. Linking Chains: Comanche Captivity, Black Chattel Slavery, and Empire in Antebellum Central Texas   197
   Mark Allan Goldberg

PART III. Links to Legacies of Slavery   223

9. *Cautivos y criados:* Cultural Memories of Slavery in New Mexico   229
   Enrique R. Lamadrid

10. Relocation Revisited: Twentieth-Century Considerations   257
    Sarah Deer

11. Slavery and Prostitution: A Twenty-First-Century Abolitionist Perspective   283
    Melissa Farley

References   317
Index   365

Figures

5.1	Slave-raiding networks in Alta and Native California, 1780s–1850s	126
5.2	Documented victims of forced bondage by group, 1700–1860	129
7.1	Daguerreotype of the main plaza in Saltillo, Coahuila, 1847–1848	182
8.1	Texas, 1855	199
9.1	Gertrudis Gallegos de Valdés	233
9.2	"Los Comanches" performers, Ensenada, New Mexico, c. 1932	234
9.3	Los Comanches de la Serna, 2003	235
11.1	Lip tattoo from pimp Richey, 2011	284
11.2	Bar code on woman's wrist, 2012	290
11.3	Woman reveals tattoo, showing that she was owned by her pimp, 2013	293

Acknowledgments

Collaborative projects like this one depend on the assistance of so many people in so many places. We owe a special debt to our two sponsors, the William P. Clements Center for Southwest Studies at Southern Methodist University (SMU) in Dallas, Texas, and the School for Advanced Research (SAR) in Santa Fe, New Mexico. Not only did SAR fund a workshop for the contributors in the fall of 2012, SAR Press has published the resulting volume. Our warmest thanks to everyone from the kind hospitality team at the Santa Fe campus, Nicole Taylor, Leslie Shipman, and Carla Toscano and the gracious editorial staff, including Lynn Thompson Baca, former director of SAR Press; its interim managing editor, Sarah Soliz; former managing editor Lisa Pacheco; and editorial assistant, Ellen Goldberg. We also would like to thank our copy editor, Diana Rico, for her generous help.

We deeply appreciate the insights and support we received from Andrew Graybill and Sherry Smith, codirectors of the William P. Clements Center for Southwest Studies, and from the center's former executive director Andrea Boardman, who urged us to expand our ideas into a book and symposium. Ruth Ann Elmore, the current executive director, worked tirelessly on the complex logistics that this enterprise demanded and, in particular, on organizing the open symposium held in Dallas in April 2013. We extend our thanks, too, to the William P. Clements Department of History at SMU for providing that opportunity (and many others) for a conversation among researchers and the interested public.

We would like to thank our contributors for the energy, patience, and passion they poured into this project and, finally, the late David J. Weber, who was the first director of the Clements center. David's vision of a place devoted to the study of Texas, the American Southwest, and the US-Mexico borderlands has become a reality. He encouraged us to pursue the idea for this collection of essays, just as he nurtured the endeavors of many other researchers. For that and so much more, we dedicate this volume to him.

Introduction

Bonnie Martin and James F. Brooks

When we picture slavery in North America in the decades before the Civil War, this is not what we usually imagine:

> A Delaware trader, in 1850, brought into the settlements [in Central Texas] two negro girls which he had obtained from the Comanches. It appeared that they had been with a number of Seminole negroes who attempted to cross the Plains to join Wild Cat [a Seminole chief] upon the Rio Grande. The party had been intercepted by the Indians, and every one, with the exception of these two girls, put to death. They were taken to the camp, where the most inhuman barbarities were perpetrated upon them. Among other fiendish atrocities, the savages scraped through their skin into the flesh, believing that beneath the cuticle the flesh was black like the color upon the exterior. They burned them with live coals to ascertain whether fire produced the same sensations of pain as with their own people, and tried various other experiments which were attended with most acute torture. The poor girls were shockingly scarred and mutilated when I saw them.[1]

This disturbing scene comes to us from the journal of Randolph B. Marcy, a US Army officer and explorer who traveled widely on Indian frontiers from Florida to Utah in the decade before the Civil War.[2] His eyewitness account does not match the images we typically hold of slavery in North America. In our minds, slavery's story unfolds on cotton plantations in southern states east of or close to the Mississippi River—an image reinforced by the powerful 2013 film based on the life of Solomon Northup, *12 Years a Slave*.[3] African Americans sweat in cotton fields under the brooding presence of white overseers and sadistic owners. The cast of characters that populates the typical dramas of slavery does not include mutilated Negro girls purchased from Comanche captors by a Delaware Indian trader. Accounts like Marcy's raise the questions this volume addresses. The chapters that follow introduce more unexpected scenes to such stories and challenge assumptions about how slavery worked across North America. One of our goals is to expand the perspective on slavery that we gain from narratives of commercial slavery in the United States in the decades before the Civil War. We showcase less familiar slave systems and less recognizable consequences of slavery across what would become the United States, Mexico, and Cuba, from the days before the Europeans arrived and into the twentieth and twenty-first centuries.[4] We want to encourage our readers and fellow researchers to examine the links among the many histories of slavery that constitute a continental epic, stretching across centuries. Some of these links are actual connections among peoples through networks of trade and migration. Others are the analytical links we ourselves create across time and space.

This collection is the culmination of a joint endeavor of the School for Advanced Research (SAR) and the William P. Clements Center for Southwest Studies at Southern Methodist University. The project brought together scholars from anthropology, history, psychology, and ethnic studies. Over the course of two workshops and a public symposium held in the autumn of 2012 and the spring of 2013, the participants shared their original research into lesser known stories of slavery in North America. The result showcases examples of cutting-edge work that builds upon the kinds of analytical and methodological breakthroughs urged by scholars in the 1970s, scholars who believed that we should investigate more diverse sources in order to better understand the tensions and the compromises within working slave systems.[5] Our collaboration has revealed surprising parallels in slave cultures across North America. The same forces that transformed peoples and places east of the Mississippi River fostered Comanche equestrianism and migration to the southern Great Plains in the late seventeenth century; created genízaro (mixed ethnic) communities in colonial

New Mexico on the Indian/Spanish frontier from descendants of captives in the late eighteenth century; and turned the Klamath people in the Pacific Northwest from smaller-scale captive raiding to commercial slaving in the 1830s.[6] In fact, Native Americans everywhere adapted their institutions and slave practices to fit evolving conditions. While indigenous peoples tried to preserve traditional cultural norms even as the level of warfare increased and the geographical range of slaving expanded, they also modified some customs in response to new realities. Access to European trade goods and more chattel slaves created new economic and ceremonial opportunities within traditional Indian societies, and indigenous peoples made the most of them—as Marcy's Comanche traders and others highlighted in these chapters illustrate.[7] Unless we expand our view to reach across the continent, we miss striking similarities between the dynamics of slavery in these western shatter zones and in Euro-American societies.[8]

Although the focus of our collection is North America, we join those who take a broad view of slavery as a global historical phenomenon. Until the modern era, bondage was almost universally understood as essential to a well-functioning society and economy. Slaves worked the kitchens, fields, and business districts of ancient Japan, Athens, and Rome.[9] In the late Middle Ages and Renaissance, *fotzati* (enslaved oarsmen) powered the commercial and war galleys that sliced through the Mediterranean, and Arab pirates scored high profits auctioning off Byzantine women.[10] Beginning in the early modern era, Christian janissary (enslaved) soldiers fought on Ottoman frontiers in southwest Asia, while slave women cooked, cleaned, played instruments, did acrobatics, and were prostituted in households of the lords of Rajput, what is now northern India and Pakistan.[11] Contemporaneously, in North America we find kidnapped mestizas (women of mixed Indian and Spanish descent) and Apache women grinding corn near Navajo hogans or scraping hides outside Comanche tipis on the Great Plains. The region's own caste of janissaries, the genízaros, were guarding the frontiers of New Mexico. Meanwhile, across the Atlantic, at the same time that the black female slaves were bought by Marcy's Delaware trader, orphaned children were forced to labor in British textile mills, spinning thread and weaving fabric from the cotton grown in fields like the ones worked by Solomon Northup and other African Americans in the United States.[12]

The literature from global systems of slavery and bondage reminds us that the torture and sale of the two black girls encountered by Marcy reflected a long-standing cross-cultural pattern: raiding parties targeted women and children from "alien" ethnic groups. Typically, men defending the attacked villages were killed, while young women, girls, and prepubescent boys were taken captive. As in most societies, indigenous peoples of

North America placed great social and economic value on the capture and forced incorporation of women and children during the pre-Columbian period. Only when Europeans arrived with the enslaved Africans did the demographics of slavery in North America suddenly shift, first to a preference for male slaves, and then to one that was more gender balanced, in order to foster reproduction of the slave force.[13] Although boys and men would come to be the human commodity of choice in the well-publicized transatlantic trade and at times in the Southwest borderlands, the capture and abuse of the Negro girls shows that the more prevalent, ancient custom of enslaving and exploiting women and children continued across the continent. The chapters highlight examples of this older pattern, the exploitation of women and children sexually and economically, showing how it persisted in the United States after emancipation and into the present.[14] Events in 2014 confirm that this practice continues around the globe. More than two hundred girls from a Christian school in Chibok, Nigeria, were captured by the Islamist rebel group Boko Haram. The girls, designated as slaves, were forced to convert to Islam. Some, it seems, were sold to guerillas in Chad, Cameroon, and Niger.[15] Yazidi women and girls captured by ISIL fighters in Iraq and others seized by members of a madrassa in the Hapur district in northeastern India found themselves threatened with a similar fate.[16]

The forced conversions of women kidnapped in Nigeria, Iraq, and India in 2014, and by many ethnic groups in the past, lead us to another of the common challenges faced by enslavers across time and space: the tension between the need to control and yet absorb captives. Marcy portrays the Comanches as ignorant barbarians who kept two Negro girls alive for the curiosity and the thrill of torture and then sold them as chattels to another Indian slave trader. But note that Marcy saw the girls only after the branding and torture. Was this gratuitous violence? Could this also be evidence that the Comanches were testing the suitability of the girls for incorporation into the group? How often were captives fully accepted into Indian communities? For example, how many of the "Seminole negroes" slaughtered by the Comanches had been accepted as full-fledged Seminoles, and how many were slaves traveling with their Seminole owners? Recent research suggests that patterns of absorption were complex and nuanced, more so than Marcy could have appreciated, and these patterns had roots deep in the slave systems designed by indigenous North American cultures. Counter to the presumption that kinship and slavery were distinct social categories, these roles blended together in many indigenous North American cultures. As in Africa and Asia, norms of kinship and slavery operated as much along a "continuum of coercion" as they did in opposition to one another.[17]

As mentioned above, most cultures validated coercion, enabling and supporting it throughout the larger society. Slavery was condoned and enforced not just by the bureaucratic empires of Rome, Asia, and early modern Europe but also by the community consensus of indigenous American peoples in the centuries before the Europeans arrived. The enforcement mechanisms differed in complexity, but each of these societies gave its citizens power to inflict physical and psychological stress on the enslaved and to restrict their social and economic opportunities. Such powers inhered within the group, although the harshness of mores governing slave treatment in North America varied over places and periods. For example, in precontact times slaves had fewer chances for social and economic mobility if they lived among coastal Indian peoples in present-day Washington and Oregon. The same was true for captives of the pastoral sheepherding Navajos of the Southwest in the eighteenth century and for African Americans on plantations in the antebellum South.[18] Oddly enough, slaves living among some of the most successful indigenous slave-raiding groups, like the Iroquois and the Comanches, enjoyed greater possibilities of raising their status and power. Such opportunities were pragmatic cultural reactions to conditions of endemic warfare and slaving. It was critical to replace warriors killed or women and children stolen in counter-raids with captives.[19]

The chapters to follow highlight another global theme inherent in Marcy's description. Both enslaving and enslaved peoples were migrating in cross-cultural trading networks. In Randolph Marcy, we have the agent of the United States, a young nation whose government was engineering large in-migrations of free whites and African American slaves to the new cotton South, and at the same time the forced out-migrations of Indians—some of them slaveholders—to the West. Each of these migrations was triggered by private and public agendas to produce capital and cotton. The Marcy incident involves Native American slavers trading Negro girls and illustrates the intersection of these multiple slaving cultures in North America. The encounter expands the dimensions of human trafficking in the US antebellum era and offers more opportunities for cross-cultural comparisons and intercultural dynamics. For example, what were African Americans doing on the plains? Why was Wild Cat, a Seminole chieftain, leading a band toward the Rio Grande and not to the allotted Oklahoma reservation? We suggest that overlapping slave trades spurred migration across the continent in the nineteenth century, as they had in the colonial period and just as other slaving networks had moved peoples across the Atlantic Ocean, Africa, and Southeast Asia.[20] The Marcy incident provides multiple examples of ethnic migrants. Some were free; some were enslaved;

some were slavers. There was Marcy's traveling party of Euro-American soldiers. There were the Seminoles with their slaves crossing the same plains to escape the expulsion from Florida to Oklahoma forced on them by the US government. The Delaware Indian trader represented a group that itself was pushed out of its homelands after the Europeans arrived. In turn, he was buying and transporting Negro slave girls trafficked across the plains by Comanches, girls who were descended from Africans previously forced to migrate. The Comanches also were migrants, albeit voluntary ones, who chose to leave the Great Basin in order to take advantage of the new horse technology brought by the Spaniards. They used those horses to make themselves powerful and wealthy by raiding and trading, while actively buying and selling women and children as human chattels. They also kept and at times incorporated some female slave laborers to process hides for the American market and, in time, Mexican boys to manage the vast herds of cattle they plundered from Chihuahua and Durango.

The volume also features other cases of slaving and enslaved peoples migrating in cross-cultural trading networks. Some Apaches found themselves forcibly moved to Cuba by the Spanish. Other groups, like the Erie Indians displaced by Iroquois raiders and traders from New York, became slavers themselves, supplying British colonists with Indian captives taken from Virginia to Florida. Many, like the Choctaws of Mississippi and Alabama, were both slavers and victims of slavers.[21] Episodes of interethnic exchanges of captives, like the one Marcy documented, happened time and again, as demand for slaves in North America pulled captives and captors across the continent and into Caribbean islands like Cuba, Jamaica, and Barbados—the marine borderlands of North America.

Both economic and social incentives drove indigenous and Euro-American slave systems and migrations from the earliest contacts into the nineteenth century. The idea that Indian slavery was "economic" runs against common conceptions of slavery in North America. Older studies often depicted indigenous bartered exchanges as highly local, permeated with ritual, and economically unsophisticated. Such duality is artificial and unnecessary. A number of Indian peoples managed to straddle both customary and new rules of trade for more than a century.[22] Slavery among livestock-herding pastoralists, like the Comanches or Navajos, fits neatly into the global dynamics of slavery, in which pastoral economies utilize slave labor far more than any other mode of production. Fully 73 percent of pastoral societies include some form of slavery in their social organization, compared with 43 percent of agriculturalists and 17 percent of horticulturalists.[23] The Comanches actively assembled a labor force of captive women to dress bison hides for the lucrative Saint Louis market. Certainly, some Indian groups, like the Quechans on the lower Colorado River, were less profit oriented. Recent research suggests, however, that many Indian groups manipulated their human resources much as southern plantation owners did. Precontact cultures did value captive women and children as kin replacements, prestige goods, or diplomatic gifts, but these societies also appreciated the economic reality that domestic slave labor enhanced subsistence and increased the production of marketable commodities for their owners.[24]

Although contact with European markets did accelerate and expand Native American slaving, indigenous household production had long been valued for the lucrative economic opportunities provided by the items slaves made, as well as for the social status and spiritual benefits slave ownership conferred.[25] As in industrialized societies, slave labor increased the food supply in Indian communities, but slaves had value far beyond that single use, shading the lines between a European-style chattel slavery and indigenous chattel slavery. Captives held by Indians farmed, cooked, herded, and made clothes, structures, and tools. Like plantation slaves, they were last and least fed. Also like plantation slaves, they adapted to and made the most of social and economic opportunities available within captor societies. In the process of working for slaveholders, people in bondage inevitably modified the nature of the very cultures trying to absorb them—whether these cultures were Indian or Euro-American. Slaves added new foods, as well as new artistic and practical designs to the cooking, crafts, and rituals they fashioned. Moreover, like their western counterparts, indigenous slave owners traded their slaves as chattels, in addition to using them to sustain cultural norms and rituals.[26] In both Euro-American and Indian communities, economic and social needs were met through slave ownership and the domestic labor and trade production that accompanied it.[27]

The standard commercial story line of African American peoples enslaved on Euro-American plantations becomes more diverse and nuanced as we add these histories of indigenous North Americans.[28] By examining slave systems across time, cultures, and the continent, we discover continuities and discontinuities in social patterns.[29] This collection expands our understanding of slavery in North America by exploring how eastern cultures and networks linked with slaving cultures and networks west of the Mississippi, both on the continent and in its Caribbean island borderlands.[30] North America was a vast, pulsing map of trading, raiding, and resettling. Whether the systems were pre- or postcontact indigenous, European colonial, or US national, they grew into complex cultural matrices in which the economic wealth and the social power created using slavery proved indivisible.[31] Indigenous and Euro-American slave systems evolved and innovated in response to each other.

We who research slavery face the challenge of formulating a general definition. There were and are many kinds of bondage practiced around the globe, and it remains a matter of debate which particular points on the continuum of coercion should be defined as "slavery." Were the *criados*, the Apache children bought at the New Mexico trade fairs and "raised up" by the Spanish, slaves?[32] Were the captives called *awakaan* (dogs) held by the Algonquians of the Great Lakes slaves?[33] How do we define the condition of the *panis* in New France or the African "servants" in the British Caribbean?[34] The *lúgsh* of the Klamath in the Pacific Northwest?[35] In this volume, we anchor our definition in four patterns that we have found in the literatures of history and anthropology.

Slavery is
1. a coerced state of living, a limitation on basic human choices including movement, work, family, and reproduction;[36]
2. enforced by the threat of violence and often accompanied by actual physical and psychological abuse;
3. forced labor to produce both economic and social wealth. Cultural slave systems demand, support, or tolerate coerced labor through law or custom (including coerced domestic and sexual labor) that produces wealth, status, and/or power for the slaveholder; and
4. not gender neutral but depends on cultural values and economic circumstances. Although male adults have been the targets of slavers in certain periods and places—in the Atlantic African slave trade, for example—over the broad expanse of history, women of reproductive age and children have most often been the targets of slavers and their cultures.[37]

This definition of slavery suits the continental scope of this collection. We want to expand the conversation about how the coercers, the coerced, and outside observers understood what it meant to be a "slave" in various times and cultures—including the connotations of the term in the twentieth and twenty-first centuries. What people considered slavery differed not only *among* the many cultural groups we address but also *within* a cultural group over time.[38] Inevitably, our attempt to define slavery also finds influence in our own cultural memories and norms—including the various perspectives of individual academic disciplines. This diversity sparked a lively discussion among the contributors. We debated whether we were talking about linking histories of "slavery" or histories of "slaveries" in North America. It seemed most helpful for our volume to distinguish between "slavery" as an abstract concept, the one defined above, and "slave systems" as expressions of that concept. Slavery as a cultural institution manifests itself in many forms, that is, as many distinct slave systems. Each system shares some characteristics with others, and each has its own history that traces changes over place and time. This underlines "slavery" as an almost universal social phenomenon, while "histories" stresses the many ways peoples have woven slavery into particular cultural templates.

The chapters that follow examine a range of cultural responses that incorporate many of the fundamental elements of slavery. As noted earlier, every slave system had to cope with the challenge of successfully incorporating outsiders. Slaves had to learn their roles within that system—what they must do and what they were forbidden to do—but they were taught in ways that reflected particular internal and external economic and social conditions. In part I, "Links to Early Slavery," anthropologists Catherine M. Cameron and Eric E. Bowne provide an overview of slave systems operating in North America during pre-Columbian and early contact periods. While taking us on a tour of precontact North America, Catherine M. Cameron (chapter 1) challenges assumptions that Indian slave systems were nearly interchangeable. They were not, not in the roles assigned to slaves and not in the opportunities available to them. Nor should we assume that Indian slave systems had little in common with "modern" European slavery. Cameron notes the striking similarity between the treatment of slaves by Indian groups in the Northwest and Euro-Americans in the plantation South. Next, Eric E. Bowne (chapter 2) maps the migration streams created by Indian slave traders and their victims—plus Indian slave-traders-turned-victims—during the early postcontact period. Bowne begins by showing the linked networks of slavers and slaves moving from north to south in the Atlantic East. He then shifts to a wide satellite-like view of the Caribbean and regions west of the Mississippi River.

In part II, "Links to Expanding Slave Networks," six historians explore the dynamic intersections of Indian, European, Euro-American, and African cultures and economies in the late eighteenth and nineteenth centuries. Paul Conrad (chapter 3) tracks the movement of Apache laborers transported from the Spanish Southwest into Mexico and Cuba. Conrad shows how the kinetic energy of slaves and slave traders in transit continued from the earlier periods described by Cameron and Bowne. Similarly, Boyd Cothran (chapter 4) takes the story to the Pacific Northwest, where the raids of Klamath groups illustrate similar cross-cultural and entrepreneurial qualities of slaving. In chapter 5, Natale Zappia further exposes the links between the Pacific coastal trade and internal networks, but this time in the far Southwest. Multiple Indian and Euro-American groups generated significant commercial connections in the trade of livestock and slaves. Zappia sketches out these less familiar routes of trafficking and the slave diaspora through North America's internal and external borderlands. Calvin Schermerhorn (chapter 6) sees parallels in the forced migrations of black Americans *into* and Indians *out of* the western edges of the cotton South—and therefore into the slaving networks of the West described in earlier chapters. Schermerhorn underlines the complicity of modern state action in shaping economic cycles of slavery in North America. Andrew J. Torget (chapter 7) follows Schermerhorn's political and economic links to the philosophical and economic debates over slavery in the nineteenth century in Saltillo, Mexico, where just such a modern state was emerging. On the northern frontier of that new republic, legislators argued over the imperatives of national independence and individual freedoms in light of the pragmatic challenges caused by the rapid immigration of American slaveholders from Schermerhorn's cotton South into Mexican Texas. In chapter 8, Mark Allan Goldberg takes us to antebellum Texas, where he traces the links between two slave systems, the Comanche empire and the expanding United States, and the ways they clashed, collaborated, and extended the continental patterns of slavery's violent commerce and coercion. With Goldberg's chapter, we come full circle to the circumstances of our opening scene—R. B. Marcy's account of Indians and Anglo-Americans operating overlapping slave trades in Texas, networks overlooked in traditional histories of North American slavery.

Part III, "Links to Legacies of Slavery," focuses on the legacies of slavery in North America. In chapter 9, ethnomusicologist Enrique R. Lamadrid explores the long resonance of intercultural slavery in the life of villages and pueblos in New Mexico. Songs and dances blend histories of coercion and kinship in public performances—poignant evidence of the ways people in New Mexico managed the trauma of endemic slave raiding. The victims of murderous attacks and violent kidnappings and their descendants managed to turn cultural memories of family separation and forced incorporation into communal coping strategies. Today this sense of shared history, identity, and discrimination—but also healing—reinforces a sense of pride in genízaro (mixed) heritage.

Tragically, coercion remained a prominent part of the human experience across the continent during the twentieth century, and it continues into the twenty-first. Violence and abuse, especially of women and children, add new faces and places to the histories of slavery in North America. The final two chapters push us into that nether zone between coercion and consent and ask us to ponder how strongly the legacies of North America's slave systems endure. Sarah Deer and Melissa Farley explore the blurred lines between exploitation and compulsion. It can be difficult to distinguish between conditions that meet the definition of illegal slavery and brutal but legally tolerated social circumstances produced by past slavery and colonialism. Law professor Sarah Deer (chapter 10) explores the

INTRODUCTION

sexual exploitation of Native American children and women in the late nineteenth and early twentieth centuries. Deer argues that persistent socioeconomic realities linked to the colonial past created a proclivity for the exploitation of indigenous people as groups and individuals. In chapter 11, psychologist Melissa Farley presents historical and contemporary examples of legal and illegal prostitution bondage, juxtaposing them against a number of cultural and legal definitions of slavery. Farley then asks us to consider whether recent data show that prostitution in the twenty-first century is tantamount to slavery.

Asking researchers from such disparate fields to compare indigenous and Euro-American slave systems in their own times and on their own terms is challenging and rewarding in itself, but with this collaboration, SAR and the Clements center also wanted to illustrate how studying the past can enrich our understanding of present social issues. To that end, each of the three parts of the volume has its own introduction. In the notes there are recommendations for sources that encourage further comparisons and discussions. These sources include works of fiction, autobiography, music, and film, as well as scholarly articles that suggest how patterns of past slavery might deepen our understanding of exploitation in the present.

Taken together, the chapters in this volume provide a wide sampling of North American slave systems over time: slavery both within distinct culture groups and across networks linking many cultures—like that evidenced by the Comanche trading of African American slaves recorded in R. B. Marcy's journal. Much is to be learned from exploring these links: from indigenous customs of coercion before European contact to those of the tumultuous colonial era, to less familiar paradigms of slavery before the Civil War, and, finally, to coercion in the hazy legal borders between voluntary and involuntary servitude today. This breadth complements and enhances traditional scholarship that has focused on slavery in the colonial and nineteenth-century South. If we make a conscious effort to find the links among the many histories of slavery across disciplines, cultures, time, and space, we will better understand the many ways coercion and slavery worked (and works) across North America.

Notes

1. R. B. Marcy, *Thirty Years of Army Life on the Border* (New York: Harper and Brothers, 1866), viii, 35–36. The editors would like to thank Claudio Saunt for bringing this journal excerpt to their attention. "Wild Cat," whose Seminole name was Coacoochee (c. 1810–1857), was a Seminole chieftain during the Second Seminole War. In 1850 he led approximately three hundred Seminoles, African Americans (some free Seminoles, some slaves), and Kickapoos from reservations in the United States to Coahuila, Mexico.

BONNIE MARTIN AND JAMES F. BROOKS

Donald A. Swanson, "Coacoochee [Wild Cat]," *Handbook of Texas Online*, Texas State Historical Association, accessed September 9, 2013, http://www.tshaonline.org/handbook/online/articles/fcoaz. Also in the *Handbook*, see Jeffrey D. Carlisle, "Seminole Indians," accessed September 9, 2013, http://www.tshaonline.org/handbook/online/articles/bms19. On the historical interaction of African Americans and Seminoles that began in Florida, see Jane Landers, *Black Society in Spanish Florida* (Urbana: University of Illinois Press, 1999); Daniel F. Littlefield, Jr., *Africans and Seminoles: From Removal to Emancipation* (Westport, CT: Greenwood Press, 1977); and the new edition of Kenneth W. Porter's classic work, *The Black Seminoles: History of a Freedom-Seeking People*, ed. Alcione M. Amos and Thomas P. Senter (Gainesville: University Press of Florida, 2013).

2. Edward S. Wallace, "Introduction," in Marcy, *Thirty Years of Army Life*, v–ix.

3. The film is based on the memoir of Solomon Northup, *Twelve Years a Slave: Narrative of Solomon Northup, a Citizen of New York, Kidnapped in Washington City in 1841 and Rescued in 1853, From a Cotton Plantation near the Red River in Louisiana* (Buffalo, NY: Derby, Orton, and Mulligan, 1853). The film, *12 Years a Slave*, was written by John Ridley and directed by Steve McQueen (Los Angeles: Fox Searchlight Pictures, 2013). For more on the film, see the review by Manohla Dargis, "The Blood and Tears, Not the Magnolias: '12 Years a Slave' Holds Nothing Back in Show of Suffering," *New York Times*, October 17, 2013, accessed January 7, 2014, http://www.nytimes.com/2013/10/18/movies/12-years-a-slave-holds-nothing-back-in-show-of-suffering.html?_r=0&pagewanted=2.

4. Examples of recent scholarship following traditional geographical boundaries include a monograph by Walter Johnson, which does stretch the dimensions of slavery in the nineteenth century beyond the traditional South into its Atlantic borderlands. It does not, however, reach to regions west of the Mississippi River. Walter Johnson, *River of Dark Dreams: Slavery and Empire in the Cotton Kingdom* (Cambridge, MA: Harvard University Press, 2013). For a recent traditional political history of slavery, see John Craig Hammond, *Slavery, Freedom, and Expansion in the Early American West* (Charlottesville: University of Virginia Press, 2007) and "Slavery, Settlement, and Empire: The Expansion and Growth of Slavery in the Interior of the North American Continent, 1770–1820," *Journal of the Early Republic* 32 (Summer 2012): 175–206. In the monograph, Hammond defines "the West" as the new territories in the northern Midwest and Mississippi. In the article, Hammond refers to Native Americans as "nations" resisting the migrations of Euro-Americans and African Americans from the Atlantic and Caribbean colonies. With the exception of a brief reference to Indian slaves in the Illinois country, Indians are not portrayed as migrating slaver traders, slaveholders, or slaves west of the Mississippi. There are no indications of the networks that predated and also fed the expansion of slavery in both indigenous and European societies. Hammond,

Introduction

"Slavery, Settlement, and Empire," 178, 181, 183, 185, 188, 190, 200. See also Gary J. Kornblith, *Slavery and Sectional Strife in the Early American Republic, 1776–1821* (Lanham, MD: Rowman & Littlefield, 2009). On migration and slavery that focus on African American versus Indian slaves, see Ira Berlin, *The Making of African America: The Four Great Migrations* (New York: Penguin, 2010) and *Many Thousands Gone: The First Two Centuries of Slavery in North America* (Cambridge, MA: Harvard University Press, 1998). For contrasts in the migrations and labor laws from early colonial times to the Civil War, but within the English settlements, see Christopher Tomlins, *Freedom Bound: Law, Labor, and Civic Identity in Colonizing English America, 1580–1865* (New York: Cambridge University Press, 2010). This is an in-depth treatment of the circumstances of indentured servants, African slaves, and free whites. There is little discussion of Native Americans.

5. For example, see "AHR Forum: Crossing Slavery's Boundaries," *American Historical Review* 105 (2000): 451–484; David Brion Davis, "Looking at Slavery in a Broader Perspective," *American Historical Review* 105 (2000): 452–466; Peter Kolchin, "The Big Picture: A Comment on David Brion Davis, 'Looking at Slavery in a Broader Perspective,'" *American Historical Review* 105 (2000): 467–468; Stanley L. Engerman, "Slavery at Different Times and Places," *American Historical Review* 105 (2000): 480–484; Rebecca J. Scott, "Small-Scale Dynamics of Large-Scale Processes," *American Historical Review* 105 (2000): 472–479. Donald M. MacRaild and Avram Taylor, *Social Theory and Social History* (New York: Palgrave Macmillan, 2004). See also Daniel Lord Smail and Andrew Shyrock, "History and the 'Pre,'" *American Historical Review* 118 (2013): 709–737. With roots in the post–World War II Annales school and the methods urged by historians like Marc Bloch in *The Historian's Craft: Reflections on the Nature and Uses of History and the Techniques and Methods of Those Who Write It* (Toronto: Knopf, 1953), the new social history blossomed in the work of British Marxist labor historians like E. P. Thompson, *The Making of the English Working Class* (London: V. Gollancz, 1963), and the interpretation of cultural expressions of ordinary people, as exemplified by work of American historians like Herbert Gutman in *The Black Family in Slavery and Freedom, 1750–1925* (New York: Vintage Books, 1977). The challenges involved in meaningfully counting and interpreting the statistics of such historical evidence were addressed by historians in the generation that followed. See, for example, Gary B. Nash, *The Urban Crucible: Social Change, Political Consciousness, and the Origins of the American Revolution* (Cambridge, MA: Harvard University Press, 1979); Sean Wilentz, *Chants Democratic: New York City and the Rise of the American Working Class, 1788–1850* (New York: Oxford University Press, 1984). For a fine recent example of the use of statistics to give voice to ordinary working people, including slaves, see Seth Rockman, *Scraping By: Wage Labor, Slavery, and Survival in Early Baltimore* (Baltimore, MD: Johns Hopkins University Press, 2011).

6. On transitions to commercial slave raiding across the continent, see the chapters in this volume by Eric E. Bowne (chapter 2), Paul Conrad (chapter 3), Boyd

BONNIE MARTIN AND JAMES F. BROOKS

Cothran (chapter 4), Natale Zappia (chapter 5), and Mark Allen Goldberg (chapter 8). Also see Pekka Hämäläinen, *The Comanche Empire* (New Haven, CT: Yale University Press, 2009); James F. Brooks, *Captives and Cousins: Slavery, Kinship, and Community in the Southwest Borderlands* (Chapel Hill: University of North Carolina Press, 2002); and Robbie Ethridge, "Introduction: Mapping the Mississippian Shatter Zone," in *Mapping the Mississippian Shatter Zone: The Colonial Indian Slave Trade and Regional Instability in the American South*, ed. Robbie Ethridge and Sheri M. Shuck-Hall (Lincoln: University of Nebraska Press, 2009), 43. See the following chapters in *Mapping the Mississippian Shatter Zone*: Stephen Warren and Randolph Noe, "'The Greatest Travelers in America': Shawnee Survival in the Shatter Zone," 163–187; William A. Fox, "Events as Seen from the North: The Iroquois and Colonial Slavery," 63–80; Sheri M. Shuck-Hall, "Alabama and Coushatta Diaspora and Coalescence in the Mississippi Shatter Zone," 250–271; John E. Worth, "Razing Florida: The Indian Slave Trade and the Devastation of Spanish Florida," 295–311. These texts provide evidence for the argument that what happened in the far Northeast had a tremendous impact on the Southeast and the Great Plains. All these regions saw an expansion of the traditional trades in slaves, pelts, and luxury goods. Increased demand prompted greater movement of each of these across transcontinental networks. Disease and European debt institutions spread along with trade. Recent studies broaden this picture to include the Southwest, the Northwest, Mexico, and the Caribbean. Among Indian peoples, competition intensified for guns, for trade goods, and for key roles as middlemen—those who managed the flow of slaves, animal pelts, and European goods.

7. Matthew H. Jennings, "Violence in a Shattered World," in Ethridge and Shuck-Hall, *Mapping the Mississippian Shatter Zone*, 272–294. Jennings does not see the dynamics as consistent with a Richard White–styled "middle ground," but rather that slave raiding reinforced relations that remained particularly violent. Richard White, *The Middle Ground: Indians, Empires, and Republics in the Great Lakes Region, 1650–1815* (Cambridge: Cambridge University Press, 1991).

8. Ethridge, "Introduction," generally and especially at 2, 4, 6.

9. Herman Ooms, *Imperial Politics and Symbolics in Ancient Japan: The Tenmu Dynasty, 650–800* (Honolulu: University of Hawaii Press, 2009), 262–263; Timothy Taylor, "Believing the Ancients: Quantitative and Qualitative Dimensions of Slavery and the Slave Trade in Later Prehistoric Eurasia," *World Archaeology* 33 (June 2001): 27–43; Alan Watson, *Roman Slave Law* (Baltimore, MD: Johns Hopkins University Press, 1987); M. I. Finley, ed., *Classical Slavery* (Totowa, NJ: F. Cass, 1987); W. W. Buckland, *The Roman Law of Slavery: The Condition of the Slave in Private Law from Augustus to Justinian* (New York: AMS Press, 1969).

10. Angus Konstam, *Renaissance War Galley, 1470–1590* (Oxford: New Vanguard, 2002), 34, 35, 38, 46. On Arab pirates, see Youval Rotman, *Byzantine Slavery and the*

INTRODUCTION

Mediterranean World, trans. Jane Marie Todd (Cambridge, MA: Harvard University Press, 2009), 74–75. On the enslaved soldiers of the Abbasid caliphs, see Peter Jackson, "Turkish Slaves on Islam's Indian Frontier," in *Slavery and South Asian History*, ed. Indrani Chatterjee and Richard M. Eaton (Bloomington: Indiana University Press, 2006), 63–82. For examples of slavery in Japan, see Thomas Nelson, "Slavery in Medieval Japan," *Monumenta Nipponica* 59 (Winter 2004): 463–492; at 481 for the sale of a woman and her unborn children in 1324; at 468 for an account of men executed for debt or crimes and the subsequent enslavement of their wives and children; and at 479–481 on captive taking in raids in the sixteenth century, like the Japanese invasion of Korea led by the samurai warrior Toyotomi Hideyoshi.

11. Ramya Sreenivasan, "Drudges, Dancing Girls, Concubines, Female Slaves in Rajput Polity," in Chatterjee and Eaton, *Slavery and South Asian History*, 136–161.

12. Jane Humphries, *Childhood and Child Labour in the British Industrial Revolution* (Cambridge: Cambridge University Press, 2010).

13. Once again, much has been written on this topic. See, for example, Philip D. Morgan, *Slave Counterpoint: Black Culture in the Eighteenth-Century Chesapeake and Lowcountry* (Chapel Hill: University of North Carolina Press, 1998); Jennifer Morgan, *Laboring Women: Reproduction and Gender in New World Slavery* (Philadelphia: University of Pennsylvania Press, 2004); Wilma King, *Stolen Childhood: Slave Youth in Nineteenth-Century America*, 2nd ed. (Bloomington: Indiana University Press, 2011); Gwyn Campbell, Suzanne Miers, and Joseph C. Miller, eds., *Children in Slavery through the Ages* (Athens: Ohio State University Press, 2009). On the persistence of traditional customs of coercion after 1865 in the US Southwest, see James F. Brooks, *Captives and Cousins*.

14. Jacqueline Jones, *Labor of Love, Labor of Sorrow: Black Women, Work, and the Family, from Slavery to the Present*, rev. ed. (Philadelphia: Basic Books, 2009); Eric Arnesen, ed., *The Black Worker: Race, Labor, and Civil Rights since Emancipation* (Champaign: University of Illinois Press, 2007); Sharon Harley, ed., *Sister Circle: Black Women and Work* (Piscataway, NJ: Rutgers University Press, 2002). See also the classic monograph by Thomas Dublin, *Transforming Women's Work: New England Lives in the Industrial Revolution* (Ithaca, NY: Cornell University Press, 1995).

15. For example, see the report by Ted Thornhill, Jack Doyle, Jason Groves, and Andrew Malone, "Paraded by a Blood-Crazed Fanatic, the Terrified Schoolgirl Captives: Boko Haram Release Chilling Videos of Missing Nigerian Girls as They Reveal They Have All Been Forced to Convert to Islam," *Daily Mail* (UK), May 12, 2014, accessed September 6, 2014, http://www.dailymail.co.uk/news/article-2626019/We-know-Nigerian-governor-claims-intelligence-missing-schoolgirls-leader-Anglican-church-says-talks-need-start-Boko-Haram-back.html.

16. Martin Chulov, "Yazidis Tormented by Fears for Women and Girls Kidnapped by Isis Jihadists," *The Guardian* (UK), August 11, 2014, accessed September 6, 2014,

BONNIE MARTIN AND JAMES F. BROOKS

http://www.theguardian.com/world/2014/aug/11/yazidis-tormented-fears-for-women-girls-kidnapped-sinjar-isis-slaves; Piyush Srivastava, "Tensions Brew in Meerut as Woman, 20, Is Kidnapped, Gang Raped, and Forced to Change Religion," *Daily Mail India*, August 4, 2014, accessed September 6, 2014, http://www.dailymail.co.uk/indiahome/indianews/article-2715890/Tensions-brew-Meerut-woman-20-kidnapped-gang-raped-forced-change-religion.html.

17. Pierre Bonte, "Ecological and Economic Factors in the Determination of Pastoral Societies," in *Change and Development in Nomadic and Pastoral Societies*, ed. John G. Galaty and Philip Carl Salzman (Leiden: Brill, 1981), 33–49; Gerald Betty, "'Skillful in the Management of the Horse': Comanches as Southern Plains Pastoralists," *Heritage of the Great Plains* 30, no. 1 (1997): 5–31; George Peter Murdock, "Ethnographic Atlas: A Summary," *Ethnology* 6 (April 1967): 109–236; Igor Kopytoff, "Slavery," *Annual Review of Anthropology* 11 (1982): 207–230. For overviews and debates around kinship and slavery relationships, see Suzanne Miers and Igor Kopytoff, eds., *Slavery in Africa: Historical and Anthropological Perspectives* (Madison: University of Wisconsin Press, 1977); Claude Meillassoux, *The Anthropology of Slavery: The Womb of Iron and Gold* (Chicago: University of Chicago Press, 1991); Paul E. Lovejoy, *Transformations in Slavery: A History of Slavery in Africa* (Cambridge: Cambridge University Press, 1983); Tiya Miles, *Ties That Bind: The Story of an Afro-Cherokee Family in Slavery and Freedom* (Berkeley: University of California Press, 2005); Martin A. Klein, ed., *Breaking the Chains: Slavery, Bondage, and Emancipation in Modern Africa and Asia* (Madison: University of Wisconsin Press, 1993); James F. Brooks, "Reflections and Refractions from the Southwest Borderlands," in *Native American Adoption, Captivity, and Slavery in Changing Contexts*, ed. Max Carocci and Stephanie Pratt (New York: Palgrave Macmillan, 2012), 185–195; Joaquín Rivaya-Martínez, "Becoming Comanches: Patterns of Captive Incorporation into Comanche Kinship Networks, 1820–1875," in *On the Borders of Love and Power: Families and Kinship in the Intercultural American West*, ed. David Wallace Adams and Crista DeLuzio (Berkeley: University of California Press, 2012), 47–70.

18. For example, see Catherine M. Cameron, "Captives and Slaves in Indigenous North America," chapter 1 in this volume. See also Kenneth M. Ames, "Slavery, Household Production, and Demography on the Southern Northwest Coast: Cables, Tacking, and Ropewalks," in *Invisible Citizens: Captives and Their Consequences*, ed. Catherine M. Cameron (Salt Lake City: University of Utah Press, 2008), 138–158; Brooks, *Captives and Cousins*, 241–250.

19. Kurt A. Jordan, "Incorporation and Colonization: Postcolumbian Iroquois Satellite Communities and Processes of Indigenous Autonomy," *American Anthropologist* 115 (March 2013): 29–43; Christina Snyder, *Slavery in Indian Country: The Changing Face of Captivity in Early America* (Cambridge, MA: Harvard University Press, 2010), 46; Fox, "Events as Seen from the North," 63–80; Brett Rushforth, "'A Little Flesh We

Offer You': The Origins of Slavery in New France," in *Indian Slavery in Colonial America*, ed. Allan Gallay (Lincoln: University of Nebraska Press, 2009), 353–389, at 366–369; Hämäläinen, *The Comanche Empire*; Brooks, *Captives and Cousins*. In contrast, raiding societies like the Chickasaws were more likely to sell than to incorporate captives. See Jay K. Johnson et al., "Measuring Chickasaw Adaptation on the Western Frontier of the Colonial South: A Correlation of Documentary and Archeological Data," *Southeastern Archaeology* 27 (Summer 2008): 1–30; Robbie Ethridge, "The Making of a Militaristic Slaving Society: The Chickasaws and the Colonial Indian Slave Trade," in *Indian Slavery in Colonial America*, ed. Allan Gallay (Lincoln: University of Nebraska Press, 2010), 251–276; Wendy St. Jean, "Trading Paths: Mapping Chickasaw History in the Eighteenth Century," *American Indian Quarterly* 27 (Summer/Fall 2003): 758–780.

20. Samples from the large literature on this topic can be found in Toyin Falola and Matt D. Childs, eds., *The Yoruba Diaspora in the Atlantic World* (Bloomington: Indiana University Press, 2005); Berlin, *Many Thousands Gone*; John Thornton, *Africa and Africans in the Making of the Atlantic World, 1400–1800* (Cambridge: Cambridge University Press, 1992); Gwyn Campbell, Suzanne Miers, and Joseph C. Miller, eds., *Women and Slavery*, vol. 2, *The Modern Atlantic* (Athens: Ohio University Press, 2007); Chatterjee and Eaton, *Slavery and South Asian History*.

21. Eric E. Bowne, "'Caryinge awaye their Corne and Children': The Effects of Westo Slave Raids on the Indians of the Lower South," in Ethridge and Shuck-Hall, *Mapping the Mississippian Shatter Zone*, 104–114. See also Daniel H. Usner, Jr., *Indians, Settlers, and Slaves in a Frontier Exchange Economy: The Lower Mississippi Valley before 1783* (Chapel Hill: University of North Carolina Press, 1992).

22. See Eric E. Bowne, "From Westo to Comanche: The Role of Commercial Indian Slaving in the Development of Colonial North America," chapter 2 in this volume; Brett Rushforth, *Bonds of Alliance: Indigenous and Atlantic Slaveries in New France* (Chapel Hill: University of North Carolina Press, 2012); Patricia Galloway, "Choctaws at the Border of the Shatter Zone: Spheres of Exchange and Spheres of Social Value," in Ethridge and Shuck-Hall, *Mapping the Mississippian Shatter Zone*, 333–364.

23. Bonte, "Ecological and Economic Factors," 33–49; Betty, "'Skillful in the Management of the Horse,'" 5–31; Murdock, "Ethnographic Atlas," 109–236; Kopytoff, "Slavery," 207–230.

24. Natale A. Zappia, *Traders and Raiders: The Indigenous World of the Colorado Basin, 1540–1859* (Chapel Hill: University of North Carolina Press, 2014), and "Captivity and Economic Landscapes in California and the Far West, 1769–1850," chapter 5 in this volume; Hämäläinen, *The Comanche Empire*.

25. For revisionist challenges to this interpretation, see Walter Johnson, "Agency: A Ghost Story," in Walter Johnson, Eric Foner, and Richard Follett, *Slavery's Ghost: The Problem of Freedom in the Age of Emancipation* (Baltimore, MD: Johns Hopkins University

Press, 2011), 8–30; Ames, "Slavery, Household Production, and Demography"; E. A. S. Demers, "John Askin and Indian Slavery at Michilimackinac," in Gallay, *Indian Slavery in Colonial America*, 391–416, especially at 391, 400–411.

26. Brett Rushforth, "A Little Flesh We Offer You," 353–389, especially at 353–354, 360, 372, 374, and *Bonds of Alliance*.

27. For examples of regional and micro studies, see the chapters in the current volume and Brooks, *Captives and Cousins*; Hämäläinen, *The Comanche Empire*; Ames, "Slavery, Household Production, and Demography"; Walter Johnson, *Soul by Soul: Life inside the Antebellum Slave Market* (Cambridge, MA: Harvard University Press, 1999).

28. James F. Brooks, "'We Betray Our Own Nation': Indian Slavery and Multi-ethnic Communities in the Southwest Borderlands," in Gallay, *Indian Slavery in Colonial America*, 320–323, and *Captives and Cousins*; Bonnie Martin, "Slavery's Invisible Engine: Mortgaging Human Property," *Journal of Southern History* 76 (2010): 817–866.

29. On shipping Indians to the Caribbean, see Alan Gallay, "Introduction: Indian Slavery in Historical Context," in Gallay, *Indian Slavery in Colonial America*, 1–32, and Juliana Barr, "A Spectrum of Indian Bondage in Spanish Texas," in same volume, 277–317; also, Paul Conrad, "Indians, Convicts, and Slaves: An Apache Diaspora to Cuba at the Start of the Nineteenth Century," chapter 3 in this volume.

30. See the chapters in this volume, plus Brooks, *Captives and Cousins*, and Rushforth, *Bonds of Alliance*.

31. Brooks, "We Betray Our Own Nation," 320–323, and *Captives and Cousins*; Martin, "Slavery's Invisible Engine"; Edward E. Baptist, "Toxic Debt, Liar Loans, Collateralized and Securitized Human Beings, and the Panic of 1837," in *Capitalism Takes Command: The Social Transformation of Nineteenth-Century North America*, ed. Michael Zakim and Gary J. Kornblith (Chicago: University of Chicago Press, 2012), 69–92, especially 75–90.

32. Brooks, *Captives and Cousins*, and see the story of the enslavement sexual abuse of the criada Indian woman "Maria" in Barr, "A Spectrum of Indian Bondage in Spanish Texas," 306–308.

33. Rushforth, *Bonds of Alliance*, 35. Also see Ramon A. Gutiérrez, *When Jesus Came, the Corn Mothers Went Away: Marriage, Sexuality, and Power in New Mexico, 1500–1846* (Stanford, CA: Stanford University Press, 1991).

34. Rushforth, *Bonds of Alliance*, generally. For example, see Susan Dwyer Amussen, *Caribbean Exchanges: Slavery and the Transformation of English Society, 1640–1700* (Chapel Hill: University of North Carolina Press, 2007). Of particular interest are the illustrations of "owners" and "servants."

35. See Boyd Cothran, "*Lúgsh* and *Laláki*: Slaves, Chiefs, Medicine Men, and the Indigenous Political Landscape of the Upper Klamath Basin, 1820s–1860s," chapter 4 in this volume.

36. On slavery as only one form of coerced labor, see Gwyn Campbell and Edward Alpers, "Introduction: Slavery, Forced Labour, and Resistance in Indian Ocean Africa and Asia," in *Slavery and Resistance in Africa and Asia*, ed. Edward Alpers, Gwyn Campbell, and Michael Salman (New York: Routledge, 2005), 1–19.

37. See Jeremy Black, *A Brief History of Slavery: A New Global History* (London: Constable and Rutherford, 2011), 7, 16, 25, 45, 58, 70–73, 86; Joseph C. Miller, *The Problem of Slavery as History: A Global Approach* (New Haven, CT: Yale University Press, 2012); Berlin, *Many Thousands Gone*; Campbell and Alpers, "Introduction," 7–8. On women and young girls making up the majority of slaves in the trade, see the chapters in this volume and Brooks, *Captives and Cousins*. On forced marriages of prepubescent girls, plus demands on local populations for labor that fall between plantation and *encomienda* slavery, see Francesca Declich, "Unfree Labour, Forced Labour, and Resistance among the Zigula of the Lower Juba," in *Resisting Bondage in Indian Ocean Africa and Asia*, ed. Edward Alpers, Gwyn Campbell, and Michael Salman (New York: Routledge, 2007), 24–39. On slavery, war, and non-European capitalism, including sexual slavery in early modern Asia and China, see James Francis Warren, *The Sulu Zone, 1768–1898: The Dynamics of External Trade, Slavery, and Ethnicity in the Transformation of a Southeast Asian Marine State* (Singapore: Singapore University Press, 1981); Warren, "The Balangingi Samal: The Global Economy, Maritime Raiding, and Diasporic Identities in the Nineteenth-Century Philippines," *Asian Ethnicity* 4 (March 2003): 7–29; Warren, *Iranun and Balangingi: Globalization, Maritime Raiding, and the Birth of Ethnicity* (Honolulu: University of Hawaii Press, 2003); Black, *A Brief History of Slavery*, 70–73. See also the following essays, which focus on women in slavery, in Chatterjee and Eaton, *Slavery and South Asian History*: Daud Ali, "A Study of Palace Women in the Chola Empire," 44–62; Sreenivasan, "Drudges, Dancing Girls, Concubines"; Sylvia Vatuk, "Bharattee's Death: Domestic Slave-Women in Nineteenth-Century Madras," 210–233. Also see Gwyn Campbell, Suzanne Miers, and Joseph C. Miller, eds., *Women and Slavery*, vol. 1, *Africa, the Indian Ocean World, and the Medieval North Atlantic* (Athens: Ohio University Press, 2007), and *Women and Slavery*, vol. 2, *The Modern Atlantic*.

38. David Brion Davis, *Inhuman Bondage: The Rise and Fall of Slavery in the New World* (New York: Oxford University Press, 2006); Lovejoy, *Transformations in Slavery*; James H. Sweet, *Recreating Africa: Culture, Kinship, and Religion in the African-Portuguese World, 1441–1770* (Chapel Hill: University of North Carolina Press, 2006); Stuart B. Schwartz, ed., *Tropical Babylons: Sugar and the Making of the Atlantic World, 1450–1680* (Chapel Hill: University of North Carolina Press, 2004); Chatterjee and Eaton, *Slavery and South Asian History*; James Francis Warren, *The Sulu Zone*, "The Balangingi Samal," and *Iranun and Balangingi*. As in North America, these slave systems varied in their openness to incorporating enslaved people. We also can compare resistance in Japanese work camps in Java during World War II and on Australia ranches between 1920 and 1940. In Alpers,

Campbell, and Salman, *Resisting Bondage in Indian Ocean Africa and Asia*, see Shigeru Sato, "Forced Labourers and Their Resistance in Java under Japanese Military Rule, 1942–45," 82–95, and in the same volume, Robert Castle, James Hagan, and Andrew Wells, "'Unfree' Labour on the Cattle Stations of Northern Australia, the Tea Gardens of Assam, and the Rubber Plantations of Indo-China, 1920–50," 96–113. In addition, patterns of *marronage*, that is, escapes from slavery, offer many insights into the conditions of bondage. There are strong parallels between resistance via "small-scale, short-term marronage" in Asia and Africa and what was typical in Euro–North American settlements. For example, Richard B. Allen argues that marronage rates of 4 to 5 percent in Mauritius during the late eighteenth century grew to 11 to 13 percent by the early 1820s, whereas reports of marronage in New World societies suggest rates of "often less than 1 percent per year." Underreporting may account for this low percentage. Richard B. Allen, "A Serious and Alarming Daily Evil: *Marronage* and Its Legacy in Mauritius and the Colonial Plantation World," in Alpers, Campbell, and Salman, *Slavery and Resistance in Africa and Asia*, 20–36, at 24–25. Also see "Out of the House of Bondage: Runaways, Resistance, and Marronage in Africa and the New World," special issue, *Slavery and Abolition* 6, no. 3 (1985), "Part 2: Runaways and Resistance in the New World," 37–128, and "Part 3: Marronage," 131–184.

Linking the Histories of Slavery

PART I

Links to Early Slavery

Before the arrival of Europeans and Africans, slavery was already a key component in many indigenous North American societies. When we link the discoveries of research on precontact slavery to the results of studies on European American slave systems, we see new patterns and parallels. This provides us an opportunity to sketch the kind of "big picture" of slavery that historian David Brion Davis and others have encouraged.[1]

In chapter 1, "Captives and Slaves in Indigenous North America," anthropologist Catherine M. Cameron presents a survey of indigenous slave systems operating across precontact North America. The social restrictions imposed on slaves, the agency available to them, and the levels of abuse they were likely to experience varied among cultural groups. Yet the evidence shows that Native slave societies shared general characteristics with those that would be introduced later. For example, skeletal remains exhibit signs of slavery, that is, certain individuals were selected for food deprivation, more intense labor, and violent physical abuse. Some studies suggest that the treatment of Indian slaves was similar to the semistarvation diets and physical battery found on Euro-American plantations.[2] Whether kidnapped, traded, or offered as gifts, Indian captives (like kidnapped Africans) found themselves traveling with traders and captors, sometimes over great distances. Cameron reminds us, however, that

3

PART I

wherever they went and however harshly their captors tried to strip away their identities, captives carried and spread their own traditions. Women in particular introduced new techniques and fresh ideas to their captors, especially in domestic crafts like food preparation, pottery manufacturing, and child rearing—just as when Africans and African Americans were trafficked across the plantation South.[3] Contrary to the demographics of the European Atlantic slave trade, however, most indigenous American cultures targeted women and children. Cameron's chapter provokes questions about the human relationships that develop within cultures of coercion, questions that transcend time and place. In the sweep of human history, the incorporation of captives through marriage, childbearing, adoption, and fictive kin systems served to enhance the labor capacity and economic success of households and communities, and each of these personal interactions wove emotional ties of varying strength. Whether we are examining slavery in the distant past, the recent past, or the present, how do we distinguish between strategic cooperation and true consent between captors and slaves?

In chapter 2, anthropologist Eric E. Bowne moves the stories forward from Catherine Cameron's overview of precontact indigenous slave systems. Bowne tracks routes of the slave trade from the days of early encounters between Indians and Europeans into the eighteenth and nineteenth centuries. As in the precontact period, indigenous peoples continued to take slaves to augment labor pools in their communities, to avenge or replace dead relatives, to satisfy rites of passage into manhood, or to sell as commodities. Further, as Bowne demonstrates, the migration of Europeans into North America intensified the demand for slaves. The growth in trafficking (selling for profit) accelerated Indian slaving attacks and, therefore, the free and forced migrations of indigenous peoples throughout the continent. For example, pressure from Iroquois Covenant nations forced Erie Indians to move south from the Great Lakes. On their migration from Virginia to South Carolina, the Eries survived by kidnapping and selling Indian captives to the British. Other groups, like the Chickasaws, were able to preserve their homeland base, but only by raiding their southern neighbors and traveling east to exchange Choctaw captives for British imports. The Comanches followed a third migration and slaving pattern, moving seasonally and raiding across what would become the US Southwest and northern Mexico. Bowne shows that slave raiding, commerce, and military alliances became inextricably linked.[4] Groups like the Eries, the Choctaws, and the Comanches could operate skillfully within mercantile, capitalist, and traditional systems of exchange. Indians also required their Euro-American commercial partners to accept certain Native trading traditions. Historians have stressed the economic importance to colonial economies of the export trade in animal skins supplied by Indians and the rice and tobacco produced by Africans, but in general they have undervalued the economic impact of the slave trade as a distinct economic engine that operated locally and internationally. Similarly, for the nineteenth century, the profits from cotton cargoes have proved to be distractions in economic interpretations of North American slavery. Recently, scholars have begun to reevaluate how much capital and growth were generated by the circulation of cash, credit, and enslaved human assets produced from both within and without the colonies and the new nation.[5]

The chapters by Cameron and Bowne in part I indicate the insights we gain by linking our evaluations of the conditions of slavery in early Indian societies and Euro-American communities. Both authors provide comparative perspectives challenging the perception that Indian slave systems were less disruptive, less violent, and less degrading than nineteenth-century plantation slavery. Both authors argue that although slaves did serve as prestige goods in Indian societies, they were vital economic assets in both indigenous and Euro American communities, in both state and nonstate societies.[6]

With these two chapters in mind, we can go further and consider links between the histories of slavery in the past and slavery in the present. The reality is that women and children continue to be kidnapped and traded in North America. In 2010, Nick Martin of the British newspaper *The Guardian* exposed particularly horrendous examples in Ciudad Juárez, just south of El Paso, Texas. Grim evidence began to accumulate of the sexual abuse and murder of thousands of young women and girls locally and of customers in the United States placing orders for young children.[7] We can compare and contrast the circumstances of these kinds of contemporary coercion to the slave systems described by Catherine Cameron and Eric Bowne. There are also conceptual links from Cameron and Bowne to chapters later in the volume, those by Sarah Deer (chapter 10) and Melissa Farley (chapter 11), for example. Their accounts of Indian children forced to attend Anglo-American schools and women trapped in prostitution raise difficult questions about slavery and the legacies that persist in North America today. Linking these chapters allows us to compare kidnappings across ethnic borders in the North American past with the trafficking of women and children as sex and domestic slaves in the twentieth and twenty-first centuries. This also helps place North American bondage within the context of world slavery.[8]

Part I

Notes

1. See "AHR Forum: Crossing Slavery's Boundaries." *American Historical Review* 105 (2000): 451–484, especially David Brion Davis, "Looking at Slavery in a Broader Perspective," 452–466.

2. Debra L. Martin, "Ripped Flesh and Torn Souls: Skeletal Evidence for Captivity and Slavery from the La Plata Valley, New Mexico, AD 1100–1300," in *Invisible Citizens: Captives and Their Consequences*, ed. Catherine M. Cameron (Salt Lake City: University of Utah Press, 2008), 159–180; also in *Invisible Citizens*, see Susan M. Alt, "Unwilling Immigrants: Culture, Change, and the 'Other' in Mississippian Societies," 205–222.

3. See Judith A. Habicht-Mauche, "Captive Wives? The Role and Status of Nonlocal Women on the Protohistoric Southern High Plains," in Cameron, *Invisible Citizens*, 181–204. This kind of influence continues in North American borderlands today. For example, see the work of Gloria Anzaldúa in which she contends that women in the Southwestern borderlands today survive both as ethnic mediators and as the targets of exploitation, finding creative ways to preserve the traditions of their natal groups and their sense of self-worth despite deprivation and degradation. Gloria Anzaldúa, *Borderlands: La Frontera, the New Mestiza* (San Francisco: Spinsters / Aunt Lute, 1987), 27–31, 77–82.

4. A number of studies exist that can take readers deeper into those places beyond the traditional southeastern Atlantic locus of slavery. In this volume, Paul Conrad (chapter 3) follows the forced migration of Apache captives to Havana. Elsewhere, Brett Rushforth traces Apache captives along northern trade circuits to New France. Brett Rushforth, "'A Little Flesh We Offer You: The Origins of Slavery in New France,'" in *Indian Slavery in Colonial America*, ed. Alan Gallay (Lincoln: University of Nebraska Press, 2010), 353–389, and *Bonds of Alliance: Indigenous and Atlantic Slaveries in New France* (Chapel Hill: University of North Carolina Press, 2012).

5. Robbie Ethridge, "Introduction: Mapping the Mississippian Shatter Zone," in *Mapping the Mississippian Shatter Zone: The Colonial Indian Slave Trade and Regional Instability in the American South*, ed. Robbie Ethridge and Sheri M. Shuck-Hall (Lincoln: University of Nebraska Press, 2009), 1–63, at 2. On the significance for local and regional economies of raids and sales of slaves, see E. A. S. Demers, "John Askin and Indian Slavery at Michilimackinac," in Gallay, *Indian Slavery in Colonial America*, 400–411, at 405. On the financial importance of the slave trade in Euro-American colonial and antebellum economies, see Calvin Schermerhorn, chapter 6 in this volume; Bonnie Martin, "Slavery's Invisible Engine: Mortgaging Human Property," *Journal of Southern History* 76 (November 2010): 817–866; Edward E. Baptist, *The Half Has Never Been Told: Slavery and the Making of American Capitalism* (New York: Basic Books, 2014).

6. In his article on indigenous peoples living on the Northwest Coast during the

early contact period, Kenneth M. Ames estimates that slaves comprised between 5 and 25 percent of the Indian population. As in the Euro-American South, slave ownership was not evenly distributed, which actually increased its economic and cultural impact. Kenneth M. Ames, "Slavery, Household Production, and Demography on the Southern Northwest Coast: Cables, Tacking, and Ropewalks," in Cameron, *Invisible Citizens*, 138–158. See also the classic work on slavery in the Pacific Northwest, Leland Donald, *Aboriginal Slavery on the Northwest Coast of North America* (Berkeley: University of California Press, 1997). See also Claudio Saunt, *A New Order of Things: Property, Power, and the Transformation of the Creek Indians, 1733–1816* (Cambridge: Cambridge University Press, 1999). For additional evidence on this point, see Rushforth, *Bonds of Alliance*, especially chapter 1.

7. Nick Martin, "Mexican Woman Tells of Ordeal with Cross-Border Child Traffickers," *The Guardian* (UK), January 11, 2010, accessed December 12, 2013, http://www.theguardian.com/world/2010/jan/11/mexican-woman-border-child-traffic.

8. In *Invisible Citizens*, Catherine M. Cameron assembled scholarly studies that lay out a more expansive understanding of slavery in North America and beyond. In that volume, see Laura Lee Junker, "The Impact of Captured Women on Cultural Transmission in Contact-Period Philippine Slave-Raiding Chiefdoms," 110–137, and Brenda J. Bowser, "Captives in Amazonia: Becoming Kin in a Predatory Landscape," 262–282.

1

Captives and Slaves in Indigenous North America

Catherine M. Cameron

Captive taking and enslavement have been found in almost every society in the world and in ancient, as well as modern, times.[1] As an archaeologist, my purpose in studying slavery has been a concern that my discipline has overlooked the presence of a significant category of social person in prehistoric societies—captives, many of whom became slaves. I have used ethnohistoric, historic, ethnographic, and archaeological data to investigate the roles captives may have played in prehistoric societies and especially their contributions to those societies.[2] I have argued that archaeologists ignore an important vehicle for the transmission of cultural practices by overlooking the presence of captives in the prehistoric small-scale societies they study. Here I explore the nature of captive taking and enslavement among indigenous small-scale societies in North America. I hope to further the goals of this volume by widening our view of the slave and slavery in North America.

I examine indigenous enslavement in four regions of Native North America: the Northeast, the Southeast, the Southwest Borderlands, and the Northwest Coast. In all of these regions, warfare and captive taking have been well documented in the ethnohistoric record (which I access primarily through secondary sources), and there is archaeological evidence for these practices prehistorically. These regions show substantial similarities in captive taking and enslavement across North America, but also some important differences. The ethnographic and ethnohistoric sources I use, of course, document postcontact captive taking and enslavement, which makes their application to the prehistoric past problematic. The entry of Europeans into North America caused dramatic changes to indigenous societies, including significant increases in warfare, captive taking, and enslavement among these groups. Still, these accounts are the best source of analogy we have for a class of people who have, until recently, been largely invisible in the archaeological record.

I begin by describing each of the four North American regions and then discuss three intertwined topics. First, I explore how captives/slaves (the words combined to suggest the origin of most indigenous slaves) were created and incorporated into captor societies. The violence that created captives/slaves was an integral part of male status striving in indigenous societies. Ideologies of exclusion were based on kinship and in some cases included the belief that slaves could be transformed into kin. Next, I examine how slaves were valued by their owners. Slaves in indigenous societies tended to be valued for social and symbolic reasons, as well as for their labor.[3] Finally, I examine the ways that captives/slaves affected the social boundaries of the societies they joined. In three of the four regions examined here, the presence of slaves as a degraded social class tended to strengthen social boundaries.

CAPTIVE TAKING IN FOUR REGIONS OF NORTH AMERICA

Historic and prehistoric groups in the Northwest, Southeast, Southwest Borderlands, and Northwest Coast can be characterized as *small-scale societies*, a term that includes a wide range of social forms typically glossed as "chiefdoms," "bands," or "tribes."[4] As is typical of small-scale societies, warfare and raiding were common and linked to male status striving. Captive taking was often a primary goal of aggression. Captives in the indigenous small-scale societies of North America (as in many societies around the world) were most frequently women and children.[5] For the captive taker, captured males were dangerous and difficult to control, while women and children were more manageable and more readily incorporated into captor society. This section provides a general overview of these societies and background on their warfare and captive-taking practices. Although these descriptions are not meant to imply homogeneity in practices across regions or through time, I note that warfare and captive taking were not activities introduced by Europeans but had considerable antiquity in each region.

Northeast

The Northeast includes both the Iroquoian groups of the eastern Great Lakes and the diverse groups of central Algonquians and Sioux in the western Great Lakes (or Pays d'en Haut).[6] Horticulturalists, hunters, and fishermen, northeastern people lived in longhouses or lodges clustered into settlements of varying size, with the largest settlements holding fifteen hundred to two thousand people.[7] Longhouses were occupied by kin groups and their affines. Widespread warfare and captive taking were described by early-seventeenth-century visitors to the area, especially Jesuit missionaries and French explorers. Warfare increased dramatically in the second half of the seventeenth century as a result of European contact, but it had clearly been important prior to this time.

Warfare in the Northeast was an integral part of social life and an essential avenue for young men to follow in order to gain prestige and status; in fact, success in war determined much of a young man's future life path.[8] Called "mourning wars," these violent encounters had a number of social values, including restoring lost population, confronting the deaths of group members, and ensuring the continuity of the social group. Captive taking was of utmost importance, as indicated by early ethnographic accounts, iconography, and linguistic analysis.[9] "The act of enslavement dominated and defined Natives' thinking about slavery far more than the long-term status of those they enslaved."[10] There is archaeological evidence that patterns of warfare described for the postcontact period also existed prehistorically.[11]

Southeast

The Southeast was, at the time of European contact, an area with a sizeable indigenous population organized into dozens of chiefdoms.[12] Discrete territories consisted of towns and villages of varying sizes, and each chiefdom had at least one town with a ceremonial center of mounds or open space around which houses were built. Towns were typically built on high ground along rivers or streams, and some were surrounded by a palisade.[13] Unoccupied areas between chiefdoms apparently served as buffer zones.[14] The earliest Spanish explorers, in the sixteenth century, described the southeastern chiefdoms as ranked and hierarchical societies, with rulers carried around on litters, surrounded by retainers and deferential commoners.[15] The rulers dressed, ate, and lived considerably better than the commoners, and they also seem to have kept large numbers of slaves.[16] Warfare and captive taking were widespread in the postcontact Southeast, but there is also considerable archaeological evidence for prehistoric warfare and captive taking.[17]

Chiefdoms are unstable political formations, and warfare among competing chiefdoms is common. The chronicles of Hernando de Soto, who led the first European expeditionary force to traverse the Southeast, described indigenous warfare as constant and unceasing, an established element of social interactions among the chiefdoms of the region.[18] Warfare was motivated by revenge, as well as by the desire of some powerful chiefs to control outlying districts and demand tribute from them.[19] Perhaps the most important motive, however, was status striving among young men. Captives were the most prestigious prizes of war, and for a young man, the taking of a captive was an enormous accomplishment that was celebrated by the entire community in song and ceremony.[20]

Southwest Borderlands

When the Spaniard Francisco Vásquez de Coronado led the first major European expedition into the Southwest Borderlands in 1540, he encountered a range of indigenous people. Some were sedentary agriculturalists, some were nomadic hunters, and others used a combination of strategies to stay alive in this arid region. Pueblo villages were strung out along the Rio Grande as far north as Taos and in a line that extended west to the Hopi mesas. North and west of the pueblos were the Utes and Navajos, respectively, and on the eastern plains were the Comanches, Kiowas, and Apaches, among other groups.[21] Some were recent arrivals in the region. The Navajos and Apaches were Athapaskans who had moved from Canada and entered the Southwest about the same time as the Spanish. The Comanches were a Shoshonean group who reestablished themselves in the southern plains during the late seventeenth century.

All of these groups, including the Spanish intruders, were involved in raiding, captive taking, and enslavement.[22] Spanish desire for labor and the opening of a globalized market for slaves dramatically increased the frequency and violence of raiding and captive taking, yet there is good evidence, including ethnohistory, iconography, and bioarchaeology, that captive taking also predated the Spanish entrada.[23] Here I focus primarily on the Comanches and Navajos, as they are the groups among which captive taking and enslavement have been best documented.[24] As in the other regions, raiding and captive taking created status and wealth for Comanche and Navajo warriors.

Northwest Coast

The Northwest Coast comprises the Pacific coast of North America from southern Alaska to northern California, bounded on the east by coastal mountain ranges.[25] When first contacted by Europeans in the late eighteenth century, the Northwest Coast was a densely populated area whose people spoke a diversity of languages.[26] Focusing on marine and terrestrial resources, Northwest Coast people lived in large, permanent villages and towns, varying in population from a few dozen to as many as one thousand people. Although there was no overarching political organization and each village operated independently, the region had a surprisingly hierarchical social organization. The major social division was that between free individuals and slaves. Within the free class were chiefs, who held many titles; other elites, who held few titles; and commoners.[27]

Warfare in this region was undertaken for the protection of status, to exact revenge for the loss of status, and for the capture of slaves, who provided labor and represented wealth.[28] Captive taking was common between neighboring groups, but long-distance maritime attacks were also reported.[29] Women and children were preferred captives, and while many males were killed during raids, others were enslaved.[30] Slave labor was important in the production of food and its use in the maintenance of elite status.[31] A number of lines of evidence, including ethnohistoric, bioarchaeological, and archaeological, suggest that warfare, captive taking, and enslavement were practiced on the Northwest Coast prior to European contact.[32]

INCORPORATION INTO CAPTOR SOCIETY

> "Slavery…is but a temporary status in a process through which enemy others are civilized and transformed into intimate consanguines."[33]

Captives were taken through violence, but "captive" was a temporary role. Once they reached the captors' settlement, a social location had to be opened for these alien individuals. In many—but not all—indigenous societies, captives faced a range of fates, and their status and that of their children were not necessarily fixed. Indigenous captives could be killed, enslaved, married, or adopted, and their fates depended in part on the age, gender, and personal characteristics of each captive, as well as the needs and caprice of captors.[34] This section explores factors that affected the social locations offered to captives in the regions under consideration, including the ways slaves were obtained, as well as captor ideology with regard to "others" and its effect on whether captives could ever become kin.

CATHERINE M. CAMERON

The Creation and Incorporation of Captives

> They set up a theater on the hill and went into the woods in search of sticks or thorns, whatever they fancied. Thus armed, they formed two lines, a hundred on one side and a hundred on the other, and forced us, all naked as we were, to pass in between along that path of fury and anguish. There was rivalry among them to see who could land the most blows and the heaviest.[35]

Captives in the indigenous societies of the Americas were typically members of an enemy group that had been vanquished in battle. As they entered the village of their captors, captives often encountered a wave of anger, despair at the death of hometown warriors, and a desire for vengeance. These feelings subsided with time, but initially they structured relations between captives and their captors. Groups in the Northeast and Southeast had formal rituals in which some captives were tortured to death to atone for earlier deaths in captor families.[36] Even those not slated for death generally underwent rituals of "social death,"[37] in which the captive's prior social identity was erased and the victim was recast as a member of the new social group.

As the quote above indicates, captives in the Northeast were likely to undergo brutal treatment that either resulted in their death or ended in their adoption. Captives were killed to avenge the death of captor kin or adopted to replace deceased members of the group. Among the Iroquois of the eastern Great Lakes region, after hours of torture, "headmen apportioned [captives] out to grieving families, whose matrons then chose either to adopt or to execute them."[38] Women and children were most likely to be spared torture and death and be adopted, and the easy assimilation of young children made them especially sought after captives,[39] but no options were completely closed for captives of any age or sex. Adopted captives were given the name and identity of a deceased member of the captor's social group, but this did not ensure them treatment as full kin and the actual status of adoptees was variable. In the western Great Lakes region, "indigenous slaves lived under a wide range of conditions, some dehumanizing and others nearly familial, and a particular slave's place in the community could change over time."[40] Arguing for the slavelike situation of Iroquoian adoptees, Starna and Watkins point out that the initial torture meted out to captives often left them permanently marked; especially common was the amputation or mutilation of the fingers.[41] This meant that their slave status would always be obvious. Captives were assigned the most menial and difficult tasks, including gathering firewood, fetching water, and serving as porters. Young female captives were subject to sexual abuse.[42] Yet some captives could attain positions of prominence in northeastern captor groups, reflecting the fluidity and flexibility of captive status.

Captives experienced similar brutal treatment among the Comanches of the Southwest Borderlands. The Comanches took captives of all ages and sexes,[43] although in a sample of Mexican citizens redeemed from the Comanches, more than two-thirds were males, mostly captured as children or teenagers.[44] Young boys were desired as tenders for the large herds of horses the Comanches had acquired, but Hämäläinen notes that women were increasingly desired as wife-laborers, especially in the early nineteenth century, as an increasingly larger labor force was needed to care for livestock and produce buffalo robes.[45] Captives underwent horrible abuse during their first days of captivity in an attempt to strip them of their previous identity through the process of "natal alienation."[46] Although some captives were eventually incorporated into Comanche society as wives or subsidiary kin, others remained in a servile position until they died, escaped, or were redeemed. The youngest children were most readily incorporated into captor societies, and those below age five were especially desired.[47]

Less is known about the initial treatment of captives among the Navajos. Like the Comanches, they were involved in raiding for captives to sell to the Spanish and other groups, primarily the Utes and Paiutes.[48] They often took women and children in raids and kidnapped young boys who were herding their family's flocks in isolated areas. The Navajos called the Paiute people *báyodzín*, synonymous with "slave."[49] Efforts to assess the slavelike status of Navajo captives turn up mixed results,[50] with some captives well treated and others not. For example, in Spanish reports of five Mexican males who were taken as teenagers or preteens during the mid-nineteenth century and were later either recovered or had their experiences described to Spanish authorities, four seem to have been satisfied with their treatment, and one who had been captive for seventeen years had two wives and no desire to return to Spanish society. A fifth male captive reported beatings and generally bad treatment. Franciscan clergy described Navajo slaves forced into hard labor. Female captives were not taught the highly valued art of weaving, and captives could be killed at the whim of their masters.[51]

Treatment of captives was somewhat softer in the Southeast. They were generally not abused on the return journey to the captor's village, where the successful warrior handed over his captives to the community after a giddy celebration of his remarkable accomplishment.[52] At that point, as in the Northeast, it was women who decided a captive's fate: "Beloved [high-ranking] women sorted through the captives, deciding whose fiery

15

deaths would atone for past murders, who would take the place of deceased clan members, and whose labor would enrich the clan's wealth and prestige."[53] As in the Northeast, captured women and children were most often adopted, while men were beaten and prodded by "beloved women" in an effort to assess their health, strength, and prior crimes against the captor group. Captives selected for death were generally tied to a stake, tortured, and burned alive.[54] Those adopted went through a series of purification rituals that involved singing, taking ceremonial baths, ingesting cleansing herbs, and donning the clothes and hairstyles typical of the captor group.[55] Captives not killed or adopted became slaves.[56] Slavery was apparently a common fate for captives, and William Bartram, an eighteenth-century visitor to the Creek and Seminole territories, reported male slaves in every town,[57] although Bartram likely overlooked women captives incorporated into the captor groups as slaves or wives.

Captives taken by Northwest Coast warriors had far fewer options than those in the other regions. Except for the occasional slave redeemed by his or her family or freed (see below), slave status was the only social location open them.[58] Interestingly, Northwest Coast societies do not seem to have had the elaborate rituals signaling the death of a captive's previous social identity that were common in the Northeast and Southeast.[59] As both captives and captors shared a common understanding of slavery and how slaves were produced, seizure in a raid may have been all that was necessary to transform a victim into a slave. In some groups, slaves could be identified by the short hair they were forced to wear or by the presence or absence of cranial deformation practiced by some groups.[60]

In the Northwest Coast, the control of locations where spawning salmon could be easily procured was the primary source of wealth, and this kept the Northwest Coast elite from ever permitting captives to become kin.[61] There were other limited resources in the Northwest Coast that elite families were also reluctant to share: songs, dances, ritual paraphernalia, myths, and names.[62] Desire to maintain absolute family control of this intellectual property prevented slaves in the Northwest Coast from ever being invited into the kinship system of their masters.[63]

The Ideology of Captivity and Opportunities for Transformation

Whereas race was the key defining characteristic for slaves in class-based Euro-American society, among indigenous groups *kinship* was the central fact that structured all social relationships. Because captives in small-scale societies were outside the kinship system of their captors, they were defined as nonhuman, at least initially. Yet the boundary separating captives from captor kin networks was not always fixed and could sometimes be altered, at times not only allowing humans to change into animals, but also allowing slaves to transform into humans.

Slaves in the Northeast and Southeast were often classed with tamed or domesticated animals. For example, the Iroquois use the same word for capturing and taming an animal as they use for taking and enslaving a captive.[64] Captives in the western Great Lakes were equated with dogs and considered a form of property that existed at the pleasure of their masters.[65] In the Southeast, the term for slaves ("owned people") translated for some groups as "domesticated animal" or "tamed."[66] For example, among the Cherokee, human and nonhuman possessions were given the same terms, and slaves were in the same social position as animals—outside the kinship system.[67]

Many indigenous societies in North America and elsewhere were confident in their ability, Pygmalion-like, to transform their captives into useful members of their society—perhaps not in the first generation, but eventually. Captors' concepts of their captives in tropical America (an area that comprises southern Florida, the Caribbean, and parts of South America) are apt for the regions discussed here as well: "War captives were seen both as quasi animals to be domesticated and as quasi humans to be civilized."[68]

The ability of captives to become kin may have been easiest in the Northeast, as indicated by the debate among scholars of this region concerning whether adoptees achieved real kinship with their adoptive families.[69] Although many adopted captives functioned as slaves, some were able to become valued and prominent members of captor society. Captives could improve their social position by working assiduously to please their masters, and some became war leaders or other influential members of society. But "if they displeased, they were quietly and unceremoniously killed."[70] Slave status, however, was not hereditary. Children of captives were free members of captor society.[71] This suggests both the importance of the process of enslavement, which the children of captives had not experienced, and the transformative powers captors believed they held.

In the Southeast and the Southwest Borderlands, there is no doubt that some captives were slaves and remained forever outside the kinship system of their captors. But in both areas, marriage was one avenue out of slavery and into at least a semblance of membership in the captor's group. In the Southeast, "marriage did not bind captives to their host societies as tightly as did adoption. They did not become members of a clan, but they did gain some protection from their spouse's clan.... Kin ties enhanced their status, moving them from society's bottom tier into the category of people who belonged."[72] As in groups in the Northeast, slave status was confined to a single generation, and the children of slaves were free members of the society into which they were born. Even the child of a pregnant white woman captured by the Creek Indians in the late eighteenth century was adopted into a Creek clan and considered a member of their nation.[73]

In the Southwest Borderlands, Comanche captives occupied a variety of statuses based on their sex, age at capture, length of captivity, and their personal characteristics, especially their ability to learn the Comanche language.[74] Although in a sample of more than eight hundred Mexican captives, there were far more males than females, female captives were also common and were more easily incorporated into Comanche society.[75] Girls and women were involved in women's daily practices, while boys sent out as herders had far less opportunity to learn language and customs.[76] Still, captives of either sex could be incorporated through adoption, marriage, or simply acceptance as a member of Comanche society. "Incorporation was not a communal decision, nor was it marked by a ceremony. Instead, it was realized in practice through private and public interactions (for example, addressing the captive as kin) that made evident to the larger Comanche community the captive's new status."[77] Whether female or male, captives could become valued members of Comanche society. Adult male captives were rarely assimilated into Comanche society; those who were typically underwent a replacement ceremony in which they took on the identity of a deceased Comanche—much like incorporation of outsiders as kin members in northeastern societies.[78] But as in northeastern societies, incorporated outsiders almost always retained a stigma of the foreigner and were referred to using special terms.[79]

Among the Navajo, captives also faced a variety of possible statuses ranging from adoption as kin to full slavery.[80] Apache, Ute, Paiute, or Spanish women captured by an ambitious young Navajo man might be adopted into his matrilineal clan, which increased the pool of potential wives; men captured in the same raids could be sold to affluent Navajos who needed herders.[81] The status of captives in Navajo society was mutable. As among the Comanches, a captive who was immediately addressed using a proper kinship term was instantly recognized as a tribal member,[82] but not all captives were so lucky: "Few firm lines delineated the semiservile or dependent categories of kinship and quasi kinship from the harsher condition of the slave, nor did time or circumstance prohibit mobility between statuses."[83] In fact, the Navajos themselves apparently disagreed about exactly who qualified for slave status, some including as slaves those poor Navajos who labored for others.[84] There seems to be no doubt, however, that captives taken by Navajos could be bought and sold and that hard labor was often their lot. Captive women labored in fields, tending flocks, or as domestic workers; at least some male captives, though, could hold personal property and marry.[85]

In contrast to the ability of slaves in the Northeast, Southeast, and Southwest Borderlands to gain some or all of the privileges of kinship in the society of their captors, captives in the Northwest Coast had no such options. "War captives became slaves, and neither they nor their children (if any) could normally expect amelioration of this status. Neither captives nor their children could expect to be adopted into their master's kin group or to be gradually transformed into commoners."[86] Captives could be redeemed if their families paid a large ransom, but this applied almost exclusively to titleholders whose families could afford the high cost.[87] Slaves were occasionally freed by their masters on ritual occasions as part of the giving away of property. Among the Tlingits, slaves tended to be freed on "happy" occasions, such as the birth of a child to high-ranking parents.[88] Many ritual occasions, such as the death of a titleholder, called for the sacrifice of slaves, but freeing slaves (also a destruction of property from the owner's perspective) became more common as Europeans began to intervene to halt slave sacrifice.[89] With these few exceptions, slavery on the Northwest Coast was strictly bounded and did not admit the sorts of transformation found in other regions.

THE VALUE OF CAPTIVES

Trade in captives was common among indigenous societies in North America. While European demand for labor clearly increased the capture and trade of captives among Native American groups,[90] there are indications that slave trading also existed prior to European contact, including evidence of extensive trade routes over which captives were moved.[91] Although the labor of slaves was important to indigenous American societies, this section highlights the social values of indigenous captives. Captives were valued as evidence of success in warfare, of the high social rank of their owners, as prestige items that could be given as gifts to create bonds between people or groups, and as gifts to the gods, given through sacrifice. The economic value of captives was important, but their social value was more important.

A slave's symbolic value derived from the connection between warfare, captive taking, and male status striving that is found in most regions of North America and elsewhere. Once captives were returned to the captor's home, their mere presence enhanced the status of the captor—the high status of the captor was evident as a striking contrast with the low, degraded, and subservient position of the captive. Captives of all ages and genders could become retainers or household servants, constantly at the beck and call of their master or mistress; such master/slave interactions were in part a public display of the power of the slave owner. Captives could be given as gifts, and the humanity of this gift had special meaning in many indigenous societies.

In the Northeast, participation in a war party was a significant aspect of a young man's development, and his stature in his clan and village was increased by his success in battle.[92] "No honor was more important to a young man than capturing slaves. His success was celebrated in public ceremonies, etched into his war clubs, and displayed on his body with tattoos representing each enemy he had captured."[93] Once captives had been paraded through the village, brutalized, and "domesticated," their primary purpose as symbols of the triumph of captors over their enemies was largely fulfilled. Still, many continued to serve as retainers, burden carriers, and agricultural workers, relieving their masters of household tasks.[94] A seventeenth-century Seneca woman lamented to a Jesuit priest that her recently deceased daughter had had twenty slaves to accomplish her domestic duties.[95] The mother feared that unless one of these slaves died soon to follow her, her daughter might be forced to do her own work in the afterlife.

Captives/slaves in the Northeast not only enhanced captor status, but also were symbolically potent and valuable gifts in peacemaking and alliance building.[96] When antagonists sued for peace, a gift of captives signified the giving of life, rather than the taking of it. During peacetime, captives were part of diplomatic offerings intended to develop mutually profitable alliances for trade and defense. There is evidence that the use of captives to build alliances between groups was ancient. The earliest European explorers in the Northeast were often offered captives as signs of friendship from the Native American groups they encountered,[97] and enslavement and the use of captives as diplomatic tools were deeply embedded in ritual systems here.[98]

In the Southeast, as in the Northeast, warfare was one of the most important ways for young men to enhance their social status and to acquire material goods, especially captives.[99] "The society of warriors was a strictly ranked hierarchy wherein a man achieved status through accumulation of plunder, scalps, and captives."[100] Those captives who became slaves were set to work, and slave production of agricultural and tributary goods enriched their masters.[101]

Slaves enhanced the reputation of southeastern chiefs by becoming personal servants. Captives belonged to the man who had captured them and performed menial tasks for him. The captive's "primary value to his 'master' seems to have been prestige—the captive was a sort of living scalp."[102] William Bartram, traveling among the Seminoles during the late eighteenth century, reported a chief with many Yamasee captives who "served and waited upon him with signs of the most abject fear."[103] When Hernando de Soto traversed the Southeast in the mid-sixteenth century, he was often given hundreds of *tamemes* by chiefs with whom he stayed. Described by Bourne as "Indians that carry burdens," tamemes were likely captives/slaves, the word having this meaning in the Nahuatl-Mexica language.[104] At Cofitachequi (thought to be located in modern South Carolina[105]), the chieftainess whom de Soto briefly kidnapped was also described as traveling with her "female slaves."[106] Among the Calusas of southern Florida, captives functioned almost exclusively as retainers for high-ranking men and women, rather than as economically productive laborers.[107] Personal attendants to the paramount Calusa chief carried him on their shoulders on special occasions or carried his guests. Captives were also assigned to fetch water and firewood, serve as messengers, row burial canoes, and guard burial houses from predators. The importance of captives as elements of wealth and status for prominent members of Calusa society was most evident in their role as human sacrifices. Special captives (sometimes Spaniards) were selected and prepared for the annual harvest ceremony, when the paramount chief demonstrated his control over life and death by having the captives beheaded. Other captives were killed at funeral ceremonies to accompany their masters to the afterworld.[108]

As in the Northeast, captives in the Southeast were also important in establishing relationships between groups or soothing over conflicts. "An exchange of captives commonly accompanied peace between former enemies."[109] Historic accounts report a number of such exchanges during the eighteenth century between Chickasaws, Creeks, and Cherokees.[110] Native Americans also offered captives to establish peace with Europeans and demanded payment for the return of European captives. Hernando de Soto was offered women by southeastern chiefs in an effort to gain an alliance with him, evidence of the antiquity of use of captives in establishing political relationships.[111]

In the Southwest Borderlands, captives had considerable social value, and, as elsewhere, the most effective avenue toward gaining social status was success in war. Among the Comanches, men who had not gone on a raid were poorly regarded.[112] Comanche men who owned no horses or women were at the lowest end of the social strata, and raids allowed them to steal these symbols of success and masculinity.

If there was an all-embracing internal force behind the rise of the Comanche empire, it was the relentless competition for social prestige among Comanche men. Violent seizure of livestock and captives through pillage represented for men the main path to social acceptance: it gave them access to wealth and women and lifted them toward full manhood.[113]

Not only was warfare the primary avenue toward status for Comanche males, it also offered one of the only opportunities for male captives to improve their social standing. Male captives who showed respect for their captors and demonstrated courage, especially those who were successful in war, were generally able to gain the same rights as Comanche men.[114]

Among the Navajos during the late eighteenth and early nineteenth centuries, raiding was often undertaken by men from poor communities or those from wealthier communities who were dependent on their more affluent kin.[115] As among the Comanches, in order to gain status and reach full adulthood in Navajo society, young men had to acquire wives and animals. Men who had become wealthy through amassing large flocks of sheep also controlled most marriageable women. Raiding for women and animals was often the only avenue toward success open to young men who lacked the means to purchase wives or animals. The women they captured increased the number of available wives in these men's matrilineal outfits, and any male captives could be sold to wealthy Navajos or to the Spanish for profit.

On the Northwest Coast, slave labor created wealth for slave owners.[116] Slaves were involved in all major areas of food production, they performed all or almost all of the household chores for titleholder households, and they built houses and made craft goods.[117] Slaves were vital for producing the wealth necessary for titleholders to host status-enhancing feasts, including helping to amass the food and other goods that were necessary for these events.[118] Yet equally important was the slave's symbolic value as a prestige good. They enhanced the status of their owner by serving as personal retainers.[119] They attended to menial tasks at ceremonial occasions, assisted their master in enforcing social control, and were assigned as personal maids to a titleholder's female relatives. Slaves were held almost exclusively by elite titleholders and were an important indicator of the owner's status, including the individual's spiritual power—a good person was one with many slaves.[120]

Northwest Coast slaves were given as gifts to other titleholders invited to status-enhancing feasts; they could be traded for furs and other goods to be given away at such feasts; and they might be sacrificed at feasts to demonstrate the wealth and power of the titleholder host.[121] Highly valued captives/slaves were moved along ancient trade routes.[122] Historic records have permitted the reconstruction of major northern and southern slave-trading routes in the Northwest Coast on which slaves could be moved hundreds of miles.[123] These routes closely correspond to the prehistoric routes by which obsidian moved, supporting the notion of their antiquity.[124]

CAPTIVES AND SOCIAL BOUNDARIES

In spite of being abject "others," slaves had significant effects on the social boundaries of the societies they joined. Social categories of race, class/status, or ethnicity are imagined communities subject to constant manipulation and redefinition, yet the boundaries of such groups can also be firmly defended, and captives are often integral to this process. For example, strong feelings of difference *between* ethnic groups are just as important as the common "ways of doing" that define them.[125] In fact, ethnic groups must have ways of interacting with other groups that prevent ethnic modification. Even where captives made up a large proportion of captor society, they did not necessarily dissolve or change social boundaries; instead, they could strengthen them.

Overdeveloped feelings of superiority by slave owners are common in societies of all social levels around the world.[126] Of most interest here is how these attitudes were constructed through interactions with captives and how they could maintain social boundaries even in multiethnic societies. In all four areas under consideration, captives arrived as despised others. Slaves in the Southeast, Southwest Borderlands, and the Northwest Coast strengthened boundaries between ethnic groups or status classifications by being exemplary of "incorrect" ways of behaving. In contrast, captives in the Northeast were often forced to become careful and assiduous replicators of captor cultural practices if they hoped to live. However, the result in the northeastern example was also the strengthening of boundaries around the social group.

In the Southeast, slaves acquired by the Cherokees (called *atsi nahsa'i*) were vital to the Cherokee sense of group identity because their presence allowed free members of the society to calibrate "correct" behavior by observing the incorrect behavior of their atsi nahsa'i.[127] As in many small-scale societies, membership in a clan was far more important than identification as Cherokee, and clan membership is what atsi nahsa'i lacked. Because slaves could not adopt the manners and comportment of a proper kinsman or kinswoman (not having any kin), they were daily reminders of improper ways of conducting oneself. "The presence of a deviant, an atsi nahsa'i, in Cherokee society reaffirmed the norm. By clearly demonstrating inconveniences and dangers of not being a member of a Cherokee clan, the atsi nahsa'i helped establish and strengthen group identity among the Cherokee."[128]

The presence of captives also aided in the policing of social boundaries among the Navajos and Comanches. Because captive women in Navajo communities could not be taught the sacred art of weaving, they were always marginal, even if they married or were adopted into a clan. "By the nineteenth century, some female binaalté [slaves] might have begun to serve as social boundary markers, especially those adopted or born into ancillary captive or slave clans, where institutional marginalization solidified in-group identities while retaining for the slave some assimilative benefits of kinship."[129] Furthermore, the practice of Enemy Way Ceremonies, which focus on driving out alien ghosts, suggests that outsiders in Navajo society were used to cement Navajo social solidarity in ways similar to the use of atsi nahsa'i among the Cherokees.[130] Among the Comanches, captives never completely lost their status as outsiders, and the slur *kwuhupu* (which conveyed the ideas of "captive" and "wife") hurled at an incorporated male captive not only reminded him that he remained an outsider but also strengthened the positions of in-group Comanche men and enhanced their sense of masculinity.[131]

Among the Tlingits of the Northwest Coast, as in many Northwest Coast societies, slaves were important to the process of social differentiation. Tlingit nobles considered themselves knowledgeable and moral in contrast with the lowest tiers of society, which included slaves and other marginal people who were called *nichkakáawu yahaayí*, or "dried fish slaves."[132] The *nichkakáawu* (a group including illegitimate children, criminals, and the incompetent) were incomplete and profane people, their lazy and immodest behavior a stark contrast to the proper comportment of the aristocrats. True slaves, on the other hand, were so far beyond the bounds of society that they were not considered people at all. "The *nichkakáawu* and the slaves existed not only as a social category but as a moral imperative as well. Their existence was a constant reminder to those above them of the consequences of not showing respect to others and of having no self-respect."[133]

Captives in the Northeast who were allowed to live were adopted, even though their day-to-day existence might be much like that of slaves.[134] Because slave status in northeastern societies was varied and changeable, rather than serve as daily reminders of incorrect social behavior, captives were required to studiously replicate the cultural behavior of their captors. Their place in society was at least partially dependent on how successful they were at accurate cultural replication. Captives in the Northeast were taken in part to build up group membership that had been depleted by warfare. "Policing the boundaries of slave status was thus less important than it would be in Atlantic societies that demanded slaves primarily for their productive and perpetual labor."[135] The effectiveness of captives in strengthening social group boundaries is evident in the fact that, toward the end of the seventeenth century, perhaps two-thirds of the people calling themselves Oneidas were non-Iroquois captives,[136] yet the cultural practices of the Oneidas continued. In other words, the boundaries of the social group were maintained in spite of a massive turnover in personnel. The large number of captives present in Iroquois settlements was a result of the intense warfare that engulfed the Northeast at this period. In spite of the many problems of accommodating so many captives, the Iroquois had great success in erasing their natal allegiances and incorporating them as members of Iroquois groups.[137]

CONCLUSIONS

This chapter has explored aspects of the role of captives/slaves in indigenous societies in four regions of North America. Captives/slaves arrived in captor society with an alien identity and one that was generally associated with a detested enemy. They were then either eliminated or assigned a social location, albeit most often on the lowest rungs of the captor society. Indigenous small-scale societies constructed "others" on the basis of kin group membership. The ideology of social group membership among some groups permitted captives or their offspring to become kin, but this was not always the case. The Northwest Coast, because of emphasis on control of land-based resources and intellectual property, created a slave status from which few slaves ever escaped. In the other three regions discussed (and in other parts of North America), captor ideology allowed for the transformation of captive to kin. In the Northeast, the Southeast, and the Southwest Borderlands, social group size was an important avenue toward power, and captives added to group size. This is one reason that captives—or at least their offspring—might become kin group members. The mutability of human, animal, and object forms in indigenous ideology opened a space where captor social location could be negotiated.

Although slaves worked for their masters and their labor created wealth, it was the social or symbolic values of slaves that tended to be foregrounded in indigenous societies. The presence of slaves allowed masters to see themselves as superior beings (an almost universal pattern).[138] Slaves served as a social counterpoint, a daily reminder of the power of their masters. Slaves were retainers, litter carriers, burden bearers, concubines, drudge wives; they fanned, fed, and dressed their masters and mistresses. They were given away as gifts and party favors; they were presented to seal alliances. The arrival of Europeans in North America was transformative to these small-scale societies. They were swiftly linked to a global market for slaves, which dramatically increased warfare and imparted a strong economic value to captives. I investigate this transformation elsewhere,[139] but here I attempt to explore the place captives may have occupied in indigenous societies prior to extensive European influence (at least to the extent possible using ethnohistorical data).

The display of superiority by slave masters also played an important role in maintaining social boundaries. Among the indigenous societies discussed here, the public display of the captive/slave's degraded position and the superiority of the captor were effective in maintaining the social boundaries even in the absence of formal laws. This was not the only avenue through which social boundaries were upheld. In the Northeast, where slave status was a less important social category, captives might become assiduous replicators of captor culture, creating another avenue through which social boundaries could be maintained. Captives in the Northeast were acting in their own self-interest, because lack of compliance and conformity could result in death, but there were also other reasons, including a strong desire to leave the outcast status, for following captor social rules to the letter.

The argument of this chapter is that captives were common in small-scale societies in the Americas and that their presence had important effects on these groups. Captives are a category of social person that has been overlooked by archaeologists, a point I make elsewhere.[140] In this chapter, I hope to contribute to the goals of *Linking the Histories of Slavery: North America and Its Borderlands* by highlighting the fundamental role that warfare and captive taking played in small-scale societies. Captives may have been marginal individuals, but they were an active part of the social organization of these societies.

Notes

1. David Brion Davis, *The Problem of Slavery in Western Culture* (Ithaca, NY: Cornell University Press, 1966); Davis, *Inhuman Bondage: The Rise and Fall of Slavery in the New World* (Oxford: Oxford University Press, 2006); Moses I. Finley, *Ancient Slavery and Modern Ideology* (New York: Viking Press, 1980); Milton Meltzer, *Slavery: A World History*,

updated ed. (Boston: DeCapo Press, 1993[1971–1972]); Orlando Patterson, *Slavery and Social Death* (Cambridge, MA: Harvard University Press, 1982).

2. Catherine M. Cameron, "Introduction: Captives in Prehistory: Agents of Social Change," in *Invisible Citizens: Captives and Their Consequences*, ed. Catherine M. Cameron (Salt Lake City: University of Utah Press, 2008), 1–24; Cameron, "Captives and Culture Change: Implications for Archaeology," *Current Anthropology* 52, no. 2 (2011): 169–209; Cameron, "Captives in the Past: Contexts for Prehistory" (unpublished manuscript).

3. For contrast, see Joaquín Rivaya-Martínez, "Becoming Comanches: Patterns of Captive Incorporation into Comanche Kinship Networks, 1820–1875," in *On the Borders of Love and Power: Families and Kinship in the Intercultural American Southwest*, ed. David Wallace Adams and Crista DeLuzio (Berkeley: University of California Press, 2012), 50.

4. David G. Anderson, *The Savannah River Chiefdoms: Political Change in the Late Prehistoric Southeast* (Tuscaloosa: University of Alabama Press, 1994); Marvin Jeter, "Ripe for Colonial Exploitation: Ancient Traditions of Violence and Enmity as Preludes to the Indian Slave Trade," in *Native American Adoption, Captivity, and Slavery in Changing Contexts*, ed. Max Carocci and Stephanie Pratt (New York: Palgrave Macmillan, 2012). For discussion of chiefdoms, see Robbie Ethridge, "Introduction: Mapping the Mississippian Shatter Zone," in *Mapping the Mississippian Shatter Zone: The Colonial Indian Slave Trade and Regional Instability in the American South*, ed. Robbie Ethridge and Sheri M. Shuck-Hall (Lincoln: University of Nebraska Press, 2009). For discussion of anthropological understandings of tribes, see Severin Fowles, "From Social Type to Social Process: Placing 'Tribe' in a Historical Framework," in *The Archaeology of Tribal Societies*, ed. W. Parkinson (Ann Arbor, MI: International Monographs in Prehistory, 2002).

5. Cameron, "Introduction: Captives in Prehistory" and "Captives and Culture Change."

6. Brett Rushforth, "'A Little Flesh We Offer You': The Origins of Indian Slavery in New France," *William and Mary Quarterly* 60, no. 4 (2003): 777–809; Rushforth, *Bonds of Alliance: Indigenous and Atlantic Slaveries in New France* (Chapel Hill: University of North Carolina Press, 2012); Peter Peregrine, "Social Death and Resurrection in the Western Great Lakes," in Cameron, *Invisible Citizens*.

7. William N. Fenton, "Northern Iroquoian Culture Patterns," in *Handbook of North American Indians*, vol. 15, *Northeast*, ed. Bruce G. Trigger (Washington, DC: Smithsonian Institution, 1978); Bruce G. Trigger, *The Children of Aataentsic I: A History of the Huron People to 1660* (Montreal: McGill-Queen's University Press, 1976).

8. Daniel K. Richter, "War and Culture: The Iroquois Experience," *William and Mary Quarterly* 40, no. 4 (1983): 528–559; Trigger, *Children of Aataentsic*, 145–146.

9. Richter, "War and Culture"; Rushforth, *Bonds of Alliance*; Trigger, *Children of Aataentsic*, 70.

10. Rushforth, *Bonds of Alliance*, 95.

11. Ibid., 21–22; Trigger, *Children of Aataentsic*, 144–145, 159; James A. Tuck, "Northern Iroquoian Prehistory," in Trigger, *Handbook of North American Indians*, vol. 15, *Northeast*, 326.

12. Anderson, *Savannah River Chiefdoms*; Ethridge, "Introduction," 8; Robbie Ethridge, "The Emergence of the Colonial South: Colonial Indian Slaving, the Fall of the Precontact Mississippian World, and the Emergence of a New Social Geography in the American South, 1540–1730," in Carocci and Pratt, *Native American Adoption*, 49; Alan Gallay, *The Indian Slave Trade: The Rise of the English Empire in the American South, 1670–1717* (New Haven, CT: Yale University Press, 2002), 10–19.

13. Charles Hudson, *The Southeastern Indians* (Knoxville: University of Tennessee Press, 1976), 210–211.

14. For example, Edward G. Bourne, *Narratives of the Career of Hernando de Soto* (New York: A. S. Barnes, 1904), 60–64.

15. Anderson, *Savannah River Chiefdoms*, 57; Bourne, *Hernando de Soto*; Hudson, *Southeastern Indians*, 203–210.

16. Anderson, *Savannah River Chiefdoms*, 57. Bourne, *Hernando de Soto*; Gallay, *The Indian Slave Trade*, 29.

17. Susan Alt, "Unwilling Immigrants: Culture, Change, and the 'Other' in Mississippian Societies," in Cameron, *Invisible Citizens*; David H. Dye, "Art, Ritual, and Chiefly Warfare in the Mississippian World," in *Hero, Hawk, and Open Hand: American Indian Art of the Ancient Midwest and South*, ed. Richard F. Townsend and Robert V. Sharp (New Haven, CT: Yale University Press, 2004); David H. Dye and Adam King, "Desecrating the Sacred Ancestor Temples: Chiefly Conflict and Violence in the American Southeast," in *North American Indigenous Warfare and Ritual Violence*, ed. Richard J. Chacon and Rubén G. Mendoza (Tucson: University of Arizona Press, 2007); Hudson, *Southeastern Indians*, 241–242; Matthew H. Jennings, "Violence in a Shattered World," in Ethridge and Shuck-Hall, *Mapping the Mississippian Shatter Zone*; Jeter, "Ripe for Colonial Exploitation."

18. Bourne, *Hernando de Soto*.

19. Anderson, *Savannah River Chiefdoms*, 99; Chester B. DePratter, *Late Prehistoric and Early Historic Chiefdoms in the Southeastern United States* (New York: Garland Press, 1991); Hudson, *Southeastern Indians*, 240.

20. Christina Snyder, *Slavery in Indian Country: The Changing Face of Captivity in Early America* (Cambridge, MA: Harvard University Press, 2010), 91.

21. James F. Brooks, *Captives and Cousins: Slavery, Kinship, and Community in the Southwest Borderlands* (Chapel Hill: University of North Carolina Press, 2002), 33.

22. Ibid.

23. Ibid.; Ryan P. Harrod, "Centers of Control: Revealing Elites among the Ancestral Pueblo during the 'Chaco Phenomenon,'" *International Journal of Paleopathology* 2, nos. 2–3 (2012):123–135; Timothy A. Kohler and Kathryn K. Turner, "Raiding for Women in the Prehispanic Northern Pueblo Southwest? A Pilot Examination," *Current Anthropology* 47, no. 6 (2006): 1035–1045; Debra L. Martin, "Ripped Flesh and Torn Souls: Skeletal Evidence for Captivity and Slavery from the La Plata Valley, New Mexico, AD 1100–1300," in Cameron, *Invisible Citizens*; Polly Schaafsma, "Head Trophies and Scalping: Images in Southwest Rock Art," in *The Taking and Displaying of Human Body Parts as Trophies by Amerindians*, ed. Richard J. Chacon and David H. Dye (New York: Springer, 2007).

24. Brooks, *Captives and Cousins*; David M. Brugge, *Navajos in the Catholic Church Records of New Mexico, 1694–1875* (Santa Fe, NM: School for Advanced Research Press, 2010[1968]); Brugge, "The Spanish Borderlands: Aboriginal Slavery," in *Encyclopedia of the North American Colonies*, ed. Jacob Ernest Cooke (New York: Charles Scribner's Sons, 1993); Pekka Hämäläinen, *The Comanche Empire* (New Haven, CT: Yale University Press, 2008); Rivaya-Martínez, "Becoming Comanches." As Brugge, *Navajos in the Catholic Church*, notes at 128, under Spanish domination, the Pueblos held few captives, and those whom they did have were generally treated much like those in Spanish households.

25. Kenneth M. Ames and Herbert D. G. Maschner, *Peoples of the Northwest Coast: Their Archaeology and Prehistory* (London: Thames and Hudson, 1999); Leland Donald, *Aboriginal Slavery on the Northwest Coast of North America* (Berkeley: University of California Press, 1997).

26. Ames and Maschner, *Peoples of the Northwest Coast*.

27. Ibid., 27.

28. Ibid.; Donald, *Aboriginal Slavery*.

29. Ames and Maschner, *Peoples of the Northwest Coast*, 199; Donald, *Aboriginal Slavery*, 106.

30. Donald, *Aboriginal Slavery*, 112–113.

31. Ibid.

32. Kenneth M. Ames, "Slavery, Household Production, and Demography on the Southern Northwest Coast: Cables, Tacking, and Ropewalks," in Cameron, *Invisible Citizens*; Ames and Maschner, *Peoples of the Northwest Coast*, 190; Jerome S. Cybulski, *A Greenville Burial Ground: Human Remains and Mortuary Elements in British Columbia Prehistory* (Hull, QC: Canadian Museum of Civilization, 1992); Donald, *Aboriginal Slavery*, 201–213.

33. Fernando Santos-Granero, *Vital Enemies: Slavery, Predation, and the Amerindian Political Economy of Life* (Austin: University of Texas Press, 2009), 174–175.

34. Cameron, "Introduction: Captives in Prehistory" and "Captives and Culture Change."

35. Allan Greer, *The Jesuit Relations: Natives and Missionaries in Seventeenth-Century North America* (Boston: Bedford / St. Martin's, 2000), 162. This passage references Father Isaac Jogues's captivity among the Iroquois in 1642.

36. Rushforth, "A Little Flesh We Offer You"; Snyder, *Slavery in Indian Country*.

37. Patterson, *Slavery and Social Death*.

38. Richter, "War and Culture," 533.

39. William A. Starna and Ralph Watkins, "Northern Iroquoian Slavery," *Ethnohistory* 38, no. 1 (1991): 34–57.

40. Rushforth, "A Little Flesh We Offer You," 19.

41. Starna and Watkins, "Northern Iroquoian Slavery."

42. Ibid., 50.

43. Hämäläinen, *The Comanche Empire*, 250.

44. Rivaya-Martínez, "Becoming Comanches."

45. Hämäläinen, *The Comanche Empire*, 251–252; Rivaya-Martínez, "Becoming Comanches," 48, 57–58. However, Rivera-Martínez feels that materialistic considerations have been overstated.

46. Patterson, *Slavery and Social Death*; Hämäläinen, *The Comanche Empire*, 254; Rivaya-Martínez, "Becoming Comanches," 50.

47. Rivaya-Martínez, "Becoming Comanches," 52.

48. Brooks, *Captives and Cousins*, 80–116.

49. Ibid., 242.

50. Brugge, *Navajos in the Catholic Church Records*, 127–144.

51. Ibid., 133–134. "National Capital Topics: Slavery in the Navajo Indian Tribe; Agent Riordan Discovers That Slavery Exists among the Savages—His Efforts to Break Up the Evil," *New York Times*, May 15, 1883.

52. Snyder, *Slavery in Indian Country*, 90–97.

53. Ibid., 93.

54. Ibid., 94–95.

55. Ibid., 103–105.

56. Ibid., 127–151.

57. Gregory A. Waselkov and Kathryn E. Holland Braund, eds., *William Bartram on the Southeastern Indians* (Lincoln: University of Nebraska Press, 1995), 58.

58. Donald, *Aboriginal Slavery*; Donald Mitchell, "Predatory Warfare, Social Status, and the North Pacific Slave Trade," *Ethnology* 23, no. 1 (1984): 39–48.

59. Donald, *Aboriginal Slavery*, 105.

60. Ibid., 76–78, 94–95; Sergi Kan, *Symbolic Immortality: The Tlingit Potlatch of the Nineteenth Century* (Washington, DC: Smithsonian Institution, 1989), 62.

61. Donald, *Aboriginal Slavery*, 100–102.

62. Ibid., 101–102.

63. For discussion of "open" and "closed" systems of slavery, see James L. Watson, "Slavery as an Institution: Open and Closed Systems," in *Asian and African Systems of Slavery*, ed. James L. Watson (Berkeley: University of California Press, 1980).

64. Starna and Watkins, "Northern Iroquoian Slavery," 49.

65. Rushforth, "A Little Flesh We Offer You," 51–55.

66. Snyder, *Slavery in Indian Country*, 128.

67. Theda Perdue, *Slavery and the Evolution of Cherokee Society, 1540–1866* (Knoxville: University of Tennessee Press, 1979), 16.

68. Santos-Granero, *Vital Enemies*, 174–175.

69. Starna and Watkins, "Northern Iroquoian Slavery."

70. Richter, "War and Culture," 533.

71. Starna and Watkins, "Northern Iroquoian Slavery," 52.

72. Snyder, *Slavery in Indian Country*, 146–147.

73. Ibid., 149.

74. Rivaya-Martínez, "Becoming Comanches," 52.

75. Ibid., 52–53.

76. Ibid., 52.

77. Ibid., 53.

78. Hämäläinen, *The Comanche Empire*, 257.

79. Ibid., 257; Rivaya-Martínez, "Becoming Comanches," 55.

80. Brooks, *Captives and Cousins*, 242; Brugge, *Navajos in the Catholic Church Records*, 127–244.

81. Brooks, *Captives and Cousins*, 243.

82. Ibid., 245.

83. Ibid., 244.

84. Ibid., 244.

85. Ibid., 246–247.

86. Donald, *Aboriginal Slavery*, 95.

87. Ibid., 95–98; Kan, *Symbolic Immortality*, 133.

88. Kan, *Symbolic Immortality*, 133.

89. Donald, *Aboriginal Slavery*, 168.

90. Ethridge, "Introduction"; Gallay, *Indian Slave Trade*; Alan Gallay, "Introduction: Indian Slavery in Historical Context," in *Indian Slavery in Colonial America*, ed. Alan

CATHERINE M. CAMERON

Gallay (Lincoln: University of Nebraska Press, 2010); Rushforth, "A Little Flesh We Offer You"; Daniel H. Usner Jr., *Indians, Settlers, and Slaves in a Frontier Exchange Economy* (Chapel Hill: University of North Carolina Press, 1992).

91. Ames, "Slavery, Household Production, and Demography"; Carl J. Ekberg, *Stealing Indian Women: Native Slavery in the Illinois Country* (Urbana: University of Illinois Press, 2007), 16–17.

92. Richter, "War and Culture," 530; Trigger, *Children of Aataentsic*, 70.

93. Rushforth, *Bonds of Alliance*, 4.

94. Starna and Watkins, "Northern Iroquoian Slavery," 51.

95. Ibid., 51.

96. Rushforth, "A Little Flesh We Offer You" and *Bonds of Alliance*.

97. Ekberg, *Stealing Indian Women*, 11; Rushforth, "A Little Flesh We Offer You" and *Bonds of Alliance*.

98. Rushforth, *Bonds of Alliance*, 30–34.

99. Ethridge, "Introduction," 22; Claudio Saunt, "History until 1776," in *Handbook of North American Indians*, vol. 14, *Southeast*, ed. Raymond D. Fogelson (Washington, DC: Smithsonian Institution, 2004), 136; Snyder, *Slavery in Indian Country*, 84–85.

100. Ibid., 85.

101. Anderson, *Savannah River Chiefdoms*, 101.

102. Hudson, *Southeastern Indians*, 253–254.

103. Waselkov and Braund, *William Bartram*, 51.

104. Bourne, *Hernando de Soto*, 57.

105. Anderson, *Savannah River Chiefdoms*, 58.

106. Bourne, *Hernando de Soto*, 70.

107. Santos-Granero, *Vital Enemies*, 138–139.

108. Hudson, *Southeastern Indians*, 76–77; Santos-Granero, *Vital Enemies*, 139.

109. Snyder, *Slavery in Indian Country*, 135.

110. Ibid., 136–139.

111. Charles Hudson, *Knights of Spain, Warriors of the Sun: Hernando de Soto and the South's Ancient Chiefdoms* (Athens: University of Georgia Press, 1997), 227; Christina Snyder, "Conquered Enemies, Adopted Kin, and Owned People: The Creek Indians and Their Captives," *Journal of Southern History* 73, no. 2 (2007): 276.

112. Hämäläinen, *The Comanche Empire*, 266.

113. Ibid., 269.

114. Rivaya-Martínez, "Becoming Comanches," 58.

115. Brooks, *Captives and Cousins*, 243–244.

116. Donald, *Aboriginal Slavery*, 128.

117. Ibid., 126–128.

118. Ibid., 297.

119. Ibid., 127.

120. Ibid., 86–88.

121. Ibid., 297.

122. Ames, "Slavery, Household Production, and Demography"; Donald, *Aboriginal Slavery*, 139–147; Mitchell, "Predatory Warfare."

123. Donald, *Aboriginal Slavery*, 139–156.

124. Ames, "Slavery, Household Production, and Demography," 144–146.

125. Fredrik Barth, *Ethnic Groups and Boundaries: The Social Organization of Culture Difference* (Long Grove, IL: Waveland Press, 1998[1969]), 15–16.

126. Patterson, *Slavery and Social Death*, 79–94.

127. Perdue, *Slavery and the Evolution*, 17–18.

128. Ibid., 18.

129. Brooks, *Captives and Cousins*, 246–247.

130. Ibid., 246–247.

131. Rivaya-Martínez, "Becoming Comanches," 61.

132. Kan, *Symbolic Immortality*, 98.

133. Ibid., 98.

134. Starna and Watkins, "Northern Iroquoian Slavery."

135. Rushforth, "A Little Flesh We Offer You," 65.

136. Ruben G. Thwaites, *The Jesuit Relations and Allied Documents* (Cleveland: Burrows Brothers, 1896–1901), 51:123, cited in Trigger, *Children of Aataentsic*, 826.

137. Trigger, *Children of Aataentsic*, 831.

138. Patterson, *Slavery and Social Death*, 77–101.

139. Cameron, "Captives in the Past."

140. Cameron, "Introduction: Captives in Prehistory," "Introduction: Captives and Culture Change," and "Captives in the Past."

2

From Westo to Comanche

The Role of Commercial Indian Slaving in the Development of Colonial North America

Eric E. Bowne

In the last decade scholars have begun to recognize the central importance of the Native slave trade in the development of colonial North America. Much of that scholarship has focused on the Eastern Woodlands, but some important recent studies have been undertaken regarding the trans-Mississippi West and the Southwest Borderlands.[1] Understanding the importance of the Indian slave trade is complicated by the fact that legal and moral issues surrounding the activity were interpreted in complex and changing ways throughout the colonial period and across the regions mentioned above. At times, such commerce was legal, and records, though sparse, remain. Indian slavery was often illegal, however, and was, therefore, a clandestine activity that left little direct evidence. Despite this limitation, it has become clear that virtually every Native group in colonial North America fell victim to Indian slavers at one time or another, even those groups that went on to pursue commercial slaving themselves. Yet to date, there have been few attempts to contextualize and analyze Indian slavery on a continental scale, even though European demand crosscut regions and colonizing strategies. Native slaves were desired in both plantation and nonplantation colonies, and they were traded within North America in addition to being exported.

Native polities throughout North America reacted to this demand in remarkably similar ways despite having come from diverse cultural and political backgrounds and having practiced disparate forms of aboriginal slavery (a number of examples of which are discussed by Catherine Cameron, chapter 1 in this volume). One of those reactions was to pursue slaving as a primary mode of production by developing an economic and military relationship with one or more European colonies in which indigenous peoples hunted and captured other Native peoples, who were then exchanged for European-manufactured goods, particularly arms and ammunition. Under certain circumstances, these types of relationships, though often short-lived, had a tremendous impact on the shape of colonial history. The intrusion of European commerce into the New World had the ability to transform Native polities at great distances from Euro-American beachheads, and the driving force behind such transformations was the influence of this new commercial slaving livelihood.[2] My own research has shown that in the South this economic strategy developed as a result of a set of circumstances that allowed the Westo Indians to seize almost complete control of the market for several decades during the seventeenth century. These circumstances included their own experiences in the Beaver Wars of the Northeast, Euro-American inexperience with Native languages and with the geography of the interior Southeast, privileged access to European arms and ammunition, an easily exploitable resource—mission Indians in Florida and so-called pagan Indians along the Spanish frontier—and access to European markets.[3]

As I have argued elsewhere, Westo depredations were one of the major factors that led to the formation of a number of Native confederacies, including those of the Yamasee and Creek peoples.[4] Of course, the targets of Westo slave raids sought the protection afforded by European firearms and were thus forced to participate in the burgeoning slave trade themselves. As the trade expanded, the Westos could no longer satisfy the European demand for captives, though they attempted to maintain their preeminent position. From the perspective of their English trading partners, the once indispensable Westos had become an obstacle to economic growth. In response, a group of Carolina planters financed a secret war against the group, which was effectively destroyed within two years. Without the Westos' interference, Carolina merchants were able to further expand the market in slaves, entangling every Native polity in the region as a consequence. Over the next century and a half, as a result of the deadly combination of Old World diseases and the slave trade, the social and political diversity of the region plummeted, and only large, confederated groups, such as the Creeks, remained. Was the story of the Westos unique or simply a local manifestation of a phenomenon that repeated itself everywhere

European commerce intruded into Native America, from the Great Lakes to the Gulf of Mexico and from the Atlantic Coast to the Rocky Mountains and Southwest Borderlands?

EUROPEAN COLONIZING STRATEGIES AND OTHER IMPORTANT DYNAMICS

Spain was the first European power to establish permanent colonies in North America, founding La Florida in the Southeast during the sixteenth century and New Mexico and Texas in the Southwest during the seventeenth. They followed an age-old prescription for empire building, attempting to conquer new lands with armies and turn the inhabitants into Christian peasants through the mission system. Previously, in Mexico, the Spaniards had exploited the existing Native hierarchical political system in order to control their new imperial subjects, the Aztecs, and they hoped to use the same blueprint for their North American colonies.[5] Although they soon discovered that Native chiefs in Florida and New Mexico could not exercise the same level of coercive power as the Aztec emperor, Spain was able to create long-lasting relationships with both Mississippian and Puebloan leaders. A recent study (discussed further below) suggests that despite regularly sending out exploratory parties in the hopes of extending their influence, the Spaniards did not have a tremendous impact on Native peoples beyond their colonial settlements and outposts. To be sure, mission Indians contracted Old World diseases throughout the late sixteenth and early seventeenth centuries, but it is quite possible that they suffered the brunt of the damage without spreading epidemics to the interior.

In the days before the English arrived in La Florida and French influence penetrated the Southwest, interactions between "Spanish" Indians and those of the interior were much less frequent than they would become. Both Mississippians in the South and Puebloans in the Southwest traded with politically and culturally distinct neighbors on a regular but infrequent basis, and European-manufactured goods were simply added to the items already exchanged. Some of the new goods were substitutions for aboriginal products, as in the case of glass beads and other items of jewelry. Other items were clear upgrades—for example, metal hoe blades, axes, and knives. Yet because the Spaniards did not supply their Native allies with firearms or alcohol, none of these goods were truly transformational (with the exception of horses and sheep in the Southwest, discussed below), and their availability does not seem to have stimulated market growth. This was due in part to the fact that the Spaniards were less concerned with Indian trade than with other aspects of their colonial endeavors.[6]

In contrast, the French, despite attempting to establish a mission system of their own, were quite interested in developing a commercial exchange with their Native hosts in the Northeast. What began as a way to increase profits on fishing expeditions in the sixteenth century turned into a thriving trade in beaver pelts in the first decades of the seventeenth.[7] The traders of New France had competition from the Dutch at New Netherland, as well as from the merchants of New England, and by 1630 the Dutch West India Company, the Company of New France, and the Massachusetts Bay Company were all in operation.[8] The proximity of multiple European colonies and the economic rivalries between them led to intense interactions among their Native allies. These interactions created a context in which diseases could readily spread within and between Native groups. New England Indians, the Hurons, and the Five Nations Iroquois all suffered multiple disease outbreaks by midcentury.[9]

Meanwhile, the struggle to develop and maintain Native trading partners led Europeans to illegally exchange guns and ammunition in an effort to gain or keep Indian alliances.[10] By the mid-1640s, the Mohawks alone were said to possess as many as four hundred Dutch firearms.[11] In response, the French began to arm their primary Native allies in New France, the Hurons. An arms race also began among New England Indians following the Pequot War of 1636–1637, and forty years later, the Natives were better armed than colonial militias. Coupled with diseases, guns added a frightening new element to the mourning war complex.[12] Tremendous loss of life during epidemics prompted survivors to launch raids to capture ever larger numbers of enemies who could be adopted to replace the dead.[13] Those who possessed firearms tended to target groups that had yet to acquire them. The reverberations from this chaotic mix of guns, diseases, and slaving were soon felt throughout all of eastern North America.

Farther south, the lengthy Atlantic coast between New Netherland and Spanish Florida was claimed entirely by the English, with the exception of a small Swedish settlement along the Delaware River. But this did not prevent a similarly competitive economic situation from arising. By 1629, a trade had developed between Virginians and Susquehannas in the Chesapeake Bay.[14] That trade was challenged when both Marylanders and Swedes attempted to enter the market in the 1630s. As had occurred in the Northeast, in less than a decade a bidding war for the allegiance of Native groups led Europeans to begin exchanging guns with Indians. Until midcentury, the Chesapeake was the southernmost European market for firearms, but in the 1650s a number of entrepreneurs financed explorations of the Piedmont with the intent of further developing the Indian trade.[15] They successfully expanded the market to the south and west in the 1660s and introduced a new "product" as well—Indian slaves. Virginia had recently developed tobacco as an export crop, and the colony could not meet labor demands or afford to import sufficient numbers of Africans and indentured servants.[16] In response, merchants armed their Native trading partners with guns and sent them south to capture slaves among groups that did not possess firearms.

At the same time Virginians were developing trade on the southern Piedmont, the French influence was expanding to the west.[17] During the second half of the seventeenth century, much of the Ohio Valley and the eastern Great Lakes area was abandoned as a result of Iroquois mourning wars.[18] Refugees headed west, where dozens of Native groups lived in nucleated villages in present-day Wisconsin under conditions that left them extremely vulnerable to epidemic diseases. The Hurons had been so harried by Iroquois slavers and Old World diseases that their population plummeted, and the Ottawas took over as the primary trading partner of the French.[19] In response to Iroquois aggression, in the 1660s the French built several missions in the western Great Lakes region that served as trading posts and refugee camps, locales that were particularly important to the development of the "middle ground."[20] The capture of prisoners who could be exchanged during calumet ceremonies was an integral part of Native-French alliance building and maintenance but also served to stimulate the growth of the Indian slave trade.[21] Slaves taken from the Pays d'en Haut (as the French referred to the Great Lakes region), including those given to the French during diplomatic exchanges, were sent to New France. Some remained there as servants to the colonists, but others were exported to the Caribbean.[22]

English commercial expansion began in earnest with the founding of Carolina in 1670.[23] Carolina was intimately connected with Barbados, one of England's Caribbean colonies, to which it provided timber, beef, and a large percentage of the Natives captured by its primary trading partners, the Westos.[24] The desire for unfree labor in the Caribbean was insatiable, however, and by 1680, even as England's Atlantic trade in African slaves expanded, the Westos could no longer meet the continuing demand for Indian slaves to export from Charles Town. Over the next two decades, therefore, the influence of the commercial slavers who helped to supply the growing Caribbean labor market spread across the lower South, pulling every Native group into a complex web of interactions that offered new opportunities to some but threatened the very existence of most. By connecting Native groups across wide geographic areas and increasing the frequency of contact between them, the market system created a context in which epidemic diseases could easily spread across the region.[25] In part as a result of depopulation, the search for victims took commercial slavers west to the Mississippi and beyond.

After more than two decades of exploration in the Mississippi River valley, the French founded Louisiana on the Gulf Coast in 1699 and soon began to explore the western tributaries of the great river in the hopes of expanding both their commercial interests and their Native alliance network while simultaneously thwarting English westward expansion. Unfortunately for the peoples of the Mississippi River valley and the trans-Mississippi West, diseases followed European-manufactured goods and commercial slavers into the region, with devastating results. In the more southerly reaches of the continent, France was able to befriend recent victims of English-sponsored slave raids, such as the Quapaws and the Caddos, who sought military assistance in the form of firearms to protect themselves from slavers.[26] Meanwhile, in the midcontinent soon after the turn of the eighteenth century, French guns provided an opportunity for the Osages of the Missouri River valley to develop a commercial slaving livelihood at the expense of Native groups without strong connections to European markets.[27] As France's Indian allies probed west in search of hides and slaves, they encountered Native groups within Spain's sphere of influence and consequently connected Spanish markets in the Southwest with English and French markets in the East, adding horses to the already lethal mix of guns and slaving.

Horses were introduced to the Southwest and southern Great Plains early in the seventeenth century and were widespread there by the beginning of the eighteenth.[28] At first, access to horses drew diverse Native groups to the plains and lessened their dependence on European and indigenous markets, but the introduction of guns from the East and an increased demand for Indian slaves changed the dynamics in the West.[29] Native groups who practiced a mixed hunting and farming economy, because they spent a predictable part of the year gathered around their agricultural fields, became potential victims of slavers.[30] Those groups who were able to obtain both arms and horses fought for control of the market system that now connected the pueblos of the Rio Grande valley, the horse cultures of the southern plains, and the villages of the Red River valley with New France, Louisiana, and the Atlantic colonies. The Jumanos acted as middlemen in a long-distance trade before the Spanish arrived in the region, but after the introduction of the horse, they lost their preeminent position in the exchange network to Plains Apache groups.[31] In the early decades of the eighteenth century, however, the Comanches acquired French guns to go with their large horse herds, and they used the combination not only to usurp the Apaches but also to develop perhaps the most influential of all the commercial slaving societies.[32]

Within the context of these diverse European colonizing strategies and Native foreign policies, a number of interwoven dynamics were at play, four of which were extremely important: the development of the Atlantic market system, the introduction of Old World diseases to North America, the dislocation and consequent migrations of scores of Native groups, and their coalescence into new social and political forms. The introduction of guns and horses was transformational and forced groups in contact with those who had acquired these items to use all available effort to acquire them as well, a fact that forged the political economy of Native North America during the colonial period. Old World diseases have long been recognized as having had a tremendous impact on Native populations, and recent studies have shown that the more developed a trading network, the more readily epidemic diseases spread between populations.[33] The effects of the market system and diseases caused the dislocation of many Native groups, and migrations, sometimes across vast distances, were a regular part of the colonial world. Dislocated groups routinely joined with others to form coalescent societies—polities composed of previously unrelated peoples (sometimes speaking different languages) who formed new social and political institutions, often in new locations—in the hopes of maintaining cultural viability. Coalescence was so common, in fact, that the majority of Native societies in the eighteenth century, especially throughout the Eastern Woodlands and Great Lakes regions, were products of this process.[34] The engine that drove these monumental changes was commercial slaving, a livelihood made possible by a combination of factors at play within the subregions of the continent at various times during the colonial period.

FACTORS THAT MADE COMMERCIAL SLAVERS POWERFUL AND INFLUENTIAL

A Decided Military Advantage

No matter the region, the commercial slaving strategy could be pursued only under the right set of circumstances. A decided military advantage was absolutely necessary, and the key to such an advantage in the Eastern Woodlands was privileged access to European firearms. Native groups with such access were almost invariably successful in military campaigns against groups who lacked it. Although a bow could fire arrows rapidly and was useable in inclement weather, guns inflicted terrible wounds beyond the abilities of indigenous medical practitioners to treat.[35] The Natives' desire for firearms and ammunition was universal, and in every region of the continent, they went to great lengths to obtain them.[36]

Native access to firearms was almost invariably the result of multiple European nations vying for control of the Indian trade in the same region, despite laws that commonly forbade the exchange of guns with Indians.[37] Such competition between European powers gave Natives access to firearms in the seventeenth century in New England, New France, New Netherland, Virginia, Maryland, and Carolina.[38] By the turn of the eighteenth century, virtually every Native group in eastern North America possessed guns, even those that had little or no direct contact with European traders, a fact noted by a number of intrepid explorers.[39] This glut of firearms forced commercial slavers across the Mississippi in search of victims, but in the trans-Mississippi West and the Southwest Borderlands, the mobility and power of the horse were additional requirements for military success.

Once a military advantage was gained, it had to be maintained by either controlling access to the market in order to keep guns out of the hands of others or by traveling to areas that did not yet have guns in search of victims. The Five Nations Iroquois blocked their western neighbors' access to English and Dutch markets and were thereby able to systematically enslave, sell, and adopt thousands of Hurons and others in the 1640s and 1650s.[40] The Westos also maintained a near monopoly on guns coming out of Carolina between 1674 and 1680, during which time they, too, captured hundreds, perhaps thousands, of Indian slaves.[41] When it was not possible to keep neighbors from acquiring firearms, slavers had to travel, sometimes hundreds of miles, to find groups vulnerable to capture. Englishman Gabriel Arthur spent several months in 1673–1674 with the Tomahitans and accompanied them when they journeyed from Virginia to Spanish Florida on a slave raid.[42] Once the Illinois acquired guns in 1686, they began raiding south and west against people who did not yet possess firearms.[43] The Chickasaws, too, crossed the Mississippi River before the turn of the eighteenth century in search of bow-and-arrow Indians to enslave.[44]

A Strategic Geo-economic Location

Occupying an advantageous geo-economic location was only slightly less important than maintaining a clear military advantage and often required a migration of some sort and violence to procure and maintain. Although the Mohawks did not have to move to develop a relationship with the traders in New Netherland, they did have to displace the Mahicans, whose villages were located between the Mohawks and the Dutch.[45] The Westos traveled from the shores of Lake Erie to the Virginia backcountry and then on to the Savannah River on the border of present-day Georgia and South Carolina, ostensibly to procure a stable market for arms and Indian slaves.[46] Henry Woodward, Carolina's principal Indian trader over the first decade and a half of the colony's existence, encountered a group of Shawnees on the Savannah who had traveled from the Ohio Valley to Spanish Florida and back to Carolina in search of an exchange partner.[47] Similar long-distance migrations also occurred west of the Mississippi River, as evidenced by the Comanches' move from New Mexico's far northern frontier to the southern plains, where they violently displaced the Plains Apaches, who had previously dominated trade in the region.[48] Not all economically motivated migrations covered such long distances. The Lower Creeks moved from the Apalachicola River valley to the Ocmulgee in the 1690s to take advantage of a newly built English trading establishment and to put some distance between themselves and their former Spanish allies.[49] The Yamasee traveled an even shorter distance to establish a partnership with the English when they moved from the northern frontier of the Spanish mission system to Port Royal when Scots founded a short-lived colony there in 1685.[50]

An Easily Exploitable Resource

In addition to military and geo-economic advantages, commercial slavers needed access to an easily exploitable resource, that is to say, Native groups that did not possess European arms and ammunition and, by implication, lacked European friendship and military support. If possible, traditional enemies were targeted, but the new dynamics of the market system often set strangers upon one another with little cause beyond the need to acquire "currency" to exchange. As the availability of firearms increased in a given region, potential victims were found in the hinterlands or in small, isolated pockets near colonial settlements. Europeans referred to the latter remnant groups by a variety of names—including "settlement Indians," "*les petit nations*," "praying Indians," and "mission Indians"—and benefited from their presence in a variety of ways but could provide them only limited protection from commercial slavers. The Five Nations Iroquois, the most aggressive and successful slavers in the Northeast, targeted primarily other Iroquoian-speaking peoples during the 1640s and 1650s but extended their raids into the Ohio Valley and the Pays d'en Haut in the following decades. The mid-Atlantic region beyond the Appalachian Mountains was a potential source of slaves for other groups besides the Five Nations, especially after Virginians expanded their markets to the south and west in the third quarter of the seventeenth century. The Westos, working first with Virginians and later with Carolinians, raided extensively along the northern borders of Spanish Florida beginning in 1659, and the region remained a favorite target for commercial slavers into the eighteenth century. As Native groups that did not possess firearms became scarcer in the East, slavers began raiding across the Mississippi River, putting people at risk in the northern plains; the large river valleys of the midcontinent, such as the Missouri, Arkansas, and Red; the Gulf Coast; and the southern plains.

Access to Markets

Once slaves had been procured, their captors needed access to a market in which to dispose of their "goods." Often that market was located within the region, but as the sale of Apache captives to merchants in French Louisiana attests, the slave trade connected vastly divergent areas in real and meaningful ways.[51] Although far from any colonial settlement in the seventeenth century, the Chickasaws of northeastern Mississippi were nevertheless positioned to access a number of European markets (see Boyd Cothran, chapter 4 in this volume, for a detailed example of a similar geo-economic situation in the Klamath region).[52] To the north and east, the Mississippi River provided a route to the French posts of the Pays d'en Haut, and its tributary, the Ohio, led to traders in the mid-Atlantic region. To the south in the Lower Mississippi River valley were potential victims who could be taken to the Caddo traders along the western tributaries of the Mississippi or east to Indians who had trade connections with Spanish Florida.[53] The Chickasaws launched commercial slave raids along all the routes mentioned above, and their captives were likely sold at markets in New France, Louisiana, Texas, and New Mexico, as well as Charles Town.[54]

Obtaining access to markets or blocking other groups from attaining such access was a regular and important part of the geo-economic warfare that characterized much of the conflict between Native groups in the seventeenth and eighteenth centuries. The Mohawk-Mahican War mentioned above is a classic example of such conflicts, but similar ones occurred in every region. Indians also attempted to keep European traders from bypassing them to make direct contact with other Native groups. When French explorers and traders first encountered the Quapaws near the mouth of the Arkansas River, the group was quite receptive to creating an alliance with the European newcomers, but they worked tirelessly to prevent the French from making similar alliances with their neighbors.[55] The Osages were equally adamant about keeping the French from traveling beyond them up the western tributaries of the Mississippi, where they might trade with Osage enemies.[56]

For their part, Europeans also engaged in geo-economic warfare, but with the opposite goal in mind. They wanted to open up access to their markets in order to increase the flow of goods in both directions. Therefore, there was an inherent tension between slavers, who were alienating, disturbing, and reducing Native peoples, and traders, who needed stability and large, friendly nations in order to establish and expand commerce. Although European traders certainly benefited from the activities of commercial slavers, especially in the early stages of trade in a particular region, such groups were inevitably seen as a hindrance to market expansion. This tension between slavers and traders often resulted in violent confrontations that played themselves out on a number of levels, from the killing of individual traders on one hand to trade wars aimed at removing entire nations of Native peoples on the other. William Byrd was all too familiar with the former when he reported in 1684 that traders in his employ "were killed by the Indians in their return from the westward, about 30 miles beyond Ochanechee, what great predujice [sic] it is to me you may guesse, they having made a very advantageous [trading] journey."[57] The Westo War of 1680, in which the Goose Creek traders of Carolina essentially destroyed their Native trading partners, provides an example of the latter.[58]

Lack of European Military Interference

Europeans were rarely in the position to drastically affect the geopolitics of the market in the seventeenth century, and their inability to interfere directly with the activities of slavers is an often overlooked, but sometimes critically important, advantage enjoyed by successful commercial slaving groups. For the first generation or two in any given locale, most European colonists were unable to travel in the uncharted interior beyond their small beachheads without Natives willing to act as guides and interpreters.[59] Obviously, these Natives had the ability to take their European guests only where they wanted them to go and communicate to them only the things they wanted them to know. Indian companions were also necessary to keep Europeans safe when they traveled away from the settlements, though some involved in trade still met violent ends.[60] Europeans who failed to follow Native diplomatic protocol and who lacked the proper respect for other Native customs and rituals often met with dire consequences.[61] European impotence in the interior, particularly among the English, was perhaps most directly related to their relative military incompetence in the North

American theater of war. In the seventeenth century, Europeans had not yet adopted the guerilla style of warfare necessary to succeed in forest combat; colonial militias generally had poorer quality firearms than Indians, who obtained guns through private traders; and the military presence of Europeans was thin at best.[62]

All of the factors that made commercial slavers powerful—a decided military advantage, a strategic geo-economic location, an easily exploitable resource, access to markets, and lack of European military interference—were strengthened, weakened, or destroyed on the basis of the changing context created by the complex interplay of European colonizing strategies and Native responses. For example, Spanish policy in Florida forbade arming Native allies with guns and encouraged them to congregate at widely spread missions only nominally protected by soldiers. At the same time, the newly developing plantation economies of Virginia and Carolina demanded a significant supply of unfree labor, but neither was yet a significant port of call in the African slave trade. Meanwhile, the ubiquitous European demand for beaver pelts pitted English, French, and Dutch traders against one another in the Northeast, resulting in a region-wide arms race that ultimately saturated the area with firearms. In the ensuing chaotic scramble to secure access to European markets, groups were bounced around the Eastern Woodlands like pool balls after a break. Some of those groups traveled south with their firearms and used their experiences in the so-called Beaver Wars to help them create a successful commercial slaving livelihood hundreds of miles from their traditional homelands. Similar tales can be told about much of North America, and in all regions the actions of commercial slavers had a tremendous effect on European and Native groups alike.

EFFECTS OF THE ACTIONS OF COMMERCIAL SLAVERS

Provided the Impetus behind Coalescence

Commercial slavers, more than any other factor, provided the impetus behind coalescence, a phenomenon nearly as ubiquitous in North America as the Indian slave trade. On the one hand, although the reduction of population numbers due to disease has often been noted as a primary factor behind coalescence, disease episodes by themselves did not compel people to join together with other groups until population loss was severe enough to threaten individual or cultural survival. On the other hand, the presence of slavers forced people to congregate for protection, flee the area, or acquire the necessary military presence to dissuade their would-be captors. Contemporary accounts of Chickasaw slave raids describe villages stealthily set upon by large numbers of gun-wielding warriors who, after killing the adult males, marched scores of captives to slave pens in Chickasaw towns to await exportation.[63] Chickasaw raids and others like them clearly provided a strong incentive to join forces with neighboring groups. As I have argued elsewhere, only confederated polities managed to pass through the crucible of Old World diseases and commercial slaving and remain viable political and military players in the contest for the continent.[64] Not all groups, however, found it acceptable to throw in their lot with outsiders, cultural and linguistic similarities notwithstanding.

Take, for instance, a number of groups along the Gulf Coast, including the Acolapissas, Bayogoulas, Mougalouchas, and the Taensas, all of whom either joined other groups or allowed other groups to join them, only to violently turn against them when cultural accommodation could not be reached.[65] Groups that clung tenaciously to the idea of their own cultural superiority and refused to join with others often sought alliances with Europeans, alliances that left cultural boundaries more or less intact. Some southeastern Native leaders used their relationships with the Spaniards to bolster their own authority in an attempt to retain traditional chiefly governance.[66] More often, however, small Native groups that formed alliances with Europeans were reduced to performing for them a number of tasks for which colonists were initially unsuited, such as hunting, collecting wood and other forest resources, or tracking down and returning runaway slaves.[67] Both the former neo-traditional and the latter Euro-dependent polities were vulnerable to the raids of commercial slavers, however, and untold numbers of their members were captured and sold into slavery. In other words, commercial slavers forced other Native groups to decide upon one of a limited number of political strategies and then preyed on those groups that chose wrongly.

Helped Develop Markets

Commercial slavers helped develop markets by increasing demand for European products, particularly arms and ammunition, among their potential victims. During the seventeenth century in eastern North America, "participation in the slave trade became one of the structural principles of life around which most everything else revolved."[68] As the slave trade expanded in the late seventeenth and early eighteenth centuries, the same became true in the trans-Mississippi West, the southern plains, and the Southwest. For those without access to European firearms, the prospect of facing Indian warriors who had guns and were intent on carrying away loved ones to be sold into slavery was terrifying. When English colonists arrived on the Carolina coast in 1670, they discovered that the coastal Native groups greatly feared the gun-wielding Westos and hoped that by bringing Carolinians meat and dressed deerskins, they would receive protection from the Europeans.[69] Across the continent, similar descriptions and requests were made in reference to the Five Nations Iroquois, Chickasaws, Osages, Apaches, Comanches, and other commercial slavers. Most colonial governments attempted to regulate the Indian trade by placing restrictions on exchange, requiring a license to operate, and other measures. Often it was illegal to trade in guns or slaves. Yet the high demand for European arms and ammunition that resulted from the presence of slavers provided the context and opportunity for the development of a thriving black market.

Quantifying the exchanges in this market is made difficult by two facts. First, the majority of traders, both legal and illegal, left few written records, despite having been involved in one of the most widespread and lucrative businesses in colonial North America. In addition, the worst demographic effects of the slave trade occurred in the hinterlands, away from all but the most intrepid European adventurers. French coureurs de bois and voyageurs traveled the entire length and breadth of the continent, extending French trading interests as they sought personal gain and providing alternative options to Native groups without access to permanent European trading posts.[70] Spain and England produced traders and travelers analogous to those of France, who journeyed extensively in the American wilderness and served as vital connection points to European markets for harried Native groups made desperate by the presence of commercial slavers. These all but forgotten men played an important role in the expansion of the market by exchanging firearms for furs, pelts, skins, and slaves with any Native group, regardless of the intentions of colonial governments or commercial slavers. As potential victims of slavers obtained firearms, their would-be captors were forced to extend their raids, and European traders followed in their wakes, developing routes that would soon be crowded with humans, the barter they trucked, and a host of microscopic organisms that brought disaster to Indian country.

Facilitated the Spread of Epidemics

Commercial slavers unintentionally helped facilitate the spread of epidemics by stimulating the development of markets and forcing potential captives to live in nucleated settlements, where they often suffered from malnourishment and unsanitary conditions.[71] The effects of Old World diseases on Native populations of the Southeast during the sixteenth and seventeenth centuries, when only the Spanish had a colonial presence in the region, seem to have been overstated. Although diseases certainly claimed many lives among mission Indians during that time, it has been argued that disease epidemics did not severely affect Native groups in the interior before the development of a widespread trade network. It has generally been assumed that the dramatic decrease in Native population in the South between 1685 and 1715 was epidemiological in nature.[72] But this period also represents the height of the Indian slave trade in the region, which contributed significantly to the demographic decline, in part because European commercial interest exacerbated indigenous practices related to the capture of enemies. The first major recorded outbreak of smallpox in the region did not begin until 1696 in Virginia. It quickly spread from the mid-Atlantic region into the Southeast, eventually reaching the Mississippi River valley and traveling south to the Gulf Coast and north to the Ohio Valley. Aftershocks followed on the heels of the Great Southeastern Smallpox Epidemic, and indigenous peoples suffered the worst biological consequences of colonialism "as the deadly synergism of Columbian Exchange diseases, aboriginal germs, and malnourishment took a truly horrific toll."[73]

In the Northeast, the barriers that kept diseases from spreading to the interior were broken down earlier but were also likely introduced along trade routes.[74] The Five Nations Iroquois faced epidemics regularly during the middle decades of the seventeenth century, including during the years 1633, 1640–1641, 1647, 1656–1657, 1661–1663, 1668, 1673, and 1676.[75] In response to these disease outbreaks, the Five Nations almost invariably launched raids designed, at least in part, to procure captives for adoption.[76] By the end of the seventeenth century, the Iroquois had captured thousands of people, some of whom passed into the hands of others but many of whom eventually became accepted as citizens of the Five Nations.[77] Those who escaped Iroquois raids were forced to join with other refugees and seek access to firearms and ammunition or risk falling prey to new assaults. In other words, throughout eastern North America a positive feedback loop existed between disease epidemics and slave raids that heightened Native vulnerability to both. As these twin hammers battered North America, Indian populations were pushed and pulled across the continent by a growing vortex of violence and uncertainty.

Forced the Migration of Scores of Populations

Scores of populations were forced to migrate, sometimes repeatedly, in response to fluctuations in the market, the changing fortunes of particular commercial slaving groups, the movement of other Native populations, and a host of other factors equally beyond their control. Commercial slavers provided an important push factor for this movement, since one strategy for avoiding enslavement was to migrate outside the range of the slavers. The Quapaws appear to have left their original home in the Ohio Valley sometime during the seventeenth century as a result of recurrent raids against them by Five Nations Iroquois groups armed with Dutch guns from New Netherland.[78] The Quapaws ended up near the mouth of the Arkansas River, where they encountered the French in 1673, whom they soon solicited for firearms to protect them from Chickasaw slaving expeditions.[79] European settlements served as pull factors in migration because they offered the possibility of market access. The Comanches, after acquiring horses and transforming their culture as a result, migrated onto the southern plains, where they began an aggressive campaign to oust the Apache groups already living there in order to gain access to both Spanish and French markets.[80] In addition to the possibility of exchange, European settlements offered the promise of protection from commercial slavers, and many groups that moved as a result of slave raids sought new homes near colonial outposts or towns. The French posts in the Pays d'en Haut became multicultural, polyglot communities composed of myriad groups attempting to avoid becoming slaves while at the same time acquiring the means (guns) to enslave others.[81] The Westos successfully followed such a strategy when they fled their home near Lake Erie as a response to Iroquois aggression and migrated to Virginia, where they were able to gain access to a source of arms and ammunition.[82]

Increased the Level of Hostile Interactions

Competition to obtain firearms and slaves increased the level of hostile interactions between Native groups and hindered the creation of Indian alliances. "Slave raids were acts of war [and] required retaliation," regardless of political and economic consequences.[83] Whenever possible, the targets of slave raids were chosen in accord with cultural, as well as political and economic, imperatives. That is to say, slave raids were often launched against old enemies, as when the Five Nations targeted various northern Iroquoian speakers who might be more readily adopted by their captors.[84] Yet the realities of the exchange system regularly conspired to help create new enemies, as when the Savanna Indians turned on their erstwhile friends, the Westos, in an attempt to become the preeminent trading partners of Carolina's Goose Creek men.[85] Sometimes, as in the case of the Savannas and the Westos, conflicts between Indian groups served colonial purposes by increasing market demand. In fact, European traders in every region were at times accused of fomenting war to increase their profits. Other times, however, these enmities ran counter to European desires and imperial plans. The Great Peace of Montreal, negotiated by the French in 1701, was an amazing feat of diplomacy, considering that in order to reach an agreement the Five Nations, on the one hand, and a number of Algonquin-speaking groups, on the other, had to put aside bad feelings resulting from generations of endemic violence.[86] The peace accord provided for an exchange of prisoners taken in previous raids but, ironically, also required the participants in Montreal to capture new slaves from groups not represented at the treaty negotiations, which they could exchange among themselves as a sign of friendship and alliance.[87] No matter peace or war, slaving was a widespread and persistent activity in colonial North America, but such a disruptive force could not be sustained indefinitely.

THE DECLINE OF THE INDIAN SLAVE TRADE AND COMMERCIAL SLAVING

Declining Supply of Potential Captives

A number of factors converged in the eighteenth century to decrease the overall traffic in Indian slaves, even though they continued to be exploited in North America into the 1800s. The positive feedback loop between diseases and slaving severely diminished the supply of potential captives. In the Northeast, epidemics and Iroquois raids combined to create a vacant quarter from the Ohio River north to the Great Lakes.[88] In the South, within fifty years of the founding of Carolina, the century-and-a-half-old Spanish mission system was effectively destroyed, and much of the population of the peninsula of Florida had already been enslaved.[89] Within thirty years of the establishment of French Louisiana, virtually all the Native peoples of the Lower Mississippi River valley had been reduced to remnant groups of refugees known as "les petite nations."[90] Epidemics and commercial slavers took their toll west of the Mississippi, spreading up its western tributaries and claiming new victims while simultaneously stimulating the expansion of trade networks and enflaming competition between France, Spain, and their respective Indian allies and exchange partners.[91] Whether the potential victims of commercial slavers attempted to congregate for protection or to flee an area for safety, they were forced to seek access to firearms to ensure their continuing liberty.

Increased Availability of Guns

Slaves were the currency generally exchanged for arms and ammunition, so as the market for Indian captives increased, the availability of guns increased as well. Whenever a group of sufficient population that had previously been victimized by commercial slavers was able to obtain access to firearms, it stood a chance of changing its fortunes. After having been battered back and forth between Iroquois and Sioux raiders from the east and west, respectively, the Ottawas were able to step into the breach left by the Huron diaspora and become major trading partners of the French.[92] Similarly, the Osages turned access to French firearms into a commercial slaving livelihood, but only after they had been forced west from the Ohio Valley area, like their Dhegiha Siouan cousins the Quapaws.[93] In the Southeast, in part as a result of falling victim to slave raids, the Lower Creek peoples ended their alliance with the Spanish (who knew them as Apalachicolas); concluded a peace between themselves and the Westos, with Henry Woodward acting as mediator; and moved to the Ocmulgee River to obtain English firearms.[94] The Yamasee Indian polity was composed of the remnants of several Native peoples from present-day central Georgia and the sea islands of Georgia and South Carolina, who were forced to coalesce and seek an alliance with Spain in response to Virginia-sponsored slave raids. When a chance came in 1684 to instead align themselves with the English, the Yamasee took the opportunity, received guns from their new trading partners, and changed their status from captive to captor virtually overnight.[95] As more and more groups obtained arms and ammunition, the supply of vulnerable potential victims decreased.

Increased European Military Interference

While the effects of diseases and slave raids combined with the availability of guns to increase the difficulty of locating suitable captives, colonists also began to impinge more directly upon the affairs of their Native neighbors. The experiences gained in the interior of the continent by European traders in the preceding decades better equipped them to bypass Native blockades, decipher Indian intentions and actions, and understand and manipulate the politics of exchange. Europeans throughout North America had also become more potent militarily, partly as a result of an increased ability to travel and communicate without absolute dependence on Native guides and interpreters, but also because they adopted the forest combat strategies of the Indians. Along the eastern seaboard, the ever-growing colonial population posed perhaps the biggest threat to Native societies, increasing potential exposure to lethal microbes, intensifying the contest for possession of the continent, and adding demand for Indian captives. Now every group, even those with sufficient arms and ammunition, feared enslavement. Just as it had been in the Pays d'en Haut before the Great Peace of Montreal, the situation in the Southeast had become untenable.

The plantation economies of the mid-Atlantic and lower South were the biggest consumers of Indian slaves outside of the Caribbean and provided the largest markets for their exportation. In the mid-seventeenth century, as the market for Indian captives developed in these regions, small commercial slaving groups became powerful, but a number of other strategies—the neo-traditional, Euro-dependent, and confederated approaches—were pursued by Native groups as well. As the trade expanded, however, slaving became essential to survival, and followers of other strategies soon became slaves. Eventually, even commercial slaving groups with small populations, like the Westos and the Tuscaroras, became vulnerable to enslavement, a situation that ultimately resulted in the Yamasee War.[96] After three decades as commercial slavers, the Yamasees (rightly) feared that they would soon be enslaved by their former trading partners the Carolinians, and they killed the traders and officials visiting them on April 15, 1715, igniting an epidemic of violence against the English that spread along the same trading paths as the diseases that had ravaged Native groups. Every major Indian trading partner of the English murdered traders living among them in the weeks following the Yamasees' initial attack, and their combined efforts exacted a terrible toll in English lives, forcing the English to reevaluate their economic policies regarding Native slavery.[97]

Expanded Markets for African Slaves

After the Yamasee War, the primary markets for Indian slaves in the mid-Atlantic and southeastern regions of the continent dried up; at the same time, the markets for Africans, who were universally preferred over Natives or indentured Europeans as chattel slaves, were expanding. The plantation economies of Virginia and the Carolinas had somewhat stabilized, and in the hopes of expanding the system, the English turned their focus toward expelling their French and Spanish rivals from the South. As this imperial contest in the East heated up, Native allies became much more important as military auxiliaries than as producers for the market, and, therefore, colonial officials could not afford to allow the effects of the slave trade to alienate potential Indian allies. Native societies that had been able to maintain large populations, either because of comparative geographic isolation, as in the cases of the Cherokees and Choctaws, or through the incorporation of refugee groups and adoption of captives, as in the cases of the Creeks and the Five Nations Iroquois, were able to survive the era of commercial slaving in the East to become important political and military players in the European contest for the continent.[98] As a result of new demographic realities among Native societies and new political goals of European empire, the Indian slave trade declined east of the Mississippi after the first couple of decades of the eighteenth century, quelling to a certain degree the unprecedented loss of social and cultural diversity that had resulted in great part from the practice.

CONCLUSION

Spanish markets in Texas and New Mexico and French markets in the Pays d'en Haut and Louisiana together created enough demand for Native captives to maintain commercial slaving as a viable strategy not only in the trans-Mississippi West, southern plains, and Southwest but even as far west as Alta California (the captive and livestock trade networks of which are discussed in detail by Natale Zappia, chapter 5 in this volume). Additionally, the factors that made slavers powerful were still in operation in the West. A true military advantage could be maintained in the region by coupling possession of large horse herds with access to European firearms and ammunition, which were still available only in limited numbers, unlike in the East. Those who were able to acquire both horses and guns found a number of easily exploitable targets from the river valleys of the western tributaries of the Mississippi across the northern and southern plains and on to the Great Basin and the Pueblo communities in the Rio Grande valley, as well as their pastoral neighbors the Navajos. Good geo-economic locations with access to multiple European markets could still be controlled by Native groups, which ensured that there was always a place to exchange their goods, no matter the political climate in Europe. In the West, there were far fewer Spanish, French, and English colonists than there were east of the Mississippi, their outposts were widely scattered and only nominally protected, and the most essential items necessary for pursuing a raiding lifestyle, horses, could not be kept from Natives by Europeans in the same way powder and shot could be withheld.

After having completely altered their way of life during the sixteenth and seventeenth centuries by developing a dependence on the European-introduced horse, the Comanches decided to migrate from the northern frontier of Spanish New Mexico to the heart of the southern plains, where they obtained access to European markets through which horses, Native captives, and firearms could all be exchanged. Beginning at the turn of the eighteenth century, when the Indian slave trade in the East was reaching its violent crescendo, the Comanches used the above-mentioned advantages to break into and ultimately dominate the trade in captives on the southern plains by midcentury, in the process displacing, and in some cases enslaving, Plains Apache groups (whose diaspora from Apachería between the seventeenth and nineteenth centuries is traced by Paul Conrad, chapter 3 in this volume).[99] Between approximately 1750 and 1850, the Comanches used their preeminent place in the regional exchange system to create an empire and become, as some scholars have put it, "Lords of the South Plains."[100] They were able to forestall attempts by Europeans and Americans to oust them or in any way gain control of Comanche lands, at the same time plundering colonial resources virtually at will. They kept their population high by willingly incorporating large numbers of foreign Native groups and were able, for more than a century, to maintain the advantages that allowed them to develop a hegemonic influence over the other polities in the region, both Indian and European.[101]

Like the Westos and other commercial slaving groups before them, the Comanches had a tremendous but little recognized role in determining the political, economic, and military development of the colonial world. For more than two hundred years, such groups arose wherever the interplay of European colonizing strategies and Native responses provided the opportunity. By exploiting European inexperience and their own military and geo-economic advantages, commercial slaving groups provided a major impetus for social and political coalescence, facilitated the spread of disease as they expanded the market, and increased the level of hostile interactions between Native and European groups. Everywhere this strategy was implemented, a positive feedback loop between slaving and the spread of diseases developed, the availability of firearms increased dramatically, and the search for victims sent slavers into the colonial hinterlands. Although the influence of particular commercial slaving polities was often short-lived and the demographic effects of their raids were less severe than those related to European-introduced diseases, the consequences of their actions reverberated throughout colonial history. The further study of these groups promises to enrich and unite our understanding of the histories of slavery in North America.

Notes

1. Juliana Barr, *Peace Came in the Form of a Woman: Indians and Spaniards in the Texas Borderlands* (Chapel Hill: University of North Carolina Press, 2007); Ned Blackhawk, *Violence over the Land: Indians and Empires in the Early American West* (Cambridge, MA:

ERIC E. BOWNE

Harvard University Press, 2006); Eric E. Bowne, *The Westo Indians: Slave Traders of the Early Colonial South* (Tuscaloosa: University of Alabama Press, 2005); James F. Brooks, *Captives and Cousins: Slavery, Kinship, and Community in the Southwest Borderlands* (Chapel Hill: University of North Carolina Press, 2002); Robbie Ethridge and Sheri M. Shuck-Hall, eds., *Mapping the Mississippian Shatter Zone: The Colonial Indian Slave Trade and Regional Instability in the American South* (Lincoln: University of Nebraska Press, 2009); Alan Gallay, ed., *Indian Slavery in Colonial America* (Lincoln: University of Nebraska Press, 2010); Gallay, *The Indian Slave Trade: The Rise of the English Empire in the American South* (New Haven, CT: Yale University Press, 2002); Joseph M. Hall, *Zamumo's Gifts: Indian-European Exchange in the Colonial Southeast* (Philadelphia: University of Pennsylvania Press, 2009); Paul Kelton, *Epidemics and Enslavement: Biological Catastrophe in the Native Southeast, 1492–1715* (Lincoln: University of Nebraska Press, 2007); Christina Snyder, *Slavery in Indian Country: The Changing Face of Captivity in Early America* (Cambridge, MA: Harvard University Press, 2010).

2. Ethridge and Shuck-Hall, *Mapping the Mississippian Shatter Zone.*

3. Bowne, *Westo Indians.*

4. Eric E. Bowne, "'Caryinge awaye their Corne and Children': The Effects of Westo Slave Raids on the Indians of the Lower South," in Ethridge and Shuck-Hall, *Mapping the Mississippian Shatter Zone*, 104–114.

5. Jerald Milanich, *Laboring in the Fields of the Lords: Spanish Missions and Southeastern Indians* (Washington, DC: Smithsonian Institution, 1999).

6. Gregory Waselkov, "Seventeenth Century Trade in the Colonial Southeast," *Southeastern Archaeology* 8, no. 2(1989):117–133.

7. Bruce G. Trigger, "Early Iroquoian Contacts with Europeans," in *Handbook of North American Indians*, vol. 15, *Northeast*, ed. Bruce G. Trigger (Washington, DC: Smithsonian Institution Press, 1978), 346.

8. Daniel K. Richter, *The Ordeal of the Longhouse: The Peoples of the Iroquois League in the Era of European Colonization* (Chapel Hill: University of North Carolina Press, 1992), 58.

9. Patrick M. Malone, *The Skulking Way of War: Technology and Tactics among the New England Indians* (Baltimore, MD: Johns Hopkins University Press, 1991), 34–36; Colin G. Calloway, *One Vast Winter Count: The Native American West before Lewis and Clark* (Lincoln: University of Nebraska Press, 2003), 224; Richter, *Ordeal of the Longhouse*, 58–59.

10. Trigger, "Early Iroquoian Contacts," 354.

11. José António Brandão, *Your Fyre Shall Burn No More: Iroquois Policy toward New France and Its Native Allies to 1701* (Lincoln: University of Nebraska Press, 1997), 100.

12. Richter, *Ordeal of the Longhouse*, 32–38.

13. Ibid., 58.

14. Frederick J. Fausz, "Present at the Creation: The Chesapeake World That Greeted the Maryland Colonists," *Maryland Historical Magazine* 79 (1984):7–20.

15. Alan V. Briceland, *Westward from Virginia: The Exploration of the Virginia-Carolina Frontier, 1650–1710* (Charlottesville: University Press of Virginia, 1987).

16. Alan Taylor, *American Colonies: The Settling of North America* (New York: Penguin, 2001), 94–106.

17. Claiborne A. Skinner, *The Upper Country: French Enterprise in the Colonial Great Lakes* (Baltimore, MD: Johns Hopkins University Press, 2008).

18. Penelope B. Drooker, "The Ohio Valley, 1550–1750: Patterns of Sociopolitical Coalescence and Dispersal," in *The Transformation of the Southeastern Indians, 1540–1760*, ed. Robbie Ethridge and Charles Hudson (Jackson: University of Mississippi Press, 2002), 115–134.

19. Calloway, *Winter Count*, 228–229.

20. Richard White, *The Middle Ground: Indians, Empires, and Republics in the Great Lakes Region, 1650–1815* (Cambridge: Cambridge University Press, 1991).

21. Brett Rushforth, "'A Little Flesh We Offer You': The Origins of Indian Slavery in New France," in Gallay, *Indian Slavery in Colonial America*, 353–390.

22. Brett Rushforth, *Bonds of Alliance: Indigenous and Atlantic Slaveries in New France* (Chapel Hill: University of North Carolina Press, 2012).

23. Verner W. Crane, *The Southern Frontier, 1670–1732* (Tuscaloosa: University of Alabama Press, 2004).

24. Bowne, *Westo Indians*, 13–16.

25. Kelton, *Epidemics and Enslavement*.

26. Kathleen DuVal, *The Native Ground: Indians and Colonists in the Heart of the Continent* (Philadelphia: University of Pennsylvania Press, 2006), 67–78; Calloway, *Winter Count*, 250–254.

27. DuVal, *Native Ground*, 103–110.

28. Calloway, *Winter Count*, 267–269.

29. Ibid., 276.

30. Pekka Hämäläinen, *The Comanche Empire* (New Haven, CT: Yale University Press, 2008), 28–37.

31. Thomas A. Britten, *The Lipan Apaches: People of Wind and Lightning* (Albuquerque: University of New Mexico Press, 2009), 54–56.

32. Hämäläinen, *The Comanche Empire*.

33. Henry F. Dobyns, *Their Number Become Thinned: Native American Population Dynamics in Eastern North America* (Knoxville: University of Tennessee Press, 1983); Alfred W. Crosby, *Ecological Imperialism: The Biological Expansion of Europe, 900–1900*

(Cambridge: Cambridge University Press, 1986); Kelton, *Epidemics and Enslavement.*

34. Stephen Kowalewski, "Coalescent Societies," in *Light on the Path: The Anthropology and History of the Southeastern Indians,* ed. Thomas J. Pluckhahn and Robbie Ethridge (Tuscaloosa: University of Alabama Press, 2006), 94–122.

35. Bowne, *Westo Indians,* 65–69; William Strachey, *The Historie of Travell into Virginia Britania,* ed. Louis Wright and Virginia Freund (London: Hakluyt Society, 1953), 110.

36. John Lederer, *The Discoveries of John Lederer,* ed. William P. Cumming (Charlottesville: University of Virginia Press, 1958), 41; Dean Snow, Charles T. Gehring, and William A. Starna, eds., *In Mohawk Country: Early Narratives about a Native People* (Syracuse, NY: Syracuse University Press, 1996), 209.

37. Snow, Gehring, and Starna, *In Mohawk Country,* 209.

38. Malone, *Skulking Way of War;* Brandão, *Your Fyre Shall Burn No More;* Bruce G. Trigger, "The Mohawk-Mahican War (1624–28): The Establishment of a Pattern," *Canadian Historical Review* 52 (1971):276–286; Frederick J. Fausz, "Fighting 'Fire' with Firearms: The Anglo-Powhatan Arms Race," *American Indian Culture and Research Journal* 3, no. 4 (1979):33–50; Fausz, "Present at the Creation"; Gallay, *The Indian Slave Trade.*

39. John Lawson, *A New Voyage to Carolina,* ed. Hugh Talmage Lefler (Chapel Hill: University of North Carolina Press, 1967), 33, 38, 175; Thomas Nairne, *Nairne's Muskogean Journals: The 1708 Expedition to the Mississippi River,* ed. Alexander Moore (Jackson: University of Mississippi Press, 1988), 37–38; Snow, Gehring, and Starna, *In Mohawk Country,* 209.

40. Richter, *Ordeal of the Longhouse,* 60–65.

41. Bowne, *Westo Indians,* 82–85.

42. Clarence W. Alvord and Lee Bidgood, eds., *The First Explorations of the Trans-Allegheny Region by Virginians, 1650–1674* (Cleveland, OH: Arthur H. Clark, 1912), 210–226; Briceland, *Westward from Virginia,* 147–170; Kelton, *Epidemics and Enslavement,* 115–118.

43. Calloway, *Winter Count,* 247.

44. Robbie Ethridge, "The Emergence of the Colonial South: Colonial Indian Slaving, the Fall of the Precontact Mississippian World, and the Emergence of a New Social Geography in the American South, 1540–1730," in *Native American Adoption, Captivity, and Slavery in Changing Contexts,* ed. Max Carroci and Stephanie Pratt (New York: Palgrave Macmillan, 2012), 47–64.

45. Trigger, "The Mohawk-Mahican War."

46. Bowne, *Westo Indians,* 1–4.

47. Langdon Cheves, ed., "The Shaftesbury Papers and Other Records Relating to Carolina and the First Settlement on the Ashley River Prior to the Year 1676," in *Collections of the South Carolina Historical Society,* vol. 5 (1897), 460–661; Stephen Warren

and Randolph Noe, "'The Greatest Travelers in America': Shawnee Survival in the Shatter Zone," in Ethridge and Shuck-Hall, *Mapping the Mississippian Shatter Zone*, 163–187.

48. Hämäläinen, *The Comanche Empire*, 1.

49. Gregory Waselkov, "The Macon Trading House and Early European-Indian Contact in the Colonial Southeast," in *Ocmulgee Archaeology, 1936–1986*, ed. David J. Hally (Athens: University of Georgia Press, 1994), 190–195.

50. Gallay, *Indian Slave Trade*, 73–91.

51. Barr, *Peace Came in the Form of a Woman*.

52. Robbie Ethridge, *From Chicaza to Chickasaw: The European Invasion and the Transformation of the Mississippian World, 1540–1715* (Chapel Hill: University of North Carolina Press, 2010); Edward Cashin, *Guardians of the Valley: Chickasaws in Colonial South Carolina and Georgia* (Columbia: University of South Carolina Press, 2009).

53. Ethridge, "Emergence of the Colonial South," 56–58.

54. Ibid., 59–62.

55. DuVal, *Native Ground*, 91–93.

56. Ibid., 110–111.

57. Marion Tinling, ed., *The Correspondence of the Three William Byrds of Westover, Virginia, 1684–1776*, 2 vols. (Charlottesville: University of Virginia Press, 1977), 1:16.

58. Bowne, *Westo Indians*, 99–100.

59. Ibid., 58–61.

60. Lederer, *Discoveries of John Lederer*, 39; Alvord and Bidgood, *First Explorations*, 215–218.

61. DuVal, *Native Ground*, 89.

62. Malone, *Skulking Way of War*, 67–87.

63. Nairne, *Muskogean Journals*, 43; Patricia Galloway, "Henri de Tonti du Village des Chacta, 1702: The Beginning of the French Alliance," in *LaSalle and His Legacy: Frenchmen and Indians in the Lower Mississippi Valley*, ed. Patricia Galloway (Jackson: University of Mississippi Press, 1983), 159.

64. Eric E. Bowne, "Southeastern Indian Polities of the Seventeenth Century: Suggestions toward an Analytical Vocabulary," in *Native American Adoption, Captivity, and Slavery in Changing Contexts*, Max Carocci and Stephanie Pratt, eds. (New York: Palgrave Macmillan, 2012), 65–78.

65. Kelton, *Epidemics and Enslavement*, 193–194.

66. John Worth, "Spanish Missions and the Persistence of Chiefly Power," in *The Transformation of the Southeastern Indians, 1540–1760*, ed. Robbie Ethridge and Charles Hudson (Jackson: University of Mississippi Press, 2002), 39–64.

67. Bowne, "Southeastern Indian Polities," 73–75; Daniel H. Usner, Jr., *Indians, Settlers, and Slaves in a Frontier Exchange Economy: The Lower Mississippi Valley before 1783*

(Chapel Hill: University of North Carolina Press, 1992).

68. Robbie Ethridge, "Creating the Shatter Zone: Indian Slave Traders and the Collapse of the Southeastern Chiefdoms," in *Light on the Path: The Anthropology and History of the Southeastern Indians*, ed. Thomas Pluckhahn and Robbie Ethridge (Tuscaloosa: University of Alabama Press, 2006), 209.

69. Cheves, "Shaftesbury Papers," 168, 200–201.

70. Carolyn Podruchny, *Making the Voyageur World: Travelers and Traders in the North American Fur Trade* (Lincoln: University of Nebraska Press, 2006).

71. Kelton, *Epidemics and Enslavements*.

72. Peter Wood, "The Changing Population of the Colonial South: An Overview by Race and Region, 1685–1790," in *Powhatan's Mantle: Indians in the Colonial Southeast*, ed. Peter Wood, Gregory Waselkov, and Thomas Hatley (Lincoln: University of Nebraska Press, 1989), 35–103.

73. Kelton, *Epidemics and Enslavements*, xx.

74. Richter, *Ordeal of the Longhouse*, 58.

75. Ibid., 59.

76. Brandão, *Your Fyre Shall Burn No More*, 75.

77. Ibid., 73.

78. DuVal, *Native Ground*, 67–68.

79. Morris Arnold, *The Rumble of a Distant Drum: The Quapaws and Old World Newcomers, 1673–1804* (Fayetteville: University of Arkansas Press, 2000), 18–19.

80. Calloway, *Winter Count*, 283–287.

81. Ibid., 228–230.

82. Bowne, *Westo Indians*, 49–53.

83. Ethridge, "Emergence of the Colonial South," 61.

84. Richter, *Ordeal of the Longhouse*, 60–66.

85. Bowne, *Westo Indians*, 99–100.

86. Rushforth, *Bonds of Alliance*, 155–156.

87. Ibid., 157–160.

88. Calloway, *Winter Count*, 228–229.

89. John Worth, "Razing Florida: The Indian Slave Trade and the Devastation of Spanish Florida, 1659–1715," in Ethridge and Shuck-Hall, *Mapping the Mississippian Shatter Zone*, 295–311.

90. Kelton, *Epidemics and Enslavement*, 188–195.

91. Calloway, *Winter Count*, 276–293.

92. Ibid., 228–231.

93. DuVal, *Native Ground*, 104–105.

94. Eric E. Bowne, "Dr. Henry Woodward's Role in Early Carolina Indian

Relations," in *Creating and Contesting Carolina: Proprietory Era Histories*, ed. Michelle LeMaster and Bradford Wood (Columbia: University of South Carolina Press, 2013), 73–93; Steven C. Hahn, *The Invention of the Creek Nation, 1670–1763* (Lincoln: University of Nebraska Press, 2004), 49–52.

    95. Kelton, *Epidemics and Enslavement*, 130–131.

    96. Ibid., 165–168; William Ramsey, *The Yamasee War: A Study of Culture, Economy, and Conflict in the Colonial South* (Lincoln: University of Nebraska Press, 2008); Bowne, "Southeastern Indian Polities."

    97. Kelton, *Epidemics and Enslavement*, 202–220.

    98. Ibid., 152–155.

    99. Calloway, *Winter Count*, 283–285.

    100. Ernest Wallace and E. Adam Hoebel, *The Comanches: Lords of the South Plains* (Norman: University of Oklahoma Press, 1987); T. R. Fehrenbach, *Comanches: The History of a People* (New York: Random House, 1974).

    101. Hämäläinen, *The Comanche Empire*, 1–4.

PART II

Links to Expanding Slave Networks

Slave trading multiplied across North America and the Caribbean during the eighteenth century and into the nineteenth, and the migrations of enslavers and enslaved swelled. This movement through overlapping indigenous and European slaving cultures is the theme of part II. Six historians suggest how the links among the many histories of relocation during this period add depth and breadth to traditional plantation stories. In chapter 3, Paul Conrad tracks the forced migrations of Apache slaves in a diaspora from northern New Spain (Spanish Texas and New Mexico) into Spanish Mexico and then east to Havana. Cuba's growing demand for women as domestics and men as field workers fueled the diaspora, just as similar labor scarcities built the slave trade in the North American South. Also, as in the South, slaves sent to Cuba resisted. There were subtle work slowdowns, sabotage, and theft. Like the bandits and rebels on the mainland, slaves escaped into the countryside. Some became roving bandits, while others organized in more formal armed rebellions.[1]

Chapter 4 takes us to southern Oregon in the years of the gold rush. Boyd Cothran shows how Klamath Indian entrepreneurs took advantage of the opportunities presented by the gold fever's new markets. Slaves had long been a significant part of the Klamath population, but like many of the Indians in the Atlantic southeast (see Eric E. Bowne, chapter 2), the

Part II

Klamaths adjusted when local, continental, and global economies converged in California. They altered their traditions of slavery and social hierarchy and began kidnapping and selling their neighbors in the Columbia River slave fairs.

In chapter 5, we move with Natale Zappia from the Pacific Northwest to a story of cultural adaptation in the Pacific Southwest. During the late eighteenth and into the mid-nineteenth centuries, the region developed a dynamic trade in slaves and livestock. Much as in other contact zones, Native peoples chose to relocate, coming from as far inland as Utah and New Mexico in order to take advantage of new trade opportunities near the coast. Ambitious Indian slavers found that they themselves could become targets, however, compelled to join other involuntary migrants who were trafficked and sold as chattels.[2]

Calvin Schermerhorn (chapter 6) shifts the scene to the heart of the cotton kingdom. Schermerhorn follows the streams of three major ethnic migrations—Indian, African American, and Euro-American—as these peoples moved west from the Old South. Some Indian slaves and many slaves of African descent were driven on forced marches to Mississippi, Alabama, and Louisiana. Others were pressed onto trains and steamships. This chapter highlights a particular element of our definition of slavery. Whether legally enshrined as an institution in Euro-American colonies or states or endorsed by cultural consensus within Indian groups, slaveholding brought the force of law and custom to support the ownership and marketing of slaves. Schermerhorn argues that the migrations were linked, with state and federal governments organizing some removals directly while indirectly facilitating private trafficking by slave traders, land speculators, and plantation investors—the free white migrants. Schermerhorn joins those historians who are not reluctant to delve into the history of financial markets and their connections to slavery and capitalism.[3]

As economic and political engines relentlessly propelled migrations westward, another phenomenon spread across the Americas: the cascade of colonial liberation movements called the Age of Revolutions. In chapter 7 Andrew J. Torget explores the debate over liberty, slavery, and migration in newly independent Mexico, where the pressures of demography and political philosophy collided. The governing assembly of the state of Coahuila y Tejas struggled to strike a balance between liberal ideals grounded in fundamental human rights and the practical need to grow the economy in its remote Texas district. Allowing American plantation entrepreneurs to migrate and settle with their African American slaves in Texas would bolster the non-Indian population and stimulate lucrative markets with the

Old South. The philosophical cost would be high, however, since the new national constitution forbade slavery.[4]

In chapter 8, the migration streams and slaving networks described in chapters 6 and 7 converge. Mark Allan Goldberg brings us to Torrey Trading House, a key contact point between Indian and Anglo-American slave-trading networks in north central Texas, near present-day Waco. There are clear parallels between the stories of African American slaves living on the frontier of the Comanche empire and those in the rest of the cotton South. Enslaved people in Texas faced the same trials of plantation slavery as their counterparts in the settled South, enduring the physical and psychological demands of a forced labor system that divided their families with chattel sales. On the other hand, Goldberg helps us appreciate that, unlike those working in the antebellum East, Texas slaves had to withstand the challenges of life in a borderland shared with powerful indigenous slavers. African Americans in Texas knew that they and their children were prize targets for Indian raiders. If they were kidnapped, like the women in Marcy's journal entry, they might be tortured, killed, held for life, or resold to Anglo-Americans or other Indians.[5]

Each chapter in part II adds to the map of expanding, intersecting, cross-cultural slave trade networks. Taken together, these linked histories reveal the fearful continental reach of North American slavery.

Notes

1. On the subject of resistance and revolts in Cuba, see also Stephen Chambers, "At Home among the Dead: North Americans and the 1825 Guamacaro Slave Insurrection," *Journal of the Early Republic* 33 (Spring 2013): 61–86.

2. Two recent monographs give readers the opportunity to expand Zappia's sketch of slaving in the Southwest. Ned Blackhawk lays out a broad study of the cultural and economic evolution of peoples in the Great Basin after the arrival of Euro-Americans, showing how imperial expansion escalated and reshaped slaving. Ned Blackhawk, *Violence over the Land: Indians and Empires in the Early American West* (Cambridge, MA: Harvard University Press, 2006). Pekka Hämäläinen traces the challenges and changes faced by the powerful Comanche confederation, which dominated the territory and economic traffic of slaves and other commodities across the southern plains from early in the eighteenth century until after the US Civil War. Pekka Hämäläinen, *The Comanche Empire* (New Haven, CT: Yale University Press, 2009).

3. On the growing significance of slaves in generating development capital in Euro-American societies, see Edward E. Baptist, *The Half Has Never Been Told: Slavery and the Making of American Capitalism* (New York: Basic Books, 2014). On the reluctance of

Part II

historians, see Baptist, "Toxic Debt, Liar Loans, Collateralized and Securitized Human Beings, and the Panic of 1837," in *Capitalism Takes Command: The Social Transformation of Nineteenth-Century North America*, ed. Michael Zakim and Gary J. Kornblith (Chicago: University of Chicago Press, 2012), 69–92, at 72, 89; Walter Johnson, *River of Dark Dreams: Slavery and Empire in the Cotton Kingdom* (Cambridge, MA: Harvard University Press, 2013); Kenneth Morgan, *Slavery, Atlantic Trade, and the British Economy, 1660–1800* (Cambridge: Cambridge University Press, 2000). On the funding of slave economies and on the liquidity of slaves, see Schermerhorn, chapter 6 in this volume; Baptist, "Toxic Debt," 79, 81, and generally, 90–91. On the financial importance of the slave trade in Euro-American colonial and antebellum economies, see Bonnie Martin, "Slavery's Invisible Engine: Mortgaging Human Property," *Journal of Southern History* 76 (November 2010): 817–866.

4. Readers will find a good complement to Torget's chapter in a study by Sean M. Kelley that explores the emancipation question from the perspective of those actually enslaved in Texas. Kelley combines compelling snapshots of the work routines on nineteenth-century cotton and sugar plantations with updated interpretations of the traditional images of slavery in the South. Sean M. Kelley, *Los Brazos de Dios: A Plantation Society in the Texas Borderlands, 1821–1865* (Baton Rouge: Louisiana State University Press, 2010), chapters 2 and 3. On the debate in the settled South, see Lacy K. Ford, *Deliver Us from Evil: The Slavery Question in the Old South* (New York: Oxford University Press, 2009). For those interested in the earlier development of the slavery debate in Mexico, Frank Proctor provides a fascinating tour of the emancipation question in the colonial period. Frank Proctor, *Damned Notions of Liberty: Slavery, Culture, and Power in Colonial Mexico, 1640–1769* (Albuquerque: University of New Mexico Press, 2010). Finally, law students and undergraduates majoring in political science will appreciate William Suarez-Potts's detailed study on the development of labor jurisprudence in Mexico. William Suarez-Potts, *The Making of Law: The Supreme Court and Labor Legislation in Mexico, 1875–1931* (Stanford, CA: Stanford University Press, 2012). See also Ben Vinson and Matthew Restall, eds., *Black Mexico: Race and Society from Colonial to Modern Times* (Albuquerque: University of New Mexico Press, 2009).

5. Another link to explore is the research that contrasts the working conditions of imported Chinese contract laborers and African American slaves. Both ethnic groups built railroads in Texas and chopped sugarcane in Louisiana, and both are part of current populations that have had to confront the legacies of slavery, including poverty and racism. See, for example, Kelley, *Los Brazos de Dios*; Moon-Ho Jung, *Coolies and Cane: Race, Labor, and Sugar in the Age of Emancipation* (Baltimore, MD: Johns Hopkins University Press, 2006); Theresa A. Case, *The Great Southwest Railroad Strike and Free Labor* (College Station: Texas A&M University Press, 2010), 88–96.

3

Indians, Convicts, and Slaves

An Apache Diaspora to Cuba at the Start of the Nineteenth Century

Paul Conrad

They came aboard the *Brujula* and *Polonia* in August 1802, two dozen survivors of a convoy of Apache war captives that had originally numbered more than eighty when it left the northern interior of New Spain. The governor of Cuba, the Marqués de Someruelos, had probably already prepared the announcement of their arrival for the Havana newspaper, informing residents that Indians would be given to "proper persons to instruct them in religion" and that those who wished to "have the advantage of their service [and] contribute to this pious work" should apply to him. Within days, petitions from residents eager to receive an Indian man or woman began to arrive in the governor's office, citing both religious objectives and excitement at the prospect of an unpaid domestic to help with household chores. If we can only speculate about what these Apache captives knew of the fates awaiting them as they neared shore, we do know that to be sent away had become a well-known and feared experience during the last two decades of war in the North American West, as Native men and women were routinely transported to central New Spain and the Caribbean.[1]

Apache Indians embarking to Cuba at the start of the nineteenth century navigated a world characterized by what one scholar has termed "a spectrum of bondage."[2] Native prisoners of war were not the most common of cargo unloaded in the Havana harbor, but their presence illustrates the far-flung imperial and commercial networks that drew captives of varied origins and statuses into forced labor in the Caribbean and the Atlantic World. Hundreds of convicts from distant parts of the Spanish empire also made the journey, sometimes in the same ships as Apaches, as courts in Spain, Spanish America, and the Philippines sentenced individuals convicted of serious crimes to servitude in overseas military forts and public works projects. Thousands more enslaved men and women of African descent also arrived in Havana during these years, some born on neighboring islands, others in Africa. Because Cuba was a slave society that also served as an island prison for convicts and prisoners of war, multiple forms of bondage intersected here. Legal and racial distinctions influenced people's life trajectories and the way they were perceived within the community; to be an Indian prisoner of war was not the same thing as being a black slave. Some Apaches, for example, came to understand and exploit Spanish interests in promoting their "instruction in religion" and in distinguishing between their status and that of enslaved Africans. At first, however, the best of Spanish intentions likely presented little solace to men and women who had endured an arduous journey into forced labor in circumstances not of their choosing.[3]

This journey and its meaning for understandings of slavery in North America and its borderlands is the subject of this chapter. In tracing the lives of the men and women aboard the *Brujula* and *Polonia* from the roots of their captivity through their arrival in Cuba in 1802, I pursue two primary aims. First, a microhistorical approach to the life trajectories of these Apache captives and their captors in 1802 lends a human face to a history usually addressed in broader or more speculative terms. The fact that Indian slavery was often illegal within colonial societies has served to limit or obscure its documentation in Euro-American archives. The transport of Apache captives—who were legally termed "prisoners of war," not "slaves"—was officially sanctioned, documented, and orchestrated by Spanish officials and soldiers. This history thus allows for a closer examination of captives' experiences than is often possible in other contexts.[4]

Second, tracing Apaches from Southwestern America to a center of chattel slavery, the Caribbean, furthers considerations of the ways in which practices of captivity and slavery differed across space and time in North America and its borderlands. This Apache diaspora illustrates, for example, how the correlations that European and Euro-American regimes drew between categories like "Indian" and "prisoner" or "black" and "slave" did not necessarily correspond to the understandings of ordinary people on the ground, including captives themselves. Such categories and associations proved unstable as Apaches journeyed south from the present-day US-Mexico border region to the Caribbean basin. Native captives from the same family might be labeled as "orphans" to be purchased for the price of a horse in Chihuahua, "prisoners" to be housed in the royal jail in Mexico City, or "slaves" to be eagerly adopted into households in Cuba "because blacks [were] too expensive."[5]

Apaches were not simply passive vessels for such imaginings. Deemed uncontrollable on New Spain's frontiers, they proved beyond the control of Spanish imperial schemes in the Caribbean as well. Even as some residents of Cuba continued to request Apaches for their homes, the escape of Native captives and their collaboration with runaway slaves of African descent eventually led local magistrates and the governor in Havana to demand that no more Apaches be sent to the island. In sum, like captives and slaves throughout North America and its borderlands, Apaches navigated harsh circumstances creatively, through adaptation, resistance, and violence. Their story thus illuminates both the overlapping histories of bondage that characterized North America and the Caribbean at the turn of the nineteenth century and the diverse strategies that captives and slaves employed to make the best of their lives wherever they found themselves.[6]

ROOTS OF CAPTIVITY AND THE EXPERIENCE OF FORCED MIGRATION

The fate of Apaches uprooted from kin and homeland at the turn of the nineteenth century was not unique, but it was rooted in a particular historical context. In the interests of securing core territories and thwarting the advances of imperial adversaries, a new generation of Spanish policymakers in the 1760s and 1770s had sought fresh approaches to Indians who had long thwarted their military and missionary endeavors. In North America, the Comanches, Utes, and Navajos proved receptive to Spanish peace entrées or initiated treaty negotiations for their own reasons. For many neighboring groups, including Apaches, such efforts proved disastrous, as they found themselves caught between newly aggressive Spanish forces and long-standing Indian enemies. With the cooperation of Native allies, the Spanish pursued a two-pronged approach in the last decades of the eighteenth century. If Apaches laid down their arms and agreed to live around presidios (military forts), they would be offered regular gifts and rations. Alternatively, if they refused, they would face offensive war and permanent exile to central Mexico and the Caribbean. The exile of captives had become routine by the late 1770s, affecting not only Apache groups but also other Native groups across the region, from Seris on the Pacific coast to Coahuiltecan bands near the Gulf of Mexico. More than two thousand Apache Indians and as many as five thousand Natives in total were sent south in the process. Any discussion of such statistics must be placed in the context of the relatively sparse population of harsh Southwestern landscapes. For Apache groups in particular—estimated during this period to have numbered in the thousands, not tens of thousands—these forced migrations involved a significant proportion of their total populations.[7]

In seeking to move entire groups of people and exploit them for their labor, Spanish military officers and governors echoed similar schemes orchestrated by their predecessors and by imperial competitors during the eighteenth century. One historian has described this period as a "wide-ranging world of imperial experimentation" characterized by creative solutions to the demands of "a vast market for colonial labor." The British, French, and Spanish each pursued their own plans to colonize distant lands with convicts, Acadians, or Canary Islanders or draw upon the labor of enslaved Africans, smugglers, or Apaches for arduous construction projects, military service, and imperial defense. Sometimes such plans were successful in the sense that imperial dreams translated fairly well into colonial realities. More often, the schemes of empires did not align with their power to put them into practice.[8]

The Apache diaspora to the Caribbean provides an example of just such a rift between theory and practice, vision and reality. The transport of Native war captives from the present-day US-Mexico border region to Cuba was paid for by the royal treasury, orchestrated by soldiers and militiamen, and explained in the interests of the "public good" as a means of securing North American frontiers and incorporating non-Christian Indians into the folds of a Catholic monarchy. Officials imagined that in the Caribbean, where there was an insatiable demand for labor, Apaches could surely be put to good use. If Spanish governors and viceroys envisioned the forced removal of Apaches to be in the best interests of captors and captives alike, in practice, deaths, escapes, and resistance en route consistently frustrated their expectations.[9]

The coerced migration of sixteen Apache men and seven women who boarded the *Polonia* and *Brujula* bound for Havana in the summer of 1802 had begun months earlier in the rugged mountains of the North American West. The captives were most likely Gileño or Chiricahua Apaches, who lived with their extended families in mountain camps they chose for their access to water, security, and food sources. They designed camps to be temporary so that they could abandon them easily if necessary, but they often returned to the same locations at specific times of the year to hunt, harvest plants, or perform ceremonial functions. They knew these lands by names that referenced natural features or past events, and they recognized borders that divided their territory from enemies and outsiders. Though many "Apache" groups shared similar ways of life, recognized degrees of kinship, and spoke related and even mutually intelligible languages, they were not united by a pan-Apache identity or tribal structure. While Spaniards often misunderstood relationships within what they called "Apachería," or Apache country, they nonetheless recognized divisions between Apache groups that influenced Spanish military and diplomatic strategies.[10]

In fact, military officials employed their knowledge of Apache groups to try to turn them against one another and toward an alliance with the Spanish. Promises of gifts and rations and the specter of exile had led hundreds of Apaches to ally with the Spanish and agree to aid them in their ongoing military campaigns by the early 1800s. Throughout 1801, for example, the captain of the Spanish presidio at Janos, Nueva Vizcaya, reported that a number of Gileño Apache headmen were "at peace" in his district and were out on campaigns against other Indians who remained at war. It was likely with the aid of these Native allies that the Spanish targeted the camps of Apache families who later would compose the cargo of the *Brujula* and *Polonia*.[11]

Though the precise moments of their capture elude the historical record, we know that Spanish and Native warriors usually stormed their enemies' camps at daybreak, seeking to catch them by surprise and capture as many women and children as possible. In the event that the captives were kin of an influential headman, presidio captains might try to leverage them to bring men to the negotiating table. The ability to petition for return of kin was a key motivating factor for some Apaches to negotiate peace agreements at Spanish presidios in the late 1700s and early 1800s.[12]

The captives gathered in campaigns in the fall and winter of 1801 would not be so lucky, though the Spanish did claim that the success of these campaigns helped lead three Gileño Apache headmen—Concha, Chafalote, and Naranjo—to request peace the following summer.[13] If it was common for entire families to enter into captivity together, military officers sometimes separated young captives from their kin and kept them in the North. On occasion, they gave them to local families as "orphans" to raise. Other times, it was the very Spanish and Native warriors who had captured them who also petitioned to receive them, as when the commandant general in Chihuahua City, Pedro de Nava, explained that the little Apache girls that Sergeant Nicolás Madrid and Mariano Varela had chosen could be left to them and that other soldiers should be given the same opportunity, "to select a little Indian girl, to their satisfaction." The image of soldiers selecting girls for "their satisfaction" suggests the range of productive and reproductive labor that "adopted" young people might be expected to perform.[14]

Such trafficking of Native children was commonplace, and it endured well into the twentieth century in the North American West. Indians deemed "orphans" because their parents had been either killed or exiled might be adopted into Hispanic families and become like kin, just as Hispanic youths were sometimes incorporated into Native communities. Intimacy and exploitation blurred, as the documentary record evinces evidence of Apache boys and girls "sold as slaves for the price of a horse" or used to pay off gambling debts. In this way, the particular case of this group of Apache war captives gathered in 1801 and 1802 evokes a broader characteristic of bondage evident in the borderlands of Southwestern America: potential masters coveted children in particular because of the perception that they were more controllable and assimilable into Christian society than adults. The promise of conversion and acculturation served to justify the removal of children from their natal communities and their exploitation even as it buttressed masters' sense of themselves as charitable people who were helping to "raise up" indigenous people from their "barbarism."[15]

In this particular case, officials appear to have endorsed this customary practice, for when soldiers surveyed the captives in the jail at the presidio of Conchos in Chihuahua in early February 1802, they reported none under the age of fifteen. Among twenty-one men and sixty-five women, most were young adults or middle aged. Two ninety-year-old women also awaited the long journey south, including one who later arrived in Havana. In fact, the presence of elderly captives in convoys was not uncommon, indicating how the instilling of fear as much as concern for frontier security or demand for labor influenced the forced migration campaigns of this era.[16]

As the captives waited in jail, Sergeant Joseph Antonio Uribe made preparations to escort them south. He was a veteran convoy conductor, and his experience and reputation for maintaining good security may help explain why all but three of the Apache captives who departed Chihuahua arrived in Mexico City at the end of March 1802, after a journey of nearly two months. The viceroy of New Spain commended Uribe for his track record of preventing escapes and asked him to report his methods to the troops that he had commissioned to transport the captives on to the coastal port of Veracruz. Uribe explained that he shackled men two by two on muleback and encircled the convoy with soldiers whenever they came to a stop. At night, when it was common for them to house the captives in a roadside inn, he posted two guards inside and one at the door, taking care that the guards inside be armed only with clubs. If guards inside carried guns, Uribe explained, Indians might be able to use them to their advantage in an escape attempt. Of course, such attention to security responded to the reality that escapes were frequent and had motivated officials to mandate that all Apache prisoners of war be exiled overseas to Havana rather than remain in New Spain.[17]

Uribe's emphasis on shackling men, but not women, suggests that not only age but also gender shaped captives' fates. In the 1770s and 1780s, convoys had sometimes left Indian women behind in households in Mexico City as "criadas." The term literally means "one who is raised up," suggesting the understanding that by Christianizing these captives, masters would save their souls and make them useful to themselves and society as laboring subjects of the king. Many criadas had little interest in either the salvation or servitude their masters offered, however. When Native women, like their male counterparts, proved adept at escaping and making the long journey home, they, too, were more commonly sent on to the Gulf Coast and the Caribbean.[18]

Apache captives in 1802, like others before them, spent several months in confinement in Mexico City before continuing on to the coast, which helps explain why many of them did not make it all the way to Havana. In fact, for a variety of reasons—illness, age, perceived behavior, escape—many Indians never arrived in the Caribbean but instead remained in jails, poorhouses, or Catholic parishes or returned to their homelands. In the spring of 1802, Uribe and his men transported male captives to the royal jail, as was common. They left female captives at either the poorhouse or the collection house, an institution that focused especially on housing and "reforming" prostitutes. Wherever captives were housed, space was at a premium. In places like the collection house, for example, Apache women were usually confined alongside thirty or forty prostitutes. Given that they were cramped in close quarters with strangers, it is unsurprising that house directors complained that Native women not only picked fights with the prostitutes but also quarreled among one another.[19]

If Apache men and women may have felt some physical relief in the temporary end to their march in Mexico City, they faced new psychological challenges in these prisons and poorhouses. After years of diaspora, the return of escapees north had likely given Apaches some sense of what it meant to be sent away. Perhaps they even knew from the stories of runaways that their march would continue to the sea and that they might be embarked on boats leading onward to some unknown destination.[20] If these and other possibilities occupied their thoughts as the days and weeks passed in confinement in Mexico City, they may have found some comfort in their kin. Because the Spanish targeted extended family camps in their military campaigns, it was common for groups of captives to include mothers and daughters, sisters and brothers. But the presence of family brought new torments when sickness spread through these jails, as it did in the spring of 1802 and other occasions. Traditionally, Apaches abandoned any place where death had occurred, because they believed that ghosts could continue to dwell among the living and do them harm. The inability to respond appropriately to deaths on April 10, May 14, May 16, May 30, and June 11—to flee prisons where their kin had died from smallpox, cholera, and other illnesses—must have made incarceration all the more terrifying.[21]

Unfamiliar landscapes and uncertain futures beckoned when Natives finally continued their journey from Mexico City toward the Gulf Coast in late June. If Indians sometimes rode on muleback from the north to the capital, they always marched on foot on the 250-mile journey from Mexico City to the coast. Soldiers chained Indian men and women two by two, with one of the pair shackled to the chain that bound together the whole group.[22] They traveled eight to twelve miles a day (four to six leagues) across rugged terrain. Soldiers described the attitude of Indians on the march as "die first, walk tomorrow." Natives sometimes threw themselves to the ground and refused to march any further. After beating an Indian with a rod, for example, one soldier managed to get him to walk another half mile, until, "seeing his resistance, and insistence on throwing himself to the ground," he had to put him on muleback. When three or four other Indian men started throwing themselves to the ground, the conductor explained, he could tell that one of them "did it with such ostentation that [the conductor] knew his resistance was rooted not in exhaustion, but in furor." In fact, the man inclined his head to the ground as he fell eight or nine times, and any one of these impacts would have cracked his skull, "but for the fortune that [they] were traveling through land with soft, loamy soil."[23]

When the chain gang arrived on the coast, Natives again faced confinement. They were housed in the castle of San Juan de Ulúa until the next ship was available to carry them on to Cuba. In the meantime, Spanish captors continued efforts to ascribe new identities to them, even if they could not forcibly alter their captives' self-understandings. Because soldiers complained that Native names were virtually impossible to determine—one explained that even those with Christian names claimed to be "Peter today and then John tomorrow"—they identified most of them by numbers. In central Mexico and the Caribbean alike, residents commonly referred to these Indian captives not as "Gileño Apaches" or even "Apaches," but by the term *meco*, which derived from the term *chichimeco*, long applied to allegedly "uncivilized" or "nomadic" Indians. This meant that individual Indians might be referred to as "Meco number 3" or "Meca number 134."[24] In the case of these captives in July 1802, officials in Veracruz also planned a mass baptism to prepare them for shipment to Havana and to give them new Christian names. Some Apaches apparently did see an opportunity for salvation in baptism, but not in the way their captors intended. In the midst of the ceremony, they "fled in all directions," which may explain why only sixteen men and seven women continued on to Havana.[25]

ARRIVAL AND LIFE IN CUBA

When the captives boarded the *Brujula* and *Polonia* in early August 1802, they had already lived through months of incarceration and forced migration. The historical record contains no accounts from an Apache perspective of how they viewed their impending transport to Cuba. Conversations they may have had about what it would mean to cross the sea are thus unknowable. Their actions, however, suggest the desperation with which some sought to avoid this fate, however they may have understood it. The governor of Veracruz noted, for example, that Apaches had "such disregard for life" that they often threw themselves into the water from the castle of San Juan de Ulúa with their chains still attached. He described how their bodies sometimes washed up on shore, even as other times they succeeded in escaping into the countryside. In fact, the belief that such escapees fomented resistance to Spanish rule back in the Southwest Borderlands buttressed the argument that the only way to secure Apache war captives would be to "put water in between them" and their homelands.[26]

The harrowing escapes Apache men and women carried out in order to return home after arriving on the coast suggest that it was not life they disregarded but rather captivity and servitude. If some took advantage of opportunities to leap into the sea, others faced another forced passage, joining a motley cargo of Native war captives and Hispanic convicts bound for forced labor in the Caribbean, including murderers and thieves sentenced by courts in Mexico City to terms of forced labor overseas. The ship captain carried the sentences of these convicts and information about their crimes to report to officials in Havana; for the Indians, he carried no such documentation, only a count of the number of men and women on board.[27]

The fact that Havana residents had little specific knowledge of these captives' origins or identities does not mean that they did not have preconceptions about Indians that influenced their reception of them. Years earlier, when the viceroy of Mexico had first inquired about sending Apaches to Havana, the governor of Cuba had responded enthusiastically. Diego José Navarro imagined that after they baptized and catechized them, large numbers of Apaches might form a separate neighborhood in Havana from which they could provide labor useful to the king and their Spanish neighbors. Navarro was not alone in believing that separation from home might help alter the Indians' character. One of his successors wrote that "he knew about the perversity of these people in their own lands, but he did not believe them to be ferocious once taken away from home." He was convinced that Apaches in Cuba "would not exercise their bloody passions."[28]

If some Spaniards believed that the process of forced migration itself could transform Apaches, others were more skeptical. When the brigantine *General Gálvez* and the packet boat *Oliba-blanca* arrived in March 1784 carrying eighteen Indian women and thirty-three Indian men, Navarro's successor, Governor Luis de Unzaga y Amezaga, sent a missive to his counterpart in Veracruz to explain that he had received no news about these Indians, where they had come from, or what he should do with them. Moreover, he was deeply concerned about the presence of these "unbelievers" in his jurisdiction, given what he perceived to be their "fierce and indomitable" character. Unzaga y Amezaga contrasted his views with those of his predecessor. If Navarro had welcomed the transport of Indians to Cuba because he believed them to be "less corrupt" in their customs than convicts and more likely to work hard, Unzaga y Amezaga disagreed, explaining that far from hardworking, these Indians' character was "savage." His colleague in Veracruz responded by noting that the viceroy had decided to send Native war captives to Cuba to prevent their escape and return to their country by placing them in "decent homes, where they might be taken care of and educated." Like it or not, he noted, the governor would need to make the most of the situation.[29]

Even as royal officials compared and debated the merits of Indians, convicts, and slaves as laborers, many residents of Cuba proved perfectly happy to employ any laboring body they could get their hands on. When the first shipments of Apaches arrived in Havana in March, May, and August 1784, residents welcomed captives into their homes and workshops. The governor noted that local citizens "requested them enthusiastically." He distributed the captives within days to individuals asking for them.[30] Subsequent shipments of Apache captives in the 1780s and 1790s made this process routine. After the newspaper *Papel periódico de la Habana* was founded in 1790, the governor at the time posted an announcement to let local residents know about the impending arrival of "indios mecos." Subsequent governors may have posted announcements similar to this one, as extant petitions from Havana residents reproduce similar language:

> *Meca* girls...will be placed under the care of persons of their sex who are proper persons to instruct them in Religion, [and said] persons may have the advantage of their services. Those who wish to contribute to this pious work should apply to the Governor and Captain General, and they will receive the girls on the condition that they give a receipt for them and assume the obligation to report to the said Superior authority in case the girls die or run away.[31]

Of course, such official rhetoric and Havana residents' views of Apaches arriving in August 1802 did not always align. Extant petitions are often formulaic and usually adhere closely to the tropes of pious charity reflected in advertisements of the arrival of Indians. Others deviate enough to provide more of a sense of how different residents viewed Apaches they received and what they expected from them. In this regard, petitions illustrate that even if Spanish officials claimed that Natives were not legally slaves, slavery shaped residents' understandings of them. Since the late 1700s, slavery had been booming in Cuba as the island imported thousands of enslaved Africans both to labor in urban centers like Havana and to work on the growing number of sugar plantations dotting the countryside. The presence of slaves of African descent thus provided a point of comparison through which residents of Cuba sought to make sense of Indian captives.[32]

References to expensive slaves in petitions indicate that many residents viewed Indians equivalently, even if they may also have been motivated by interest in the "pious work" of converting non-Christians. Ana María Gamonales, for example, a widow originally from Cádiz, Spain, explained that she was supported by three sons who as army officers did not make enough for them to be able to purchase slaves to help maintain her household. She thus asked for one of the Indian women who had just arrived, promising to "treat her like a daughter" and noting that "the addition of this girl" to their home would be a "great relief."[33] Lorenzo de Ávila, a sergeant in the infantry regiment, echoed Gamonales's argument in explaining that his wife was ill and because she was unable to attend to the home, they were in need of the help of a slave. They could afford neither to buy nor to rent one, and he thus asked for an Indian woman to "assist his wife and [care for his three children]."[34]

Enslaved Africans were expensive, so the possibility of receiving an unpaid domestic must have tantalized a widow or young military officer.

In fact, Havana residents had greeted prior shipments of Indians with petitions making similar comparisons between black slaves and Indians. Six months earlier, Josefa de Castro, the wife of an attorney, had explained that she was sick, that she had children, and that her husband was absent. She regrettably did not have the means to support a "*negra*" and thus requested a "meca" who, she heard, had recently arrived among others. The same was true of Sergeant Major Manuel Cavello, who asked for an Indian woman to serve his daughter Josefa, given that the black slave he had given her "had gone crazy."[35]

One Havana resident slipped from comparing slaves and Indians to calling Indians "slaves." None of the petitioners did so in August 1802, but when a shipment of Apaches had arrived five years earlier, Domingo Correa, a supervisor of public works projects, had explained that "he did not have a slave for the service of his family, because of the small salary he received and the fact that slaves were so expensive." Having received word of the arrival of Indian women, he hoped that the governor of Havana would be willing to "grant him one of said slaves, and he would maintain her and instruct her in the Christian doctrine." Correa had his supervisor write a note testifying to his good conduct, and he was granted an Indian woman for his service.[36]

Comparison to enslaved Africans may not have been the only means through which Havana residents understood the arrival of these Indians, however. One petitioner, María Josefa Martely, for example, explained that she had received word that "conquest Indians" (*indios de conquista*) had arrived from Veracruz. She asked for two females and a male, promising to teach them "and raise them like children with charity." Though conclusions from a single petition should not be overdrawn, at least one Havana resident in the summer of 1802 echoed the long-standing custom that war was a legitimate means through which the forced labor of Natives might be acquired.[37]

The interests of Havana residents in acquiring Native domestics open a window onto the local customs and cultural expectations of potential masters that shaped Apaches' experiences in Cuba upon arrival. Drawing upon the familiar example of elite households with enslaved African women as domestics, middling Havana widows and military officers saw the incorporation of a Native woman or youth as a similar, if perhaps more affordable, symbol of status. An Indian not only provided productive labor but also served as an illustration of the "charity" and decency of a family in helping to Christianize and educate mecos—uncivilized Indians—from a distant land.[38]

The specific fates of Apache Indians aboard the *Brujula* and *Polonia* thus reflected an interplay between imperial policy and the local understandings of race, gender, and slavery. When the ships docked in the Havana harbor on August 2, 1802, the Indians and convicts aboard disembarked at La Cabaña, a fortress complex that served as both a military base and a prison. Here or in the plaza of Casablanca nearby, Indians' first encounters with Havana residents were often with enslaved Africans, as it was royal slaves or members of the black artillery company who orchestrated the transport of Native captives. They delivered them to the petitioners who had requested them and returned them to jail at the fortress if they did not suit their masters, as happened on occasion.[39] Given the urban setting of Havana, most residents who had heard about the arrival of Indians desired domestics, a role commonly fulfilled by women, and it is thus unsurprising that they requested them first in this instance. As residents' petitions for Indian women make clear, they intended them to perform the same labor as black slaves would have in their households—caring for children, cleaning, and preparing food. Records also reveal that some captives served in institutional settings rather than individual households, working for the Charity House (Casa de Beneficencia), the city hospital, or the tobacco factory. By the end of August, petitioners had asked for all but one of the female captives.[40]

Manuel Cavello, the sergeant major in charge of the plaza of Casablanca (who had also requested an Indian for his daughter), provided more details to Someruelos about the distribution of captives at the end of August. Sending along a carefully crafted chart, he detailed for the governor the new names that subjects had given to the captives they had received. "Meca number 1" had become "María Dolores," "Meca number 4," "María Antonia," and so on. Three of these women were now living in area households, while three others were serving at the Hospital of San Francisco de Paula. He noted that one woman remained in prison because she was "very old." This captive was likely one of the ninety-year-old women noted by officials in northern New Spain when they surveyed the convoy before its departure.[41]

By royal decree, Apache men were to work indefinitely on fortification projects and in shipyards. When the English had captured Havana during the Seven Years' War in 1762, the stunning loss of the city had illustrated that it was not adequately defended and had helped spark the construction of new fortresses at key Spanish coastal cities throughout the Caribbean basin. Reflecting broader imperial practices of the era, the Spanish made use of convict labor, rented slaves, and prisoners of war to maintain and expand such sites. In this way, it is striking that they exploited the labor of the same Apache men deemed too dangerous to be allowed to remain in the Southwest Borderlands to help maintain and expand imperial defenses in another region of the empire.[42]

Such men would have helped with any number of tasks requiring manual labor at the fortress complex. They might have cut and transported lumber needed for the shipyard, formed work gangs for construction projects in and around the port, or manned crews for the pontoons and barges that dredged the harbor. Criminals convicted of the most serious crimes were designated specifically for the arduous task of moving the chain pumps that kept the dry docks from flooding, though it is unclear if any Native captives were ever employed in this function. Across the Caribbean in Veracruz, Native men who had avoided shipment to Cuba performed similar labor: working at limekilns and in shipyards.[43]

In practice, Apache men were sometimes also given to local residents. In this particular case in August 1802, for example, the ship surgeon aboard the *Brujula* submitted a petition to receive both a man and a woman after the ship docked in the harbor. Don José Muñoz asked for special consideration because he had "assisted them in their journey." Perhaps because the governor had already received a number of petitions, he granted Muñoz only one captive, "Meco number 3," whom Muñoz renamed "José María." In the case of this shipment, then, the governor appears to have given residents the opportunity to receive both men and women, though it is striking that by the end of August, Manuel Cavello reported to him that a number of Indian men remained in the plaza of Casablanca "because of their physique or age." This was not the first time that captives' age, gender, bodily appearance, or perceived behavior led Havana residents to pass on the opportunity to incorporate them into their households. Though it is unclear precisely what officials did with the remaining men in this instance, they likely transported them to La Cabaña to work alongside convict laborers maintaining this fortress, as they had in the past.[44]

In sum, Apache men and women did not form a separate neighborhood, as one governor had once envisioned, but rather dispersed into different parts of Havana and beyond. The tendency to divide captives along gendered lines shaped distinct life trajectories for women and men. Women's placement in individual households scattered across the city would have made it difficult, for example, for them to reunite with friends or relatives. Women's isolation may have lessened the appeal of setting off into an unknown urban landscape in search of some alternative to a life of servitude. For women, more than for men, familiarity with forms of bondage

INDIANS, CONVICTS, AND SLAVES

practiced in the Southwest Borderlands—Native servitude in New Mexican households, for example—may have played a role in their ability to adapt to their circumstances and the labor their masters expected of them.[45]

If Apache women's status may not have been entirely foreign to them, this does not mean that it was desirable. Like enslaved Africans in domestic settings, they were uniquely vulnerable to the whims and moods of their masters. As was true in the Southwest Borderlands, intimacy and exploitation could go hand in hand. One man, Juan Manuel del Pilar, wrote with affection about his Indian servant María Vincenta, lamenting in a note to the governor that she had experienced a "violent convulsion of blood" and that he had brought in three doctors and an apothecary to care for her, "sparing no costs to contribute to her cure." In the end she had died, and he had buried her outside the Havana Cathedral. Submitting similar notes blending affection for Native servants with attention to suffering and death, masters also noted how their parish priests recorded the deaths of Indians in the same ledgers with those of mulatto and black slaves. As with the enslaved to whom people in Cuba compared them, some Apaches likely experienced a range of treatment characterized as often by abuse as by warmth or attachment.[46]

The fact that captives' life events were recorded in the same ledgers with those of mulattos and blacks also helps to explain the difficulty of tracking Apaches' experiences in Cuba through time. Like enslaved Africans, they may have borne the children of their masters, incorporated Catholicism into their worldviews and spiritual practices, or even married and started families.[47] Children likely had the greatest ability to forge new lives as part of Hispanic society in the Caribbean. In April 1799, a Havana resident forwarded to Governor Someruelos a letter he had received from his brother that hints at just such a possibility. Jacinto de Porras explained that a group of bandits had recently killed a young Indian boy—"un indiecito meco"—in his neighborhood. He noted that the boy had learned shoemaking, played the violin, and had "lived honorably."[48]

Some Apaches learned to draw upon Spanish religious sentiment or legal distinctions between their status and that of enslaved Africans to try to exit captivity and a life of forced labor. In March 1805, for example, two "Meco Indians" petitioned the viceroy of New Spain for their freedom. With the aid of a Spanish notary, Carlos and Manuel explained that they had worked in the ports of Veracruz and Havana for twenty-two years alongside convict laborers and enslaved Africans. Citing their good behavior, baptism into the Catholic faith, old age, and the fact that they had not committed any crimes, they asked the viceroy to "lift their chains" and

81

allow them some rest for what remained of their lives. "We suffer," they explained, "only because the Almighty chose to raise us among heathens." Six months later, the men petitioned a second time because the viceroy had not answered them, and they continued to labor in exile.[49]

For these men and others, neither conversion, learning Spanish, nor "honorable" labor necessarily presented a way out of circumstances not of their choosing, however. In this sense, it is unsurprising that some Apaches, including some of the men who arrived in the summer of 1802, defied Spanish hopes that "putting the sea between" them and their home would end their resistance to Spanish imperial aims. Less than two weeks after the arrival of the *Brujula* and *Polonia* in August 1802, six Indian men escaped from the plaza of Casablanca and fled into the countryside. Their story, like those of others, highlights another means through which Apache men and women navigated diaspora, even upon arrival in Cuba: escape. Native men's escapes and cooperation with runaways of African descent occupied the attention of the highest levels of government in Havana and ultimately helped fuel demands by Governor Someruelos and others that no more Apaches be sent there.[50]

RUNAWAYS AND THE END OF THE APACHE DIASPORA TO CUBA

Though it is unclear precisely when or how six Indian men escaped from the port of Havana in August 1802, we know that they fled south approximately ten leagues toward the mountainous district known as San José de las Lajas, likely in pursuit of food and horses. It was on a sugar plantation in this district that they were reported to have killed a black slave named Pasqual. This slave's death sparked a frantic manhunt to track the runaways, changing the lives of all involved. The captain of the party sent in pursuit and his men spent the next three years hunting Indians in the Cuban countryside. As for the surviving escapees, they would be tried for the murder of the slave, imprisoned, and shipped overseas again.[51]

It was in mid-August 1802 that the Native runaways first came to the attention of area residents. The overseer of a local ranch observed that he was missing an ox, and in searching for it, he had discovered six saddleless horses tied up on the mountainside. Assuming that bandits must be hiding nearby, he informed the district captain, José Gavilán, who formed a party of men to investigate. Before nightfall they had discovered six "indios mecos" on the top of a cliff. As they tried to capture them, the Indian men resisted "fiercely and barbarously." They were on higher ground and threw so many rocks that by nightfall Gavilán and his men had managed to capture only one of them. They sent him back to Havana the next day, continuing their hunt for the remaining five runaways. After this skirmish with the Indian runaways, Gavilán received an official commission from Governor Someruelos to pursue and apprehend them. If Gavilán lamented the "harm" that the runaways were causing to area farms, the stolen corn and a half-eaten horse he described indicate more than anything the basic means through which the Indians survived on the lam.[52]

The discovery of the body of a slave in a corral on a nearby plantation lent new urgency to Gavilán's pursuit in late August. By following the tracks from Pasqual's body all the way to the abandoned mountain camp of the Indians, Gavilán became convinced that they had committed this homicide. Days later, he finally located the runaways, and, as he explained, though he tried "the most humanitarian methods to attract them, they made the cruelest resistance that their barbarity made possible." The fight continued off and on through the next day until, Gavilán reported, he had killed or captured all six of the runaways. He wrote proudly to the governor that the planters of the area "could now relax and live in peace, free of the kinds of harm they had been experiencing since the Indians first set foot in these mountains." With a potential monetary reward in mind, he also reminded the governor that he had endangered his own life for the public good, "without fear of sacrificing himself in order to stop in their tracks these enemies of humanity."[53]

While the four surviving runaways awaited trial for the murder of Pasqual in Havana, Gavilán took up a commission to track other Native escapees. For more than five years, the governor had received reports about Indians in the countryside in the district of Filipinas, sixty leagues west of Havana. Though he had commissioned parties to track them, they had yet to be apprehended. On the basis of Gavilán's recent success near Havana, Someruelos was hopeful that he was the best man for the job. Though Gavilán later claimed that he was interested only in "the public good," he was likely influenced as well by the bounties on the heads of the alleged leaders of this gang of runaways: two Indian men named El Chico and El Grande. Someruelos, the City of Havana, and the Royal Consulate, which regulated slave commerce on the island, had joined together to offer rewards of three thousand pesos for the apprehension of El Chico or El Grande alive or two thousand pesos dead. This they would pay in addition to any costs that the men who captured them accrued in their expedition.[54]

Less than a month after apprehending runaway Apaches near Havana, Gavilán and his party set off for the western tip of Cuba to begin this new expedition to locate an Indian-led runaway gang, or *palenque*, as they were commonly known in Spanish America. Locals around the town of Pinar del Río may have shared stories with them about the "indios mecos" they believed had committed more than twenty homicides and dozens of robberies on area plantations in recent years. They may have told the tale of a party of men who had briefly captured three such Indians, for example. They had explained that they needed directions to the coast to "find a way to disembark," and by conveying a desire for religious instruction, they had managed to get the men to provide them with food and water before they escaped again into the mountains.[55] Residents may have also told Gavilán about Governor Someruelos's own failed scheme to capture the Indians by luring them onto abandoned farms with residents painted in blackface pretending to be slaves tending livestock. Perhaps the local magistrate in Pinar del Río mentioned his own theory for the strange absence of black runaways in recent years: the Indians had killed them all.[56]

Governor Someruelos believed these Indians to be Apaches transported to Cuba from New Spain. The long-distance escapes orchestrated by Apaches on the mainland lend plausibility to the idea that captives from the Southwest Borderlands may have been among these and other reported palenques. At the same time, it should be noted that Euro-Americans transported a broad range of Native groups to the Caribbean, members of which could have comprised the palenques rustling livestock from Cuban plantations. British contraband traders had carried Indian captives to the island in the past, and Yucatec Mayans had arrived in Cuba at times as well. Even more common was the presence of *guachinangos*, a term drawn from Nahuatl that people in Cuba used to describe "Mexicans." At times, contemporary descriptions of palenques that included "wild Indians" and guachinangos seem to embody rumors and fears more than actual firsthand observation; the presence and escape of Apache Indians and other Natives fueled fears of Indians in some contexts where no Indians may have actually been present. Attention to Spanish efforts to track and apprehend such palenques nonetheless casts light on the broader presence and influence of Indians in Cuba beyond Havana during this period and their influence in shaping ideas about the transport of Apache captives to the island.[57]

Gavilán's immediate task in western Cuba in October and November 1802 was to deal with the mess his predecessors had left. From what he could gather, the motley crew of convicts and other men whom Someruelos had sent to apprehend the runaways had been worse than the runaways themselves, scaling walls, breaking into homes, and setting fire to fields. Having sent these men back to Havana, Gavilán and his own men set to work tracking El Chico and El Grande and the members of their palenque.

For more than forty days, they explored the mountains and coasts along the western tip of the island without finding any sign of Indians. Finally, in January 1803, a group of Gavilán's men encountered the palenque face-to-face. They later described how they had observed two Indians, El Chico and El Grande, along with five other men, "two *pardos*, one *negro*, and another two like guachinangos."[58] Gavilán's lieutenant, Eugenio Malvar, had ordered that the party's attack dogs be let loose, and one of them grabbed El Grande and knocked him to the ground. This gave Malvar time to reach him and stab him to death with his machete. In the meantime, the other members of the palenque had managed to wound Malvar and some of his men before escaping into the mountains. If Malvar and Gavilán lamented the escape of El Chico and his companions, they nonetheless had killed El Grande and made preparations to claim the two thousand peso reward. As proof of their success, they shipped his head in a vat of brandy to Governor Someruelos in Havana and presented sworn statements of witnesses that attested to their version of events, as well as to the crimes allegedly committed by the Indians and their companions in recent days. On the same day of the encounter, for example, witnesses reported that the Indians had attacked a local farm, killed seven dogs, stolen furniture and clothes from area homes, profaned the holy water of the local parish, and broken off the hand of a statue of the Virgin Mary.[59]

Ultimately, we can only speculate about the aims of El Chico and El Grande and their companions. Perhaps, like the group of Indian men who claimed to be seeking "to disembark" two years prior, they were looking for some route off the island. More likely, they sought an alternative to the servitude required of them within society in Cuba, creatively improvising a life on the lam through association with other runaways, including slaves of African descent, that may have echoed their past lives raiding ranches and rustling livestock on the mainland. This palenque was not alone, either, as Gavilán and members of his party continued to track reports of Indian runaways in the coming years, conducting expeditions to apprehend various Afro-Indian palenques in 1803, 1804, and 1805.[60]

These palenques and the runaway Apaches who had sparked Gavilán's entry into the business of slave hunting in the first place fueled efforts by Governor Someruelos to end the transport of Apaches to Cuba altogether. Even as the trials of the four surviving men for the murder of Pasqual unfolded, Someruelos levied evidence of such escapes and runaway gangs to lobby the Crown to stop the shipment of Apaches from New Spain to Cuba. He sent missives to the viceroy in Mexico City and the Spanish monarch demanding that no more of these "*indios feroces*"—ferocious Indians, as he called them—be sent to Cuba from Mexico, unless they were children. In the meantime, officials in Havana produced dozens of pages of documents as they investigated the murder case, even employing an interpreter to collect testimony from the men involved. Unfortunately, to date, only references to such documents, rather than the actual trial transcripts, have been located. What is known, however, is that after Gavilán captured the four men, he sent them back to jail in Havana. In their cells, the men learned of their sentences nine months later, in September 1803. While the court had originally sentenced them to a public execution, officials decided to commute this sentence for each of the surviving Indian men and replace it with a ten-year term of forced labor at an overseas presidio.[61]

In a startling turn of events, one of the men, named Rafael, was ordered by the court to complete his sentence at the castle of San Juan de Ulúa in Veracruz, back on the mainland. When officials in Cuba shipped him there, the governor of Veracruz had to remind officials in Havana that by royal decree Apache Indians were never allowed to return to Mexico, given the risk that they might escape and make it back home. Rafael did not survive to serve his full sentence.[62] Shipped multiple times between Veracruz and Havana, he died awaiting shipment overseas again, this time to Cartagena de Indias in present-day Colombia. His life and long journey—from capture in the Southwest Borderlands through shipment to Havana, forced labor, escape, incarceration, and death—speak to the complex interplay between imperial aims and local understandings of race, caste, and bondage that influenced his and other Native captives' lives in diaspora during this period. In one sense Rafael was the victim of larger processes of colonialism and empire that uprooted thousands of people like him during the early modern era. Unknowingly perhaps, he and his companions also shaped this history by illustrating that even "putting the sea between" them and their homelands would not prove sufficient to ensure their submission to Spanish designs. Although royal advisors officially denied Someruelos's demands to stop shipping Apaches to Cuba, neither do they appear to have transported any more Native captives to Havana until perhaps 1810 or 1816, the last extant references to Apaches en route to Cuba before Mexican independence.

CONCLUSION

What do we make of a world in which Native runaways banded with enslaved Africans in palenques hunted by Spanish militiamen in Cuba? What does it mean to find Apaches from the North American West imprisoned, laboring, or escaping far from home, in the heart of the Spanish empire? The story of an Apache diaspora charted here provides one illustrative example of how histories of slavery in North America and the Atlantic World included a diverse cast of characters from far-flung places of origin. In the Caribbean, as in the borderlands of the North American West, cross-cultural relations of captivity and bondage proved complex and variable.[63]

The fates of eighty-six Apache men and women in diaspora in 1802 reveal how the protean nature of race and slavery in North America and its borderlands affected a specific group of people in a particular historical moment. The experiences of Apache men and women carried into unfamiliar social and cultural contexts by continental and transoceanic networks of empire and commerce illustrate how understandings of "slavery" and who could be subjected to it shifted across space and time. Spanish visions of orphans to adopt, prisoners to confine, or slaves to exploit tell only part of the story, however. Apaches, like captives and slaves elsewhere, shaped history through their resistance, adaptation, and escape. In the process, they proved to be more than the pawns of imperial schemes, whether adapting creatively to a new life in diaspora or raiding sugar plantations and stoking fear in the hearts of Caribbean planters.

Notes

1. Documents related to the transport of captives aboard the *Brujula* and *Polonia* are contained in files 1716 and 1721, Papeles de Cuba, Archivo General de Indias, Seville (hereafter cited as AGI-Cuba file #). See especially "Relación de los presidiarios q.e conduce de transporte este Buq.e desde el Puerto de Veracruz," August 2, 1802, AGI-Cuba 1716. For quotes from the announcement of Indians' arrival in the Havana newspaper, see Duvon C. Corbitt, "Immigration in Cuba," *Hispanic American Historical Review* 22, no. 2 (1942): 285, as cited in Jason M. Yaremko, "Colonial Wars and Indigenous Geopolitics: Aboriginal Agency, the Cuba-Florida-Mexico Nexus, and the Other Diaspora," *Canadian Journal of Latin American and Caribbean Studies* 35, no. 70 (2010): 182. On broader experience of exile during this period, see Paul Conrad, "Captive Fates: Displaced American Indians in the Southwest Borderlands, Mexico, and Cuba, 1500–1800" (PhD diss., University of Texas–Austin, 2011), 248–254.

2. Juliana Barr, "A Spectrum of Indian Bondage in Spanish Texas," in *Indian Slavery in Colonial America*, ed. Alan Gallay (Lincoln: University of Nebraska Press, 2010), 277–309; Barr, "From Captives to Slaves: Commodifying Indian Women in the Borderlands," *Journal of American History* 92, no. 1 (June 2005): 19–46. I employ the category of "bondage" here to encompass slavery, incarceration, and involuntary servitude. I do not view chattel slavery as just another form of forced labor, but neither did legal categories like "slave" and "prisoner of war" necessarily correspond neatly

to the lived experience of captives, particularly, indigenous peoples like Apaches at the turn of the nineteenth century. Moreover, historical actors themselves made comparisons between categories like "slave," "convict," and "prisoner" in order to make sense of each, which makes uniting analyses of them under the category of "bondage" useful.

    3. For the broader context of Native transport to the Spanish Caribbean, see Yaremko, "Colonial Wars and Indigenous Geopolitics"; Christon I. Archer, "The Deportation of Barbarian Indians from the Internal Provinces of New Spain, 1789–1810," *Americas* 29 (January 1973): 376–385; Conrad, "Captive Fates," 211–247; Sigfrido Vázques Cienfuegos and Antonio Santamaria Garcia, "Indio foráneos en Cuba a principios del siglo XIX: Historia de un suceso en el contexto de la movilidad poblacional y la geoestrategia del imperio español," *Colonial Latin American Historical Review*, 2nd series, vol. 1, no. 1 (Winter 2013): 1–34. The Spanish convict labor system is described in Ruth Pike, "Penal Servitude in the Spanish Empire: Presidio Labor in the Eighteenth Century," *Hispanic American Historical Review* 58, no. 1 (1978): 21–40. For the boom in slavery in Cuba during this period, see especially Matt Childs, *The 1812 Aponte Rebellion in Cuba and the Struggle against Atlantic Slavery* (Chapel Hill: University of North Carolina Press, 2006).

    4. For examples of the varied legal contexts of Indian slavery in North American colonial societies, see Gallay, *Indian Slavery in Colonial America*; for Spanish America more specifically, see James F. Brooks, *Captives and Cousins: Slavery, Kinship, and Community in the Southwest Borderlands* (Chapel Hill: University of North Carolina Press, 2002), 123–124.

    5. In utilizing "diaspora" broadly as a category describing the forced removal and dispersal of people into new communities, I draw from Nancy Van Deusen, "Diasporas, Bondage, and Intimacy in Lima, 1535 to 1555," *Colonial Latin American Review* 19, no. 2 (August 2010): 247–277, and Christopher Hodson, *The Acadian Diaspora: An Eighteenth Century History* (New York: Oxford University Press, 2012), 3. My thinking about the "mercurial" nature of categories of race and bondage is influenced by both Nancy Shoemaker, "Race and Indigeneity in the Life of Elisha Apes," *Ethnohistory* 60, no. 1 (Winter 2013): 27–44, and Brett Rushforth, *Bonds of Alliance: Indigenous and Atlantic Slaveries in New France* (Chapel Hill: University of North Carolina Press, 2012), especially 3–14.

    6. My approach to Apaches' life trajectories in diaspora draws inspiration from the introductory essay by the volume editors, Emma Christopher, Cassandra Pybus, and Marcus Rediker in *Many Middle Passages: Forced Migration and the Making of the Modern World* (Berkeley: University of California Press, 2007), especially 3, where they discuss

"the threefold process of violence, resistance, and creativity" characterizing forced migrations.

7. For Spanish approaches to mobile Indians, see David J. Weber, *Bárbaros: Spaniards and Their Savages in the Age of Enlightenment* (New Haven, CT: Yale University Press, 2005). On geopolitical shifts in the North American West during this period, see Brian DeLay, *War of a Thousand Deserts: Indian Raids and the US-Mexican War* (New Haven, CT: Yale University Press, 2008); Matthew Babcock, "Turning Apaches into Spaniards: North America's Forgotten Indian Reservations" (PhD diss., Southern Methodist University, 2008); Juliana Barr, *Peace Came in the Form of a Woman: Indians and Spaniards in the Texas Borderlands* (Chapel Hill: University of North Carolina Press, 2007); Pekka Hämäläinen, *The Comanche Empire* (New Haven, CT: Yale University Press, 2008); Conrad, "Captive Fates," 167–210. For the "deportation," or exile, of Apaches south through New Spain, see Max L. Moorhead, "Spanish Deportation of Hostile Apaches: The Policy and the Practice," *Arizona and the West* 17, no. 3 (Autumn 1975): 205–220; Archer, "Deportation of Barbarian Indians"; Mark Santiago, *The Jar of Severed Hands: Spanish Deportation of Apache Prisoners of War, 1770–1810* (Norman: University of Oklahoma Press, 2011); Conrad, "Captive Fates," especially 211–247.

8. Quotes on labor markets and imperial experimentation are from Hodson, *The Acadian Diaspora*, 7. For convicts, see, for example, Clare Anderson, "Convict Passages in the Indian Ocean, 1790–1860," in Christopher, Pybus, and Rediker, *Many Middle Passages*, 129–149; Pike, "Penal Servitude." For Canary Islanders, see David J. Weber, *The Spanish Frontier in North America* (New Haven, CT: Yale University Press, 1992), 192–194.

9. For a summary of these arguments, see Hugo O'Connor to Viceroy, March 8, 1774, Provincias Internas, vol. 54, Archivo General de la Nación, Mexico City (hereafter cited as AGN-PI); Moorhead, "Spanish Deportation of Hostile Apaches"; Archer, "Deportation of Barbarian Indians"; Santiago, *Jar of Severed Hands*, 42.

10. Morris Opler, *Apache Lifeway: The Economic, Social, and Religious Institutions of the Chiricahua [Apache] Indians* (New York: Cooper Square Publisher, 1965). On the diversity of Apache groups and their cultural traditions, see also relevant entries in Alfonso Ortiz and William C. Sturtevant, eds., *Handbook of North American Indians*, vol. 10, *Southwest* (Washington, DC: Smithsonian Institution, 1978). On Indian territoriality, see Juliana Barr, "Geographies of Power: Mapping Indian Borders in the 'Borderlands' of the Early Southwest," *William and Mary Quarterly* 68, no. 1 (January 2011): 5–46; Keith H. Basso, *Wisdom Sits in Places: Landscape and Language among the Western Apache*, 6th ed. (Albuquerque: University New Mexico Press, 2000).

11. "Padrón que manifiesta el numero de Apaches de Paz establecidos en este Puesto y su Ynmediación," January 1, 1801, April 1, 1801, and October 1, 1801, in Janos

Paul Conrad

Presidio Collection, folder 16, section 1C, Benson Latin American Collection, Austin, Texas (hereafter cited as Janos Collection, F# [folder], S# [section]). On Apache motivations for entering peace agreements with the Spanish, see Matthew Babcock, "Rethinking the Establecimientos: Why Apaches Settled on Spanish-Run Reservations, 1786–1793," *New Mexico Historical Review* 84 (Summer 2009): 363–397.

12. On leveraging headmen to bring them to the negotiating table, see Paul Conrad, "*Bárbaros* into Soldiers: Violence, Reciprocity, and Identity on New Spain's Northern Frontier" (master's thesis, University of Texas–Austin, 2007); Conrad, "Captive Fates," 248–254; Babcock, "Turning Apaches into Spaniards." On daybreak raids, see Karl Jacoby, *Shadows at Dawn: An Apache Massacre and the Violence of History* (New York: Penguin Books, 2008).

13. De Nava to S.or D.n José Man.l de Ochoa, August 11, 1802, Janos Collection, F16, S2D.

14. De Nava to Casanova, March 20, 1794, and September 23, 1794, Janos Collection, F10, S1. By 1804, 10 percent of the population of the presidio of Janos was comprised of Indian "orphans" or *criados*; see "Padron que manifiesta el numero de Tropa, Imbalidos, y Vecinos de este Puesto," December 31, 1804, Janos Collection, F17, S2. Such dynamics reflect broader cultural convergences that help explain captive exchange complexes across the Southwest Borderlands; see James F. Brooks, *Captives and Cousins* and "'This Evil Extends Especially…to the Feminine Sex': Negotiating Captivity in the New Mexico Borderlands," *Feminist Studies* 22, no. 2 (1996): 279–309.

15. For the sale of Apache children and the paying of gambling debts with them, see Antonio Garcia de Aexada to Viceroy, April 16, 1816, AGN-PI, vol. 239; Ramón Gutiérrez, *When Jesus Came, the Corn Mothers Went Away: Marriage, Sexuality, and Power in New Mexico, 1500–1846* (Stanford, CA: Stanford University Press, 1991), 152–153. For the broader trafficking of children in the borderlands of the North American Southwest and the relationship between intimacy and exploitation, I draw from Brooks, *Captives and Cousins*; Katrina Jagodinsky, "Territorial Bonds: Indenture and Affection in Intercultural Arizona, 1864–1896," and Margaret Jacobs, "Breaking and Remaking Families: The Fostering and Adoption of Native American Children in Non-Native Families in the American West, 1880–1940," both in *On the Borders of Love and Power: Families and Kinship in the Intercultural American Southwest*, ed. David Wallace Adams and Crista DeLuzio (Berkeley: University of California Press, 2012), 255–277 and 19–46, respectively.

16. For the 1802 convoy makeup, see "Estado que manifiesta el numero de Piezas Prisioneras de Guerra, que ha recivido en este Quartel el Sargento Joseph Antonio Uribe p.a conducir a Mexico," AGN-PI, vol. 238, exp. 12. On broader makeup of such

convoys, see Conrad, "Captive Fates," 255–260; Santiago, *Jar of Severed Hands*, 201–203.

17. Uribe to Viceroy, April 7, 1802, AGN-PI, vol. 238, exp. 12. On Indian escapes, see Conrad, "Captive Fates," 225–233 and 259–260. For royal decrees at the turn of the nineteenth century and officials citing such decrees, see Viceroy to Regente de la Real Acordada, January 10, 1798, AGN-PI, vol. 208, f. 490; "Que se guarde lo ordenado sobre remision de Mecos," Council of Indies to Viceroy of New Spain, July 16, 1803, AGN–Reales Cedulas, vol. 188, exp. 169.

18. Domingo Valcarcel to Viceroy, December 4, 1778, AGN-PI, vol. 146, f. 414: "por averse experimentado el mal servicio de las Mecas, su genio indocil, y la facilidad con que se huien no se encuentran en el dia casas en que quieran recivirlas."

19. Del Corral to Viceroy, July 14, 1790, AGN-PI, vol. 155, f. 97; on the imprisonment of this particular group of captives in Mexico City in 1802, see AGN-PI, vol. 238, exp. 12. For broader practices, see Conrad, "Captive Fates," 211–247.

20. For discussion of Indians returning from the coast to their homelands, see Roque de Medina to Commandant General of Interior Provinces, June 8, 1796, AGN-PI, vol. 238, f. 448.

21. This analysis draws from Stephanie Smallwood's approach to the experience of African captives in *Saltwater Slavery: A Middle Passage from Africa to American Diaspora* (Cambridge, MA: Harvard University Press, 2008), especially 60–63. For Apache responses to death, see Opler, *Apache Lifeway*, 41. For deaths in jail, see AGN-PI, vol. 238, exp. 12, especially f. 362–363.

22. On the route between Mexico City and Veracruz, see "Ytinerario que debe observar el oficial que conduce la cuerda de Mecos (1810)," AGN-PI, vol. 238, f. 285. On shackles, see, for example, "Sobre haber intentado hacer fuga en Apan 27 Indios Apaches Prisioneros de Guerra (1801)," AGN–Presidios y Carceles, vol. 6, exp. 11, especially f. 170.

23. Testimony of Franquilino Vitado, August 20, 1801, AGN–Presidios y Carceles, vol. 6, exp. 11, f. 205–206: "ellos havian resuelto morir antes que caminar el siguiente dia." Testimony of D. Pedro Paez, August 13, 1801, AGN–Presidios y Carceles, vol. 6, exp. 11, f. 172: "biendo su resistencia, e insistiendo en tirarse al suelo…se huviera roto la caveza, pero la fortuna de haver encontrado un suelo blando y humedo le preservó de esta desgracia."

24. Diego de Lasaga to Viceroy, September 5, 1781, AGN-PI, vol. 123, f. 55: "de cuios nombres como tan variables, por que el que oy es Pedro, mañana es Juan, no se ha podido hazer lista formal; ni tampoco conseguir noticia cierta de los que sean baptizados." On the use of numbers for prisoners, see Juan Antonio de Araujo to Viceroy, February 13, 1798, AGN-PI, vol. 208, f. 525.

25. For baptism and escape, see "Sobre haberse aprehendido en Calpulalpa

dos Mecas Apaches de las que hicieron fuga en la ultima Cuerda," AGN–Presidios y Carceles, vol. 10, exp. 1 (1802), especially f. 17–18.

26. Joseph de Carrion y Andrade to Luis Unzaga y Amezaga, April 30, 1784, AGI-Cuba 1335: "desprecio de la vida," "poniendoles agua de por medio."

27. Documents related to the transport of captives aboard *Brujula* and *Polonia* are contained in AGI-Cuba 1716, 1720, and 1721, which also contain correspondence related to the transport of convicts, usually referred to as *forzados* or *presidiarios*.

28. On the Apache neighborhood in Havana, see Governor Diego José Navarro, as cited in Luis Unzaga y Amezaga to Viceroy, September 20, 1783, AGN–Archivo Histórico de Hacienda, vol. 1083, exp. 38: "y con el tiempo, juntandose algun numero destinarseles sitio en q.e hiciesen Poblaciones capaces de rendir al Rey y al Publico [ventajas y conveniencias]…juzgando ademas dificil la desercion de ellos y el regreso a sus territorios." For his successor's similar view, see Cabello y Robles to Pedro Corbalan, January 14, 1790, AGI-Cuba 1429: "Conosco la perversidad de estas gentes en estando en sus terrenos, pero no los tengo por feroces quando salen de ellos, por cuyo principio creo no exercitaran aqui su pasion sanguinolenta."

29. Havana Governor Unzaga y Amezaga to Veracruz Governor Carrion, April 14, 1784, AGI-Cuba 1335: "por su carácter fiero e indomable"; "Este dictamen se apoyó en la reflexion de que los Yndios aunque infieles no estan tan viciados en sus costumbres como los Presidiarios; son de indole docil, y por consequencia se aplicarian mejor al trabajo…lexos de tener estas circunstancias, son de un carácter fiero."

30. On shipments arriving in Havana, see Unzaga y Amezaga to Viceroy of Mexico, May 14, 1784, AGI-Cuba 1335: "en efecto quedan ya todos empleados en estos terminos, pues estos Vecinos los solicitan con empeño."

31. The quote from the announcements is drawn from Corbitt, "Immigration in Cuba," 285, as cited in Jason M. Yaremko, "Colonial Wars and Indigenous Geopolitics," 182.

32. On the boom of chattel slavery during this period, see Childs, *The 1812 Aponte Rebellion in Cuba*.

33. Ana María Gamonales to Someruelos, August 4, 1802, AGI-Cuba 1716: "carezen de Esclabos para el servicio mecanico de su Casa…suplica se digne mandar se le entregue una de dichas Mecas…ofreciendo enseñarla los Dogmas de Nuestra S.ta Religion Catolica, y tratarla como a hija con el mayor cariño, como que conseguiria un gran consuelo en la incorporacion de dicha indibidua."

34. Lorenzo de Avila to Someruelos, August 6, 1802, AGI-Cuba 1716: "suplica se sirva hacerle la gracia de proporcionarle una Meca de las que han venido de Mexico, a fin de que pueda asistir a su muger, y cuidar de sus tres hijos menores."

35. Maria Josefa de Castro to Governor of Havana, February 11, 1802, AGI-Cuba

1716: "D.a Josefa de Castro Esposa del Licenciado D.n Rafael Binelo con el devido respecto hace presente a V.S. hallarse enferma, con hijos, y el Marido ausente, y sin proporcion de sostener una negra q.e le es indispensable p.a su servicio"; S.or Brigadir D.n Vicente Nieto to Governor of Havana, February 11, 1802, AGI-Cuba 1716: "haversele vuelto loca una Negra que la tenia señalada."

36. Domingo Correa to Governor of Havana, March 16, 1797, AGI-Cuba 1516A: "que no teniendo esclava p.a el servicio de su familia, por el corto sueldo que disfruta y estar sumamente caras, dhas esclavas, y teniendo noticia de que en S.n Ysidro se allan depositadas alg.s Yndias Mecas por tanto Supp.ca a v.e. se digne conzederle una de dhas esclavas, a la que mantendra, y enseñara en la doctrina cristiana."

37. D.a María Josefa Martely to Governor of Havana, August 6, 1802, AGI-Cuba 1716: "ha llegado a su noticia haver arribado a este P.to de la Beracruz Indios de Conquista"; "criarlos como hijos con caridad."

38. My analysis here benefits from Nancy Van Deusen's consideration of the ways in which Castilians understood Native peoples arriving in Castille in the sixteenth century by comparing them with what was familiar. See Van Deusen, "Seeing Indios in Sixteenth-Century Castile," *William and Mary Quarterly* 69, no. 2 (April 2012): 205–235.

39. For the role of royal slaves in transport, see, for example, Félix González to Governor of Havana, March 28, 1791, AGI-Cuba 1516A. On the "slaves of his majesty" more broadly, see Maria Elena Diaz, *The Virgin, the King, and the Royal Slaves of El Cobre: Negotiating Freedom in Colonial Cuba, 1670–1780* (Stanford, CA: Stanford University Press, 2000).

40. For institutional settings, see for example, Francisco José de Bassave to Someruelos, February 12, 1802, AGI-Cuba 1721; on distribution by the end of August, see Manuel Cavello to Someruelos, August 31, 1802, AGI-Cuba 1721.

41. Manuel Cavello to Someruelos, August 31, 1802, AGI-Cuba 1716: "Noticia que demuestra el reparto de siete Yndias meca que vinieron de Veracruz en las Vrcas de S.M. S.ta Polonia y S.ta Brujula."

42. Ruth Pike, "Penal Servitude." For an example of dueling over convict laborers, see Matias de Galvez to Luis de Unzaga y Amezaga, March 12, 1784, AGI-Cuba 1335.

43. On these labor tasks, see Pike, "Penal Servitude." On Native labor in Veracruz, see "Arresto de dos Indios Mecos," November 24, 1784, AGN–Archivo Histórico de Hacienda, vol. 723, exp. 17; D.a Beatriz del Real to Viceroy, February 16, 1786, AGN–Archivo Histórico de Hacienda, vol. 723, exp. 28.

44. On Indians not distributed because of age or "disfigure," see Cabello, Casablanca to Someruelos, August 31, 1802, AGI-Cuba 1716: "Queda una mui vieja en Casa Blanca," "Quedan en casa blanca treze los que nadie los apeteze por su mala figura, y carga de años." For "perverse inclination," see D.a Clara Maria de Sierra to

Governor, n.d. (March 1791, from context), AGI-Cuba 1516A: "aun que se ha heforsado a su enseñansa, no hacido posible poderla persuadir, p.r ser de perversa indole."

45. On the trafficking of Native women in the New Mexican borderlands, see James Brooks, "'This Evil Extends Especially.'" For a perspective placing greater emphasis on the coercive aspects of such trades in the Louisiana borderlands, see Barr, "From Captives to Slaves."

46. Juan Manuel del Pilar y Manzano to Governor of Havana, January 28, 1791, AGI-Cuba 1429: "Fue acometida de un violento escorbuto de sangre…no habiendo excusado gastos para contribuir a su alivio." Similar notices in AGI-Cuba 1716 and 1720 describe Native life events being recorded in the ledgers of "pardos y mulatos."

47. In making these comparisons and speculations, I draw from Christopher Schmidt-Nowara, *Slavery, Freedom, and Abolition in Latin America and the Atlantic World* (Albuquerque: University of New Mexico Press, 2011), and Herbert S. Klein and Ben Vinson III, *African Slavery in Latin America and the Caribbean*, 2nd ed. (New York: Oxford University Press, 2007). See also Patrick J. Carroll, *Blacks in Colonial Veracruz: Race, Ethnicity, and Economic Development* (Austin: University of Texas Press, 1991); Herman L. Bennett, *Africans in Colonial Mexico* (Bloomington: Indiana University Press, 2003); Jane G. Landers and Barry M. Robinson, eds., *Slaves, Subjects, and Subversives: Blacks in Colonial Latin America* (Albuquerque: University of New Mexico Press, 2006).

48. "Parrafo de la carta que el Teniente D.n Jacinto de Porras que lo es del Partido de Guanes escrivio a su Hermano D.n Mauricio Esno. de Guerra de esta Plaza, su fha 26 de Abril anterior (1799)," AGI-Cuba 1510A.

49. Carlos and Manuel, "Mecos," to Viceroy José de Iturrigaray, October 14, 1805, AGN–Indiferente Virreinal, box 5908, exp. 50 (hereafter cited as AGN-IV). Documents contained in this file reveal that their first petition arrived and was brought to the viceroy's attention in March 1805; they petitioned again in October. Although the file contains several petitions from these two Indian men and documents investigating their history, there is no evidence in the file that they were in fact freed. Original quotes: "alsandoles la prisión"; "Confiesan, para mas explicar su dolor que no han cometido delito civil, ni criminal, y asi solo padecen por haver querido el todo Poderoso criarlos entre Gentiles."

50. Several files related to the escape of these six captives are contained in AGI-Cuba 1716 and 1720, as well as AGN-PI, vol. 238, especially f. 475, as cited below.

51. Ibid.

52. José Gavilán to Someruelos, September 18, 1802, AGI-Cuba 1720.

53. Ibid.: "aunque se valió de los medios mas prudentes que pide la humanidad para atraerlos hicieron la mas cruel resistencia que a su barbarie les fue posible"; "los vecinos Hacendados…ya descansan y viven pasificos y libres de toda clace de daños que

iban experimentando p.r momentos desde el instante que se posaron los Yndios en aquellas montañas"; "he sido el autor de esta empresa, que expuse mi vida, quebrante mi salud en esta campaña, y que no tube temor de sacrificarme por el bien publico para cortar en los principios los pasos agigantados de unos individuos enemigos de la humanidad."

54. On the actions of Indian runaways in Filipinas, see "Noticia que manifiesta los Muertos, Heridos, Robos, destrozo de Animales, Yncendios de Casas, y demas atrosidades que han cometido los Yndios feroces en el territorio de esta Jurisdiccion de Filipina, desde el año de 1796," Josef de Aguilar to Someruelos, April 2, 1803, AGI-Cuba 1720. On the bounties for El Chico and El Grande, see Real Consulado to Someruelos, October 14, 1802, AGI-Cuba 1720.

55. Rudesindo de los Olivios to Someruelos, May 16, 1800, AGI-Cuba 1720: "lo que querian era saber el camino de la buelta de arriba para solicitar modo de embarcarse."

56. Josef de Aguilar to Someruelos, April 2, 1803, AGI-Cuba 1720.

57. Someruelos used the case of Indian runaways in Filipinas to argue that Apache prisoners of war should no longer be sent to Cuba. See Someruelos to Viceroy of New Spain, October 6, 1802, AGI-Cuba 1720. On contraband trade, see Gregorio Guazo y Calderón to His Majesty, March 16, 1722, AGI–Santo Domingo 379. On Yucatec Mayans, see Yaremko, "Colonial Wars and Indigenous Geopolitics," 179.

58. "Extracto formado por D. Josef Lopez Gavilán," Lopez Gavilán to Someruelos, January 22, 1803, AGI-Cuba 1720.

59. Ibid.: "habian los Yndios asaltado la Hacienda la chorrera, matado siete perros, rompido la losa, robado varios muebles y ropas y por ultimo violado la Yglesia Parroquial rompiendo una mano a la imagen de nuestra señora y profanado los vasos y avios del sagrario."

60. For these expediciones, see "Comision de D.n Joséf Gabilan para la aprension del Yndio Chico," September 6, 1804, AGI-Cuba 1720.

61. "Autos crimin.s seguido de oficio contra los Yndios Rafael, Vitaque, Oste, y Cle s.re la muerte del Negro Pasqual esclabo," AGI-Cuba 1716, with additional references to the case in AGI-Cuba 1720.

62. A fragment amid documentation related to Rafael's case in AGI-Cuba 1720 reads, "Murió en hospital segun informó el alcalde."

63. See also Barr, "From Captives to Slaves."

4

Lúgsh and Laláki

Slaves, Chiefs, Medicine Men, and the Indigenous Political Landscape of the Upper Klamath Basin, 1820s–1860s

Boyd Cothran

In the summer of 1843, Marcus Gunn, a missionary at the Hudson's Bay Company outpost of Oregon City, reported the arrival of a group of Klamath *laláki*.[1] They were transporting twenty *lúgsh* (slaves), he observed, captured earlier that spring when a large war party of Klamaths and Modocs set out from their villages along the banks of Klamath Lake in southern Oregon and headed south into the Pit River territory of the Achomawis and Atsugewis.[2] After a three-day journey, these raiders located a small village and camped nearby. In the morning they attacked, mounted upon horses, with bows and arrows and perhaps a gun or two. The battle was brief. They captured the women and younger children. They drove off or killed the men. And they collected all the bows, arrows, blankets, beads, dentaliums, and anything else of trade value remaining in the destroyed village.[3] They then returned to the Upper Klamath Basin to sell their captives to the laláki, a newly emerged, entrepreneurial class of wealthy and powerful trader-chieftains who undertook the journey north to the slave markets of the lower Columbia River. Crossing over the Cascades and following the north fork of the Santiam River through the territory of the Northern Molalas, the laláki arrived at Oregon City a few weeks later. In exchange for their human cargo, these Klamath entrepreneurs received on average three horses for each lúgsh. And these horses, in turn, could be exchanged for a variety of goods.[4] Occasionally, a laláki would remain for a year or two among the *yámakni*[5]—the Klamath name for the Indian communities of the Columbia River—to learn the regional trade jargon, Chinuk Wawa.[6]

This incident is the earliest archival account we have of Upper Klamath Basin Indians participating directly in the sprawling indigenous trade network centered around Celilo Falls on the Columbia River.[7] And on its face, it might seem insignificant: merely the Euro-American recording of a widespread indigenous socioeconomic practice. Indeed, as Marcus Gunn reported, "Slavery has existed from time immemorial. The stronger tribes make war upon the weaker, take prisoners and enslave them. They are frequently taken to other parts of the country and sold to other tribes.... [They] are not considered *tillicum*, that is, people, but as dogs. They do the principal part of the work and drudgery.... [They are fed and clothed,] but the epithet—slave—is fixed upon them never or seldom to be removed."[8] But perhaps Gunn was a bit too cavalier in his assessment. Indeed, while it is true that, as Catherine Cameron observes in chapter 1 of this volume, many, if not virtually all, Northwest Coast Indian communities practiced slavery, the arrival of Klamath entrepreneurial laláki with their enslaved lúgsh did not represent an immemorial practice. Rather, it represented a profound reshaping of life in the Upper Klamath Basin that historians of North American Indian slavery have yet to fully grasp.[9]

Throughout the eighteenth and nineteenth centuries, epidemic diseases, ecological change, systemic violence, and exploitative labor practices all affected Indian communities in the Pacific Northwest.[10] Indians suffered from the effects of Euro-American imperialism, but the competition nonetheless played out on a predominately indigenous political landscape. As Juliana Barr, Kathleen DuVal, Pekka Hämäläinen, Ned Blackhawk, and other historians of the southern plains and the intermountain West have demonstrated, Indian communities employed a dizzying array of tactics as they sought to incorporate Euro-Americans into their Native-dominated world. In the process, they sometimes absorbed the violence of colonialism and sometimes displaced it onto their neighbors, making and remaking their political and economic realities while coping with the effects of Euro-American trade, disease, and warfare.[11]

Examining the ways in which colonial violence moved outward from small enclaves of Euro-American settlements through Oregon's indigenous political and economic landscape, this chapter investigates the expansion of the Pacific Northwest's Indian slave trade into the Upper Klamath Basin of southern Oregon and northern California in the early nineteenth century. Beginning around 1800, the arrival of European trade goods along established indigenous trade routes significantly altered inter- and intratribal economic and political relationships in the region. As the competition for access to trade goods intensified, captive taking took on new meanings and significance. Prior to the 1820s and 1830s, Upper Klamath Basin Indians only occasionally took captives in war or in the course of community feuds. Those few who were taken were often returned or let go after a period of time or else were forcibly adopted as kin, and social taboos tended to protect them against abuse and extreme violence.[12] But around 1830, the nature of captivity and the nature of authority began to change in tandem in the Upper Klamath Basin. Modoc, Klamath, and Paiute laláki turned to commercial slavery as they maneuvered for economic advantage, fundamentally restructuring tribal political identities. The arrival of horses and guns in the Upper Klamath Basin increased the importance of slaves to the region's economy and to political leadership. Whereas before, spiritual *kíuks* (shamans) held the highest position in Upper Klamath Basin society, entrepreneurial Klamath laláki claimed more power as they gained wealth and prestige through their associations with the north.[13] Significantly, this generation of cosmopolitan Klamath laláki co-opted authority in the region to forge alliances with other indigenous peoples and to broker agreements with American colonial officials that further reinforced their power and prestige. Increasing their raids on neighboring communities, leveraging and protecting their position as middlemen, and transporting their newly acquired captives hundreds of miles to the slave markets on the Columbia River, these entrepreneurial laláki reshaped the Upper Klamath Basin's indigenous political landscape long before Euro-American settler colonies took hold in the region. Pulling their communities ever deeper into a political economy of violence, these laláki transformed their neighbors into captives and their captives into lúgsh, creating a new kind of wealth in the Upper Klamath Basin in the form of portable and fungible human commodities.

"Captivity and its most exploitative form—slavery—was indigenous to North America," Christina Snyder observed in her book *Slavery in Indian Country*.[14] And while that is certainly true, the development of cultural practices of captive taking and slave making within isolated and marginal regions of indigenous North America is not ahistorical. Indeed, as Eric Bowne (chapter 2), Natale Zappia (chapter 5), and others observe elsewhere in this volume, Indian communities developed particular cultures of slavery in response to specific historical forces, and their decisions often had political, social, and cultural ramifications. My aim in this chapter, then, is to reconstruct the complicated history of slavery and the slave trade in the Upper Klamath Basin in order to explain how waves of Euro-American colonialism shaped and reshaped the indigenous political and economic world there. Cameron and others have considered slavery in the Pacific Northwest in more sweeping and comparative detail, but my goal here is to demonstrate how Euro-American settler colonialism in the larger region dramatically reshaped the political and economic landscape of the Upper Klamath Basin long before Euro-American colonists arrived to settle. To tell that story, however, I must first provide a general sketch of what life for Indian people in the Upper Klamath Basin was like before Euro-American settlers arrived, and we must also consider how the relative remoteness of the Upper Klamath Basin shaped life during the initial stages of Euro-American colonization of the broader region in the late eighteenth and early nineteenth centuries.

* * *

The Upper Klamath Basin of southern Oregon and northern California is far removed from the extensive trade network of the Columbia River. Nonetheless, Upper Klamath Basin Indians had been indirectly involved in trade with the Columbia River tribes for centuries. Indeed, centered on the Dalles-Celilo area along the Columbia River, this sprawling indigenous network of trade was a long-established part of the Plateau economy. From the north, elaborately decorated coiled baskets, furs, and berries were traded for wapatoo (sometimes called "Indian potato"), whale oil, and dentaliums from the west. Southern traders brought obsidian, bows, and, eventually, slaves to trade for camas bulbs (a kind of editable lily), buffalo hides, and, by the mid-eighteenth century, horses from the east. At the heart of this network was a staggering trade in pemmican, dried and pulverized salmon packed in salmon-skin-lined baskets. According to one estimate, the Indians around the Dalles-Celilo area prepared approximately one million pounds of pemmican solely for the purpose of trade each year. Indeed, pemmican became so popular that it could be found regularly as far north as Fort Thompson in what is now British Columbia, as far east as Wyoming, and as far south as the Upper Klamath Basin, where local tastes so preferred the durable trade good that entrepreneurial traders fashioned their own unique kind of pemmican from local whitefish. Favoring local specialization, this sprawling trade network encouraged many regional economies to concentrate on the production of certain trade commodities.[15]

Although archival evidence is nonexistent for the precontact era, archaeological and ethnographic reconstructions suggest that few resources were desirable enough to sustain long-distance trade in the remote Upper Klamath Basin, where trade privileged light, easily transportable, and highly valuable commodities. Beginning around 600 CE, Upper Klamath Basin Indian traders began exporting obsidian obtained from the Warner Mountains along the basin's eastern edge and Glass Mountain to the south. Hard, light, and capable of holding a razor-sharp edge, obsidian quickly came to dominate the region's export economy as Plateau residents valued it for their arrowheads, hatchets, and knives.[16] In exchange for obsidian, Upper Klamath Basin traders received a variety of foodstuffs, as well as dentaliums, the shells of a tubular mollusk found along the western coast of Canada, especially around Vancouver Island and Quatsino Sound; these shells were prized throughout the Pacific Northwest as international trade items and soon assumed special value among the tribes of northern California, who viewed them as a display of wealth.[17]

Dentaliums seem to have represented a significant form of wealth in the region prior to the arrival of European trade goods, but it remains uncertain how much of the regional dentalium trade Upper Klamath Basin Indians controlled. Ethnologist John Peabody Harrington reported that the Karoks of the Lower Klamath River believed that their upriver neighbors were its only source. They thought that "all good things...come down the Klamath River" and that the Indians of the Klamath Basin were "famed as warriors and as holders of the Klamath Lakes in the mud of which dentalium money was believed to grow and be obtained."[18] Others report that Wishram and Wasco Indians living near the Dalles had from time to time obtained dentaliums from the Achomawis of the Pit River drainage, with the Klamaths acting as intermediaries.[19] However, as significant as these trade relations likely were, life in the Upper Klamath Basin at the end of the eighteenth century was shaped more by extensive exploitation of local resources than by participation in wide-ranging trade networks.

Located on the fringes of the Columbia River trade network, Upper Klamath Basin Indians relied predominantly on their local environment for everyday needs. With an average elevation above 4,000 feet, the Upper Klamath Basin was plagued by a short and unpredictable growing season and the possibility of frost year-round. Situated within the moderate rain shadow east of the southern Cascades on the California-Oregon border, it was a land of little rain but covered by sprawling marshes and dotted by numerous lakes. Originating in the spring-fed creeks around Mount Thielsen, Mount McLoughlin, and Crater Lake, these waters spread out to form the Upper and Lower Klamath Lake complex, the largest lake by area west of the Rocky Mountains, from which flows the Klamath River, California's second-longest river. Today a land of scarcity and fierce conflict over water rights, the Upper Klamath Basin had such an abundance of water in the nineteenth century that it won the moniker "District of the Lakes" or "Land of Lakes," leading one early visitor to exclaim, "The Country as far as the eye can reach [is] one continuous Swamp and Lakes."[20]

This profusion of water gave rise to the Upper Klamath Basin's diverse plants and wildlife. Woca (*Nuphar polysepalum*), tule (*Schoenoplectus acutus*), cattail (*Typha latifolia*), and other edible plants were cultivated and harvested along the shores of lakes around which Klamath Basin Indians built their villages. In these wetlands, birds abounded. The region's verdant forests offered abundant large and small game. And to the south and east, in the arid lava beds around Tule Lake, mountain sheep, antelope, and jackrabbit were plentiful.[21] But the foundation of the Upper Klamath Basin Indians' diet was by far the region's numerous species of fish. And although fish could be taken year-round from swift-moving creeks or springs that never froze, the great seasonal runs of the spring and fall dictated an annual cycle of activities.[22]

Essentially a linguistically homogenous region before the arrival of Euro-American settlers, the Upper Klamath Basin was home to three semi-autonomous, though culturally similar, groups of people: the Klamaths, the Modocs, and, by the mid-nineteenth century, at least one community of Northern Paiutes. To the south and east were the Achomawis and other Pit River tribes. And to the south and west were the Shastas, Karoks, Yuroks, and other tribes of the Lower Klamath River. The limits of early-twentieth-century salvage anthropology and the notorious inaccuracy of contemporary Euro-American labeling of Indian communities render a definitive description of indigenous political structures problematic. However, on the basis of evidence provided by informants around the turn of the twentieth century, it appears that by the end of the eighteenth century, all communities within the Upper Klamath Basin were bound together to various degrees by marriage, political alliances, and a shared sense of peoplehood.[23]

On the edges of Spanish, American, British, and Russian imperial activities, the Upper Klamath Basin and its surrounding areas did not directly encounter Euro-American colonization efforts throughout the eighteenth century. To be sure, these Indians had marginal access to Euro-American trade goods, and successive waves of epidemic diseases, such as the smallpox outbreaks of the 1770s and 1780s, almost certainly changed the demographic landscape of southern Oregon and northern California, though we lack even general population figures for the region.[24] But the beginning of the nineteenth century would bring swift changes to the political, economic, and social world of the Upper Klamath Basin.

The gradual arrival of Euro-American trade goods throughout the eighteenth and early nineteenth centuries brought new forms of wealth and violence to the Plateau. The first significant Euro-American trade good to arrive along indigenous trade networks was the horse. Introduced to the Plateau by the Northern Shoshonis around 1730, the horse accelerated Indian raids even as it expanded their capacity for trade. By the mid-eighteenth century, the superb herds of the Nez Percés and Salishes proved to be a tempting target for their numerically superior and better armed enemies to the east. Controlling their monopoly over access to firearms from Hudson's Bay and North West Company traders along the Saskatchewan River and Euro-American traders along the Missouri, the Blackfeet and their Piegan and Blood allies made war on their Crow neighbors to the southeast and raided the Interior Salishes for their horses with impunity for nearly fifty years. Around 1780, the Crows received firearms from the Hidatsas and, in an attempt to break the control of the Blackfeet Confederacy over the trade, began supplying weapons to the Bannocks, Nez Percés, and Salishes. By 1810, the Blackfeet Confederacy was suing for peace, while the Salishes continued to hunt buffalo in the Blackfeet country. Warfare such as that between the Blackfeet Confederacy and the Bannocks, Nez Percés, and Salishes soon spilled into the southern Plateau, though Indian leaders often tried to tightly control the flow of horses and guns to their enemies. The result was that in the first two decades of the nineteenth century, guns and horses spread unevenly throughout the southern Plateau. Those communities with horses began to increase raiding on those with none, altering settlement patterns throughout the Great Basin, southern Plateau, and Upper Klamath Basin and disrupting the region's social, economic, and political relations.[25]

As a result of these changing political and economic relations, when Euro-American fur trappers and traders first arrived in the Upper Klamath Basin in the 1820s, they encountered communities in the midst of dramatic change. Consider, for example, what Peter Skene Ogden, a Hudson's Bay Company factor and the creator of the earliest archival record we have pertaining to the region, observed when he entered the Upper Klamath Basin in the early winter of 1826. Upon a close reading of his journals, we get the sense that he encountered a people under siege. He described the first village he saw as a small settlement of twenty structures "built on the water and surrounded on all sides by water and from its depth impossible to approach them on foot or on Horseback but with Canoes…[they were] constructed for defense…[for] they have many enemies to apprehend and are constantly guarded."[26] Perched as they were over water that would soon freeze, the Klamaths had apparently abandoned their traditional subterranean winter dwellings for more defensible structures. The Klamaths, moreover, seem to have viewed Ogden's arrival as both a blessing and a curse. They were very eager to trade with his starving men but also feared the violence Ogden's arrival surely heralded.

> They express themselves well pleased to see us on their Lands still they could not but regret we had open'd a communication, for many years past they informed us the Nez Percey Indians have made different attempts to reach our Village but could not succeed...but now they will have in [the] future your road.[27]

While this may have been a veiled attempt on the part of the Klamaths to cajole Ogden into trading with them for guns, they had nonetheless good reasons to fear invasion. The Klamath Basin Indians were in the earliest stages of adopting horses. And their herd, possibly stolen from Northern Paiute settlements around Surprise Valley the previous year, had been reduced to a single miserable animal. This left them susceptible to attack.[28]

The Klamaths' vulnerability may have been a recent development. But anthropologist Thomas Layton speculates that mounted raiders had subjected the Klamaths to periodic attacks from the north for nearly two decades prior to Ogden's visit. There is evidence that the Wallawalla, Cayuse, and Nez Percé traders might have traversed the Klamath Basin sometime after 1800 en route to the Sacramento River delta to obtain horses stolen from the California missions.[29] If incursions from the north were not enough, mounted raiders from the Great Basin were increasing pressure on Paiute settlements around Surprise Valley, either pushing them deeper into the Upper Klamath Basin or forcing them to abandon the area altogether.[30] In other words, at the time of Ogden's arrival in the region, Upper Klamath Basin Indians were under increasing pressure from their mounted neighbors to the north and east, whose violent raids were beginning to strain their communities. As an old Klamath song recorded a half century later ran, "*Kó-i ak a nä'pka Yámatni gatpam'nóka*" (Disastrous times we had when the northern Indians arrived).[31]

The opening of the Upper Klamath Basin to Euro-American trappers spurred Klamath traders to begin making the long journey to the international markets on the Columbia River, creating the opportunity for them to emerge as influential nodes in the regional slave trade. Anthropologists and ethnohistorians disagree over precisely when this change in trade patterns occurred. Speaking with informants in 1930, Edward Spier reported that the first Klamath traders to journey to the Dalles did so in the company of some French Canadian trappers who arrived in the Upper Klamath

Basin around 1835.[32] However, Spier is almost certainly mistaken about the date. It is much more likely that the first Klamaths to travel to the Dalles did so with Ogden in 1827. According to Spier's informants, during their stay, the French Canadians who introduced the Klamaths to the Dalles had "bought fat dogs of the Klamath, which to the latter's amazement, they ate. For these they gave buttons and metal disks with a central perforation."[33] But the memory of French Canadian trappers eating dogs before traveling north with a group of would-be Klamath traders dates back not to 1835, but to the winter of 1826–1827. On December 6, 1826, Ogden recorded in his journal, "[We] succeeded in trading at a cheap rate 40 Dogs and some small Fish not more than two inches in length and far from being good."[34] And shortly after Ogden's arrival in the Upper Klamath Basin, Klamath traders seem to have begun making regular trips north to the Columbia River trading outposts, where they gained greater access to Euro-American goods. The pursuit of these would bring important changes to the indigenous political landscape of the Upper Klamath Basin.

The probability of a late 1820s opening of the northern markets to Klamath Basin Indians is further suggested by the effect it had on the Achomawis of the Pit River drainage. Visiting the area with two Klamath guides in 1827, Peter Skene Ogden found the Achomawis willing to help and not fearful of a large party of men on horses wandering around their villages.[35] Five years later, however, when Hudson's Bay Chief Trader John Work traveled to the same area, he observed very different behavior, suggesting that the Achomawis had been subjected to Klamath and Modoc slave raids in the recent past. "There are tracks of Indians quite fresh, but they fly on our approach and none of them are to be seen," he reported on November 2, 1832. For the next several days, his party encountered several encampments of Achomawis, but each time, the Indians fled before them, assembling on hills far away, and they were reluctant to approach the strangers.[36] If the opening of the Upper Klamath Basin to raids from the north and east brought increased violence to the region, this sudden change in the Achomawis suggests that shortly after Ogden's 1826–1827 journey, Upper Klamath Basin Indians began displacing the violence of colonialism, leveraging their new access to horses to terrorize Indian communities to the south.

On the basis of data collected by anthropologists around the turn of the twentieth century, it seems likely that direct access to the international markets of the Columbia River altered the nature of slavery in the Upper Klamath Basin. Linguistic evidence seems to suggest that slavery existed prior to the 1820s and that captives were taken in warfare or during community feuds. Indeed, the word *lû'gshla* (from which *lúgsh*, or "slave," is derived) means "to capture in war."[37] But most often it seems that captives were returned or let go after a period of time or were forcibly adopted as kin. In fact, some informants from the 1920s reported that abusing a captive was frowned upon as socially unacceptable, while marriages to captives were viewed favorably as a convenient way to avoid strict kinship bans on marriage. To be sure, captives existed in a degraded position in society. Archaeological evidence from the Upper Klamath Basin suggests that domiciles for the enslaved were smaller than and often ancillary to those of their masters. Moreover, by Klamath custom, lowly individuals and those bereaved of prestige or spiritual power were often characterized as "having nothing, being no better than a slave." But in general, practices of captivity and slavery seem not to have been highly commercialized, and there exists no archival or other evidence suggesting that Upper Klamath Basin Indians exported captives north to the Dalles prior to the 1820s.[38] By the 1830s and 1840s, the experience of being made captive by the Klamaths, however, was changing, as lúgsh came to represent wealth in the form of portable and fungible commodities.

Taking advantage of their direct access to the international markets of the Columbia River, entrepreneurial Klamaths used violence to secure a niche in the region's trade. They turned to slavery either in emulation of their Great Basin neighbors to the east, where a brutal and lucrative slave trade had cropped up among the Ute, New Mexican, and Euro-American slavers, or as a response to increased demand among the Columbia River tribes.[39]

Northwest Coast indigenous communities, including the Kwakiutls, Tlingits, Haidas, and many others, had, as Cameron discusses in chapter 1 of this volume, practiced slavery for hundreds, if not thousands, of years. And although historians and anthropologists have debated the relative economic value of slaves, Leland Donald has traced the central role of slavery in Northwest Coast indigenous cultures. Indeed, far from being merely prestige and ceremonial objects or external indicators of wealth, slaves in many Northwest Coast communities performed a dizzying array of tasks for their masters, and their labor produced considerable surpluses, allowing for the maintenance of rigidly hierarchical societies. The demand for slaves, moreover, was not inelastic. The establishment of Fort Vancouver in 1824 increased the availability of Euro-American trade goods, virtually eliminating the market for obsidian. But the increase in Euro-American trade goods also increased the demand for slaves among northwestern tribes, because those slaves were instrumental to the production of surplus in the region's indigenous economy. Euro-American settler colonists, in other words, increased the demand for slaves. And these market forces created opportunities within the Columbia River slave trade. Upper Klamath Basin entrepreneurs were well positioned to fulfill this need.[40]

The opening of trade to the north corresponded with a substantial increase in slave raids by the Klamaths and Modocs upon the Shastas, Achomawis, and Atsugewis of the Pit River drainage to the south and, to a lesser extent, the Takelmas and Latgawas of the Rogue River valley. As Chiloquin, a prominent reservation-era Klamath leader, later recalled:

> When the Snakes [Northern Paiute] made war on us...that made us keen to fight other Indians and we made war without provocation on the Pitt Rivers, Shastas, and Rogue Rivers, but they never made willing war on us. Those wars lasted a great many years. We found we could make money by war, for we sold the provisions and property captured for horses and other things we needed. It was like soldiers nowadays who fight for money. *We made war because we made money by it, and we rather got to like it anyhow.* The Snakes provoked us to make war on them.[41]

With horses and guns they could make money by raiding their neighbors.

Slave raiding soon became an annual or semiannual activity, and with it came significant profits. Upper Klamath Basin slavers constructed a series of fortified sites where they could safely rest during the raiding season, and within a generation, raiding parties of more than one hundred warriors were pillaging enemy villages and returning with as many as fifty-six captives bound for the Columbia River slave markets.[42] As David Hill (Wawa'liks), a mid-level headman during the early reservation era, recalled years later, "Never [did the other Indians of the region make] slaves of the Lake tribe conquering by war those from tribe all-around; the Lake men alone enslaved all surrounding Indians in this country."[43]

In addition to enslaving their neighbors, Klamath traders bolstered their position as middlemen in the regional slave trade by controlling local markets, thereby ensuring their monopoly on the transportation of slaves to the north. A key characteristic of the Columbia River trade network was the existence of several lesser interregional and secondary trade centers, feeding into the primary inter- and intraregional trade center of the Dalles. The major nodes were the fishery at Kettle Falls on the Upper Columbia and the mouths of the Okanogan and Snake Rivers. The introduction of horses into the Columbia River trade network only increased the importance of these trade centers.[44]

In the Upper Klamath Basin, there is evidence that Klamath powerbrokers controlled a periodic, minor trade center at Yainax Butte, some thirty miles east of Klamath Lake. According to Samuel A. Clarke, a journalist who spoke with many Upper Klamath Basin Indians in the 1870s, Indians from "hundreds of miles about sent annual delegations for various purposes of trade and festival. Here they exchanged products, sold horses, and carried on all manner of native commerce…. Here, also, was the great slave mart of the mid-mountain region."[45] Through kinship ties with influential members of certain Northern Paiute communities, the Yainax Butte trading center may have provided opportunities for the Klamaths to incorporate their region into the Great Basin's robust slave economy throughout the 1830s and 1840s.[46] In other words, the opening of trade to the north destabilized the Klamath Basin politically even as it enriched and empowered a new class of Klamath entrepreneurs who controlled the region's slave trade—the so-called laláki.

The acceleration of trade with the north brought Euro-American ideas, as well as trade goods, into the region long before settlers arrived. Throughout the 1830s and 1840s, ambitious young laláki spent several years outside the Upper Klamath Basin, developing their skills in commerce, establishing important alliances with outsiders, and returning with new cultural and material innovations to the Upper Klamath Basin. For example, living and working at the first Euro-American colonial settlement in the Willamette Valley for nearly a decade, a laláki named Charlie Preston returned home to the Upper Klamath Basin in the late 1850s as one of the few Klamaths fluent in English, a skill he used when he served as the tribe's official interpreter during the treaty negotiations in 1864.[47] Another Klamath laláki, named Link River Jack, recalled that as a young man he had traveled to the Columbia River, where he met "good men [who] told him about the Holy Spirit that was to come to the whole world and visit its remotest parts. When he came back from the Dalles he told his people about it but found them groping in perfect darkness…he tried to tell them about the mission of the Holy Spirit preached by the white men…[but they] would not believe him and told him he lied."[48] If new religious ideas were seemingly rejected, numerous satirical songs likewise record the derision of Upper Klamath Basin Indians toward the perceived excesses of the laláki nouveaux riches. One collection of satirical songs taunts:

> Kátchkal û'yank amníyamna / Get geno'la tsiálash patso'k Yamakî'shamkshi…. Ká tal hû'k mû shétaluatk?/ Ke' lish tok walxátchkatko gûlí.

He goes around giving away sticks of tobacco and is very noisy about it. / This man starts out to feed on salmon among the northern Indians.... Who is he, the allegedly wealthy man? / She [the laláki's wife] has entered the house of a poorly dressed husband.[49]

Met with derision at home, those who traveled nonetheless controlled the introduction of new items and ideas to the Upper Klamath Basin. The role Klamath laláki played in this period of intertribal acculturation has led anthropologist Theodore Stern to conclude, "Change was mediated in those years [more] by Klamath, visiting beyond their homeland, than by strangers in the Klamath country."[50]

The rise of a class of prominent entrepreneurial laláki with control over the region's political economy of violence in the capture and transportation of enslaved lúgsh disrupted long-established social and political arrangements in the Klamath Basin. Prior to the opening of trade with the north, wealth and power were concentrated in the hands of those who could claim close associations with the sacred. So-called shamans or medicine men, known as "kíuks," stood at the top of the social order. But kíuks never traveled far, generally staying in the villages where they lived, and they accumulated wealth by charging fees to heal and remove or place curses and perform other religious services.[51] The primacy of shamans over chiefs is further suggested by the fact that Albert Gatschet, a member of the Bureau of American Ethnology, reported in the 1880s that his Klamath and Modoc informants could remember no pre-trading-era chiefs, but numerous shamans from the same era could be named.[52]

But the historic primacy of kíuks was undermined by the beginning of direct exchange with the Columbia River tribes. With wealth obtained through the slave trade, young, cosmopolitan laláki returned to the Upper Klamath Basin and, by the 1840s and 1850s, began exercising greater power over local affairs. Anthropologist Leslie Spier argues that the laláki imported notions of social stratification based on wealth from Pacific Northwest tribes like the Klallams, Snohomishes, Chinooks, Wishrams, Wascos, and Alseas, whose societies were highly stratified along class lines and whose hereditary chiefs exercised significant power. Indeed, the use of the Chinuk Wawa honorific *hyas tyee* (big king) among Upper Klamath Basin chiefs further supports a Columbia River origin for the practice of chieftaincies.[53] Although emerging laláki seem to have had to moderate the model of a rigorously class-based society, they nonetheless quickly usurped the spiritual-economic control of the kíuks.

A Klamath story about Chiloquin, a historical figure but in this story probably a composite character representing all of the slave-trading nouveaux riches, records the historic replacement of kíuks by laláki. In the story, the northern shamans challenge their Klamath visitors to endure the sweat lodge, but none of the Klamath kíuks had traveled to the north. So the Klamath visitors put forward Chiloquin—a laláki—to represent them. "One after the other each northern shaman sprinkled water on the hot rocks as he sang his song, hoping to force the other out." And one by one, each northern shaman was overcome and had to be dragged out. As the story goes, "Once outside they wondered what had become of Chiloquin; he was nowhere to be seen. They thought he must have died. After a long time he began to talk, throwing water on the rocks. When he was quite ready he came out and walked to his own people. He had bested the shamans."[54] The ordeal of the sweat lodge, a common theme in Klamath storytelling, here is employed to commemorate Chiloquin's triumph over the northern shamans and to explain the rise of slave-trader wealth, supplanting the traditional authority of the shamanistic kíuks.

Although the story tells of Chiloquin winning over the shamans by outlasting them in the sweat lodge, it is more likely that the laláki gained power by forming alliances with and buying the support of the kíuks, usurping the religious leaders' former monopolies on political power through their newly acquired wealth. In the 1880s, Henry Blow—a prominent reservation-era headman—recalled just such transference of authority: "Years ago when there was no law [the kíuks were] used by the chiefs to get rid of rivals and there are some of us old enough to remember of doctors [the kíuks] being paid to kill certain persons and of their foretelling of the exact day they would die."[55] It seems likely, then, that as new forms of wealth and cultural experiences flowed into the Upper Klamath Basin and as laláki gained power and influence over Klamath society, the political landscape of the region changed.

Participation in the slave trade provided social mobility for entrepreneurial laláki. But what were the experiences of the lúgsh in this changing society? And what effect did the presence of slaves have on these developments? On the basis of accounts of traditional practices and complaints by tribal members to early reservation-era government agents, it seems that captivity and slavery became harsher as the laláki imported notions of corporal punishment from beyond the Upper Klamath Basin. Indeed, according to a letter sent to Superintendent J. W. P. Huntington in 1866, imprisonment, whipping, and corporal punishment had all became more common as a result of the slave trade.[56] Ironically, mistreating the enslaved may have undermined their value, but it also corresponded with changes in the place of the lúgsh in Upper Klamath Basin society as many people began to view the lúgsh more strictly as property. William Pickett, a prominent Oregon settler in 1869 recounted the story of Charlie, a Pit River Indian lúgsh enslaved by a Klamath laláki and sold to a Warm Springs Indian:

> Their condition is too lowly for their oppressions to reach the notice of the most benevolent intentions so long as they are compelled to live with or near their former owners.... In appearance, all the Indians here are upon the same social legal plane; but the law of caste rules here upon the former and present slaves—no intermarriage or social intercourse...these people *are their property*.[57]

In 1873, journalist Stephen Powers reported as much when he recounted the Klamath practice of burning a deceased man's property, including his slaves.[58] And the Klamaths were not alone in this. Indeed, the Modocs seem to have adopted the ritual practice of destroying the property of the dead, including lúgsh.[59] These practices may have stemmed from the interaction of laláki with Northwest Coast cultures, whose intense interests in ownership are well documented.[60] But if so, the harsh treatment of the lúgsh would not constitute the only cultural practice Upper Klamath Basin Indians adopted as a result of their integration into the northern slave trade.

The northern slave trade also brought Klamath Basin Indians into direct contact with Euro-American settlers. As it did so, however, prominent laláki like Lileks, Chiloquin, and Link River Jack worked to strengthen their indigenous political, economic, and military alliances. One particularly illuminating example is the adoption of an unofficial treaty between the laláki and Elijah White in the summer of 1844, during their annual visit to the slave markets along the Columbia River.[61] White, a medical doctor from New York, had been appointed to the position of subagent of the still disputed Oregon Territory in 1842. In a misguided and unnecessary attempt to establish what he called "order" among the Natives, White devised a series of agreements known as the "Nez Perce Laws"—after the first tribe to agree to them. The "laws" served mainly to protect colonists' property and provided a justification for extending American judicial power to Indian subjects, if not exactly over them. For example, in addition to mandating hanging for arson and murder and whippings of various amounts for trespassing, thievery, larceny, and wanton destruction, the laws established an unambiguous separation of jurisdiction but also a subtle double standard. "If an Indian raises a gun or other weapons against a white man, it shall be reported to the chiefs, and they shall punish him. If a white man do the same to an Indian, it shall be reported to Dr. White, and he shall punish or redress it." And "if an Indian break these laws, he shall be punished by his chief; if a white man break them, he shall be reported to the agent, and punished at his instance." In other words, Indian transgressors were to be punished immediately by their leaders as prescribed by the laws, whereas whites were to be dealt with at the discretion of the subagent.[62] In 1844, after a day or two of considerable debate, the Klamaths and Molalas agreed to White's commandments.[63]

Why would the Klamaths agree to accept such laws? The draconian requirements and apparent inequality of the Nez Perce Laws have led some scholars to suggest that Oregon Natives misunderstood or were willfully misled. It seems as likely, however, that the entrepreneurial Klamath laláki who met with Elijah White saw political advantage in accepting his system of laws. In particular, the concentration of legal authority in the hands of chiefs and the use of whipping as a form of punishment probably would have been appealing to the rising laláki, who at that moment were usurping control from the kíuks, or spiritualists. Whipping was not commonly practiced in the Upper Klamath Basin prior to 1844, though it was a widely observed form of punishment among Plateau tribes, who possibly adopted it from Southwest Indians via the eighteenth-century horse and slave trade.[64] It was also common among many Northwest Coast tribes, including the Makahs, Klallams, and Chinooks.[65] Did the Klamath laláki consider White's so-called laws an opportunity to extend the use of corporal punishment? Possibly. The infamous reservation-era headman Lileks—who spent the first half of the 1840s in continuous residency at the Dalles—was known for using public whipping as a form of punishment after his assent to power in the 1850s.[66] Moreover, Nancy Philip—a 1930s-era informant of Spier's—recalled that many "laws" were said to have come from the north in the prereservation days.[67] It seems likely, then, that the laláki who agreed to White's laws in 1844 viewed them as a means to bolster their own power and influence over Upper Klamath Basin society and to shore up their control of the northern slave trade.

Throughout the 1830s and 1840s, the laláki gained power and authority by means of the wealth and the technologies of control they acquired as a result of the northern slave trade. But by the late 1840s, Upper Klamath Basin Indians increasingly had to contend with Euro-American settler colonialism. Between 1843 and 1850, the Euro-American population of the fertile Willamette Valley exploded from approximately 160 inhabitants to more than 23,000. This tremendous demographic shift resulted in an intense period of settler-colonial environmental, economic, and social transformation, disrupting indigenous trade networks along which the laláki had traveled with their lúgsh.[68] At the same time, massive disease epidemics devastated Indian populations. In 1847, for instance, a severe outbreak of smallpox or possibly measles killed an estimated 40 percent of the Upper Klamath Basin Indian population.[69] These disruptions corresponded with the killing of Marcus and Narcissa Whitman and the destruction of their Presbyterian mission at Waiilatpu on November 29, 1847, which in turn enraged Euro-American settler-colonists and became the rationale for years of government-backed vigilante justice and militia offensives against Natives throughout Oregon. The Cayuse War, a campaign of retribution carried out between 1847 and 1855, fueled numerous calls for the extermination of Indians throughout the Pacific Northwest. Armed with genocidal rhetoric and a determination to kill Indian people, many Oregonians brought their destructive views to the goldfields of northern California after 1848 and to Yreka in the Upper Klamath Basin after 1851. Murdering Natives in the mining towns of Mariposa, Siskiyou, and Lake Counties, they repaid a thousandfold any violence possibly perpetrated by Indian peoples.[70] And this violence was particularly acute in the Upper Klamath Basin. Between 1854 and 1861, the region witnessed a conflagration of state-sponsored Indian killing, including the notorious Ben Wright massacre and the murderous Crosby or Modoc Expedition of 1856, which resulted in the death of scores, if not hundreds, of Upper Klamath Basin Indians and may have been the most lethal of all California militia expeditions in a very bloody era.[71]

Throughout this period of colonial violence, captive taking and slave trading with the north may have been disrupted, but slavery increased to the south of the Upper Klamath Basin in California. In 1850, the California state legislature passed the Act for the Government and Protection of Indians, which established vagrancy laws for Indians, empowering authorities to enslave Native Californians found loitering. The law also created a slave market for Indian children, who could be indentured until adulthood, sometimes without parental consent. The act was later amended to allow for the indenture of orphaned Native children, which, of course, led to a brutal epidemic of kidnappings. Indeed, as Round Valley superintendent George Hanson recalled, when he asked a Euro-American slaver how he knew the children he was transporting were orphans, he replied, "I killed some of [their parents] myself."[72]

Euro-American slavers dominated the California slave trade. But Upper Klamath Basin Indians participated in this new market to at least some degree. As within the Columbia River market, slaves fetched on average three horses apiece in the 1850s and anywhere from $50 to $200 in the 1860s.[73] Comparable to the northern market, California was simply another market for the Klamath laláki and their enslaved lúgsh. And as a result, slave raiding continued. Indeed, during a visit to the Pit River Indians in the summer of 1857, E. A. Stevenson, Indian agent at Red Bluff, California, reported that the Pit River Indians had been attacked by a large Klamath war party led by none other than the powerful laláki Lileks, who had taken their women and children to sell as slaves.[74]

But trade with the north did not completely end. A few years later, in 1860, Alexander Piper, commander at Fort Umpqua, reported after visiting the upper Klamath country that Lileks, along with two other laláki, was on his way to the Columbia River to trade a number of female lúgsh for horses.[75] Attesting to the importance of the newly ascendant laláki as the powerbrokers and authority figures in the region through whom Euro-American colonial administrators had to negotiate, Piper waited nearly a month to secure an audience with these men, knowing that it was essential to obtain their support to ensure peace in the region.[76]

The slave trade persisted throughout the tumultuous 1850s. But American federal officials in the Upper Klamath Basin did seek to reduce its economic and political importance. Emos Rogers, subagent for the area around Jacksonville, underscored this point in a letter to J. W. P. Huntington, superintendent of Indian affairs of Oregon, in 1863. He called for Huntington to negotiate a treaty with the Klamaths and Modocs and to establish a military fort in the region. But he also expressed his concern that the Klamath laláki had cemented their position in southern Oregon as the middlemen of the region's trade. Through trade with newly arrived Euro-American settlers in the Upper Klamath Basin, they had gained immediate access to the horse and gun trade so vital to the Great Basin economy. "By this intercourse," Rogers explained, "they obtain ammunition and arms not only for themselves...carry[ing] on quite a brisk trade in this line with the tribes east of the mountains who rarely venture into the settlements, but who, they boast, will at any time unite with them to make war upon the settlement."[77] With the beginning of Euro-American settlement in the Upper Klamath Basin, the laláki began to rely, it seems, less on the northern slave trade and instead used their access to local Euro-American settlements to forge political alliances and foster the economic dependency of their neighbors.

Access to Euro-American settlements in the Upper Klamath Basin also provided the laláki with a more ready market for their lúgsh under the noses of federal officials. Often portrayed by Euro-American commentators at the time simply as "the prostitution of their women," the sexual relations of Indian women with various colonists were a bit more complicated than that phrase implies. Many Klamath and Modoc women, of course, intermarried with Euro-American settlers, as well as with African Americans and Hawaiians—as Rogers reports: "I refer to a certain class of our mining population, including Kanakas and Negroes, many of these do not hesitate to intermarry and cohabit with and raise children by squaws." And for these unions, dowry gifts followed long-established Klamath customs. Yet many lúgsh, it seems, were also employed in an illicit sex trade for which laláki received commodities such as whiskey, ammunition, guns, or, in the words of Rogers, "whatever their terms of contract require[d]." Indeed, it seems that by the early 1860s, entrepreneurial Klamath laláki became so adept at the arms trade that one Indian agent complained, "[The trade] is so adroitly managed that it cannot be traced; yet its truth is apparent. The Indians making the contract [for sale of slaves] will so shift the Property that by the time it may be discovered it will have passed through a half-dozen hands."[78]

Slavery remained essential to the maintenance of the laláki throughout the 1860s, a fact confirmed by the October 14, 1864, treaty between the United States and the Klamath, Modoc, and Yahooskin Paiute nations. The Treaty of 1864 reserved over one million acres of land from their original claim of more than twenty million acres in the Klamath Basin in exchange for thousands of dollars in supplies over the next fifteen years. Crucially, however, it contained no provision calling for the freeing of slaves or ending the slave trade in the Upper Klamath Basin. Earlier versions of the treaty may have included such provisions.[79] But efforts on the part of the federal government to manumit Upper Klamath Basin lúgsh faced stiff opposition from the laláki. For instance, an 1865 proposal by Lindsay Applegate, the newly appointed and provisional agent of the Klamath reservation, resulted in threats from Lileks that he would "kill all of the Pit River Indians among them" rather than see them freed.[80] Indeed, it would not be until after Lileks was deposed as chief headman in 1869 that all lúgsh in the Klamath Basin were freed.

Contested and contentious as the ending of slavery may have been in the Upper Klamath Basin, once they decided to end the practice, citizens of the Klamath Tribes chose a path of political and social inclusion, an alternative to the more divisive approaches to integration practiced by some former slave-owning tribes. In 1871, former slaves were invited to elect their own representatives to the reservation tribal councils and courts.[81] Discrimination also seems to have been minimal or nearly nonexistent.

By the mid-1880s and 1890s, after the devastation wrought by the Modoc War of 1872–1873, former slaves seem to have integrated into reservation life in most ways, freely intermarrying and inheriting property. Indeed, a former slave of laláki chief Lilu named Henry Jackson became one of the wealthiest landowners and ranchers on the reservation before he died. And perhaps most telling of all, the powerful laláki Chiloquin himself, the one who famously bested the northern kíuks, or spiritualists, in their own sweat lodge, even married a former Shasta slave. Distinctions seem to have remained well into the twentieth century. But today descendants of the laláki, the lúgsh, and the kíuks are all citizens of the Klamath Tribes.[82]

* * *

The role of slavery and the slave trade in Upper Klamath Basin history is complicated and has often been excluded from the larger history of the Northwest Coast slave cultures. Prior to the 1820s and 1830s, captives were rarely taken and often viewed as potential kin. After 1830, they became more common and were counted as a form of wealth. By the mid-1840s, moreover, participation in the Columbia River slave trade deeply influenced Upper Klamath Basin power structures. The arrival of horses and guns in the region led to the increasing importance of slaves to the region's economy, transforming the nature of political leadership in the Upper Klamath Basin. Where before, spiritual kíuks held the highest position in Upper Klamath Basin society, entrepreneurial Klamath laláki claimed more power as they co-opted authority in the region. Gaining wealth and prestige through their associations with the north and their lucrative trade of the enslaved lúgsh, a generation of cosmopolitan Klamath laláki leveraged its alliances with other Indian peoples to broker agreements with American colonial officials that pulled the Upper Klamath Basin ever deeper into a political economy of violence. Understanding how shifting forms of violence and the Indian slave trade made and remade the indigenous political landscape of the region long before settlers ever arrived is crucial to untangling the dynamics of American settler colonialism and empire in the Upper Klamath Basin and beyond, something Marcus Gunn was completely unaware of when he observed the arrival in Oregon City of a party of entrepreneurial Klamath laláki and their lúgsh cargo in the summer of 1843.

Notes

1. In the mid-nineteenth century, terms like *laláki* seem to have been undergoing change. Gatschet most often translates *laláki* as "chief," "commander," or even occasionally as "commissioner." But it also could be translated as "slave trader" or "one

who acquires wealth through trade." This is suggested by Barker's translation of *lagi*, his representation of *laláki*, as "to be rich, powerful, have prestige; chief, boss." In this chapter, Klamath terminology is presented as rendered in Albert Samuel Gatschet, *Klamath Indians of Southwestern Oregon*, 2 vols. (Washington, DC: US Department of the Interior, 1890). The Klamath Tribes prefer the system employed by Muhammad Abd-al-Rahman Barker in his *Klamath Dictionary* (Berkeley: University of California Press, 1963) as more accurately representing all the sounds of the Klamath language. Where possible, I will also provide Barker's representations. However, for the sake of consistency, I will use Gatschet's renderings in the text.

2. Barker represents *lúgsh* as *lo·g*.

3. Robert Carlton Clark, *History of the Willamette Valley, Oregon* (Chicago: S. J. Clarke, 1927), 56–57; Elsie Frances Dennis, "Indian Slavery in Pacific Northwest (in Three Parts, I)," *Oregon Historical Quarterly* 31, no. 1 (March 1, 1930): 80; Gatschet, *Klamath Indians of Southwestern Oregon*, 1:lix, 19–27.

4. Leslie Spier, *Klamath Ethnography*, vol. 30, *University of California Publications in American Archaeology and Ethnology* (Berkeley: University of California Press, 1930), 41.

5. Barker represents *yámakni* as *ya·makni·*. It translates most directly as "northern people," and it was a term applied to all of the Columbia River tribes.

6. Leslie Spier and Edward Sapir, *Wishram Ethnography* (Seattle: University of Washington Press, 1930), 227.

7. Theodore Stern, "Columbia River Trade Network," in *Handbook of North American Indians*, vol. 12, *Plateau*, ed. William C. Sturtevant and Deward E. Walker (Washington, DC: Smithsonian Institution, 1998), 641–652, especially 641; Luther S. Cressman, "Contrastive Features of Native North American Trade Systems," in *For the Chief: Essays in Honor of Luther S. Cressman*, ed. Fred W. Voget and Robert L. Stephenson (Eugene: University of Oregon, Department of Anthropology, 1972), 153–169.

8. Clark, *History of the Willamette Valley*, 56–57.

9. Leland Donald, *Aboriginal Slavery on the Northwest Coast of North America* (Berkeley: University of California Press, 1997); Robert H. Ruby and John A. Brown, *Indian Slavery in the Pacific Northwest* (Spokane, WA: A. H. Clark, 1993), especially 253–277; Andrew C. Isenberg, *Mining California: An Ecological History* (New York: Hill and Wang, 2005), especially 131–163; Stephen Most, *River of Renewal: Myth and History in the Klamath Basin* (Seattle: University of Washington Press, 2006); Nathan Douthit, *Uncertain Encounters: Indians and Whites at Peace and War in Southern Oregon, 1820s–1860s* (Corvallis: Oregon State University Press, 2002); Patricia Nelson Limerick, *Something in the Soil: Legacies and Reckonings in the New West* (New York: W. W. Norton, 2001); Richard H. Dillon, *Burnt-Out Fires: California's Modoc Indian War* (Englewood Cliffs, NJ: Prentice-Hall, 1973); Keith A. Murray, *The Modocs and Their War* (Norman: University

of Oklahoma Press, 1959); William S. Brown, *California Northeast: The Bloody Ground* (Oakland, CA: Biobooks, 1951).

10. Robert Boyd, *The Coming of the Spirit of Pestilence: Introduced Infectious Diseases and Population Decline among Northwest Coast Indians, 1774–1874* (Seattle: University of Washington Press, 1999).

11. Juliana Barr, *Peace Came in the Form of a Woman: Indians and Spaniards in the Texas Borderlands* (Chapel Hill: University of North Carolina Press, 2007); Kathleen DuVal, *The Native Ground: Indians and Colonists in the Heart of the Continent* (Philadelphia: University of Pennsylvania Press, 2006); Pekka Hämäläinen, *The Comanche Empire* (New Haven, CT: Yale University Press, 2008); Ned Blackhawk, *Violence over the Land: Indians and Empires in the Early American West* (Cambridge, MA: Harvard University Press, 2006).

12. Spier, *Klamath Ethnography*, 39–43.

13. Barker represents *kíuks* as *qyogs*.

14. Christina Snyder, *Slavery in Indian Country: The Changing Face of Captivity in Early America* (Cambridge, MA: Harvard University Press, 2010), 4.

15. Stern, "Columbia River Trade Network," 641; Cressman, "Contrastive Features," 153–169.

16. James Davis, *Trade Routes and Economic Exchange among the Indians of California* (Ramona, CA: Ballena Press, 1974), 7; Douglas Deur, *In the Footprints of Gmukamps: A Traditional Use Study of Crater Lake National Park and Lava Beds National Monument* (Seattle: US National Park Service, Pacific West Region, 2008), 162–163.

17. Spier and Sapir, *Wishram Ethnography*, 227.

18. John Harrington, *Tobacco among the Karuk Indians of California* (Washington, DC: US Government Printing Office, 1932), 3–4.

19. Spier and Sapir, *Wishram Ethnography*, 208.

20. Jeffrey M. LaLande and Peter Skene Ogden, *First over the Siskiyous: Peter Skene Ogden's 1826–1827 Journey through the Oregon-California Borderlands* (Portland: Oregon Historical Society Press, 1987), 10.

21. Spier, *Klamath Ethnography*, 155–160.

22. Ibid., 148–149; Theodore Stern, *The Klamath Tribe: A People and Their Reservation* (Seattle: University of Washington Press, 1965), 11.

23. Alfred Kroeber, *Handbook of the Indians of California* (New York: Dover Publications, 1976), 318–335; Theodore Stern, "Klamath and Modoc," in Sturtevant and Walker, *Handbook of North American Indians*, 12:446–466.

24. Elizabeth A. Fenn, *Pox Americana: The Great Smallpox Epidemic of 1775–82* (New York: Hill and Wang, 2001), 224–258; Robert Boyd, "Demographic History until 1990," in Sturvetan and Walker, *Handbook of North American Indians*, 12:467–483.

25. Theodore Binnema, *Common and Contested Ground: A Human and Environmental History of the Northwestern Plains* (Norman: University of Oklahoma Press, 2001), 86–106; Francis Haines, "The Northward Spread of Horses among the Plains Indians," *American Anthropologist* 40, no. 3 (September 1938): 429–437; Herbert J. Spinden, "Nez Perce Tales," part 2, *Journal of Folk-Lore* 21, no. 81 (1908): 158; Laura Peers, "Trade and Change on the Columbia Plateau, 1750–1840," *Columbia Anthology* 10, no. 4 (Winter 1996–1997): 6–12; Donald E. Worcester and Thomas F. Schilz, "The Spread of Firearms among the Indians on the Anglo-French Frontiers," *American Indian Quarterly* 8, no. 2 (Spring 1984): 103–115, especially 111–112; Thomas N. Layton, "Traders and Raiders: Aspects of Trans-Basin and California-Plateau Commerce, 1800–1830," *Journal of California and Great Basin Anthropology* 3, no. 1 (1981): 127–137.

26. K. G. Davies, ed., *Peter Skene Ogden's Snake Country Journal, 1826–27* (London: Hudson's Bay Record Society, 1961), 33. For a discussion of traditional Klamath winter lodging, see Spier, *Klamath Ethnography*, 197–205.

27. Davies, *Peter Skene Ogden*, 33.

28. Ibid., 33; Isabel T. Kelly, "Ethnography of the Surprise Valley Paiute," *University of California Publications in American Archaeology and Ethnology* 31 (1932): 67–210. It is likely that these horses came from the Columbia River, though it is possible they came up from California. See Haines, "The Northward Spread of Horses," 430. Anthropologist Thomas Layton has speculated that the Klamath may have hidden their herds from Ogden, but there seems to be little evidence supporting this claim. Layton, "Traders and Raiders," 127–130.

29. Layton, "Traders and Raiders," 128; Robert F. Heizer, "Walla Walla Indian Expedition to the Sacramento Valley, 1844–47," *California Historical Society Quarterly* 21 (1942): 1–7; Davis, *Trade Routes and Economic Exchange*, 10.

30. Mark Q. Sutton, "Warfare and Expansion: An Ethnohistoric Perspective on the Numic Spread," *Journal of California and Great Basin Anthropology* 8, no. 1 (1986): 65–82.

31. Gatschet, *Klamath Indians of Southwestern Oregon*, 1:192.

32. Spier, *Klamath Ethnography*, 7. Philleo Nash reiterates Spier's claim with greater detail; see Nash, "The Place of Religious Revivalism in the Formation of the Intercultural Community on Klamath Reservation," in *Social Anthropology of North American Tribes*, ed. Fred Eggan (Chicago: University of Chicago Press, 1955), 380–381.

33. Spier, *Klamath Ethnography*, 7.

34. Davies, *Peter Skene Ogden*, 36.

35. Ibid., 38–42.

36. Alice Bay Maloney, "The Fur Brigade to the Bonaventura: John Work's California Expedition, 1832–1833, for the Hudson's Bay Company," *California*

Historical Society Quarterly 22, no. 3 (September 1943): 193–222, at 207. Also see Erminie Wheeler-Voegelin, *Pitt River Indians of California* (New York: Garland, 1974), 19–56.

37. Gatschet, *Klamath Indians of Southwestern Oregon*, 1:315, 2:198. *Lúgsh* has been inaccurately translated as meaning "to carry a load"; Ruby and Brown, *Indian Slavery in the Pacific Northwest*, 27. *Éna* means "to carry," and *kshéna* means "to carry something," like a load of sticks. There are many variations on this word but none connected to *lúgsh*. Gatschet, *Klamath Indians of Southwestern Oregon*, 2:29.

38. Luther S. Cressman, "Klamath Prehistory: The Prehistory of the Culture of the Klamath Lake Area, Oregon," *Transactions of the American Philosophical Society* 46, no. 4 (January 1, 1956): 375–513, at 435–436; Spier, *Klamath Ethnography*, 22, 32; Theodore Stern, "Ideal and Expected Behavior as Seen in Klamath Mythology," *Journal of American Folklore* 76, no. 299 (January 1, 1963): 27. Verne F. Ray supports the idea that slaves married into Klamath and Modoc families, and he also suggests that male slaves, taken as boys, became essentially free, retaining little stigma, if they married a Modoc woman; see Ray, *Primitive Pragmatists: The Modoc Indians of Northern California* (Seattle: University of Washington Press, 1963), 138, 144–145.

39. Ned Blackhawk, *Violence over the Land*, 140–144.

40. Donald, *Aboriginal Slavery on the Northwest Coast*, 35–40, 121–138, 214–252.

41. Emphasis added. Samuel A. Clarke, "Early Klamath History" (unpublished manuscript, n.d.), CB C556h, 5 folders, University of Oregon Special Collection, Eugene (hereafter cited as OrColl). Albert Gatschet recorded a similar description of the raids from David Hill in Klamath during one of his research trips for the Bureau of American Ethnology: "The Lake men [Klamath] not often warred against the Shasti; continually however fought and (many) killed [the] Pit River men [Achomawi]. The Lake men enslaved also many every spring-time. Not (are) they bellicose, very despondent at the mere sight of Lake men they ran away, never they scalped, killed only they; many then they killed Pit River men. Never massacred the Lake men the Pit Rivers." Gatschet, *Klamath Indians of Southwestern Oregon*, 1:19.

42. Spier, *Klamath Ethnography*, 29; Gatschet, *Klamath Indians of Southwestern Oregon*, 1:ix–x, 16. For the existence of fortified sites, see Wheeler-Voegelin, *Pitt River Indians of California*, 33; Fred B. Kniffen, "Achomawi Geography," *University of California Publications in American Archaeology and Ethnology* 23 (1928): 297–332, especially 317.

43. Gatschet, *Klamath Indians of Southwestern Oregon*, 1:17.

44. Stern, "Columbia River Trade Network," 642–645.

45. Samuel A. Clarke, *Pioneer Days of Oregon History* (Portland: J. K. Gill, 1905), 119–120, 123.

46. Layton, "Traders and Raiders," 129–131.

47. Theodore Stern, "The Klamath Indians and the Treaty of 1864," *Oregon Historical Quarterly* 57 (December 1956): 229–273, especially 246.

48. Samuel A. Clarke, "Scenes on the Reservation" (unpublished manuscript, n.d.), Oliver Cromwell Applegate Papers, Ax 005, box 25, folder 3, University of Oregon Special Collections & University Archives, Eugene (hereafter cited as OCAP).

49. Gatschet, *Klamath Indians of Southwestern Oregon*, 1:189–191.

50. Stern, "The Klamath Indians," 232–233.

51. "Medicine Man's Widow Dies at 108," *San Francisco Chronicle*, January 19, 1956; Spier, *Klamath Ethnography*, 35–39, 107–112; Stern, *The Klamath Tribe*, 24; Nash, "The Place of Religious Revivalism," 380; Ray, *Primitive Pragmatists*, 136–137.

52. Gatschet, *Klamath Indians of Southwestern Oregon*, 1:xli.

53. Spier, *Klamath Ethnography*, 308–310.

54. Ibid., 37–38. I have replaced Spier's phonetic spelling of *Tcî'lokîn* with *Chiloquin*.

55. Samuel A. Clarke, "Tyee Blowe of Klamath on Doctors" (unpublished manuscript, n.d.), CB C556h, 5 folders, OrColl.

56. W. V. Rinehart to J. W. P. Huntington, July 9, 1866, Lindsay Applegate Papers, Ax 004, box 1, folder 1, University of Oregon Special Collections & University Archives, Eugene (hereafter cited as LAP); Edward S. Curtis, *The North American Indian; Being a Series of Volumes Picturing and Describing the Indians of the United States, and Alaska* (Seattle: E. S. Curtis, 1907), 13:175.

57. Emphasis added. William Pickett to unknown, June 4, 1869, *Letters Received at Bureau of Indian Affairs, Oregon*, in Wilkinson, Boyden, Cragun and Barker, and United States, eds., *Klamath, Modoc, and Yahooskin Documents in Connection with Litigation before the Indian Claims Commission Dkt. no. 100*, KMY-ICC-100, roll 1-A, frames 00584–00586, University of Oregon Special Collections & University Archives, Eugene (originally from National Archives and Record Administration, Washington, DC, n.d.).

58. Stephen Powers, "The California Indians," *Overland Monthly* 10, no. 6 (June 1873): 541.

59. Ray, *Primitive Pragmatists*, 113, 116, 122.

60. Donald, *Aboriginal Slavery on the Northwest Coast*, 80–81, 165–175, 311.

61. US Senate, *Annual Report of the Commissioner of Indian Affairs to the Secretary of the Interior for the Year 1844–1845* (Washington, DC: US Government Printing Office, 1845), 194; Frances Victor, *The River of the West: Life and Adventure in the Rocky Mountains and Oregon* (Hartford, CT: Columbian Book Company, 1870), 347–349; Gatschet, *Klamath Indians of Southwestern Oregon*, xxvi; US Senate, *Annual Report of the Commissioner of Indian Affairs to the Secretary of the Interior for the Year 1900* (Washington, DC: US Government Printing Office, 1900), 359.

62. US Senate, *Annual Report of the Commissioner of Indian Affairs to the Secretary of the*

BOYD COTHRAN

Interior for the Year 1843 (Washington, DC: US Government Printing Office, 1843), 443–455; Elliott West, *The Last Indian War: The Nez Perce Story* (New York: Oxford University Press, 2009), 30–34.

63. US Senate, *Annual Report of the Commissioner of Indian Affairs, 1844–1845*, 194; Victor, *The River of the West*, 347–349.

64. Thomas R. Garth, "The Plateau Whipping Complex and Its Relationship to Plateau-Southwest Contacts," *Ethnohistory* 12, no. 2 (Spring 1965): 141–170.

65. Donald, *Aboriginal Slavery on the Northwest Coast*, 79–80.

66. Gatschet, *Klamath Indians of Southwestern Oregon*, 58–69; Spier, *Klamath Ethnography*, 35, 307; Garth, "The Plateau Whipping Complex," 141–170.

67. Spier, *Klamath Ethnography*, 27.

68. Gray Whaley, *Oregon and the Collapse of Illahee: US Empire and the Transformation of an Indigenous World, 1792–1859* (Chapel Hill: University of North Carolina Press, 2010), 161–189.

69. Stephen Powers, *Tribes of California* (Berkeley: University of California Press, 1977), 254–255; Isenberg, *Mining California*, 144–145.

70. Whaley, *Oregon and the Collapse of Illahee*, 177–182; Stephen Beckham, *Requiem for a People: The Rogue Indians and the Frontiersmen* (Norman: University of Oklahoma Press, 1971).

71. Brendan C. Lindsay, *Murder State: California's Native American Genocide, 1846–1873* (Lincoln: University of Nebraska Press, 2012). Benjamin Madley has meticulously documented the more than seventy-eight hundred incidents of California Indian death by violence in his recent dissertation. Madley, "American Genocide: The California Indian Catastrophe, 1846–1873" (PhD diss., Yale University, 2009), 212–315.

72. Albert L. Hurtado, *Indian Survival on the California Frontier*, Yale Western Americana Series (New Haven, CT: Yale University Press, 1988), 129–131; James J. Rawls, *Indians of California: The Changing Image* (Norman: University of Oklahoma Press, 1986), 93. For the slaver's quote, see William J. Bauer, Jr., *We Were All like Migrant Workers Here: Work, Community, and Memory on California's Round Valley Reservation* (Chapel Hill: North Carolina Press, 2009), 51–52.

73. Bauer, *We Were All like Migrant Workers*, 34, 52.

74. "Indian Claims Commission Case Documents: Docket Materials, Docket 100: Draft on Klamath, Modoc, and Yahooskin Band of Snake Indians," box 9, folder 90, p. 48, Erminie Wheeler-Voegelin Papers, Edward E. Ayer Manuscript Collection, Newberry Research Library, Chicago.

75. Alexander Piper, "Reports and Journal," *Oregon Historical Quarterly* 69, no. 3 (September 1, 1968): 245.

76. Ibid., 245–249.

77. Emos E. Rogers to J. W. P. Huntington, May 1, 1863, in Wilkinson et al., *Letters Received at Bureau of Indian Affairs, Oregon*, KMY-ICC-100, roll 1-A, frames 00485–00489.

78. Ibid.

79. Elijah Steele to his brother, n.d. [c. May 1873], in US House of Representatives, *Official Copies of Correspondence Relative to the War with the Modoc Indians in 1872–73*, 43rd Cong., 1st Sess., 1874, House Executive Document 122 (Washington, DC: Adjutant General's Office, 1874), 297–309.

80. Hiroto Zakoji, "Klamath Culture Change" (master's thesis, University of Oregon, 1953), 77.

81. O. C. Applegate to Frank Applegate, May 3, 1869, OCAP, box 3, folder 2; E. S. Belden to Lindsay Applegate, May 1868, OCAP, box 3, folder 1. Also see Stern, *The Klamath Tribe*, 77–79.

82. Stern, *The Klamath Tribe*, 70–99.

5

Captivity and Economic Landscapes in California and the Far West, 1769–1850

Natale Zappia

In 1781, Spanish captives helplessly observed the Quechan *kwoxot* Olleyquotequiebe triumphantly adorn the *protector* (shield) of his slain enemy, the Spanish Captain Fernando Rivera y Moncada.[1] Hundreds of his warriors cheered as Olleyquotequiebe placed every last accoutrement of La Misión de la Purísima Concepción del Río Colorado and of a second mission, San Pedro y San Pablo, including gospels, missals, crosses, and other sacramental items, in a wooden box and tossed them into the Lower Colorado River. As witnesses later reported in Sonora, Olleyquotequiebe and his men rounded up more than one hundred Spanish captives, who would later serve as pawns in peace negotiations or become slaves for Quechan families.

To Spanish missionaries and military officials, the destruction of their settlements and crushing defeat at the hands of the Quechans and their Mojave allies proved a decisive blow, cutting short the century-long effort to connect the pueblos, missions, and presidios of Sonora and Las Californias via the Colorado River, strategically located at the midpoint between the two colonies (figure 5.1).[2] A culmination of factors explains the attack, ranging from the ecological strain caused by scores of settlers to at least one thousand head of overgrazing livestock and a lack of promised material benefits like clothes, tools, and seeds. Perhaps more important, though, the Quechan revolt reflected their frustration with Spanish partners who

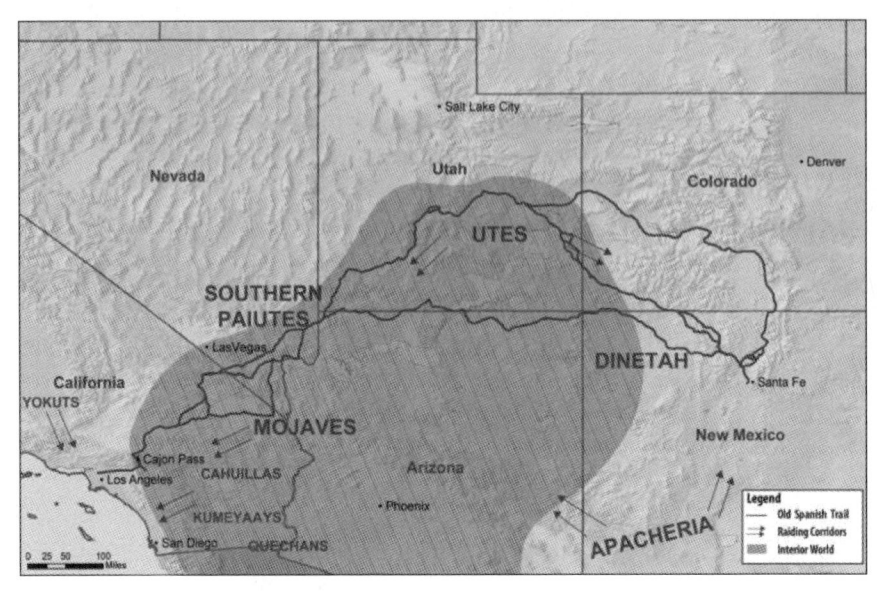

FIGURE 5.1
Slave-raiding networks in Alta and Native California, 1780s–1850s.

had promised access to the market in indigenous captives that had rapidly expanded during the eighteenth century.

Eight decades later, after Spaniards and Mexicans failed to colonize the Quechans, Euro-Americans attempted to control the same indigenous borderlands that Olleyquotequiebe fought to preserve in 1781. As these new arrivals observed, the indigenous slave trade continued unabated, and Native networks—rather than Euro-American links—stitched together California and Sonora. In 1839, for example, Thomas J. Farnham, an American fur trader who mapped parts of this vast interior region, described the systematic raiding and trading of Southern Paiutes between Los Angeles and Santa Fe: "These poor creatures are hunted in the spring of the year, when weak and helpless, by a certain class of men, and when taken are fattened, carried to Santa Fe and sold as slaves during their minority."[3] A few years later, in 1851, California governor John McDougal similarly reflected on the continued dominance of indigenous raiders:

> If the Indians of the Gila and Colorado should destroy the United States troops and ferryman, they would probably advance in order to form a junction with the Agua Caliente and Cohauilla [*sic*] Indians. If this junction should be effective, it would present an Indian force of four or five thousand warriors. It would strain

the energies of this country to their utmost tension, to resist so formidable a combination if it could be resisted at all.[4]

Seeing from opposite vantage points of borderlands history, these Spanish and Euro-American witnesses revealed the long-standing political-economic influence of indigenous captive and livestock networks in California and the Far West.[5] Since the seventeenth century in northwest New Spain, a shared Indian-Spanish practice of borderlands slavery expanded because of several economic trends, including frontier mining, ranching, agriculture, and missionary efforts, as well as Indian demand for labor and livestock. Native women and children served as the victims in this trade, and almost every part of northern Sonora and the Californias engaged in their capture and enslavement. By the time of the Quechan revolt, this vigorous market for captives engulfed a vast stretch of the Indian and colonial worlds.

During the eighteenth and nineteenth centuries, the indigenous borderlands between Sonora and Alta and Baja California facilitated complex networks of captivity. To be sure, captive labor meant very different things across the Far West. In Sonora, for example, Native captives served either as lifelong household servants in colonial presidios like Tucson, where a large proportion of the population consisted of *nijoras* (Indian captives from the Colorado–Gila River region), or as laborers in more hazardous mining environments, where epidemics and certain early death lurked. In contrast, the missions of coastal California (as well as those of the Gila River valley in northern Sonora) relied on a more seasonal form of coerced labor that granted degrees of autonomy much greater than those experienced by nijoras. In between Alta California and Sonora, interior indigenous communities utilized captive slaves to work alongside families to raise crops, produce goods, and fight against enemies (many times their own ethnic group). Within Indian country, captives sometimes had the opportunity to become adopted kin and to be allowed some relative flexibility in their social relationships. Similar forms of indigenous bondage existed in earlier periods and across different regions.[6]

Thus, restrictive and more dynamic forms of slavery all intermingled in California and Sonora between the eighteenth and nineteenth centuries, even as chattel slavery expanded into Indian country from the US cotton belt farther east. Olleyquotequiebe's adopted Spanish name, Salvador Palma, evinced these overlapping systems in the coastal and desert worlds. It derived from two different encounters during the 1770s. "Salvador" originated with a fugitive slave from the San Gabriel Mission in Alta California named Sebastián Tarabal. Tarabal was from a Tongva village in the Los

Angeles basin, where the San Gabriel Mission produced wine, wheat, corn, and cattle for both Spanish and Indian settlements near the coast. He most likely worked as part of a village quota arranged between missionaries needing labor and *alcaldes* (village leaders) who served as the appointed authorities who joined Spanish and indigenous worlds. Alcaldes typically held political sway over Indian villages and influence among missionaries and soldiers. These leaders essentially contracted out Indian labor while promising tangible benefits (such as a steady supply of food) for workers.

Tarabal's work revolved around the predictable seasonal agricultural patterns in Los Angeles that increasingly mimicked Mediterranean food systems imported from southern Europe. His form of servitude may have been less onerous than that of a captive slave in Sonora attached to a family or forced to work in hazardous mining conditions, but the labor he performed reflected its own form of brutality. The harsh conditions ultimately compelled him to flee into the interior. Tarabal most likely knew about frequent indigenous kidnappings occurring at San Gabriel. Since the establishment of the mission economy, interior raiders, like the Mojaves, had increasingly targeted San Gabriel's laborers and livestock. Despite the risk that his flight might actually lead him into a life of slavery, he evidently regarded his situation as desperate enough to cause him to flee. Olleyquotequiebe found Tarabal lost in the desert and rescued him. In gratitude to Olleyquotequiebe, Tarabal called his rescuer "Salvador" (savior).

Olleyquotequiebe's other name, "Palma," originated from his friendship with a slave trader in Caborca, northern Sonora, with the same moniker in the 1770s. *Rescates* (redeemers) like the Carborcan Palma trafficked in nijoras throughout Sonora. During the eighteenth and nineteenth centuries, hundreds of nijoras were sold into slavery, and Olleyquotequiebe may have also been involved in the trade (figure 5.2).[7] The name "Salvador Palma," then, quite aptly illustrates these intersections through varying forms of slavery that existed within and across colonial-indigenous worlds. These connections remained in some form as the Far West moved from Spanish to Mexican to Euro-American labor systems.

Indian captivity networks simultaneously linked these disparate systems. Captives followed one of several different paths shared by thousands of others during this period. The first path included "adoption" into a family as a wife, sister, and/or servant. In the years after her capture, a female captive might be married, bear children, and live out the rest of her life along the Colorado River. A similar fate may have awaited surviving captive children adopted into the tribe. These were the possibilities for captured women and children for the next one hundred years, until the Apache Wars

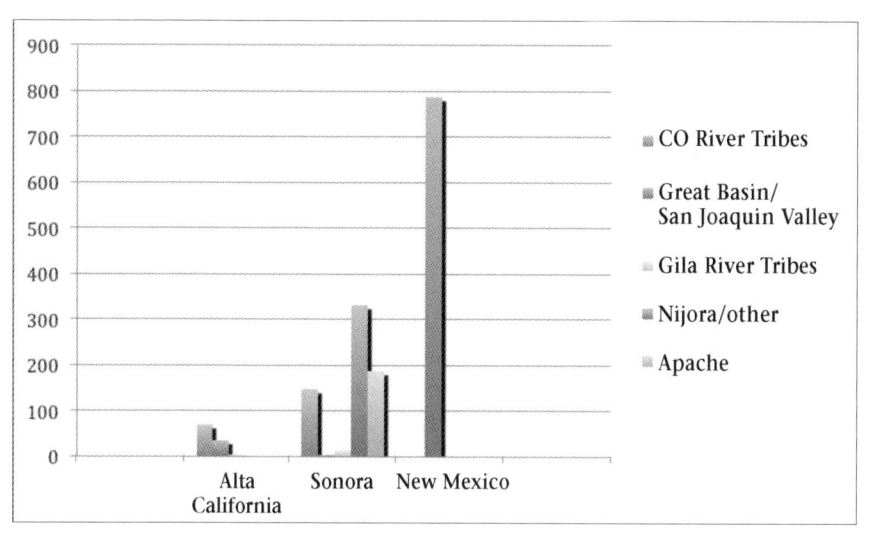

CAPTIVITY AND ECONOMIC LANDSCAPES IN CALIFORNIA AND THE FAR WEST

FIGURE 5.2
Documented victims of forced bondage by group, 1700–1860.

of the 1870s and 1880s.[8] Male captives, usually warriors from the Apachería abducted by Spanish or Mexican soldiers, were marched to coastal Mexico and even taken farther away, to places like Cuba.[9] Another path for the men would be even more arduous, following the route of *los rescatín*, moving east to Sonora, north into Ute territory, or, increasingly after 1800, west into Alta California. In the coming century, slave raiding indeed became the most likely fate as livestock economies expanded in Alta California, linking the Colorado River with the Pacific coast in more direct ways than they had been earlier.[10]

By closely looking at these interior indigenous borderlands that remained on the edge or outside of European and Euro-American control between the 1770s and the 1840s, I attempt in this chapter to understand and unify fluid slave networks that defined different coastal and desert economies. Although forced labor at missions, ranchos, and mines have rightly seized the attention of scholars exploring the economies and ecologies of early California, the act of more directly connecting these regimes with Indian networks of captivity reveals further layers of history intersecting coastal California with the borderlands of the Far West and Southwest.[11]

ECOLOGIES AND SLAVERIES IN ALTA CALIFORNIA

For many scholars studying Alta California, the great majority of archival material focuses on a small geographic wedge hugging the coastline within the mission system. Missionaries kept meticulous baptismal records that have greatly enriched our understanding of indigenous-Spanish interactions. However, most of the people of Alta California and almost all of its Native inhabitants lived outside of Spanish control and thus lurked on the edges of historical records. Nonetheless, these individuals and communities exerted an inordinate (if usually unrecognized) influence on the development of the colony. Particular regions (like the Lower Colorado River) even expanded their economic reach alongside the Spanish-Mexican coast.[12]

As in other borderlands, raiders expressed indigenous economic and cultural power through kin- and gender-based networks based on the local needs of villages, clans, and powerful kwoxots like Olleyquotequiebe. But these borderlands also experienced the predictable and irrevocable marks of foreign influence, including epidemics, horses, cattle, and other Mediterranean biota that spilled into the region during the eighteenth and nineteenth centuries and spread into almost every Native space in North America as Spaniards, Mexicans, and Euro-Americans created dynamic economies based on livestock, furs, and agriculture. Yet, it also paralleled other indigenous-defined borderlands across the West and expanded even as Euro-Americans became the dominant ruling classes. Through the formation and expansion of indigenous raiding, Native contours of economic and military power forged "Native grounds," "middle grounds," Apacherías, and Comancherías that connected local economies and shaped the larger designs of state power. In all of these Native spaces, captivity influenced complex cultural geographies.[13]

The Spanish colonies of New Mexico, Sonora, and California also practiced forms of bondage that evolved alongside the Indian slave trade. In many parts of Alta California between 1769 and 1848, for example, coerced labor regimes existed throughout the missions and ranchos, despite the official edicts issued in Mexico City and Spain.[14] These earlier systems overlapped with forms of slavery (called "apprenticing" by American rancheros and miners) that survived California's entry into the United States as a nonslavery state in 1850, resulting in often genocidal military campaigns and exploitive labor systems.[15]

The California gold rush further introduced some of the most insidious forms of indigenous slavery practiced in the state.[16] The dramatic influx of aggressive non-Native settlers, miners, and ranchers, with their accompanying diseases, coupled with extensive droughts, all undermined the power and control that Native Californians had over their territory by the 1850s.[17] When the US government negotiated a series of treaties establishing reservations away from population centers in California in order to protect Natives from kidnapping by rancheros or miners, the citizens of the state rejected ratification and refused to acknowledge any Indian rights. Policies imposed by the state legislature, particularly "apprenticeship" acts and vagrancy laws passed between 1850 and 1861, irrevocably altered Indian country but left standing older forms of oppression.

In the eighteenth century, when many of these earlier captivity networks had proliferated, Spanish goods and biota also infiltrated every corridor of this vast region, where disease, horses, slave raiding, and exogenous plants moved along Native roads.[18] Despite these invasions, Natives fought direct Spanish intervention into the slave-trading networks. Farther west along the coast, Natives migrated, adopted new food systems, succumbed to disease, converted to Christianity, and produced new commodities for regional and even global networks. Indirectly, changes initiated by the coastal mission economy began to shape Indian lives in places like the Lower Colorado River on the edge of Alta California.

Villages within Native California and Sonora held divergent strategies, resulting from very different indigenous histories, that in turn shaped Indian-Spanish interactions. In Sonora, for example, Native farmers had cultivated corn, cotton, and even wheat before missionization. Along the coast, Chumash, Tongva, and Kumeyaay communities did not engage in similar intensive forms of agricultural production until the first wave of Spanish Franciscans arrived in 1769. By the nineteenth century, corn and livestock raised by coastal communities quickly replaced earlier Native staples at the missions along the Alta California coast, with profound disruptions. Disease outbreaks, for example, including a major flu epidemic in 1798, spread across mission settlements alongside other Mediterranean biota, shaking both the Spanish and Indian economies in Alta California. Reactions to these deadly contagions varied. Healthy Chumash and Tongva neophytes fled farther into the interior to avoid doing the debilitating work involved in raising crops or contracting illnesses. By 1817, close to 10 percent of all San Gabriel converts had left the mission for Indian country.[19] The Luiseños, in contrast, invited Franciscans to settle nearby in the hopes that the priests would protect them from waves of epidemics. For some Native groups, the missions afforded food security and even some space for control over their labor, despite the efforts of priests to control cultural practices. For others, though, the Franciscans only promised a harsh life of restrictive and backbreaking work.[20]

At the mission farms and pastures, Franciscans appointed Indian alcaldes to supervise labor output. Chumash alcaldes like Sulumigieguit, for example, intensified production at the Santa Barbara Mission.[21] While his efforts and those of other alcaldes varied from village to village and between mountain and coastal towns, the Chumash decision to neglect interior trade dissolved many coastal-inland connections that had existed for several centuries. The relative economic stability of some missions, numerous construction projects (churches, ranches, irrigation canals), and regular church attendance (assisted in part by the increasing importation of ritualistic crosses, statues, and books) hardened the boundary between the coast and the interior, paradoxically fueling the demand for Indian captives provided by interior raiders.[22] As Indian labor produced vast stores of agricultural commodities, livestock simultaneously fed demands by Yokuts, Ute, and Mojave raiders. By 1800, a complex, symbiotic relationship had emerged that connected coastal Indian labor with interior Indian raiding.[23]

The Yokuts illustrate this complexity. Located on the edge of the mission frontier, Yokuts continued to trade with some Chumash and Serrano villages. Fleeing converts, called "fugitives" by the Franciscans, made their way into the San Joaquin Valley. Spanish (and later Mexican) soldiers pursued runaway neophytes and livestock. Similarly, authorities issued ordinances outlawing Indian horseback riding, which the governor, Don Diego de Borica, thought was "liable to bring grave consequences."[24] Natives working near the missions also sold horses and firearms to Yokuts raiders. In many ways, then, Yokuts territory became a new borderland where overlapping economies, property, and agendas clashed.[25] In the face of Yokuts opposition, Spanish intentions to replicate the coastal economy made up of valley Indian laborers quickly failed, and the rapid expansion of Yokuts horse herds (considered "wild" horses by Spaniards) competed with livestock for coveted grasslands.[26] Like their more domesticated relatives, by the 1820s these horses dramatically affected the composition of the San Joaquin Valley grasses. Yokuts began to incorporate horses into their diet, economy, and culture.

The Yokuts, in fact, made frequent attacks on the missions and ranchos during the nineteenth century. With their strategic location just beyond the Tejon Pass and the Bay Area watershed, northern and southern Yokuts bands raided almost the entire chain of settlements, sometimes with the assistance of mission Indians fleeing from captivity, other times in spite of Native opposition. In several documented cases, coastal Chumashes allied themselves with the Yokuts by colluding in horse and cattle raids, kidnapping, and burning mission property.[27] By the early 1800s, several costly expeditions across the mission chains made their way into the interior to retrieve runaways who refused to work in the mission or, after 1821, the rancho system.[28] Most of these expeditions proved costly in lives, money, and time, as did the pan-Indian revolts that the Yokuts participated in, particularly in 1824 at San Luis Obispo, Santa Ynez, and La Purísma. This major assault resulted in more than one thousand exiles into Yokuts territory who defied the coastal economy.[29] Yokuts remained a military power that kept Spanish and Mexican settlers close to the coast.[30] In failing to establish missions among the Yokuts, Franciscans suspiciously viewed them as agents of the expanding Apachería, even though Apache raiders lived hundreds of miles to the east. This association reflected the fear commonly felt by foreigners that Indian slave and horse raiding evoked.[31]

Located farther east and closer to the Colorado River, the Mojaves also expanded their reach through raiding trails into Alta California. Raids stimulated, in part, the establishment of Serrano and Cahuilla ranching settlements east of San Gabriel Mission that buffered attacks. Franciscans and soldiers viewed the Mojaves in the same way as the Yokuts—as agents of the expanding Apachería. In 1819, Spanish soldiers clashed with Mojave traders at the Mission San Buenaventura, resulting in the death of one Mojave and two soldiers. Later that year, Mojaves attacked San Gabriel Mission, stealing livestock. Fifty soldiers unsuccessfully pursued the raiders into the Mojave Desert.[32] Mojave power now clearly reached into Spanish territory and caused alarm on the coast. José de la Guerra, a prominent Californio, even discussed the possibility of establishing a *vigía* (defensive watchtower) near the Colorado River in 1819.[33] Limited funds withheld by officials skeptical of controlling raiders (as demonstrated in the Apachería) halted the establishment of the outpost. With the help of their Tongva and Serrano allies, Mojaves continued to raid.

In many instances, vaqueros and other workers on ranchos became victims of kidnappings alongside livestock. Serrano ranchers bore the brunt of these raids, leading to formal petitions to establish a garrison to shield them. In 1819, Natives petitioned for the establishment of an *asistencia* (mission rancho) near present-day Redlands in order to provide protection from Mojaves and extend grazing land away from San Gabriel. While it never received the status of an asistencia (which required the full-time residence of a priest), an *estancia* (smaller rancho) outpost was developed by Serranos and Cahuillas working with San Gabriel Franciscans, and it survived for the next four decades. Despite the antagonistic relationship between Spanish and interior groups and the deleterious impacts of forced labor on the coastal side of the frontier, though, the Mediterranean ecology introduced by Spaniards remained, irrevocably replacing Native food systems and autonomy in Alta California. Even as political instability and mission secularization in 1834 reconfigured some labor relationships, many coastal Natives continued to live as virtual slaves on ranchos in an emerging Californio economy.

CALIFORNIO-ANGLO-INDIAN NETWORKS OF CAPTIVITY ALONG THE OLD SPANISH TRAIL

During the late eighteenth century, ecological systems and labor regimes at the missions of Alta California and Sonora overlapped because of the corresponding expansion of interior indigenous borderlands centered largely on the Colorado River. By the mid-nineteenth century, though, Mexican Californios had initiated their own efforts to link the former Spanish colonies of New Mexico, Alta California, and Sonora through a trading corridor known as the Old Spanish Trail (see figure 5.1).[34] Beginning around 1829, the Old Spanish Trail linked New Mexico and California along a northerly route, bypassing the strategic indigenous junction on the Lower Colorado River where Spaniards had disastrously failed fifty years earlier. Jedediah Smith dubbed the trail "Spanish," but it is more accurate to say that it served the interests of Mexican ranchers and Euro-American overland migrants.

Proponents of the Old Spanish Trail envisioned a lucrative exchange of sheep, processed wool, and blankets (from New Mexico) for mules and horses (raised in California). The connection of Los Angeles with Santa Fe further linked maturing colonial production centers. At the same time, it provided New Mexico with access to international trade through the coastal economy. By 1800 the Pacific Rim already brimmed with economic activity and exploration. Fueled in part by Chinese demand for pelts, the otter fur trade, for example, allowed Russians to expand into northern California, British sailors to travel into the Pacific Northwest and to Hawaii, and Euro-Americans from Boston and New Mexico to get to Mexican ports.

But the Old Spanish Trail also cut through the heart of preexisting indigenous captivity networks.[35] In greater numbers then ever, two powerful Native groups, in fact, came to dominate the trail: Mojaves and Utes. Violence perpetrated by these raiders on the trail spilled outward from its narrow course, engulfing Alta California. A more disruptive, even horrific expansion of slavery thus resulted from increased trade on the Old Spanish Trail. The Utes who lived and traveled along the trail had already emerged as important economic partners with many New Mexicans by the time Mexico achieved independence from Spain in 1821. During the eighteenth century, in fact, Ute raiders dramatically shaped the New Mexican borderlands, providing a steady supply of slaves (usually kidnapped Southern

Paiute women and children) for colonial New Mexican *obrajes* (factories) in exchange for horses.[36]

Even before the Mexican period, many Spanish settlers valued this lucrative relationship and sought to maintain partnerships, whereas colonial officials felt threatened and in 1778 attempted to ban the Ute trade. Despite the *bando* (ban), the slave trade flourished, and Utes continued raiding.[37] Many of those Spaniards who defied these orders also searched for ways to penetrate other markets. Ute traders guided them on trails that moved northwest (and out of the reach of the Quechans) from Santa Fe before cutting southwest, following the course of the Colorado River and through present-day Utah, Arizona, and Nevada. As many Spaniards observed, Utes used these trails to kidnap Southern Paiutes for slave markets in New Mexico but also increasingly in California. In the coming decades, they would navigate these trails to steal horses from Californio ranchos as well.[38]

Alongside these interior developments, a regional California hide and tallow trade also increased in importance, reaching even global dimensions along the eastern Pacific Basin. Californios met demand by dramatically expanding livestock production. Native vaqueros (both free and captive) shaped the trade by raising, tanning, and preparing hides for export.[39] Cattle and horse herds expanded steadily, reaching close to five hundred thousand head along the coast.[40] Thus, thousands of heads of livestock crisscrossed the trading corridor soon after Mexican independence, further expanding indigenous interregional raiding between California, Sonora, and New Mexico.[41] Using the Old Spanish Trail, Ute and Mojave raiders entered California and stole mostly horses and mules. Horse populations escaping from ranchos also supplied raiders with steady transportation and food. Horse theft quickly engulfed the Far West borderlands, also expanding Native slave raiding. Violence and ethnic tension increased alongside multiethnic raids. This greatly disrupted some communities while forging links among others. Some groups, like the Southern Paiutes, bore increasing hardship, becoming the frequent victims of slave raids.

As herd numbers reached their peak between the 1830s and 1840s, Utes also undertook the largest thefts of horses, sometimes amassing thousands in a single sweep.[42] With their great prowess on horseback, Utes easily outmaneuvered ranchers and vaqueros across Southern California. Located near the Cajon Pass, San Bernardino and San Gabriel Valley settlements (but also those within the Los Angeles basin) bore the brunt of Ute raids. Exact figures on the number of horses and captives stolen during this period remain unclear, but the archival material that does exist speaks to the prevalence of Ute raids in Southern California. Perhaps blamed for attacks in which Utes never participated, Ute raiding (real or imagined) became an ingrained part of the geography of the Far West.

Like the Utes, Mojaves capitalized on their strategic position along the Old Spanish Trail in the Mojave Desert. With their superior knowledge of crisscrossing trade routes, warriors easily overtook and captured horses, goods, and slaves. As traffic between New Mexico and California increased, Mojaves grew proficient at hit-and-run strategies. Reported thefts by raiders along the trail occurred as early as 1833.[43] Even before the Old Spanish Trail became a familiar trading route, Mojaves clashed with encroaching fur trappers venturing from the north and the east for beaver pelts and captives.[44] Several fur traders, including Jedediah Smith (in 1826), James Pattie (1826), George C. Yount (1828, 1831), Ewing Young (1829), and William Wolfskill (1830), experienced attacks while squatting in Mojave territory.[45]

Mojave raiders not only kept potential squatters out of their territory but also expanded their economic reach, riding through the Cajon Pass to organize raids into the Los Angeles basin from the 1820s through the 1840s. On the eve of the Mexican-American War, both Californios and Euro-Americans credited Mojaves and Utes for almost every raid that took place. In 1842, rumors of a Paiute-Mojave attack on San Bernardino alarmed the Los Angeles Prefecture, which granted a request to fund an expedition into the Mojave Desert in order to stop raiding:

> This prefecture trusts you will attend efficiently to this matter, as it is only by taking a strong stand that you will be able to stop the harm and damage constantly being caused by these marauding Indians. Considering that this service will be a (638) public benefit, this Prefecture shall lend all the means in its power to ensure success to this enterprise.[46]

A few years later, Benjamin D. Wilson, a ranchero who owned part of Rancho Jurupa (near present-day Riverside), recalled that "Mojave and other Indians were constantly raiding upon the ranches in this part of the country." George Yount also commented on the perceived Mojave power along the Old Spanish Trail, claiming that "the Mohaves [sic] [were] said to number 5,000 warriors and they [held] the neighboring tribes in perpetual fear and dread."[47] Ranchos from as far away as Santa Barbara, San Gabriel, and San Diego all underwent Mojave attacks. These raids intensified during and after the Mexican-American War. In an 1847 letter from San Diego to the military governor of California, S. W. Kearney, H. D. Fitch reported the effects of these raids: "It is my unpleasant duty to communicate to you that...these people will very soon lose every head of cattle and every horse which they possess."[48]

Such attacks continued even after California became part of the United States. In a similarly alarming petition received by Major General J. H. Bean of the California Militia in 1850, Los Angeles County officials requested protection from what rancheros perceived as a multiethnic and multiregional front. The petition speculated, "The Indians of the Tulare valley seem determined to wage [war] against the settlements; while the Yotahs [sic], encouraged and excited as their several bands must be by the news of their late success, can and will descend upon our plains." The petition viewed the Tejon and Cajon Passes as the gateways for raiders. In response, Governor John MacDougal quickly authorized Bean to raise a militia.[49] Despite the militia reinforcements, raiding continued. One militiaman stationed at Cajon Pass observed the persistent dominance of the raiders: "They have become very bold; entering the valleys at night; they collect and drive off large herds of horses before a sufficient force can be assembled to overtake them. The Eutaws and the 'Piutes' are the two principal tribes engaged in these plunders."[50]

Farther south, Kumeyaays and Cahuillas attacked San Diego and other towns periodically, even through the Mexican-American War.[51] These raiders, in turn, traded captives on the Colorado River. Recollecting the 1838 kidnapping of two children, Tomasa and Romona, for example, Apolinaria Lorenzana said that "the Indians went to sell the children to the Colorado River."[52] It is not known where these children ended up, but Lorenzana's remarks both illustrate the indigenous connections between the coast and the interior and reveal how coastal settlers thought about indigenous raiders. While Natives could not defeat Euro-Americans in Los Angeles and San Diego, they threatened the steady flow of commerce that tenuously maintained settlements. The raiding strategy thrived on hit-and-run tactics rather than all-out confrontation. Moreover, if raiders destroyed settlements and removed the Euro-American presence, they would have no target populations to steal from. As in Sonora during the eighteenth century, horses also facilitated an increase in slave trafficking along the Old Spanish Trail during this period. The violent and brutal practice of slave raiding altered households, local communities, and labor regimes across Indian country, further reconfiguring gender roles in ways that greatly undermined the economic power of Native women.

GENDERED CAPTIVITY NETWORKS IN THE CALIFORNIA BORDERLANDS

Throughout the seventeenth and eighteenth centuries, women played a vital role in production and trade in the interior world. Their role as household producers of pottery, shell beads, baskets, and textiles facilitated exchange. By the beginning of the nineteenth century, almost two hundred years of exposure to disease had undermined their power. As a result, the roles shared by men, women, and children dramatically changed. Women and children became commodified as slaves, alongside horses and cattle. By the 1830s the Old Spanish Trail was being used to funnel slaves between New Mexico and California as Mojave and Ute raiders continued kidnapping to meet demand. Raiders forced captives into Sonora, New Mexico, and occasionally Los Angeles for sale.[53]

Many women and children captives labored in Southern California, tanning cattle hides both on the ranchos and in the raiding communities. Crucially, they also replaced local populations that had been decimated by disease and war. In California, children in particular bore the brunt of kidnapping and trade among ranchers, who preferred to use them as servants and couriers. The practice became so pervasive that the legislature enacted the Act for the Government and Protection of Indians in 1850 to clarify the legality of (although not entirely eliminate) the kidnapping of Indians. Ranchers found loopholes so that they could "apprentice" children and release them after they turned fifteen. Others chose to "rent" the children from their parents.[54] At the same time, section 17 of the act punished Natives who engaged in raiding horses and other livestock with lashings and/or a fine of up to $200. In stark contrast, section 4 stated that any white settler caught abusing Indian children would be fined only $10. This disparity clearly reflected the paradoxes and pervasiveness of raiding and Indian slavery in early California. On the one hand, lawmakers were determined to stop raiding and eventually to eliminate captivity. On the other hand, they relied on the labor of Indian slaves, who shaped daily life in California.[55]

Native communities like the Southern Paiutes (who lived northeast of Los Angeles along the Old Spanish Trail) bore the biggest brunt of raiding and slavery. The Southern Paiutes had had very little contact with foreigners until the 1850s, although indirectly they had long felt the painful consequences of the colonial demand for slaves. When the priest Silvestre Vélez de Escalante led one of the first Spanish expeditions into Ute country in 1776, the Spanish-Ute slave connection had already preceded him. It took "a thousand gestures" to convince five young Paiutes to come down from a tree into which they had fled upon seeing the Spanish entourage. By the nineteenth century this trepidation pervaded all Southern Paiute territory. Edward Beale, the superintendent of Indian Affairs, made a similar observation during his 1857 expedition through the Mojave Desert: "So common is it to make a raid for this purpose [kidnapping for slavery], that it is considered as no more objectionable than to go on a buffalo or a mustang hunt."[56] Upon being approached in their settlements, women commonly hid their children.

This Southern Paiute fear, especially of their Ute neighbors, intensified during the mid-nineteenth century. Ute raiders traded Southern Paiutes to both the east and the west, so the latter found themselves as slaves in both New Mexico and Alta California.[57] Southern Paiute women sold for as much as $150 in Santa Fe (boys for $100 and girls for $200) and for somewhat less in Los Angeles.[58] Without direct access to horses, Southern Paiutes failed to withstand the onslaught of raiders. Increasingly, Utes referred to all Southern Paiutes in gendered terms as "women." By the 1830s the Ute raider Wakara assumed that he had total control over Southern Paiutes and their territories. As Martha Knack has argued in her study on Southern Paiutes, "Utes not only threatened Paiutes bodily but also claimed the right to move freely over Paiute territory."[59]

To the Utes, Southern Paiutes became an exploitable commodity. Recall the fur trader Thomas J. Farnham's comment about the systematic raiding and trading of Southern Paiutes at the start of this chapter. His observations proved commonplace during this time period. Yet another migrant, a Mormon named Anson Call, remarked on the relative ease with which slaves were bought and sold in Utah in 1853: "We were surrounded in every direction by different tribes who annoyed us much by a constant begging...occasionally small bodies of Spaniards were passing who were buying up Indian children for the purpose of making slaves of them."[60]

The treatment of Southern Paiutes changed in the 1850s. The establishment of Fort Yuma in 1849 and Fort Mojave in 1859 initiated the decline of Ute and Mojave raiding. Instead of raiders, migrants on wagons now disrupted the Southern Paiute territory, destroying crops and large livestock herds. Southern Paiutes initially welcomed the cessation of Ute raiding, but they quickly grew weary of Mormons redeeming Paiute children from Utes.[61] In response, Southern Paiutes either sporadically attacked herds, forts, and settlements or joined their Mojave and Chemehuevi neighbors along the Colorado River to the south.[62]

While women and children suffered most from the violent exchanges unfolding during the nineteenth century, they continued to shape the raiding economy. Even as captives, women often introduced new traditions and influenced local traditions while producing textiles, baskets, and pottery. Multilingual women captives conversant with neighboring practices served as negotiators between friendly or antagonistic communities. With the exception of the well-documented story of Olive Oatman (a teenaged Mormon girl who was traded for horses to Mojaves and lived among them as a captive between 1851 and 1857), only sporadic archival material about women captives has surfaced that illustrates similar roles women played in the borderlands of the Far West.[63] But a closer look at household economic activity in the region shows that women helped shape the landscape of the raiding economy.[64]

Along the Old Spanish Trail and other overland migration routes, Mojave and Ute raiding thus represented a formidable economic force in the burgeoning trade linking California with the interior. Mojaves and Utes, as well as many Yokuts and Kumeyaays, attacked Mexican and Euro-American settlements and migrants at will, with little fear of retaliation. Ranching communities remained on the defensive until the demise of the livestock economy, never gaining control of or subduing raiding, which continued even after the onset of the gold rush and the resulting demographic influx into California after 1849. At the same time, indigenous raiders periodically supplied slaves to these same settlements. These trends continued until the devastating droughts of the early 1860s.

CONCLUSION

Virtually all of the Far West felt the environmental and social impacts of increased overland migration, the Mexican-American War, and the California gold rush beginning in 1848.[65] Along the coast and in Northern California in particular, outright theft, destruction, and (as some scholars have argued) genocidal onslaught devastated Native communities.[66] The indigenous borderlands also experienced their demise, in part, as a result of the demographic influx that radically altered local agricultural and livestock production. Yet during this period, raiders continued to wield some power. This held true throughout the borderlands between the United States and Mexico. Natives frequently at odds with Mexico and the United States acted as interethnic adversaries with their own objectives.[67] To raiders, distinctions between "American" and "Mexican" meant little.

In parallel yet devastatingly divergent ways, Indian laborers in California also saw no difference between Spanish, Mexican, American, or even indigenous oppressors. Regime changes, new political-economic trends, even antislavery "protection" laws—these bore few differences to

Captivity and Economic Landscapes in California and the Far West

Indian communities forced to serve in dramatically transformed ecological landscapes shaped by corn and wheat cultivation, mining, and livestock raising. Somewhat uniquely in Native America, coastal California Indians experienced the brunt of two overlapping forms of indigenous and Euro-American colonialism for almost a century. Indians labored on vast estates defined by Mediterranean biota and its accompanying agricultural methods, closely managed by alcaldes who acted as overseers, not unlike those of other slave societies in the Americas. But in other ways, Natives also worked in an isolated frontier partially controlled by Indian groups who exploited this vulnerability. Indian raiding of horses and people forced Spaniards to restrict the freedom of its neophyte converts, who in turn fled and/or revolted against harsh labor practices. At the same time, raiders afforded the coastal economy some success, since it relied so heavily on livestock production for horse-for-slave trading farther north and east. Collectively, interior Natives and coastal Spaniards shared the margins of claimed territories that perpetuated Indian slavery. As California became an American state, the threat of Indian raiding allowed rancheros to justify enslaving coastal Indian communities, just as their Spanish and Californio predecessors had.

After 1850, land tenure became the central focus of Indian policy in Anglo California as hundreds of thousands of migrants flooded into the state and dramatically altered the demography and ecology of the landscape. But those deep Indian-Spanish landscapes remained, in many ways shaping the contours of modern agriculture that came to dominate all of California. As for the Quechans, who were ultimately forced onto a reservation set aside by executive order in 1865, they still remain, more than two centuries after the revolt of Olleyquotequiebe. And the Colorado River where they continue to farm today also flows onto vast fields tended by migrants struggling within the evolving, yet still oppressive, systems of labor initiated by Indians and foreigners long ago.

Acknowledgments

The author would like to thank Bonnie Martin, James Brooks, and all of the participants of the SMU-SAR seminar for their revision suggestions and advice. Sections of this chapter appear in my book *Traders and Raiders: The Indigenous World of the Colorado Basin, 1540–1859* (Chapel Hill: University of North Carolina Press, 2014).

Notes

1. Quechans and other Colorado River tribes relied on the leadership of *kwoxots* (roughly translated as "the good"), who competed for allegiance of their people

NATALE ZAPPIA

through success on the battlefield, compelling dreams, and material benefits. See Mark Santiago, *Massacre at the Yuma Crossing: Spanish Relations with the Quechans, 1779–1782* (Tucson: University of Arizona Press, 1998).

2. The revolt occurred near present-day Yuma, Arizona. For a report on the revolt, see "Sublevacion de los Yumas," Mexican Manuscripts Collection, MS 1, C697M3, William Andrews Clark Memorial Library, UCLA. Several studies footnote the Quechan revolt. See Vladimir Guerrero, "Lost in the Translation: Chief Palma of the Quechan," *Southern California Quarterly* 92, no. 4 (2010): 327–350; Hubert Howe Bancroft, *Works of H. H. Bancroft*, vol. 18 (San Francisco: History Company Publishers, 1886), 380–383; Jack Forbes, *Warriors of the Colorado: The Yumas of the Quechan Nation and Their Neighbors* (Norman: University of Oklahoma Press, 1965); Selden E. Stone, "California's Twenty-Second and Twenty-Third Missions: The Colorado Missions" (master's thesis, La Verne College, 1972); Santiago, *Massacre at the Yuma Crossing*, which provides the most comprehensive account.

3. As quoted in Carling Malouf and A. Arline Malouf, "The Effects of Spanish Slavery on the Indians of the Intermountain West," *Southwestern Journal of Anthropology* 1 (1945): 381. Original quote in T. J. Farnham, "Travels in the Great Western Prairies, Part I," in *Early Western Travels, 1748–1846*, vol. 28, ed. R. G. Thwaites (Cleveland: A. H. Clark, 1906), 249.

4. Bean to McDougal, November 30, 1851, 140, MS F3753, Indian War Papers, California State Archives, Sacramento.

5. The "Far West" is usually defined to include California, Nevada, and the coastal Pacific regions of Oregon, Washington, British Columbia, Alaska, and Hawaii. See Earl Pomeroy, *The American Far West in the Twentieth Century* (New Haven, CT: Yale University Press, 2009). My chapter adopts a view of the Far West that includes the indigenous borderlands of southeastern California, southern Nevada, Utah, Arizona, New Mexico, and Sonora, Mexico.

6. See, for example, chapters 1 and 2 by Catherine Cameron and Eric Bowne, respectively, in this volume.

7. More than four hundred nijoras appear in the Sonoran and Alta California mission records between 1700 and 1830. See Tumacácori National Historical Park, Mission 2000 Spanish Missions Database, personal ID 23855, http://www.nps.gov/tuma/learn/historyculture/mission-2000.htm. Similar phenomena occurred in New Mexico and the Great Plains. First published in 1968, David M. Brugge's foundational *Navajos in the Catholic Church Records of New Mexico, 1694–1875*, 2nd ed. (Santa Fe, NM: SAR Press, 2010), exhaustively documented captivity networks through mission baptism records. Also see James Brooks's exploration of Southwest Borderlands slavery in

Captivity and Economic Landscapes in California and the Far West

Captives and Cousins: Slavery, Kinship, and Community in the Southwest Borderlands (Chapel Hill: University of North Carolina Press, 2002).

8. For indigenous forms of captivity in Arizona during the late nineteenth century, see Victoria Smith, *Captive Arizona, 1851–1900* (Lincoln: University of Nebraska Press, 2009).

9. As described by Paul Conrad in chapter 3 of this volume.

10. Various forms of Indian slavery existed throughout North America. See Alan Gallay, *The Indian Slave Trade: The Rise of the English Empire in the American South, 1670–1717* (New Haven, CT: Yale University Press, 2002), and his more recent collection of essays surveying Indian slavery across the continent, *Indian Slavery in Colonial America* (Lincoln: University of Nebraska Press, 2010); Brett Rushforth, *Bonds of Alliance: Indigenous and Atlantic Slaveries in New France* (Chapel Hill: University of North Carolina Press, 2012); Christina Snyder, *Slavery in Indian Country: The Changing Face of Captivity in Early America* (Cambridge, MA: Harvard University Press, 2010). Colin G. Calloway's *One Vast Winter Count* masterfully surveys Indian slave trading across the North American West. See Calloway, *One Vast Winter Count: The Native American West before Lewis and Clark* (Lincoln: University of Nebraska Press, 2003).

11. This chapter focuses on pre–gold rush California, but several recent innovative works explore overlapping forms of bondage after 1848. See Michael Magliari, "Free Soil, Unfree Labor," *Pacific Historical Review* 73 (2004): 349–390; Stacy L. Smith, *Freedom's Frontier: California and the Struggle over Unfree Labor, Emancipation, and Reconstruction* (Chapel Hill: University of North Carolina Press, 2013).

12. A remarkably diverse group of communities between Sonora and Alta California included Mojaves, Quechans, Cahuillas, Yokuts, Kumeyaays, Maricopas, Akimel O'odhams, Utes, Cocopas, Yavapais, Southern Paiutes, and Apaches.

13. See Pekka Hämäläinen, *The Comanche Empire* (New Haven, CT: Yale University Press, 2008); Juliana Barr, *Peace Came in the Form of a Woman: Indians and Spaniards in the Texas Borderlands* (Chapel Hill: University of North Carolina Press, 2007); Brian DeLay, *War of a Thousand Deserts: Indian Raids and the US-Mexican War* (New Haven, CT: Yale University Press, 2008); Richard White, *The Middle Ground: Indians, Empires, and Republics in the Great Lakes Region, 1650–1815* (Cambridge: Cambridge University Press, 1991); Kathleen DuVal, *The Native Ground: Indians and Colonists in the Heart of the Continent* (Philadelphia: University of Pennsylvania Press, 2006).

14. Works by several authors have revealed the powerful role that California Native laborers (both captive and free) played in creating the mission/Californio and the Pacific Rim economies, challenging historians to connect Alta California's history with other colonial histories. Steve Hackel and Lisbeth Haas have made this point most poignantly in Steven W. Hackel, *Children of Coyote, Missionaries of Saint Francis:*

NATALE ZAPPIA

Indian-Spanish Relations in Colonial California, 1769–1850 (Chapel Hill: University of North Carolina Press, 2005), 5, and Lisbeth Haas, *Saints and Citizens: Indigenous Histories of Colonial Missions and Mexican California* (Berkeley: University of California Press, 2013). Also see George Harwood Phillips, *Vineyards and Vaqueros: Indian Labor and the Economic Expansion of Southern California, 1771–1877* (Norman: University of Oklahoma Press, 2010); James A. Sandos, *Converting California: Indians and Franciscans in the Missions* (New Haven, CT: Yale University Press, 2004); David Igler, *The Great Ocean: Pacific Worlds from Captain Hook to the Gold Rush* (Oxford: Oxford University Press, 2013). Also see Robert H. Jackson and Edward Castillo, *Indians, Franciscans, and Spanish Colonization: The Impact of the Mission System on California Indians* (Albuquerque: University of New Mexico Press, 1995). For recent comparison of colonial interactions at missions in the Californias, see Lee M. Panich, "Missionization and the Persistence of Native Identity on the Colonial Frontier of Baja California," *Ethnohistory* 57, no. 2 (2010): 225–262. For similar influential works from California and Great Basin anthropologists, see Jack Forbes, *Warriors of the Colorado*; Martha C. Knack, *Boundaries Between: The Southern Paiutes, 1775–1995* (Lincoln: University of Nebraska Press, 2001); M. Kat Anderson, *Tending the Wild: Native American Knowledge and the Management of California's Natural Resources* (Berkeley: University of California Press, 2006).

15. For transitional economic and Indian policies in California history, see Magliari, "Free Soil, Unfree Labor"; Gerald Thompson, *Edward F. Beale and the American West* (Albuquerque: University of New Mexico Press, 1983). For the shift to industrial agriculture in the San Joaquin Valley, see David Igler, *Industrial Cowboys: Miller & Lux and the Transformation of the Far West, 1850–1920* (Berkeley: University of California Press, 2005). Also see Albert L. Hurtado, "Hardly a Farm House—A Kitchen without Them: Indian and White Households on the California Borderland Frontier in 1860," *Western Historical Quarterly* 13, no. 3 (1982): 245–250.

16. Recent studies have chronicled the devastating impacts of post–gold rush era policies on Native California, many of which aimed to annihilate Indian communities. For early statehood and Indian policies in California, see Andrew C. Isenberg, *Mining California: An Ecological History* (New York: Hill and Wang, 2005); Benjamin Madley, "Reexamining the American Genocide Debate: Meaning, Historiography, and New Methods," *American Historical Review* 120, no. 1 (February 2015): 98–139; Albert L. Hurtado, *Indian Survival on the California Frontier* (New Haven, CT: Yale University Press, 1988); Clifford E. Trafzer and Joel R. Hyer, *Exterminate Them! Written Accounts of the Murder, Rape, and Enslavement of Native Americans during the California Gold Rush* (East Lansing: Michigan State University Press, 1999); Laurence M. Hauptman, *Tribes and Tribulations: Misconceptions about American Indians and Their Histories* (Albuquerque:

Captivity and Economic Landscapes in California and the Far West

University of New Mexico Press, 1995); also see Philip J. Wilke, *The Expedition of Capt. J. W. Davidson from Fort Tejon to the Owens Valley in 1859* (Socorro, NM: Ballena Press, 1976).

17. These effects continue to shape contemporary public perceptions of Indian country in the state. Only recently, thanks to a considerable economic and cultural resurgence among Native communities, have recognition and some reconciliation occurred. See Trafzer and Hyer, *Exterminate Them!*; Robert F. Heizer, ed., *The Destruction of California Indians* (Santa Barbara, CA, and Salt Lake City, UT: Peregrine Smith, 1974); see also George E. Tinker, *Missionary Conquest: The Gospel and Native American Cultural Genocide* (Minneapolis, MN: Fortress Press, 1993).

18. For a discussion of how Native trading networks across the Americas facilitated the spread of smallpox, see Elizabeth A. Fenn, *Pox Americana: The Great Smallpox Epidemic of 1775–82* (New York: Hill and Wang, 2001). Also see Daniel T. Reff, *Disease, Depopulation, and Culture Change in Northwestern New Spain, 1518–1764* (Salt Lake City: University of Utah Press. 1991). For disease dispersal within interior California, see William Preston, "Serpent in Eden: Dispersal of Foreign Diseases into Pre-Mission California," *Journal of California and Great Basin Anthropology* 18, no. 1 (1996): 2–37.

19. William McCawley, *The First Angelinos: The Gabrielino Indians of Los Angeles* (Banning, CA: Ballena Press, 1996), 196–197.

20. Lisbeth Haas, "Luiseño Scholar Pablo Tac," in *Alta California: Peoples in Motion, Identities in Formation, 1769–1850*, ed. Steven W. Hackel (San Marino: Huntington Library / University of California Press, 2010), 81.

21. Marie Duggan, *The Chumash and the Presidio of Santa Barbara: Evolution of a Relationship, 1782–1823* (Santa Barbara, CA: Presidio Research Center, 2004), 65–68.

22. Competition between missions also shaped colonial boundaries, as evidenced by Franciscans who pleaded poverty when asked to contribute resources to fellow missionaries. When the San Fernando and San Luis Rey missions were established in 1797, the five neighboring missions (Santa Barbara, San Diego, San Juan Capistrano, San Gabriel, and San Buenaventura) scraped together just twenty horses as a contribution. See "Contribución de cinco misiones para la fundación de las San Fernando Rey y España y San Luis Rey de Francisco," Documentos para la historia de California, Academy of American Franciscan History Microfilm Collection, MSS 2005/262, carton 3, roll 1061-3, 201–202, Bancroft Library, University of California, Berkeley (hereafter cited as BL). See also Phillips, *Vineyards and Vaqueros*, chapter 4, and Duggan, *The Chumash and the Presidio*, 229–231.

23. For grain (corn, wheat, barley) and livestock production at the Alta California missions, see Jackson and Castillo, *Indians, Franciscans, and Spanish Colonization*, appendix 1, 113–131.

24. Hermenegildo Sal to Alcalde of San Jose, April 29, 1796, Landon Fellom San Jose Document Transcriptions, 3145, California State Library, Sacramento.

25. George Harwood Phillips has argued in his landmark study of the San Joaquin Valley, "While undergoing extensive social and economic change, they [Yokuts] maintained their political independence and exhibited an aggressiveness that hindered foreign occupation and later damaged coastal settlements." See Phillips, *Indians and Intruders in Central California, 1769–1849* (Norman: University of Oklahoma Press, 1993), 157.

26. Ibid., especially chapters 4 and 5. Also see Brook S. Arkush, "Yokuts Trade Networks and Native Culture Change in Central and Eastern California," *Ethnohistory* 40 (Autumn 1993): 619–641.

27. See Gabriel Moraga, "Diarios de exploraciones de misiones al interior de California, 1808," MS C-C 224, BL. Gabriel Moraga counted more than thirty-three "rebel" villages in the San Joaquin Valley in 1808.

28. In stark contrast to these expeditions, one of the earliest (the Moraga Expedition of 1806) was, according to the priest Pedro Martínez, amicable. Martínez estimated that they encountered roughly 5,000 Yokuts from twenty-five villages. He also claimed to have baptized 141. Most were not interested, although they apparently asked for missions. See Fray Pedro Muñoz, "The Gabriel Moraga Expedition of 1806: The Diary of Fray Pedro Muñoz," ed. Robert Glass Cleland and Haydée Noya, *Huntington Library Quarterly* 9, no. 3 (1946): 223–248, especially 245–248.

29. For analysis of the revolt, see James Sandos, *Converting California*, and Lisbeth Haas, "Indigenous Ethnic and Interethnic Relations in the Spanish/Mexican Borderlands: The Chumash Revolt," in *Journey into Otherness: Essays in North American History, Culture, and Literature*, ed. Ada Savin (Amsterdam: VU University Press, 2005), 135–148.

30. For complaints about "Tulare" raiders, see Anastasio Carrillo to Jose de la Guerra, February 21, 1822, MS FAC 667, Huntington Library, San Marino, CA (hereafter cited as HL). For complaints about exiles in Yokuts territory, see José Palomares, "Memoria relatada por José Francisco Palomares," MS C-D 135, reel 18, BL. See also Haas, "Indigenous Ethnic and Interethnic Relations," 135–148.

31. Haas, "Luiseño Scholar Pablo Tac," 80.

32. Lowell Bean and William Mason, *Diaries and Accounts of the Romero Expeditions in Arizona and California, 1823–1826* (Palm Springs, CA: Palm Springs Desert Museum, 1962), 7.

33. See José de la Guerra, Guerra Family Collection, June 1, 1819, and April 24, 1821, MS box 20, folder 904, HL. For discussion of the "watch tower" on the Colorado River, see Guerra Family Collection, June 6, 1819, MS box 23, folder 923, HL.

Captivity and Economic Landscapes in California and the Far West

34. Several studies have explored the history of the Old Spanish Trail, and these works parallel historiographic shifts from triumphalist to more multicultural accounts of western history. Ann Hafen and LeRoy Hafen, *Old Spanish Trail: Santa Fe to Los Angeles* (Glendale, CA: Arthur H. Clark, 1954), represents the former, while more recent works take the latter approach, such as Peter Gough, "Continuity, Convergence, and Conquest: A New History of the Old Spanish Trail" (master's thesis, California State University–Long Beach, 1997), and Joseph P. Sanchez, *Explorers, Traders, and Slavers: Forging the Old Spanish Trail, 1678–1850* (Salt Lake City: University of Utah Press, 1997). Also see Harlan Hague, *The Road to California: The Search for a Southern Overland Route, 1540–1848* (Los Angeles: Arthur C. Clark, 1978).

35. As early as 1788, Spanish officials became wary of transporting animals overland between settlements because of captive raiding near the Colorado River. See Clodomino Soberanos to Antonio Bexar, January 8, 1788, MS C-B 98, Documentos para la historia de California, BL.

36. See Brooks, *Captives and Cousins*, 116. For colonial policies and the Utes, see Ned Blackhawk, "The Displacement of Violence: Ute Diplomacy and the Making of New Mexico's Eighteenth-Century Northern Borderlands," *Ethnohistory* 54 (2007): 723–755, and *Violence over the Land: Indians and Empires in the Early American West* (Cambridge, MA: Harvard University Press, 2006), 70–87.

37. A bando was a "ban" on goods. Sanchez, *Explorers, Traders, and Slavers*, chapter 8.

38. The Bourbon Reforms, implemented in northern New Spain by Visitador General José de Gálvez, influenced Alta California's production of horses and cattle. Some scholars argue that the shift did not occur until 1805, while others point to the changes ushered in by Gálvez in the 1770s. See Robert H. Jackson and Edward Castillo, "The Changing Economic Structure of the Alta California Missions: A Reinterpretation," *Pacific Historical Review* 61 (1992): 387–415; Scott Mensing and Roger Byrne, "Pre-Mission Invasion of *Erodium Cicutarium* in California," *Journal of Biogeography* 25 (1998): 757–762.

39. Calloway, *One Vast Winter Count*, 293–300, provides an innovative look at the development of export markets from the Native perspective.

40. MS C-C, 63A, 64–65, California Mission Manuscripts, BL. In 1831 Alexander Forbes estimated more than 216,000 cattle grazing among the former missions. See Alexander Forbes, *California: A History of Upper and Lower California from Their First Discovery to the Present Time* (1839; repr., New York: Arno Press, 1973), 266.

41. S. Houck to Manuel Alvarez, February 25, 1853, folder 25, box 2, Manuel Alvarez Papers, New Mexico State Records and Archives, Santa Fe.

42. The most infamous raid by the Ute leader Walkara (which netted between three thousand and five thousand horses) is discussed below in the text.

43. "Notas Californianas por Juan Avila," 9–10, reel 8, MS C-D 31–41, BL.

44. For Mojave raids on the Old Spanish Trail, see "Diary from Aug. 16, 1849," Whiting Papers, HL.

45. See John Phillip Reid, "Principles of Vengeance: Fur Trappers, Indians, and Retaliation for Homicide in the Transboundary North American West," *Western Historical Quarterly* 24 (1993): 21–43.

46. Santiago Arguello to unnamed recipient, June 6, 1842, Los Angeles Prefecture, 1839–1854, vol. 1, MFilm 00382, reels 1 and 2, 636–38, HL.

47. Statement made in 1845. See MS 10422, Benjamin D. Wilson Papers (hereafter cited as BDW), 1877, HL; MS 1061, George C. Yount diary, in BDW, 1877, HL. For increased traffic on the Old Spanish Trail in the 1830s and 1840s, see Edward L. Lyman, *The Overland Journey from Utah to California: Wagon Travels from the City of Saints to the City of Angels* (Reno: University of Nevada Press, 2004), especially chapter 2. Also see Gerald A. Smith and Clifford Walker, *The Indian Slave Trade along the Mojave Trail* (San Bernardino, CA: San Bernardino County Museum, 1965).

48. H. D. Fitch to S. W. Kearney, April 19, 1847, MS C-B 81–82, Documentos para la historia de California, BL.

49. McDougal, of course, would become increasingly alarmed at indigenous raiding in 1851. See his admonition at the start of the chapter. Governor John McDougal to J. H. Bean, March 1, 1851, 124, MS F3753, Indian War Papers, California State Archives (hereafter cited as CSAS).

50. James Schurman to his sister, March 31, 1851, MS 84/73c, BL.

51. Apolinaria Lorenzana, "Memorias de Dona Apolinaria Lorenzana 'La Beata' Vieja de unos setenta y cinco anos," 30–39, MS C-D 111–122, reel 16, in MS C-D 146–156, BL.

52. "Los tiempos pasado de la Alta California," 15–16, MS C-D 119, reel 16, in MS C-D 146–156, BL.

53. See MS 742, De Valle Family Papers, 1818–1920, Los Angeles County Natural History Museum. Five Navajo slaves were identified as "Navajas/Cajon Navajas" on a list of merchandise purchased in 1828 by Manuel Gutiérres and Juan Ygnacio Mancisidor from Carílo C. Lebnicoff. Exact numbers for indigenous captives in Los Angeles and other California towns are frustratingly difficult to quantify, but recent work has estimated the number in the hundreds. See Michael J. González, *This Small City Will Be a Mexican Paradise: Exploring the Origins of Mexican Culture in Los Angeles, 1821–1846* (Albuquerque: University of New Mexico Press, 2005). Also see Los Angeles Prefecture, 1839–1854, vol. 1, MFilm 00382, reel 1, HL, for the inclusion of "Yuma servants" in property deeds.

54. For "renting" children among ranchers, see letter from Cave Couts, April 20,

Captivity and Economic Landscapes in California and the Far West

1855, MS CT 193, Cave J. Couts Collection, HL. For the "Act for the Government and Protection of Indians" and reported instances of Indian kidnapping, see Heizer, *The Destruction of California Indians*, 219–241.

55. See Phillips, *Vineyards and Vaqueros*.

56. Ted J. Warner, ed., *The Dominguez-Escalante Journal: Their Expedition through Colorado, Utah, Arizona, and New Mexico in 1776* (Provo: University of Utah Press, 1976), 84–86. For the Edward Beale quote, see Stephen Bonsal, *Edward Fitzgerald Beale: A Pioneer in the Path of Empire, 1822–1903* (New York: G. P. Putnam's Sons, 1912), 150.

57. See "Journal of 1849," 22, MS 1747, Benjamin Butler Harris Papers, HL. The Maricopas and O'odhams also filtered slaves from the Great Basin into Sonora at annual trading fairs that served as slave markets; this continued into the 1840s. See Henry Dobyns, "Thematic Changes in Yuman Warfare," in Verne F. Ray, *Proceedings of the 1957 Annual Spring Meeting of the American Ethnological Society* (Seattle: American Ethnological Society, 1957), 150.

58. See letter from Lafayette Head, April 30, 1852, MS RI 2150, box 7, William G. Ritch Collection, HL, for a statement of set policies regarding the buying and selling of Southern Paiute children. No clear economic data has emerged on the prices of Native slaves sold in Los Angeles. Gerald Smith argued that secularization in 1834 undercut the need for slaves, and yet slavery increased during the mid-1800s. This period of rampant kidnapping and massacres in California may have made the purchasing of slaves unnecessary. Los Angeles Plaza Church records indicate the presence of Southern Paiute and Ute slaves in 1831 (Maria Yuta, Indian child); 1843 (Dolores Palluche, of the Colorado River); 1845 (Santiago, Indian child of Maria de la Luz, Indian from New Mexico); 1846 (Maria Conception, Indian adult "de nacion Palluche" and "Hija politica" of Don Ignacio Coronel); and 1848 (Maria de Jesus, Palluche, adult). Smith and Walker, *The Indian Slave Trade*, 13–14.

59. Knack, *Boundaries Between*, 54.

60. "The Life Record of Anson Call," 45, MS 67/56, BL.

61. During the 1850s, Mormons purchased captives from Utes in order to free them from bondage while adopting them and attempting to convert them. Many Southern Paiutes complained that redemption actually meant reenslavement by Mormon captors. See Leonard J. Arrington and Davis Bitton, *The Mormon Experience: A History of the Latter-Day Saints* (Urbana: University of Illinois Press, 2006), 150–156.

62. See Brigham Young to Jacob Hamblin, August 4, 1857, MS 1317, Jacob Hamblin Collection, HL, for efforts to sustain Mormon alliances with Southern Paiutes. For Mormon-Ute interactions, see Ronald W. Walker, "Walkara Meets the Mormons, 1848–52: A Case Study in Native American Accommodation," *Utah Historical Quarterly* 70 (2002): 215–237. Also see Stephen P. Van Hoak, "Waccara's Utes: Native American

Equestrian Adaptations in the Eastern Great Basin, 1776–1876," *Utah Historical Quarterly* 67 (1999): 309–330.

63. For Olive Oatman's experiences with Mojaves, see "Susan Thompson Parrish Account," MS 16760, HL. Also see E. J. Pettid Papers, Special Collections, University of Arizona, Tucson. Also see Brian McGinty, *The Oatman Massacre: A Tale of Desert Captivity and Survival* (Norman: University of Oklahoma Press, 2005); Margot Mifflin, *The Blue Tattoo: The Life of Olive Oatman* (Lincoln: University of Nebraska Press, 2009).

64. Although not directly related to the slave trade, the Toypurina Revolt serves as a good example of how women could shape the political dynamic of Southern California. See Steven W. Hackel, "Sources of Rebellion: Indian Testimony and the Mission San Gabriel Uprising of 1785," *Ethnohistory* 50 (2003): 643–669; Rose Marie Beebe and Robert M. Senkewicz, eds., *Testimonios: Early California through the Eyes of Women, 1815–1848* (Berkeley: University of California Press, 2006); Albert L. Hurtado, *Intimate Frontiers: Sex, Gender, and Culture in Old California* (Berkeley: University of California Press, 1999); Virginia M. Bouvier, *Women and the Conquest of California, 1542–1840: Codes of Silence* (Tucson: University of Arizona Press, 2001), 116–141; Miroslava Chávez-García, *Negotiating Conquest: Gender and Power in California, 1770s to 1880s* (Tucson: University of Arizona Press, 2004). For gender and the gold rush, see Susan Lee Johnson, *Roaring Camp: The Social World of the California Gold Rush* (New York: W. W. Norton, 2000), especially 92–94 on the role of Miwok women leaders. Also see Stephen Silliman, *Lost Laborers in Colonial California: Native Americans and the Archaeology of Rancho Petaluma* (Tucson: University of Arizona Press, 2004), for Native women and their assertion of identity through production and labor.

65. See Richard J. Orsi and Kevin Starr, eds., *Rooted in Barbarous Soil: People, Culture, and Community in Gold Rush California* (Berkeley: University of California Press, 2000); Albert L. Hurtado, "Sex, Gender, Culture, and a Great Event: The California Gold Rush," *Pacific Historical Review* 68 (1999): 1–19. For indigenous strategies at the household level in the post–gold rush era, see Albert L. Hurtado, "'Hardly a Farm House," 245–270.

66. Heizer, *The Destruction of the California Indians*; Hurtado, *Indian Survival on the California Frontier*; Madley, "California's Yuki Indians," 303–332.

67. DeLay, *War of a Thousand Deserts*; Andrés Reséndez, *Changing National Identities at the Frontier: Texas and New Mexico, 1800–1850* (Cambridge: Cambridge University Press, 2005); Tomás Almaguer, *Racial Fault Lines: The Historical Origins of White Supremacy in California* (Berkeley: University of California Press, 1994), 17–41.

6

"The Time Is Now Just Arriving When Many Capitalists Will Make Fortunes"

Indian Removal, Finance, and Slavery in the Making of the American Cotton South

Calvin Schermerhorn

The forced removal of southeastern Indians and the forced relocation of African-descended enslaved people helped to develop the political economy of the early United States republic. Euro-Americans' forced movement of nonwhite peoples across the landscape of the American South was integral to the process of nation building and economic growth. This chapter investigates two microcosms of that anguished history, juxtaposing two stories illustrating the tragedy of ambition in the early republic. It details land speculation and Indian removal through the eyes of an upstart speculator and removal agent from Vermont and the interstate slave trade through one of the largest slave-trading firms of the 1830s. Together their stories put into view two processes that seem at first glance to be unrelated.

Southeastern Indians occupied lands that promised great agricultural wealth, primarily from slave-grown cotton, in an age when great transatlantic chains of cotton and credit accounted for the largest financial interests in the republic. The timing of Indian removal in the 1830s coincided with the apex of the US interstate slave trade, and both took place during a time of unprecedented economic expansion. The federal government forced out Indians on lands unavailable to slaveholders, but the bonanza in Indian lands in the southeastern region of North America is exceptional in that Euro-Americans pushed out nonwhite inhabitants and forcibly relocated other nonwhites, most of whom were enslaved agricultural workers. The development of finance accelerated the process of expropriating Indian lands, converting them to private ownership, and putting enslaved African-descended Americans to work growing export staples. Ghastly outcomes for the Choctaws, Chickasaws, Creeks, Cherokees, and Seminoles appeared as glittering opportunities for Euro-Americans.

William Beattie was among the opportunists. After failing to make a living in New York City early in 1830, Beattie decided to strike out for the South. "I have about made up my mind to go to Alabama," he wrote a friend, "and try for a fortune amongst the natives." The eighteen- or nineteen-year-old had contracted Alabama fever. The oldest of ten children of James and Margaret Beattie of Ryegate, in east-central Vermont, he had no special preparation to traffic in the miseries of others. "My own property is gone," Beattie moaned to a friend as he prepared to board a ship sailing from New York City. His few possessions, including money, had burned in a fire. After a tumultuous sea voyage, Beattie arrived in Mobile, where he found work as a clerk in a store. That situation lasted a short time, and by late summer, he was in Williamston, Pike County, Alabama, in the eastern part of the state. A friend from Vermont had written that eastern Alabama seemed "a good place to make money."[1]

Money was at the center of Beattie's anxious pursuits, and in his time and place, land, slaves, and cotton represented a trinity of moneymaking means. But that was not merely a matter of taking out a mortgage on a farm and driving a gang of bonds people to labor in a field. It involved a large process of converting Native American homelands into private property and making arable lands into plantations by moving in bound workers to shoulder the burdens of construction and production. That required a great deal of political will, market development, and financial technology.

In the early republic, finance was highly politicized, and politics were deeply commercialized. The 1830s witnessed extensive expansion of banking, especially in the lower South. Agriculturalists required substantial capital to start commercial farms and plantations. Besides buying land, planters demanding enslaved workers had to pay labor costs up front, which required them to borrow heavily in the initial phases of production and continue borrowing right up to the limits of their abilities. Cotton became the basis of an international financial system in the late 1820s as British capital flowed like a river into American enterprises connected to the crop.[2]

Federal trade and Indian removal policies supported that financial development. The Jackson administration liberalized trade, making cotton cheaper to transport and therefore to sell to customers in Great Britain.

"The Time Is Now Just Arriving..."

The administration removed reciprocal duties and inspection regimes with Britain. At the same time, the Jackson administration made Indian removal a top policy priority, committing resources and coordinating efforts already underway. The American South became tied ever more firmly to industrial England at the same time that the federal government committed itself to using tax revenues to clear Indians out of critical areas of the southern interior river complex and open it for Euro-American exploitation.[3]

The numbers can but hint at the processes underlying them. Between 46,000 and 52,000 Indians were removed as a consequence of federal policies. In 1832, free Creeks numbered 21,780 (along with 914 who were enslaved), mainly in eastern Alabama and western Georgia. In 1836, the federal government forcibly removed some 15,000 Creeks, who followed another 3,500 who had moved on their own. Many hundreds died in the process. In Beattie's adopted home of Alabama, census takers counted 117,549 African-descended slaves in 1830 and 253,532 in 1840, an increase of more than 115 percent, while the free white population of Alabama increased 76 percent. The social destruction left in the wake of those movements of people would resound down the generations.[4]

Uprooting and forcibly removing Native Americans did not begin with the Andrew Jackson administration's Indian Removal Act of 1830, but the law sanctioned the process within a federal legal framework. Congress initially appropriated half a million dollars for removal, or about 5 percent of the annual military budget. The removal process did more than just force people out of their homelands. It also opened Indian lands to private acquisition by Americans. The Jackson administration attempted to make removal pay for itself. The 1830 Treaty of Dancing Rabbit Creek was supposed to be a model, granting Choctaws allotments of ceded land that were subject to sale. In most cases, recipients were supposed to sell allotments to pay for their own removal, using the market for lands to accomplish government policy goals.

But federal policy had nasty consequences for Choctaws who sought to register treaty allotments. Nearly immediately, speculators bought up their allotments, while government agents refused to register Choctaw claims. Because of fraud, waste, and delays, Choctaw removal cost the federal government an unexpectedly large $5 million, ten times the initial cost, much of it going to contractors who were supposed to provision and transport groups of Choctaws. But the United States eventually collected $8 million from sales of the Choctaw cession (and later paid the Choctaws some $3 million). Between 1833 and 1846 the lands ceded in the Treaty of Dancing Rabbit Creek—a great swath of Mississippi, from the Mississippi

River southeast to the headwaters of the Big Black River to the Alabama state line—came on the market. Most was part of the Black Belt, some of the most fertile and productive agricultural lands for cotton.[5]

Besides causing staggering fatalities and epochal miseries, Indian removal turned out to be an expensive policy. The United States military budget in the era of removal and the Seminole Wars took up between 50 and 60 percent of federal spending. Yet sales of expropriated land filled federal coffers as well. The War Department's revenues from sales of Chickasaw lands in Mississippi constituted the capital that made possible the start-up phase of Arkansas's banks. Land speculation in Alabama was big business as well. By the 1850s the United States had collected $11.25 million selling lands taken from the Creeks in the 1814 Treaty of Fort Jackson. The Cherokees—who had been allies against the Red Sticks in the 1814 campaign that led to the Treaty of Fort Jackson—had, themselves, been uprooted and removed, their lands redistributed to white Georgians.[6]

William Beattie entered that environment with no money, no friends, no family, and little else besides a few introductions and the drive to make his fortune. Beattie reinvented himself in Alabama at the same time that Congress passed the Indian Removal Act. Beattie's father and sister, Jane, registered disapproval over federal Indian policy. "The general opinion," they wrote from Vermont, "is that government is violating the treaties made with the Indians.... If that is so government is doing wrong." Citizens were bitterly divided along party and geographic lines, with opponents of Andrew Jackson and New Englanders most staunchly against Indian removal.[7]

Whatever residual New England hesitation Beattie may have possessed on his trip from New York melted in the heat of his ambition to make money in the land market. In eastern Alabama, Beattie was at the heart of the Creek land cession. The Creeks had been forced to cede their Georgia lands in the 1820s but held fast to lands in eastern Alabama that were home to Muskogee-speaking people and other members of the Creek confederation.[8] They were compelled to sign a cession treaty similar to the Treaty of Dancing Rabbit Creek. The Third Treaty of Washington, signed in March 1832 and ratified nearly immediately, ceded five million acres in exchange for allotments of land, an initial payment, subsequent payments, and provisions, plus the cost of removal. Creeks who did not consent to move were permitted allotments of lands, although Alabama's extension laws virtually outlawed Creek politics and their livelihoods.

Speculators began buying up Creek allotments. Timing was critical, and buyers who arrived early snapped up lands that they could resell at a profit. But these speculators faced difficulties similar to those encountered by buyers who had sought Choctaw lands. Aggrandizement of Creek lands in eastern Alabama hinged on buyers' abilities to pry ownership away from individual holders. The initial grab was a disorganized convulsion of speculation.[9]

As if on cue, in April Beattie entered into partnership with two men from Georgia, one from Arkansas, and a Pike County neighbor, as soon as word of the treaty reached Alabama. All agreed to become "equal copartners together in the purchase of Lands claims, titles, reserves, or anything pertaining to Lands." One was Siah Hardage. He was a Creek and an erstwhile supporter of William McIntosh, part of a faction that had been removed earlier. Like others, Hardage's heritage did not inoculate him from making a profit at the expense of fellow Creeks. Divisions among Native Americans reflected varying strategies and opportunities. Creeks, Cherokees, and other Indians owned slaves and behaved in nearly every market-savvy way that Euro-Americans did. As Euro-Americans sought Indian lands, however, they also sought to drive out nonwhite competitors.[10]

From Irwinton (now Eufaula), Beattie planned to acquire lands of the Eufaula Indians near the Chattahoochee River, which borders Alabama and Georgia. He wrote Captain John Page, an officer in charge of treaty enforcement in the area, with a request to expedite the transfer of Eufaula lands to Indians so that his company might buy them. "It is generally understood with the Indians that their lands are ceded to Government," Beattie wrote, "but the stipulations are not known."[11] In the normal run of things, a card player parking himself at the gaming table might use guile when asking the dealer to help him cheat other players. In this case, the dealer was openly complicit in the swindle.

The treaty signed in Washington was not technically a removal treaty. But it subjected Creeks to two kinds of victimization: Speculators attempted to defraud holders of real estate that was now transferable. At the same time, would-be removal agents vied for contracts to escort beleaguered Creeks out of their homelands. William Beattie intended to do both. Land companies such as Beattie's were swift, sharp, and ravenous. Speculators did not wait for permission to overrun Creek lands. Men like Beattie flooded in, founded Irwinton, and started trading. Many began planting cotton, often on fields cleared by vacating Indians.[12]

Beattie framed that onslaught in ringing terms to his father. "Since I left your parental roof I have labored diligently to improve my poor education to gain a knowledge of mankind and to better my present condition," he reported. The going was hard. "Since my arrival in this country," he moaned, "I have suffered everything but death with a hope that I may obtain the means to compensate myself together with my friends." Speaking of his diligence with regard to his "red brothers, the Creek Indians," Beattie bragged, "I have gained their affection and their confidence and by some [am] considered a super natural being, this having originated from several of my prophecies, all of which has befallen them as I told them." The upstart in his early twenties informed his father that he was "their correspondent with government."[13]

The state legislature ratified those perceptions and gave Beattie and those like him legal sanction. Alabama had "passed laws affording opportunities to speculate on lands," he reported, from which he had already made $400, eight times the monthly salary he had earned upon arriving in Mobile a year and a half before. "And by the late treaty another speculation is offered into which I shall go all that I can," he assured his family. "Had I the means," Beattie summarized, "I could make a fortune."[14]

But such fortune seeking tended to undermine treaty provisions. Alabamians' enthusiasm for Creek lands conflicted with federal policy, and the army began expelling illegal speculators and squatters. Locals, including the sheriff, defied that pressure. "All intruders are now ordered out of the nation and all the whites' improvements will be destroyed," Beattie sulkily wrote to his family from the vicinity of Eufaula. "I have improvements to the amount of one thousand dollars which I am fearful of losing." He contemplated "hav[ing] them reserved by the Indians consent but whites would be so much enraged that they would privately destroy them."[15] In the frenzied atmosphere, anyone who appeared to make common cause with either the Indians or the federal government was subject to violent reprisals.

As Indians were being forced out, African-descended Americans were being forced in. Would-be planters entering that volatile landscape were developing lands into cotton plantations. Eufaula and its vicinity were part of the Black Belt. New owners put enslaved people to work cutting wood, digging furrows, planting cotton, and toiling at innumerable other tasks, all with the aim of making owners' fortunes. That process took place within a federal framework as well. Since 1808 the United States had prohibited the importation of foreign captives, conferring a legal monopoly on sales of slaves to American slaveholders. Instead of hailing slave ships sailing from the African coast, Alabamians in search of slaves journeyed to Virginia or South Carolina to buy enslaved people they could bring into the state to clear land and build plantations. Over time, they turned to slave traders who furnished them bonds persons in abundance. The importations of American slaves through the port of Mobile was so great that in 1837 citizens estimated that $10 million worth of slaves had been brought into the state in each of the four previous years.[16]

Eastern Alabama was becoming slave country. Populations in Beattie's backyard increased fourfold between 1830 and 1840. In 1830, census takers counted 1,878 slaves in Pike County, who made up more than 26 percent of a population of 7,108. In 1840, Barbour County, which had been carved from Pike County and Creek lands, including Eufaula, contained 5,548 slaves, or about 46 percent of a population of 12,024. Combined, Pike and Barbour Counties had an enslaved population of 7,659 people in 1840, more than four times the number of ten years before. Not coincidentally, Barbour County became known for its proslavery extremism and rabid states' rights partisanship. As the initial wave of squatters and small, illegal operators was forced out, more well-financed firms moved in.[17]

By the spring of 1833, Beattie was chagrined that honor ran short among his class of entrepreneur. He became incensed at the towering frauds of the Columbus Land Company, one of the firms that were buying up Creek allotments. "To my utter astonishment," he fumed to its president, Eli S. Shorter, in April 1833, "I find my plans frustrated by a party that I had heretofore been friendly [with].... My objects were merely that of emigration and I presumed yours to be wholly that of the Land," Beattie insisted, fatuously, "but I find through the acts of...John Scott that you are grasping at all." Beattie had partnered with Scott, who now seemed to be conniving with Shorter to hire Indians to impersonate owners. Columbus Land Company agents paid straw buyers to register false allotment claims with certifying agents, who recorded the legitimized fraudulent transactions. Actual owners were left with nothing.[18]

Shorter's company was among the more notorious speculators in Creek lands and defrauders of Indians. The Third Treaty of Washington allotted lands to Creek heads of households and Creek leaders, but regulations and measures to prevent fraud were scarce. The Jackson administration initially left it to certifying agents to interpret treaty provisions. The result was disastrous for Creek landholders. Shorter himself admitted, "Stealing is the order of the day...and out of the host of Indians at the agency, I don't think there are ten *true* holders of land."[19]

Cheated by former allies in the land business, Beattie looked elsewhere for opportunities. He took a job removing Indians in Florida. "Am now busily engaged in emigrating the Apalachicola Indians and am trying to get the Creek Nation in a mind to accept the western country for a home," Beattie wrote his family from southwest Georgia in May 1833. He conducted the party across the Mississippi River and through Arkansas to

Indian Territory in what would become Oklahoma. On the way, he apparently undertook a fraudulent scheme of his own, filing suit in New Orleans for $6,500 the Apalachicolas supposedly owed him. Beattie took an out-of-court settlement of $2,000 and two enslaved people worth another $1,000. Beattie returned to Alabama and continued to search for a way to speculate in Creek lands.[20]

Raising capital was still a problem, but his experience moving the Apalachicola party was marketable. "The want of ready cash capital prevents me from making an immense fortune," he explained to his mother, "but I must keep on striking." He apologized for not returning to Vermont for a visit: "The time is now just arriving when many Capitalists will make fortunes." Beattie was slowly building real estate holdings while burrowing his way into the Indian removal business. By 1833, he was collecting debts and buying plots of land from Creek holders. In late 1834, the United States government began its Creek removal, and Beattie again became an agent.[21]

Land speculation and Indian removal were becoming more closely related, and larger firms were now forming to take advantage of lucrative removal contracts. The Alabama Emigrating Company (AEC) formed to meet the demands of moving thousands of unwilling Native Americans from their homelands west across the Mississippi River. The AEC was a reorganized version of the John W. A. Sanford Company, a firm headed by Sanford. Beattie had worked as an agent of the Sanford company, composed of Columbus, Georgia, speculators in Indian lands. Sanford had curious credentials for a job to deport Creeks. He had been complicit in the widespread fraud in Russell and Barbour Counties after the scramble for Creek land, and he was also president of a failed Georgia bank that had gone under partly as a result of rampant land speculation.[22]

With Beattie acting as a guide, the AEC undertook the first federally sponsored removal of 600 Lower Creeks. In the winter of 1834, they set out from Fort Mitchell in Russell County, Alabama, walking nearly 200 miles to Tuscaloosa. From there, they marched another 60 miles to Columbus, Mississippi, turned to the northwest, and marched an additional 160 miles to Memphis. As was becoming common, the forced migrants were embarked on steamboats for the slog up the Mississippi and Arkansas Rivers. Under the supervision of Captain John Page, Beattie led the group on what became a death march. Just 469 Creeks survived Beattie's forced relocation, a 22 percent fatality rate.[23]

Far from disqualifying him, Beattie's neglect or brutality demonstrated his aptitude for the business, a reflection of the AEC's strategy. Yale-educated Sanford won a seat in the US House of Representatives as a

Jackson supporter in 1834. It was not as rewarding as removing Indians and grabbing their land, and he resigned in July 1835. Officials in Washington charged the fox with reporting on predations in the henhouse. After receiving numerous reports of fraud in Creek territory, Secretary of War Lewis Cass appointed Sanford to investigate the matter.

The Trail of Tears was lengthening. In December 1835, Beattie led more than five hundred Creeks from Wetumpka, Alabama. Their path led through Montevallo, Elyton, Moulton, and Tuscumbia, Alabama, and from there the group boarded a steamboat towing a pair of keelboats on the Tennessee River. Steamers carrying Indians were notoriously overcrowded, and ad hoc arrangements, such as towing auxiliary craft, were both uncomfortable and dangerous—so much so that some Indians chose the punishing overland march over steamboat travel. Beattie's party reached Indian Territory by late January 1836.[24]

Between Wetumpka and Tuscumbia, Beattie and his forlorn party trod over a landscape that was becoming one of extirpation and speculation. Sanford's company was one among many. In northwestern Alabama, for instance, planters and other speculators gobbled up Chickasaw allotments after they were surveyed in 1835. Some included agents for northeastern joint-stock companies, such as the Boston and Mississippi Cotton Land Company, the Boston and New York Chickasaw Land Company, and the New York, Mississippi, and Arkansas Land Company. One of the more well capitalized was the American Land Company, organized in New York and capitalized at a million dollars. Metropolitan investors a thousand miles from the banks of the Tennessee River acquired much of the land. Such eastern joint-stock companies aggrandized 35 percent of Chickasaw allotments.[25]

Practically speaking, Beattie and removal agents like him were settling the question of slavery's extension in the West. Indians who were removed along with slaves violated the Missouri Compromise when they settled north of the line. That congressional compromise, which was supposed to prohibit the expansion of slavery north of Missouri's southern border, was abrogated during Indian removal—more than a decade before the issue of slavery extension in Kansas became a catalyst for disunion. Cherokees were among the Indians forced to occupy lands north of the 36° 30´ latitude line that was supposed to be the border between slaveholding and nonslaveholding territories. That is not to say that Native American slaveholders preserved their property on the Trail of Tears. Creek slaveholders lost perhaps two-thirds of their bonds people during the era of removal, and Georgians stripped many Cherokee slaveholders of their slaves as well. Those bonds people were more often reenslaved or sold than freed.[26]

By the time Beattie reached Indian Territory in 1836, the Creek War had broken out, which gave the United States a pretext for enforced removal. That promised more work for removal agents. In the summer of 1836, Beattie led a group of Creeks through Arkansas. "Our route will be up the north side of the Arkansas river," Beattie reported to Captain Jacob Brown in Little Rock, disbursing agent for Indian removal west of the Mississippi River. "The Indians are in good health and spirits, and easily managed," he boasted. "Other parties may be daily expected."[27] In the fall of 1836, Beattie again conducted a party of Creeks while working for the AEC. By that time, Beattie was a seasoned agent to whom others looked for guidance, although the US Marine officer observing the removal contended that profit overrode considerations of humanity. Historians have since called the process "genocide."[28]

The following year, Beattie beckoned his family to join him. "I have plenty of land in Alabama that is good and Father can take his choice of 600 acres," he crowed in the spring of 1837. By the late 1830s he owned 3,854.25 acres in Tallapoosa County. Some members of his old Ryegate neighborhood were interested, but Beattie did not manage to lure them to Alabama. It is unclear how Beattie was paid, but the federal government regularly disbursed hard currency. In a land awash in cheap paper money, silver coins stood out and commanded a substantial premium over most bank notes. Beattie's disbursement officer, Jacob Brown, submitted a voucher for expenses in 1838, including "for transportation of $8 or $9,000 in Specie funds belonging to the Dept" from Fort Gibson to Fort Coffee to pay agents. If in silver, that amount would have weighed about 560 pounds. Brown at the time was injured in the leg, and locals gouged him for a horse and wagon. It is little coincidence that some of the wealthier landowners in Arkansas amassed a fortune in the provisioning trade.[29] The removal market created opportunities for a variety of entrepreneurs. As thousands upon thousands of acres were transferred to private ownership, demand for enslaved laborers increased dramatically.

Franklin and Armfield met much of the new demand for slaves. The firm was an interregional, interlocking partnership of professional slave traders operating in the Chesapeake Bay and Lower Mississippi River valley. They were perhaps the largest such firm in the 1830s and supplied thousands of bound workers to buyers in the cotton- and sugar-growing regions of the lower South. In the flush times of the 1830s, slave-trading firms rationalized an interregional market for bound laborers, taking advantage of federal prohibitions on the importation and sale of foreign captives. Their most important financial innovation was to use the chain of credit and debt that extended from southern ports to northern financial centers and across the Atlantic Ocean to British and European merchants, bankers, and manufacturers.

Like the land companies that aggressively sought Indians' allotments, Franklin and Armfield seized competitive advantages on account of its purchasing power and financial and organizational strategy. John Armfield in Alexandria (then in the District of Columbia) ran the firm's shipping operation. Sales directors in the lower South, like Isaac Franklin and his nephew James Franklin, cooperated with purchasing directors, like Rice C. Ballard in Richmond, to build an expansive firm that funneled enslaved captives to the lower South and remitted the proceeds of their sales northward.[30]

As it grew in scope, the firm also grew in sophistication. In order to assemble shiploads of captives, the firm's purchasing directors in cities like Richmond, Alexandria, and Baltimore hired agents to scour the countryside and buy enslaved people, whom they jailed and embarked aboard merchant vessels for the saltwater passage to New Orleans (although the firm also transported one coffle, or caravan of bound forced migrants, of up to 300 bonds persons overland from Alexandria to Natchez each summer). Ballard was a partner and one of the firm's largest purchasing managers. Of 350 captives whose ages Ballard recorded between 1831 and 1833, the median age of the enslaved people he shipped was eighteen and a half. Neither he nor his partners wanted families, the very young, or the elderly at a time when slaves' life expectancy at birth was just over thirty years.[31]

Ballard took advantage of surging demand and a federally protected slave market. The Jackson administration's liberalized trade policies, increasing prices for agricultural commodities, and foreign demand for commodities grown chiefly by enslaved Americans were helping fuel demand for slaves. Farm product prices rose almost 51 percent between 1829 and 1836, during which time overall prices increased 18 percent. In the 1830s the slave trade surged nearly 84 percent above what it had been the previous decade. Perhaps two-thirds of slaves were transported in the interstate trade. Most would end up in cotton fields, but the sugar industry expanded in the 1820s, and sugar masters demanded young, predominantly male slaves to perform some of the most arduous and dangerous work in North America. Meanwhile, the number of banks in the United States more than doubled between 1827 and 1837, from 333 to 729, and while most banks lent to commercial rather than agricultural customers, agriculturalists benefited from the expansion of credit through factors acting as retail bankers.[32]

The growth and development of finance was the decisive factor in

Franklin and Armfield's strategy. Captives served a North Atlantic market for slave-produced commodities, but the money that paid for them traveled from Louisiana to Virginia on a chain of credit that linked New Orleans with New York and other northern financial centers. Franklin and Armfield attempted to finance its operations internally but used debt instruments and financial relationships that spanned its thousand-mile commodity chain in enslaved people. Because the early republic was made up of smaller networks and regions within which money traveled, exchanging money within the United States was like foreign exchange today. American slave traders preferred bills of exchange to specie or trade in kind, like remittance procedures in the eighteenth-century British slave trade. In the summer and fall of 1831, for instance, Franklin and Armfield sought to lower transaction costs by remitting bills of exchange from Louisiana to Richmond, Virginia. Those were the proceeds of slave sales to be invested in more slaves.[33]

The tyranny of distance threatened to overwhelm the magic of returns. Once slaves were sold in Natchez or New Orleans, the partners could not merely send cash without incurring costly expenses. Simply put, Louisiana bank notes did not spend well back in Virginia, and Chesapeake sellers of slaves insisted on cash from interstate traders. A Louisiana bank note might be discounted 5 percent below its face value in Virginia, which represented a corresponding cost to the firm. But Ballard was able to put Virginia bank notes in the hands of his purchasing agents because of remittances of other kinds of financial paper from his partner Isaac Franklin, the firm's managing partner in New Orleans.

To minimize the cost of sending money over long distances, the proceeds of sales were remitted as bills and bank drafts primarily. Instead of paying what amounted to a 5 percent tax on the distance between New Orleans and Richmond, sending bills drawn by merchants in New Orleans and payable in New York or Philadelphia decreased that by half. Between June and August 1831, Franklin had sent Ballard four bills of exchange totaling $20,000, which was his branch's pool of working capital. Bills of exchange were orders to pay a certain sum at a certain place and time, usually sixty days after the bill was accepted for payment. Those debt instruments linked East Coast merchants to their New Orleans counterparts. They paid for cotton in New Orleans and imported manufactures in New York. For instance, Franklin sent Ballard a $2,000 bill on Bache McEvers, a New York City commission merchant, shipper, and insurer who sold Louisiana cotton and sugar. Neither McEvers nor the drawer in New Orleans need have known that the bill paid for slaves on its route north.

The funds arrived in Richmond along with exhortations to practice thrift. Franklin instructed Ballard, "A fine negro well purchased will always make more money than the many badly purchased."[34] Franklin bought New York bills at a small discount in New Orleans and sent them through the post office to his partner. Such transactions were essential to domestic exchange. US and foreign bills drawn on merchants such as McEvers were the primary interregional commercial medium. They were close to what central bankers today call "narrow money." When he received them in Richmond, Ballard cashed those bills at the Bank of Virginia, the Richmond branch taking a percent or percent and a half, depending on the prevailing exchange market.[35]

Such remittances were the firm's lifeblood. Ballard laid out nearly $8,900 for a shipment of twenty-five bonds persons in late September 1831, more than $10,000 for the subsequent shipment of thirty captives two weeks later, and nearly $25,000 for the shipment of sixty-nine captives in late October. To keep those captives coming, Franklin sent refreshers, including $10,000, which Ballard entered as cash, and a $5,000 bill of exchange in early November, which he entered as "return capitol," supplemented by another $4,000 bill of exchange entered two days later.[36]

Responding to demand from buyers along the river corridor between New Orleans and Natchez, Franklin and Armfield became a nonbank creditor. Few customers outside New Orleans actually paid in cash. The firm extended credit to buyers the way automobile manufacturers would a century later, which helped to amplify the expansion of bank money and credit. In the winter of 1832, Franklin sought to compete with other slavers by extending long credit to buyers at 10 percent interest, a strategy that took advantage of his firm's scope and capitalization. Meanwhile, he instructed his Chesapeake partners to borrow to cover their operating margins should they need to.[37]

Credit expansion was the market's magic and slavery's mainstay. The agriculturalists who typically bought Franklin and Armfield's slaves were already deeply in debt to factors and preferred to pay with what merchants called "long paper," bonds, promissory notes, or bills maturing at ninety days or longer. But the paper Franklin took as payment could not be remitted to his Chesapeake purchasing directors without punishing discounts. Promissory notes authored by indebted planters in Louisiana or Mississippi and endorsed by their factors were worth considerably less in Baltimore or Richmond, where planter and factor were unknown, than in Natchez or New Orleans. Besides, planters were used to renewing debts rather than paying them. Debt ballooned in a healthy market, and as cotton planters bought Indian allotments and other agricultural lands, they took on a staggering amount of it.

Franklin's business boomed in Natchez, but buyers wanted ever more credit. He needed to remit funds to his Chesapeake partners and needed credit himself. Franklin looked to a new kind of financial institution for help: property banks. Most banks refused to lend directly to agricultural customers and slaveholders, preferring commercial customers instead. The difference had to do with liquidity. If a loan to a planter went bad, the bank would have to sell real and personal property—lands and slaves—which could take a long time and result in severely diminished returns. But a bank lending on the strength of a shipment of cotton could easily sell the collateral if the debt was not paid. Property banks attempted to lend directly to agriculturalists and slaveholders, reasoning that upwardly spiraling land, farm product, and slave prices would generate sound returns for all and minimize risk.

Mississippi property banks were beneficiaries of outside investment and state bond guarantees, which served both planters and slave traders simultaneously—and left taxpayers on the hook should the bank fail. From Natchez, purchasing director James Franklin reported to Ballard in March 1832, "All the negroes we have sold commanded fair prices," but he moaned that sellers "had to take all sorts of paper in payment for negroes." Natchez had its share of merchants with connections to New York or Philadelphia, but a newly chartered property bank made available drafts payable in New York.[38] Isaac Franklin became a client of Samuel Gustin, one of the founders of the Planters Bank of Natchez, chartered in 1830. Gustin had raised initial capital by selling the bank's bonds to Philadelphia and New York investors. In May and June 1832, Isaac Franklin was able to remit Ballard three Planters Bank drafts totaling $23,000, payable at the Phenix Bank of New York, which had correspondent ties with southern banks like Planters. Franklin became a commercial customer of a bank that was in the business of lending to his customers. But the strategy soon unraveled.

The local reputation of Franklin's firm was damaged that fall during a cholera outbreak, when hastily buried bodies of dead slaves were discovered to have been unceremoniously tossed into shallow graves on bayous of the Mississippi River. Furious citizens expelled slave traders from Natchez, and even rival slave-trading firms blamed Franklin and Armfield. Their Natchez agents were implicated, and Isaac Franklin's explanations did not wash away suspicion that he was leading midnight burials on the banks of local bayous.[39]

Franklin then turned to Louisiana property banks and their relationships with New York banks. Instead of bills or Mississippi checks on New York, Franklin used a correspondent tie between the Union Bank of Louisiana and the Merchants Bank of New York to lower the firm's transaction costs. Franklin was a business insider, but he did not travel in the elevated circles of New Orleans's merchant elite. In order to use the Union Bank's financial services, he cultivated a relationship with Richard L. Booker, cashier of the Bank of Louisiana. Booker acted as Franklin's financial agent, and in late December 1832, Franklin sent Ballard a check for $15,000, payable at the Merchants Bank of New York, obtained by Booker. Franklin did not rely exclusively on such arrangements. In Natchez, Franklin bought two checks from Yeatman Woods and Company of New Orleans, agents of Baring Brothers and Company of London.

As the slave trade intensified and the firm's business grew, Franklin increasingly relied on drafts from the Union Bank. Booker, "at the request of Mr. I. Franklin," sent Ballard a $10,000 draft in April 1833, issued by the Union Bank of Louisiana and payable at the Merchants Bank of New York. Union Bank cashier J. B. Perrault signed that draft in favor of Rice Ballard, which passed through Booker's hands. Ballard cashed it to buy captives in Virginia. As Franklin became a regular customer of the Union Bank, it became his financial savior. "I can get money when no other trader can obtain a dollar," Franklin crowed during a national credit crisis in 1834. The firm had solved one of the major problems facing any interregional company of its scope and scale, thanks to a massive expansion in state banking that was in turn dependent on the cotton economy.[40]

The timing of Indian removal and the surge in the interstate slave trade was not, therefore, coincidental. Euro-Americans like Beattie seized what they considered their democratic entitlements to speculate in Indian lands in the flush times of the 1830s, and slave traders like Franklin and Armfield innovated ways to supply bound workers. A potent combination of a rise in agricultural prices, liberalized trade and finance, and aggressive seizures of Indian lands made land speculating and slave trading profitable. On a regional level, the Indian removal market employed, profited, and in some cases enriched citizens who oversaw the Trail of Tears. Contracting was a dicey business, and when contractors' accounts arrived in Washington, DC, War Department auditors often recoiled at unexpected costs and surcharges, waste, and fraud and other irregularities. But disbursing funds to the frontier areas of the republic was good politics. Congressmen and other federal officials zealously pursued payment to removal agents, even fraudulent ones. Land speculators' and removal agents' actions were part of a volatile and violent process that benefited more well organized capitalists, including cotton and shipping merchants who tied them to metropolitan investors in the United States and abroad.[41]

Acknowledgments

Brett Andersen, Ryan Evans, and Justin Weiss helped to transcribe Beattie correspondence as student assistants at Arizona State University, and Paul Carnahan of the Vermont Historical Society was instrumental in making the materials available. Special thanks to Joshua D. Rothman and Daniel F. Littlefield Jr. for their suggestions.

Notes

1. William Beattie to Jacob Covert, January 6, 1830, Mss. 158:3, part 1, Beattie Family Papers, Vermont Historical Society (hereafter cited as VHS) (first quotation); Mr. [?] Cameron to William Beattie, August 1830, Mss. 158:3, part 2, Beattie Family Papers, VHS (second quotation); see also Brett E. Whalen, "A Vermonter on the Trail of Tears," *Proceedings of the Vermont Historical Society* 66, nos. 1–2 (Spring 1998): 31–38.

2. Martijn Konings, *The Development of American Finance* (New York: Cambridge University Press, 2011), chapters 1–4.

3. Scott Reynolds Nelson, *A Nation of Deadbeats: An Uncommon History of America's Financial Disasters* (New York: Knopf, 2012), chapter 2.

4. David A. Chang, *The Color of the Land: Race, Nation, and the Politics of Landownership in Oklahoma, 1832–1929* (Chapel Hill: University of North Carolina Press, 2010), 29; Anthony F. C. Wallace, *The Long, Bitter Trail: Andrew Jackson and the Indians* (New York: Hill and Wang, 1993), chapter 4; Russell Thornton, *American Indian Holocaust and Survival: A Population History since 1492* (Norman: University of Oklahoma Press, 1987), chapter 5; Steven Deyle, *Carry Me Back: The Domestic Slave Trade in American Life* (New York: Oxford University Press, 2005), 288; Michael Tadman, *Speculators and Slaves: Masters, Traders, and Slaves in the Old South* (Madison: University of Wisconsin Press, 1989), chapter 2; Historical Census Browser, University of Virginia, Geospatial and Statistical Data Center, accessed August 6, 2014, http://mapserver.lib.virginia.edu/.

5. Francis Paul Prucha, *The Great Father: The United States Government and the American Indians*, vol. 1 (Lincoln: University of Nebraska Press, 1984), 206–219; Katherine M. B. Osburn, *Choctaw Resurgence in Mississippi: Race, Class, and Nation Building, 1830–1977* (Lincoln: University of Nebraska Press, 2014), chapter 1; Arthur H. DeRosier, *Removal of the Choctaw Indians* (Knoxville: University of Tennessee Press, 1970), 163; Mary Elizabeth Young, *Redskins, Ruffleshirts, and Rednecks: Indian Allotments in Alabama and Mississippi, 1830–1860* (Norman: University of Oklahoma Press, 1961), 22–36, 47–72.

6. Daniel F. Littlefield Jr., "Arkansas and Indian Removal," in *Encyclopedia of*

American Indian Removal, ed. Daniel F. Littlefield Jr. and James W. Parins (Santa Barbara, CA: ABC-CLIO, 2011), 1:15; Stephen J. Rockwell, *Indian Affairs and the Administrative States in the Nineteenth Century* (New York: Cambridge University Press, 2010), 141; Ira Katznelson, "Flexible Capacity: The Military and Early American Statebuilding," in *Shaped by War and Trade: International Influences on American Political Development*, ed. Ira Katznelson and Martin Schefter (Princeton, NJ: Princeton University Press, 2002), 92–93; Claudio Saunt, "Taking Account of Property: Stratification among the Creek Indians in the Early Nineteenth Century," *William and Mary Quarterly* 57, no. 4 (October 2000): 733–760.

7. James Beattie to William Beattie, February 16, 1831, Mss. 158:3, part 2, Beattie Family Papers, VHS.

8. J. Leitch Wright Jr., *Creeks and Seminoles: The Destruction and Regeneration of the Muscogulge People* (Lincoln: University of Nebraska Press, 1987), 246.

9. Young, *Redskins, Ruffleshirts, and Rednecks*, chapter 4; Francis Paul Prucha, *American Indian Treaties: The History of a Political Anomaly* (Berkeley: University of California Press, 1994), 173.

10. Partnership agreement between Henry Allen and W. Beattie of Pike County, State of Alabama, John Scott and Dan Nevis of Stewart Country, State of Georgia, and Siah Hardage of the Territory of Arkansas, April 1832, Mss. 158:5, part 1, Beattie Family Papers, VHS; R. Halliburton Jr., "Chief Greenwood Leflore and His Malmaison Plantation," in *After Removal: The Choctaw in Mississippi*, ed. Samuel J. Wells and Roseanna Tubby (Oxford: University Press of Mississippi, 1986), 56–63; Theda Perdue, *Slavery and the Evolution of Cherokee Society, 1540–1866* (Knoxville: University of Tennessee Press, 1979), chapter 4.

11. William Beattie to John Page, April 10, 1832, Mss. 158:3, part 4, Beattie Family Papers, VHS; Grant Foreman, *Indian Removal: The Emigration of the Five Civilized Tribes of Indians* (Norman: University of Oklahoma Press, 1932), chapter 9.

12. Wright, *Creeks and Seminoles*, 246–247; Prucha, *American Indian Treaties*, 173–174.

13. William Beattie to James Beattie, April 29, 1832, Mss. 158:3, part 4, Beattie Family Papers, VHS.

14. Ibid.

15. Ibid. (quotation); Wright, *Creeks and Seminoles*, 247; Prucha, *American Indian Treaties*, 274.

16. Tadman, *Speculators and Slaves*, 36; Deyle, *Carry Me Back*, 45.

17. Historical Census Browser, accessed September 7, 2012, http://mapserver.lib.virginia.edu/.

18. William Beatty to Eli S. Shorter, April 28, 1833, Mss. 158:3, part 5, Beattie Family Papers, VHS.

CALVIN SCHERMERHORN

19. Michael Paul Rogin, *Fathers and Children: Andrew Jackson and the Subjugation of the American South* (New York: Alfred A. Knopf, 1975), 229.

20. William Beattie to Alex Harvey, May 2, 1833, Mss. 158:3, part 5, Beattie Family Papers, VHS (quotation); Daniel F. Littlefield Jr., "Apalacicola Removal," in Littlefield and Parins, *Encyclopedia of Indian Removal*, 2:12.

21. William Beattie to Margaret Beattie, April 29, 1833, Mss. 158:3, part 5, Beattie Family Papers, VHS (quotation); James Whitcomb to James Beattie, April 1, 1840, Mss. 158:6A, part 1, Beattie Family Papers, VHS.

22. Carolyn Yancey Kent, "Deas, Edward (1812–1849)," in Littlefield and Parins, *Encyclopedia of Indian Removal*, 2:59; Daniel F. Littlefield Jr., "Sanford, John W. A. (1798–1870)," in same work, 2:198.

23. Robert H. Gudmestad, *Steamboats and the Rise of the Cotton Kingdom* (Baton Rouge: Louisiana State University Press, 2011), chapter 4.

24. Littlefield, "Sanford," 198; Gudmestad, *Steamboats and the Rise*, 84–86.

25. Young, *Redskins, Ruffleshirts, and Rednecks*, 117–121.

26. See Andrew Torget's essay, chapter 7 in this volume; I am indebted to Daniel F. Littlefield Jr. for this insight. Littlefield, *Africans and Creeks: From the Colonial Period to the Civil War* (Westport, CT: Greenwood Press, 1979); Quintard Taylor, *In Search of the Racial Frontier: African Americans in the American West, 1528–1990* (New York: W. W. Norton, 1998), chapter 2.

27. *Arkansas Gazette*, August 16, 1836, 1.

28. John T. Sprague, "Journal of 1836 Creek Emigration Party," *Encyclopedia of Indian Removal*, 1:212; Rogin, *Fathers and Children*, 248 (quotation); Brian Loveman, *No Higher Law: American Foreign Policy and the Western Hemisphere since 1776* (Chapel Hill: University of North Carolina Press, 2010), 83; Lenore A. Stiffarm, "The Demography of Native North America: A Question of American Indian Survival," with Phil Lane Jr., in *The State of Native America: Genocide, Colonization, and Resistance*, ed. M. Annette Jaimes (Norman: University of Oklahoma Press, 1988), 34, passim.

29. William Beattie to [?], May 6, 1837, Mss. 158:4, part 2, Beattie Family Papers, VHS (first quotation); US Bureau of Land Management, Alabama Land Records, document nos. 519, 1493, 1494, 1549, 1573, 1575, 1591, 1593, 1594, 1642, 1727, and 7682, Ancestry.com, accessed September 8, 2012, http://www.ancestry.com; Gouverneur Morris, Account for 4th quarter 1837 and 1st quarter 1838 by Captain Jacob Brown, US Army, Bureau of Indian Affairs, National Archives and Records Administration, microfilm 239 (second quotation).

30. Robert H. Gudmestad, *A Troublesome Commerce: The Transformation of the Interstate Slave Trade* (Baton Rouge: Louisiana State University Press, 2003), chapter 1; Jonathan

B. Pritchett and Herman Freudenberger, "A Peculiar Sample: The Selection of Slaves for the New Orleans Market," *Journal of Economic History* 52 (1992): 109–128.

31. "Ledger: Ballard and Co., 1831–1834," vol. 38, subseries 5, folder 463, and "R. C. Ballard and Co. Invoice Book," vol. 2, series 5, folder 417, both in Rice C. Ballard Papers, Southern Historical Collection, University of North Carolina, Chapel Hill (hereafter cited as UNC); Herbert S. Klein, *A Population History of the United States* (New York: Cambridge University Press, 2012), chapters 3–4.

32. Howard Bodenhorn, *State Banking in Early America: A New Economic History* (New York: Oxford University Press, 2003), 289; Nelson, *A Nation of Deadbeats*, chapters 5–6; Deyle, *Carry Me Back*, appendix A; Richard Follett, *The Sugar Masters: Planters and Slaves in Louisiana's Cane World, 1820–1860* (Baton Rouge: Louisiana State University Press, 2005), 20–22; George D. Green, *Finance and Economic Development in the Old South: Louisiana Banking, 1804–1861* (Stanford, CA: Stanford University Press, 1972), chapters 1–2.

33. Ronald Michener and Robert E. Wright, "Development of the US Monetary Union," *Financial History Review* 13, no. 1 (April 2006): 19–41; Bodenhorn, *State Banking in Early America*, chapter 10; Green, *Finance and Economic Development*, chapter 3.

34. Isaac Franklin to Rice C. Ballard and Company, May 30, 1831, series 1, folder 1 (quotation), and "R. C. Ballard and Co. Invoice Book," vol. 2, series 5, folder 417, both in Ballard Papers, UNC; *New York Evening Post*, May 17, 1831, 3.

35. "Ledger: Ballard and Co., 1831–1834," vol. 38, subseries 5, folder 463, Ballard Papers, UNC; Walter Johnson, *River of Dark Dreams: Slavery and Empire in the Cotton Kingdom* (Cambridge, MA: Harvard University Press, 2013), chapters 9–10; Robert E. Wright, *The Wealth of Nations Rediscovered: Integration and Expansion of American Financial Markets, 1780–1850* (Cambridge: Cambridge University Press, 2002), chapters 5–8.

36. "Ledger: Ballard and Co., 1831–1834," vol. 38, subseries 5, folder 463, Ballard Papers, UNC (quotation); David L. Lightner, *Slavery and the Commerce Power: How the Struggle against the Interstate Slave Trade Led to the Civil War* (New Haven, CT: Yale University Press, 2006), 8; Deyle, *Carry Me Back*, 98–100.

37. Edward E. Baptist, "'Cuffy,' 'Fancy Maids,' and 'One-Eyed Men': Rape, Commodification, and the Domestic Slave Trade in the United States," *American Historical Review* 106 (2001): 1619–1650; Jim Barnett and H. Clark Burkett, "The Forks of the Road Slave Market at Natchez," *Journal of Mississippi History* 63, no. 3 (September 2001): 168–187.

38. James R. Franklin to Rice C. Ballard, March 27, 1832, series 1, folder 5, Ballard Papers, UNC (quotation); Bodenhorn, *State Banking in Early America*, chapter 10.

39. "Ledger: Ballard and Co., 1831–1834," vol. 38, subseries 5, folder 463, Ballard

Papers, UNC; Gudmestad, *A Troublesome Commerce*, 93–96; Larry Schweikart, *Banking in the American South from the Age of Jackson to Reconstruction* (Baton Rouge: Louisiana State University Press, 1987), 69–71.

40. Isaac and James Franklin to Rice C. Ballard, December 20, 1832, series 1, folder 9; Richard L. Booker to Rice C. Ballard, April 18, 1833, series 1, folder 11 (first quotation); Isaac Franklin to Rice C. Ballard, March 30, 1834, series 1, folder 13 (second quotation); and "Ledger: Ballard and Co., 1831–1834," vol. 38, subseries 5, folder 463, all in Ballard Papers, UNC; Howard Bodenhorn, *A History of Banking in Antebellum America: Financial Markets and Economic Development in an Era of Nation-Building* (New York: Cambridge University Press, 2000), chapters 2–5.

41. Thomas Abbot to T. Hartley Crawford, Commissioner of Indian Affairs, US War Dept., March 30, 1840, *Records of the Bureau of Indian Affairs, 1793–1999*, National Archives and Records Administration, microfilm 240; Donald L. Fixico, *Bureau of Indian Affairs* (Santa Barbara, CA: ABC-CLIO, 2012), chapter 1.

7

The Saltillo Slavery Debates

Mexicans, Anglo-Americans, and Slavery's Future in Nineteenth-Century North America

Andrew J. Torget

During the winter of 1826–1827, an unprecedented debate took place in northern Mexico over the future of slavery in North America. In the small town of Saltillo, nestled into the foothills of the Sierra Madres, the legislature of the recently formed state of Coahuila-Texas hammered away at a new state constitution intended to promote the growth and prosperity of both Mexicans and Anglo-American immigrants in northeastern Mexico. The constitution, everyone hoped, would organize a vast stretch of Mexico's far-northern frontier, as well as determine how a steady stream of new immigrants from the United States would be integrated into Mexican society. Although most aspects of the constitution had been easily resolved, the question of slavery's future in the region soon sparked fierce debates at the constitutional convention. As legislators struggled to reconcile conflicting visions for slavery and freedom in North America, Mexicans and Anglo-Americans confronted each other in heated exchanges about what they believed slavery meant for the development of the continent and the fate of liberalism in Mexico and the United States.

The debates came because of a terrifying problem confronting Mexicans at their moment of independence from Spain: how to secure their sparsely populated northeastern border with the United States. Over the course of several centuries, Spanish authorities had utterly failed to wrest the region they called "Texas" away from the powerful Indian nations that controlled it and thus had never managed to convince their fellow countrymen to move into the violent territory. When Mexicans began building a new nation in 1821 from the rubble of New Spain, they found the underpopulated Mexican settlements in Texas teetering along the edge of collapse—the victims of relentless waves of Comanche and Apache raiding—and feared that the wayward province would become a security threat to the rest of the Mexican nation. "The most important problem is the security of the Province of Texas," reported a Mexico City commission in December 1821. "It would be an irreparable loss to the Empire if this beautiful Province is lost. In order to save it there remains only one recourse—to populate it."[1]

It was not hard to see why Mexicans feared for Texas. During the 1810s, as Spanish settlements in the region languished, an explosion in American migration to the southern United States had brought more than 350,000 people into the territories bordering northeastern Mexico. In Arkansas and Louisiana alone, more than 167,000 Americans crowded up against the border with Mexico, with another 220,000 in nearby Mississippi and Alabama.[2] In stark contrast, authorities in San Antonio reported that only 2,500 Mexicans made their homes in Texas—most of them several hundred miles from the border—and Mexico's entire military presence in the region amounted to a mere 186 soldiers.[3] Leaders in Mexico City recognized the alarming vulnerability of their northeastern border: there was simply nothing to stop the Americans from forcing their way into Texas and claiming the region for the United States.

With few options available, leaders in Mexico City therefore turned toward an unlikely solution: they would invite Americans to settle in Texas in exchange for vast tracts of nearly free land. Reasoning that a growing population of Anglo-American colonists (who would become Mexican citizens) might bring some measure of stability and prosperity into the Mexican frontier, Mexican leaders hoped that building settlements of Anglo-Mexicans would allow Mexico's far north to resist aggressive Indian raiders and an ever-expanding United States. And so, with reluctance, they threw open the gates of Texas to American migration during the early 1820s.

Anglo-Americans, in turn, proved eager to migrate into northern Mexico in order to take advantage of the region's potential for cotton farming. The great migrations to Louisiana, Mississippi, and Alabama that so worried Mexican officials had been sparked by a dramatic rise in cotton prices during the 1810s, when British industrialists began buying as much of the crop as they could. Prices for cotton doubled to thirty cents per pound by 1815, prompting hundreds of thousands of Americans to race to the Gulf Coast in hopes of growing rich by growing cotton. US cotton production exploded: the number of cotton bales exported by the United States increased tenfold during the 1810s, and by 1820 the southern United States surpassed India as the world's leading cotton producer.[4] The result was nothing less than the rapid transformation of the southwestern United States into one of the most profitable places in the world. And because Mexico's northern frontier stood along the western edge of that development, waves of American migrants began making their way into Texas during the 1820s in search of new cotton lands along the Gulf Coast of North America.

When those Americans insisted, however, that slavery serve as the labor system of cotton farming in northeastern Mexico, battles erupted among Mexicans and Americans about the future of the US-Mexican borderlands. Because Gulf Coast agriculture was—in the minds of US farmers—inseparable from slave labor, Anglo-Americans fought to defend a vision for slavery's place in northern Mexico that mirrored its development in the southern United States. Yet among Mexicans there was no single position on slavery; different groups with varying levels of investment in the institution held different perspectives. For some, slave-based agriculture seemed to offer the best hope for the rapid development of the region, while others vehemently opposed slavery as incompatible with the establishment of a liberal democracy in Mexico. These contrasting visions came to a head during the winter of 1826–1827, when the state legislature of Coahuila-Texas began writing a constitution that would define the future of Mexico's far northeastern territories.

BUILDING A MEXICAN NATION

Mexico's extreme poverty when it achieved independence meant that there were few available options for shoring up the nation's weak hold on the Texas borderlands. Without the funds to send an army into the region, leaders in Mexico City acknowledged that opening Texas to foreign colonization appeared to be the only viable option. Most members of the national congress in Mexico City remained leery of inviting foreigners of unknown loyalties to settle in Mexico, preferring to offer the lands to poor Mexicans from the nation's interior. But if they could not convince their own people to move to an isolated and violent frontier (and, as experience would show, they could not), most were also willing to take a chance on foreign colonists. The risks of doing nothing, moreover, seemed too great to chance. Mexico thus began drafting a national colonization law in March 1822, and soon dozens of would-be colonization agents—known as *empresarios*—

besieged Mexico City in hopes of securing the lucrative right to transport foreign settlers into northern Mexico.[5]

The vast majority of these would-be empresarios hailed from the United States, and nearly all of them hoped to capitalize on the strong desire among Americans for cheap lands along the North American Gulf Coast. The spectacular rise of global cotton prices during the 1810s had transformed such acreage into a highly valuable commodity. By the time of Mexican independence, the best cotton lands in the United States sold at auction for fifty dollars an acre.[6] The Panic of 1819 and its aftermath, however, bankrupted countless American farmers and put nearly all cotton lands beyond their financial reach. Northern Mexico, it seemed, might become the next place to go for those displaced farmers, since the Texas borderlands shared the same long growing season, rich soils, and ready access to Gulf Coast shipping ports that had made Mississippi acreage so appealing. As Calvin Schermerhorn shows in chapter 6, there was no shortage of Anglo-Americans looking to profit from the rapid expansion of Gulf Coast agriculture during the 1820s and 1830s, and the same forces that brought Indian removal to Mississippi and Alabama soon converged on northern Mexico.

As Mexicans debated colonization, it was not the prospect of bringing Anglo-Americans into the country that proved controversial. It was, instead, the insistence of those Americans that chattel slavery accompany them into Mexico that sparked heated debates. For the overwhelming majority of white Americans of the era, slavery was considered the indispensable engine for running a successful cotton economy, and petitioners from the United States seeking colonization contracts pushed hard for the continued sanction of slavery in Mexico. Stephen F. Austin, who would become the most successful of the empresarios, lobbied fiercely on behalf of preserving slavery as indispensable for encouraging American farmers to immigrate into Mexico. "The primary product that will elevate us from poverty is Cotton," Austin explained, "and we cannot do this without the help of slaves."[7] Leaders in Mexico City, as a result, soon found themselves embroiled in debates over slavery and American colonization, exposing the major fault lines within Mexico regarding the institution.

Much to their dismay, Anglo-Americans such as Austin discovered that most Mexicans hoped to abolish slavery from the nation during the early years following independence. For some Mexicans, antislavery convictions grew out of the fervor of the revolution itself. Father Miguel Hidalgo y Costilla, whose protest had begun the movement for independence from Spain, decreed an end to enslavement at the outbreak of his rebellion in 1810.[8] In leading the final charge toward overthrowing Spanish rule, Agustín de Iturbide declared everyone in Mexico to be social equals as one of the Three Guarantees of his Plan de Iguala. In neither case did slavery appear to fit the ideals that had animated the War for Independence. And for Mexican legislators taken with the ideals of the Enlightenment, enslavement clashed violently with liberal concepts of the natural rights of human beings. Thus, the opportunity to create a new nation in Mexico based on principles consistent with the revolution and liberalism seemed to present a unique opportunity to abolish the institution from Mexican territory.[9]

There were also practical reasons for Mexicans to outlaw slavery. Although chattel slavery had once been an important part of the Mexican economy, the institution had withered to near insignificance in almost every Mexican province by 1821. As Paul Conrad demonstrates in chapter 3, the enslavement of Indians had a long history in northern Mexico, and over the centuries, Indian labor had proven far cheaper than enslaved African labor. By the nineteenth century, most of Mexico's unfree laborers were Indians or mestizos working as indebted peons, rather than enslaved Africans considered chattel. In a nation of more than six million, there were perhaps only eight thousand enslaved Africans still toiling in Mexico by the early 1820s.[10]

Because the Mexican economy no longer relied on chattel slavery in any meaningful way, abolishing the institution appeared to require no significant sacrifice on the part of the country's industry, agriculture, or trade. Similarly, there were few incentives for Mexico to involve itself in the international slave trade. Both Great Britain and the United States had recently abolished the practice, and the British navy had even begun intercepting ships that trafficked in slaves. By the early 1800s, indeed, Great Britain had become home to an increasingly powerful abolitionist movement, whose leaders hoped to use London's political power to enact gradual emancipation worldwide.[11] As a new nation setting itself up on the world stage, Mexico would do well to avoid conflicts with Great Britain—which, at the time, was both the dominant global power and the biggest foreign investor in Mexico's economy—over an institution that had little salience for the national economy. For most politicians in the nation's capital, there appeared to be no meaningful advantage to keeping the institution of slavery legal in Mexico.[12]

The prime exception, however, was the Mexicans who lived in the Texas borderlands. In the eyes of most Mexican Texans—usually called *Tejanos*—the greatest challenge facing northeastern Mexico remained the sheer absence of any sizeable non-Indian population, a problem whose persistence seemed poised to doom the region to remain underdeveloped and impoverished for the foreseeable future. Without more people, there could be no growth of Tejano commerce or trade, no means for developing Tejano villages like San Antonio into prosperous towns, and—most menacing—no way to counter the violent raids of nearby Indian nations. The Comanches and Apaches had waged a merciless war against Tejano outposts in Texas during the late 1810s, and by 1820 the situation had devolved into such chaos that the governor of Texas warned of the imminent collapse of Tejano settlements.[13] For Tejanos, American colonization appeared to offer the only realistic option for developing the region—and thus the fact that these Americans would bring chattel slavery with them proved to be a far lesser concern for Tejano leaders than the dire necessity of finding some means of populating northeastern Mexico.

Because of their proximity to the American South, Tejanos also had compelling economic ties to the southern United States. Nearly every Tejano leader made his living by trading in merchandise imported from New Orleans, where men like Juan Martín de Veramendi, Erasmo Seguín, José Casiano, and Ramón Músquiz built enduring relationships with US traders. Some Tejanos, such as José Antonio Navarro and José Francisco Ruiz, had spent much of the late 1810s living in the southern United States, where they saw firsthand the transformations that cotton had wrought on the region. Tejanos desperately wanted that same transformation to come to Texas, which made them ardent supporters of allowing Anglo-Americans—and therefore slavery—into northern Mexico. One Tejano later put it this way to Stephen F. Austin: "I cannot help seeing the advantages which, to my way of thinking, would result if we admitted honest, hard-working people, regardless of what country they come from...even hell itself."[14]

Such deep divisions among Mexicans over the institution ensured that slavery would not appear in the final version of the 1824 constitution. The new federal constitution, in fact, made no mention of slavery, delegating the matter to the individual states, a decision with profound implications. State legislators could now write their own laws on slavery, and so the majority of states quickly outlawed the institution. Yet the strongest reverberations of this approach would be felt in northeastern Mexico. Because the Mexican Congress had also grafted the province of Texas onto its more populated southern neighbor Coahuila, it would now be up to the new state legislature of Coahuila-Texas to determine the future of American colonization and slavery along Mexico's northeastern frontier.

By the time the new congress convened, around three thousand American farmers had already begun building homes and plowing fields in Texas. As Austin and the Tejanos had hoped, the colonies had become a rapid success. By the mid- to late 1820s Austin estimated that his fledgling colony annually shipped several hundred bales, probably around 200,000 pounds of cotton.[15] That meant that the Anglo colonies constituted only a tiny fraction of the cotton commerce coming out of the Gulf of Mexico. Mississippians, by comparison, produced 10 million pounds of cotton in 1826, while Louisiana and Alabama planters shipped 38 million and 45 million pounds, respectively.[16] Yet Austin and the Tejanos saw these small Texas shipments as the first fruits of a booming new industry in northern Mexico. In letters to Mexican officials, Austin cited the massive scale of cotton exportation in places like Alabama and Mississippi, arguing that Texas—given the right support from the Mexican government—could one day exceed the southern United States in cotton production.[17] All of that, however, depended on slavery, and an 1825 census of Austin's colony revealed that a full quarter of the new population was enslaved.[18]

ARTICLE 13

During the spring of 1826, the congress of Coahuila-Texas convened in Saltillo and began work on the state's constitution. When drafts of various sections began circulating among the eleven members of the legislature—ten from Coahuila, one from Texas—the Texas representative learned that an antislavery faction had formed among Coahuilans to write abolition into the new constitution. Drafted as Article 13, their antislavery proposal was bold: "The state prohibits absolutely and for all time slavery in all its territory, and slaves that already reside in the state will be free from the day of the publication of the constitution in this capital."[19] The Texas representative, the Baron de Bastrop, sent an emergency message to the Tejano leadership in San Antonio, warning that something had to be done immediately to counter the antislavery faction in Saltillo or their efforts to bring Americans into Texas would "be completely ruined."[20]

Article 13 had been drafted by Manuel Carrillo, one of three representatives from Saltillo in the state legislature and a leading voice for liberalism in Coahuilan politics during the late 1820s. Liberals in Coahuila tended toward a sympathetic view of the United States, generally favored the adoption of American-style federalism in their own government, and often supported inviting foreign colonists into the new Mexican nation. Slavery, however, was a practice that put men like Carrillo at odds with colonization efforts in Texas. While Mexican liberals frequently pointed to the United States as a model for liberal democracy, chattel slavery stood out for many as a glaring contradiction in how Anglo-Americans practiced their liberal creed. For some liberals in the state—such as Dionisio Elizondo, a representative from northern Coahuila—developing the Texas colonies was less important than ensuring that the state protect the "universal rights of men" that they recognized as the foundation of a liberal democracy.[21] Conservatives in the state, far fewer in number, generally opposed foreign colonization (often out of fear of economic competition from foreign merchants) and thus joined Carrillo's antislavery effort largely as a means of countering the potential dangers of American immigration. Seizing the constitution as an opportunity, this antislavery cabal moved swiftly to abolish the institution.[22]

Recognizing that an emancipation article in the state constitution could destroy the new American colonies, Tejanos in San Antonio immediately began building their own countercoalition in order to contain the potential damage of Article 13. San Antonio's town council sent an emergency appeal to the state congress in Saltillo declaring slavery "to be *indispensable* to the prosperity of this Department" and demanded that further debate on Article 13 be halted until Texas could weigh in on the matter. Texas political chief José Saucedo then forwarded news of the antislavery article to Stephen F. Austin in the Anglo colonies, lamenting "the deathblow that Texas receive[d] with the constitution's article on slavery."[23]

Following the Tejano lead, Austin launched his own intense lobbying campaign, sending numerous petitions to the state congress offering every defense he could imagine to dissuade legislators from abolishing the institution. His central argument—and the main theme of Tejano protests—was that any attack on slavery would decimate Anglo-American migration into northern Mexico. "I made efforts to persuade rich men who owned slaves to emigrate because with them the country would make swift progress," Austin protested. "I told them that the Government would never take away slaves brought by them for their own use.... What would the world say," he asked, "if in direct violation of that law and that guarantee, the Government were to take away that property from those colonists against their will?" Such an act, he insisted, would drastically undermine the new government's credibility, and "the mistrust which is certain to follow will destroy all hope of further emigration."[24]

As Austin and the Tejano elite scrambled, rumors began spreading among Anglo colonists that demonstrated their fears were well founded. Wild stories of impending emancipation spread rapidly among the colonists' farms throughout the late summer of 1826, and Austin warned San Antonio, "More than one half of these people are awaiting the decision of Congress in regard to their slaves, as they intend to leave the Country if emancipation is decreed."[25] Then, on October 10, 1826, the *Arkansas Gazette* printed an article reporting "the recent passage of a law by the Mexican Government for the emancipation of all the slaves in the province of Texas, and that orders had been received for carrying it into immediate effect."[26] The *Gazette* had long served as an organ for anti-Texas propaganda (hoping to discourage Americans from abandoning places like Arkansas for northern Mexico), and its editor apparently harbored no reservations about claiming—falsely—that Article 13 was already in effect.

With publication in the *Gazette*, the story of Mexico forcibly freeing the slaves of American colonists soon found its way into newspapers across the United States, discouraging potential settlers. Travelers from Arkansas carried issues of the *Gazette* to trading hubs such as Saint Louis, Missouri, and New Orleans, Louisiana, while other copies moved through the mails to destinations farther east. By the beginning of November, the *Gazette*'s story had traveled to Kentucky, where the editor of the *Louisville Public Advertiser* reprinted the full article under the headline "Emancipation of Slaves at Texas."[27] Ten days later the story appeared in both Richmond, Virginia, and Washington, DC, as copies of the *Advertiser* joined those already circulating of the *Arkansas Gazette*.[28] Tales of Mexican abolition soon made their way up the Atlantic seaboard, and by the end of the week, newspapers as far away as Massachusetts had reprinted the story.[29] By reprinting the same story throughout November 1826, newspaper editors across the United States made an alarming account of Mexican antislavery legislation available to tens of thousands of Anglo-Americans.

Debates within the Saltillo legislature thus became part of discussions within the US press about the future of slavery in North America. During the early nineteenth century, antislavery activism among white Americans remained largely confined to proposals of state-sponsored schemes—known collectively as "colonization"—to deport people of African descent to Africa. Such schemes had emerged as the most popular approach to antislavery, primarily because "colonization" offered a slow, voluntary means for slaveholders to help solve the problems of race and slavery in American society. Yet the seeds for a more militant and confrontational antislavery movement had already taken root in the United States by the late 1820s as concerns about the institution's future in the country continued to grow in certain—mostly northeastern—communities. Some of these burgeoning antislavery sentiments came from the evangelical revivals that swept across portions of the United States during the 1810s and 1820s; some emerged from the dogged abolitionist efforts of free African Americans in northern cities. The dramatic rise of a politically powerful abolitionist movement in

Great Britain during these years played the greatest role, helping to crystallize American antislavery thought. Although full-blown emancipationist antislavery would not emerge as a significant political force in the United States until the early 1830s, a rising tide of antislavery sentiments had nonetheless taken root in portions of the United States during the late 1820s. When the *Arkansas Gazette*'s story reached the eastern seaboard, several US editors therefore seized upon rumors of Mexican abolition as an opportunity to voice their general displeasure with both slavery and American slaveholders.[30]

SALTILLO DEBATES I

While rumors spread across the United States about antislavery laws in Mexico, the Anglo-Tejano alliance worked feverishly to amend the effects of Article 13. Stephen F. Austin sent his brother, James "Brown" Austin, to Saltillo to join the Baron de Bastrop's lobbying effort. Upon his arrival in Saltillo, Brown Austin learned that efforts to thwart Manuel Carrillo's antislavery coalition had produced mixed results. If they were lucky, explained the baron, they might be able to secure an exemption for Austin's existing colonists to retain ownership of slaves already held in Texas. But there would likely be no other concessions: "Further introduction of slaves is out of the question."[31] Carrillo's antislavery faction in the congress outnumbered the baron's meager countercoalition, and its members seemed largely unwilling to yield on the issue of slavery's future in the region.

Brown Austin recognized that the political situation in Saltillo promised short-term relief to the American colonists while presenting more troubling, long-term challenges. The possibility that slaveholders might be allowed to retain ownership of slaves already in Texas might help stave off an immediate exodus of settlers from the colonies. Yet Brown also knew that if new settlers were barred from bringing slaves with them into Mexican territory, empresarios such as Austin could no longer recruit slaveholders from the southern regions of the United States. And since empresarios relied heavily on the lure of cotton profits to entice Anglo-American settlers onto Mexican land, a ban on slavery in Texas seemed to promise a rapid end to colonization efforts. The best that the Anglo colonies could hope for, Brown Austin realized, was to convince the Saltillo legislature to extend the period of legally sanctioned slavery beyond the life-spans of the enslaved men and women already living in Texas, which might buy them enough time to secure more favorable laws from a future legislature.

Brown Austin decided to focus on convincing state legislators that the children of Texas slaves should not be deemed free upon birth, detailing "every *reason* I could invent" for why freeing those children would be detrimental to the interests of the state and of the slaves themselves. Playing on the sentiments of antislavery legislators, Brown argued that freeing children too young—before they could develop skills with which to support themselves—would force those children to depend on handouts and thievery for survival, causing each of them to become "a Public pest and continually a subject of correction." The more humane alternative, he told legislators, would be to enslave those children until they reached at least fourteen years of age, when they would be "possessed of some useful branch of industry whereby they might gain a livelihood—instead of becoming *vagabonds*." Pitching enslavement as a benefit to the enslaved, Brown Austin and the Baron de Bastrop lobbied every legislator who would listen.[32]

When Article 13 finally came up for debate on the floor of the state congress in late November 1826, Austin and Bastrop remained unsure what their backroom wrangling of the preceding few months would bring. All the legislators, with the exception of antislavery leader Manuel Carrillo, had given the Texans their word that they would vote so that the slaves in the state would remain slaves. Yet, as the baron noted, the further importation of slaves seemed certain to be banned, and the age at which children of enslaved parents should be freed remained a point of fierce debate within the congress. Although the Texans appeared on the verge of preventing the emancipation of enslaved men and women already in northeastern Mexico, it remained to be seen whether they could also continue to enslave the children of their laborers.[33]

Anglo and Tejano lobbying, it turned out, had succeeded in convincing most Coahuilans to abandon the idea of immediate abolition. On November 30, 1826, Article 13 was read before the congress—along with the petitions of the Tejanos in San Antonio and Stephen F. Austin—and opened to formal debate. José María Viesca, serving as president of the congress, began the discussion by pointing out that immediate emancipation was impossible since the dismal financial condition of the state meant that it could not compensate slaveholders for their confiscated property. And so Viesca opened the floor to new proposals for how best to handle the future of slavery in the region.[34] Informal agreements forged in backroom negotiations during the preceding several months were now to be tested on the floor of Congress (figure 7.1).

Some legislators had come to doubt that the state's constitution would serve as the best venue for handling issues as vexing as slavery and emancipation. Dionosio Elizondo, a liberal representative from northern Coahuila, offered his support for the abolition of the slave trade, but he

FIGURE 7.1
Rare daguerreotype of the main plaza in Saltillo, Coahuila, taken during the 1847–1848 US invasion of northern Mexico. The Saltillo slavery debates likely took place in a building facing this plaza. (Yale Collection of Western Americana, Beinecke Rare Book and Manuscript Library)

came down hard against writing emancipation into the state constitution. Elizondo had been taken with the legal writings of Jeremy Bentham, an English jurist and philosopher, and proposed an approach to abolition patterned after Bentham's arguments in favor of gradual emancipation. Forcing emancipation on the Anglo colonies in Texas, Elizondo predicted, would be "a violent operation" that "would bring tremendous ills upon the state" by destroying vast amounts of personal property. Elizondo recommended that Congress instead "adopt softer means" of emancipation by passing a series of laws—such as limiting the right of slaveholders to pass slaves down to their heirs and setting a standard price for compensating slaveholders for the freeing of a slave, both Bentham-inspired proposals—that would eliminate the institution from the region gradually and without onerous consequences for the state. "Because the legislator cannot cut the tether of slavery all at once," Elizondo counseled, "he unties it little by little over time, and the march of liberty is no less safe for being slow."[35]

Most legislators agreed—the British model of gradual emancipation apparently resonated in Coahuila—and the discussion quickly moved toward when to free the children of the enslaved. Viesca recommended that Article 13 be rewritten to ensure that slaves already in Texas would remain enslaved for life and to include a six-month extension for Anglo-American colonists to import new slaves after the publication of the constitution, suggestions that met no challenges. As for the children of those enslaved men and women, Viesca proposed that they be held as slaves themselves until they reached twenty-five years of age, "when they [could] think with judgment and maturity." Most legislators hoped to emancipate the children of slaves by the age of fourteen, acknowledged Viesca, but he spoke out against the idea by invoking Brown Austin's argument that such a move would free children before they developed the ability to support themselves. "If you give them freedom at fourteen years of age," reasoned Viesca, "it would not accomplish anything but to fill the state with corrupt men who will be parasites on society." Apparently swayed by Brown Austin's backroom arguments, Viesca now deployed the American's logic on the floor of the state congress.[36]

The precise timing of emancipation for the second generation of Texas slaves quickly became the flashpoint of debate among legislators. Santiago de Valle, a representative from northern Coahuila, challenged Viesca's contention that twenty-five years was the proper age for freedom. "The children of slaves should not be made to suffer the enormous imprisonment of slavery for so long," insisted de Valle, who offered his own proposal for how Article 13 might be rewritten. This version would free enslaved children at the age of fourteen, when, de Valle believed, they would still be young enough to devote a few years of work toward purchasing the freedom of their parents. Dionisio Elizondo eagerly seconded the proposal as a clever scheme for enlarging the reach of freedom throughout Coahuila and Texas. Viesca, however, objected to the enterprise as wholly unrealistic, pointing out that de Valle's proposal rested on the assumption that fourteen-year-olds would voluntarily take it upon themselves to work for the freedom of their parents. "If the children are ingrates," as Viesca argued that boys and girls just entering puberty were likely to be, "they would serve nothing to their parents."[37]

With no one willing to yield on the matter, Article 13 was sent back to the drafting committee for rewriting without a consensus on the age at which enslaved children should be freed. Most of the important details over how the constitution would deal with slavery and freedom, however, appeared to be settled. Those already enslaved in Texas, legislators agreed, would remain the lifelong property of their masters. Yet slavery in the region was on a slow road to extinction. Six months after the publication of the state constitution, the importation of slaves into Texas would become illegal. The congress also agreed that children of enslaved parents in the region should eventually be freed, even if legislators continued to bicker over when that should happen. This meant that the closing of the international slave trade to northeastern Mexico would be fundamentally different from what had happened in the United States. There would be no self-reproducing class of enslaved laborers in the Texas colonies—the current generation of slaves in northeastern Mexico would be the last to be enslaved for life.

RUMORS AND REBELLION

As the Coahuila-Texas legislature began rewriting Article 13, an uprising among Anglo-American colonists dominated US newspaper coverage of events in northeastern Mexico, revealing the extent to which the Saltillo debates had entangled questions of slavery and emancipation within the American imagination of Mexico's northern territories. The man at the center of the revolt, Haden Edwards, was a land speculator recently arrived from Mississippi who secured an empresario contract in 1825 from the Saltillo legislature. Covering much of the easternmost portion of Texas, the Edwards grant included the town of Nacogdoches and a motley band of squatters—French, Spanish, Mexican, and American—who had long made their homes on lands near the US-Mexican border. When Edwards arrived in Nacogdoches in the fall of 1825, he posted notices declaring that anyone already living within the boundaries of his grant must present valid titles for their land. Those who could not, warned Edwards, would have their land confiscated and sold. Although many of these settlers had lived in the territory surrounding Nacogdoches for decades, most did not possess legal titles to their homes. Edwards soon found himself locked in a fierce struggle with longtime residents of eastern Texas.

Complaints about Edwards began pouring into San Antonio and eventually reached the desk of the president of Mexico, Guadalupe Victoria, who revoked the Edwards empresario grant and ordered his expulsion from Mexico. Edwards reacted by taking over Nacogdoches with a small band of armed men, who then declared Texas free of Mexican rule and proclaimed themselves the "Republic of Fredonia."[38]

The news sent Stephen F. Austin into a panic, fearing that the uprising might destroy Anglo-Tejano efforts to carve out protections for slavery in the state constitution. Austin immediately sent messages to rebels he knew personally, warning that the insurrection could extinguish all hope of preserving the right of Anglo colonists to hold slaves in northeastern Mexico. "The slave question is now pending in the Legislature, the constitution now forming," Austin seethed. "What influence are acts of this outrageous character calculated to have on the minds of the members and on the decission of the slave or any other question involving the interests and prosperity of the new Settlements?" Fearing that the Fredonian Rebellion could give Manuel Carrillo's antislavery coalition control of the ongoing slavery debate in Saltillo, Austin urged the rebels to surrender themselves immediately to Mexican authorities as the "one way for you all to save yourselves and *only one*."[39]

News of the Fredonian Rebellion soon made its way into the United States. Reporting on the rebellion in early January 1827, the *Louisiana Advertiser* in New Orleans interwove rumors of the uprising with unconnected reports that "slavery shall be abolished" in the new Coahuila-Texas constitution. The editor of the *Advertiser* made clear his own doubts that Mexican moves toward abolition had motivated the Fredonians, calling slavery "the pretended cause of the revolution," although he acknowledged that many in New Orleans believed that the two were somehow related.[40] When copies of the New Orleans story arrived in New York City three weeks later, they were rushed to the offices of local newspapers. The editor of the *New York Daily Advertiser* decided to reprint the New Orleans report of the rebellion, but he cut out the sections disclaiming slavery as a cause of the uprising as he fit the story into the space available for the next day's edition. As a result, the *New York Daily Advertiser* hit the streets on February 8, 1827, with an article that tightly connected news of the Fredonian revolt with reports of the Coahuila congress's attempts to outlaw slavery in northeastern Mexico.[41] As copies of the *Daily Advertiser* began circulating throughout the northeastern United States, where the story was subsequently reprinted by other newspapers, it was left to readers to somehow discern that the Fredonian Rebellion and controversies over slavery in Texas were not related.[42]

Soon US editors began asserting that the Fredonians had revolted in order to preserve slavery within Mexican Texas. When the *Niles' Weekly Register* published news of the rebellion on March 17, 1827, the newspaper reported that "the objection of the *Fredonians* to the Mexican government was, that it would not admit of slavery."[43] The *New York Observer* published a similar piece—asserting that the rebellion "appears to have been occasioned by the new law prohibiting the importation of slaves into the Mexican dominions; or as some accounts say, abolishing slavery altogether"—that was soon reprinted by newspapers in Vermont, Massachusetts, and New Hampshire.[44] At least one newspaper, confused by the various second- and third-hand accounts circulating, even reported that the Fredonians themselves had abolished slavery.[45] Mistaken though they were, by the spring of 1827 many US newspapers had combined reports of the Fredonian uprising with rumors of abolition in Mexican Texas, encouraging readers to imagine the revolt as an uprising of American slaveholders to preserve the future of slavery in northeastern Mexico.

The disputes that led to the Fredonian Rebellion were not about slavery, and the revolt itself failed within a matter of weeks because so few Anglo-Americans rallied to its cause. Yet the timing of the insurrection, coming upon the heels of debates over the future of slaveholding in Coahuila and Texas, meant that many in the United States understood the uprising as a stand by Anglo-Americans against antislavery in Mexico. Such stories would prove highly effective at dissuading potential colonists in the southern United States from considering migration to Mexico.

SALTILLO DEBATES II

As Americans read alarming reports about Mexican abolitionism, the debates over slavery resumed in Saltillo. On January 31, 1827, the newly revised version of Article 13 was read before the congress: "In the state no one is born a slave and six months after the publication of this constitution in each center of the state the introduction of slaves will not be permitted under any pretext."[46] The revisions represented a significant shift from the article's original thrust, in that it no longer promised to free slaves already present in northeastern Mexico. It would, however, end the importation of slaves into the region following a six-month period, and it promised freedom upon birth to the children of enslaved parents.

The proslavery bloc in Texas had continued its relentless lobbying during the winter, focusing on selling the extension of slavery as a humanitarian effort. Before debate could resume, the congress read a new petition from Stephen F. Austin urging the Saltillo congress to permit the continued importation of slaves as a means for expanding liberty and freedom. The slaves whom Anglo-American colonists brought to Mexico, Austin pointed out, were already enslaved in the United States. As such, "to extend the time for introducing slaves [was] not to make new slaves of free people" but would instead, he insisted, grant those slaves "the consolation of seeing their descendants freed." If the Saltillo legislature truly wanted to extend liberty in North America, he argued, then the congress should permit colonists to continue importing new slaves into Texas, because that would guarantee freedom to future generations and thereby "serve the cause of humanity." With similar reasoning, Austin pushed for the children of enslaved parents to remain slaves until they reached twenty-five years of age, so that they could be trained "to be laborers and servants" in order to survive.[47] If adopted wholesale, Austin's proposals promised to push back emancipation in northeastern Mexico by at least thirty years, giving Anglo-American settlers time to develop the region's agricultural promise and secure more favorable slave laws from a future legislature.

Once debate over Article 13 resumed, however, it became clear that Anglo-Tejano efforts to extend the enslavement of black children had lost support among legislators. During the November 1826 debates, Dionisio Elizondo had argued for gradual emancipation and supported proposals to keep those children enslaved until they were fourteen years old. But Elizondo had since reconsidered the matter, arguing now that the congress should not endorse slavery any more than absolutely necessary. The source of Elizondo's shift in thinking was his commitment to liberalism as the foundational framework of the state constitution. If the constitution was to be founded on "the gentle principles of the most liberal philanthropy," as Elizondo believed it should, that document could not embrace an institution that was fundamentally opposed to liberalism's principles. Slavery was the polar opposite of what he believed the new state constitution should embody, so Elizondo decided that if Article 13 endorsed enslaving anyone—even temporarily—it would undermine the concept of human liberty that served as the foundation of the constitution.

Elizondo, and perhaps others, had also come to be frustrated by what he saw as the undue political influence wielded by Anglo-American colonists in the rewriting of Article 13. The legislator recognized that the Anglo-Tejano alliance had succeeded in blunting much of the immediacy in the original draft of Article 13. One of the greatest coups on that front, and a frustration to Elizondo, was the opening of a six-month window during which Texans could import new servants into the state, who would then remain enslaved for life. "That, it seems to me, was very much arranged in consideration for the many individuals in Austin's colony," Elizondo grumbled. Although he wanted to make the constitution's ban on slave trafficking immediate, Elizondo recognized that he could not overcome the political coalition supporting Anglo-Tejano efforts to allow further slave importations for at least a short period of time. That did not stop Elizondo from making his disdain evident when he mocked Austin's arguments in favor of extending the six-month window to five years as an indirect means of increasing freedom. "Citizen Austin says that to delay the end of introducing slaves is not to create new slaves of free men," he announced to his fellow legislators. "The same would be a reason for us to never prohibit slavery, since until now everyone is aware that admitting new slaves is not to enslave free men."[48]

As no other legislator supported Texan proposals to extend the period for legal slave importations, the debates again centered on when to free the children of enslaved parents. Elizondo asked his fellow legislators to imagine themselves in the position of those unfortunate children, arguing that the congress should do the right thing "even though the laws may demand means for maintaining and educating the orphaned." José María Viesca finally brought the impasse to an end by suggesting that the congress defer to a future legislature the question of how to care for the freed children of the enslaved. Weary of the debate and with few objecting to the central thrust of the revised version, the legislators finally approved Article 13. Published in Saltillo with the completed constitution on March 11, 1827, the final version remained unchanged from the revisions that took place between November 1826 and January 1827: "In the state no one is born a slave, and six months after the publication of this constitution in the centers of each part of the state neither will the introduction of slaves be permitted under any pretext."[49]

The position on slavery adopted by the 1827 constitution of Coahuila and Texas was, at base, a compromise. By lining up strategic support in the congress through the Baron de Bastrop, Anglo-Texans and Tejanos had managed to wield greater influence in the state legislature than their single representative could have managed alone, and the end result was an Article 13 far different from its original design: instead of immediately abolishing slavery outright, the constitution established a long-term framework for gradual abolition to come to northeastern Mexico. In the process, the constitution implicitly endorsed the continued lifelong enslavement of African people already in the region by making no provision for their freedom and by opening a six-month window for future slave importations.

Yet, despite its compromises, the constitution's provisions leaned more heavily toward the goals of antislavery Mexican legislators than they did toward the wishes of proslavery forces in Texas. The institution itself was on a course to be eliminated from all of Coahuila and Texas, and within a matter of months, slave importation would become illegal. For antislavery Coahuilans, the original goal of immediate abolition had been traded away in exchange for provisions that committed the state to embracing freedom within a generation. For empresarios like Stephen F. Austin and the Tejano leadership in San Antonio, the constitution's slave provisions presented daunting long-term challenges. Although there would be no widespread confiscation of enslaved property by the state, officials in Texas would now be hard pressed to convince US farmers to move with their slaves to Mexican territory.

DECREE 56

The battle over slavery in northern Mexico did not end with the 1827 state constitution, and antislavery Coahuilans continued to fight to abolish slavery. José Francisco Madero, a liberal from northern Coahuila close to the antislavery Elizondo family, continued to push the state congress for more strident antislavery laws. "If all knew like me the hard and cruel treatment with which the Anglo Americans treat the slaves," Madero told his fellow legislators, "they would provide a means for saving them and perhaps would have written differently the second part of Article 13 of the constitution." Madero acquired his mistrust of American slaveholders from his travels to New Orleans, where he spent time along the docks of the largest shipping and slave-trading port in the southern United States. While in a New Orleans café one day, Madero overheard some Americans arguing that "negroes were the same as mules and should be treated as such." The comment stuck with Madero, who realized that Americans' famous devotion to liberty was entirely contingent upon race and did not extend to "the unhappy men who only for being colored black [had] been sold as if they were things." "These ideas that so much degrade the men who proclaim so greatly liberalism," Madero grumbled, "I do not think the colonists of Austin, the Colorado, and Guadalupe have abandoned them on the other side of the Sabine."[50]

In concert with two fellow Coahuilans, Madero managed to pass a law requiring the Texas colonies to keep a census of enslaved people (to ensure that their children would be freed on schedule), instituted a 500-peso fine for anyone exporting a pregnant slave to the United States (also to ensure that children of the enslaved would be freed), and mandated that whenever a master died, at least 10 percent of his slaves be freed by the state. As they laid out their proposal, the three legislators drew heavily upon the work of European philosophers, such as the French Enlightenment thinker Charles-Louis Montesquieu and the British jurist Jeremy Bentham (whose proposals for gradual emancipation clearly continued to hold weight among Coahuilans).[51] The passage of this law, despite strenuous objections from Texas, demonstrated the resilience of antislavery sentiment in certain quarters of northern Mexico.

Anglos and Tejanos in Texas, however, refused to back away from their support of the institution. A steady stream of letters from the United States made Stephen F. Austin painfully aware that the Saltillo slavery debates had slowed American migration to Mexico. James Davis had been on the road to Texas but promptly turned back when he read about Article 13 in a Tennessee newspaper, warning Austin that neither he nor his neighbors could now move to Mexico: "The prohibition of slavery in your country will be a bar to most of them."[52] Searching desperately for a way around the slavery ban, Austin came up with an ingenious scheme to ask the Saltillo legislature for a new law guaranteeing that labor contracts signed in foreign countries also be honored in Mexico. The proposal sounded innocent, but it masked a sinister intent: this would create a legal loophole that would enable American slaveholders to force their slaves into ninety-nine-year labor contracts, thereby allowing slavery to continue in Texas under the name of indentured servitude.[53]

The Anglo colonists, in effect, planned to adopt the language of Mexican debt peonage as a means of protecting chattel slavery. Peonage had a long history in northern Mexico, stretching far back into the Spanish colonial era, and provided the majority of the labor needs for large ranches and haciendas in Coahuila. Mexican peasants who worked on these ranches invariably became indebted to their masters—for room, board, and other necessities—and became tied to the land as they attempted to work off their debts. While nominally free, these men and women lost control of their labor and freedom to leave the ranch as their masters came to control nearly every aspect of their lives. Coahuila's wealthiest and most powerful family, the Sánchez Navarros, used thousands of peons to run their expansive haciendas that sprawled out around Monclova. These peons often suffered forms of physical abuse and coercion (such as chaining, beatings, and whipping) not much different from practices on US plantations, although most Coahuilans nonetheless saw meaningful differences between peonage and chattel slavery. Austin's colonists hoped to blur those distinctions, however, as a means of providing legal cover for American slaveholders to continue coming into northern Mexico.[54]

The Tejano leadership in San Antonio immediately endorsed the plan, and José Antonio Navarro and José Miguel Arciniega—the two Texas representatives in Saltillo—brought the proposal before the state legislature. When the law passed in May 1828 as Decree 56, Austin wasted no time in drafting a template contract for Anglo-American migrants to follow as they crafted legal agreements that would allow them to bring new slaves into Mexican territory. In Austin's example, the contract listed each slave's value and promised those same slaves their freedom after they paid their master for the cost of emancipating them. But since the contract set the slave's wages at twenty dollars a year and mandated annual deductions for the costs of food, clothing, and housing, freedom would never come. Austin's contract was nothing more than an attempt to redefine slavery as indentured servitude, and he began sending letters to the United States explaining how to circumvent Mexican statutes against slave importations. Within a month, a New Orleans newspaper proclaimed, "The law of Mexico, prohibiting slavery, is evaded by having negroes bound to serve an apprenticeship of 99 years."[55]

The Saltillo slavery debates exposed the fractious fault lines that separated Mexicans and Americans over the issues of slavery, yet they settled almost nothing. For the rest of the late 1820s and early 1830s, Coahuilans, Tejanos, and Anglo-Americans continued to battle one another over the future of slavery and freedom in northeastern Mexico. Those fights, in turn, produced a state that neither fully embraced nor fully rejected slavery, ensuring that neither vision for the future of the Texas borderlands would be realized under Mexico. Coahuilan legislators found that they could outlaw the name of slavery but could not stop Anglo planters and Tejano politicians from continuing the practice. Yet Texans discovered that they could not force the state to openly embrace the institution of slavery, a problem that continued to undermine American migration into the region. Although they could carve out a place for slavery to endure in northern Mexico, the members of the Anglo-Tejano alliance came to realize that they could not build a thriving slave society while in conflict with their state government. What the debates had done, more than anything, was to foster a growing sense among Anglo-Americans that Mexicans opposed the expansion of chattel slavery in North America.

The failure of the debates to solve the intertwined issues of slavery and migration led to enduring instability in the US-Mexican borderlands as questions of American colonization eventually became entangled in larger fights within Mexico over federalism during the 1830s. The result was the secession of Texas from Mexico and the establishment of the Republic of Texas, which emerged in 1836 as the most unlikely creation: a republic of American slaveholders built beyond the borders of the United States. The Texas Republic then set out to undo every restriction that the Saltillo congress had placed on slavery in 1827, publishing a new constitution for the region that established—at least on paper—the most stridently proslavery government in North America. It was, indeed, everything the Confederate States of America would later attempt to create during the 1860s, and it represented the full realization of all the proslavery arguments that both Anglos and Tejanos had made in Saltillo during the 1826–1827 debates. The full Americanization of northeastern Mexico that resulted, in turn, would transform the territory by the 1850s into the western outpost of the US cotton South. And, as Mark Allan Goldberg shows in chapter 8, the needs of this US slave economy soon remade both space and power in Texas in the same ways it had in Alabama and Mississippi.

Notes

1. "Dictamen presentado a la Soberana Junta Gobernativa del Imperio Mexicano, por la Comisión de Relaciones Exteriores," December 29, 1821, quoted in Joseph Carl McElhannon, "Imperial Mexico and Texas, 1821–1823," *Southwestern Historical Quarterly* 53 (October 1949): 138.

2. All census material on Alabama, Mississippi, and Louisiana comes from the Historical Census Browser, Geospatial and Statistical Data Center, University of Virginia, accessed October 16, 2012, http://fisher.lib.virginia.edu/. Census statistics on 1820 Arkansas are from Orville W. Taylor, *Negro Slavery in Arkansas* (1958; repr., Fayetteville: University of Arkansas Press, 2000), 25.

3. Antonio Martínez to Gaspar López, February 6, 1822, in Eugene C. Barker, ed., *Annual Report of the American Historical Association for the Year 1919: The Austin Papers*, 3 vols. (Washington, DC: US Government Printing Office, 1924, 1928; Austin: University of Texas Press, 1927), 1:472–475. *The Austin Papers* will hereafter be cited as *AP*.

4. Historical Census Browser; Adam Rothman, *Slave Country: American Expansion and the Origins of the Deep South* (Cambridge, MA: Harvard University Press, 2005), 182–183; Robert V. Haynes, *The Mississippi Territory and the Southwest Frontier, 1795–1817* (Lexington: University Press of Kentucky, 2010), 133; Daniel Walker Howe, *What Hath God Wrought: The Transformation of America, 1815–1848* (New York: Oxford University Press, 2007), 128–131.

5. Ricki S. Janicek, "The Development of Early Mexican Land Policy: Coahuila and Texas, 1810–1825" (PhD diss., Tulane University), 1985, 92; Herbert Bolton, *Guide to Materials for the History of the United States in the Principal Archives of Mexico* (Washington, DC: Carnegie Institution of Washington, 1913), 350–361.

6. Howe, *What Hath God Wrought*, 127; Stuart Bruchey, *Cotton and the Growth of the American Economy: 1790–1860* (New York: Harcourt, Brace & World, 1967), 29–30.

7. Stephen F. Austin to Gaspar Flores [answering the letter of December 6, 1824], *AP*, 1:984–985 (quotation). Stephen F. Austin will hereafter be cited as SFA. On SFA's lobbying efforts in Mexico City, see SFA to Edward Lovelace, November 22, 1822, *AP*, 1:554–555.

8. No. 80, "Bando aboliendo la esclavitud," December 6, 1810, in Manuel Dublán and José María Lozano, *Legislación mexicana; o, Colección completa de disposiciones legislativas expedidas desde la independencia de la República* (Mexico City: Imprenta del Comercio, 1876), 1:339–340.

9. See, for example, sessions of October 18, 1821, and November 26, 1822, *Diario de las sesiones de la Soberana Junta Provisional Gubernativa del Imperio Mexicano, instalada según previene el Plan de Iguala y los Tratados de la Villa de Córdova*, in *Actas constitucionales mexicanas (1821–1824)* (Mexico City: Instituto de Investigaciones Jurídicas, Universidad Nacional Autónoma de México, 1980), 1:124, 7:64.

10. Timothy Henderson, *A Glorious Defeat: Mexico and Its War with the United States* (New York: Hill and Wang, 2007), 10; Gonzalo Aguirre Beltrán, *La población negra de México* (1946; repr., Mexico City: Fondo de Cultura Económica, 1972), 232–234.

11. For the origins of British abolitionism, see Christopher Leslie Brown, *Moral Capital: Foundations of British Abolitionism* (Chapel Hill: University of North Carolina Press, 2006).

12. On England's influence on early Mexico, see Stanley Green, *The Mexican Republic: The First Decade, 1823–1832* (Pittsburgh: University of Pittsburgh Press, 1987), 119, 129–133, 151–152.

13. Martínez to Arredondo, August 18, 1818, and April 1, 1819, in Virginia H. Taylor, ed. and trans., *The Letters of Antonio Martínez: Last Spanish Governor of Texas, 1817–1822* (Austin: Texas State Library, 1957), 163, 217–218; Martínez to Apodaca, April 5, 1820, in Félix D. Almaráz Jr., ed., *Letters from Governor Antonio Martínez to the Viceroy Juan Ruíz de Apodaca* (San Antonio: Research Center for the Arts and Humanities, University of Texas–San Antonio, 1983), 43.

14. José Francisco Ruiz to SFA, November 26, 1830, quoted in David J. Weber, *The Mexican Frontier, 1821–1846: The American Southwest under Mexico* (Albuquerque: University of New Mexico Press, 1982), 176.

15. SFA to Manuel de Mier y Terán, September 20, 1828, *AP*, 2:116. At an average weight of 450 pounds each, 500 bales would equal 225,000 pounds of cotton.

16. Bruchey, *Cotton and the Growth*, 18.

17. SFA to Ceballos, September 20, 1828, *AP*, 2:114–115; SFA to Manuel de Mier y Terán, September 20, 1828, *AP*, 2:116.

18. Eugene C. Barker, "Notes on the Colonization of Texas," *Mississippi Valley Historical Review* 10 (September 1923): 149–152.

19. Coahuila-Texas Congressional Session of November 30, 1826, Congreso Constituyente, 1824–1827, Actas de Primera Sesión Ordinaria (hereafter cited as APSO), August 15, 1824, to March 22, 1827, Archivo del Congreso del Estado de

Andrew J. Torget

Coahuila (hereafter cited as ACEC), Saltillo, Mexico. The initial draft of Article 13 can also be found in SFA to the Coahuila-Texas Congress, August 11, 1826, *AP*, 2:1407.

20. José Antonio Saucedo to SFA, June 29, 1826; Baron de Bastrop to Robert Leftwich, about May 30, 1826; both in Malcolm D. McLean, ed., *Papers Concerning Robertson's Colony in Texas* (Fort Worth: Texas Christian University Press, 1974–1976), 2:596–597, 613.

21. See, for example, Article 11 in the Constitution of the State of Coahuila and Texas, 1827, reprinted in H. P. H. Gammel, ed., *The Laws of Texas, 1822–1897* (Austin, TX: Gammel Book Company, 1898), 1:424.

22. On political divisions within Coahuila and Texas, see Janicek, "The Development of Early Mexican Land Policy," 189–195; Andrés Tijerina, *Tejanos and Texas under the Mexican Flag, 1821–1836* (College Station: Texas A&M University Press, 1994), 113–136.

23. J. E. B. Austin to SFA, August 22, 1826, *AP*, 2:1430; José Saucedo to SFA, July 14, 1826, *AP*, 2:1371; José Saucedo to SFA, July 27, 1826, *AP*, 2:1390.

24. SFA to Coahuila-Texas legislature, August 11, 1826, *AP*, 1:1, 406–409 (quotations); SFA to Coahuila-Texas legislature, November 20, 1826, *AP*, 2:1507–1510.

25. SFA to José Saucedo, September 11, 1826, *AP*, 2:1452.

26. *Arkansas Gazette*, October 10, 1826, reprinted in the *Connecticut Courant*, November 20, 1826.

27. *Louisville Public Advertiser*, November 1, 1826.

28. *Richmond Enquirer* (VA), November 10, 1826; *Daily National Journal*, November 10, 1826.

29. *Providence Patriot* (RI), November 18, 1826; *Columbian Phenix*, November 18, 1826; *Connecticut Courant*, November 20, 1826; *Norwich Courier* (CT), November 22, 1826; *Newport Mercury* (RI), November 25, 1826; *African Repository and Colonial Journal* 2, no. 9 (November 1826): 291; *Vermont Chronicle*, December 1, 1826.

30. See, for example, *Boston Commercial Gazette*, November 16, 1826; *New York Daily Advertiser*, quoted in the *Newport Mercury* (RI), November 25, 1826. On the rise of US abolitionism, see David Brion Davis, *Inhuman Bondage: The Rise and Fall of Slavery in the New World* (Oxford: Oxford University Press, 2006), 231–267.

31. J. E. B. Austin to SFA, September 23, 1826, *AP*, 2:1461–1462.

32. Ibid.; J. E. B. Austin to SFA, October 10, 1826, *AP*, 2:1474; Baron de Bastrop to SFA, November 18, 1826, *AP*, 2:1505.

33. J. E. B. Austin to SFA, October 10, 1826, *AP*, 2:1474; Baron de Bastrop to SFA, November 18, 1826, *AP*, 2:1505 (quotation).

34. José María Viesca speech, November 30, 1826, APSO.

35. Dionisio Elizondo speech, November 30, 1826, APSO.

36. José María Viesca speech, November 30, 1826, APSO.

37. Santiago de Valle's, Dionisio Elizondo's, and José María Viesca's speeches, November 30, 1826, APSO.

38. Eugene C. Barker, *The Life of Stephen F. Austin, Founder of Texas, 1793–1836: A Chapter in the Westward Movement of the Anglo-American People* (1926; repr., Austin: University of Texas Press, 1969), 168–202; Edmund Morris Parsons, "The Fredonian Rebellion," *Texana* 5 (Spring 1967): 11–52.

39. SFA to John Williams and B. J. Thompson, December 14, 1826, *AP*, 2:1532–1533.

40. *Louisiana Advertiser*, January 12, 1827.

41. *New York Daily Advertiser*, February 8, 1827, reprinted in the *Pittsfield Sun* (MA), February 15, 1827.

42. See, for example, the *Pittsfield Sun* (MA), February 15, 1827, and the *New Hampshire Sentinel*, February 23, 1827.

43. *Niles' Weekly Register*, March 17, 1827.

44. *New York Observer*, date unknown (most likely mid-April 1827), reprinted in *The Farmer's Cabinet* (NH), April 21, 1827; *The Farmer's Cabinet*, April 21, 1827; *Berkshire Star* (MA), May 3, 1827; *Vermont Chronicle*, April 20, 1827; *Vermont Watchman and State Gazette*, May 1, 1827.

45. *The Farmer's Cabinet*, February 17, 1827.

46. Sessions of January 2–31, 1827, APSO.

47. SFA to the Coahuila-Texas legislature, November 20, 1826, *AP*, 2:1507–1510.

48. Debates of January 31, 1827, APSO.

49. Ibid.; session of March 11, 1827, APSO.

50. José Madero speech to the Coahuila y Texas Congress, July 7, 1827, Legajo 1, Expediente 43, Decreto 18, Congreso del Estado de Coahuila, Leyes, Decretos y Acuerdos (1827), Primer Congreso Constitucional (hereafter cited as PCC), Primer Periodo Ordinario, Comisión de Gobernación, ACEC.

51. Madero, González, and Tijerina to the Coahuila y Texas Congress, September 11, 1827, Congreso del Estado de Coahuila, Leyes, Decretos y Acuerdos (1827), Legajo 1, Expediente 43, Decreto 18, PCC, Primer Periodo Ordinario, Comisión de Gobernación, ACEC. In their speeches, Madero, González, and Tijerina quoted from Montesquieu's *The Spirit of the Laws*, book 15, chapters 1–2.

52. James Davis to SFA, January 30, 1827, *AP*, 2:1598.

53. Decreto 56, PCC, Segundo Periodo Ordinario, 1827–1828, Gobernación, Legajo 4, Expediente 15, ACEC; Tijerina, *Tejanos and Texas*, 116. For the full text of the law, see Decree no. 56, May 5, 1828, reprinted in Gammel, *The Laws of Texas*, 1:213.

54. The literature on debt peonage in Mexico is vast, but a helpful overview can

be found in Alan Knight, "Mexican Peonage: What Was It and Why Was It?" *Journal of Latin American Studies* 18 (May 1986): 41–74. For an in-depth treatment of the practice in Coahuila, see Charles Harris, *A Mexican Family Empire: The* Latifundio *of the Sánchez Navarros, 1765–1867* (Austin: University of Texas Press, 1975).

55. *New Orleans Halcyon and Literary Repository,* May 25, 1828, reprinted in the *Rhode-Island American and Providence Gazette,* June 20, 1828.

8

Linking Chains

Comanche Captivity, Black Chattel Slavery, and Empire in Antebellum Central Texas

Mark Allan Goldberg

In the mid-nineteenth century, Harrison Cole, a former slave, worked on the James E. Harrison plantation near Waco, in what is now central Texas. From this vantage point, Cole grew familiar with the workings of a nearby center of exchange, Torrey's Trading Post No. 2. A few miles south of Waco, on the Tehuacana Creek, John F. Torrey and his two brothers, David and Thomas, had established the trading house in the early 1840s to serve Indians, Anglo-Americans, and Europeans in the area. Torrey's Trading Post No. 2 became a place for exchange and diplomacy between Anglo-Americans and Native peoples, including Comanches, Cherokees, Wichitas, Wacos, and Tawakonis. Comanches regularly engaged in trade there, supplying the local market with buffalo and deer hides, horses, and mules, as well as Mexican, Native, Anglo-American, and African American captives whom the Indians had acquired through raids and exchange in other parts of Texas and in northern Mexico. In an interview, Cole described the general layout of the Tehuacana Creek Torrey house. The Torreys had constructed several cabins and designated each one for specific types of goods. According to Cole, "De biggest of dese wuz to keep de skins dat wuz brought by de Indians." In other cabins, traders placed their "supplies dat wuz for de Indians, to exchange for dey skins an' pelts an horses an' mules." When Comanches came to Torrey's Trading Post No. 2, they acquired guns and ammunition, wool blankets, copper, and groceries.[1] During the antebellum era, central

197

Texas became a meeting point for diverse populations in Texas and for networks of North American exchange that extended south into Mexico, throughout the Great Plains, and as far north as New York. As a result, two systems of slavery, Comanche captivity and slavery and black chattel slavery, intersected in the region, around Torrey's Trading Post No. 2.

In the wake of the establishment of Torrey's Trading Post No. 2, Natives and newcomers negotiated US conquest through trade. In antebellum central Texas, Comanches stood at the center of such negotiations, and their customs inadvertently intersected with the needs of Anglo-American settlers, many of whom owned African American slaves. By offering livestock for trade, Comanches provided the means that Anglo-Americans and slaves used to clear lands and plant crops in central Texas. They also consumed the cotton that slaves cultivated on Anglo-American farms and plantations throughout Texas at a time when the cotton economy in Texas was beginning to boom and Anglo-Americans were expanding westward.[2] These processes of exchange intertwined Indian captivity and slavery and black chattel slavery. Moreover, the trade and diplomacy that grew out of such cross-cultural encounters involved a number of Comanche, Anglo-American, and African American everyday practices—such as eating, moving about the countryside, preparing animal hides, clearing land, and cultivating crops. By examining these everyday activities, we can see how ordinary people influenced exchange and, in turn, imperial and national projects, such as geographic expansion and slavery.

Throughout the decade after the Torreys established their post, trade between Anglo-Americans and Comanches was a regular occurrence. But because Comanches provided goods that Anglo-American farmers used to establish themselves in the region, it ultimately fueled US westward expansion. By the time of the Civil War, the United States had pushed most Comanches north and west, allowing Anglo-Americans to take control of central Texas (figure 8.1). During conquest and colonization, Anglo-Americans used particular racial ideologies to justify Indian removal and African American enslavement. Even though many of these racial biases were scientifically based or discussed in broad terms, Anglo-American newcomers reframed their preconceived notions of race in ways specific to Texas, racializing Comanche practices, slave ownership, and slave labor. Thus, in addition to exploring exchange to understand how Anglo-Americans dealt with Comanche influence that initially hindered US expansion, we need to examine race to see how US imperialism was crafted on site.

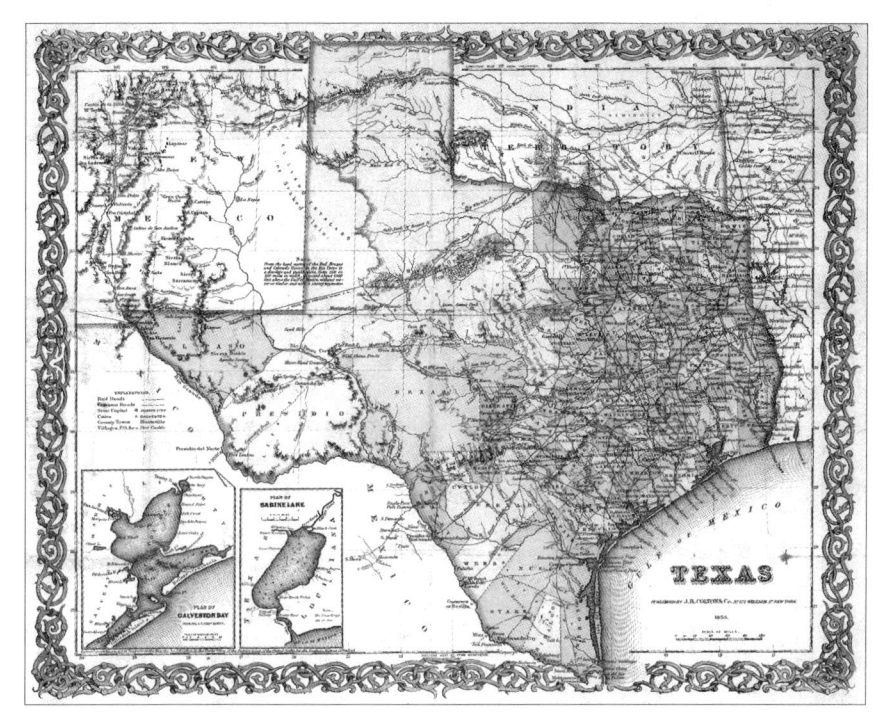

FIGURE 8.1
Texas, 1855. This map depicts the midcentury borderland between eastern Texas, which was divided into counties and incorporated into the United States, and Indian country in western Texas. Situated in McLennan County, the Torrey house was located on that borderland. The map was published by J. H. Colton and Company in 1855. (Courtesy of the David Rumsey Historical Map Collection, www.davidrumsey.com)

TRADE, WORK, AND CHATTEL SLAVERY IN ANTEBELLUM CENTRAL TEXAS

When Texas became a republic in 1836, its president, Sam Houston, ordered the construction of trade posts so that Anglo-Americans could develop economic and diplomatic relations with Texas Indians. The Torrey brothers founded posts in Austin, San Antonio, New Braunfels, and Fredericksburg, in central and south Texas. In 1843, they established Torrey's Trading Post No. 2 on Tehuacana Creek, a tributary of the Brazos River, north of Austin and near Waco. This Torrey house soon gained a monopoly over trade with Texas Indians, and Comanches traveled there regularly to exchange their processed buffalo skins, which were among the most valuable trade items.[3] In return, the Indians took blue wool blankets and fabric to make loincloths, copper wire to make ornaments, calico for shirts, knives, powder, and tobacco.[4] Comanche trade in buffalo continued into the 1850s and extended into Mexico. There, they traded the skins for hatchets, knives, calico, and mescal.[5] Some of these goods then reentered the market for further exchange. Demand for hides remained high throughout the first half of the nineteenth century, feeding Comanche trade.

Upon establishing the trade post, the Torreys entered into an existing system of exchange and diplomacy in central Texas that heavily involved the roughly twelve thousand Comanches who inhabited Texas.[6] In the mid-1840s, Torrey's Trading Post No. 2 became a major trade hub, and it also served as a site of diplomacy for the Texas republican government and Texas Indians. Working to reverse the republic's brutal Indian policy of the late 1830s, republican officials held a series of meetings in 1844 with Native peoples in central Texas, moving between the Torrey house and what was known as the Council Grounds just west of the trade post. Some Native peoples, like the Wacos and Wichitas, established peace treaties with the republic early on in the process. The Comanches had gone south to Mexico, however, missing all but the last council meeting. In 1845, the final assembly was held at Torrey's Trading Post No. 2, where the republican government and the Comanches established a truce. Soon afterward, the United States annexed Texas, and the Torrey house again served as a diplomatic space, this time for relations between Texas Indians and the US federal government.[7]

The Torrey house meetings suggest the importance of trade in Native-republic diplomacy, and the truces helped foster trade between Comanches and Anglo-Americans. Both parties offered an array of goods, and both participated in human trafficking. Comanches fueled black chattel slavery through exchange. Central Texas agriculture experienced rapid growth in the mid-nineteenth century, and Comanche trade became tied to Anglo-American farmers' agricultural pursuits.[8] According to historians Richard Lowe and Randolph Campbell, the region saw the development of more farms than most other parts of Texas during the 1850s. Farmers there primarily grew corn and wheat, some grew cotton, and others raised cattle and hogs. The majority of Anglo-American farmers in central Texas did not own slaves, and the majority of Texas slaves lived in eastern Texas, where some counties had three thousand, four thousand, and even seven thousand slaves. On the other hand, in 1855, the combined slave population of McLennan County, where Torrey's Trading Post No. 2 was located, and Travis County, directly to the south, numbered about thirty-one hundred slaves. Central Texas only began to attract Anglo-American migrants in earnest in the 1840s, accounting for many of the disparities in the slaveholding and slave populations when compared with those of the East. Out of about 750 farmers living in north-central Texas at midcentury, for example, some 140 owned slaves.[9] Despite the uneven population numbers, African American slaves did constitute a significant part of farming labor in the region. And by providing livestock and farming tools, Comanche trade shaped both Anglo-American and African American labor.

Anglo-American farmers and black slaves used horses and other animals that Comanches brought to the Torrey house to work Anglo-American-owned farms. Slaves and farmers performed the strenuous labor of corn, wheat, and cotton cultivation.[10] They employed horse-drawn plows to clear and prepare farmland. Joe Oliver, a slave in Hill County, for example, used horses to plow James Gatlin's farm.[11] Some farmers owned horse-powered machines to process crops like wheat and cotton. On the Harrison plantation near Waco, for example, slaves ran wheat through an "old fashioned thresher dat wuz driven by a horse on what dey called de treadmill, he would go roun an' roun to keep de mill goin' an' dis is why dey call hit de tread mill." Farmers from the Waco area would travel to General James Harrison's farm to process their wheat, increasing the workload for Harrison's slaves, which already included the cultivation of "cotton, corn, cane, oats, cow peas, an' wheat."[12] About sixty miles east of Waco, Burke Simpson and other slaves on Rod Oliver's farm processed the cotton they picked with a horse-powered cotton gin. According to Simpson, "Wid good steady work dey would gin 'bout four bales a day" using the device.[13] Some slaves were in charge of tending farmers' and planters' horses, a job generally performed by slaves in Comanche communities as well. For example, George Glasker, a slave on Tom Mullins's farm near Waco, recalled that a slave called Uncle Bill tended Mullins's horses. According to Glasker, Uncle Bill could tame wild horses: "[When] w'ite folks races [horses] in de later years I has often wished dat uncle Bill could have been there to tell dem a few things 'bout horses."[14] Horses played an important role in slaves' daily chores in farms and plantations around Texas.

Unlike in other parts of the state, central Texas farmers acquired their horses at Torrey's Trading Post No. 2. Joe Oliver and other slaves who worked the James Gatlin farm used horses that Indians had made available. Oliver recalled that "Indians," probably Comanches, had brought the horses "to de tradin' post called Torreys," where Gatlin had purchased them.[15] Other slaves also asserted the importance of the Torrey trade post to Anglo-Americans in the area. According to Harrison Cole, General Harrison frequented the Torrey house "because hit wuz de closest tradin place to de

Harrison Plantation."[16] And Anderson Jones, who lived in the Waco area, noted that other settlers who lived along the Brazos River in central Texas patronized the post.[17] The movement of horses from raids in northern Mexico, around Texas, to the Torrey Trading Post, and then around the plains demonstrates the value of livestock in the Texas borderlands and the magnitude of Comanche trade networks, which quite possibly linked with the exchange networks that historian Natale Zappia describes extended outward from Southern California and the North American Southwest (see chapter 5 in this volume).

In addition to the farm goods that Comanches provided for Anglo-American farmers, Comanche practices intersected with chattel slavery in another way: Comanches targeted African Americans as potential captives and introduced captured black slaves into trade markets.[18] Slaves openly feared the Indians and responded to such insecurities in a variety of ways. Living on the Gatlin plantation in Hill County, Joe Oliver described the pervasiveness of Comanche raids when he told an interviewer, "Indians... wuz de most we thought about befo' de [Civil War], for we wuz always afraid de Comanches...would cum an' steal our Massa's oxen, cattle."[19] Slaves knew that Comanches raided only at night. Jim Johnson, for example, once saw a small group of Comanches roaming around his home at Samuel Sampson's farm after nightfall.[20] African American slaves tried to protect themselves after dusk. Joe Oliver's parents advised their son to be wary and stay "awake for de Indians."[21] And at the Frierson farm in Bosque County, Alice Harwell's mother never lit lamps in her cabin after sundown, to prevent detection by Comanche and other Native raiders.[22] In interviews, none of the former slaves recalled witnessing the Comanche capture of black neighbors. But the precautionary measures taken in central Texas slave communities suggest that the prospect of captivity was very real for them.

Traders, state officials, and captives elsewhere did witness Comanches seize and trade black slaves. For example, when Caddo traders exchanged two Anglo-American women, Dolly and Patsy Webster, to the Comanches, Dolly Webster encountered an African American slave back at the rancheria. The slave had gone to south Texas with his Anglo-American master when a group of Comanches raided the area. According to Webster, the Anglo-American "was killed by these Indians in a Spanish town on the Rio-Grande," and the raiders captured his slave.[23] In addition, the Comanches and the Texas Republic signed a treaty in 1838 that directly addressed stolen property, including African American slaves. The treaty stipulated that Comanches return any stolen property to the rightful owner or to the Indian agents of the Texas Republic.[24] Indeed, Indian Agent Thomas

Western reported that a Comanche returned a black slave to Texas authorities in 1844.[25] This exchange demonstrates that some goodwill existed between Comanches and the Texas Republic, who were brought together in part by the exchange of black captives.

The Comanche capture and return of African American runaways also shows that Comanches viewed black slaves in the same way they viewed others—as potential trade commodities. And as with other goods, Comanches brought black captive slaves to the five Torrey trading houses to sell or trade. George Barnard worked as a trader for the Torreys and later purchased Trading Post No. 2, and he recorded several transactions that included Comanches selling black slaves. In 1845, Comanches sold two African American slaves, Paul and Charles, to the trade house for $100 apiece. Barnard also described two other transactions that year, one in which Comanches received $75 for a black slave and another in which they collected $325 for slaves and horses. According to Barnard, "Cases like these frequently came up in the course of ordinary trading house business."[26] Comanches saw African Americans as trade commodities and captured slaves, some of whom had been traded by whites from areas farther east and north and who might be traded by their white masters yet again. For enslaved African Americans, Comanches added another prospect for displacement and involuntary servitude.[27] The precipitous decline in buffalo in the nineteenth century hurt the Comanches' ability to sustain themselves and to engage in trade, but they continued to raid for prisoners.[28] Because of years of suffering—from famine that coincided with a series of epidemics—they adopted more captives into their families than before and traded fewer away.[29] Despite the decline in Comanche captive exchange, African American slaves in central Texas still saw the Comanche raiders as a threat.

COMANCHE CAPTIVITY AND SLAVERY IN THE TEXAS BORDERLANDS

Comanches traveled far and wide to carry out raids to obtain trade goods, captives, and food and to seek grasslands in order to nourish their extensive horse herds.[30] Raiding was central to the social, political, and economic processes and changes that occurred in the region. The practice of raiding was, by the nineteenth century, a very old one. When Spaniards introduced horses into northern New Spain and as Comanches and other Native peoples adopted equestrianism and adapted to the Spanish colonial process, violent raiding spread across the borderlands. The nomadic Utes, for example, found Spanish and Native trade partners in New Mexico, and they raided sedentary Indian communities in the Great Basin for goods and captives to exchange. The exchange economy that Spaniards and Indians developed in the colonial era continued to shape life in the borderlands after Mexican independence. A regional economy predicated on Indian raiding displaced violence throughout the North American West as Comanches and other equestrian Indians raided settlements and villages throughout the borderlands in order to participate in the exchange economy and, in the case of the Comanches, to build a trading empire.[31]

Raiding often became violent, and it involved the capture and trafficking of human bodies. Physical force helped power Comanche trade and expansion since it evoked fear among inhabitants, helping Comanches dominate the Texas landscape from Nacogdoches to the Rio Grande Valley to western Texas. After the end of Spanish rule in 1821, Mexican officials assessed the government's existing relationship with the Comanches, which forced them to address the Indians' captivity of Mexican people. José Francisco Ruíz reported, "They have over 900 prisoners with them, not counting the many who have managed to escape after suffering great hardships."[32] The Mexican state had difficulty stopping the exchange in captives, for the practice was extensive and Mexicans also participated in it. These violent attacks terrified settlers not only because of the physical pain involved but also because of the emotional pain they suffered if they were captured. After Comanches took prisoners, they often traded them in captive markets. They kept some captives and used them for slave labor, and they adopted others into their communities.

For Comanches, raids produced sustenance, tools, and in some cases wealth, prestige, and sex; for captives, raids brought torment and abuse. After Comanches took prisoners, the captives' experiences varied. In general, Comanche captors tested their prisoners' ability to adapt to rancheria life by forcing them to perform backbreaking work and suffer physical cruelties, particularly in the initial stage of captivity. Captives fell to the whims of their masters. The Anglo-American trader and traveler Josiah Gregg observed the treatment of prisoners and remarked that when a captive arrived in a Comanche rancheria, "each [Comanche] seem[ed] entitled to a blow, a kick, a pinch, a bite, or whatever simple punishment they [chose] to inflict upon the unfortunate captives.... This done," Gregg continued, "[prisoners were] delivered over to the captors as slaves, and put to the service and drudgery of the camp."[33] A captive's treatment depended largely on the personality of each individual captor. Captive women served mainly as servants and sometimes as sexual partners. They had to prepare hides, make clothes, and cook. Male prisoners generally took care of horses, and they were forced to participate in gambling contests like horse racing and fighting.[34] Oftentimes, Comanche women inflicted cruelty on female captives. Encamped along the San Saba River in what is now central Texas, for example, a few Comanche women were trying to gather honey from a hive situated in the ledge of a cliff. Unsuccessful at their attempt, they forced the Anglo-American captive Dolly Webster to try. They tied a rope around Webster and lowered her down toward the hive. Flailing wildly as the bees flew around her, Webster could not collect honey. According to the captive, the Comanche women then struck her several times and burned her hair and hands.[35] Similarly, during her long days of hauling wood, hunting, and tending to small animals, Jane Adeline Wilson claimed that the Native women were the "cause of the new cruelties…[she] began to experience." If, in their eyes, she worked slowly or poorly, they poked her with spears or whipped her.[36]

Comanche men sometimes raped captive women, further asserting power over female prisoners. The historical record reveals only a few examples of sexual abuse, and a Comanche incest taboo may have protected some women who were adopted into the community.[37] Moreover, Howard White Wolf, who was Comanche, recalled that "in the old days…if [captives] married a Comanche, they got the same rights as full bloods, children the same."[38] However, sources suggest that some male captors committed sexual violence and forced themselves onto female captives.[39] For example, Anglo-American captive Nelson Lee recalled the treatment of three English captive women. Marietta Haskins and her daughters Margaret and Harriett were on their way to Utah with a group of Mormon missionaries when Comanches at Eagle Pass, Texas, attacked them. The Indians took the women and children and distributed them upon arrival at the rancheria. Marietta "was made a common drudge in camp." Eventually, she became so ill that her captors killed and scalped her. "The daughters," Lee continued, "were appropriated by two burly warriors, and compelled to serve [the men], both in the capacity as slaves and wives."[40] Surely, by "slaves" Lee meant that Margaret and Harriett Haskins performed the labor that Comanches relegated to women. By "wives" he may have meant that the women became "chore wives," or captive women who worked in polygynous homes alongside a man's other wives and who adopted captive children.[41] Lee may also have been suggesting that, as slaves and so-called wives, the Haskins sisters forcibly "served" the two captors sexually.

Another story, concerning the daughter of the governor of Chihuahua at the turn of the nineteenth century, also suggests sexual abuse. Josiah Gregg recalled that the kidnapped governor's daughter refused to return to her home and stayed with the Comanches. According to Gregg, she sent word to her father that her captors tattooed and "disfigured her," that she was married and possibly pregnant, and "that she would be more unhappy by returning to her father under these circumstances than by remaining where she was." In her message to her father, she weighed two unfavorable scenarios: one in which she did not return home, the other in which she did return home, but disfigured, pregnant, dishonored, and ashamed.[42] Because she portrayed her decision of whether to stay or go as a lose-lose situation, she likely had little choice entering into marriage with a Comanche man. And if she did not recognize her partnership with her husband as a true marriage, then she probably would have considered sex with him as an improper act since according to Mexican gender and sexual norms, premarital sex was an act of dishonor for women.[43] Because female captives became commodities that linked different communities, captive taking reinforced exchange. At the same time, however, it reinforced male power, female subordination, and the violation of women's bodies in Comanche rancherias.

Because of the burgeoning captive market, prisoners could always become valuable trade commodities, even if marriage, adoption, and the Comanche incest taboo might have protected individual captives from certain abuses. Nelson Lee, for example, was traded twice after he entered into a covenant with Comanche Chief Big Wolf, which had stipulated that Lee remain subservient to Big Wolf in exchange for relative freedom in the community, including the rights to marry, carry a knife, participate in Comanche rituals, and accompany the chief on hunts and visits to other camps.[44] For two centuries, captives had entered the borderlands exchange economy with horses, hides, mules, and other trade goods.[45] This system of exchange continued in Texas after Spanish and Mexican rule. Captives were valuable commodities through the Mexican period and after Texas seceded from Mexico in 1836, even when the number of African American slaves in Texas was increasing. Most slaveholding Anglo-American migrants settled in east Texas, beyond the reach of the Comanches.[46] In the 1830s, Comanche peace with Mexicans, Anglo-American Texans, and Native peoples to the east and north provided security for the Comanches in Texas. After the peace, the Comanches redirected raids southward, farther away from slaveholding farms and plantations in east Texas. Comanche captive exchange continued, however, and the Texas borderlands still served as economic zones for Comanche trade, despite the flood of slaveholding settlers who established profitable farms and plantations in east Texas.

The extensiveness of Comanche and Anglo-American trade raises questions about how individuals participated in the regional economy through their daily activities and about how exchange structured life away from the trade posts. We have seen how trade shaped Anglo-Americans' and black slaves' farm work. For the Comanches, raiding and hunting directly fed trade, all of which involved other sets of cultural practices. Comanche mobility, day-to-day work, and diet influenced the development and maintenance of trade networks that linked Comanche rancherías to traders at the Torrey houses, in the Great Plains, the Rocky Mountains, and eastern Texas, and that bound together Comanche captivity and black chattel slavery.[47]

Comanches moved often and traveled long distances, which served particular social purposes: to feed the community, to sustain horse herds, to acquire useful goods, and to accumulate wealth. We can therefore think of Comanche mobility as a social and cultural phenomenon.[48] Race, class, gender, sex, nation building, and imperialism marked mobility: only men went on hunts; women prepared meats for consumption and processed hides to trade; mainly elite men enjoyed material returns on trade; economic transactions and the related violence of raiding helped the Comanches expand their influence in the region; Comanche men had sex with captives; exchange fed the Mexican, Texas republican, and US economies; and trade helped the United States achieve hegemony in central Texas by the time of the Civil War. Through constant mobility, Comanches nurtured trade, which in turn shaped Comanche communities themselves.

Comanches defined social roles around various practices. For example, Comanche foodways affected how individuals saw themselves and the people around them and helped structure their communities.[49] Eating connected diet and work. Meat, particularly buffalo, was a staple of the Comanches' diet. The Indians migrated frequently to bison-rich areas, their large collection of horses allowing them to cover extensive ground. In winter, Mexican official José Francisco Ruíz noted, "Bears, deer, wild boars, minks, and beavers descend from the north.... All these animals are hunted and eaten by the Comanches when buffaloes are scarce."[50] When Comanche men arrived in camp from a hunt, Comanche women would cut the meat into thin strips and hang them to dry.[51] Nelson Lee, a captive who lived with the Comanches in the 1850s, observed that for breakfast, the Indians mixed cooked meat, dried corn, and vegetables.[52] And Howard White Wolfe remembered that "the meat was either eaten raw or boiled. The brisket was always roasted. Ribs were removed from the side and the meat roasted."[53]

Foodways influenced gender formation in Comanchería. For example, the consumption of meat became linked with warrior identity. Comanche oral tradition from the nineteenth century illustrated the role of bison meat in ideas of Comanche manhood. Comanches believed that after death, the spirit of the dead went down one of three roads. Those who died of natural causes traveled a road strewn with signs of mourning, eliciting constant feelings of sadness. The second road, for those who died bewitched, followed a path lined with ashes and rough, prickly vegetation. This road led nowhere, and the spirits constantly wandered along it. The third road was reserved for warriors who died in battle and was flanked by lush vegetation, beautiful rivers, and "meadows abounding in fat buffaloes." It led to paradise, where the heroes became children of the sun and lived in eternal happiness.[54] The reward of abundant buffalo after death demonstrated the central importance of bison and of military bravery in Comanche culture. For Comanches, military prowess influenced a number of social interactions. Older, experienced warriors, or *lobos*, for instance, met high standards of honor and gained much prestige within Comanche communities. Lobos advised younger warriors to die in battle rather than retreat, regardless of their superiors' orders. Spurning such orders was a sign of bravery, not insubordination. Moreover, Comanche women policed Comanche male honor by demanding bravery and scorning failure. Lobos advised young women to marry only those men who proved their bravery in battle and to spurn cowardly warriors. And communities rewarded Comanche successes in battle or raids with festivities.[55] According to José Francisco Ruíz, after raids, lobos were "allowed to take all the meat they desire[d] and eat whatever else they wish[ed] without anyone hindering them," again linking meat with military honor.[56] The reward for exhibiting one's male vitality and courage was extra meat both in life and in death.

The expansion of the hide market also affected gender in Comanchería. When demand for bison hides boomed, buffalos brought wealth to Comanche communities, in addition to providing nourishment. The focus on hides reshaped Comanche manhood and reinforced gendered divisions of labor. Comanches in Texas benefited from the transformation of buffalo into commodities, particularly male elites. By the turn of the nineteenth century, an individual's horse wealth led to other forms of material wealth and political power, marking a shift from before, when military success was the primary avenue to prestige. Horses allowed men to raid for livestock, captives, and other goods and to acquire wives with gifts, all of which created opportunities for amassing more wealth. Those men with large herds formed the new aristocracy. They loaned livestock to horseless young men, rendering the latter social dependents. By acquiring wealth, moreover, elite men continually gave gifts to community members, which allowed them to become heads of their own rancherias. Horse wealth, then, was a marker of prestigious Comanche manhood, while young men without horses, women, and slaves sat at the bottom of the social ladder. Freedom from physical labor was another elite male marker, for elites' dependents performed day-to-day tasks, like cooking and the backbreaking work that successful trade ventures required.[57]

Much of the violence and physical labor of the hide trade fell on the backs of Comanche women and female captives. Women were primary targets for captivity. Inside Comanchería, moreover, the large-scale market production of skins influenced marital patterns, expanding the practice of polygyny, a marriage structure in which Comanche men had several wives. As Comanches enlarged their herds of livestock for trade, they faced shortages of labor to tend the animals. Some chose to stop amassing livestock; others turned to polygyny and slavery to increase their labor force.[58] Mexican official José María Sánchez described the women's tasks after men returned from a hunt: "[Comanche women] bring in the animals that are killed, they cut and cure the meat, tan the hides, make the clothes and arms of the men, and care for the horses."[59] Female captives also dressed animal hides. Comanches forced Sarah Ann Horn to do such work, and she detailed the process in her captivity narrative. First, she laid out the skin smoothly and shaved off all of the hair with a knife. She then dug a large hole in the ground and filled it with water. She placed the skin in the hole and tramped on it for an hour or two, depending on its toughness. Afterward, she carefully stretched the hide to dry it.[60] The growing market in buffalo hides increased grueling labor practices for Comanche women and slaves, marking them as laborers and allowing men with large herds to gain and maintain prestige. Women and captive slaves' work directly fed trade and brought material wealth to Comanche communities. Active participation in the hide trade, however, fell on the shoulders of the least empowered people in Comanche society.

RACE, REMOVAL, AND SLAVERY

Comanche participation in trade and their control of trade networks throughout the first half of the nineteenth century helped them expand their own authority and hinder US expansion for a time. But only about ten years after the construction of Torrey's Trading Post No. 2, hundreds of Comanches moved onto reservations due west of the trading firm. Backed by a significant military presence, Anglo-Americans had firmly implanted themselves in central Texas by linking regional agriculture to the US national economy at a time when Comanches were suffering from the massive decline of the bison population. Anglo-American Texans essentially ended trade relations with their Native neighbors and pushed the Comanches westward. The Comanche customs and trading practices that had driven exchange between Anglo-Americans and Comanches were the same practices that Texas lawmakers and Anglo-American settlers now characterized as threats to US civilization and were now used to justify Comanche removal. In the mid-1850s, economies that were once bound together broke apart, and many Comanches decided that their best option was to relocate onto reserves in western Texas.

Anglo-Americans who moved west felt that they were bringing "civilization" to an "uncivilized" place. They carried preconceived notions of African American, Native, and Mexican "races," which shaped how chattel slavery and westward expansion unfolded in Texas.[61] However, the racial ideologies that they crafted in scientific laboratories and popular publications back east do not tell the whole story about the role of race in US expansion. Anglo-American farmers who settled near Torrey's Trading Post No. 2 most likely shared in the popular notion that they were superior to the Comanches they encountered, and they most certainly felt superior to their African American slaves. At the same time, though, many Anglo-American farmers had to rely on so-called racially inferior Comanches for the tools to successfully farm their own lands. As Anglo-Americans encountered resident populations and made sense of how Texas would become part of the United States, they reformulated and rearticulated existing racial ideas in local terms, defining Comanche practices as improper, uncivilized, and even unhealthy. They clarified how Anglo-Americans would maintain their position of power in central Texas, how Comanches would be removed from American society, and how black slaves would be securely chained to the Texas political economy.

By painting Comanche customs as both savage and unhealthy, Anglo-American military surgeons helped lay the political groundwork for Comanche removal. In the 1850s, the US surgeon general sent military physicians to US Army posts in the West and required them to record the health of soldiers in their respective forts and the health and customs of Indians in the area, along with information on local climate, flora, fauna, and geography. He then compiled these medical topographies, as they were known, from all US forts recorded between 1839 and 1855. And in 1856, the US Congress published the *Statistical Report on the Sickness and Mortality in the Army of the United States*. All of the Texas medical topographies were written in the mid-nineteenth century when the United States was trying to prepare south and west Texas for Anglo-American settlement, linking military medical practice to US nation and empire building.

Physicians in west Texas reported that the Comanches were a weak and unhealthy people largely because their lifestyles made them susceptible to disease. The doctors injected health into notions of both civilization and savagery and saw Anglo-American sedentary agrarianism as the healthiest way to live. In 1853, for example, US Army assistant surgeon S. Wylie Crawford wrote that most of the Comanches who lived near his post at Fort McKavett had died from respiratory illnesses. He identified a number of causes for the disease: "The lungs are, no doubt, weakened by the universal habit of drawing tobacco-smoke into them.... Their low houses are heated to excess, and they lie upon the ground; and this, often when the body is relaxed and profusely perspiring. They are indolent, and, with few exceptions, they are physically weak." Crawford also commented on Comanche diet. He noted that "their food [was] often insufficient," probably because the bison population had declined by now and because the Comanches had seen their access to hunting grounds slowly diminish.[62] Images of sick and weak Comanches helped Crawford identify his Indian neighbors as inferior. Crawford surely thought that he was just doing his job as a physician in explaining why the Comanches were getting sick; however, the US military mission, as well as the notion that Comanches were living the wrong way, shaped his diagnosis. So the issue here is not whether Crawford's diagnosis was accurate. Rather, what is important for understanding how Anglo-Americans perceived their Comanche neighbors is the racial picture Crawford painted inside a medical frame. According to the doctor, Comanches were unhealthy because of their physical weakness and laziness and because their cultural practices caused disease. Comanches slept on the ground in portable dwellings because they were nomadic, and tobacco smoking was part of some rituals. Crawford was contrasting the Indians with a way of life that he deemed both proper and healthy: sedentary agrarianism. He implied that if Comanches ceased to live nomadically, altered their practices, and lived more like Anglo-Americans did, then their health could improve, despite their inherent weakness.

Some west Texas military physicians brought Anglo-Americans directly into discussions of Comanche health. In 1852, US Army assistant surgeon Alexander B. Hasson also formulated a medical argument that "proved" that Comanches' nomadic practices caused sickness. He focused on Comanche men and boys and claimed not only that infant mortalities from exposure could be prevented, presumably by living a more sedentary life, but also that "in a civilized community, [those children] would have been reared to useful manhood."[63] Hasson suggested that Comanche men, who were in charge of hunting and trade, were not "useful" in the way that "civilized" Anglo-American men who practiced farming and ranching were and who, as a result, lived healthier lives. His narrative suggests that Comanche men's labor did not constitute true productive work, and similar to Crawford, he argued that Comanche nomadism caused health problems. Coming from a US Army surgeon, this assessment praising the healthiness of sedentary life was rooted in the military's role in facilitating US expansion into the West. Moreover, Comanche hunting and nomadism were tied to trading and raiding, which threatened US domination. The state government had been working hard to minimize Comanche raiding because it increased frontier violence and clashed with the practice of sedentary agriculture, which was central to US nation and empire building.

A few of the surgeons specifically surveyed Comanche body types to assess the Indians' health. Stationed at Camp J. E. Johnston, for example, Assistant Surgeon Ebenezer Swift described the Comanches as "large and well formed." To get a sense of what Swift meant by this sketch, we can look at the statistics he took on the age, girth, height, and weight of twenty Comanche men, which he felt gave a fair representation of the Comanches who lived around the camp. Of the twenty men, the average age was about thirty-one years old, average girth was 36.6 inches, average height was about 5 feet 7 inches, and average weight was 158.7 pounds. In Assistant Surgeon Swift's eyes, these Comanche men may have been physically large, but they did not "have...great muscular strength." For the surgeon, Comanche gendered divisions of labor accounted for different body types between men and women and for men's so-called physical weakness: "The women are short, thick-set, and proportionally stronger and more muscular than the men. [The women] do all the drudgery, dress their food and skins, cook, pitch tents, take care of the horses, etc."[64] According to Doctor Hasson, though, Comanche women did not always have "hardier constitutions," even if they were more muscular than the men. And Hasson claimed that exposure to extreme heat and cold weakened all Comanches.[65] He argued that Comanche dwellings inadequately protected the Indians from severe temperatures, which made them susceptible to illness. He further claimed that exposure made women especially vulnerable to disease and too weak to survive childbirth. His interpreter claimed that "among the Comanche women he [had] frequently known and heard of cases of death in childbirth, and that he [had] seen in the tribe many cases which he called rheumatism and consumption."[66] On the basis of their observations of everyday life, west Texas physicians "proved" Comanche unhealthiness and inferiority, using Anglo-Americans' agrarian lifestyles as the health standard and the counterpoint to Comanche living.

The military medical reports influenced Indian policy in Texas. In 1854, Texas governor E. M. Pease signed legislation that established two Clear Fork reserves on the Brazos River about 200 miles northwest of Torrey's Trading Post No. 2, opening up lands for slaveholding farmers and other Anglo-American settlers. Several Comanche chiefs agreed to move there, and hunger drove other bands in. By 1855, more than five hundred Comanches inhabited Clear Fork.[67] The following year, Texas Indian agent Robert Neighbors reported, "There has been great improvement last year in the moral and physical condition of the Indians now settled. They are gradually falling into the customs and dress of the white man; and by being well clothed, having houses to live in, and relieved from the continued anxieties attending a roving life, their health has greatly improved, and they now, for the first time for several years, begin to raise healthy children."[68] Outlining the advantages of reservation life and the advances that the Comanche "settlers" made, Neighbors used similar language as the physicians had before him. He valued the Comanches' shift from a nomadic lifestyle to the practice of subsistence agriculture and other Anglo-American customs, and he claimed that it was having a positive effect on Comanche health. In their reports on the Comanches, military doctors observed local customs and depicted Comanche life as unhealthy while pushing the healthiness of the nation's agrarian vision. The US government translated this vision into imperial practice with the west Texas reservations. For Indian Agent Neighbors, reservation life would civilize the Indians and, in turn, make them healthy. And Anglo-Americans would lead the way.

For Anglo-American Texans, their position at the top of the political and economic hierarchy extended beyond improving Comanche lives while expanding the US economy in central Texas; it also meant that, as masters, they alone could get the most out of black slave labor, which would additionally strengthen the regional and national economy. As Anglo-Americans pushed Comanches west, Anglo-American and Indian slaveholders continued to live side by side in eastern Texas. During Indian removal in the 1830s, slave-owning Indians migrated from the US South to Arkansas Territory, Texas, and Indian Territory.[69] Rebecca McIntosh, the daughter of Creek chief William McIntosh, for example, moved to Arkansas and married a Creek man named Benjamin Hawkins.[70] In 1833, Rebecca, Benjamin, their daughter Louisa, and their six slaves moved to Texas. Benjamin Hawkins passed away three years later, and Louisa obtained ownership of some of the family's slaves. In 1838, Rebecca McIntosh Hawkins married Spire Hagerty, who became Louisa's guardian and administrator of her slaves.[71] When Louisa Hawkins turned eighteen, she sought to reclaim her slaves and "their material increase." Spire Hagerty passed away around this time, and the administrators of his estate refused Louisa's request. So she petitioned to recover her property. During depositions, Hagerty's slave overseer, Benjamin Kimberling, argued that the slaves in question had not garnered much profit, which he attributed to the slaves' Native owners: "They were all what was called Indian negroes. Indian negroes were different from those raised by whites. They had not been trained to labor but acted more like free negroes and did pretty much as they pleased and continued to be so till by proper training they were reduced to subjection."[72]

In his testimony, Benjamin Kimberling depicted the ideal slave owner and the ideal slave laborer in a way that reflected Texas's multiracial makeup. He felt that African American slaves who worked for Indian masters were inferior to those who worked for white masters, tying notions about what made a "good" slave to a slave owner's race.[73] White proslavery advocates often argued that blacks were biologically fit for enslavement.[74] But for Kimberling and others who subscribed to the "Indian negro" idea, African American subjugation did not simply occur because of inherent inferiority. Slave owners had to mold African Americans to fit their racial position as slave laborers, and whites were the most suited to do so because of *their* racial superiority. Since the Creek Hawkinses owned the slaves in question, the slaves could not have produced the high profits that Louisa Hawkins sought, according to this racial logic. In a place that saw both Indian and Anglo-American slaveholders, Kimberling suggested that black fitness for slavery was not absolute and it was up to white slave owners to maximize slaves' productivity. A legacy of Indian removal, the image of the inferior "Indian negro" was now localized to the US West, where Anglo-American slaveholders competed with Indian slaveholders.

As Anglo-Americans wrested control of central Texas, they articulated some of their responsibilities as the leaders of the multiracial region: to civilize Comanches away from white society and to increase slave productivity. Slavery allowed migrants to realize their imperialistic ambitions and push Indians westward. When Anglo-Americans first arrived, Comanche trade made it possible for Anglo-American slaveholders to build up their farms, reinforcing whites' authority over their slaves—masters decided where their slaves went, where they slept, and much of what they ate. Sometimes, slaves were able to assert some control over their lives, by running away, by healing other slaves, or by presenting themselves in ways that could influence slave sales slightly in their favor.[75] Nevertheless, Anglo-American Texans kept blacks in their position as enslaved laborers and removed and confined Comanches to reservations, helping Anglo-Americans consolidate rule in the region and serving the US imperial mission. The Anglo-American system of racial slavery won out.

CONCLUSION

Anglo-American hegemony expanded with black chattel slavery into central Texas, a process that dates back to the 1820s and 1830s in the US North and South and Mexican Texas, as historians Calvin Schermerhorn (chapter 6 in this volume) and Andrew Torget (chapter 7) demonstrate. In the 1840s and early 1850s, Torrey's Trading Post No. 2 brought Comanche traders and Anglo-American farmers together, symbolizing the fluidity of power relations in the midcentury borderlands, since trade simultaneously allowed Comanches to maintain their influence and enabled Anglo-Americans to establish their farms. The systems of Comanche captivity and black chattel slavery overlapped through Comanche–Anglo-American exchange. Racial slavery helped Anglo-American leaders stake geographic claims in central Texas in the name of the Texas Republic and then the United States along the ambiguous border between eastern Texas, where most Anglo-Americans lived, and Comanchería to the west. After a brief period of steady Anglo-American–Comanche exchange, the US empire embedded itself in central Texas as the state dispossessed Comanches and took control of the region, a process that occurred on the backs of enslaved African Americans.

Torrey's Trading Post No. 2 contained materials, livestock, and human captives obtained by Comanches in raids and made them available to Anglo-American slaveholders. Comanche practices unwittingly helped Anglo-Americans subjugate African American slaves and stake land claims in central Texas. Farmers who had surplus crops sold them mainly within local markets, but they also supplied markets to the east.[76] The growth of these economic links to other parts of Texas and to national markets in the 1850s attracted more Anglo-Americans to central Texas and helped the state and US governments take control of the region from the Comanches. Moreover, the Comanches' dependence on horses, which had enabled them to dominate the region for centuries, contributed to their downfall. As they added to their horse herds, they required access to more grasslands for the animals to graze and came to rely on hunting bison for food and trade. But the number of buffalo declined rapidly in the nineteenth century, and an increasing population in Texas obstructed Comanche access to land for hunting and for feeding horses. The Comanches therefore faced economic and ecological catastrophe, which reduced their ability to subsist and to negotiate politically and economically on the frontier. In the 1850s, the

US government established the Clear Fork reservations in west Texas, and many Comanches moved there either by force or by choice. By the time of the Civil War, Anglo-American hegemony in central Texas meant that Comanches could no longer maintain a steady flow of goods through hunting, raiding, and trading.

Examining everyday practices in mid-nineteenth-century central Texas reveals that the networks that connected Comanches, Anglo-Americans, and African Americans included ordinary individuals, not just elites. All Comanches consumed bison meat, and Comanche and captive women processed the skins, feeding trade in bison hides along networks that linked diverse peoples throughout the region. In addition, Comanche commodities made their way into Anglo-American and African American farm work. Yet while various day-to-day practices connected different communities, westering Anglo-Americans rewrote racial ideologies based on their perceptions of many of these practices. In the eyes of Anglo-American military doctors, for example, the nomadic customs central to exchange weakened Comanches, and removal meant that Anglo-Americans could teach reservation Indians about healthy, civilized living away from white settlements. Moreover, Anglo-American slaveholders argued that African Americans were biologically suited to perform forced labor on central Texas farms but Anglo-Americans were best fit to extract the most profit from black slaves. In addition to the bonds that grew out of material exchange, Anglo-Americans discursively linked Comanches, African Americans, and Mexicans through invectives about race and civilization, envisioning a world in which Anglo-Americans conquered the nonwhite populations of the US West. This vision shaped life in the West beyond the Civil War and into the twentieth century. And through an examination of Indo-Hispano musical traditions in New Mexico (chapter 9 of this volume), literary scholar Enrique Lamadrid shows us that the legacies of racial violence and slavery are still very much with us today.

Notes

1. Harrison Cole interview, *The American Slave: A Composite Autobiography*, ed. George P. Rawick, supplement, series 2, vol. 3, *Texas Narratives*, part 2 (Westport, CT: Greenwood Press, 1979), 766–767 (hereafter cited as Rawick). Quotations from the WPA slave narratives appear as they do in the original written version. These quotations are white interviewers' renderings of African American speech in the 1930s, and white interviewers often misrepresented and stereotyped former slaves' speech. This presents a problem that we should consider when using this source and when reading quotes from the interviews. I believe that the WPA narratives are still an incredibly rich source

for the study of African American slavery, but we need to keep an eye on the problems of memory and social context that informed these interviews. For a discussion of the WPA slave narratives as a window into the everyday lives of slaves and of the problems associated with the narratives, see Deborah Gray White, *Ar'n't I a Woman?: Female Slaves in the Plantation South*, rev. ed. (New York: W. W. Norton, 1999), 22–25.

2. For more on the growth of the cotton economy in antebellum Texas, see Randolph B. Campbell, *An Empire for Slavery: The Peculiar Institution in Texas, 1821–1865* (Baton Rouge: Louisiana State University Press, 1989), 67–95; Quintard Taylor, *In Search of the Racial Frontier: African Americans in the American West, 1528–1990* (New York: W. W. Norton, 1998), 53–62.

3. Henry C. Armbruster, *The Torreys of Texas* (Buda, TX: Citizen Press, 1968), 23–24; John Willingham, "George Barnard: Trader and Merchant on the Texas Frontier," *Texana* 12, no. 4 (1974): 306–334.

4. Ferdinand Roemer, *Texas*, trans. Oswald Mueller (San Antonio, TX: Standard Printing Company, 1935), 192–194.

5. Nelson Lee, *Three Years among the Comanches: The Narrative of Nelson Lee, Texas Ranger* (Gulford, CT: Globe Pequot Press, 2004), 112. For a discussion of the uses of and the problems associated with Indian captivity narratives, see Kathryn Zabelle Derounian-Stodola and James Arthur Levernier, *The Indian Captivity Narrative, 1550–1900* (New York: Twayne Publishers, 1993).

6. For more on Comanche-Mexican relations in Texas prior to Texas independence, see Pekka Hämäläinen, *The Comanche Empire* (New Haven, CT: Yale University Press, 2008), 191–198. For the Comanche population in Texas, see Gary Clayton Anderson, *The Conquest of Texas: Ethnic Cleansing in the Promised Land, 1820–1875* (Norman: University of Oklahoma Press, 2005), 22.

7. Walter Prescott Webb, "The Last Treaty of the Republic of Texas," *Southwestern Historical Quarterly* 25, no. 3 (January 1922): 151–173.

8. Roemer, *Texas*, 193; Armbruster, *Torreys of Texas*, 24.

9. These statistics can be found in Campbell, *An Empire for Slavery*, 264–266, and Richard G. Lowe and Randolph B. Campbell, *Planters and Plain Folk: Agriculture in Antebellum Texas* (Dallas: Southern Methodist University Press, 1987), 30–34.

10. Dr. I. R. R., "Great Facility of Raising Corn in Texas," in *Texas Almanac for 1859* (Galveston, TX: Willard Richardson, 1859), 73–74.

11. Joe Oliver interview, in Rawick, series 2, vol. 8, 2986.

12. Harrison Cole interview, in Rawick, series 2, vol. 3, 771.

13. Burke Simpson interview, in Rawick, series 2, vol. 9, 3557.

14. George Glasker interview, in Rawick, series 2, vol. 5, 1504.

15. Joe Oliver interview, in Rawick, series 2, vol. 8, 2986.

16. Harrison Cole interview, in Rawick, series 2, vol. 3, 767.

17. Anderson Jones interview, in Rawick, series 2, vol. 6, 2064–2065.

18. William Dean Carrigan, "Slavery on the Frontier: The Peculiar Institution in Central Texas," *Slavery and Abolition* 20, no. 2 (1999): 63–96.

19. Joe Oliver interview, in Rawick, series 2, vol. 8, 2985.

20. Jim Johnson interview, in Rawick, series 2, vol. 6, 2017.

21. Joe Oliver interview, in Rawick, series 2, vol. 8, 2985–2986.

22. Alice Harwell interview, in Rawick, series 2, vol. 5, 1666.

23. Benjamin Dolbeare, *A Narrative of the Captivity and Suffering of Dolly Webster among the Camanche Indians in Texas* (New Haven, CT: Yale University Library, 1986), 20.

24. Republic of Texas, Treaty between Texas and the Comanche Indians, May 29, 1838, in *Texas Indian Papers*, vol. 1, *1825–1843*, ed. Dorman H. Winfrey (Austin: Texas State Library, 1960), 50–52.

25. Thomas G. Western to Benjamin Sloat, December 14, 1844, in *Texas Indian Papers*, vol. 2, *1844–1845*, ed. Dorman H. Winfrey (Austin: Texas State Library, 1960), 152–153.

26. John K. Strecker, *Chronicles of George Barnard: The Indian Trader of the Tehuacana, and Other Bits of Texas History* (Waco, TX: Baylor University, 1928), 14.

27. For more on the slave trade within the United States, see Ira Berlin, *Generations of Captivity: A History of African-American Slaves* (Cambridge, MA: Belknap Press of Harvard University Press, 2003), 161–244; Steven Deyle, *Carry Me Back: The Domestic Slave Trade in American Life* (New York: Oxford University Press, 2005); Walter Johnson, *Soul by Soul: Life inside the Antebellum Slave Market* (Cambridge, MA: Harvard University Press, 1999); Michael Tadman, *Speculators and Slaves: Masters, Traders, and Slaves in the Old South* (Madison: University of Wisconsin Press, 1989).

28. Andrew C. Isenberg, *The Destruction of the Bison: An Environmental History, 1750–1920* (Cambridge: Cambridge University Press, 2000).

29. Hämäläinen, *The Comanche Empire*, 292–320.

30. Pekka Hämäläinen, "The Politics of Grass: European Expansion, Ecological Change, and Indigenous Power in the Southwest Borderlands," *William and Mary Quarterly* 67, no. 2 (April 2010): 173–208.

31. For more on Utes and the displacement of violence in the borderlands, see Ned Blackhawk, *Violence over the Land: Indians and Empires in the Early American West* (Cambridge, MA: Harvard University Press, 2006). For trade and the development of the Comanche empire, see Hämäläinen, *The Comanche Empire*, 141–180.

32. José Francisco Ruíz, *Report on the Indian Tribes of Texas in 1828*, ed. John C. Ewers, trans. Georgette Dorn (New Haven, CT: Yale University Library, 1972), 9.

33. Josiah Gregg, *Commerce of the Prairies; or, The Journal of a Santa Fé Trader, during*

Eight Expeditions across the Great Western Prairies, and a Residence of Nearly Nine Years in Northern Mexico, vol. 2 (New York: Henry G. Langley, 1844), 316–317.

34. For more on the variety of captives' experiences, see Joaquín Rivaya-Martínez, "Captivity and Adoption among the Comanche Indians, 1700–1875" (PhD diss., University of California–Los Angeles, 2006), 162–178, 190–243.

35. Dolbeare, *A Narrative of the Captivity*, 22.

36. Jane Adeline Wilson, *A Thrilling Narrative of the Sufferings of Mrs. Jane Adeline Wilson during Her Captivity among the Comanche Indians* (Fairfield, WA: Ye Galleon Press, 1971), 16–18, quote on 16.

37. James F. Brooks, *Captives and Cousins: Slavery, Kinship, and Community in the Southwest Borderlands* (Chapel Hill: University of North Carolina Press, 2002), 187–190.

38. Anthropologist Waldo Rudolph Wedel's interview with Howard White Wolf, August 2, 1933, in *Comanche Ethnography*, ed. Thomas W. Kavanagh (Lincoln: University of Nebraska Press, 2008), 327.

39. In his work on the Comanche empire, Pekka Hämäläinen describes Comanche traders publicly raping female captives at a trade fair in New Mexico. While this chapter focuses on less public forms of sexual abuse, this is another important example of how sexual violence became part of some captives' experiences. Hämäläinen, *The Comanche Empire*, 45.

40. Lee, *Three Years among the Comanches*, 135–138.

41. Hämäläinen, *The Comanche Empire*, 257. For more on Comanche wives, see Juliana Barr, *Peace Came in the Form of a Woman: Indians and Spaniards in the Texas Borderlands* (Chapel Hill: University of North Carolina Press, 2007), 254.

42. Gregg, *Commerce of the Prairies*, 43–44.

43. For more on gender in colonial Mexico, see Steve J. Stern, *The Secret History of Gender: Women, Men, and Power in Late Colonial Mexico* (Chapel Hill: University of North Carolina Press, 1995).

44. Lee, *Three Years among the Comanches*, 109–110, 143–145.

45. For more on captive exchange in the colonial borderlands, see Barr, *Peace Came in the Form of a Woman*, 157–196, 247–286; Blackhawk, *Violence over the Land*, 55–118; Brooks, *Captives and Cousins*, 1–207; Hämäläinen, *The Comanche Empire*, 113, 138.

46. Campbell, *An Empire for Slavery*, 50–57.

47. Available sources make it difficult to measure the extensiveness of Comanche trade in numerical terms. But measuring trade in geographic terms can help us visualize how influential Comanche trade was. Comanche trade networks moved in and out of Comanchería in Texas and New Mexico and linked directly to communities across much of the North American West. For more on the extensiveness of Comanche trade in early nineteenth-century North America, see Hämäläinen, *The Comanche Empire*, 141–180.

48. For more on the idea of mobility as a social and cultural phenomenon, see Tim Cresswell, "Embodiment, Power, and the Politics of Mobility: The Case of Female Tramps and Hobos," *Transactions of the Institute of British Geographers* 24, no. 2 (1999): 176–179.

49. For more on food and imperial identities in North America, see Rebecca Earle, *The Body of the Conquistador: Food, Race and the Colonial Experience in Spanish America, 1492–1700* (New York: Cambridge University Press, 2012); Trudy Eden, *The Early American Table: Food and Society in the New World* (DeKalb: Northern Illinois University Press, 2008).

50. Ruíz, *Report on the Indian Tribes*, 8.

51. Lee, *Three Years among the Comanches*, 111; José María Sánchez, "A Trip to Texas in 1828," trans. Carlos E. Castañeda, *Southwestern Historical Quarterly* 29, no. 4 (April 1926): 262; and Waldo Rudolph Wedel's interview with Howard White Wolf, August 1, 1933, in Kavanagh, *Comanche Ethnography*, 315.

52. Lee, *Three Years among the Comanches*, 97–98.

53. Waldo Rudolph Wedel's interview with Howard White Wolf, August 1, 1933, in Kavanagh, *Comanche Ethnography*, 315.

54. Ruíz, *Report on the Indian Tribes*, 15–16.

55. For more on Comanche male honor, see Brian DeLay, *War of a Thousand Deserts: Indian Raids and the US–Mexican War* (New Haven, CT: Yale University Press, 2008), 120–122.

56. Ruíz, *Report on the Indian Tribes*, 11, 13, quote on 11.

57. Hämäläinen, *The Comanche Empire*, 259–269.

58. Ibid., 248.

59. Sánchez, "A Trip to Texas," 262.

60. Carl Coke Rister, ed., *Comanche Bondage: Dr. John Charles Beale's Settlement of La Villa de Dolores on Las Moras Creek in Southern Texas of the 1830s, with an Annotated Reprint of Sarah Ann Horn's Narrative of Her Captivity among the Comanches, Her Ransom by Traders in New Mexico and Return via the Santa Fé Trail* (Glendale, CA: A. H. Clark, 1955), 156–157.

61. For more on how ideas of race tied together US westward expansion and slavery in the minds of Anglo-Americans, see Reginald Horsman, *Race and Manifest Destiny: The Origins of American Racial Anglo-Saxonism* (Cambridge, MA: Harvard University Press, 1981); Ronald T. Takaki, *Iron Cages: Race and Culture in Nineteenth-Century America*, 2nd ed. (New York: Oxford University Press, 1990).

62. S. Wylie Crawford, "Medical Topography and Diseases of Fort McKavett," in *Statistical Report on the Sickness and Mortality in the Army of the United States, Compiled from the Records of the Surgeon General's Office; Embracing a Period of Sixteen Years, from January, 1839, to January, 1855*, ed. Robert H. Coolidge (Washington, DC: A. O. P. Nicholson, 1856), 392.

63. Alexander B. Hasson, "Medical Topography and Diseases of Post on Clear Fork of Brazos River (Phantom Hill)," in Coolidge, *Statistical Report*, 377.

64. Ebenezer Swift, "Medical Topography and Diseases of Camp J. E. Johnston," in Coolidge, *Statistical Report*, 384–385.

65. Nineteenth-century physicians saw exposure to severe cold or heat as a cause of illness. They worked to balance cold with heat, and vice versa. For an example of how a physician in the mid-nineteenth century wrote about exposure, see William B. Carpenter, "On the Supposed Value of Alcoholic Liquors in Maintaining the Heat of the Human Body under Exposure to Severe Cold," *London Medical Gazette* 46 (1850): 510–517.

66. Hasson, "Medical Topography and Diseases," 377. In the nineteenth century, "consumption" referred to tubercular phthisis, or tuberculosis. See John Forbes, Alexander Tweedie, John Conolly, and Robert Dunglison, eds., *Cyclopaedia of Practical Medicine: Comprising Treatises on the Nature and Treatment of Disease, Materia Medica and Therapeutics, Medical Jurisprudence, Etc., Etc.*, vol. 4 (Philadelphia: Lea and Blanchard, 1850), 489.

67. Hämäläinen, *The Comanche Empire*, 308–309.

68. Robert Neighbors to George W. Manypenny, September 18, 1856, in US Office of Indian Affairs, *Report of the Commissioner of Indian Affairs* (Washington, DC: A. O. P. Nicholson, 1856), 173.

69. For more on Indians and black chattel slavery, see Daniel F. Littlefield Jr., *Africans and Seminoles: From Removal to Emancipation* (Westport, CT: Greenwood Press, 1977), and *Africans and Creeks: From the Colonial Period to the Civil War* (Westport, CT: Greenwood Press, 1979); Cynthia Cumfer, *Separate Peoples, One Land: The Minds of Cherokees, Blacks, and Whites on the Tennessee Frontier* (Chapel Hill: University of North Carolina Press, 2007); Tiya Miles, *Ties That Bind: The Story of an Afro-Cherokee Family in Slavery and Freedom* (Berkeley: University of California Press, 2005); Celia E. Naylor, *African Cherokees in Indian Territory: From Chattel to Citizens* (Chapel Hill: University of North Carolina Press, 2008); Theda Perdue, *Slavery and the Evolution of Cherokee Society, 1540–1866* (Knoxville: University of Tennessee Press, 1979); Claudio Saunt, *A New Order of Things: Property, Power, and the Transformation of the Creek Indians, 1733–1816* (Cambridge: Cambridge University Press, 1999), and *Black, White, and Indian: Race and the Unmaking of an American Family* (New York: Oxford University Press, 2005); Fay A. Yarbrough, *Race and the Cherokee Nation: Sovereignty in the Nineteenth Century* (Philadelphia: University of Pennsylvania Press, 2008).

70. Although McIntosh's husband, Benjamin Hawkins, shares the same name as US Indian agent Benjamin Hawkins, who was heavily involved with the Creeks in the late eighteenth century, historian Judith McArthur shows that McIntosh's husband was

not related to the well-known Indian agent. See Judith N. McArthur, "Myth, Reality, and Anomaly: The Complex World of Rebecca Hagerty," *East Texas Historical Journal* 24, no. 2 (Fall 1986): 22.

71. Ibid., 19–24.

72. Benjamin Kimberling's deposition in the Louisa Hawkins case can be found in *James C. Scott v. Cephus K. Andrews and James H. Hughes*, So. 5d 1849 (Nacogdoches Cty., TX, 1851). The documents of this case can be found in Petition 21585111 of the Race and Slavery Petitions Project, Series II: Petitions to Southern County Courts, 1775–1867. The Race and Slavery Petitions Project, housed at the University of North Carolina–Greensboro, has created a microfilm edition of tens of thousands of legislative and county court petitions that are only available in states' respective archives and county courthouses.

73. The label "Indian negro" was used in Texas also after the emancipation of slaves. See, for example, "The Law's Atonement," *Fort Worth Daily Gazette* (TX), January 21, 1887; "Six Men Hanged. One an Indian Negro, Four Straight-Out Mulattoes, and One a White Man—History of the Crimes," *Fort Worth Daily Gazette* (TX), April 28, 1888; "Six in One Day," *Mineola Monitor* (TX), May 5, 1888; "Given a Hundred Lashes," *Velasco Daily Times* (TX), May 13, 1892; "Went after Moonshiners," *Fort Worth Gazette* (TX), February 23, 1895.

74. See, for example, influential Texas politician and physician Ashbel Smith, January 9, 1849, folder "Journal, 1832–1857," box 2G234, Ashbel Smith Papers, 1823–1926, Briscoe Center for American History, University of Texas–Austin, and *An Oration Pronounced before the Connecticut Alpha of the Phi Beta Kappa at Yale College, New Haven, August 15, 1849* (New Haven, CT: B. L. Hamlen, 1849). This sentiment also appeared in the Texas Secession Convention, "A Declaration of Causes Which Impel the State of Texas to Secede from the Federal Union," in *Journal of the Secession Convention of Texas, 1861*, ed. Ernest William Winkler (Austin, TX: Austin Printing Company, 1912), 61–65. For more on ideas of blackness at this time, see Horsman, *Race and Manifest Destiny*, 122–127.

75. For more on slave resistance in the slave market, see Johnson, *Soul by Soul*, 162–188. For more on runaway slaves in central Texas, see Carrigan, "Slavery on the Frontier," 63–96. For different forms of running away, see Stephanie M. H. Camp, *Closer to Freedom: Enslaved Women and Everyday Resistance in the Plantation South* (Chapel Hill: University of North Carolina Press, 2004). For more on slave healing, see Sharla M. Fett, *Working Cures: Healing, Health, and Power on Southern Slave Plantations* (Chapel Hill: University of North Carolina Press, 2002), 111–192.

76. Lowe and Campbell, *Planters and Plain Folk*, 12, 22–23.

PART III

Links to Legacies of Slavery

Slaves in North America suffered and continue to endure physical and psychological violence. The final three chapters ask us to consider the cultural and economic consequences of their cumulative burdens. In chapter 9, ethnomusicologist Enrique Lamadrid examines how both indigenous and Spanish colonial peoples living in the pueblos and villages of New Mexico dealt with the traumatizing psychological repercussions of a period of endemic warfare that lasted from the mid-seventeenth century into the late nineteenth. Mestizo communities lost fathers, wives, and children to Native raiders in seasonal cycles of kidnapping and murder. At the same time, colonials captured and enslaved Indian victims, who grieved for their families and homelands. In the villages of New Mexico, bereaved mestizo families lived closely with the kidnapped Indians, often women and children, who were forced to work for them. As the decades passed, captives and colonists married and mated, sometimes voluntarily, sometimes not. Both groups, along with their mixed-heritage descendants, used music and community pageantry to help tolerate and try to make sense of the continuing violence. As happened across early North America, the languages, food ways, and musical styles of captors and captives began to blend. In poetry and song, the villagers retold and reimagined catastrophic events and the

PART III

fates of those killed or taken captive. Lamadrid illustrates how the words of *inditas* (popular ballads) like "La cautiva Marcellina" (Marcellina, the Captive) and "Santo Niño de Atocha" (Christ Child of Atocha) allowed generations of Hispano families to feel a sense of connection with those who had disappeared. The songs of captured Comanche boys and the memorial dramas inspired by battles with heroic Comanche chiefs melded trauma with an admiration for the free and fierce life of people of the plains.[1] A similar process of reimagining continues in the southwestern borderlands of the twenty-first century. We can hear echoes of the triumphs and terrors of slave raiding in the *narcocorridos*, popular songs that narrate exploits in drug and human trafficking.[2]

In the last two chapters, Sarah Deer (chapter 10) and Melissa Farley (chapter 11) draw links between slavery and more recent tragedies of exploitation. Both do research on human trafficking and sexual violence, and both argue that cultural misperceptions and assumptions remain stubborn obstacles to reducing these practices and their inherent brutality. Deer and Farley identify political and social trends that reflect surprising tolerance for ethnic oppression, racism, and the sexual exploitation of women in North America. Law professor Sarah Deer, a citizen of the Muskogee (Creek) Nation, specializes in criminal cases on Indian reservations and research on sexual assault in the wider society. In chapter 10, Deer asks us to consider two issues: federal policies that targeted Indian children and the violent manipulation of Native American women. Deer contends that after the Civil War and into the twentieth century, young Indians were systematically forced into government schools and coerced into rejecting their Native cosmologies. Many suffered sexual abuse. She also finds that there was and remains widespread acquiescence to violence against Native American women. This economic and psychological pressure still pushes many into prostitution. Deer argues that these social norms have their roots in colonialism and slavery. Indian peoples slid into desperate poverty after they were repeatedly denied promised lands and contractual payments. Privation continues to exacerbate the violence against Indian women—both those who remain on Native reservations and those who leave and try to survive as urban prostitutes in Canada and the United States.[3]

In chapter 11, Melissa Farley, a clinical psychologist and a founder of Prostitution Research & Education in San Francisco, further considers the parallels between slavery in the past and sexual exploitation in the present. Like Sarah Deer, she asks unsettling questions. For example, can women give genuine consent to prostitution—particularly if others control their access to food, lodging, toilets, and even menstrual supplies? Farley describes the prisonlike conditions in a legal Nevada brothel. The stone walls of the compound are topped with barbed wire. Women receive their food on trays passed through slots in metal doors. The price of clean sheets is deducted from the wages they keep after their pimps are paid.[4] As we look for links with coercion in the past, we find that the expenses charged to prostitutes have much in common with the fiscal realities of debt peonage in eighteenth- and nineteenth-century New England. There, the concepts of debt and slavery were tightly coupled. Money debts created a legal rationale that courts used to impose punishments of enslavement and physical abuse.[5] Farley argues that similar reasoning today allows purchasers of sex to believe that they legally own a woman's body, if only temporarily. They believe that this "ownership" gives them certain "rights" they can enforce, even with violence.[6] Meanwhile, those who profit from the sex trade bolster social tolerance for prostitution through international publicity campaigns laden with misinformation about the conditions of sex for sale. Cultural norms and deception continue to promote prostitution and the psychological trauma, physical battering, malnutrition, and disease that accompany it—the same maladies suffered by slaves across the North American past.

The chapters by Enrique Lamadrid, Sarah Deer, and Melissa Farley bring us full circle to the themes highlighted by Catherine Cameron in chapter 1: the emotional, economic, and cultural consequences of the trafficking of people, especially women and children, across North America. We ask our readers to think both narrowly and widely about slavery. We suggest that they compare slavery as it was perceived and practiced by slaves, slaveholders, and nonslaveholders and from both within and across cultures.[7] It is necessary to approach slavery from multiple perspectives because bondage was and remains intensely personal and yet broadly practiced. For this reason we have sought out both microhistories and the many links between them. Microhistories can trace the details of foodways, patterns of material culture, word use, and evidence of physical abuse, as well as the rate at which each changed in any culture. Linking local histories together allows us to map the patterns of slavery in North America over time. The advantage gained by studying both meticulous microstudies and the far-reaching linkages among them is that this approach preserves the historical motivations of enslavers and the lived experiences of the enslaved in particular places, times, and groups while also yielding fresh insights and questions about the nature of slavery as it developed and was practiced throughout North America. In the end, we gain a more complete grasp of slavery in the past, and we can better evaluate the cultural and economic pressures and the violence that continue to define the experience of slavery in North America today.

Part III

Notes

1. Enrique R. Lamadrid, *Hermanitos comanchitos: Indo-Hispano Rituals of Captivity and Redemption*, with photographs by Miguel A. Gandert (Albuquerque: University of New Mexico Press, 2003), 45, 51–79, 95–112.

2. See Elijah Wald, *Narcocorrido: A Journey into the Music of Drugs, Guns, and Guerrillas* (New York: Rayo, 2002). See also Mark Cameron Edberg, *El Narcotraficante: Narcocorridos and the Construction of a Cultural Persona on the US-Mexican Border* (Austin: University of Texas Press, 2004). A resource in which the streams of trafficked drugs, slave labor, torture, and sexual abuse converge is *Prayers for the Stolen*, the short novel by Jennifer Clement. Clement built her story partially on interviews with women who had survived kidnapping by Mexican drug lords. Jennifer Clement, *Prayers for the Stolen* (New York: Hogarth, 2014).

3. A number of sources can put contemporary faces on Sarah Deer's statistics. In his novel *Running Alone in Photographs*, Robert Mirabal drew on his Taos Pueblo heritage to create the character of Maggie May Wind. Robert Mirabal, *Running Alone in Photographs* (Taos, NM: Red Willow Press, 2008). Wind is a young Pueblo woman who escapes from a reservation where her spirit and talents are starved and debased, only to lose herself again in the self-destructive realities of the society outside. There are provocative parallels between Maggie May's reflections and the poetry and prose of Gloria Anzaldúa referenced in the endnotes of the introduction to part I. See the poem in Mirabal, *Running Alone in Photographs*, 215–216; Gloria Anzaldúa, *Borderlands: La Frontera, the New Mestiza* (San Francisco: Spinsters / Aunt Lute, 1987), 27–31, 77–82. Another Mirabal text, the autobiographical *Skeleton of a Bridge*, offers strong echoes of the days of captive taking and exchange. With parallels to Enrique Lamadrid's inditas, readers can hear the painful and enduring communal memories of slave raiding. Robert Mirabal, *Skeleton of a Bridge* (Taos, NM: Blinking Yellow Press, 1994), especially 49–54, 62, 76–78. For an example of the fusion of precontact and postcontact religions in music and ritual, see Robert Mirabal and the Rare Tribal Mob, *Music from a Painted Cave*, Red Feather Music, B00005ARF3, 2001, compact disk.

4. Melissa Farley, *Prostitution and Trafficking in Nevada: Making the Connections* (San Francisco: Prostitution Research & Education, 2007).

5. See Margaret Ellen Newell, "Indian Slavery in Colonial New England," in *Indian Slavery in Colonial America*, ed. Alan Gallay (Lincoln: University of Nebraska Press, 2010), 53–57.

6. The circumstances surrounding sexual trafficking across the US-Mexico border and beyond add to this debate over perceived ownership and consent. For example, see Grace Peña Delgado, "Border Control and Sexual Policing: White Slavery and Prostitution along the US-Mexico Borderlands, 1903–1910," *Western Historical Quarterly*

43 (Summer 2012): 157–178. Regarding drugs, prostitution, and police corruption, see the *El Paso Times* articles by Diana Washington Valdez on the discovery of the remains of eleven young women in Albuquerque: "Families Offer Clues in Albuquerque's 'Crime of the Century': Tips in Albuquerque Crimes Hint at Drug Gangs, Dirty Cops," *El Paso Times*, February 15, 2014, accessed February 16, 2014, http://www.elpasotimes.com/news/ci_25146711/families-offer-clues-albuquerques-crime-century?source=JBarTicker and "Families of Victims Received Tips about Possible Killers," *El Paso Times*, February 15, 2014, accessed February 16, 2014, http://www.elpasotimes.com/news/ci_25155150/families-victims-received-tips-about-possible-killers?IADID=Search-www.elpasotimes.com-www.elpasotimes.com. Compare the excerpts from Farley's interviews of women who escaped prostitution with Gloria Anzaldúa's passionate reflection on women living in these borderlands. Anzaldúa, *Borderlands*, 27–31, 77–82. See also Clement, *Prayers for the Stolen*. Anthropologist Brenda Bowser reveals that the historic style of slave raiding for women and children continues in the Americas of the twenty-first century, in her study of indigenous peoples of Amazonia. Brenda J. Bowser, "Captives in Amazonia: Becoming Kin in a Predatory Landscape," in *Invisible Citizens: Captives and Their Consequences*, ed. Catherine M. Cameron (Salt Lake City: University of Utah Press, 2008), 262–282. For more on the "roots, consequences, and connections" of "rethinking trafficking as contemporary slavery," see Alison Brysk and Austin Choi-Fitzpatrick, "Rethinking Trafficking," in *From Human Trafficking to Human Rights: Reframing Contemporary Slavery*, ed. Alison Brysk and Austin Choi-Fitzpatrick (Philadelphia: University of Pennsylvania Press, 2012), 1–24, quotation at 3.

    7. See Joseph C. Miller, "A Theme in Variations: A Historical Schema of Slaving in the Atlantic and Indian Ocean Regions," *Slavery and Abolition* 24 (2003): 169–194, and *The Problem of Slavery as History: A Global Approach* (New Haven, CT: Yale University Press, 2012), 4–8, 123–127.

9

Cautivos y criados

Cultural Memories of Slavery in New Mexico

Enrique R. Lamadrid

Embedded in the four-hundred-year legacy of Indo-Hispano culture in the Southwest Borderlands lies a veiled heritage of captivity and redemption, assimilation and resistance. The exposure of slavery and elucidation of its cultural memories will help eradicate the painful legacy of inequality that it spawned—debt peonage, class privilege, subordination of women, and the continuing existence of an underclass in order for the region to "prosper." This study draws out the iconic figure of the *cautivo criado* (family-raised captive) from the realm of Nuevomexicano expressive culture to complement and corroborate recent interdisciplinary, collaborative work linking the multiple histories of slavery across North America.

The comments of two visitors, a Franciscan cleric from eighteenth-century Mexico and a radical educator from twentieth-century Brazil, bracket and illuminate this discussion. In the 1776 report of his inspection of the missions of New Mexico, Fray Francisco Atanasio Domínguez wrote of complexities of cultures and ethnic identities of the slave society he encountered: "Some are masters, others servants, and others are both, serving and commanding themselves."[1] And in 1970, the same year he visited a renowned group of cultural activists in Embudo, New Mexico, Paolo Freire inscribed his decolonial vision of education as liberation, declaring, "This, then, is the great humanistic and historical task of the oppressed: to liberate themselves and their oppressors as well."[2]

Enrique R. Lamadrid

TRESCIENTOS AÑOS ESCLAVOS: SLAVERY AND ITS SHADOW LEGACY

In the hearts and minds of the Nuevomexicanos, euphemisms like "cautivos" and "criados," or domestics, have long disguised the bondage of persons who by any other name would be slaves. Such definitions were purposefully blurred for generations after the Nuevas Leyes de Indias in 1542 and the Recopilación of 1681 forbade the practice of taking or ransoming Indians as slaves. But, of course, enemy Indians defeated in battle according to the tenets of *guerra justa*, or "just war," could be taken into bondage to be "rehabilitated." They were slaves in practice, if not in name.[3]

In Spanish, the cultural vocabulary of captivity included verbs like *rescatar* (to rescue) and *redimir* (to redeem), which signaled a path to social liberation and religious redemption, both prize and price of transculturation and assimilation into the burgeoning sector of genízaros—Hispanicized Natives taken from enemy tribes.[4] The new "humanitarian" policy of ransoming encouraged even more slaving, and more young cautivos were entrusted to Spanish Mexican families *para criar*, to raise. Thus arose the doubly ambiguous meaning of criados as mentored wards and criados as household servants. Some earned their freedom, were freed upon marriage, or distinguished themselves in military service. Others, especially women, stayed with families as sister-wives, nannies, and *chichiguas*, or "mammies," whose service involved long-term lactation.[5] Every community had them on hand to ensure the survival of infants, since death in childbirth was a constant specter.

Both before and after the 1680 Pueblo Revolt, defeated Apaches were in great demand as slaves for the silver mines of Nueva Vizcaya to the south. The newly arriving Nuhmuhnuh, or tribal Comanches, soon recognized the value of human commerce and were quick to supply the demand. When the Spanish Crown learned of the abuses of the slave trade by the 1720s, the royal treasury began funding the ransom of captives. The rest of the century was consumed with trade and warfare with the Nuhmuhnuh, who were also baptized into Nuevomexicano family-style bondage and likewise incorporated plenty of captives into their own culture. During his 1775 visit, Fray Domínguez also took note of the social and linguistic complexity he found in Nuevo México, the cultural legacy of slavery:

> These settlers are people of all classes, but mostly mestizo and genízaro.... They speak the local Spanish, and most of them speak the language of the pueblos with ease, and to a considerable extent the Comanche, Ute, and Apache languages.[6]

The military conflicts of the nineteenth century brought Navajos, Utes, and Apaches into the fray and into Nuevomexicano households. Everyone had criados—common folk, clergy, officials of state, American traders, and even Washington-appointed governors after the US invasion of 1846. One of the most detailed sections of the 1848 Treaty of Guadalupe Hidalgo is Article 11, dedicated to the disposition of transnational captives and the responsibility of the United States to repatriate them, punish their captors, and pacify the borderlands.

In 1864, after their defeat by the US Army, Navajos were marched three hundred miles on the Long Walk to their concentration camp at Bosque Redondo along the Pecos River. While Union soldiers were dying on Civil War battlefields to end slavery in the United States, in the New Mexico Territory, hundreds of Navajo children were being sold and traded into bondage. Abraham Lincoln's Emancipation Proclamation and the Thirteenth Amendment were seemingly ignored in New Mexico. It took a special Executive Order of Emancipation by President Andrew Johnson on June 9, 1865, to call national attention to the nefarious practices of slavery in New Mexico, in which American officials and settlers were fully complicit.[7] Criados in servitude could be found in households across the land, from the poorest rural families' homes to the governor's mansion.

CAUTIVOS EN LA PLAZA: DOCUMENTING FESTIVAL TRADITIONS

New Mexico has its own set of apologia for all of this—cultural justifications of the regional practices of slavery, forged over more than three centuries and lasting well into the twentieth century. Community historians were willing accomplices in putting a "human face" on the institution, distinguishing it from the plantation-based chattel slavery of the South, implying that Hispanicization and Christianization somehow mitigated the human costs. However sublimated, a blurred collective memory of slavery is persistent in the upper Rio Grande region and is regularly enacted in expressive cultural practices down to the present.

The Native and mestizo peoples of northern Mexico and New Mexico dramatize their political and cultural struggles in festival and ritual display. Conquest and reconquest, resistance and transformation are recurring themes. Victory and morality plays, ritual dance, and even contemporary fiesta parades utilize mimetic portrayals of cultural selves and others, including Christians, Muslims and Jews, Aztecs and Comanches, Spaniards and Anglos. Alterity, hybridity, gender, and ultimately identity are negotiated on the plaza and in the cultural imagination.[8] To read cultural narratives and metaphors more deeply, we must follow them beyond the documents of history and into choreography, costume, ritual, and song. Collective memory is deep in a contested region at the edges of empire, where conquerors are conquered in turn and where discourses of power morph into discourses of survival.

A culture of amnesia, denial, erasure, and romanticization surrounds the long and pernicious tradition of bondage and peonage in New Mexico. One technological antidote to erasure is documentary photography and its many uses as an ethnographic research method. By sharing his photographs with his subjects, commissioner of the "Indian New Deal" and visual anthropologist John Collier extended the parameters of collaboration and inquiry, concluding, "The value of projective responses to photography is the powerful persuasion of realism. Often we think of psychological explosions in terms of symbolism; realism can be even more provocative."[9]

Photographs of actual cautivos are exceedingly rare and are usually kept close within family circles. Their enigmatic presence is usually consigned to the background and margins of the frame.[10] As some captives formally joined the families of their owners through marriage, they moved toward the center of family circles and portraits. Miguel Gandert, the photographer who illustrates the pages of this chapter, discovered in later life that his maternal great-grandmother, Gertrudis Gallegos, had joined his family as a criada. She was a young Pueblo child captured, raised, and exchanged by Navajos.[11] In a lost but well remembered family portrait, she proudly takes her place at the side of her husband, the youngest of three Valdés brothers, who posed on the portal of their house near Antonito, Colorado.[12] Figure 9.1 is a photograph of her in her last years.

Photography and documentation of contemporary expressive culture serve as subjective and qualitative counterparts to the document-based sociological and historical research that deciphers and decodes census and baptismal records to discover who are the masters and who are the slaves. Since there are so few survivals of seventeenth-century captivity stories, we begin chronologically with the eighteenth century and draw from my comprehensive study *Hermanitos comanchitos: Indo-Hispano Rituals of Captivity and Redemption*.[13]

Cautivos are present in folk drama as characters in the scenes of "Los Comanches," an equestrian victory play once performed on many village plazas across southern Colorado and northern New Mexico. The antagonists are historical figures—the wise and elderly Capitán Carlos Fernández of the Santa Fe Presidio and the young and brash Comanche war chief Cuerno Verde (Green Horn), who always invokes the power of the four

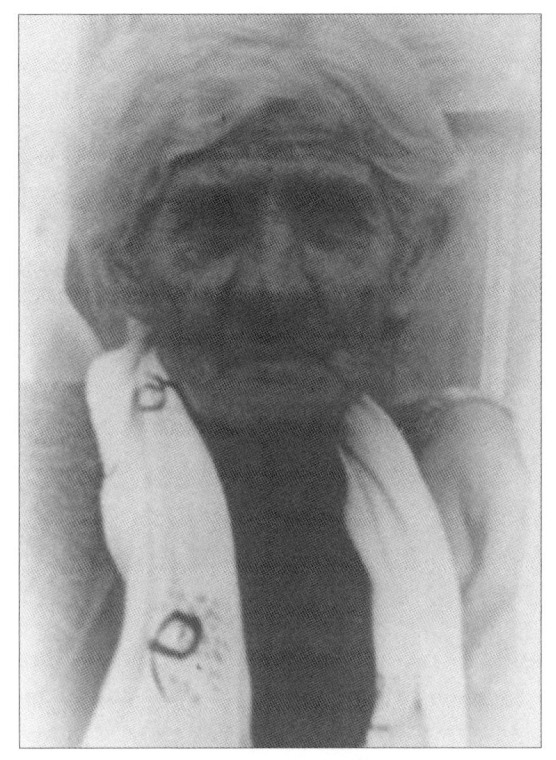

FIGURE 9.1
Gertrudis Gallegos de Valdés, born c. 1862, birthplace unknown; died 1954, Salida, Colorado. (Used with permission of the family)

directions before combat. *Arengas*, or battle harangues, resound as a pitched skirmish ends in the death of Cuerno Verde. The battle that rages in the play is fought over *las pecas*, two young female captives from Pecos (as their name indicates), a pueblo located between the Great Plains and Santa Fe on a Comanche trade route. In figure 9.2, they bear silent but anxious witness from the sidelines to the battle fought over them. They are mounted and ready to flee their captors or follow their liberators, depending on the outcome.[14]

The next layer of Hispano-Comanche celebrations moves cautivos from the margins to the center. In the ritual dance traditions from Ranchos de Taos, pantomimes represent the capture and ransoming of children and adults. With the first signal syllables of "La rueda" (the ring dance song), dancers take captives from the shivering New Year's morning audience. They are escorted under guard to the center space to be shown off and

Enrique R. Lamadrid

FIGURE 9.2
Las pecas, *or captive girls, mounted on fifth horse from left and second horse from right, are guarded by Spanish soldiers lined up with Comanche warriors in the oldest known performance portrait of "Los Comanches," in Ensenada, New Mexico, c. 1932. Mounted on the fourth horse from the right is Cuerno Verde, with his one-horned headdress. (New Mexico Records and Archives Center)*

honored by warriors dancing in a tight circle around them. They do not dance or speak but are corporeally captivated by the rhythms. Afterwards, they are "ransomed" by their families with cash or shots of *güisque* (whiskey) spirits as homage is paid to them. They command the respect of their captors. They are fought over, paid for, rescued, abused, loved. They are the *redimidos*, the redeemed ones (figure 9.3).

As Michael Taussig notes of such culturally mimetic rituals, "Mimesis plays the trick of dancing between the very same and the very different…of being like, and of being Other."[15] Symbolic inversions go a step further in the Hispano Comanche Nativity plays of western New Mexico, in which the newly born Santo Niño, or Christ Child, is taken captive and indigenized. As the story goes, a group of traveling Comanches appear on Guadalupe or Christmas or Epiphany Eve and offer to dance for the Santo Niño, then fall in love with him and later in the night kidnap him. The Santo Niño is, of course, an inert figurine. As they sing for him, the Comanche dancers animate the child in their lyrics, imagining that he watches them, smiling and waving his arms. Again, the romance of subjugation elides the violence of colonialism and conflict.

Surrounded by Hispano villagers and Comanche dancers in this same play is a captive girl who is nicknamed "Marcelina," after a famous cautiva. This little girl acquires powers from the liminal cultural space that she

FIGURE 9.3
Los Comanches de la Serna dance around their captives, New Year's morning, the Feast of Emmanuel, in Ranchos de Taos, New Mexico. (Miguel A. Gandert, 2003)

inhabits—the strength gained from surviving captivity, the knowledge of multiple cultures. Her presence is a source of blessings, and her touch can heal the sick.

In the next phase of this choreography, the cautivos are animated to become subjects rather than objects of the dance. When this dancing begins, another level of somatic cultural memory and embodied knowledge is activated.[16] North of Albuquerque, the town of Bernalillo absorbed the population of the villages of the Rio Puerco valley after the 1930s. Their pantomimes prepared children to confront their own fears. At any time during the Advent season, neighbors and family dressed as "Comanches" came and "kidnapped" children, especially disobedient children, right out of their houses. These "raids" were announced by screaming and general mayhem. Children would hide anywhere they could—under beds, in closets—where, of course, they would be found. This was the cue for parents to "plead" for them, pulling them away from their captors, promising that the children's behavior would improve. The children would obediently kneel and say the Padre Nuestro (Our Father) or another prayer before the Comanches would go away.

Since so many families moved to Bernalillo and since the Comanche Nativity plays were usually held in private houses, community elders modified the celebration and added Comanchito (little Comanche) dancers to the annual Posadas, which represent the journey of José and María to Nazareth, where they sought lodging for the birth of Jesús. These children are said to represent all the captives of the past, orphans and victims of warfare and slave raiding on all sides. The *indita* hymn they dance to asks the Santo Niño de Atocha for protection and deliverance. Only the Holy Child really knows where and how many Comanchitos there are:

ENRIQUE R. LAMADRID

> *Santo Niñito de Atocha,*   Holy Child of Atocha,
> *danos tu bendición,*   grant us your blessing,
> *cuida de tus comanchitos,*   take care of your little Comanches,
> *tú nomás sabes cuántos son.*   only you know how many there are.[17]

With such a proliferation of Comanche celebrations, it would be tempting to believe that New Mexico was totally overrun with the Nuhmuhnuh, which is not the case. They exerted a tremendous influence on commerce, politics, and culture during the eighteenth century, disproportionate to their actual numbers. They earned a level of charisma and respect both on and off the battlefield that made the term *Comanche* an emblem of independence and indomitability. In actuality, Hispano-Comanche cultural elements are an amalgam of Pueblo, Ute, Navajo, Kiowa, and Apache sources, as well as Nuhmuhnuh.

Indo-Hispano cultural practices contest erasure and challenge amnesia. People are freed to wonder again from whom and from where they come. Cautivos emerge from the margins and take their place in the center, where they begin to dance. Then they begin to sing and speak for themselves. The silence is broken first by vocable singing. Then lyrics become a part of the poetics of captivity and slavery. Commemorative and devotional indita ballads prepare a narrative field that is filled with oral histories and, eventually, literary expression as well.

CANTOS DE LOS CAUTIVOS: SONGS OF CAPTIVITY

Early visitors to Nuhmuhnuh villages reported them singing to their captives.[18] The Hispano-Comanche captivity songs are sung to captives and captors, since it is no longer clear who is who. As Fray Domínguez wrote in 1776, they assume both roles of "serving and commanding" themselves. As cautivos approach the moment of their liberation or of their transfer to new masters, they begin to sing. These songs are sung in vocables, pure vocalizations, the syllable singing style that is the most common characteristic of North American Native musical traditions. In the Indo-Hispano tradition, vocables reference and recall indigeneity and Native spirituality.[19]

Narrative voicing is the next step in the development of captivity songs, and verses alternate with vocable choruses in a series of ritual songs. The first example could be called formative in the developmental sense, in that it is a widespread *arrullo* (lullaby).

> *El comanche y la comancha*   The Comanche and his woman
> *se fueron a Santa Fe*   went to Santa Fe

pa' vender a sus hijitos	to sell their little children
por azúcar y café.	for sugar and coffee.[20]

The texts of cradlesongs are filled with implied abuse and sublimated retaliation for the sleepless nights of parents. The not-so-hidden message is a threat, "Behave, go to sleep, or I will sell you off to the Indians"—the cultural history of New Mexico in a nutshell.

Such folk poems remembered and performed are living artifacts of intangible cultural heritage, dependent on breath, voice, and memory. The culture of Greater Mexico boasts many such relics, a millennial ballad tradition through which people collectively reflect upon their historical and personal experiences. It includes several genres, all based on the venerable eight-syllable line, so mnemonically matched with *asonancia* (vowel rhyming). Stanzas are organized in sets of four lines in the ubiquitous quatrain, verso, or copla, but also in sets of six lines in the sextain and in sets of ten in the *décima*. Genres include the often philosophical décima, or complex ten-line, four-stanza poem with a keystone initial quatrain; the *cuándo* ballad, which lingers ironically on the rhetorical question "When?"; the masculine *corrido*, which "runs" right through a story, searching for definitive moments and quotes; and the female-inflected indita, with its deeply reflective, emotive choruses and powerful first-person narration.[21]

The quintessential indita about captivity, "La cautiva Marcelina," merits reconsideration here because of its role in the Comanche Nativity plays.[22] The play is not complete unless the indita is sung. Marcelina is the captive woman who witnesses the destruction of her entire community and kin; she is destined to wander the plains with her captors, with only mare's meat to eat. What concerns us here is not historicity or whether the captors were Comanches, Yutas (Utes), Navajoses, Apaches, Caiguas (Kiowas), or Pánanas (Pawnees), but rather the rhetorical structuring of the ballad. Whatever her precise historical origins, Marcelina the captive belongs to everyone as she enters both the oral and folk drama traditions. People singing and talking about her become part a narrative process that has been termed "transvaluation," or a rhetorical reframing in which her personal story of captivity and redemption acquires value and transcendent meaning to the larger community.[23]

From a third-person narrative frame that recounts the multiple tragedies of Marcelina, the anguished first-person lament of la cautiva herself emerges tearfully.

La cautiva Marcelina,	Marcelina the captive woman,
ya se va, ya se la llevan	now she goes, now they take her

para esas tierras mentadas,	*to those famous lands,*
a comer carne de yegua.	*to eat mare's meat.*
(refrán)	(refrain)
Por eso en el mundo	*That is why in this world*
no puedo más amar.	*I can love no more.*
De mi querida patria	*From my beloved country*
me van a retirar.	*they will take me away.*[24]

Stanza by stanza, she loses everything in the world that she loves, then returns to sing the heart-wrenching refrain as death knell. At the end of each successive stanza, she recounts the mounting death toll:

Mataron a mi papá...	*They killed my father...*
Mataron a mis hermanos...	*They killed my brothers and sisters...*
Mataron al Delgadito...	*They killed Skinny [a nickname]...*
Mataron a mis hijitos...	*They killed my little children...*

The intensity of pathos becomes almost unbearable. It is no wonder that the song developed a secondary performance context, sung by girls as a jump-rope rhyme in the Mora Valley, within sight of the dangers of the Great Plains:

Marcelina, Marcelina,	*Marcelina, Marcelina,*
ya se la llevaron...	*they have taken her away...*[25]

LA PASIÓN DE PLÁCIDA ROMERO: **THE POWER OF A POEM**

The voice of the *cautiva* subject moves through the narrative *indita* beyond pathos and victimhood into full and defiant agency and full-blown first-person narration in the famous and controversial case of Plácida Romero of Cubero, New Mexico. Her captivity in 1881–1882 with the Gileños, or Warm Springs Apaches—the people of the great warrior leaders Nané, Victorio, and Mangas Coloradas—had local, national, and international repercussions. Plácida witnessed the treacherous murder of her husband, Domingo Gallegos, at their remote ranch and homestead south of her home village. Within days of her kidnapping, she was forced to abandon her infant daughter, Trinidad, to strangers at a Navajo encampment. A twenty-eight-year-old mother with seven children, absorbed with the daily obligations of family and ranching, she was thrust without warning into an ordeal that tested every fiber of her being.

Romero's story is richly documented in multiple sources, from military records, depositions, and legislative memorials to newspaper accounts and editorials.[26] But compared with the extraordinary commemorative poetry composed with and for her, historical sources are ephemeral. Thanks to the power and persistence of popular verse, deep and specific dialogues on the history and culture of New Mexico continue. The nucleus of this poetry is the female engendered voice of the indita ballad, a genre of narrative folk song closely allied to the male engendered corrido. The highly emotive first-person voice of Plácida is heard in every single verse as she insists on telling and retelling her own story. She performed it herself, as do her female descendants, so many years later. The key word in her indita is *adiós*, her farewell to her children; her murdered husband, Domingo; their ranch hand and probable criado, José María; her mother, Marucasia; her father, Cayetano; her La Cebolla ranch; her town of Cubero; its plaza; her house, its walls and corners. Plácida's despair is complete. The landscape itself weeps for her. Across the variants, trees and rocks shed tears for all of Plácida's misfortunes: her captivity, the loss of her daughter, her disappointment that nobody is coming to her rescue, her total betrayal.

Adiós, rancho de la Cebolla,   Farewell, La Cebolla ranch,
¿por qué te muestras esquiva?   why have you turned away?
Los palos, las piedras lloran   The trees, the rocks are weeping
de verme salir cautiva.   to see me go into captivity.[27]

The *topos*, or commonplace of pathetic fantasy, the sympathy of the natural landscape is only part of the story. From Plácida's perspective, this is the Valle de Lágrimas, the Valley of Tears in the Salve Regina prayer from the Roman Catholic Rosary.[28] Her experience in the wilderness, her tireless work as a mule packer for the Apaches on their lightning-strike guerrilla campaign, the compassion of the Apache women who aid her escape in Mexico, her return home, her pregnancy, her unfailing devotion—all of these are the stations of her *vía crucis*, her own passion. Her descendants still meditate on the mysteries of her passion and draw strength from her pain.

La cautiva is present in her absence, and her farewells in each one of the ten variants collected are repeated dozens of times in stanzas and in the following refrain:

Adiós, ya me voy,   Farewell, I am leaving,
voy a padecer.   I am going into suffering.
Adiós, mis queridos hijos,   Farewell, my beloved children,
¿cuándo los volveré a ver?   when will I see you again?

Such extensive reiteration within such limited texts generates a metanarrative dimension where "repetition not only raises the repeated words and its referent to a different level, 'making it present,' it also calls our attention to the act of 'presenting.'"[29] More so than any of the operative verbs or verb aspects, the insistent and plaintive "adiós" makes present the voice of Plácida Romero through the voices of her descendants.

TESTIMONIOS DE LOS CAUTIVOS: NARRATION, EMPATHY, AND ENTITLEMENT

As she emerged from the deep trauma of her captivity and the frustrated attempts to recover her daughter, Plácida Romero was the first to realize how compelling her exemplary story would become to her family and community and how many people would empathize with her ordeals. The rhetorical power of the first-person narrative poem projected her voice far into the future and into the oral tradition. But in performance, folklorist John McDowell notes, the more formalized genres, like the ballad, are always preceded and followed by conversation, "anchored in a conversational flow attending to the ritual constraints of talk."[30] Performances move from what he defines as the "commemorative" modes of poetry to the "informative" modes of conversation. Using an "ethnography of speaking" approach, an analysis of these narratives and the way they are constructed and recounted reveals the dynamic contexts of memory and identification.[31]

Over months and years, Plácida's experience was entwined in the same narrative process of transvaluation as those of other *cautivas*. Exemplary stories of individuals take on emblematic meanings for an entire community. Women are awed and strengthened, and the protective instincts of men are awakened. But testimonial authority is vetted and negotiated by "empathy and entitlement."[32] Empathy flows intuitively from the deepest springs of emotion. But it can easily turn into nostalgia and appropriation of someone else's story. Entitlement is the reclaiming of narrative authenticity through linkage to direct experience and reaffirmation of subject as witness. Both happen in the testimonial narratives of the *cautivos*.

CUANDO LOS NAVAJOSES SE LLEVARON A MI ABUELO: TÍO BEN'S STORY

Much more common and current than the Comanche captivity tales of the eighteenth century and the occasional Pawnee or Kiowa stories of the nineteenth are the hundreds of cases of mutual captive raiding from the conflicts between the Hispanos and the Navajos and Apaches, which lasted into the late twentieth century. The story that Uncle Benjamín Archuleta told his family about his grandfather's abduction by the Navajos is one of many in the Rio Chama valley, where the *genízaro* town of Abiquiu was founded as a buffer zone with Utes and Navajos. These narratives relate many common themes: the capture of children, especially those engaged in herding, "adoption" into a host family, mistreatment or abuse, resistance and retaliation, and, finally, liberation. In this case, American soldiers in the mop-up operations on the Navajo reservation after the Civil War and the Long Walk are the agents of freedom. Events date to the 1870s. The story was told in English, with a minimum of rhetorical framing and dialogue.

> Two little kids, one, my grandfather, was about ten years old, and the other one was about twelve. They was taking the hobbles off of the burros to bring them back when the Indians were coming right close to them and they start to running. They kept pointing with their arrows to them that they was thought they were going to shoot them. And finally they catch him [my grandfather], but they didn't catch the other kid. And as soon as they catch him, they went back and took the two burros and then went clear up to a place we call Vallecito. They camped that night there. They killed one of them burros and had plenty of meat. The next morning they went toward the Navajo reservation. They just kept going in that direction until they got to where they live. My father, I don't know just how long he stayed with that first one, one Indian claim him like a son. He send him with that daughter of his to herd the goats and horses. And my grandfather says she was pretty mean to him. Every little bit she just whip him. And my father didn't do nothing. He just take all she give him, and finally he got tired. One day she was going to whip him, and he turned around and got in a fight with her and whip her. And as soon as she got up from the ground, she got on her horse. From there on the girl changed her ways. She never whipped him anymore. She started treating him better. Finally at that time Uncle Sam was trying to get the Indians in peace. He had some, a camp of soldiers right close to where they lived. The soldier told him, "If you don't want to go back with those Indians, don't go. Just stay here." He stayed there in the camp until this fellow got ready to come home. They said this fellow come on a horse and he put him behind the saddle and bring him over here to Abiquiu. He said the people were pretty glad to see my grandfather back here.[33]

Tío Ben was a master of understatement. In telling his grandfather's story, he avoids embellishment, allegory, moralizing, and sensationalizing. There is a wisp of humor and pride when his grandfather asserts himself and the abusive stepsister is put back in her place. And of course his family was overjoyed to see him again.

LAS CAUTIVAS DE NAMBÉ: THE LAST ORAL HISTORIES OF CAPTIVITY

Fully developed narratives of assimilation and transculturation are a challenge to find in community circles nearly a century and a half after the events in question. Pacífica García's story about the incorporation of a number of young Navajos into her community, the Hispano village of Nambé, New Mexico, is complex and nuanced. There was no escape or liberation for them, only a story of resignation and respect for the transformations that the cautivos experienced as they became family. In an animated interview with the author, the eighty-five-year-old touched on a broad range of topics—family and community history, cautivos, food ways, religious customs and songs, miracle stories, narrative ballads, folk poetry, courtship, social dance, and education! All these themes were carefully linked and integrated in a masterful performance, complete with all concomitant rhetorical features, embedded dialogues, back-channel cuing, and several renditions of music, poems, and narratives.

Through the stories she heard from her grandmother, she established a direct narrative link to early territorial days in New Mexico, from the US military invasion of 1846 to the American Civil War and the final campaigns against the Navajos and Apaches. She began in the manner of all Nuevomexicano conversations, by connecting genealogies with place to establish both autochthony—legitimacy in place—and cultural authority.[34] Here García speaks of the village patriarchs whom she met, the veterans of the Guerra de Valverde. The War between the North and South in New Mexico was named for its two major battles—Valverde and Glorieta. After the defeated Texans retreated in 1862, several companies of New Mexico volunteers continued serving in the Navajo campaign, which is why these three military conflicts are conflated in cultural memory.[35]

> Each of these old men went to the Valverde War. And in this war they fought and took away captives, Navajos. Some took males and other[s] females. They fought with the Navajos and took captives from them and brought them to their homes, as if they were family. They had servants.... The Indian that they had taken to tend to the family and they did not let her go out or anything. Very strict, very strict!.[36]

The refrain reiterated here—"¡Muy estrictos, muy estrictos!"—is a litany of authority repeated across dozens of family narratives remembering bygone patriarchs and matriarchs. The realization that severe disciplinary regimes had their origins in the practices of slaveholding is chilling. Before, during, and after the Long Walk, many hundreds of captives were taken away and likewise disciplined.[37]

Not surprisingly, memories of Navajo *sirvientas* (servant women) are deeply entwined with the tastes and aromas of food ways, since virtually all of them labored in kitchens. With enthusiasm and nostalgia, 'Mana Pacífica recalled the preparation of *machigües*, a kind of corn fritter made with dried meet, cheese, and an iconic ingredient, the *chile pasado*.[38] Once the signature taste of New Mexico, the sun-dried, roasted green chile is all but forgotten, thanks to freezers.

> What my grandma Casimira said was that all of them were cautivas, all of them.... And they were very good workers, hear. And they taught them well, see? They woke up early to cook the corn with lime and washed it and put it in a clay pot, and then it went into the metate. They had remarkable metates, there they ground it and started soaking dried chile they had roasted, the kind they call chile pasado. Like in the old times, they put it in the *horno*, ohh, what good chile!

In the excitement of the kitchen, an intriguing rhetorical shift takes place that closes the gap between captives and family. The earthy and sumptuous cooking of the criadas becomes one and the same as the cooking of the grandmothers, of her grandmother: "What a good cook my grandmother was.... They were women who had their style, those women."

No accident that the first writer to break silence on the topic of slavery used the common ground of the kitchen, Indo-Hispano food ways, and knowledge of medicinal plants to approach it. Fabiola Cabeza de Baca Gilbert began collecting recipes and compiling notes on traditional culture as a teacher and agricultural extension agent during the Great Depression. Her books told the history of New Mexico through food ways and raised consciousness and the status of regional gastronomy, from low-class cooking to the level of haute cuisine. She fully contextualized her recetas and made them available cross-culturally to American readers in *The Good Life*, in print since 1949, which portrays a year in the life of a prototypical New Mexican village over four seasons. Her use of the word *slave* in reference to Señá Martina, the genízara Herb Woman, is groundbreaking and unprecedented in its impact:

> No one remembered when she was born. She had been a slave in the García family for two generations and that was all any one knew.... She had never married, but she had several sons and daughters.... Some said the children belonged to the patrón, the master, under whom she had worked; others said they were his grandchildren. Doña Paula thought, "What right have I thinking of such things? They are children of God and they have been good sons and daughters. That is all that matters."[39]

'Mana Pacífica noted that over time and with strict discipline, when basic security was finally achieved, these young women were allowed to participate in social dancing. This was the site of the next level of community acceptance and incorporation—courtship and the forging of new layers of affinal kinship. Personal liaisons became public in a popular dancing game, the Valse Chiquiado.[40] *Valse* is "waltz," and *chiquear* is a verb that means "to baby, to coax, or to persuade." Proceedings began when a *bastonero*, or master of ceremonies, would choose a dancer, usually a woman, to sit in a chair in the middle of the dance hall. Then, with his cane (*bastón*), the dance master would single out a young contender to recite or improvise a verse to coax the potential partner out of the chair in order for the dance to resume. The attention of the entire group focused on the poetic interaction between the couple. The man would recite a verse that revealed both desires and intentions. The woman answered back with a range of cold to hot responses, having full license to reject and humiliate or accept and praise. Recited in such an intense spotlight, these verses were remembered across generations. When said by a young Navajo either in the hot seat or in the cajoling role of the pretender, the poems take on an additional level of irony. First, the young man speaks:

Te quiero como mi vida,	*I love you as I love my life,*
te estimo como el dinero,	*I esteem you like money,*
y si me da coraje,	*and if I get angry,*
te tiro p'al basurero.	*I'll throw you on the trash heap.*

Then the young woman responds:

La esquina se va cayendo,	*The corner is falling down,*
vida mía, detenla tú.	*my life, my love, go hold it up.*
Si me vas aborreciendo,	*If you go start loathing me,*
suéltame con amplitud.	*let me go free completely.*[41]

Open and public references to possessive love, money, anger, rejection, loathing, and breaking free would be especially poignant or embarrassing to a criado or criada in front of their families and neighbors. These are practical lessons on *respeto* and *vergüenza*, culturally based notions of respect and shame deeply linked to honor and character.[42]

At this humorous climax in the interview, I mustered the courage to ask the big question: "Su familia de usted, antes, o sus antepasados, ¿tenía sirvientas?" (Did your family before, or your ancestors, have servants?) 'Mana Pacífica's defensive answer was direct and unflinching: "¡Pues, no le digo, hubo una guerra, señor! Me platicaba mi abuela." (Well, am I not telling you, there was a war, sir! My grandmother told me.) With a wink, her tacit admission was that her *abuela* was indeed a criada.

BREAKING THE CULTURE OF SILENCE: SEXUAL CAPTIVITY

From the domestic and public arenas of kitchen and dance hall, we move to the most private and personal realm, where only conjecture, rumor, and innuendo have broken the silence of the forbidden zone, the intimate relations at the core of bondage. Since cautivos are deprived of their freedom, by definition they are stripped of both their honor and their shame. They are socially and sexually subordinated, vulnerable to all manner of abuse and exploitation. Historically, civil and religious institutions developed some sensitivity to these matters and left archival records to document the passage of captives into a new society. Military records and church sacramental records of baptism, marriage, and burial are a significant resource for historians, as are court cases. Genízaro men and women used the courts freely to register their complaints and seek justice for all types of abuse—physical, psychological, and sexual. Their descendants used American courts and often suffered public humiliation to achieve justice.[43]

In the cultural imagination, captivity narratives convey these concerns, and the most complex and compelling are told about women. As we have seen, the testimonials of men and boys were about defiance, perseverance, and the personal resolve necessary to stand up to the abuses of captivity. Since the unspoken and unspeakable aspects of the ordeals of women captives are implied, imagined, or assumed, their voices disappear almost immediately in a "culture of silence."[44] Although Plácida Romero transmitted her voice and example of faith and strength to her descendants, only silence surrounds her predicament of coming home pregnant from her captivity with the Apaches.

For more insight into these forbidden matters, we must turn to the lyric tradition, especially the inditas, which specialize in intercultural relations of conflict and of love. One of the most popular inditas, with many nuances and variants, is "Indita de Cochiti." This dark and disturbing version was sung in 1981 by José D. Romero, who remarked that he heard it and performed it at dances.[45]

> *Indita, indita, indita,*
> *indita de Cochiti,*
> *no le hace que seiga indita*
> *si al cabo no soy pa' ti.*
>
> *Indita, indita, indita,*
> *indita del otro lado,*
> *¿en dónde andabas anoche*
> *que traes el ojo pegado?*
>
> *Indita, indita, indita,*
> *indita del otro día,*
> *¿en dónde andabas anoche*
> *que traiga barriga fría?*

> *Indita, indita, indita,*
> *indita from Cochiti,*
> *it doesn't matter you are Indian*
> *if in the end I'm not for you.*
>
> *Indita, indita, indita,*
> *indita from the other side,*
> *where were you last night*
> *to get that swollen eye?*
>
> *Indita, indita, indita,*
> *indita of the other day,*
> *where were you last night*
> *that your belly is so cold?*

Cochiti is a Keres Pueblo south of Santa Fe, known for its close relations with surrounding Hispano villages.[46] The physical and sexual abuse implied in the lyrics is therefore all the more chilling. The Indian woman not only is rejected but also shows up the morning after with a swollen eye and an inexplicably cold belly. This variant of the song is sung in a burlesque manner, complete with winks and raucous laughter.

Until the recent archival discovery of "Indita de Juliana Ortega" (c. 1860), the taboo topic of sexual abuse has only rarely surfaced overtly in expressive culture.[47] Married off by her mother at the first signs of puberty, Juliana is held captive by a jealous and abusive husband. During this era, girls from lower social status backgrounds often lived in concubinage and experienced illicit sexual relations at early puberty. Worse yet, under the laws of the New Mexico Territory between 1865 and 1897, the age of consent for sexual relations for "a female child" in New Mexico was ten years old.[48] Juliana's bitter complaints to her family that she is being overworked and starved by her in-laws and unfaithful husband go unheeded for three years, until she convinces her father of her mistreatment:

> *Ya cumpliendo tres años*
> *de mi desgraciada vida,*
> *hice un reclamo a mis padres*
> *para salir de cautiva.*

> *And after three years*
> *of my disgraced life,*
> *I made a complaint to my parents*
> *to escape captivity.*

The first-person testimony typical of these narrative inditas invests them with resonant rhetorical power. When Juliana's husband learns of her plans, he absconds with her to the nearby village of Algodones, where he gets drunk and she escapes. She is taken into custody and deprived of her voice until her father gets a warrant for the husband. A courtroom scene ensues, after which creditors waylay her in the street and strip off her clothes, because they still are the property of her husband. Ortega returns to the safety of her family to make a fresh start on life with the following admonitions and a surprising renunciation:

Y ruego a todas las madres	I beg of all mothers
que vivan con caridad,	to live with charity,
que no casen a sus niñas	to not marry off their daughters
antes de cumplir la edad.	before coming of age.
Ya con esta me despido,	And with this I take my leave,
mi historia es bastante larga,	my story is very long,
renuncio los matrimonios	I renounce all marriage
por la vida tan amarga.	for the bitterness it brings to life.

It is rare that overt protests would achieve direct poetic expression, but inditas were the primary vehicle to carry the laments of captive women with such pathos. Whether they lose their honor and freedom as a result of warfare and enslavement or as prisoners in a bad marriage, there is always hope for redemption.

The desire for liberation is so strong that if it cannot be achieved by diplomacy or politics, then expressive culture can open creative spaces in which symbolic solutions to cruelty and conflict may be imagined. Festival drama is richly invested with scenarios of redemption and rescue. Testimonial narratives progress toward the hopeful allegories of "historical romance," where desire for reconciliation of enemies and rivals can be achieved.[49]

In the lyrics of a love song or a lullaby, the brutal contradictions of intercultural conflict can be beautifully resolved. The theme of many inditas is love between cultures, after all. The above variant of "Indita de Cochiti" burlesques the dark and abusive side of desire. This following variant of the same indita, sung to the same tune, with many of the same lyrics, imagines a more positive resolution. It was collected, adapted, and sung by Alex Chávez.[50]

Indita, indita, indita,	Little Indian girl,
indita de Cochiti,	Indian girl from Cochiti,

eres bonita, indita,	*you are beautiful, indita,*
y yo te quiero a ti.	*and I'm in love with you.*
Indita, indita, indita,	*Little Indian girl,*
yo fui a Santa Fe	*I went to Santa Fe,*
y traje un regalo	*and brought you a present*
que va a ser para usted.	*which will be for you.*

Here the "little Indian girl" is not only lover but also wife and child, the progeny of intercultural love when it is freed from oppression. The Hispano narrator goes to Santa Fe to buy a present for his precious little mestiza daughter. A new cultural synthesis is born, free of the oppression and suffering that preceded it.

INDO-HISPANO CULTURAL IMAGINARY: LITERARY EMERGENCE AND GENÍZARO RENAISSANCE

By the turn of the twenty-first century, oral histories of slavery had receded into the past. The only expressive forms left are a few ballads and a few fiestas. The story of cautivos and criados, the legacy of bondage in New Mexico, passed into the hands of writers of ethnohistory, fiction, and nonfiction.

In 1979 Alfonso Ortiz published an entry on genízaros in the Smithsonian Institution's *Handbook of North American Indians*.[51] In the same year, fellow anthropologist Gilberto Benito Córdova published his dissertation on the genízaro community of Abiquiu and how Indo-Hispano culture is still celebrated during the Fiesta de Santo Tomás Apóstol.[52] Until then, scholars had assumed that genízaro identity had been submerged for at least two centuries.[53] In 2000 Miguel Gandert published his photographic study *Nuevo México Profundo: Rituals of an Indo-Hispano Homeland*.[54] In 2002 James F. Brooks and Estevan Rael-Gálvez produced definitive studies of Indian slavery in the New Mexico region.[55] Since then, many more new studies began looking at genízaro ethnogenesis and consciousness, as well as at Indo-Hispano ethnomusicology.[56]

Laguna Pueblo writer Leslie Marmon Silko's 2010 memoir, *The Turquoise Ledge*, includes a horrific and well-documented tale of one of her ancestors from the Luna family of Los Lunas, who received four little Navajo sisters to raise after a military campaign in 1823. Josephine Romero Luna's brother was so abusive to them that they managed to poison him in revenge. The three older sisters were immediately hanged. The youngest, Juana, was raised by the family. Juana, the Navajo criada, became a beloved surrogate grandmother figure in the family.[57]

The most lyrical fictional treatment of the themes of cautivos and criados is Jim Sagel's *Always the Heart* (1998). This bilingual novella for adolescent readers is set in the Rio Chama valley and emerges from the intuitive, mystical relationship between a love-stricken teenager and her great-grandmother. The old woman speaks of the tragic love story of her own mother:

> "You see, the only way they could see each other was in secret."
>
> "But why?"
>
> "Because she was a criada."
>
> "A criada?" I ask, marveling at the thickness of my abuelita's long hair.
>
> "That's what they used to call Indian women when they were taken captive. They were kept as slaves, but since they were raised up as part of the family, they became just as Spanish as the rest of us."[58]

Sagel's novella uses the allegories of historical romance to show how people imagine symbolic solutions to otherwise unbearable situations.

The tour-de-force genízaro novel *Big Dreams and Dark Secrets in Chimayó* (2006) was written by Gilberto Benito Córdova. It is a delirious, Dionysian encyclopedia of Indo-Hispano folklore and includes characters ranging from the Iberian picaresque Pedro de Ordimalas to the Pueblo trickster 'Mano Fashico to the Navajos' Coyote and Spider Woman.[59]

Meanwhile, in plazas, *resolanas*, and public forums around New Mexico, Indo-Hispano cultural expression continues to emerge.[60] New verses are being composed for Comanche celebrations in Ranchos de Taos every year. The Comanches de la Serna, a genízaro community from Ranchos de Taos, have been invited to Abiquiu for the Fiesta de Santo Tomás (November 26) and to Alcalde for both the San Antonio and Santa Ana celebrations (December 27 and July 25, respectively) to share music and choreography. Likewise, new verses are regularly composed for the Comanche Nativity plays from San Mateo, recombining old themes of conflict with Navajos with new themes of conflict with Anglo America. Another arrullo, or lullaby, has come to light in Silver City that corresponds to its geographical origins, conflating references to both the Apache and the Comanche threats to little children who will not fall asleep. The Matachines dances of the Holy Child Parish in the Sandia Mountains east of Albuquerque have always ended with a movement called "El Comanche," in which the abuelos, or ancestral spirit clowns, kill the bull dancer, all to the same tune to which the Comanche lullabies and certain inditas are sung. A group of

Nuhmuhnuh dancers led by tribal elder and activist Ladonna Harris showed up at Placitas in 2008 to share tribal dances with the Comanchitos celebrations of Christmas, New Year's, and Epiphany Eves. Documentary films on genízaro history and culture by Cynthia Gómez and Samuel Sisneros are in production, and more research is in progress. And in the most formal public forum in the state, the New Mexico State Legislature, both the senate and house passed memorials recognizing the legacy of genízaro culture in New Mexico, including these fragments read into the public record:

> WHEREAS, indigenous people became part of New Mexican communities and households through capture in war, kidnapping, trade fairs, punishment for crimes, adoption, abandonment and the sale of children; and...
>
> WHEREAS, by 1776, genízaros comprised at least one-third of the entire population of the province; and
>
> WHEREAS, genízaros and their descendants have participated in all aspects of the social, political, military, and economic life of New Mexico during the Spanish, Mexican, and American periods; and...
>
> WHEREAS, many New Mexicans can trace their ancestry to these indigenous peoples;
>
> NOW, THEREFORE, BE IT RESOLVED...that the House of Representatives recognize the existence and importance of this indigenous group and the presence and importance of its descendants today.[61]

These almost forgotten chapters of New Mexico's cultural history were very publically proclaimed in 2007 in the legislative circles of the "Round House," the state capitol, whose design echoes that of the Great Kivas of prehistoric Chacoan culture.

CONCLUSION

Scholars of cultural hybridity and mestizo traditions in the Southwest have realized that past is still present in New Mexico. The familiar tropes and transformations of modernization, urbanization, and globalization do not fully apply here. Neither do the classic notions of residual and emergent cultural process.[62] Cultural memory is somehow more persistent in this landscape. The rituals, music, pantomimes, and dance dramas rooted in what we call Antiguo Mestizo or Indo-Hispano culture at first resemble residual traditions, heirlooms still playing a role in current cultural process.[63] Shared by Pueblo and Hispano communities across the centuries, region-wide performance complexes like the Matachines dance drama, the Comanche celebrations, and the singing and dancing of inditas still evolve across generations to mediate changing cultural conditions.[64] Since they generate such viable and varied meanings in performance, they have many features that can be considered emergent and invite continuing study on the plaza. But back in family and public archives, the methodical and sometimes serendipitous work of cultural and literary recovery regularly brings to light new texts, testimonies, and practices that further illuminate the past.

Notes

1. Fray Francisco Atanasio Domínguez, *The Missions of New Mexico, 1776: A Description by Fray Francisco Atanasio Domínguez*, ed. and trans. Eleanor B. Adams and Fray Angélico Chávez (Albuquerque: University of New Mexico Press, 1975), 113.

2. Paulo Freire, *Pedagogy of the Oppressed* (New York: Continuum International Publishing Group, 2005), 41. The activists and community organizers Freire visited were La Academia de Aztlán. To honor the visit, they renamed themselves La Academia de la Nueva Raza, in celebration of the "new humanism" of the emerging hemispheric revolutions.

3. James F. Brooks, *Captives and Cousins: Slavery, Kinship, and Community in the Southwest Borderlands* (Chapel Hill: University of North Carolina Press, 2002), 121–123.

4. Alfonso Ortiz, "Genízaros," in *Handbook of North American Indians*, vol. 9, ed. William C. Sturtevant (Washington, DC: Smithsonian Institution, 1979), 198–200.

5. Rubén Cobos, *A Dictionary of New Mexico and Southern Colorado Spanish* (Santa Fe: Museum of New Mexico Press, 1983), 45.

6. Domínguez, *Missions of New Mexico*, 113.

7. Robert Francis Castro, "After the Slavers: Law, Liberation, and Captive-Taking in the New Mexico Borderlands," *Slavery and Abolition* 28, no. 3 (December 2007): 375.

8. Discussions of hybridity (cultural synthesis between cultural groups in contact) and alterity (the construction of cultural otherness) are widely theorized in anthropology and cultural studies, as is the idea of cultural negotiation in all types of festivals. Enrique R. Lamadrid, *Hermanitos comanchitos: Indo-Hispano Rituals of Captivity and Redemption*, with photographs by Miguel A. Gandert (Albuquerque: University of New Mexico Press, 2003), 190–199; Michael Taussig, *Mimesis and Alterity: A Particular History of the Senses* (New York: Routledge, 1993). Longtime Smithsonian Folklife Festival directors Richard Kurin and Diana Parker have amply discussed the festival as a "dialogic approach to cultural interpretation" and the notion of "cultural conversations"

on the National Mall, where "cultural identity is negotiated" between participants in this carefully crafted festival setting; cited in Lamadrid, *Hermanitos comanchitos*, 195.

9. John Collier, *Visual Anthropology: Photography as a Research Method* (New York: Holt, Rinehart and Winston, 1967), 65. Collier's groundbreaking New Deal era work on the San Lorenzo Fiesta of Picurís Pueblo and its implicit commemoration of the Pueblo Revolt was one of the first collaborative uses of photographs in documenting festival traditions in the Southwest.

10. Estevan Rael-Gálvez, "Identifying Mestizo Phenomena: Representation and Reclamation of Mestizaje's Foothold," in *The Interpretation and Representation of Latino Cultures: Research and Museums Series* (Washington, DC: Smithsonian Center for Latin Initiatives, 2011), 8.

11. Miguel A. Gandert, interview with the author, Albuquerque, New Mexico, June 4, 2006.

12. Since Miguel A. Gandert's mother never shared the story with him, he actually discovered his ancestor's origins at a lecture given by Estevan Rael-Gálvez at the School for American (later, Advanced) Research in Santa Fe, New Mexico, in 2000.

13. Lamadrid, *Hermanitos comanchitos*.

14. The historical battle actually happened in August 1779 in the Green Horn Mountains of southern Colorado, near Colorado City.

15. Taussig, *Mimesis and Alterity*, 129.

16. Deirdre Sklar, "All the Dances Have a Meaning to That Apparition: Felt Knowledge and the Danzantes of Tortugas, New Mexico," *Dance Research Journal* 31, no. 2 (1999): 17–19.

17. Lamadrid, *Hermanitos comanchitos*, 127.

18. Gary Clayton Anderson, *The Indian Southwest, 1580–1830: Ethnogenesis and Reinvention* (Norman: University of Oklahoma Press, 1991), 222.

19. Vocables are the euphonic, nonlexical, nonreferential syllable sequences sung or chanted in Native music; their meaning resides in and accumulates on an associational and symbolic level. Brenda M. Romero, "Cultural Interaction in New Mexico as Illustrated in the Matachines Dance," in *Musics of Multicultural America: A Study of Twelve Musical Communities*, ed. Kip Lornell and Anne K. Rasmussen (New York: Schirmer, 1997), 163.

20. Lamadrid, *Hermanitos comanchitos*, 93.

21. Brenda M. Romero, "The Indita Genre of New Mexico: Gender and Cultural Identification," in *Chicana Traditions: Continuity and Change*, ed. Olga Nájera-Ramírez and Norma Cantú (Chicago: University of Illinois Press, 2002), 56–80.

22. Lamadrid, *Hermanitos comanchitos*; Romero, "The Indita Genre."

23. Amy Shuman, "Entitlement and Empathy in Personal Narrative," *Narrative Inquiry* 16, no. 1 (2006): 149.

24. Lamadrid, *Hermanitos comanchitos*, 98.

25. Roberto Martínez, interview with the author, Albuquerque, New Mexico, September 6, 1985.

26. Enrique R. Lamadrid, "Faith and Intercultural Relations in Two New Mexican Inditas: Plácida Romero and San Luis Gonzaga," in *Nuevomexicano Cultural Legacy: Forms, Agencies, and Discourse*, ed. Francisco A. Lomelí, Víctor A. Sorrell, and Genaro M. Padilla (Albuquerque: University of New Mexico Press, 2002), 164–184; A. E. Bob Roland, "The Ballad of Plácida Romero: History of an Apache Raid, a Captured Woman, and a Song," *New Mexico Historical Review* 86, no. 3 (Summer 2011): 279–324.

27. Lamadrid, "Faith and Intercultural Relations," 168.

28. The metaphorical Valley of Tears becomes a toponym in many areas of Latin America, especially where there was conflict with Native peoples. New Mexico's Valle de Lágrimas is on the Llano Estacado (Staked Plains) near the gorge of the Rio Colorado (Canadian River), along a Comanche trade route. Dan Flores, *Caprock Canyonlands: Journeys into the Heart of the Southern Plains* (Austin: University of Texas Press, 1990), 67.

29. Barbara Babcock, "The Story in the Story: Metanarration in Folk Narrative," in *Verbal Art as Performance*, ed. Richard Bauman (Rowly, MA: Newbury House Publishers, 1977), 72.

30. John H. McDowell, "Folklore as Commemorative Discourse," *Journal of American Folklore* 105, no. 418 (1992): 403.

31. Dell Hymes, *"In Vain I Tried to Tell You": Essays in Native American Ethnopoetics* (Philadelphia: University of Pennsylvania Press, 1981).

32. Shuman, "Entitlement and Empathy," 149.

33. Enrique R. Lamadrid, *Tesoros del espíritu: A Portrait in Sound of Hispanic New Mexico*, with Jack Loeffler, recordist, and Miguel A. Gandert, photographer (Embudo, NM: Academia / El Norte Publications, 1994), 30.

34. Charles L. Briggs, *Competence in Performance: The Creativity of Tradition in Mexicano Verbal Art* (Philadelphia: University of Pennsylvania Press, 1988), 247.

35. Rafael Chacón, *Legacy of Honor: The Life of Rafael Chacón, a Nineteenth-Century New Mexican*, ed. Jacqueline Meketa (Albuquerque: University of New Mexico Press, 1986).

36. Pacífica García, interview with the author, Nambé, New Mexico, March 21, 1987. Translation by the author. Subsequent García quotations are from this same interview.

37. David M. Brugge, *Navajos in the Catholic Church Records of New Mexico, 1694–1875* (Santa Fe, NM: SAR Press, 2010); Jennifer Denetdale, *Reclaiming Diné History: The*

Enrique R. Lamadrid

Legacies of Navajo Chief Manuelito and Juanita (Tucson: University of Arizona Press, 2007).

38. *'Mana*, abbreviated from the word *hermana*, or "sister," is an honorific title common in New Mexico.

39. Fabiola Cabeza de Baca Gilbert, *The Good Life: New Mexico Traditions and Food* (Santa Fe: Museum of New Mexico Press, 2005), 14.

40. Rubén Cobos, "The New Mexican Game of Valse Chiquiao," *Western Folklore* 15, no. 2 (April 1956): 95–101.

41. García, interview with the author.

42. Facundo Valdez, "Vergüenza," in *The Survival of Spanish American Villages*, ed. Paul Kutsche, Colorado College Research Committee Publication no. 15 (Colorado Springs: Colorado College, 1979), 100.

43. Ramón Gutiérrez, *When Jesus Came, the Corn Mothers Went Away: Marriage, Sexuality, and Power in New Mexico, 1500–1846* (Stanford, CA: Stanford University Press, 1991); Pablo Mitchell, *Coyote Nation: Sexuality, Race, and Conquest in Modernizing New Mexico, 1880–1920* (Chicago: University of Chicago Press, 2005).

44. Diana Rebolledo, "Las hijas de la Malinche: Mexicana/India Captivity Narratives in the Southwest, Subverting Voices," in *Nuevomexicano Cultural Legacy: Forms, Agencies, and Discourse*, ed. Francisco A. Lomelí, Víctor A. Sorrell, and Genaro M. Padilla (Albuquerque: University of New Mexico Press, 2002), 136.

45. Jack Loeffler, Katherine Loeffler, and Enrique R. Lamadrid, *La música de los viejitos: Hispano Folk Music of the Río Grande del Norte* (Albuquerque: University of New Mexico Press, 1999), 33.

46. Charles H. Lange, *Cochití: A New Mexico Pueblo, Past and Present* (Albuquerque: University of New Mexico Press, 1959).

47. Ortega, Juliana, "Indita de Juliana," folder 2, serial box #19831, c. 1860, Albuquerque Museum Collection of Hubbell Family Papers (Collection 2002-049), New Mexico State Records and Archives, Santa Fe. Initial research into census records places the events and people of the "Indita de Juliana Ortega" in the 1850s and 1860s in the Albuquerque area, although the legal records of court proceedings have not been located yet. Archivist historian Samuel Sisneros discovered the ballad in the Hubbell Family Papers in 2011. It did not survive in oral tradition, no doubt because it speaks the unspoken so eloquently.

48. Janet Lecompte, "Independent Woman of Hispanic New Mexico, 1821–1846," *Western Historical Quarterly* 12, no. 1 (January 1981): 29; Mitchell, *Coyote Nation*, 69.

49. Frederick Jameson, *The Political Unconscious: Narrative as a Socially Symbolic Act* (Ithaca, NY: Cornell University Press, 1981), 117.

50. Alex J. Chávez, *El Testamento: Spanish Folk Music of Northern New Mexico and*

Southern Colorado, John Donald Robb Musical Trust, 1995, compact disk.

51. Ortiz, "Genízaros," 198–200.

52. Gilberto Benito Córdova, "Missionization and Hispanicization of Santo Tomás Apóstol de Abiquiú, 1750–1770" (PhD diss., University of New Mexico, 1979).

53. In 1991, in *When Jesus Came, the Corn Mothers Went Away*, historian Ramón Gutiérrez took a fresh and innovative look at colonial marriage records and court cases for a new assessment of genízaros in the late eighteenth century as the term began to disappear from census records. In his 1985 dissertation, sociologist and community organizer Tomás Atencio speculated on the community spirit of resistance and survival he characterized as a survival of "Genízaro consciousness" into modern times; see Atencio, "The Old Town Liquor Dispute: Social Change and Conflict in New Mexico," Southwest Hispanic Research Institute Working Paper no. 112 (Albuquerque: University of New Mexico, 1985). The two most important studies on slavery in the New Mexico region are Brooks, *Captives and Cousins*, and Estevan Rael-Gálvez, "Identifying Captivity and Capturing Identity: Narratives of American Indian Slavery, Colorado and New Mexico, 1776–1934" (PhD diss., University of Michigan, 2002).

54. Miguel A. Gandert, *Nuevo México Profundo: Rituals of an Indo-Hispano Homeland*, with essays by Enrique R. Lamadrid, Ramón Gutiérrez, Lucy Lippard, and Chris Wilson (Santa Fe: Museum of New Mexico Press, 2000).

55. Brooks, *Captives and Cousins*; Rael-Gálvez, "Identifying Captivity and Capturing Identity."

56. Doris Swann Avery, "Into the Den of Evils: The Genízaros in Colonial New Mexico" (master's thesis, University of Montana, 2008); Romero, "The Indita Genre"; Peter J. García and Enrique R. Lamadrid, "Performing Indigeneity in the Nuevomexicano Homeland: Antiguo Mestizo Ritual and New Mestizo Revivals, Antidotes to Enchantment and Alienation," in *Comparative Indigeneities of the Américas: Toward a Hemispheric Approach*, ed. M. Bianet Castellanos, Lourdes Gutiérrez Nájera, and Arturo J. Aldama (Tucson: University of Arizona Press, 2012), 96–112; and Peter J. García, *Decolonizing Enchantment: Echoes of Nuevo Mexicano Popular Musics* (Albuquerque: University of New Mexico Press, 2015), 96–112.

57. Leslie Marmon Silko, *The Turquoise Ledge* (New York: Viking, 2010). Silko also includes a discussion of Plácida Romero in the memoir since Plácida was taken captive from Romero's ranch, not far south of Laguna Pueblo.

58. Jim Sagel, *Siempre el corazón/Always the Heart* (Santa Fe, NM: Red Crane Books, 1998), 12.

59. Gilberto Benito Córdova, *Big Dreams and Dark Secrets in Chimayó* (Albuquerque: University of New Mexico Press, 2006). Cultural anthropologist Michael L. Trujillo

dedicates an entire chapter to the novel in his ethnography of the Española Valley, *Land of Disenchantment: Latina/o Identities and Transformations in Northern New Mexico* (Albuquerque: University of New Mexico Press, 2009).

60. The *resolana* is the traditional space, real and metaphorical, for public dialogue, whether located along a sunny plaza wall in the winter or in other public spaces. The list of examples is from the field notebooks of the author.

61. New Mexico State House and Senate, "A Memorial Recognizing the Role of Genízaros in New Mexico History and Their Legacy," *House Memorial 40, Senate Memorial 59* (Santa Fe: New Mexico State Legislature, 2007). New Mexico state historian Estevan Rael-Gálvez, Regis Pecos, and others collaborated on the writing and passage of this historic memorial.

62. Raymond Williams, *Marxism and Literature* (Oxford: Oxford University Press, 1977).

63. García and Lamadrid, "Performing Indigeneity."

64. Sylvia Rodríguez, *The Matachines Dance: Ritual Symbolism and Interethnic Relations in the Upper Río Grande Valley* (Albuquerque: University of New Mexico Press, 1996); Lamadrid, *Hermanitos comanchitos*.

10

Relocation Revisited

Twentieth-Century Considerations

Sarah Deer

In 2000, Congress passed the Trafficking Victim Protection Act[1] and funded a comprehensive public relations campaign[2] to bring attention to modern-day slavery. As a result, there has been an unprecedented attention to sex trafficking in the United States during the past fifteen years. This attention is long overdue. The federal government claims that global sex trafficking has reached crisis proportions and urges other countries to take notice and implement immediate corrective action.[3] Congressional appropriations have funded dozens of task forces to combat sex trafficking in several metropolitan areas. At least twenty-five federally funded studies and reports on human trafficking have been published since 2000.[4]

Many of these reports assert that the United States is a world leader in the international efforts to address this crime.[5] In claiming the role of "global sheriff," the American government has suggested that the most common manifestations of human trafficking in the United States originate in foreign countries.[6] Less publicized has been the finding that the United States is not only a destination for the commercial trade in human beings but also a point of origin.[7] In cases of domestic trafficking, women and girls are transported and sold within the United States for use in the commercial sex industry (primarily pornography, stripping,

257

and prostitution).[8] Preliminary estimates reveal that domestic trafficking within the United States is as much of a problem, if not a bigger one, than international trafficking into the United States.[9]

Notably, most of the government-funded reports imply that the sex trafficking to, from, and within the United States is either a relatively new phenomenon or one that has only recently experienced sudden and dramatic growth. This assumption is mistaken. Sexual trafficking has a long and storied history within the United States, and failure to acknowledge this reality impedes the resolution of the epidemic of sexual exploitation within this country.

An honest analysis of sex trafficking in the United States must begin with recognition of the long history of the legal sex trade in the Western hemisphere. The sexual subjugation of women of color has been (and continues to be) a product of the European and American colonization projects.[10] Failure to understand this legacy makes the US government's efforts seem disingenuous, if not dishonest, in the eyes of victims' advocates around the world.[11] This chapter seeks to set the record straight. Although women from all segments of society are victims of sex trafficking and sexual violence, this chapter focuses on the sexual exploitation of American Indian and Alaska Native[12] women because they suffer sexual violence at the highest rate of any ethnic group within the United States, according to the federal government's own crime statistics.[13] Although sexual exploitation of Native women may seem randomized or isolated today, this dynamic has historical roots in formal institutions of the United States, including the military and federally funded educational programs. This chapter examines the sexual exploitation of Native women through the lens of the United States' own legal definition of trafficking.

The abolition of human slavery is a laudable goal, and though the proactive role taken by the US government in the past decade is commendable, the United States must be honest about its failings if it expects to reduce sexual slavery. As one commentator observed:

> Members of Western society see themselves on the forefront of civilization, bringing the world technology, capitalism, and democracy. However, these same individuals often fail to recognize that centuries earlier, when native people presented their Western ancestors with some of these same societal notions, particularly the valuable contributions of women, Westerners were repulsed and dismissed these ideas immediately as a savage, inferior way of functioning.[14]

In light of recent efforts by the United States to address global sex trafficking, it seems only fair to expose the long history of complicity of the United States and its colonial predecessors in sustaining the very behavior it professes to condemn.

Over the past five hundred years, American Indians have been subject to war, conquest, rape, and genocide. All of these depredations have disconnected Indian people from both the land and their own bodies.[15] In fact, it has been suggested that sexual violence can be employed as a metaphor for colonialism.[16] Alienation from one's homeland provides a strong foundation upon which sexual victimization can take place. One indigenous scholar explains the connection by asserting that colonial forces found it easy to shift "from the raping of a woman to the raping of a country to the raping of the world. Acts of aggression, of hate, of conquest, or empire-building [evolve to] Harems of women and harems of people; houses of prostitution and houses of pimps."[17] A 2008 report on sex trafficking in Minnesota explains that

> traffickers seek out persons perceived to be vulnerable for various reasons, including: age, poverty, chemical dependency, history of abuse, lack of resources or support systems, or lack of immigration status. Traffickers then use various tactics to control these persons that may include: inflicting sexual, emotional or mental abuse; confiscating documents; inducing or enabling chemical addiction; withholding money or identification documents; and violent physical assaults or threats of assaults.[18]

These tactics of traffickers are consistent with many of the tactics used by colonial and American governments to subjugate Native women and girls. Indeed, the behavior is so deeply ingrained in American history that it is often rendered invisible and thus becomes normalized.

The dispossession and relocation of indigenous peoples on this continent both necessitated and precipitated a highly gendered and sexualized dynamic in which Native women's bodies became commodities—bought and sold for the purposes of sexual gratification (or profit), invariably being transported far away from their homes. Removing Native women from their lands, homes, and families was an essential factor in depriving them of their personal liberty. The result was that the transport and sale of sex slaves throughout the Americas became widespread because it was rarely criminalized. Often, this exploitation was de jure legal (in that it was legally sanctioned by the government). Even in those instances when sex slavery was declared illegal, it continued to flourish because of official indifference and in large part institutionalized racism and prejudice. Therefore, Indian sex slavery was de facto legal.

Several different kinds of colonial-initiated physical movement of Native people have been associated with sexual mistreatment. Forced migration, mandatory boarding school education, and urban relocation are all "movements" that are correlated with sexual abuse. This chapter highlights two forms of "movement"—mandatory boarding schools and urban relocation—to illustrate how these tactics have traumatized and devastated tribal communities, with a particular focus on the lives of Native women and girls. This chapter also examines how the historic legacy of colonizing tactics continues to play a role in tribal communities today, suggesting the need for policy changes, as well as areas for further study. The factors leading to high crime rates in other contexts (drug trafficking and domestic violence) are facilitating the sexual exploitation of Native women and girls today.

The legacy of enslavement of blacks under United States law has long been the subject of legal scholarship. Enslavement of Indians is less well known but was a common practice among the Spanish, English, and French colonies. Enslavement of Indians continued to be widely practiced in many regions of the United States after the 1700s. Although human enslavement was technically abolished throughout the United States upon the passage of the Thirteenth Amendment in 1865, slave-like conditions persisted for many years. Even forty years later, little seemed to have changed for freed blacks in the Deep South. The practice of enslaving Indians also continued even after ratification of the Thirteenth Amendment. In California, for example, the Law for the Protection of the Indian, passed in 1850, allowed Indians convicted of certain crimes (including vagrancy) to be bonded out to "the best bidder." The Indian would then be compelled to work for said "best bidder" until such time as the fine was paid in full. This 1850 law remained on the books until well after the ratification of the Thirteenth Amendment.

Beginning in the nineteenth century in the United States and Canada, forcing Native people to relocate to government-selected reservations at gunpoint became common. Once Native people were sufficiently weakened and relocated onto bounded land, the wars and forced migrations ended, at least for the time being. The last major military actions on Indian land occurred near the end of the nineteenth century.[19] However, as the twentieth century began, the predatory forces at work to sexually denigrate Native women took on new forms. With the collective trauma of surviving war and relocation not yet fully addressed, new government policies launched a different kind of attack on tribal cultures: boarding schools.[20] The governments decided to "civilize" tribes by forcing their "savage" children to attend boarding schools. At boarding schools, the children learned "useful skills" that would allow them to get menial jobs working for white people in the cities. Beginning in the twentieth century, Native children were removed from tribal communities and adopted out to non-Indian families at an extraordinary rate. Unlike the nineteenth-century migrations to reservations, which were the result of overt violence, boarding schools involved official coercion of a different kind.[21] But when viewed in the context of a century of rape, murder, and starvation by soldiers and Indian agents, we may see the boarding schools strategy as a continuation of the legacy of oppression.

Exploitation of Native women began as soon as their initial contact with Europeans and continues to this day. Although warfare, boarding schools, and urban relocation have generally not been identified as forms of human trafficking, they are an inextricable part of the destruction of tribal nations, weakening these nations to the point that they could not adequately protect women and children from abduction, removal, and sexual enslavement. Time spent in boarding schools was regarded as education from the white perspective but was often regarded as kidnapping and brainwashing from an indigenous perspective. Urban relocation from the reservation was the next logical step on the agenda for "civilizing" tribes and was just another chapter in the long history of Native people being taken far from home by a hostile foreign power. Thus, the many historical acts of relocating Indians can be categorized as human trafficking. The various relocation techniques used by the United States government and settlers were designed to benefit non-Natives at the expense of Natives. Land theft, forced labor, and sexual exploitation were common results of these relocation techniques.

RELOCATION REVISITED

Colonization in the United States required the indoctrination of Indian children.[22] Once tribal nations were placed on reservations, the children of Native families were removed—which sent a variety of messages to the tribal communities, but particularly to mothers.[23] The dominant society disapproved of the way Native people parented.[24] The boarding schools can be seen as an essential step in the colonial project. In the 1950s, as tribal communities continued to make efforts to remobilize and establish roots in the prescribed space, the government again retooled its approach to tribal people—this time moving them from their reservation communities to urban centers.[25] Although other scholars have addressed the legal and social impact of these larger policies on tribal communities, they have not considered these actions as a form of human trafficking. When we view them through the lens of human trafficking, however, we can see that these relocations by the US government left Native people vulnerable to victimization, ensuring that yet another generation of Native women would be exposed to sexual abuse and degradation.

TRAFFICKING IN NATIVE CHILDREN: MANDATORY BOARDING SCHOOLS

For many Native people, the boarding school era is synonymous with sexual abuse and sexual exploitation on a grand scale. Targeting children is one of the most sinister methods of attacking a community and destroying it from the inside out. Native children were easy victims for this strategy, which reached its zenith in the early twentieth century. In an effort to promote assimilation of tribal people (after war failed to exterminate all of them),[26] the government endorsed the widespread removal of children from their communities to be "educated" in government and church-run boarding schools throughout the United States and Canada.[27] This involuntary movement of Native children was often linked to sexual exploitation. The schools were "coercive, often violent sites for forced assimilation. The history of the 'lost generation' of Native American youths, shuffled off to Bureau of Indian Affairs (BIA) boarding schools, is itself a history of violence, intimidation, and repression."[28]

> Forced attendance at boarding schools, where youth often were sexually, physically, emotionally, and verbally abused, was a traumatic event with the potential for being internalized and later manifesting as psychological symptoms. The resulting psychological symptoms may have been transmitted…onto family members (secondary traumatic stress) and passed onto subsequent generations (intergenerational transmission), in the absence of culturally appropriate ways for healing (unresolved grief).[29]

Children were sent hundreds, sometimes thousands, of miles from home on steamboats, trains, and wagons.[30] When they refused to go, their families were threatened with starvation and incarceration.[31] Some Indian schools engaged directly in abduction of Native children in order to "maintain student enrollment levels."[32] Government documents indicate that there were efforts to keep members of the same tribe apart, which was likely designed to facilitate assimilation.[33] The institutions themselves were "often harsh and repressive."[34]

Labor exploitation is often paired with sexual abuse. In the case of the boarding school era, there is evidence of labor exploitation alongside widespread sexual abuse. As part of the overall effort to remove children from their homeland and culture, many schools did not allow children to return home during the summer months.[35] Although assimilation or indoctrination was the primary goal of the boarding schools, commercialization and profit were by-products of these boarding school efforts; the local communities often benefited from cheap or free labor as a result of the process.[36] In Phoenix, for example, girls and young women were required to provide domestic services for white families—often with substandard (or no) pay.[37]

> One report noted that some girls were compelled by their mistresses "to do all the dirty work of the house, kept toiling from early to late, never given a word of encouragement, never permitted to enter the living rooms of the home, [and] compelled to always eat [their] meals from a plate in the kitchen alone." Another observed that some families cared nothing for the girls "except for the work they can get from them."[38]

Indian girls were also expected to follow strict social codes as established by Victorian-era morality.[39] "In the minds of many [V]ictorians, Indian women by nature were prone to filth, 'animal gratification,' [and] lewd, licentious, and promiscuous behavior."[40] The federal agenda was clear: "Train Indian girls in subservience and submission to authority."[41] In other words, indoctrinate the dominant paradigm of the patriarchy into Native women. Corporal punishment was acceptable and, in fact, was the subject of some well-publicized controversies in the early twentieth century.[42] The boarding school facilities often included jail cells, used to punish children who disobeyed orders.[43] Survivors of the boarding schools have disclosed that sexual abuse was common.[44] Victims often report that there was no option for filing grievances in these situations—the children were powerless to take any action to stop the abuse.[45] As Métis author and former prostitute Jackie Lynne explains: "These children were terrorized sexually with no avenues of escape. When they were allowed to visit their families during holidays, these children often felt increasing loneliness and despair due to a widening sense of cultural estrangement and abandonment."[46] The widespread sexual abuse continued well into the late twentieth century; in 2003, more than a hundred living former students of Native boarding schools in South Dakota began filing lawsuits against the Catholic Church for years of sexual abuse.[47]

SARAH DEER

URBAN RELOCATION

In the Trafficking Victims Protection Act of 2000, Congress found the following:

> Traffickers primarily target women and girls, who are disproportionately affected by poverty, the lack of access to education, chronic unemployment, discrimination, and the lack of economic opportunities in countries of origin. Traffickers lure women and girls into their networks through false promises of decent working conditions at relatively good pay as nannies, maids, dancers, factory workers, restaurant workers, sales clerks, or models. Traffickers also buy children from poor families and sell them into prostitution or into various types of forced or bonded labor.[48]

The relatively sanitized word *relocation* has often been used to refer to the Indian urbanization policies of the 1950s. In practice, "relocation" is a continuation of the colonial indifference to the inherent protection offered by one's relatives' homeland. This process created new avenues for predators to manipulate, and force or coerce Native women into the commercial sex industry.

One scholar has argued that the urbanization process is one in which "slum administration replaces colonial administration."[49] Consider that in 1940, only 7.2 percent of Native people lived in urban areas.[50] In 1943, the BIA launched a comprehensive program to transition Indian people from the reservations to the cities. A second initiative, launched in 1952, was initially called "The Voluntary Relocation Program."[51] Within a few short years, the number of Native people living away from their tribal communities had dramatically increased.[52] By 1960, 33,466 Indians had been relocated.[53] This number has steadily increased. In 1980, the bureau formally suspended the project, but the urban migration continued.[54] By 1990, the US Census indicated that nearly 60 percent of Native people resided in urban areas.[55] The intended goal was to force Native people to assimilate into mainstream society.[56]

The relocation project was often presented as a benevolent opportunity.[57] Living conditions on most reservations had deteriorated to the level of abject poverty.[58] Federal employees from the BIA traveled to reservations and recruited young Native people to move to the city, where they were promised jobs and housing. This era can be seen as a logical next step after the subjugation and forced migrations of the prior century. Indian people had been economically and emotionally subjugated by centuries of officially sanctioned violence and often had very limited options for their own well-being. Further, many Indian people were living hundreds of miles from their ancestral homelands on reservations that were places of suffering at the hands of the federal government. In order to take advantage of the small stipends available for relocation, an Indian person had to go through an interview and approval process.[59] They received no compensation or support to return home (even in cases of family illness or death).[60] It can safely be said that no comprehensive efforts existed to ensure that Native women had access to any social services should they fall victim to sexual exploitation in the cities.[61] Few programs exist even today.[62] Native people often found themselves unemployed soon after arriving in the city.[63] In 1965, one study estimated that "more than 75 percent of the Indians who ha[d] relocated would choose to return to their reservations as soon as possible."[64] One anthropologist wrote, "The physical, social, and mental costs of such prolonged stress are staggering."[65] Part of the stress came from poverty: "In 1969 the Indian unemployment rate was eight to ten times the national average, and individual incomes were less than half the national poverty level."[66] All of these "urbanization" factors created the perfect opportunity for pimps and other predators to gain a foothold in the lives of Native people.

Situating Indians within urban settings also provided more convenient opportunities for social scientists to "study" Indian culture and adaptation styles. A review of this literature is illuminating because it becomes clear that tribal culture was often blamed for causing "deviant" behavior, rather than the effects of forced acculturation, institutionalized racism, and poverty being considered.[67] One expert, for example, explained that Indians suffered poverty and other social ills in the urban locations because they were incapable of comprehending the "basic instrumental values of modern urban industrial society."[68]

While most of the studies of urban Indians focused on men, some reports did devote attention to gender dynamics, and a few focused on women. Although this body of literature often acknowledged behavior that might have indicated sexual exploitation, it was usually not labeled as such. Sexual exploitation by white men was rarely framed as predatory behavior—sometimes it was couched as "experimentation" or directly tied to drinking. Social scientists often suggested that Native women were engaging in promiscuous behavior with non-Native men. Consider the following observation from 1963: "For the young [Native] females, drinking seems to help them overcome sexual inhibitions; this is crucial to their popularity with many of the young Whites."[69] In 1968, another social scientist wrote:

> The rejection of native males, and the valuing of transient white males, results in a situation of mutual exploitation between the transients and the [Native] girls. The girls will go so far as to seek out Navy men, construction and barge workers (both single and married), gaining presents from them, most notably in the form of beer.[70]

This typical characterization of the relationships as "mutual exploitation" is directly followed by observations that reveal a more one-sided dynamic:

> Generally speaking, the [Native] girls do not profit in the long run from this mutual sexual exploitation. Many of them are burdened with illegitimate children and contract venereal diseases, which are especially prevalent. Very few of the transients marry native girls.[71]

It should come as no surprise that these Indian women, marooned in an unfamiliar urban environment, without any social support network or job skills, were easy prey for organized crime. No empirical data is available to allow us to determine the extent to which sex traffickers in the mid- to-late twentieth century may have targeted Native women. Anecdotal evidence, however, indicates that Native women who left the reservations for urban areas were vulnerable to such exploitation.[72] For instance, testimony provided to Congress by social worker Amabel Bulin in 1944 indicates that the sex trafficking of Native girls was common in Minnesota. Bulin, an activist in Minneapolis in the 1940s and 1950s, testified in front of a House committee that Indian girls in Minneapolis were illegally being sold liquor and that this made them vulnerable to "exploitation" and "immorality."[73]

A 1970 article provides some insight into the approach mainstream (that is, white male) experts had toward prostituted Native women.[74] Cowritten by a physician and a well-known biochemist, the article claims that Native prostitutes are "habitual liars" and "chronic alcoholi[cs]."[75] The authors claim that "random factors and forces" are responsible for Native women entering prostitution, ignoring the role of sexual predators (and history) in the criminal ecosystem of sexual slavery.[76]

CONTEMPORARY ISSUES

Although sex trafficking is now criminalized in the United States,[77] the legacy of enslavement, exploitation, and exportation is reflected in the lives of Native girls in the sex trade and Native women who want to leave the sex trade. The US government has ceased its official endorsement of removing Native children from their families.[78] Tribal members are no longer pressured by federal agents to leave the reservation for the city. Indeed, the federal government has provided some degree of support for tribal self-determination and cultural revitalization.[79] However, the United States has never formally acknowledged most of the reprehensible actions that contributed to the disparities in income, health, well-being, and life expectancy experienced by Native and African American people.[80] The laws of the United States have changed for the better, but the historical legacy of sexual oppression still has a considerable impact on the lives of individual Native women today. Prostitution is akin to the colonial process; the act, "through enabling men to mark the boundary between themselves and [the oppressed 'other'], and the law's treatment of it as a contract, [effectively] sustain a colonial social order."[81]

There is significantly more research on Native women in the sex trade in Canada, which shares a strikingly similar history when it comes to the oppression of its indigenous population.[82] Canadian statistics have demonstrated that aboriginal women and girls are prostituted at disproportionate rates.[83] "A study conducted in 2000 estimated that 70% of street prostitutes working in the most dangerous and lowest paying 'tracks' in the Downtown Eastside [Vancouver] were Aboriginal women."[84] In Winnipeg, one advocate reported that hundreds of teen and preteen girls, as young as eight and averaging about thirteen, were working the streets.[85] Even more were being abused behind closed doors, with about 80 percent of child prostitution taking place in gang houses and "trick pads."[86] An estimated 70 percent of these girls were aboriginal.[87]

Researchers in Canada have also found links between the historical legacy and present-day concerns.[88] A qualitative study on aboriginal women living with HIV in Winnipeg, for example, found that "relocation, through government apprehension or running away, resulted from the perceived inadequate or abusive parenting that thrived within an environment permeated with absence/loss."[89] *Displacement* is a particularly useful word in describing the experience of a person who is unable to govern what happens to her own body. Although comparable statistics are not available within the United States, it is indisputable that the legacy of relocation, chronic poverty, lack of decent education, and societal trauma significantly reduce the opportunities available to Native women and make them vulnerable to victimization and the sex trade.

Trafficking of any kind is notoriously difficult to research, and the invisibility of victims is a common problem.[90] The subject of Native women as contemporary sex trafficking victims in the United States has only recently received attention in a few select regions.[91] Native women likely are significantly overrepresented in the United States sex industry. First, Native women and girls suffer disproportionately from risk factors that social scientists have identified as correlated with prostitution.[92] Second, because of a variety of jurisdictional limitations and resource shortages, many tribal communities are currently targeted by criminal enterprises.[93] These criminal enterprises often carry benchmarks that have been correlated with sex trafficking in other contexts. These are the societal risk factors, but there are also individual risk factors.

INDIVIDUAL RISK FACTORS

The arrest rate of Native women for prostitution is understudied, but a 1983 study concluded that "70% of female inmates in American prisons were initially arrested for prostitution."[94] Recent scholarship on trafficking has explored how traffickers exploit certain kinds of social vulnerabilities.[95] A variety of risk factors have been identified as establishing a higher likelihood of an individual entering the sex industry, including sexual abuse,[96] poverty,[97] and drug/alcohol abuse.[98] Native women and girls disproportionately experience these risk factors. The US government acknowledges the high rates of sexual abuse and rape committed against Native women and girls.[99] Prostitution is also strongly correlated with drug and alcohol abuse[100]—the relationship is particularly strong in the lives of prostituted children.[101] Women and girls who are addicted to illegal drugs may be coerced to engage in prostitution (sometimes called "survival sex"[102]) both on and off the reservation in order to pay for their habits. Illegal drug distributors, for example, may put pressure on their customers to pay off debt through prostitution.

Some politicians, scholars, and activists have argued that today's prostitution is a "victimless" crime.[103] The research of Dr. Melissa Farley and Native organizations like the Minnesota Indian Women's Sexual Assault Coalition has demonstrated that women are most often engaged in prostitution because they were tricked, coerced, or forced. These studies show that women suffer unimaginable psychic and physical pain as a result of being forced into prostitution. Moreover, few deny that the prostitution of underage girls is illegal and immoral.[104] Statistics consistently indicate that most women prostitutes enter into the "profession" before the age of eighteen.[105] The US State Department has found that prostitution and related activities "fuel the growth of modern-day slavery,"[106] yet the standard American law enforcement response to prostitution continues to be to arrest and prosecute women and girls who are prostituted.[107] Incarcerating and stigmatizing the women and children engaged in prostitution further alienates these victims from networks of assistance and safety. Native women are already overrepresented in the prison population, and some common reasons are related to the intertwined issues of drug abuse and prostitution.[108]

Social service agencies sometimes fail to frame the experience of a prostitute as a form of victimization. Often women and girls are blamed for their predicament, which discourages them from seeking assistance. One Minnesota report provides an example of this victim-blaming behavior:

> An American Indian girl disclosed to a...service provider that she was trafficked into prostitution from a reservation in another state. The girl described how the service provider blamed her for the situation, as though she had "[gotten] herself into it."[109]

COMMUNITY RISK FACTORS

Global trafficking research has suggested that "poverty or political instability" can create environments conducive to a predatory criminal enterprise.[110] There is ample evidence that organized criminal behavior and gangs are common in many tribal communities.[111] Perceived and actual limitations on tribal criminal authority attract criminals, including sex traffickers. The federal government itself has acknowledged this problem and funded programs to focus on the illegal drug traffic that is associated with some tribal communities. Generally, the sex industry is inseparable from organized crime rings.[112]

The process of colonization has never truly ended in the United States, and it continues to be embedded within the American legal system. In 1978, for example, the US Supreme Court eliminated tribal criminal authority over non-Indians,[113] which means that tribal governments must depend on federal and/or state governments to prosecute non-Indian pimps and drug pushers who target tribal citizens in Indian country.[114] Tribal governments do have the legal authority to take criminal action where Indian perpetrators are involved,[115] but they have been limited in the exercise of sentencing authority.[116] Resource limitations are often cited as one of the primary causes of high crimes rates in Indian country.

Today, most tribal governments struggle with crime control, because of significant underfunding, decades of indifference, and jurisdictional limitations.[117]

SEX TRAFFICKING AND MURDER: AN UNDENIABLE LINK

Prostitution puts women and girls at a higher risk for other forms of violent victimization, including murder. As noted earlier, more investigation into the Native women trapped in the sex industry has been done in Canada than the United States. In Canada, an estimated five hundred aboriginal women and girls have disappeared (presumably abducted, most likely murdered) since the late 1980s, a fact that has caught the attention of mainstream human rights organizations, including Amnesty International.[118] At least two serial killers have been identified who targeted primarily aboriginal prostituted women.[119]

In the summer of 2009, the Federal Bureau of Investigation (FBI) announced that it believed a serial killer or killers employed in the trucking industry might be responsible for the murder of hundreds of women, several of whom were Native women trapped in prostitution.[120] This American report is quite similar to the reports from Canada. Although the FBI has not indicated the percentage of victims who were Native women, it noted that "the victims in these cases are primarily women who are living high-risk, transient lifestyles, often involving substance abuse and prostitution. They're frequently picked up at truck stops or service stations and sexually assaulted, murdered, and dumped along a highway."[121]

ENDING THE LEGACY OF TRAFFICKING AND SLAVERY OF NATIVE WOMEN

Are Native women in the United States *enslaved* today? Perhaps this is a more difficult question to answer than it seems. When there is a "market" for Native women in the sex trade, when there is evidence that Native women are targeted by pimps and traffickers, when it is clear that Native women are experiencing the highest risk factors for prostitution, then women who are victims could be said to be living a form of enslavement. Scholars and activists often talk about this dynamic in terms of widespread sexual exploitation (as opposed to slavery), but the history of the problem demonstrates that the exploitation has been a deliberate, if sometimes invisible, product of government and private enterprises for generations. So today, one can conclude that Native people have been historically enslaved and are still experiencing the ramifications of that slavery today. An honest reckoning of this history is necessary if we are to help the contemporary victims.

First, more research is needed to document the problem. Although the research in the United States is not as extensive as that in Canada, the shared history and proximity of the United States and Canada suggest that the problem with sex trafficking of Native women and girls is similar in both countries. Federally funded research found that some counties in the United States have rates of murder against American Indian and Alaska Native women that are *more than ten times* the national average.[122] In order to implement effective interventions, it is critical to have comprehensive data that focuses on the specific experiences of Native women.[123] Research that ties these contemporary problems to historical wrongs can also be helpful, because it is difficult to articulate a solution to a problem without knowing its origins.

Second, developing culturally appropriate responses to the sex trafficking of Native women and girls is necessary. However, the development of such resources presents unique challenges. Native-specific intervention models will be needed.[124] Centuries of indifference have understandably led to significant distrust of authority; many Native women may continue to feel wary of engaging with the Western criminal justice system. As of 2013, tribal recipients of funding under the Violence against Women Act will be allowed to provide direct services to victims of sex trafficking. This is a promising development because it will enhance the ability of tribal governments to think creatively about how to address the problem.

The American government has an obligation to ensure that all Native women be accorded full value and protection by the American legal system. Interventions should acknowledge the historical factors at play in the victimization of Native women and girls.[125] We need to recognize that transporting (or coercing) a Native girl or woman across sovereign lines (i.e., from a reservation to a city in the United States or Canada or from one reservation to another) for the purpose of slavery and/or sex work should be considered "international trafficking." Defining it in such a way will ensure that more appropriate and severe measures be taken by tribal, state, and federal governments to stop it.

The victimization of Native people is a story five hundred years in the making, and we cannot remedy these problems overnight, but our best chance of breaking the cycle of victimization is the development of culturally appropriate interventions to help Native women and girls break the shackles of history and prejudice.

Notes

1. Trafficking Victim Protection Act of 2006, 22 U.S.C. § 7101 (2006, amended 2008).

2. US Department of Health and Human Services, *Assessment of US Government Efforts to Combat Trafficking in Persons in Fiscal Year 2005* (Washington, DC: US Government Printing Office, 2006), explains the Department of Health and Human Services "Rescue and Restore Victims of Human Trafficking" public relations campaign.

3. Janie Chuang, "The United States as Global Sheriff: Using Unilateral Sanctions to Combat Human Trafficking," *Michigan Journal of International Law* 27 (2006): 437.

4. Tracey Kyckelhahn, Allen J. Beck, and Thomas H. Cohen, *Characteristics of Suspected Human Trafficking Incidents, 2009*, US Department of Justice (Washington, DC: Bureau of Justice Statistics, 2010). This report describes suspected human trafficking investigations and their outcomes in the United States.

5. US Department of Health and Human Services, *Assessment of US Government Efforts*, 1, claims that "the United States is among the nations leading the fight against this terrible crime."

6. Ibid., 34.

7. David R. Hodge, "Sexual Trafficking in the United States: A Domestic Problem with Transnational Dimensions," *Social Work* 53 (2008): 143–144, states that "trends in international trafficking are easier to estimate than trends in domestic trafficking."

8. Janice G. Raymond and Donna M. Hughes note that "US women are domestically trafficked across city, state, and even national borders." Janice G. Raymond and Donna M. Hughes, *Sex Trafficking of Women in the United States*, Coalition Against Trafficking in Women, National Institute of Justice (2001), 10.

9. The full extent of modern sex trafficking is extraordinarily difficult to document because the sex industry includes a combination of both legal and illegal activities. Moreover, the victims of this crime are often reluctant to come forward for fear of reprisals from the legal system or their captors. These sexual predators use violence, threats, and deception to subjugate their victims. Experts in this form of criminal enterprise have disagreed among themselves as to the true extent of the problem. In the United States, for example, the General Accounting Office has raised serious questions about the methodology used by the State Department to estimate the number of victims. See Bridget Anderson and Rutvica Andrijasevic, "Sex, Slaves, and Citizens: The Politics of Anti-trafficking," *Soundings* 40 (2009): 135, 137.

10. Gary C. Anders, "Theories of Underdevelopment and the American Indian," *Journal of Economic Issues* 14, no. 3 (1980): 681, 690: "Colonialism is a theoretical model which stresses the domination of a people by a culturally different and more powerful group over which they have little influence."

11. Vine Deloria Jr., *Custer Died for Your Sins: An Indian Manifesto* (Norman: University of Oklahoma Press, 1969): "There has not been a time since the founding of the republic when the motives of this country were innocent. Is it any wonder that other nations are extremely skeptical about its real motives in the world today?"

12. For the purposes of this article, I use "Indian," "Native," "indigenous," and "tribal" interchangeably to refer to indigenous people who live in the United States, including Alaska Native people.

13. Steven W. Perry, *American Indians and Crime: A BJS Statistical Profile, 1992–2002*, US Department of Justice, Bureau of Justice Statistics (Washington, DC: US Government

Printing Office, 2004); see also Ronet Bachman et al., *Violence against American Indian and Alaska Native Women and the Criminal Justice Response: What Is Known*, research report submitted to US Department of Justice (Washington, DC, 2008), 3.

14. Kathleen Ward, "Before and after the White Man: Indian Women, Property, Progress, and Power," *Connecticut Public Interest Law Journal* 6 (2007): 245, 247.

15. Hilary N. Weaver, "The Colonial Context of Violence: Reflections on Violence in the Lives of Native American Women," *Journal of Interpersonal Violence* 1 (2008): 1–12.

16. Andrea Smith, "Sexual Violence and American Indian Genocide," in *Remembering Conquest: Feminist/Womanist Perspectives on Religion, Colonization, and Sexual Violence*, ed. Nantawan Boonprasat Lewis and Marie M. Fortune (New York: Routledge, 1999), 31–49.

17. Jack D. Forbes, *Columbus and Other Cannibals: The Weitko Disease of Exploitation, Imperialism, and Terrorism* (New York: Seven Stories Press, 1992), 160.

18. Angela Bortel et al., *Sex Trafficking Needs Assessment for the State of Minnesota* (Minneapolis: Advocates for Human Rights, 2008), 4.

19. Mark Samels and Sharon Grimberg, executive producers, *We Shall Remain*, episode 5, "Wounded Knee," WGBH Boston, May 2009, http://www.pbs.org/wgbh/amex/weshallremain/.

20. Ibid.

21. Ibid. The episode discusses the assimilation techniques of forcing children to cut their hair, speak only English, and repress the lives they once knew.

22. Maria Yellow Horse Brave Heart and Pemyra M. DeBruyn, "The American Indian Holocaust: Healing Historical Unresolved Grief," *Journal of National Center for American Indian and Alaska Native Mental Health Research* 8, no. 2 (1998): 60, 63–64.

23. Ibid., 63. The authors note that the "messages inherent in the boarding school system…were that American Indian families are not capable of raising their own children."

24. Ibid., 63.

25. Ibid., 64–65.

26. US Senate, "Statement of Senator Beck," *Congressional Globe*, 41st Cong., 3rd Sess. 733 (1871). Congressional debates from 1871 provide some evidence that Congress moved tribes to reservations, rather than exterminating them, in part because it was less expensive than the costs of continued warfare.

27. David Wallace Adams, *Education for Extinction: American Indians and the Boarding School Experience, 1875–1928* (Lawrence: University Press of Kansas, 1995), 95–163, argues that the goal of boarding Indian children was to remove them from their savage surroundings and to place them in a purified environment in order for them to learn to look, act, and think like their white counterparts. Deloria, *Custer Died for Your Sins*,

16, recounts laws and practices that forced Indians to conform to white institutions, including kidnapping Indian children and shipping them to boarding schools. Sandra Del Valle, *Language Rights and the Law in the United States: Finding Our Voices* (Bristol, UK: Multilingual Matters, 2003), 276–286, discusses the prohibition on children speaking their native Indian languages and how this helped stigmatize and destroy Indian culture.

28. Barbara Perry, "From Ethnocide to Ethnoviolence: Layers of Native American Victimization," *Contemporary Justice Review* 5, no. 3 (2002): 231, 236.

29. Janelle F. Palacios and Carmen J. Portillo, "Understanding Native Women's Health: Historical Legacies," *Journal of Transcultural Nursing* 20, no. 3 (2009): 15, 21.

30. Adams, *Education for Extinction*, 98, describes several documented accounts of the "final farewells."

31. In 1892, the commissioner of Indian Affairs, Thomas J. Morgan, issued a rule that Indians who attempted to "prevent the attendance of children at school" were guilty of an offense and subject to imprisonment "for not less than ten days." Subsequent offense could be punished by as much as six months' incarceration. H.R. Doc. No. 52-1, pt. 5, at 28–31 (1892), reprinted in *Americanizing the American Indians: Writings by the "Friends of the Indian," 1880–1900*, ed. Francis Paul Prucha (Lincoln: University of Nebraska Press, 1973), 300. See also Adams, *Education for Extinction*, 209–214, for a discussion of parents' attempts to keep their children from being taken to the schools and their reasons.

32. K. Tsianina Lomawaima, *They Called It Prairie Light: The Story of Chilocco Indian School* (Lincoln: University of Nebraska Press, 1994), 36. See also Frank Wilson Blackmar, "The Socialization of the American Indian," *American Journal of Sociology* 34, no. 4 (1929): 653, 658. Blackmar notes that the reluctance of Indian parents to send their children away "kept the agents busy running over the country and gathering in their students."

33. US Department of the Interior, *Annual Report of the Commissioner of Indian Affairs, 1889*, Office of Indian Affairs (Washington, DC: US Government Printing Office, 1889), 422.

34. Lomawaima, *Prairie Light*, xiv.

35. Bethany Ruth Berger, "After Pocahontas: Indian Women and the Law, 1830–1934," *American Indian Law Review* 21, no. 1 (1997): 1, 49: "To ensure that the female pupils would not backslide into Indian ways, the girls were 'placed out' during vacation to give them experience with a non-Indian family."

36. Robert A. Trennert, "Victorian Morality and the Supervision of Indian Women Working in Phoenix, 1906–1930," *Journal of Social History* 20, no. 1 (1986): 113, 115. The federal government itself noted that income from the labor of Indian students could be used to help fund the establishment of additional schools. US Department of the

Interior, *Annual Report of the Commissioner*, 424.

37. Trennert, "Victorian Morality," 115. See also Berger, "After Pocahontas," 49, discussing the policy of placing Indian girls in white homes to learn domestic service, often leading to a permanent position when they were done with school.

38. Trennert, "Victorian Morality," 115.

39. Ibid., 114.

40. Ibid., 113.

41. Lomawaima, *Prairie Light*, 81.

42. Robert A. Trennert, "Corporal Punishment and the Politics of Indian Reform," *History of Education* 29, no. 4 (1989): 595, discusses American Indian Defense Association executive secretary John Collier's report on corporal punishment at Phoenix Indian School in 1930, which the author argues was undertaken to force the restructuring of the Bureau of Indian Affairs and for political gain.

43. The Phoenix Indian School building included a jail as early as 1893, three years after opening its doors; Trennert, "Corporal Punishment," 598. At Chilocco Indian School in Oklahoma, "punishment…was solitary confinement in the 'dark room,' where the only light entered through a four-inch square in the door"; Lomawaima, *Prairie Light*, 23. While attendance at boarding schools is no longer mandatory, some original punitive policies have continued with little or no modification. At least one "holding cell" in a government-run Indian boarding school was documented to exist as recently as 2003: Cindy Lou Bright Star Gilbert Sohappy, a sixteen-year-old student, died in the "holding cell" at Chemawa Boarding School in Oregon (a federally run boarding school that originally opened in 1880). See Earl E. Devaney, *Investigative Report on the Chemawa Indian School Detention Facility*, US Department of the Interior, Office of Inspector General (Washington, DC, 2005), 3–6. An official federal report on the death indicates that Cindy Lou was placed in a cell because of alcohol intoxication (p. 3). Despite regulations that required her well-being to be monitored every fifteen minutes, Cindy Lou was left alone in the cell for nearly three hours, during which time she died of alcohol poisoning (p. 5).

44. Lomawaima, *Prairie Light*, details alumni accounts of life at the Chilocco Indian Agricultural School.

45. Jackie Lynne, "Colonialism and the Sexual Exploitation of Canada's First Nations Women," paper presented at the American Psychological Association 106th Annual Convention, San Francisco, August 17, 1998, http://www.prostitutionresearch.com/colonialism.html.

46. Ibid.

47. Stephanie Woodard, "South Dakota Boarding School Survivors Detail Sexual Abuse," *Indian Country Today*, July 28, 2011.

48. Trafficking Victim Protection Act, 22 U.S.C. § 7101(b)(4) (2008).

49. Sherene H. Razack, "Gendered Racial Violence and Spatialized Justice: The Murder of Pamela George," *Canadian Journal of Law and Society* 15, no. 2 (2000): 91, 97.

50. Ann Metcalf, "Navajo Women in the City: Lessons from a Quarter-Century of Relocation," *American Indian Quarterly* 6, nos. 1–2 (1982): 71, 83.

51. Joan Ablon, "American Indian Relocation: Problems of Dependency and Management in the City," *Phylon* 26, no. 4 (1965): 362. The word "voluntary" was probably employed to differentiate the program from the involuntary "relocation program" established to imprison Japanese Americans during World War II. Dillon S. Myer, the civilian official in charge of the Japanese American internment camps in the 1940s, served as the commissioner of Indian Affairs during the pinnacle of the Indian urban relocation programs in the 1950s. See Richard Drinnon, *Keeper of Concentration Camps: Dillon S. Myer and American Racism* (Berkeley: University of California Press, 1987).

52. Metcalf, "Navajo Women," 72.

53. United Sioux Tribes of South Dakota Development Corporation Services, accessed November 18, 2009, http://unitedsioux.com/services.html.

54. Metcalf, "Navajo Women," 83.

55. Gary D. Sandefur, Ronald R. Rindfuss, and Barney Cohen, eds., *Changing Numbers, Changing Needs: American Indian Demography and Public Health* (Washington, DC: National Academy Press, 1996), 109.

56. Jennifer B. Unger, Claradina Soto, and Natalie Thomas, "Translation of Health Programs for American Indians in the United States," *Evaluation and the Health Professions* 31, no. 2 (2008): 124.

57. Ablon, "American Indian Relocation," 362, explains the perks of moving to the city as part of the relocation project.

58. Theodore D. Graves, "Urban Indian Personality and the Culture of Poverty," *American Ethnologist* 1, no. 1 (1974): 65, 66.

59. Metcalf, "Navajo Women," 73.

60. Ibid. Metcalf states that "the BIA provided one-way transportation to the selected city."

61. Ablon, "American Indian Relocation," 370: "The Bureau of Indian Affairs has had no program to follow-up relocatees except through chance encounters or by the 'grapevine,' and has not followed the progress of self-relocatees at all."

62. Yellow Horse Brave Heart and DeBruyn, "The American Indian Holocaust," 64, assert that American Indians living in urban areas "face a concerted lack of economic and health resources."

63. Ablon, "American Indian Relocation," 363. Many Native people found it difficult to secure employment because of racial prejudice. For example, a University

of Minnesota study of South Minneapolis businesses in 1970 revealed that anti-Indian sentiment was not uncommon. Richard P. Gibbons et al., "Indian Americans in Southside Minneapolis: Additional Field Notes from the Urban Slum," (Center for Urban and Regional Affairs, University of Minnesota, 1970), http://www.cura.umn.edu/publications/catalog/m1027. Among the interviewees were a flower shop owner who said that Indians "don't belong in the city but back at home on the reservation with their own people" (p. 7), a real estate agent who believed that Indians "are very dishonest and only tell you what they want to hear" (p. 10), and a gas station owner who stated, "The Indian women, they're pigs" (p. 13).

64. Ablon, "American Indian Relocation," 365.

65. Maureen Trudelle Schwarz, "Unraveling the Anchoring Cord: Navajo Relocation, 1974 to 1996," *American Anthropologist* 99, no. 1 (1997): 43, 50.

66. Graves, "Urban Indian Personality," 66.

67. Donald H. J. Clairmont, *Deviance among Indians and Eskimos in Aklavik, NWT*. (Ottawa: Department of Northern Affairs and Natural Resources, Northern Coordination and Research Centre,1963).

68. Albon, "American Indian Relocation," 368.

69. Clairmont, *Deviance among Indians,* 61.

70. A. M. Ervin, *New Northern Townsmen in Inuvik* (Ottawa: Northern Science Research Group, 1968), 11.

71. Ibid.

72. Melissa Farley, Jacqueline Lynne, and Ann J. Cotton, "Prostitution in Vancouver: Violence and the Colonization of First Nations Women," *Transcultural Psychiatry* 42, no. 2 (2005): 242, 257: "First Nations youth who leave their home communities for urban areas are particularly vulnerable to sexual exploitation in that they are both homeless and in an unfamiliar cultural environment."

73. Testimony of Mrs. Amabel K. Bulin, volunteer social worker, Minneapolis Indian Service, in US House of Representatives, *Investigative Indian Affairs: Hearings before Subcommittee of Committee of Indian Affairs,* Committee of Indian Affairs, 78th Cong. (1944), 675–677. Mrs. Bulin's testimony reflects racial prejudice against black people—particularly the "colored men" she accused of taking advantage of the Indian girls in the "slums" of Minneapolis (page 675).

74. See Robert E. Kuttner and Albert B. Lorincz, "Promiscuity and Prostitution in Urbanized Indian Communities," *Mental Hygiene* 54, no. 1 (1970): 79, for two doctors' opinions on factors promoting prostitution of Native women in an urban setting.

75. Ibid., 80, 82.

76. Ibid., 84.

77. Trafficking Victim Protection Act, 22 U.S.C. § 7101 (2006, amended 2008).

78. Child Welfare Partnership, "Disproportionality and Disparities in Oregon's Child Welfare System, State Level Data Analysis: Executive Summary," a report to the Oregon Child Welfare Equity Task Force (2009). However, reports show that Native children continue to be significantly overrepresented in the foster care system. A recent study from Oregon found that Native children are six times more likely to be placed in foster care than white children (page 4).

79. The Indian Self-Determination and Education Assistance Act, for example, transferred some federal funding to the control of tribal governments; see Public Law No. 93–638, 88 Stat. 2203 (1975). This act affected self-governance activities, including education, law enforcement, and natural resources management.

80. Rose Weston, "Facing the Past, Facing the Future: Applying the Truth Commission Model to the Historical Treatment of Native Americans in the United States," *Arizona Journal of International and Comparative Law* 18 (2001): 1017–1018. In 2000, the assistant secretary for Indian Affairs, Kevin Gover (Pawnee), did issue a comprehensive apology from the Bureau of Indian Affairs, acknowledging that agents of the US government perpetrated "acts against the children entrusted to its boarding schools, brutalizing them emotionally, psychologically, physically, and spiritually." Kevin Gover, remarks at the Ceremony Acknowledging the 175th Anniversary of the Establishment of the Bureau of Indian Affairs, Washington, DC, September 8, 2000. However, Assistant Secretary Gover was careful to explain, "I do not speak today for the United States." The Commonwealth of Virginia issued a resolution in 2007 that acknowledged "with profound regret the involuntary servitude of Africans and the exploitation of Native Americans." Virginia General Assembly, Henry L. Marsh, S.J. Resolution 332, 2007 Sess. (2007).

81. Razack, "Gendered Racial Violence," 94.

82. Yellow Horse Brave Heart and DeBruyn, "The American Indian Holocaust," 60, note that "indigenous people throughout the world can trace social pathologies and internalized oppression to similar historical legacies." Many of the official strategies in the United States have a parallel strategy in Canada. For example, the urbanization of Native people in both countries was part of an effort to find them employment. See Allison M. Williams, "Canadian Urban Aboriginals: A Focus on Aboriginal Women in Toronto," *Canadian Journal of Native Studies* 1 (1997): 179–180.

83. Farley, Lynne, and Cotton, "Prostitution in Vancouver," 245, note that "in a number of communities across Canada, Aboriginal youth [compose] 90% of the visible sex trade," quoting *Year One: 1999–2000, Out of the Shadows and into the Light: A Project to Address the Commercial Sexual Exploitation of Girls and Boys in Canada* (Vancouver, BC: Save the Children Canada, 2000), 7.

84. Dara Culhane, "Their Spirits Live within Us," *American Indian Quarterly* 27, no. 3 (2003): 593–606, citing Sue Currie, *Assessing the Violence against Street Involved Women in*

the Downtown Eastside/Strathcona Community, Ministry of Women's Equality (Vancouver, BC, 2000).

85. Mike McIntyre, "Hundreds of Kids in Sex Trade," *Winnipeg Free Press,* February 20, 2007, http://www.cyc-net.org/features/viewpoints/c-sextrade.html.

86. Ibid.

87. Ibid.

88. Ibid. McIntyre notes that the statistics indicate "the importance of placing prostitution in historical context."

89. Iris McKeown, Sharon Reid, and Pamela Orr, "Experiences of Sexual Violence and Relocation in the Lives of HIV Infected Canadian Women," *International Journal of Circumpolar Health* 63, no. 5 (2003): 399, 403.

90. Hodge, "Sexual Trafficking," 148, writes, "Traffickers deliberately seek out obscure venues to avoid detection. Victims often remain in the shadows because of the fear of arrest; reprisals from traffickers; or the fear that officials are corrupt, unconcerned, or aligned with the traffickers."

91. Alexandra (Sandi) Pierce, *Shattered Hearts: The Commercial Sexual Exploitation of American Indian Women and Girls in Minnesota* (Minneapolis: Minnesota Indian Women's Resource Center, 2009).

92. Suzanne Koepplinger, "Sex Trafficking of American Indian Women and Girls in Minnesota," *University of St. Thomas Law Journal* 6 (2008): 129, 130.

93. Christopher B. Chaney, "Overcoming Legal Hurdles in the War against Meth in Indian Country," *North Dakota Law Review* 82 (2006): 1151, 1155, notes that "drug dealers are targeting Indian country jurisdictions for drug trafficking."

94. Debra K. Boyer and Jennifer James, "Prostitutes as Victims," *Deviants: Victims or Victimizers?* 3, no. 1 (1983): 109, 131.

95. Hodge, "Sexual Trafficking," 146, states that traffickers might target "unsuspecting individuals who lack social ties."

96. Robert W. Deisher, J. A. Farrow, K. Hope, and C. Litchfield, "The Pregnant Adolescent Prostitute," *American Journal of Diseases of Children* 143, no. 10 (1989): 1162, 1164. But cf. Cathy Spatz Widom, "Victims of Childhood Sexual Abuse: Later Criminal Consequences," *National Institute of Justice Research in Brief* (Washington, DC: US Department of Justice, 1995), 2–5, http://www.ncjrs.gov/pdffiles/abuse.pdf. Widom points out, however, that "the majority of the sexually abused children in this study do not have an official criminal history as adults."

97. Linda Cusick, "Youth Prostitution: A Literature Review," *Child Abuse Review* 11, no. 4 (2002): 230, 234.

98. Cathy Spatz Widom and Joseph B. Kuhns, "Childhood Victimization and Subsequent Risk for Promiscuity, Prostitution, and Teenage Pregnancy: A Prospective

Study," *American Journal of Public Health* 86, no. 11 (1996): 1607, 1611.

99. Bachman et al., *Violence against American Indian*, 33; Perry, *American Indians and Crime*, 6.

100. In one study, the federal government determined that 85 percent of women arrested for prostitution in twenty-four cities tested positive for drugs. See US Department of Justice, "Fact Sheet: Drug-Related Crime," Bureau of Justice Statistics (Washington, DC: US Government Printing Office, 1994), 2.

101. Widom and Kuhns, "Childhood Victimization," 1607.

102. Jody M. Greene, Susan T. Ennett, and Christopher L. Ringwalt, "Prevalence and Correlates of Survival Sex among Runaway and Homeless Youth," *American Journal of Public Health* 89, no. 9 (1999): 1406, explain, "'Survival sex' refers to the selling of sex to meet subsistence needs. It includes the exchange of sex for shelter, food, drugs, or money."

103. This notion is beyond the scope of the current chapter. The focus here is on those who are prostituted as children or who wish to leave prostitution as adults.

104. David Finkelhor and Richard Ormrod, "Prostitution of Juveniles: Patterns from NIBRS," *Juvenile Justice Bulletin* (June 2004): 1–11.

105. Hodge, "Sexual Trafficking," 145. One study of aboriginal women prostitutions in Vancouver found that "the youngest age at recruitment into prostitution was ten years." Farley, Lynne, and Cotton, "Prostitution in Vancouver," 249.

106. US Department of State, "The Link between Prostitution and Sex Trafficking," Bureau of Public Affairs (Washington, DC, 2004), http://www.2001–2009.state.gov/r/pa/ei/rls/38790.htm.

107. Andrew Karmen, *Crime Victims: An Introduction to Victimology*, 7th ed. (Stamford, CT: Cengage Learning Publishing, 2009). See also Bortel et al., *Sex Trafficking Needs Assessment*, 17: "With some exceptions, the government response to sex trafficking in Minnesota currently focuses on the arrest, prosecution, and punishment of prostituted women rather than sex traffickers. This misplaced focus leads to harmful criminal and/or immigration consequences for trafficked persons."

108. Elizabeth Grobsmith, "Review of *Inventing the Savage: The Social Construction of Native American Criminality* by Luana Ross," *Great Plains Research* 9 (1999): 175, 176. See also Lori De Ravello, Jessica Abeita, and Pam Brown, "Breaking the Cycle/Mending the Hoop: Adverse Childhood Experiences among Incarcerated American Indian/Alaska Native Women in New Mexico," *Health Care for Women International* 29, no. 3 (2008): 300, 301–302. Incarceration rates are extremely high among Native populations. For example, in Alaska, Native people make up 30 to 40 percent of the incarcerated population in the state but less than 10 percent of the population overall. David Blurton and Gary D. Copus, "Alaska Native Inmates: The Demographic Relationship between

Upbringing and Crime," *Prison Journal* 83, no. 1 (2003): 90.

109. Bortel et al., *Sex Trafficking Needs Assessment*, 43.

110. Hodge, "Sexual Trafficking," 150.

111. The US Senate Committee on Indian Affairs held hearings in summer 2009 to examine the increase of gang activity on Indian reservations. US Senate, *Oversight Hearing to Examine the Increase of Gang Activity in Indian Country*, Committee on Indian Affairs, Hearing on SD 628, 111st Cong. (2009), 1.

112. Raymond and Hughes, *Sex Trafficking of Women*, 10: "Recruiters, traffickers, and pimps are involved in other criminal activity, such as fraud, extortion, migrant smuggling, theft, and money laundering, in addition to trafficking and prostitution."

113. *Oliphant v. Suquamish Indian Tribe*, 435 U.S. 191, 195 (1978).

114. The Violence against Women Act Reauthorization in 2013 provided a small restoration of tribal sovereignty in the prosecution of non-Indians, but only those who committed violence against their Native spouse or intimate partner.

115. A review of tribal codes yielded no criminal statutes that can be categorized as antitrafficking statutes. However, tribal codes often contain crimes of kidnapping, prostitution, rape, and sexual abuse, which frequently apply in trafficking cases. In *Fort Peck Tribes v. Martell*, the tribal court prosecuted a crime that could be categorized as trafficking. See *Fort Peck Assiniboine and Sioux Tribes v. Martell* (1990), Fort Peck Tribal Court, Appellate Opinion No. 090 (1990), http://www.fptc.org/appellate _opinions/090.html. In that case, the defendant (an adult tribal member) was charged with transporting a fourteen-year-old female to Havre, Montana (off reservation) and using alcohol and/or drugs to coerce the victim to have intercourse with him. The defendant raised several defenses, including a challenge to tribal jurisdiction over a crime that was alleged to have occurred, in part, outside of tribal territory. The tribal appellate court determined that since elements of the crime occurred on reservation (the coercion and initial transportation), the tribes retained criminal jurisdiction.

116. The Indian Civil Rights Act of 1968 limits tribal sentencing authority to a maximum of one-year incarceration or $5,000 fine or both. US Congress, 25 U.S.C. §§ 1301–1303 (1990).

117. For a discussion of jurisdictional issues, see Amnesty International, *Maze of Injustice: The Failure to Protect Indigenous Women from Sexual Violence in the USA* (New York: Amnesty International Publications, 2007), 27–41, http://www.amnestyusa.org /women/maze/report.pdf. Carole Goldberg-Ambrose, *Planting Tail Feathers: Tribal Survival and Public Law 280* (Berkeley: University of California Press, 1997), 45–125, discusses jurisdiction over reservation Indians. Vine Deloria Jr. and Clifford M. Lytle, *American Indians, American Justice* (Austin: University of Texas Press, 1983), 110–136, cover the Indian judicial system.

118. Amnesty International, *Stolen Sisters: Discrimination and Violence against Indigenous Women in Canada* (New York: Amnesty International Publications, 2004), 24, http://www.amnesty.ca/stolensisters/amr2000304.pdf.

119. Robert William Pickton, a Canadian pig farmer, is suspected in at least twenty-six murders and was convicted of six of them. As of this writing, his case was on appeal. Steve Mertl, "Pickton's Lawyer Wants Top Court Appeal," *CNEWS*, September 10, 2009, http://cnews.canoe.ca/CNEWS/Canada/2009/09/10/10824936-cp.html. See also Keith Bonnell, "Highways a Hunting Ground for Killers," *Vancouver Sun*, August 10, 2009, http://www.vancouversun.com/news/Highways+hunting+ground+killers/1877414/story.html, for discussion of serial killers suspected to have dumped more than thirty-two aboriginal women's bodies along one stretch of Canadian highway from Prince George to Prince Rupert. John Martin Crawford was convicted in 1996 of killing three Native women prostitutes in Saskatoon. Law enforcement failed to follow up on several initial reports of Crawford's sixteen-year violent crime spree directed toward aboriginal women; see Warren Goulding, *Just Another Indian: A Serial Killer and Canada's Indifference* (Ontario: Fifth House Publishers, 2001).

120. US Department of Justice, "Highway Serial Killings: New Initiative on an Emerging Trend," Federal Bureau of Investigation (Washington, DC, April 6, 2009), accessed November 10, 2009, http://www.fbi.gov/page2/april09/highwayserialkillings_040609.html.

121. Ibid.

122. Bachman et al., *Violence against American Indian*, 25.

123. One such research project is Melissa Farley, Nicole Matthews, Sarah Deer, Guadalupe Lopez, Christine Stark, and Eileen Hudon, *Garden of Truth: The Prostitution and Trafficking of Native Women in Minnesota*, a report sponsored by the Minnesota Indian Women's Sexual Assault Coalition and presented at William Mitchell College of Law, Saint Paul, MN, October 27, 2011.

124. Bortel et al., *Sex Trafficking Needs Assessment*, 65.

125. Palacios and Portillo, "Understanding Native Women's Health," 15–27: "Interventions to address these health disparities should be based on research findings that foster an understanding of marginalization and the context from which it arises."

11

Slavery and Prostitution

A Twenty-First-Century Abolitionist Perspective

Melissa Farley

A turning point in the British abolitionist movement was the publication of a now iconic diagram of a ship that transported slaves from Ghana to England.[1] The drawing shows slaves stacked like sardines, 482 human beings packed into the hull of the ship. It was a factual diagram carefully drawn to scale. This powerful image sparked outrage in the public. To the slave owners and traders, the image was unanswerable. Overwhelmingly, the public responded: How can we abolish slavery?

I know of places like that ship—in 2008 a California pimp transported young women, also lined up like sardines, in the trunk of his car, popping the trunk open for sex buyers to see what he had for sale.[2] One of the young women who had been in that car was the fourth generation of women in her family who had been prostituted. She had grown up with homelessness, drug abuse, racism, incest, sexualization as a child and sexual assaults by neighbors and family, overwhelming community violence, physical abuse, emotional and physical neglect, a lack of educational resources, a lack of employment opportunities, a lack of social services or legal protection, and a lack of mental health services. Because she wanted to escape her captors, she tried to get arrested by soliciting for prostitution in front of police stations. By the time she was eighteen, eight pimps had traded her, including two who put their tattooed symbols of ownership on her body (figure 11.1).

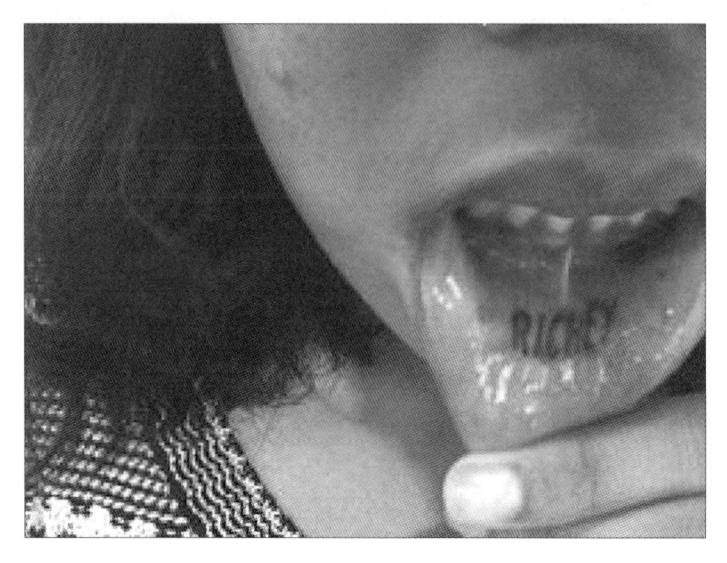

FIGURE 11.1
Woman pulling down her lip to show a tattoo of the name of her pimp, Richey. (Amita Sharma, KPBS, 2011)

According to many research studies that will be noted here, slavery and pimp-controlled prostitution are the same experience *from the perspective of the enslaved or prostituted*. The abuses of power in prostitution and the abuses of power in slavery, discussed here, are profound social injustices resulting in great harm.[3] The same arguments that justified the abolition of slavery also justify the abolition of prostitution. Pimps and traffickers are traders who own and enslave human beings. Sex buyers purchase these people, exploiting and abusing them. The adverse consequences resulting from harms inflicted by sex buyers on the women they use, rent, or own are discussed here. The inequalities and harms in prostitution are paralleled by inequalities and harms in relationships between slave owners and slaves. In the 1800s, conditions in the South and in the Atlantic African slave trade were so inhumane that they precipitated an international movement for emancipation and for abolition of legal slavery. Today, the same kinds of abuse have ignited a similar movement to abolish the global business of prostitution. As in the nineteenth century, the legal definition of slavery is today debated in some quarters, including whether or not an understanding of slavery should be applied to prostitution. The challenges of defining, understanding, and abolishing prostitution are compounded by the resistance of pimps, sex buyers, and organized criminals who campaign to romanticize or deny the realities of prostitution. In the nineteenth century, similar struggles were waged among slave owners, slave buyers, and abolitionists.

Trafficking and modern-day pimping have parallels not only in the chattel slavery practiced by the colonists of North America but also in the enslavement of indigenous women. Captive taking in warfare or civil conflict, usually with a focus on female captives, has been practiced throughout history.[4] While the hostages/slaves offered by Powhatan, the father of Pocahontas, to the British colonists are familiar, less so is the British offering to Powhatan of an English youth who was probably an indentured servant or temporary slave.[5] Like today's sales of young women by marriage brokers,[6] the prostitution of Native women by colonists who were engaged in the fur trade or military, and who often had wives in Europe, was a result of poverty and sexism on all sides.[7] James Brooks has described the enslavement and sale of peoples by both Native Americans and European Americans. At the heart of these reciprocal practices of slavery in the Southwest was the sexism of both indigenous and Spanish men. Control and ownership of women and children were proof of social status.[8] Although captives were sometimes adopted or married in the captor's culture, the experience of the captive remains very much like that of the enslaved. Similarly, pimps marry prostituted women in order to extend their control over them and to produce children. Just as the market for and trade in captives in Native American and New Mexican societies provided lower-status slavers the opportunity to accumulate power and prestige,[9] so, also, gang-controlled prostitution allows lower-status members of the culture, often ethnically marginalized men, the opportunity for significant financial gains. Some members of the Chinook and the Clatsop nations pimped enslaved women to colonists on the Northwest coast of the United States.[10]

THE RELATIONSHIP BETWEEN SELLER/MASTER AND ENSLAVED AND BETWEEN PIMP/SEX BUYER AND PROSTITUTED

Domination and Dehumanization

There are many parallels between slavery and prostitution. Prostitution is an institution of male dominance, just as transatlantic slavery was an institution of white European racial dominance. Racism drove the objectification and dehumanization of enslaved Africans, just as sexism drives the objectification and dehumanization in prostitution. Both institutions commodify human beings. Women are permitted no dignity in slavery or in prostitution. The enslaved and the prostituted are marginalized and degraded in culturally tolerated rituals that conceal deadly violations of basic human rights. Over time, the humiliation and degradation produce a core sense of incapacitating shame in the enslaved or prostituted person.

The viewpoints of buyers can be enlightening. For example, a twentieth-century planter said, "We used to own our slaves, now we just rent them,"[11] while a Nevada pimp described the temporary ownership of prostitution as being "like the time-share of a vacation home."[12] Prostitution can also be understood as renting a woman's vagina, breasts, anus, and mouth. Sex buyers' attitudes resemble those of slave buyers. Research interviews in which sex buyers were asked to define prostitution were revealing: "You get what you pay for without the 'no'"[13] and "It's like renting an organ for ten minutes."[14]

Women in both prostitution and slavery are commodities. Commodification requires objectification, changing people from humans into objects with economic value.[15] A pimp explained commodification at its most basic: "I took the kind of girl no one would miss so when they were resold, no one would look for them. It is as if I sold a kilo of bread."[16] In the same way, slave owners attributed characteristics to Africans that rationalized their intrinsic nonhumanity, thereby allowing the owners to justify any violence or abuse perpetrated against those they enslaved.

Commodification is eroticized in both slavery and prostitution. Sex buyers are aroused by the fact that they are buying or renting a "whore" who "willingly" degrades herself by submitting to her own sexual exploitation. "By taking money in exchange for sex, she strips herself of her own humanity and so 'legitimately' becomes nothing more than the embodiment of his masturbatory fantasy."[17] The temporary domination/ownership of a woman by a sex buyer is at the erotic core of prostitution. John Stoltenberg has suggested that possession is a centerpiece of men's sexual behavior.[18] Economic and sexual ownership bolsters masculinity. The intertwining of economics and sexuality in prostitution has many parallels in slavery. In reviewing letters between a slave trader and buyer from 1834, historian Edward Baptist analyzed the rape of slave women, their sexual commodification, and the fetishization of the slave trade. The economic and sexual passion for ownership of slaves was shared by traders and buyers alike. Baptist describes letters between men who owned an established slave-trading company in New Orleans and a slave buyer who was sexually obsessed with "mulatto" women slaves, that is, those women who were themselves the result of the rape of African women by slave owners. "Sexual fetishes and commodity fetishism intertwined with such intimacy that coerced sex was the secret meaning of commerce in human beings."[19] Slave sellers and buyers cataloged skin color in fetishistic detail.[20] Today sex buyers compulsively catalog details about women they buy for sex, criticizing, grading, and bragging about purchased sex via online chat boards.[21] Prostituted and enslaved women are forced to wear special clothing that identifies and advertises them.[22] If online technology had existed in the nineteenth century, slave traders would certainly have cataloged and advertised enslaved women to be sold for use in prostitution on the plantations or in brothels.

Profound Psychological and Physical Harm Resulting from Slavery and from Prostitution

Women are nonpersons in prostitution. Payment of money in prostitution, as in slavery, releases the buyer from any obligation to treat the bought person as human. A prostituted girl said, "Prostitution makes me feel like I am nothing, nothing at all."[23] To slave traders and owners, the black woman was "a fragmented commodity whose feelings and choices were rarely considered: her head and her heart were separated from…her womb and vagina."[24] The dehumanization and objectification intrinsic to enslavement and to prostitution result in a psychologically traumatized status that has accurately been described as social death.[25] The acts perpetrated on a woman in prostitution define her as a degraded object, as "cunt," as "filthy whore." Her self, her individuality, her humanity are systematically attacked and destroyed in prostitution. She is reduced to vagina, anus, breasts, and mouth. She acts the part of what men want her to be.[26] The only "plausible line in the…film *Pretty Woman*," said a prostituted woman, "is when Richard Gere, playing a client, asks Julia Roberts, playing a prostitute, what her name is, and she replies, 'Anything you want it to be.'"[27] Enslaved people at auctions said what they thought the slave traders and the slave buyers wanted to hear. "In the slave pens, the ethereal fantasies of the slaveholding regime were daily converted into the material shape of sold slaves."[28] The commodification that exists in the minds of traders, pimps, sex buyers, and slave buyers is ultimately incorporated into the identity of the prostituted or enslaved person. As a woman in strip club prostitution explained, "You start changing yourself to fit a fantasy role of what they think a woman should be. In the real world, these women don't exist. They stare at you with this starving hunger. It sucks you dry; you become this empty shell. They're not really looking at you. You're not you. You're not even there."[29]

Degradation and humiliation are central to the experience of women in prostitution and slavery. Nonslaves had difficulty understanding the depths of slavery's degradation, according to former slave Harriet Jacobs.[30]

Similarly, prostitution survivor and author Claude Jaget described the shattering experience of being selected from a brothel lineup:

> I'd freeze up inside.... It was horrible, they'd look you up and down. That moment, when you felt them looking at you, sizing you up, judging you...and those men, those fat pigs who weren't worth half as much as the worst of us, they'd joke, make comments.... They made you turn and face in all directions, because of course a front view wasn't enough for them. It used to make me furious, but at the same time I was panic-stricken, I didn't dare speak. I wasn't physically frightened, but it shook my confidence. I felt really [demeaned].... I was the thing he came and literally bought. He had judged me like he'd judge cattle at a fairground, and that's revolting, it's sickening, it's terrible for the women. You can't imagine it if you've never been through it yourself.[31]

The brothel lineup is reminiscent of the terror of the auction block.[32] Women who have survived prostitution say that the experience is so degrading, it is as if one becomes "a kind of human toilet."[33] In the language of the times, an enslaved woman explained that "a slave woman ain't allowed to respect herself."[34] Upon refusal to permit sexual assault by the owner, one sixteen-year-old was sent from the mid-Atlantic to a southern state, where she was worked to death.[35]

High rates of death from homicide are documented among slaves and among those in prostitution. Chronic health problems of enslaved and prostituted women were a result of overwhelming stress, untreated health problems, sexual assault, battering, and torture. A prostituted woman said:

> I've had three broken arms, nose broken twice, and I'm partially deaf in one ear.... I have a small fragment of a bone floating in my head that gives me migraines. I've had a fractured skull. My legs ain't worth shit no more, my toes have been broken. My feet, bottom of my feet, have been burned, they've been whopped with a hot iron and clothes hanger...the hair on my pussy had been burned off at one time...I have scars. I've been cut with a knife, beat with guns, two by fours. There hasn't been a place on my body that hasn't been bruised somehow, some way, some big, some small.[36]

In 1872 a witness described Ku Klux Klan members torturing a young African American woman using nearly identical methods:

> She stated—and I even saw the marks—that she had been whipped on her body and limbs. She also stated that while she was prostrate on the floor, one of them lit a match and burned the hair from her private parts.[37]

Neglect and malnutrition resulted in chronic health problems and reduced life expectancy for women in prostitution and slavery. Unsanitary living conditions, inadequate nutrition, and unrelenting hard labor created a susceptibility to disease.[38] Malnutrition increases susceptibility to infectious diseases and diseases of poverty, such as tuberculosis.[39] US slaves had a life expectancy of about thirty years.[40] Among those in prostitution, similar conditions—overexertion, stress, poor nutrition, and sleeplessness—create parallel vulnerability to illnesses. Like slave masters, pimps control the diets of those in prostitution. The leading causes of death among the enslaved in Virginia in 1850 were respiratory diseases, tuberculosis, nervous system disease, typhoid, diarrhea, and cholera.[41] Common medical problems of women in prostitution include tuberculosis, diabetes, cancer, arthritis, tachycardia, malaria, asthma, anemia, hepatitis, uterine infections, menstrual problems, ovarian pain, abortion complications, pregnancy, hepatitis B, hepatitis C, infertility, syphilis, and HIV.[42]

In slavery and in prostitution, the pain of relentless verbal abuse humiliates, degrades, and causes lasting emotional damage. Enslaved in nineteenth-century North Carolina, Harriet Jacobs wrote, "For my master, whose restless, craving, vicious nature roved about day and night, seeking whom to devour, had just left me, with stinging, scorching words; words that scathed ear and brain like fire. O how I despised him."[43] Using drugs and alcohol to mitigate the pain of the verbal assaults from sex buyers, a woman said, "You get extra extra high so you don't have to deal with those words they call you. They hurt so much, if it was a knife, it would cut you."[44] A survivor's description of the psychological damage of prostitution also applies to slavery: "It is internally damaging. You become in your own mind what these people do and say with you. You wonder how could you let yourself do this and why do these people want to do this to you?"[45]

Coerced rejection of family and community ties are tools of domination and control in slavery and in prostitution. Pimps convince young women who are already likely to be alienated from or abused by their families that the family is the enemy and not to be trusted. The woman's attachments to family and friends are carefully undermined and ultimately destroyed, leaving the pimp as the only available source of support, protection, or validation. In slavery the destruction of family bonds was also

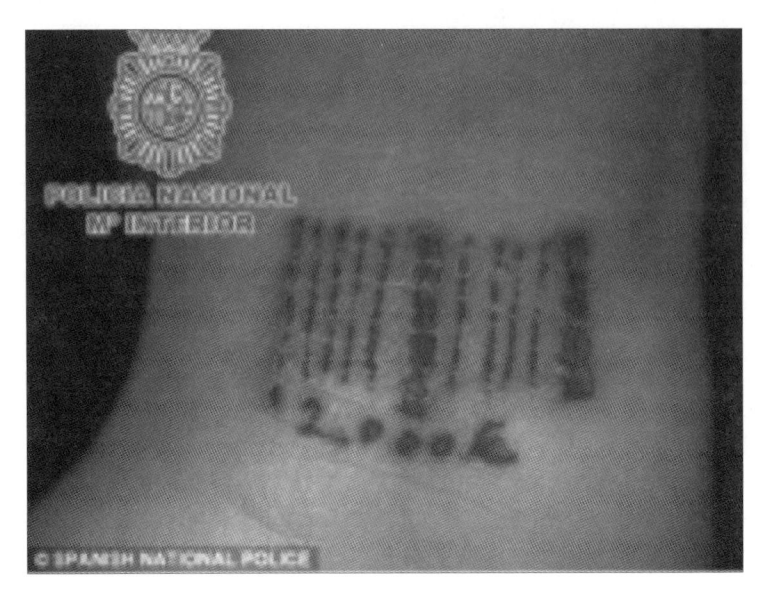

FIGURE 11.2
Bar code on woman's wrist. (Spanish National Police, 2012)

brutal. The ability to separate families at will was at the heart of the social and economic power of the slave buyers and traders.[46] Family members, parents, husbands, and children were sold to different owners.

Change of name is a ritual of enslavement.[47] In prostitution, names also change, along with a new hypersexualized identity. A mark of servitude could be inflicted on the slave, just as pimps and traffickers routinely tattoo their marks on women in prostitution. A Spanish trafficking ring inflicted a bar code branding/tattoo on a woman who tried to escape.[48] She was also beaten. The bar code symbol functioned as the young woman's coerced identity and as a certificate of ownership by a prostitution ring (figure 11.2).

Slave owners' and prostitute buyers' fantasies about slavery and prostitution drive the real lives of those enslaved or prostituted. Planters sometimes mimed the conventions of romance, enabling them to temporarily forget that they owned slaves.[49] Sex buyers today seek a "girlfriend experience" in which prostituted women are paid to mimic a love relationship. The performance is required to be one that fools the sex buyer. From the moment of sale, the purchased or rented person is measured against the buyer's fantasies—the "happy, hardworking Negro from New Orleans" or "the prostitute who loves to have sex with strangers." Failure to live up to these fantasies led to brutal beatings by slave owners. Violence by slave owners was

> the natural result of slaveholders' inevitable failure to live through the stolen bodies of their slaves. In the face of the frailty or resistance of those whom they had bought—publicly caught between their own fantasies of self-amplification and the reality of their dependence—slaveholders often responded with shocking brutality.[50]

Similar failures led to similar violence by sex buyers who rationalized:

> When there is violence, it is mostly the prostitute's fault. See, I am going to buy something. If I am satisfied with what I am buying, then why should I be violent? I will be violent when I am cheated, when I am offered a substandard service.... Sometimes violence is because the prostitute wants the client to use condoms. They force it on the client. He will naturally be disgruntled and there will be altercations.[51]

Suicidal thoughts and actual suicide are consequences of slavery and of prostitution. In two studies at an agency that assisted women in prostitution, a majority of women had made suicide attempts.[52] Equating prostitution with death, one woman stated, "Why commit suicide? I'll work in prostitution instead."[53] Some of the factors that have been connected with suicide by the enslaved include kidnapping, rape and other physical brutality, starvation, family separation, violation of religious beliefs, and unendurable physical pain.[54] Violence, the threat of violence, and psychological coercion ensure that the enslaved and the prostituted do not escape. Today's pimps, like transatlantic slave owners, have bounty hunters to capture women who try to escape.[55] But physical violence is not required for controlling women in prostitution. "They come to perceive their situation not as a deliberate action taken to harm them but as part of the normal, if regrettable, scheme of things."[56] The violent control used by pimps causes feelings not only of terror but also of helplessness and dependence. A prostituted trafficking victim in the United Kingdom explained, "Sometimes I don't see the point in doing anything. It seems useless. When someone has controlled you and made decisions for you for so long, you can't do that for yourself anymore."[57] This same dynamic existed in slavery, with contemporary historians noting the vacant look of despair in the eyes of the enslaved as she was about to be sold.[58] Mental control is accelerated by social isolation and sensory deprivation, which can include locking up victims for long periods of time in windowless rooms to keep them disoriented about time and place, deprived of sunlight, and more vulnerable to the pimp's or master's influence. The social isolation may be so profoundly stressful and disorganizing that the victim will acquiesce to any form of contact, even rape.[59] Pimps and slave owners deliberately traumatize women and children in order to establish control over them. They use starvation, sleep deprivation, protein deprivation, unexpected sexual violence, and learned helplessness.[60] The pimp's total control over young women in prostitution includes what she wears, when and where she can sleep, what and how much she can eat, whether she can use a toilet or access menstrual supplies, if and how much emergency medical care she receives, even how much air and light she is allowed to have. The same survival needs were similarly controlled and manipulated by slave owners.

Coercive subjugation in slavery or prostitution always contains the threat of violence, which is periodically inflicted under conditions that maximize its effects: unpredictably and with an overwhelming intensity. Any move toward autonomy, any attempt on the part of the woman to exert more control over her body or even to use her own critical thinking, is viewed as insubordination.[61] Whenever violence is not inflicted on her, the enslaved or prostituted person is grateful. This coerced gratitude is an essential element of the pimp-prostitute or master-slave relationship. Although it is a dynamic of domination and subordination, it is nonetheless an intimate relationship. Emotional bonding to an abuser under conditions of captivity has been described as Stockholm syndrome.[62] Attitudes and behaviors that are part of this syndrome include intense gratefulness for small favors when the captor holds life-and-death power over the captive, denial of the extent of violence and harm that the captor has inflicted or is obviously capable of inflicting, hypervigilance with respect to the captor's needs, identification with the captor's perspective on the world (an example of this was kidnapped heiress Patty Hearst's identification with her captors' ideology), the perception of those trying to assist in escape as enemies and the perception of captors as friends, and extreme difficulty leaving one's captor/pimp even after physical release has occurred.[63] Paradoxically, women in prostitution or enslaved women may feel that they owe their lives to pimps or to slave owners (figure 11.3).

Enslaved women were sold by slave traders who functioned as pimps to plantation owners for sexual use by the slave master, his friends, and his family. Traders wrote of a "great demand for fancy maids," that is, enslaved

SLAVERY AND PROSTITUTION

FIGURE 11.3

A woman reveals a tattoo showing that she was owned by King Koby, the alias of her pimp, Vincent George, who was convicted of promoting prostitution and money laundering in 2013. (Anthony Delmundo, New York Daily News, *2013)*

women who were sold as prostitutes to pimps who ran brothels.[64] Light-skinned women—born of rapes by slave owners—were valued as prostitutes and domestically trafficked. Commenting on this, a South Carolina man said, "The availability of slave women for sex avoided the horrors of prostitution...men could satisfy their sexual needs while increasing their slave property."[65] Slaves were also exploited as wet nurses and substitute mothers.

Slave owners benefited from slaves' impregnation because children born to slave women became slaves themselves. After the United States banned the importing of slaves in 1808, the breeding of enslaved women became big business, with some plantations devoted exclusively to the heinous practice.[66]

> They would buy a fine girl and a fine man and just put them

> together like cattle.... If she was a good breeder, they was proud of her.... I had an aunt in Mississippi and she had about twenty children by her marster.[67]

The harvesting of children from women in prostitution in order to produce the next generation of "sex workers" parallels the breeding of slaves. Rapes of prostituted women confer similar economic benefits on pimps, some of whom deliberately impregnate women. Prostitution survivors have described breeding programs run by trafficking syndicates. By "raising his own ho," one pimp said, he created a population of the most malleable prostitutes, since he was able to control them from birth onward.[68] The adult woman is easier to control via her child and is an easy target for threats, blackmail, and coerced choices of all kinds.

Torture

Torture is "any act by which severe pain or suffering, whether physical or mental, is intentionally inflicted on a person for such purposes as punishing him...or intimidating or coercing him or a third person, or for any reason based on discrimination of any kind."[69] According to recent definitions, torture can be a private event, as well as one that is state sponsored. There are many accounts of women's torture under slavery[70] and under prostitution.[71] Most of the psychological, sexual, and physical coercion used by slave owners and pimps meets legal definitions of torture.[72]

As in slavery, the use of well-known torture methods ensures that women will comply with any demands of sex buyers or pimps. Specific acts commonly perpetrated against prostituted women are the same acts that define torture: forced nudity, sexual mocking, rape, verbal sexual harassment, physical sexual harassment, and not permitting basic hygiene. In California, a girl described pimps' torture methods:

> When a pimp says he's going to torture you, what I've seen is girls in dog cages, girls being waterboarded, stripped down naked and put in the rain and cold outside and having to stand there all night, and if you move, you'll get beaten. I've seen girls get hit by cars and stunned with stun guns.... I've seen girls burned and strangled.[73]

Enforced nudity in slavery, torture, and prostitution is not only humiliating, it also marks its victims with shame, dehumanization, and vulnerability to rape.[74] Rape is used in torture and in prostitution as the primary method of control. The intimate, aggressive domination of rape drives home the massive inequality between the dominator and the subordinated. Describing the utter destruction of dignity and self, a man told Human Rights Watch that prison rape was "being made into a person of no self-worth, re-made into whatever the person or the gang doing the raping wants you to be."[75] In 2001, rape was designated a crime against humanity by the International Criminal Court. In prostitution or slavery, rape must be understood as an act of torture that has the goal of dominating an entire class of people.[76]

The same sexual humiliation used in slavery and in state-sponsored torture is inflicted in prostitution. Historian Joanna Bourke described the photographs of US military torture at Abu Ghraib:

> Torture aims to undermine the way the victim relates to his or her own self, and thus threatens to dissolve the mainsprings of an individual's personality.... The sexual nature of these acts shows that the torturers realise the centrality of sexuality for their victims' identity. The perpetrators in these photographs aim to destroy their victim's sense of self by inflicting and recording extreme sexual humiliation.[77]

Many viewed this torture of prisoners by the United States at Abu Ghraib with shock and horror, yet when the same acts are paid for by men who use prostituted women, torture is redefined as sexual entertainment.

CHOICE VERSUS CHOICELESSNESS AND LAWS REGARDING SLAVERY AND PROSTITUTION

Slavery removes freedom and imposes choicelessness, backed up by violence or the threat of violence. The elements of slavery are present in the relationship between pimps/traffickers and those they prostitute, including gross power inequity, physical abuse, and lack of free will.[78] Yet some assert that most adult women in prostitution freely consent to it.[79] Others point out that if a woman in prostitution is physically or mentally controlled by a pimp, then she is enslaved and without freedom. According to a survey of eighteen sources, including research studies and both governmental and nongovernmental reports, on average, 84 percent of all women in prostitution are pimped, trafficked, or under the control of third parties.[80] Two research studies found that while 89 to 90 percent of women wanted to escape prostitution, they did not feel free to exit, because of a lack of alternatives for survival.[81] One man explained:

> I don't think prostitution is quite the same as rape. Rape is worse. But it's close to the rape end of the spectrum. It's not rape, because there is superficial consent.... On the face of it, the prostitute is agreeing to it. But deeper down, you can see that

life circumstances have kind of forced her into that.... It's like someone jumping from a burning building—you could say they made their choice to jump, but you could also say they had no choice.[82]

Prostitution has been described as "the choice made by those who have no choice."[83] A woman in a Nevada legal brothel said, "No one really enjoys being sold. It's like you sign a contract to be raped."[84] Another woman characterized Dutch legal prostitution as "volunteer slavery."[85] The pimp, trafficker, or slave owner behind the practice remains invisible. Studying histories of captive taking, Cameron noted that "the distinction between voluntary (and likely desperate) refugee and violently acquired captive is difficult to discern."[86]

Less visible factors contribute to women's enslavement. Hunger combined with a lack of education or job training can compel a woman into prostitution, from which it then becomes difficult, if not impossible, to escape. Poor women exchanged sex acts for hamburgers[87] and gas money.[88] The more financially desperate she is and the more her life has been limited by racist inequality or by sexual assaults, then the less freedom she has and the more limited her resources for escape from prostitution. Yet a debate is waged over whether hunger and sexism are factors that coerce women into prostitution.

Throughout history, poverty and sexism and racism have compelled prostitution, as in the dire situation of starving Coos women in 1850 in what is now southern Oregon. Historian Gray Whaley describes the context of their prostitution:

> A broad range of colonial activities decimated traditional economic activities such as mining sluices, which clogged and polluted streams, inhibiting fish runs and spawning activity, and raising cattle, which trampled and devoured camas fields. Some Native bands literally faced starvation as a result. In this desperate state some Indian women prostituted themselves for food and, increasingly, whiskey.[89]

This lack of alternatives for survival is a crucial element of slavery.

> In interpreting the Thirteenth Amendment in contemporary peonage contexts, courts have been far less concerned with whether the condition was voluntarily entered and far more with whether the subsequent service was involuntary. That victims believe they have no viable alternative but to serve in the ways

in which they are being forced has also supported a finding of coercion, and with it the conclusion that the condition is one of enslavement. Involuntary servitude has embraced situations in which a person has made a difficult but rational decision to remain in bondage.[90]

Many of the factors described by Whaley as affecting Coos women in 1850 have a devastating impact on the lives of Native women today. Native women continue to be trafficked into prostitution. Ninety eight percent of 105 Native prostituted women in a 2011 Minnesota study were currently or previously homeless. Most had been raped and had suffered violent physical assaults. A majority of these women saw a connection between their history of colonization and present-day sexual colonization in prostitution.[91] As noted by Sarah Deer in chapter 10 of this volume, their trafficking by the United States government and others has been misnamed "relocation" and has not been recognized as trafficking.

When there is a failure to understand the lack of choice, slaves have been blamed for their own enslavement, children have been blamed for being sexually abused, Jews have been blamed for not escaping the death camps, and women in prostitution have been blamed for having made a choice to be prostituted. Philosopher Elaine Scarry, who has written about physical and mental pain, torture, and war, explained:

> It is a universal fate of those from whom the power to author their own fate has been retracted that later populations attribute to them the power of authorship and speak of them as "permitting" it.[92]

Because of the human need to name something in order to understand and then challenge it, one cannot fight slavery unless it is named slavery.[93] Harriet Jacobs wrote, "The secrets of slavery are concealed like the Inquisition."[94] Some human rights observers who go to Mauritania see people whom they understand to be working in the fields in exchange for food and shelter, rather than intergenerational slaves.[95]

As in the Mauritanian example, slavery exists in multiple configurations. Its original definition in the United States included unjust domination and subordination by either the state or private parties. Chattel slavery was simply the most extreme form of slavery. It is important to understand slavery and prostitution from the perspective of the enslaved and the prostituted and not only via legal definitions, which can be excessively restrictive. Slavery is characterized by control of movement, control of the physical environment, psychological control, measures taken to prevent or deter escape, force, threat of force or coercion, assertion of exclusivity, subjection to cruel treatment and abuse, control of sexuality, and forced labor.[96] These modes of control are also characteristic of pimp and sex buyer relationships with women in prostitution. Slavery-like conditions coexist with slavery as it has been legally defined. An undocumented agricultural worker in the United States said, "First, you had slaves. Then you had freed slaves. Then you had poor whites and sharecroppers. Now you have immigrants. It is all part of a continuum we have to break."[97] A Thirteenth Amendment scholar noted that "social movements in the nineteenth century were sometimes more honest than Americans today in recognizing unfreedom in bedrock institutions of market and family and daring to call this unfreedom slavery."[98]

In 1865 the Thirteenth Amendment legally abolished slavery and involuntary servitude, which were defined as "legal or physical force, used or threatened, to secure service, which must be distinctly personal service… in which one person possesses virtually unlimited authority over another." All of the forms of coercion recognized under the Thirteenth Amendment are common in prostitution, such as being deprived of food, sleep, and money, being beaten, and being raped, tortured, and threatened with death.[99] Vulnerabilities that have been recognized as contributing to coercion include mental retardation, poverty, being undocumented, and not speaking the dominant language.[100] A Florida state law that provides civil remedies for damages inflicted by sex buyers and pimps against prostituted women articulates these vulnerabilities. Women who are coerced into prostitution via exploitation of their social vulnerability can sue sex buyers and pimps for damages. Coercion is defined in the Florida law as restraint of speech or communication with others or exploitation of a condition of developmental disability, cognitive limitation, affective disorder, or substance dependence; exploitation of prior victimization by sexual abuse; exploitation during the making of pornography; and exploitation of the human needs for food, shelter, safety, or affection.[101]

Referring to trafficking in persons as modern slavery, the US Department of State further specified that trafficking includes obtaining or holding a person in compelled service, forced labor, sex trafficking, bonded labor, and debt bondage.[102] The US Department of Justice prohibited involuntary servitude, making it unlawful to "hold a person in a condition of slavery, that is, a condition of compulsory service or labor against his/her will."[103] To be convicted under this law, "the victim must be held against his/her will by actual force, threats of force, or threats of legal coercion." Additionally, Section 1584 "prohibits compelling a person to work against his/her will by creating a 'climate of fear' through the use of force, the threat of force, or the threat of legal coercion which is sufficient to compel service against a person's will."[104] A shortcoming of this law is its failure to mention prostitution that is under the control of a third party such as a pimp or trafficker. Today's abolitionists define trafficking as any form of prostitution controlled by a third party such as people commonly defined as pimps, but they can also be pornographers, strip club managers, or escort agency operators if these persons exercise ownership-like control over their victims.[105]

Some international laws that address prostitution's lack of freedom and choice strongly oppose prostitution and trafficking.[106] Understanding trafficked women to be victims, not criminals, the 2000 Palermo Protocol made consent irrelevant to determining whether trafficking has occurred and encouraged states to develop legislative responses to men's demand for prostitution. The protocol stated that payment of money for prostitution is a means of coercing a person into being sexually used, and it closed loopholes that had been used to define prostitution and trafficking as labor.[107] The International Criminal Court (ICC) in 1998 named enslavement a crime against humanity. The ICC statute defines enslavement as "the exercise of any or all of the powers attaching to the right of ownership over a person [including] the exercise of such power in the course of trafficking in persons, in particular women and children."[108] A 2006 report by the United Nations Special Rapporteur on the Human Rights Aspects of the Victims of Trafficking in Persons, Especially Women and Children, noted that prostitution as it is practiced in the world "usually satisfies the legal elements for the definition of trafficking" and therefore legalization of prostitution is "to be discouraged."[109] Supporting this observation, a study of trafficking in 150 countries has shown that where prostitution is legalized, trafficking increases.[110] Using someone in prostitution, the special rapporteur observed, was "directly inflicting an additional and substantial harm upon the trafficking victim, tantamount to rape, above and beyond the harmful means used by others to achieve her entry or maintenance in prostitution." Targeting the sex buyer, the 1999 Swedish law on prostitution imposed strong penalties on the person buying sex but decriminalized the person being sold (the prostituted) and provided for exit support and services. This focus on the sex buyer—assumed to be the driver of the sex trafficking industry—has resulted in Sweden's low rate of trafficking.[111]

How can slavery be distinguished from harsh and exploitive employment? Proposing that we consider the socioeconomic and gender-based foundations of relationships that are de facto slavery, attorney Rachel Harris and policy analyst Katharine Gelber explain that "slavery exists where individuals inhabit powerless subject positions, positions which exist within a complicit, if not actively exploitative, international community."[112] Australian courts, they note, have struggled to define the extent of the similarity between pimping and trafficking, on the one hand, and chattel slavery, on the other. Section 270.1 of the Australian Criminal Code defines slavery as "the condition of a person over whom any or all of the powers attaching to the right of ownership are exercised, including where such a condition results from a debt or contract made by the person."[113]

The diverse forms of domination and coercion have resulted in some unfortunate rankings of "real slavery" above practices defined as "not-quite-slavery." For example, although most prostitution includes choicelessness, Skinner contrasted "real" slavery, where physical force is used, with presumably "fake" slavery, in which hunger, abuse, brainwashing by pimps, lifetimes of lethal racism, and sexism drive women into prostitution.[114] These crushing oppressions are dismissed as factors compelling prostitution. I once had an argument with a US government official at a postconference reception. "Oh come on," he said, "you mean to tell me that you *don't think* high-priced escorts on silk sheets at the Hyatt Regency have it pretty good?" It is my experience that he is not alone in this naïve perception. The paid rapes of prostitution are camouflaged by a coerced smile, a silk sheet, and a hotel with a familiar name. The public and sex buyers alike are taken in by pimps' advertising: pay more for high-priced escorts on satin sheets, with this subtext: they are making lots of money, and they are happy. Survivors of prostitution have made it clear that alleged high-class prostitution is deeply abusive and often controlled by organized crime, as in the case of Stella Marr, described below, who was controlled by Mafia pimps in a brothel in New York. Much of the business of prostitution today is controlled by organized crime operating globally—for example, from Poland to the United Kingdom, from Nigeria to Italy, from Ukraine to the United States, from Thailand to the Netherlands. Thus, modern abolitionists acknowledge the importance of international law in ending prostitution and trafficking.

HISTORICAL AND CONTEMPORARY ABOLITIONIST MOVEMENTS

Today's movement against slavery has been informed by the seventeenth- and eighteenth-century abolitionists. The fight against slavery today includes the same problems: cultural and legal definitions, tolerance for injustice perpetrated against the marginalized and vulnerable, and outright denial. Regulationist laws were proposed to reduce the harms of slavery, if not eliminate it. The argument was that a regulatory law was better than none at all. One such English law was passed in the eighteenth century over the objection of abolitionists. The bill proposed to limit the number of slaves based on a ship's weight, to require every ship to have a doctor, and to record all crew and slave deaths. Many abolitionists feared that the bill would establish "the Principle that the Trade was in itself just but had been abused."[115] A similar harm reduction approach is seen today in public health programs that fail to provide escape from prostitution, although they improve medical care by distributing condoms.[116] There is a parallel debate today regarding the legalization or regulation of prostitution. It is widely but incorrectly assumed that prostitution is inevitable, just as proponents once argued that US slavery was inevitable. Legal prostitution is said to be safer than illegal prostitution, although much evidence to the contrary exists in Australia, the Netherlands, Germany, and Nevada.[117]

For political reasons, a narrowed definition of slavery was used during the fight for the abolition of chattel slavery. In order to pass the Thirteenth Amendment, the original and broader definitions of slavery as economic injustice and discriminatory and exploitive abuse of women were excluded. Moderate abolitionists chose to define the differences between chattel slavery and other injustices as differences in kind, not degree.[118]

> Once chattel slavery was abolished, labor activists and suffragists sought to revive the older, broader concept of "slavery." But emancipation allowed defenders of the status quo to insist that American society was now "free." Everyday aspects of economic and family life could not be "slavery," which was by definition the worst of evils and had already been eradicated by law. Even today, calling an injustice "slavery" is generally seen as overheated hyperbole and even a presumptuous insult to the memory of the victims of African American chattel slavery.[119]

Despite this focus on the most extreme type of slavery, the early abolitionists did not focus exclusively on children, as too often happens in the modern antislavery movement. Instead, they focused on the institution of slavery itself, which included both adults and children. In fact, the vast majority of children in prostitution, like children in slavery, are fully integrated into the mainstream sex industry, which serves all sex buyers, rather than in an isolated market niche catering to pedophiles.[120]

As in the past, some words are used to hide the truth. Just as torture is named "enhanced interrogation" and logging of old-growth forests is named the "Healthy Forest Initiative," words that lie about prostitution leave people confused about what it really is: "flexible laborer," "irregular migrant," "sex worker," "transnational migrant worker," "erotic entrepreneur." Human cruelties are placed into separate categories that imply they are unrelated phenomena; for example, "voluntary" is juxtaposed with "forced" prostitution. These falsehoods about prostitution are much like attempts to cover up what Patterson called the "beastliness" of slavery.[121] Slavery is presented as paternalistic, protective. Pimps are said to be protectors. Just as enslaved women trafficked into prostitution (for example, from Albania to Italy) are described as "migrant sex workers," so, also, African slave traders delivered people who were described as "recruits" or "volunteers" to the European slave traders.

In the eighteenth century, the British moved enslaved Africans to sugar plantations in the West Indies. The proslavery West India Committee consisted of two overlapping interest groups: slave traders and ship owners who transported and sold the slaves and the influential plantation owners who bought them. This lobbying alliance spent millions on proslavery propaganda. At one point, they offered tours to visitors to the West Indies, showing them the homes of the elite slaves, drivers, carpenters, and masons, rather than the crowded quarters of the field slaves. They also used words to hide the reality of slavery, at one point suggesting that slaves be called "assistant planters."[122]

Like the global prostitution industry, the slave system was strengthened by myths and lies. While Belgian King Leopold was colonizing, enslaving, torturing, and murdering millions of Congolese on rubber plantations in the eighteenth century, he was also president of the Aboriginese Protection Society.[123] Leopold hosted an antislavery conference in 1889, posing as a humanitarian who was building infrastructure in the Congo—roads, railways, steamboats—all of which was used by his troops to pursue new and escaped slaves.[124] The Belgian king formed the International African Association of the Congo, a political entity that covered up his real activities. This was a calculated lie, because at the time, there was a philanthropic organization named the International African Association. Leopold instructed his aides, "Care must be taken not to let it be obvious that the Association of the Congo and the International African Association are two different things. The public doesn't grasp that."[125] After English abolitionists published exposés of the conditions of slavery in Leopold's Congo, he counterattacked with a musical play, *The Benevolent Planters*, in which two black lovers, separated from each other in Africa, end up living on adjoining plantations in the West Indies. They are reunited and saved from the African darkness by their kindly owners. On another occasion, slave ship

Slavery and Prostitution

owners argued that "the most crowded ships [were] the most healthy" and that "the time passed on board a ship while transporting from Africa to the colonies, [was] the happiest part of a negro's life."[126]

Similar cover-ups have been deployed in opposition to the twentieth-century abolitionist movement. Sex industry apologists calculatedly appropriate the titles of human rights or public health organizations. For example, although the names are similar, the Global Alliance Against Trafficking in Women (GAATW) promotes prostitution as sex work, whereas the Coalition Against Trafficking in Women (CATW) works for the abolition of prostitution and other forms of discrimination against women.

When the ideological camouflage is removed from slavery, a crisis occurs.[127] "The victim who is able to articulate the situation of the victim has ceased to be a victim: she has become a threat."[128] When the activities of pimps, traffickers, and men who buy sex are exposed, it becomes clear that a devalued class of women has been set aside for men's sexual use. And it becomes clear that the activities of sex buyers and pimps are predatory in the extreme.

Autobiographical descriptions of what slavery was really like were powerful weapons of the abolitionists. These slave narratives exposed the elaborate lies of the slave traders. Today, the abolitionist battle, like the sex trade itself, is located on the Internet. Most prostitution today—some estimates are as high as 90 percent—is advertised on the Internet, which functions as a virtual auction block. This electronic sex market serves as a floodgate controlling the supply of women and children for prostitution tourism and commercial marriages—both forms of slavery.[129] Sex worker blogs—"secret diaries" of escorts and call girls—abound, designed to promote prostitution as a positive job choice. Pimps do not call themselves pimps—they call themselves "sex workers."[130]

The response to lies about prostitution also happens online. Survivors of prostitution and trafficking have begun to counter these myths and distortions with narratives on their own Internet sites. Those who challenge the disinformation promoted by the sex industry advocates are verbally attacked, even threatened. Formerly prostituted in a Mafia-owned New York brothel, activist Stella Marr wrote:

> I had no idea how threatening my voice was until I started to make it heard. None of us trafficking and prostitution survivors did, until we started to write about the brutality we've experienced and these big players within these pimp-dominated "sex worker activist" groups started to do everything they could to silence us and deny we exist. Survivor bloggers are cyber-stalked

via Facebook, email, Twitter, and hateful blog comments. Our email accounts are hacked and private information that could endanger us is tweeted or revealed elsewhere online. Spiteful emails about us are sent to people we work with. Supportive activists who feature our writing on their blogs are similarly swarmed with vilifying emails and comments.[131]

Slaves who resisted or spoke out against slavery were tortured and/or killed. Women in prostitution who resist or speak out are often treated similarly. In 2011, pimps tortured and killed a woman in front of another woman to frighten the survivor and her friends into cooperating with the traffickers.[132] In slavery, masters tortured, raped, and punished black women who rejected their sexual advances. In prostitution, women who resist the orders of pimps/traffickers and many of those who resist johns are tortured. Aileen Wuornos, an emotionally harmed and disturbed woman, killed six men who had raped and tortured her (of the thousands who used her for sex in prostitution). She was executed by the state of Florida.[133]

CONCLUSION

The failure to undo the legacies of slavery is a continuation of the degradation of human life caused by slavery.[134] "Following the Civil War little changed for African Americans as white plantation owners turned to violence, legal constraints, and debt peonage to keep African Americans impoverished and trapped in the fields. They were slaves in all but name."[135] Pimp-controlled prostitution today is characterized by the same violence, legal constraints, and debt peonage that occurred following the Civil War. Pimp-controlled prostitution, estimated at 84 percent of all prostitution, continues as one form of slavery today, yet most prostitution of adults is still not recognized as slavery.[136]

The legacies of the enslavement of indigenous peoples in the United States that occurred during their colonization by English settlers also continues with pervasive trafficking of Native women and the same violence, cultural degradation, and lack of adequate legal response.[137] Women have few options for escape. Without financial, emotional, and political support to permit healing, even out of prostitution, people cannot avoid the various iterations of modern slavery, including prostitution.[138] Modern-day slaveholders no longer legally own slaves, but they continue to exploit and benefit from womens' and children's poverty, which channels people into prostitution.[139] It seems that apologists for prostitution are stuck in their own illogic. In their support for prostitution, they have at the same time rejected opposition to all the elements that constitute slavery: exploitation, sex trafficking, violence, commodification, and lack of freedom.[140] In order to reverse the human rights violations of trafficking, we must first define the buying of sex as a serious criminal act. Antiprostitution laws should be enforced against sex buyers *but not* against women who are sold for sex and are themselves victims of trafficking, as in the 1999 Swedish law.[141] Public education is needed regarding the humanity of the bought, the devastation in the experience of being bought for sex, and the criminality of the buyer, not the seller, of sex.

It is necessary to look at the structural origins of social injustice in order to challenge the human rights violations of slavery and prostitution. If we ask the question "What freedom do trafficked, pimped, or enslaved women have?" then we are more likely to focus on the essential sex, race, and economic inequalities on which slavery and prostitution are built.[142] Unless *both* the intrinsic violence of prostitution *and* the intersection of sexism, racism, and poverty in prostitution are understood, it is impossible to understand why abolitionists view prostitution as such a miserably oppressive institution. Former Swedish Minister for Gender Equality Margareta Winberg asked, "Shall we accept the fact that certain women and children, primarily girls, often those who are most economically and ethnically marginalized, are treated as a lower class, whose purpose is to serve men sexually?"[143] Anthony Gumbs, whose relatives were enslaved, objected to prostitution, which he understood as a version of slavery:

> The current practice in Jamaica of the widespread use of the sanitised or politically correct terms "sex workers" when referring to prostitutes, and "sex industry" when referring to prostitution, sends a clear message of a trend towards acceptance or legitimisation, if not outright legalisation. Jamaicans have had a long, hard history of brave struggle and sacrifice to lift our people out of the quagmires of slavery, poverty, indignity, ignorance, and exploitation. Are we ready to give up now? Surely those who must earn their living by renting their genitals, instead of by using their brains or hands, are little better off than the slaves of yore in terms of human dignity. Is this what we want to be "accepted"…in our beautiful home called Jamaica? Is this what we want for any of our people?[144]

Gumbs and Winberg challenge all of us to answer those questions, informed by an understanding of the history of slavery and the facts about prostitution.

Melissa Farley

Notes

1. Thomas Clarkson, *The History of the Rise, Progress, and Accomplishment of the Abolition of the Slave-Trade, by the British Parliament* (London: British Parliament, 1839), accessed November 25, 2013, http://www.gutenberg.org/files/10633/10633-h/10633-h.htm.

2. For the past eighteen years, the author, a research and clinical psychologist, has studied prostitution and trafficking in ten countries on five continents. Twenty-four peer-reviewed publications have resulted from this work.

3. According to a survey of eighteen sources, including research studies and governmental and nongovernmental reports, on average, 84 percent of all women in prostitution are pimped, trafficked, or under third-party control. Melissa Farley, Kenneth Franzblau, and M. Alexis Kennedy, "Online Prostitution and Trafficking," *Albany Law Review* 77, no. 3(2014), fn.

4. Catherine M. Cameron, "Captives and Culture Change: Implications for Archaeology," *Current Anthropology* 52, no. 2 (April 2011): 169–209.

5. Christopher Clausen, "Between Two Worlds: The Familiar Story of Pocahontas Was Mirrored by That of a Young Englishman Given as a Hostage to Her Father," *American Scholar* 76, no. 3 (Summer 2007): 80–90.

6. Bay Fang and Mark Leong, "China's Stolen Wives," *U.S. News & World Report* 125, no. 14 (1998): 35.

7. Jacqueline A. M. Lynne, "Street Prostitution as Sexual Exploitation in First Nations Women's Lives," master's thesis, University of British Columbia–Vancouver, 1998.

8. James F. Brooks, *Captives and Cousins: Slavery, Kinship, and Community in the Southwest Borderlands* (Chapel Hill: University of North Carolina Press, 2002).

9. Ibid., 364.

10. Sexism and Eurocentric cultural prejudice taint colonial history such that prostitution was assumed when it often did not exist. European colonists surmised that Native women who had sex outside of marriage were prostituting. A woman selling vegetables was presumed by one colonist to also be selling sex. Gray Whaley, *Oregon and the Collapse of Illahee: US Empire and the Transformation of an Indigenous World, 1792–1859* (Chapel Hill: University of North Carolina Press, 2010), 49.

11. Chris Hedges and Joe Sacco, *Days of Destruction, Days of Revolt* (New York: Nation Books, 2012), 192, citing Edward R. Murrow and Fred W. Friendly's November 26, 1960, *CBS News* report "Harvest of Shame."

12. Rebecca Mead, "Letter from Nevada—American Pimp—How to Make an Honest Living from the Oldest Profession," *New Yorker*, April 23, 2001.

13. Melissa Farley et al., "Comparing Sex Buyers with Men Who Don't Buy Sex: 'You Can Have a Good Time with the Servitude' vs. 'You're Supporting a System of Degradation'" (paper, Psychologists for Social Responsibility Annual Meeting, Boston, July 15, 2011).

14. Melissa Farley, "'Renting an Organ for 10 Minutes': What Tricks Tell Us about Prostitution, Pornography, and Trafficking," in *Pornography: Driving the Demand for International Sex Trafficking*, ed. David Guinn and J. DeCaro (Los Angeles: Captive Daughters Media, 2007), 145.

15. Lesley Sharp, "The Commodification of the Body and Its Parts," *Annual Review of Anthropology* 29, no. 1 (2000): 287–328.

16. Michael Serrill, "Prostitution: Defiling the Children," *Time* 141, no. 25 (June 21, 1993): 52–55.

17. Julia O'Connell Davidson, *Prostitution, Power, and Freedom* (Ann Arbor: University of Michigan Press, 1998).

18. John Stoltenberg, "Male Sexuality: Why Ownership Is Sexy," *Michigan Journal of Gender and Law* 1 (1993): 61.

19. Edward E. Baptist, "'Cuffy,' 'Fancy Maids,' and 'One-Eyed Men': Rape, Commodification, and the Domestic Slave Trade in the United States," *American Historical Review* 106 (December 2001): 1633.

20. Walter Johnson, *Soul by Soul: Life inside the Antebellum Slave Market* (Cambridge, MA: Harvard University Press, 1999).

21. Chester Brown, *Paying for It: A Comic-Strip Memoir about Being a John* (Montreal: Drawn and Quarterly Press, 2011).

22. Orlando Patterson, *Slavery and Social Death: A Comparative Study* (Cambridge, MA: Harvard University Press, 1982.

23. Sixteen-year-old Jessenia Ramirez from San Jose, Costa Rica, eloquently explained how she felt while prostituting. James Varney, "Child Prostitution Is a Flourishing Business in Costa Rica, a Business Some Activists Are Trying to Stamp Out," *New Orleans Times-Picayune*, May 7, 2000, A1.

24. Barbara Omolade, "Hearts of Darkness," in *Powers of Desire: The Politics of Sexuality*, ed. Ann Snitow, Christine Stansell, and Sharon Thompson (New York: Monthly Review Press, 1983), 354.

25. Patterson, *Slavery and Social Death*.

26. Andrea Dworkin, "Prostitution and Male Supremacy," in *Life and Death*, ed. Andrea Dworkin (New York: Free Press, 1997), 139–151.

27. O'Connell Davidson, *Prostitution, Power, and Freedom*.

28. Johnson, *Soul by Soul*, 213.

29. Melissa Farley et al., "Prostitution and Trafficking in Nine Countries: Update on Violence and Posttraumatic Stress Disorder," in *Prostitution, Trafficking, and Traumatic Stress*, ed. Melissa Farley (New York: Routledge, 2003), 33–74.

30. Frederick Douglass and Harriet Jacobs, *Narrative of the Life of Frederick Douglass, an American Slave, and Incidents in the Life of a Slave Girl* (New York: Modern Library, 2000).

31. Claude Jaget, *Prostitutes—Our Life* (Bristol, UK: Falling Wall Press, 1980).

32. Johnson, *Soul by Soul*.

33. Ceilie Hoigard and Liv Finstad, *Backstreets: Prostitution, Money, and Love* (University Park: Pennsylvania State University Press, 1986).

34. John W. Blassingame, *Slave Testimony: Two Centuries of Letters, Speeches, Interviews, and Autobiographies* (Baton Rouge: Louisiana State University Press, 1977).

35. Blassingame, *Slave Testimony*.

36. Evelina Giobbe, "Juvenile Prostitution: Profile of Recruitment," in *Child Trauma: Issues and Research*, ed. Ann W. Burgess (New York: Garland Publishing, 1992), 126.

37. Klan report cited in Lisa Cardyn, "Sexualized Racism/Gendered Violence: Outraging the Body Politic in the Reconstruction South," *Michigan Law Review* 100, no. 4 (2002): 742.

38. Diana Paton, "Enslaved Women and Slavery before and after 1807," *History in Focus*, issue 12 (Spring 2007), Institute of Historical Research, University of London, http://www.history.ac.uk/ihr/Focus/Slavery/articles/paton.html.

39. Patricia M. Lambert, "Infectious Disease among Enslaved African Americans at Eaton's Estate, Warren County, North Carolina, ca. 1830–1850," *Memorías do Instituto Oswaldo Cruz, Rio de Janeiro* 101, suppl. 2 (2006): 107–117.

40. Calvin Schermerhorn, "The Everyday Life of Enslaved People in the Antebellum South," *OAH Magazine of History* 23, no. 2 (April 2009): 31–36.

41. Lambert, "Infectious Disease among Enslaved."

42. Melissa Farley et al., "Prostitution: Health Consequences of Physical Violence and Psychological Trauma" (paper, Eleventh International Congress on Women's Health Issues, University of California College of Nursing, San Francisco, January 28, 2000).

43. Douglass and Jacobs, *Narrative of the Life*, 147.

44. Anonymous woman who prostituted, interview by Melissa Farley, 2002.

45. Melissa Farley, "Prostitution and the Invisibility of Harm," *Women & Therapy* 26, nos. 3–4 (2005): 247–280.

46. Baptist, "'Cuffy,' 'Fancy Maids,' and 'One-Eyed Men.'"

47. Patterson, *Slavery and Social Death*.

48. Michael Martinez, "Prostitution Ring in Madrid Tattooed Nineteen-Year-Old

Woman with Bar Code," *CNN World*, March 24, 2012, accessed May 2, 2012, http://articles.cnn.com/2012-03-24/world/world_europe_spain-prostitution-tattoo_1_prostitution-ring-ring-leader-bar-code?_s=PM:EUROPE.

49. Baptist, "'Cuffy,' 'Fancy Maids,' and 'One-Eyed Men.'"

50. Johnson, *Soul by Soul*, 206.

51. Bridget Anderson and Julia O'Connell Davidson, *Is Trafficking in Human Beings Demand Driven? A Multi-country Pilot Study* (Geneva: International Organization for Migration, 2003), 24.

52. Council for Prostitution Alternatives, *Annual Report, 1991*, Portland, OR, 3.

53. Farley et al., *Prostitution and Trafficking in Nine Countries*.

54. Terri L. Snyder, "Suicide, Slavery, and Memory in North America," *Journal of American History* 97, no. 1 (2010): 39–62.

55. The passage of the Fugitive Slave Law of 1850 required anyone in the United States to assist in returning a fugitive slave to the owner. Evelina Giobbe also documents pimps' captures of women escaping prostitution. See Evelina Giobbe, "An Analysis of Individual, Institutional, and Cultural Pimping," *Michigan Journal of Gender and Law* 1, no. 1 (1993): 33–57.

56. Kevin Bales, "The Social Psychology of Modern Slavery," *Scientific American* 286, no. 4 (April 2002): 80–87.

57. Cathy Zimmerman et al., *Stolen Smiles: A Summary Report on the Physical and Psychological Health Consequences of Women and Adolescents Trafficked in Europe* (London: London School of Hygiene & Tropical Medicine, 2006), http://www.lshtm.ac.uk/php/ghd/docs/stolensmiles.pdf.

58. Johnson, *Soul by Soul*.

59. Harvey L. Schwartz, Jody Williams, and Melissa Farley, "Pimp Subjugation of Women by Mind Control," in *Prostitution and Trafficking in Nevada: Making the Connections*, by Melissa Farley (San Francisco: Prostitution Research & Education, 2007), 49–84.

60. Schwartz, Williams, and Farley, "Pimp Subjugation of Women."

61. Judith Herman, *Trauma and Recovery: The Aftermath of Violence from Domestic Violence to Political Terror* (New York: Basic Books, 1992); Harvey L. Schwartz, *Dialogues with Forgotten Voices: Relational Perspective on Child Abuse Trauma and Treatment of Dissociative Disorders* (New York: Basic Books, 2000); Schwartz, Williams, and Farley, "Pimp Subjugation of Women."

62. Dee L. R. Graham, *Loving to Survive: Sexual Terror, Men's Violence, and Women's Lives* (New York: New York University Press, 1994).

63. Graham, *Loving to Survive*.

64. Baptist, "'Cuffy,' 'Fancy Maids,' and 'One-Eyed Men.'"

65. A. F. Scott, *Southern Lady: From Pedestal to Politics, 1830–1930* (Chicago: University of Chicago Press, 1970).

66. The popular cultural story of slavery is seen through the lens of economics, color, labor, and men's experiences. Women's experiences of slavery, like women's experiences of the Holocaust, have been minimized or ignored. Although women sometimes outnumbered men in the US enslaved population, they tended to be seen as mammies or privileged mistresses. Yet the US slave system depended on slaves as reproducible raw material, not just laborers. Women's reproductive systems were under the control of the slave buyer and seller. See JoAnn Wypijewski, "Reproductive Rights and the Long Hand of Slave Breeding," *The Nation*, March 21, 2012, accessed April 8, 2012, http://www.thenation.com/article/166961/reproductive-rights-and-long-hand-slave-breeding.

67. Omolade, "Hearts of Darkness," 354.

68. Anonymous pimp, interview by Melissa Farley for a research study on prostitution, Chicago, 2007.

69. United Nations, Convention against Torture and Other Cruel, Inhuman, or Degrading Treatment or Punishment, 1465 U.N.T.S. 85, December 10, 1984.

70. Catherine Clinton, *The Plantation Mistress: Woman's World in the Old South* (New York: Pantheon, 1982); Angela Davis, "Reflections on the Black Woman's Role in the Community of Slaves," *The Black Scholar* 3, no. 4 (1971): 2–15; Douglass and Jacobs, *Narrative of the Life*; Thelma Jennings, "Us Colored Women Had to Go Through a Plenty: Sexual Exploitation of African American Slave Women," *Journal of Women's History* 1 (Winter 1990): 45–74.

71. Kathleen Barry, *Female Sexual Slavery* (New York: New York University Press, 1979); Dworkin, "Prostitution and Male Supremacy"; Giobbe, "An Analysis of Individual, Institutional, and Cultural Pimping"; Hoigard and Finstad, *Backstreets*.

72. For a discussion of international legal definitions of torture as the same as acts commonly perpetrated against women in prostitution, see Melissa Farley, "Prostitution, Trafficking, and Cultural Amnesia: What We Must *Not* Know in Order to Keep the Business of Sexual Exploitation Running Smoothly," *Yale Journal of Law and Feminism* 18 (2006): 109–144.

73. Steve Lopez, "The 'Repugnant, Vile Truth' about Sex Trafficking in L.A. County," *Los Angeles Times*, August 31, 2013, accessed September 10, 2013, http://www.latimes.com/local/la-me-0901-lopez-prostitution-20130901,0,4024210.column51.

74. Kristian Williams, *American Methods: Torture and the Logic of Domination* (Cambridge: South End Press, 2006).

75. Human Rights Watch, *No Escape: Male Rape in US Prisons* (New York: Human Rights Watch, 2001).

76. Catharine A. MacKinnon, *Toward a Feminist Theory of the State* (Cambridge, MA: Harvard University Press, 1989).

77. Joanna Bourke, "Torture as Pornography," *London Guardian*, May 7, 2004, accessed May 20, 2004, http://www.guardian.co.uk/women/story/0,3604,1211261,00.html.

78. Neal K. Katyal, "Men Who Own Women: A Thirteenth Amendment Critique of Forced Prostitution," *Yale Law Journal* 103 (December 1993): 791.

79. See, for example, Nicole Constable, "International Marriage Brokers, Cross-Border Marriages, and the US Anti-trafficking Campaign," *Journal of Ethnic and Migration Studies* 38, no. 7 (2012): 1137–1154; Denise Brennan, *What's Love Got to Do with It? Transnational Desires and Sex Tourism in the Dominican Republic* (Durham, NC: Duke University Press, 2004); Svati Shah, *Street Corner Secrets: Sex, Work, and Migration in the City of Mumbai* (Durham, NC: Duke University Press, 2014).

80. Farley, Franzblau, and Kennedy, "Online Prostitution and Trafficking."

81. Elizabeth Fry Society of Toronto, "Streetwork: Outreach with Adult Female Street Prostitutes" (unpublished report, Toronto, May 1987); Farley et al., "Prostitution and Trafficking in Nine Countries."

82. Farley et al., "Comparing Sex Buyers."

83. Christa Wichterich, *The Globalized Woman* (North Melbourne: Spinifex Press, 2002).

84. Melissa Farley, *Prostitution and Trafficking in Nevada: Making the Connections* (San Francisco: Prostitution Research & Education, 2007).

85. Ine Vanwesenbeeck, *Prostitutes' Well-Being and Risk* (Amsterdam: VU University Press, 1994).

86. Cameron, "Captives and Culture Change."

87. "Fla. Woman Allegedly Offers Sex for Two Cheeseburgers," *Bradenton Herald* (FL), April 3, 2012, accessed May 22, 2012, http://thetimes-tribune.com/news/fla-woman-offers-sex-for-2-cheeseburgers-1.1294528.

88. Nathan Hardin, "Woman Charged with Prostituting for Gas," *Salisbury Post* (NC), July 21, 2011, accessed January 15, 2012, http://www.salisburypost.com/Crime/072111-WEBcouplechargedwithprostitution-qcdChristopher%20Riddle.

89. Whaley, *Oregon and the Collapse*, 174.

90. Catharine A. MacKinnon, "Prostitution and Civil Rights," *Michigan Journal of Gender and Law* 1 (1993): 23–24.

91. Melissa Farley, Nicole Matthews, Sarah Deer, Guadalupe Lopez, Christine Stark, and Eileen Hudon, *Garden of Truth: The Prostitution and Trafficking of Native Women in Minnesota* (report sponsored by Minnesota Indian Women's Sexual Assault Coalition and presented at William Mitchell College of Law, Saint Paul, MN, October 27, 2011).

92. Elaine Scarry, *The Body in Pain: The Making and Unmaking of the World* (New York: Oxford University Press, 1985), 157.

93. Pieter C. Smit, "Slavery on World Bank Projects Mauritania," November 27, 2002, https://openlibrary.org/works/OL5293036W/Slavery_on_World_Bank_projects _in_Mauritania.

94. Douglass and Jacobs, *Narrative of the Life*, 167.

95. Elinor Burkett, "God Created Me to Be a Slave," *New York Times Magazine*, October 12, 1997, 56–60.

96. Rachel Harris and Katharine Gelber, "Defining 'De Facto' Slavery in Australia: Ownership, Consent, and the Defence of Freedom," *International Criminal Law Review* 11, no. 3 (June 2011): 561–578.

97. Hedges and Sacco, *Days of Destruction*.

98. Jack M. Balkin and Sanford Levinson, "The Dangerous Thirteenth Amendment," *Columbia Law Review* 112 (2012): 1459.

99. MacKinnon, "Prostitution and Civil Rights."

100. Ibid.

101. Margaret Baldwin, "Strategies of Connection: Prostitution and Feminist Politics," *Michigan Journal of Gender and Law* 1, no. 1 (1993): 72.

102. US Department of State, *Trafficking in Persons Report* (Washington, DC, June 2007), http://www.state.gov/documents/organization/82902.pdf.

103. US Department of Justice, U.S. Code Title 18, Chap. 77, Sects. 1581, 1584, 1589, 1590, and 1591, 2012, http://www.justice.gov/crt/about/crm/1581fin.php.

104. US Department of Justice, U.S. Code Title 18.

105. Farley, Franzblau, and Kennedy, "Online Prostitution and Trafficking," fn. 14.

106. The United Nations 1949 convention declared that trafficking and prostitution are incompatible with individual dignity and worth. The convention addressed the harms of prostitution to consenting adult women, whether transported across national boundaries or not. The UN convention defined slavery as "the status or condition of a person over whom any or all of the powers attaching to the right of ownership are exercised." The slave trade was defined to include "all acts involved in the capture, acquisition or disposal of a person with intent to reduce him to slavery; all acts involved in the acquisition of a slave with a view to selling or exchanging him; all acts of disposal by sale or exchange of a slave acquired with a view to being sold or exchanged, and, in general, every act of trade or transport in slaves." United Nations Convention for the Suppression of the Traffic in Persons and of the Exploitation of the Prostitution of Others, 96 U.N.T.S. 271, December 1949, http://www.ohchr.org/EN /ProfessionalInterest/Pages/TrafficInPersons.aspx.

107. Janice G. Raymond, "The New UN Trafficking Protocol," *Women's Studies International Forum* 25, no. 5 (2002): 491.

108. United Nations, Rome Statute of the International Criminal Court, 1998, http://legal.un.org/icc/statute/99_corr/cstatute.htm. The United States is not one of the 139 signatories to the ICC.

109. United Nations, *Report of the Special Rapporteur on the Human Rights Aspects of the Victims of Trafficking in Persons, Especially Women and Children*, Commission on Human Rights, UN Doc. E/CN.4/2006/62, February 20, 2006, 7, 9, 17.

110. Seo-Young Cho, Axel Dreher, and Eric Neumayer, "Does Legalized Prostitution Increase Human Trafficking?" *World Development* 41, no. 1 (2013): 67–82.

111. Max Waltman, "Prohibiting Sex Purchasing and Ending Trafficking: The Swedish Prostitution Law," *Michigan Journal of International Law* 33 (2011): 133–157, and "Sweden's Prohibition of Purchase of Sex: The Law's Reasons, Impact, and Potential," *Women's Studies International Forum* 5 (2011): 449–474.

112. Harris and Gelber, "Defining 'De Facto' Slavery in Australia."

113. Ibid.

114. Benjamin Skinner, *A Crime So Monstrous* (New York: Free Press, 2009).

115. Adam Hochschild, *Bury the Chains: Prophets and Rebels in the Fight to Free an Empire's Slaves* (New York: Houghton-Mifflin, 2005).

116. Harm reduction programs such as free condom distribution (of female and male condoms) can save lives, but these programs' advocates often suggest that this Band-Aid solution is sufficient. Programs that offer support groups and condoms but fail to offer exit programs contribute to a denial of the harms of prostitution. Almost all women in prostitution seek the option of escape, as well as free condoms and emotional support. In addition to the option of harm reduction, they deserve the right to harm elimination (by leaving prostitution). Parallels with slavery are evident: although improved medical care for the enslaved was welcomed, abolition of slavery was preferable.

117. Mary L. Sullivan, *Making Sex Work: A Failed Experiment with Legalized Prostitution* (North Melbourne: Spinifex Press, 2007); Farley, *Prostitution and Trafficking in Nevada*.

118. Balkin and Levinson, "The Dangerous Thirteenth Amendment," 37. Restricting the definition of slavery to its worst manifestation—the evil of chattel slavery—has been compared by Balkin and Levinson to John Yoo's infamous definition of "torture" as requiring a degree of pain and debilitation equal to facing the risk of death or organ failure. Certainly, the conditions Yoo described are understood to be torture. The problem is that Yoo felt his definition was complete whereas others think that many types of torture do not approach risking death or organ failure. Many of

these are psychological torture. Similarly, chattel slavery does not exhaust the meaning of slavery.

119. Balkin and Levinson, "The Dangerous Thirteenth Amendment," 40.

120. About 14 percent of all slaves sent by the British to the New World were children under the age of fourteen from Senegambia and Sierra Leone. About twice as many men were enslaved compared with women; see Herbert S. Klein, *The Atlantic Slave Trade* (New York: Cambridge University Press, 2010), 165.

121. Patterson, *Slavery and Social Death*.

122. Hochschild, *Bury the Chains*, 160.

123. Adam Hochschild, *King Leopold's Ghost: A Story of Greed, Terror, and Heroism in Colonial Africa* (Boston: Houghton-Mifflin, 1998).

124. Ibid.

125. Ibid.

126. Hochschild, *Bury the Chains*.

127. Patterson, *Slavery and Social Death*.

128. James Baldwin, *The Devil Finds Work* (New York: Dial Press, 1976).

129. Wichterich, *The Globalized Woman*.

130. Examples of pimping masqueraded as sex work include Margo St. James, Robyn Few, Maxine Doogan, and Norma Jean Almodovar. All of these individuals have mounted campaigns to legalize the sex industry. St. James was convicted of running a disorderly house or a brothel in 1962. Robyn Few founded the Sex Workers' Outreach Project after being convicted of conspiracy to promote interstate prostitution. The Erotic Service Providers Union is led by Maxine Doogan, who has been convicted of running an escort prostitution agency. The executive director of COYOTE/Los Angeles, Norma Jean Almodovar, was convicted of pandering. Stella Marr, "Pimps Will Be Pimps, Part 2," *The Survivor's View Blog*, June 28, 2012, http://prostitutionresearch.com/pre_blog/2012/06/28/pimps_will_be_pimps_part_2_of/.

131. Marr, "Pimps Will Be Pimps."

132. Christine Roberts, "Victim of Torture Murder in Oklahoma May Have Been Alive When She Was Dismembered," *New York Daily News*, July 25, 2012, accessed July 30, 2012, http://www.nydailynews.com/news/national/victim-torture-murder-oklahoma-alive-dismembered-article-1.1121416#ixzz254a87p00.

133. Phyllis Chesler, "A Woman's Right to Self-Defense: The Case of Aileen Carol Wuornos," *St. John's Law Review* 66, no. 4 (Fall–Winter 1993): 933–977.

134. Orlando Patterson, *The Ordeal of Integration* (Washington, DC: Counterpoint, 1997).

135. Hedges and Sacco, *Days of Destruction*, 195.

136. Farley, Franzblau, and Kennedy, "Online Prostitution and Trafficking," fn. 14.

137. See Sarah Deer, chapter 10 in this volume.

138. Today there is a lack of services for those who want to escape prostitution and in particular a lack of culturally relevant services, for example, for African American and Native American women escaping prostitution. Women of color continue to be arrested more often and given longer criminal sentences than other women in prostitution. Vednita Nelson, "Prostitution: Where Racism and Sexism Intersect," *Michigan Journal of Gender and Law* 1 (1993): 81–89. Once in prostitution, African American women have more difficulty escaping it, largely a result of a lack of resources for them. African American homeless young adults were significantly more likely to be prostituted than white Euro-Americans. Kimberly Tyler, "Risk Factors for Trading Sex among Homeless Young Adults," *Archives of Sexual Behavior* 38, no. 2 (2009): 290–297. There is an urgent need for trauma-informed services, especially for young women of color.

139. A man in debt bondage earned enough money to be free from a hereditary slave system in India but then returned to slavery because he was overwhelmed with the fear that he could not care for his family if they became sick or if he could not find food. Bales, "The Social Psychology of Modern Slavery."

140. Kajsa E. Ekman, *Being and Being Bought: Prostitution, Surrogacy, and the Split Self* (North Melbourne: Spinifex Press, 2013).

141. Waltman, "Prohibiting Sex Purchasing" and "Sweden's Prohibition."

142. Harris and Gelber, "Defining 'De Facto' Slavery."

143. Melissa Farley, "Unequal," Prostitution Research & Education, 2005, http://prostitutionresearch.com/2005/09/13/unequal/.

144. Anthony G. Gumbs, "Prostitution: A Return to Slavery," *Jamaica Gleaner*, April 24, 2006, accessed April 26, 2006, http://www.jamaicagleaner.com/gleaner/20060424/letters/letters1.html.

References

Ablon, Joan. "American Indian Relocation: Problems of Dependency and Management in the City." *Phylon* 26, no. 4 (1965): 362–371.

Adams, David Wallace. *Education for Extinction: American Indians and the Boarding School Experience, 1875–1928*. Lawrence: University Press of Kansas, 1995.

Aguirre Beltrán, Gonzalo. *La población negra de México*. 1946. Reprint, Mexico City: Fondo de Cultura Económica, 1972.

"AHR Forum: Crossing Slavery's Boundaries." *American Historical Review* 105 (2000): 451–484.

Ali, Daud. "A Study of Palace Women in the Chola Empire." In *Slavery and South Asian History*, edited by Indrani Chatterjee and Richard M. Eaton, 44–62. Bloomington: Indiana University Press, 2006.

Allen, Richard B. "A Serious and Alarming Daily Evil: *Marronage* and Its Legacy in Mauritius and the Colonial Plantation World." In *Slavery and Resistance in Africa and Asia*, edited by Edward Alpers, Gynn Campbell, and Michael Salman, 20–36. New York: Routledge, 2005.

Almaguer, Tomás. *Racial Fault Lines: The Historical Origins of White Supremacy in California*. Berkeley: University of California Press, 1994.

Almaráz, Félix D., Jr., ed., *Letters from Governor Antonio Martínez to the Viceroy Juan Ruíz de Apodaca*. San Antonio: Research Center for the Arts and Humanities, University of Texas–San Antonio, 1983.

Alpers, Edward, Gwyn Campbell, and Michael Salman, eds. *Resisting Bondage in Indian Ocean Africa and Asia*. New York: Routledge, 2007.

———, eds. *Slavery and Resistance in Africa and Asia*. New York: Routledge, 2005.

Alt, Susan M. "Unwilling Immigrants: Culture, Change, and the 'Other' in Mississippian Societies." In *Invisible Citizens: Captives and Their Consequences*, edited by Catherine M. Cameron, 205–222. Salt Lake City: University of Utah Press, 2008.

Alvord, Clarence W., and Lee Bidgood, eds. *The First Explorations of the Trans-Allegheny Region by Virginians, 1650–1674*. Cleveland, OH: Arthur H. Clark, 1912.

Ames, Kenneth M. "Slavery, Household Production, and Demography on the Southern Northwest Coast: Cables, Tacking, and Ropewalks." In *Invisible Citizens: Captives and Their Consequences*, edited by Catherine M. Cameron, 138–158. Salt Lake City: University of Utah Press, 2008.

Ames, Kenneth M., and Herbert D. G. Maschner. *Peoples of the Northwest Coast: Their Archaeology and Prehistory*. London: Thames and Hudson, 1999.

REFERENCES

Amnesty International. *Maze of Injustice: The Failure to Protect Indigenous Women from Sexual Violence in the USA.* New York: Amnesty International Publications, 2007. http://www.amnestyusa.org/women/maze/report.pdf.

———. *Stolen Sisters: Discrimination and Violence against Indigenous Women in Canada.* New York: Amnesty International Publications, 2004. http://www.amnesty-usa.ca/stolensisters/amr2000304.pdf.

Amussen, Susan Dwyer. *Caribbean Exchanges: Slavery and the Transformation of English Society, 1640–1700.* Chapel Hill: University of North Carolina Press, 2007.

Anders, Gary C. "Theories of Underdevelopment and the American Indian." *Journal of Economic Issues* 14, no. 3 (1980): 681–701.

Anderson, Bridget, and Rutvica Andrijasevic. "Sex, Slaves, and Citizens: The Politics of Anti-trafficking." *Soundings* 40 (2009): 135–146.

Anderson, Bridget, and Julia O'Connell Davidson. *Is Trafficking in Human Beings Demand Driven? A Multi-country Pilot Study.* Geneva: International Organization for Migration, 2003.

Anderson, Clare. "Convict Passages in the Indian Ocean, 1790–1860." In *Many Middle Passages: Forced Migration and the Making of the Modern World*, edited by Emma Christopher, Cassandra Pybus, and Marcus Rediker, 129–149. Berkeley: University of California Press, 2007.

Anderson, David G. *The Savannah River Chiefdoms: Political Change in the Late Prehistoric Southeast.* Tuscaloosa: University of Alabama Press, 1994.

Anderson, Gary Clayton. *The Conquest of Texas: Ethnic Cleansing in the Promised Land, 1820–1875.* Norman: University of Oklahoma Press, 2005.

———. *The Indian Southwest, 1580–1830: Ethnogenesis and Reinvention.* Norman: University of Oklahoma Press, 1991.

Anderson, M. Kat. *Tending the Wild: Native American Knowledge and the Management of California's Natural Resources.* Berkeley: University of California Press, 2006.

Anzaldúa, Gloria. *Borderlands: La Frontera, the New Mestiza.* San Francisco: Spinsters / Aunt Lute, 1987.

Archer, Christon I. "The Deportation of Barbarian Indians from the Internal Provinces of New Spain, 1789–1810." *Americas* 29 (January 1973): 376–385.

Arkush, Brooke S. "Yokuts Trade Networks and Native Culture Change in Central and Eastern California." *Ethnohistory* 40 (1993): 619–640.

Armbruster, Henry C. *The Torreys of Texas.* Buda, TX: Citizen Press, 1968.

Arnesen, Eric, ed. *The Black Worker: Race, Labor, and Civil Rights since Emancipation.* Champaign: University of Illinois Press, 2007.

Arnold, Morris. *The Rumble of a Distant Drum: The Quapaws and Old World Newcomers, 1673–1804.* Fayetteville: University of Arkansas Press, 2000.

Arrington, Leonard J., and Davis Bitton. *The Mormon Experience: A History of the Latter-Day Saints.* Urbana: University of Illinois Press, 2006.

Atencio, Tomás. "The Old Town Liquor Dispute: Social Change and Conflict in New

References

    Mexico." Southwest Hispanic Research Institute Working Paper no. 112. Albuquerque: University of New Mexico, 1985.

Avery, Doris Swann. "Into the Den of Evils: The Genízaros in Colonial New Mexico." Master's thesis, University of Montana, 2008.

Babcock, Barbara. "The Story in the Story: Metanarration in Folk Narrative." In *Verbal Art as Performance,* edited by Richard Bauman, 61–80. Rowly, MA: Newbury House Publishers, 1977.

Babcock, Matthew. "Rethinking the *Establecimientos:* Why Apaches Settled on Spanish-Run Reservations, 1786–1793." *New Mexico Historical Review* 84 (Summer 2009): 363–397.

———. "Turning Apaches into Spaniards: North America's Forgotten Indian Reservations." PhD diss., Southern Methodist University, 2008.

Bachman, Ronet, Heather Zayowski, Rachel Kallmyer, Margarita Poteyeva, and Christina Lanier. *Violence against American Indian and Alaska Native Women and the Criminal Justice Response: What Is Known.* Research report submitted to US Department of Justice, Washington, DC, 2008.

Baldwin, James. *The Devil Finds Work.* New York: Dial Press, 1976.

Baldwin, Margaret. "Strategies of Connection: Prostitution and Feminist Politics." *Michigan Journal of Gender and Law* 1, no. 1 (1993): 65–79.

Bales, Kevin. "The Social Psychology of Modern Slavery." *Scientific American* 286, no. 4 (April 2002): 80–87.

Balkin, Jack M., and Sanford Levinson. "The Dangerous Thirteenth Amendment." *Columbia Law Review* 112 (2012): 1459–1506.

Bancroft, Hubert Howe. *Works of H. H. Bancroft.* San Francisco: History Company Publishers, 1886.

Baptist, Edward E. "'Cuffy,' 'Fancy Maids,' and 'One-Eyed Men': Rape, Commodification, and the Domestic Slave Trade in the United States." *American Historical Review* 106 (December 2001): 1619–1650.

———. *The Half Has Never Been Told: Slavery and the Making of American Capitalism.* New York: Basic Books, 2014.

———. "Toxic Debt, Liar Loans, Collateralized and Securitized Human Beings, and the Panic of 1837." In *Capitalism Takes Command: The Social Transformation of Nineteenth-Century North America,* edited by Michael Zakim and Gary J. Kornblith, 69–92. Chicago: University of Chicago Press, 2012.

Barker, Eugene C., ed. *Annual Report of the American Historical Association for the Year 1919: The Austin Papers.* 3 vols. Washington, DC: US Government Printing Office, 1924, 1928; Austin: University of Texas Press, 1927.

———. *The Life of Stephen F. Austin, Founder of Texas, 1793–1836: A Chapter in the Westward Movement of the Anglo-American People.* 1926. Reprint, Austin: University of Texas Press, 1969.

———. "Notes on the Colonization of Texas." *Mississippi Valley Historical Review* 10 (September 1923): 141–152.

References

Barker, Muhammad Abd-al-Rahman. *Klamath Dictionary*. Berkeley: University of California Press, 1963.

Barnett, Jim, and H. Clark Burkett. "The Forks of the Road Slave Market at Natchez." *Journal of Mississippi History* 63, no. 3 (September 2001): 168–187.

Barr, Juliana. "From Captives to Slaves: Commodifying Indian Women in the Borderlands." *Journal of American History* 92, no. 1 (June 2005): 19–46.

———. "Geographies of Power: Mapping Indian Borders in the 'Borderlands' of the Early Southwest." *William and Mary Quarterly* 68, no. 1 (January 2011): 5–46.

———. *Peace Came in the Form of a Woman: Indians and Spaniards in the Texas Borderlands*. Chapel Hill: University of North Carolina Press, 2007.

———. "A Spectrum of Indian Bondage in Spanish Texas." In *Indian Slavery in Colonial America*, edited by Alan Gallay, 277–317. Lincoln: University of Nebraska Press, 2010.

Barry, Kathleen. *Female Sexual Slavery*. New York: New York University Press, 1979.

———. *The Prostitution of Sexuality*. New York: New York University Press, 1996.

Barth, Fredrik. *Ethnic Groups and Boundaries: The Social Organization of Culture Difference*. Long Grove, IL: Waveland Press, 1998.

Basso, Keith H. *Wisdom Sits in Places: Landscape and Language among the Western Apache*. 6th ed. Albuquerque: University New Mexico Press, 2000.

Baucom, Ian. *Specters of the Atlantic: Finance Capital, Slavery, and the Philosophy of History*. Durham, NC: Duke University Press, 2005.

Bauer, William J., Jr. *We Were All like Migrant Workers Here: Work, Community, and Memory on California's Round Valley Reservation*. Chapel Hill: University of North Carolina Press, 2009.

Bean, Lowell, and William Mason. *Diaries and Accounts of the Romero Expeditions in Arizona and California, 1823–1826*. Palm Springs, CA: Palm Springs Desert Museum, 1962.

Beck, Robin J., Jr. "Catawba Coalescence and the Shattering of the Carolina Piedmont, 1540–1675." In *Mapping the Mississippian Shatter Zone: The Colonial Indian Slave Trade and Regional Instability in the American South*, edited by Robbie Ethridge and Sheri M. Shuck-Hall, 115–141. Lincoln: University of Nebraska Press, 2009.

Beckert, Sven. *The Monied Metropolis: New York City and the Consolidation of the American Bourgeoisie*. New York: Cambridge University Press, 2001.

Beckham, Stephen. *Requiem for a People: The Rogue Indians and the Frontiersmen*. Norman: University of Oklahoma Press, 1971.

Beebe, Rose Marie, and Robert M. Senkewicz, eds. *Testimonios: Early California through the Eyes of Women, 1815–1848*. Berkeley: University of California Press, 2006.

Begum, Guvenc. "Women and Slavery: The Popularity of Female Slave Trade in Africa, Its Causes and Consequences." *Journal of Academic Studies* 7, no. 26 (August–October 2005): 221–230.

References

Bennett, Herman L. *Africans in Colonial Mexico*. Bloomington: Indiana University Press, 2003.

Berger, Bethany Ruth. "After Pocahontas: Indian Women and the Law, 1830–1934." *American Indian Law Review* 21, no. 1 (1997): 1–55.

Berlin, Ira. *Generations of Captivity: A History of African-American Slaves*. Cambridge, MA: Belknap Press of Harvard University Press, 2003.

———. *The Making of African America: The Four Great Migrations*. New York: Penguin, 2010.

———. *Many Thousands Gone: The First Two Centuries of Slavery in North America*. Cambridge, MA: Harvard University Press, 1998.

Bessel, Richard, Nicholas Guyatt, and Jane Rendall, eds. *War, Empire, and Slavery, 1770–1830*. New York: Palgrave Macmillan, 2010.

Betty, Gerald. "'Skillful in the Management of the Horse': Comanches as Southern Plains Pastoralists." *Heritage of the Great Plains* 30, no. 1 (1997): 5–31.

Binnema, Theodore. *Common and Contested Ground: A Human and Environmental History of the Northwestern Plains*. Norman: University of Oklahoma Press, 2001.

Black, Jeremy. *A Brief History of Slavery: A New Global History*. London: Constable and Rutherford, 2011.

Blackhawk, Ned. "The Displacement of Violence: Ute Diplomacy and the Making of New Mexico's Eighteenth-Century Northern Borderlands." *Ethnohistory* 54 (2007): 723–755.

———. *Violence over the Land: Indians and Empires in the Early American West*. Cambridge, MA: Harvard University Press, 2006.

Blackmar, Frank Wilson. "The Socialization of the American Indian." *American Journal of Sociology* 34, no. 4 (January 1929): 653–669.

Blansett, Kent. "Intertribalism in the Ozarks, 1800–1865." *American Indian Quarterly* 34 (2010): 475–497.

Blassingame, John W. *Slave Testimony: Two Centuries of Letters, Speeches, Interviews, and Autobiographies*. Baton Rouge: Louisiana State University Press, 1977.

Bloch, Marc. *The Historian's Craft: Reflections on the Nature and Uses of History and the Techniques and Methods of Those Who Write It*. Toronto: Knopf, 1953.

Blurton, David, and Gary D. Copus. "Alaska Native Inmates: The Demographic Relationship between Upbringing and Crime." *Prison Journal* 83, no. 1 (2003): 90–104.

Bodenhorn, Howard. *State Banking in Early America: A New Economic History*. New York: Oxford University Press, 2003.

———. *A History of Banking in Antebellum America: Financial Markets and Economic Development in an Era of Nation-Building*. New York: Cambridge University Press, 2000.

Bolton, Herbert. *Guide to Materials for the History of the United States in the Principal Archives of Mexico*. Washington, DC: Carnegie Institution of Washington, 1913.

References

Bonnell, Keith. "Highways a Hunting Ground for Killers." *Vancouver Sun*, August 10, 2009. http://www.vancouversun.com/news/Highways+hunting+ground+killers/1877414/story.html.

Bonsal, Stephen. *Edward Fitzgerald Beale: A Pioneer in the Path of Empire, 1822–1903.* New York: G. P. Putnam's Sons, 1912.

Bonte, Pierre. "Ecological and Economic Factors in the Determination of Pastoral Societies." In *Change and Development in Nomadic and Pastoral Societies*, edited by John G. Galaty and Philip Carl Salzman, 33–49. Leiden: Brill, 1981.

Bortel, Angela, Mary Ellingen, Mary C. Ellison, Robin Phillips, and Cheryl Thomas. *Sex Trafficking Needs Assessment for the State of Minnesota.* Minneapolis: Advocates for Human Rights, 2008.

Bourke, Joanna. "Torture as Pornography." *London Guardian*, May 7, 2004. Accessed May 20, 2004. http://www.guardian.co.uk/women/story/0,3604,1211261,00.html.

Bourne, Edward G. *Narratives of the Career of Hernando de Soto.* New York: A. S. Barnes, 1904.

Bouvier, Virginia M. *Women and the Conquest of California, 1542–1840: Codes of Silence.* Tucson: University of Arizona Press, 2001.

Bowne, Eric E. "'Caryinge awaye their Corne and Children': The Effects of Westo Slave Raids on the Indians of the Lower South." In *Mapping the Mississippian Shatter Zone: The Colonial Indian Slave Trade and Regional Instability in the American South*, edited by Robbie Ethridge and Sheri M. Shuck-Hall, 104–114. Lincoln: University of Nebraska Press, 2009.

———. "Dr. Henry Woodward's Role in Early Carolina Indian Relations." In *Creating and Contesting Carolina: Proprietory Era Histories*, edited by Michelle LeMaster and Bradford Wood, 73–93. Columbia: University of South Carolina Press, 2013.

———. "Southeastern Indian Polities of the Seventeenth Century: Suggestions toward an Analytical Vocabulary." In *Native American Adoption, Captivity, and Slavery in Changing Contexts*, edited by Max Carocci and Stephanie Pratt, 65–78. New York: Palgrave Macmillan, 2012.

———. *The Westo Indians: Slave Traders of the Early Colonial South.* Tuscaloosa: University of Alabama Press, 2005.

Bowser, Brenda J. "Captives in Amazonia: Becoming Kin in a Predatory Landscape." In *Invisible Citizens: Captives and Their Consequences*, edited by Catherine M. Cameron, 262–282. Salt Lake City: University of Utah Press, 2008.

Boyd, Robert. *The Coming of the Spirit of Pestilence: Introduced Infectious Diseases and Population Decline among Northwest Coast Indians, 1774–1874.* Seattle: University of Washington Press, 1999.

———. "Demographic History until 1990." In *Handbook of North American Indians*, vol. 12, *Plateau*, edited by William C. Sturtevant and Deward E. Walker, 467–483. Washington, DC: Smithsonian Institution, 1998.

References

Boyer, Debra K., and Jennifer James. "Prostitutes as Victims." *Deviants: Victims or Victimizers?* 3, no. 1 (1983): 109–146.

Brandão, José António. *Your Fyre Shall Burn No More: Iroquois Policy toward New France and Its Native Allies to 1701.* Lincoln: University of Nebraska Press, 1997.

Brennan, Denise. *What's Love Got to Do with It? Transnational Desires and Sex Tourism in the Dominican Republic.* Durham, NC: Duke University Press, 2004.

Briceland, Alan V. *Westward from Virginia: The Exploration of the Virginia-Carolina Frontier, 1650–1710.* Charlottesville: University Press of Virginia, 1987.

Bridgewater, Pamela D. *Breeding a Nation: Reproductive Slavery, the Thirteenth Amendment, and the Pursuit of Freedom.* Chicago: South End Press, 2014.

Briggs, Charles L. *Competence in Performance: The Creativity of Tradition in Mexicano Verbal Art.* Philadelphia: University of Pennsylvania Press, 1988.

Britten, Thomas A. *The Lipan Apaches: People of Wind and Lightning.* Albuquerque: University of New Mexico Press, 2009.

Brooks, James F. *Captives and Cousins: Slavery, Kinship, and Community in the Southwest Borderlands.* Chapel Hill: University of North Carolina Press, 2002.

———. "Reflections and Refractions from the Southwest Borderlands." In *Native American Adoption, Captivity, and Slavery in Changing Contexts*, edited by Max Carocci and Stephanie Pratt, 185–195. New York: Palgrave Macmillan, 2012.

———. "'This Evil Extends Especially…to the Feminine Sex': Negotiating Captivity in the New Mexico Borderlands." *Feminist Studies* 22, no. 2 (1996): 279–309.

———. "'We Betray Our Own Nation': Indian Slavery and Multi-ethnic Communities in the Southwest Borderlands." In *Indian Slavery in Colonial America*, edited by Alan Gallay, 319–351. Lincoln: University of Nebraska Press, 2009.

Brown, Chester. *Paying for It: A Comic-Strip Memoir about Being a John.* Montreal: Drawn and Quarterly Press, 2011.

Brown, Christopher Leslie. *Moral Capital: Foundations of British Abolitionism.* Chapel Hill: University of North Carolina Press, 2006.

Brown, William S. *California Northeast: The Bloody Ground.* Oakland, CA: Biobooks, 1951.

Bruchey, Stuart. *Cotton and the Growth of the American Economy: 1790–1860.* New York: Harcourt, Brace & World, 1967.

Brugge, David M. *Navajos in the Catholic Church Records of New Mexico, 1694–1875.* 2nd ed. Santa Fe, NM: SAR Press, 2010[1968].

———. "The Spanish Borderlands: Aboriginal Slavery." In *Encyclopedia of the North American Colonies*, edited by Jacob Ernest Cooke, 91–101. New York: Charles Scribner's Sons, 1993.

Brysk, Alison, and Austin Choi-Fitzpatrick. "Rethinking Trafficking." In *From Human Trafficking to Human Rights: Reframing Contemporary Slavery*, edited by Alison Brysk and Austin Choi-Fitzpatrick, 1–24. Philadelphia: University of Pennsylvania Press, 2012.

References

Buckland, W. W. *The Roman Law of Slavery: The Condition of the Slave in Private Law from Augustus to Justinian.* New York: AMS Press, 1969.

Burkett, Elinor. "God Created Me to Be a Slave." *New York Times Magazine,* October 12, 1997, 56–60.

Cabeza de Baca Gilbert, Fabiola. *The Good Life: New Mexico Traditions and Food.* Santa Fe: Museum of New Mexico Press, 2005.

Calloway, Colin G. *One Vast Winter Count: The Native American West before Lewis and Clark.* Lincoln: University of Nebraska Press, 2003.

Cameron, Catherine M. "Captives and Culture Change: Implications for Archaeology." *Current Anthropology* 52, no. 2 (2011): 169–209.

———. "Captives in the Past: Contexts for Prehistory." Unpublished manuscript.

———. "Introduction: Captives in Prehistory as Agents of Social Change." In *Invisible Citizens: Captives and Their Consequences,* edited by Catherine M. Cameron, 1–24. Salt Lake City: University of Utah Press, 2008.

———, ed. *Invisible Citizens: Captives and Their Consequences.* Salt Lake City: University of Utah Press, 2008.

Camp, Stephanie M. H. *Closer to Freedom: Enslaved Women and Everyday Resistance in the Plantation South.* Chapel Hill: University of North Carolina Press, 2004.

Campbell, Gwyn, and Edward Alpers. "Introduction: Slavery, Forced Labour, and Resistance in Indian Ocean Africa and Asia." In *Slavery and Resistance in Africa and Asia,* edited by Edward Alpers, Gwyn Campbell, and Michael Salman, 1–19. New York: Routledge, 2005.

Campbell, Gwyn, Suzanne Miers, and Joseph C. Miller, eds. *Children in Slavery through the Ages.* Athens: Ohio State University Press, 2009.

———. *Women and Slavery,* vol. 1, *Africa, the Indian Ocean World, and the Medieval North Atlantic.* Athens: Ohio University Press, 2007.

———. *Women and Slavery,* vol. 2, *The Modern Atlantic.* Athens: Ohio University Press, 2007.

Campbell, Randolph B. *An Empire for Slavery: The Peculiar Institution in Texas, 1821–1865.* Baton Rouge: Louisiana State University Press, 1989.

Cardyn, Lisa. "Sexualized Racism/Gendered Violence: Outraging the Body Politic in the Reconstruction South." *Michigan Law Review* 100, no. 4 (2002): 675–867.

Carlisle, Jeffrey D. "Seminole Indians." *Handbook of Texas Online,* Texas State Historical Association. Accessed September 9, 2013. http://www.tshaonline.org/handbook/online/articles/bms19.

Carocci, Max, and Stephanie Pratt, eds. *Native American Adoption, Captivity, and Slavery in Changing Contexts.* New York: Palgrave Macmillan, 2012.

Carpenter, William B. "On the Supposed Value of Alcoholic Liquors in Maintaining the Heat of the Human Body under Exposure to Severe Cold." *London Medical Gazette* 46 (1850): 510–517.

Carrigan, William Dean. "Slavery on the Frontier: The Peculiar Institution in Central Texas." *Slavery and Abolition* 20, no. 2 (1999): 63–96.

References

Carroll, Patrick J. *Blacks in Colonial Veracruz: Race, Ethnicity, and Economic Development.* Austin: University of Texas Press, 1991.

Case, Theresa A. *The Great Southwest Railroad Strike and Free Labor.* College Station: Texas A&M University Press, 2010.

Cashin, Edward. *Guardians of the Valley: Chickasaws in Colonial South Carolina and Georgia.* Columbia: University of South Carolina Press, 2009.

Castle, Robert, James Hagan, and Andrew Wells. "'Unfree' Labour on the Cattle Stations of Northern Australia, the Tea Gardens of Assam, and the Rubber Plantations of Indo-China, 1920–50." In *Resisting Bondage in Indian Ocean Africa and Asia,* edited by Edward Alpers, Gwyn Campbell, and Michael Salman, 96–113. New York: Routledge, 2007.

Castro, Robert Francis. "After the Slavers: Law, Liberation, and Captive-Taking in the New Mexico Borderlands." *Slavery and Abolition* 28 (December 2007): 369–386.

Chacón, Rafael. *Legacy of Honor: The Life of Rafael Chacón, a Nineteenth-Century New Mexican,* edited by Jacqueline Meketa. Albuquerque: University of New Mexico Press, 1986.

Chambers, Stephen. "At Home among the Dead: North Americans and the 1825 Guamacaro Slave Insurrection." *Journal of the Early Republic* 33 (Spring 2013): 61–86.

Chaney, Christopher B. "Overcoming Legal Hurdles in the War against Meth in Indian Country." *North Dakota Law Review* 82 (2006): 1151–1155.

Chang, David A. *The Color of the Land: Race, Nation, and the Politics of Landownership in Oklahoma, 1832–1929.* Chapel Hill: University of North Carolina Press, 2010.

Chaplin, Joyce. *Capitalism and a New Social Order: The Republican Vision of the 1790s.* New York: New York University Press, 1984.

Charles, Christopher A. D. "Skin Bleaching, Self-Hate, and Black Identity in Jamaica." *Journal of Black Studies* 33, no. 6 (2003): 711–729.

Chatterjee, Indrani. "Renewed and Connected Histories: Slavery and the Historiography of South Asia." In *Slavery and South Asian History,* edited by Indrani Chatterjee and Richard M. Eaton, 17–43. Bloomington: Indiana University Press, 2006.

Chatterjee, Indrani, and Richard M. Eaton, eds. *Slavery and South Asian History.* Bloomington: Indiana University Press, 2006.

Chávez, Alex J. *El Testamento: Spanish Folk Music of Northern New Mexico and Southern Colorado.* John Donald Robb Musical Trust, 1995, compact disk.

Chávez-García, Miroslava. *Negotiating Conquest: Gender and Power in California, 1770s to 1880s.* Tucson: University of Arizona Press, 2004.

Chesler, Phyllis. "A Woman's Right to Self-Defense: The Case of Aileen Carol Wuornos." *St. John's Law Review* 66, no. 4 (Fall–Winter 1993): 933–977.

Cheves, Langdon, ed. "The Shaftesbury Papers and Other Records Relating to Carolina and the First Settlement on the Ashley River Prior to the Year 1676." *Collections of the South Carolina Historical Society,* vol. 5 (1897).

REFERENCES

Child Welfare Partnership. "Disproportionality and Disparities in Oregon's Child Welfare System, State Level Data Analysis: Executive Summary." A report to the Oregon Child Welfare Equity Task Force, 2009.

Childs, Matt. *The 1812 Aponte Rebellion in Cuba and the Struggle against Atlantic Slavery.* Chapel Hill: University of North Carolina Press, 2006.

Cho, Seo-Young, Axel Dreher, and Eric Neumayer. "Does Legalized Prostitution Increase Human Trafficking?" *World Development* 41, no. 1 (2013): 67–82.

Christopher, Emma, Cassandra Pybus, and Marcus Rediker. Introduction to *Many Middle Passages: Forced Migration and the Making of the Modern World,* edited by Emma Christopher, Cassandra Pybus, and Marcus Rediker, 1–19. Berkeley: University of California Press, 2007.

Chuang, Janie. "The United States as Global Sheriff: Using Unilateral Sanctions to Combat Human Trafficking." *Michigan Journal of International Law* 27 (2006): 437–494.

Chulov, Martin. "Yazidis Tormented by Fears for Women and Girls Kidnapped by Isis Jihadists." *The Guardian* (UK), August 11, 2014. Accessed September 6, 2014. http://www.theguardian.com/world/2014/aug/11/yazidis-tormented-fears-for-women-girls-kidnapped-sinjar-isis-slaves.

Clairmont, Donald H. J. *Deviance among Indians and Eskimos in Aklavik, NWT.* Ottawa: Department of Northern Affairs and Natural Resources, Northern Co-ordination and Research Centre, 1963.

Clark, Robert Carlton. *History of the Willamette Valley, Oregon.* Chicago: S. J. Clarke, 1927.

Clarke, Samuel A. *Pioneer Days of Oregon History.* Portland, OR: J. K. Gill, 1905.

Clarkson, Thomas. *The History of the Rise, Progress, and Accomplishment of the Abolition of the Slave-Trade, by the British Parliament.* London: British Parliament, 1839. http://www.gutenberg.org/files/10633/10633-h/10633-h.htm.

Clausen, Christopher. "Between Two Worlds: The Familiar Story of Pocahontas Was Mirrored by That of a Young Englishman Given as a Hostage to Her Father." *American Scholar* 76, no. 3 (Summer 2007): 80–90.

Clement, Jennifer. *Prayers for the Stolen.* New York: Hogarth, 2014.

Clinton, Catherine. *The Plantation Mistress: Woman's World in the Old South.* New York: Pantheon, 1982.

———. "'With a Whip in His Hand': Rape, Memory, and African-American Women." In *History and Memory in African American Culture,* edited by Genevieve Fabre and Robert O'Meally, 205–218. New York: Oxford University Press, 1994.

Cobos, Rubén. *A Dictionary of New Mexico and Southern Colorado Spanish.* Santa Fe: Museum of New Mexico Press, 1983.

———. "The New Mexican Game of Valse Chiquiao." *Western Folklore* 15, no. 2 (April 1956): 95–101.

Collier, John. *Visual Anthropology: Photography as a Research Method.* New York: Holt, Rinehart and Winston, 1967.

References

Conrad, Paul. "*Bárbaros* into Soldiers: Violence, Reciprocity, and Identity on New Spain's Northern Frontier." Master's thesis, University of Texas–Austin, 2007.

———. "Captive Fates: Displaced American Indians in the Southwest Borderlands, Mexico, and Cuba, 1500–1800." PhD diss., University of Texas–Austin, 2011.

Constable, Nicole. "International Marriage Brokers, Cross-Border Marriages, and the US Anti-trafficking Campaign." *Journal of Ethnic and Migration Studies* 38, no. 7 (2012): 1137–1154.

Corbitt, Duvon C. "Immigration in Cuba." *Hispanic American Historical Review* 22, no. 2 (1942): 280–308.

Córdova, Gilberto Benito. *Big Dreams and Dark Secrets in Chimayó*. Albuquerque: University of New Mexico Press, 2006.

———. "Missionization and Hispanicization of Santo Tomás Apóstol de Abiquiú, 1750–1770." PhD diss., University of New Mexico, 1979.

Council for Prostitution Alternatives. *Annual Report, 1991*. Portland, OR.

Crane, Verner W. *The Southern Frontier, 1670–1732*. Tuscaloosa: University of Alabama Press, 2004.

Crawford, S. Wylie. "Medical Topography and Diseases of Fort McKavett." In *Statistical Report on the Sickness and Mortality in the Army of the United States, Compiled from the Records of the Surgeon General's Office; Embracing a Period of Sixteen Years, from January, 1839, to January, 1855*, edited by Robert H. Coolidge, 386–393. Washington, DC: A. O. P. Nicholson, 1856.

Cressman, Luther S. "Contrastive Features of Native North American Trade Systems." In *For the Chief: Essays in Honor of Luther S. Cressman*, edited by Fred W. Voget and Robert L. Stephenson, 153–169. Eugene: University of Oregon, Department of Anthropology, 1972.

———. "Klamath Prehistory: The Prehistory of the Culture of the Klamath Lake Area, Oregon." *Transactions of the American Philosophical Society* 46, no. 4 (January 1, 1956): 375–513.

Cresswell, Tim. "Embodiment, Power, and the Politics of Mobility: The Case of Female Tramps and Hobos." *Transactions of the Institute of British Geographers* 24, no. 2 (1999): 175–192.

Crosby, Alfred W. *Ecological Imperialism: The Biological Expansion of Europe, 900–1900*. Cambridge: Cambridge University Press, 1986.

Culhane, Dara. "Their Spirits Live within Us." *American Indian Quarterly* 27, no. 3 (2003): 593–606.

Cumfer, Cynthia. *Separate Peoples, One Land: The Minds of Cherokees, Blacks, and Whites on the Tennessee Frontier*. Chapel Hill: University of North Carolina Press, 2007.

Curtis, Edward S. *The North American Indian; Being a Series of Volumes Picturing and Describing the Indians of the United States, and Alaska*, vol. 13. Seattle: E. S. Curtis, 1907.

References

Cusick, Linda. "Youth Prostitution: A Literature Review." *Child Abuse Review* 11, no. 4 (2002): 230–251.

Cybulski, Jerome S. *A Greenville Burial Ground: Human Remains and Mortuary Elements in British Columbia Prehistory.* Hull, QC: Canadian Museum of Civilization, 1992.

Dargis, Manohla. "The Blood and Tears, Not the Magnolias: '12 Years a Slave' Holds Nothing Back in Show of Suffering." *New York Times*, October 17, 2013. Accessed January 7, 2014. http://www.nytimes.com/2013/10/18/movies/12-years-a-slave-holds-nothing-back-in-show-of-suffering.html?_r=0&pagewanted=2.

Davies, K. G., ed. *Peter Skene Ogden's Snake Country Journal, 1826–27.* London: Hudson's Bay Record Society, 1961.

Davis, Angela. "Reflections on the Black Woman's Role in the Community of Slaves." *The Black Scholar* 3, no. 4 (1971): 2–15.

Davis, David Brion. *Inhuman Bondage: The Rise and Fall of Slavery in the New World.* Oxford: Oxford University Press, 2006.

———. "Looking at Slavery in a Broader Perspective." *American Historical Review* 105 (2000): 452–466.

———. *The Problem of Slavery in Western Culture.* Ithaca, NY: Cornell University Press, 1966.

Davis, James. *Trade Routes and Economic Exchange among the Indians of California.* Ramona, CA: Ballena Press, 1974.

De Ravello, Lori, Jessica Abeita, and Pam Brown. "Breaking the Cycle/Mending the Hoop: Adverse Childhood Experiences among Incarcerated American Indian/Alaska Native Women in New Mexico." *Health Care for Women International* 29, no. 3 (2008): 300–315.

Declich, Francesca. "Unfree Labour, Forced Labour, and Resistance among the Zigula of the Lower Juba." In *Resisting Bondage in Indian Ocean Africa and Asia*, edited by Edward Alpers, Gwyn Campbell, and Michael Salman, 24–39. New York: Routledge, 2007.

Deisher, Robert W., J. A. Farrow, K. Hope, and C. Litchfield. "The Pregnant Adolescent Prostitute." *American Journal of Diseases of Children* 143, no. 10 (1989): 1162–1165.

Del Valle, Sandra. *Language Rights and the Law in the United States: Finding Our Voices.* Bristol, UK: Multilingual Matters, 2003.

DeLay, Brian. *War of a Thousand Deserts: Indian Raids and the US-Mexican War.* New Haven, CT: Yale University Press, 2008.

Delgado, Grace Peña. "Border Control and Sexual Policing: White Slavery and Prostitution along the US-Mexico Borderlands, 1903–1910." *Western Historical Quarterly* 43 (Summer 2012): 157–178.

Deloria, Vine, Jr. *Custer Died for Your Sins: An Indian Manifesto.* Norman: University of Oklahoma Press, 1969.

Deloria, Vine, Jr., and Clifford M. Lytle. *American Indians, American Justice.* Austin: University of Texas Press, 1983.

References

Demers, E. A. S. "John Askin and Indian Slavery at Michilimackinac." In *Indian Slavery in Colonial America*, edited by Alan Gallay, 391–416. Lincoln: University of Nebraska Press, 2010.

Denetdale, Jennifer. *Reclaiming Diné History: The Legacies of Navajo Chief Manuelito and Juanita.* Tucson: University of Arizona Press, 2007.

Dennis, Elsie Frances. "Indian Slavery in Pacific Northwest (in Three Parts, I)." *Oregon Historical Quarterly* 31, no. 1 (March 1, 1930): 69–81.

DePratter, Chester B. *Late Prehistoric and Early Historic Chiefdoms in the Southeastern United States.* New York: Garland Press, 1991.

DeRosier, Arthur H. *Removal of the Choctaw Indians.* Knoxville: University of Tennessee Press, 1970.

Derounian-Stodola, Kathryn Zabelle, and James Arthur Levernier. *The Indian Captivity Narrative, 1550–1900.* New York: Twayne Publishers, 1993.

Deur, Douglas. *In the Footprints of Gmukamps: A Traditional Use Study of Crater Lake National Park and Lava Beds National Monument.* Seattle: US National Park Service, Pacific West Region, 2008.

Devaney, Earl E. *Investigative Report on the Chemawa Indian School Detention Facility.* US Department of the Interior, Office of Inspector General, Washington, DC, 2005.

Deyle, Steven. *Carry Me Back: The Domestic Slave Trade in American Life.* New York: Oxford University Press, 2005.

———. "Rethinking the Slave Trade: Slave Traders and the Market Revolution in the South." In *The Old South's Modern Worlds: Slavery, Region, and Nation in the Age of Progress*, edited by L. Diane Barnes, Brian Schoen, and Frank Towers, 104–119. New York: Oxford University Press, 2011.

Diario de las sesiones de la Soberana Junta Provisional Gubernativa del Imperio Mexicano, instalada según previene el Plan de Iguala y los Tratados de la Villa de Córdova. In *Actas constitucionales mexicanas (1821–1824).* Mexico City: Instituto de Investigaciones Jurídicas, Universidad Nacional Autónoma de México, 1980.

Diaz, Maria Elena. *The Virgin, the King, and the Royal Slaves of El Cobre: Negotiating Freedom in Colonial Cuba, 1670–1780.* Stanford, CA: Stanford University Press, 2000.

Dillon, Richard H. *Burnt-Out Fires: California's Modoc Indian War.* Englewood Cliffs, NJ: Prentice-Hall, 1973.

Dobyns, Henry F. *Their Number Become Thinned: Native American Population Dynamics in Eastern North America.* Knoxville: University of Tennessee Press, 1983.

Dolbeare, Benjamin. *A Narrative of the Captivity and Suffering of Dolly Webster among the Camanche Indians in Texas.* New Haven, CT: Yale University Library, 1986.

Domínguez, Fray Francisco Atanasio. *The Missions of New Mexico, 1776: A Description by Fray Francisco Atanasio Domínguez*, edited and translated by Eleanor B. Adams and Fray Angélico Chávez. Albuquerque: University of New Mexico Press, 1975.

References

Donald, Leland. *Aboriginal Slavery on the Northwest Coast of North America*. Berkeley: University of California Press, 1997.

Douglass, Frederick, and Harriet Jacobs. *Narrative of the Life of Frederick Douglass, an American Slave, and Incidents in the Life of a Slave Girl*. New York: Modern Library, 2000.

Douthit, Nathan. *Uncertain Encounters: Indians and Whites at Peace and War in Southern Oregon, 1820s–1860s*. Corvallis: Oregon State University Press, 2002.

Drinnon, Richard. *Keeper of Concentration Camps: Dillon S. Myer and American Racism*. Berkeley: University of California Press, 1987.

Drooker, Penelope B. "The Ohio Valley, 1550–1750: Patterns of Sociopolitical Coalescence and Dispersal." In *The Transformation of the Southeastern Indians, 1540–1760*, edited by Robbie Ethridge and Charles Hudson, 115–134. Jackson: University of Mississippi Press, 2002.

Dublán, Manuel, and José María Lozano. *Legislación mexicana; o, Colección completa de disposiciones legislativas expedidas desde la independencia de la República*. Mexico City: Imprenta del Comercio, 1876.

Dublin, Thomas. *Transforming Women's Work: New England Lives in the Industrial Revolution*. Ithaca, NY: Cornell University Press, 1995.

Duggan, Marie. *The Chumash and the Presidio of Santa Barbara: Evolution of a Relationship, 1782–1823*. Santa Barbara, CA: Presidio Research Center, 2004.

Duguid, Paul. "Networks and Knowledge: The Beginning and End of the Port Commodity Chain, 1703–1860." *Business History Review* 79 (2005): 493–526.

DuVal, Kathleen. *The Native Ground: Indians and Colonists in the Heart of the Continent*. Philadelphia: University of Pennsylvania Press, 2006.

Dworkin, Andrea. "Prostitution and Male Supremacy." In *Life and Death*, edited by Andrea Dworkin, 139–151. New York: Free Press, 1997.

Dye, David. "Art, Ritual, and Chiefly Warfare in the Mississippian World." In *Hero, Hawk, and Open Hand: American Indian Art of the Ancient Midwest and South*, edited by Richard F. Townsend and Robert V. Sharp, 191–206. New Haven, CT: Yale University Press, 2004.

Dye, David H., and Adam King. "Desecrating the Sacred Ancestor Temples: Chiefly Conflict and Violence in the American Southeast." In *North American Indigenous Warfare and Ritual Violence*, edited by Richard J. Chacon and Rubén G. Mendoza, 160–181. Tucson: University of Arizona Press, 2007.

Earle, Rebecca. *The Body of the Conquistador: Food, Race and the Colonial Experience in Spanish America, 1492–1700*. New York: Cambridge University Press, 2012.

Edberg, Mark Cameron. *El Narcotraficante: Narcocorridos and the Construction of a Cultural Persona on the US-Mexican Border*. Austin: University of Texas Press, 2004.

Eden, Trudy. *The Early American Table: Food and Society in the New World*. DeKalb: Northern Illinois University Press, 2008.

Eggan, Fred, ed. *Social Anthropology of North American Tribes*. Chicago: University of Chicago Press, 1955.

References

Ekberg, Carl J. *Stealing Indian Women: Native Slavery in the Illinois Country.* Urbana: University of Illinois Press, 2007.

Ekman, Kajsa E. *Being and Being Bought: Prostitution, Surrogacy, and the Split Self.* North Melbourne: Spinifex Press, 2013.

Elizabeth Fry Society of Toronto. "Streetwork: Outreach with Adult Female Street Prostitutes." Unpublished report, Toronto, May 1987.

Engerman, Stanley L. "Slavery at Different Times and Places." *American Historical Review* 105 (2000): 480–484.

Ervin, A. M. *New Northern Townsmen in Inuvik.* Ottawa: Northern Science Research Group, 1968.

Ethridge, Robbie. Afterword to *Mapping the Mississippian Shatter Zone: The Colonial Indian Slave Trade and Regional Instability in the American South*, edited by Robbie Ethridge and Sheri M. Shuck-Hall, 418–424. Lincoln: University of Nebraska Press, 2009.

———. "Creating the Shatter Zone: Indian Slave Traders and the Collapse of the Southeastern Chiefdoms." In *Light on the Path: The Anthropology and History of the Southeastern Indians,* edited by Thomas Pluckhahn and Robbie Ethridge, 207–218. Tuscaloosa: University of Alabama Press, 2006.

———. "The Emergence of the Colonial South: Colonial Indian Slaving, the Fall of the Precontact Mississippian World, and the Emergence of a New Social Geography in the American South, 1540–1730." In *Native American Adoption, Captivity, and Slavery in Changing Contexts*, edited by Max Carocci and Stephanie Pratt, 47–64. New York: Palgrave Macmillan, 2012.

———. *From Chicaza to Chickasaw: The European Invasion and the Transformation of the Mississippian World, 1540–1715.* Chapel Hill: University of North Carolina Press, 2010.

———. "Introduction: Mapping the Mississippian Shatter Zone." In *Mapping the Mississippian Shatter Zone: The Colonial Indian Slave Trade and Regional Instability in the American South*, edited by Robbie Ethridge and Sheri M. Shuck-Hall, 1–63. Lincoln: University of Nebraska Press, 2009.

———. "The Making of a Militaristic Slaving Society: The Chickasaws and the Colonial Indian Slave Trade." In *Indian Slavery in Colonial America*, edited by Alan Gallay, 251–276. Lincoln: University of Nebraska Press, 2009.

Ethridge, Robbie, and Sheri M. Shuck-Hall, eds. *Mapping the Mississippian Shatter Zone: The Colonial Indian Slave Trade and Regional Instability in the American South.* Lincoln: University of Nebraska Press, 2009.

Falola, Toyin, and Matt D. Childs, eds. *The Yoruba Diaspora in the Atlantic World.* Bloomington: Indiana University Press, 2005.

Fang, Bay, and Mark Leong. "China's Stolen Wives." *U.S. News & World Report* 125, no. 14 (1998): 35–38.

Farley, Melissa. "Prostitution and the Invisibility of Harm." *Women & Therapy* 26, nos. 3–4 (2005): 247–280.

References

———. *Prostitution and Trafficking in Nevada: Making the Connections.* San Francisco: Prostitution Research & Education, 2007.

———. "Prostitution, Trafficking, and Cultural Amnesia: What We Must *Not* Know in Order to Keep the Business of Sexual Exploitation Running Smoothly." *Yale Journal of Law and Feminism* 18 (2006): 109–144.

———. "'Renting an Organ for 10 Minutes': What Tricks Tell Us about Prostitution, Pornography, and Trafficking." In *Pornography: Driving the Demand for International Sex Trafficking*, edited by David Guinn and J. DeCaro, 144–152. Los Angeles: Captive Daughters Media, 2007.

———. "Unequal." Prostitution Research & Education, 2005. http://prostitutionresearch.com/2005/09/13/unequal/.

Farley, Melissa, Isin Baral, Karina Gonzales, Merab Kiremire, Ufuk Sezgin, Frida Spiwak, and Toy Taylor. "Prostitution: Health Consequences of Physical Violence and Psychological Trauma." Paper presented at the Eleventh International Congress on Women's Health Issues, University of California College of Nursing, San Francisco, January 28, 2000.

Farley, Melissa, Ann Cotton, Jacqueline Lynne, Sybil Zumbeck, Frida Spiwak, Maria E. Reyes, Dinorah Alvarez, and Ufuk Sezgin. "Prostitution and Trafficking in Nine Countries: Update on Violence and Posttraumatic Stress Disorder." In *Prostitution, Trafficking, and Traumatic Stress*, edited by Melissa Farley, 33–74. New York: Routledge, 2003.

Farley, Melissa, Kenneth Franzblau, and M. Alexis Kennedy. "Online Prostitution and Trafficking." *Albany Law Review* 77, no. 3 (2014): 1039–1094.

Farley, Melissa, Jacqueline Lynne, and Ann J. Cotton. "Prostitution in Vancouver: Violence and the Colonization of First Nations Women." *Transcultural Psychiatry* 42, no. 2 (2005): 242–271.

Farley, Melissa, Nicole Matthews, Sarah Deer, Guadalupe Lopez, Christine Stark, and Eileen Hudon. *Garden of Truth: The Prostitution and Trafficking of Native Women in Minnesota.* Report sponsored by Minnesota Indian Women's Sexual Assault Coalition and presented at William Mitchell College of Law, Saint Paul, MN, October 27, 2011.

Farley, Melissa, Emily Schuckman, Jacqueline M. Golding, Kristen Houser, Laura Jarrett, Peter Qualliotine, and Michelle Decker. "Comparing Sex Buyers with Men Who Don't Buy Sex: 'You Can Have a Good Time with the Servitude' vs. 'You're Supporting a System of Degradation.'" Paper presented at Psychologists for Social Responsibility Annual Meeting, Boston, July 15, 2011.

Farnham, T. J. "Travels in the Great Western Prairies, Part I." In *Early Western Travels, 1748–1846*, vol. 28, edited by R. G. Thwaites. Cleveland, OH: A. H. Clark, 1906.

Fausz, Frederick J. "Fighting 'Fire' with Firearms: The Anglo-Powhatan Arms Race." *American Indian Culture and Research Journal* 3, no. 4 (1979): 33–50.

———. "Present at the Creation: The Chesapeake World That Greeted the Maryland Colonists." *Maryland Historical Magazine* 79 (1984): 7–20.

Fehrenbach, T. R. *Comanches: The History of a People.* New York: Random House, 1974.

REFERENCES

Fenn, Elizabeth A. *Pox Americana: The Great Smallpox Epidemic of 1775–82.* New York: Hill and Wang, 2001.

Fenton, William N. "Northern Iroquoian Culture Patterns." In *Handbook of North American Indians*, vol. 15, *Northeast*, edited by Bruce G. Trigger, 296–321. Washington, DC: Smithsonian Institution, 1978.

Fett, Sharla M. *Working Cures: Healing, Health, and Power on Southern Slave Plantations.* Chapel Hill: University of North Carolina Press, 2002.

Finkelhor, David, and Richard Ormrod. "Prostitution of Juveniles: Patterns from NIBRS." *Juvenile Justice Bulletin* (June 2004): 1–11.

Finley, Moses I. *Ancient Slavery and Modern Ideology.* New York: Viking Press, 1980.

———, ed. *Classical Slavery.* Totowa, NJ: F. Cass, 1987.

Fixico, Donald L. *Bureau of Indian Affairs.* Santa Barbara, CA: ABC-CLIO, 2012.

"Fla. Woman Allegedly Offers Sex for Two Cheeseburgers." *Bradenton Herald* (FL), April 3, 2012. Accessed May 22, 2012. http://thetimes-tribune.com/news/fla-woman-offers-sex-for-2-cheeseburgers-1.1294528.

Flores, Dan. *Caprock Canyonlands: Journeys into the Heart of the Southern Plains.* Austin: University of Texas Press, 1990.

Follett, Richard. *The Sugar Masters: Planters and Slaves in Louisiana's Cane World, 1820–1860.* Baton Rouge: Louisiana State University Press, 2005.

Forbes, Alexander. *California: A History of Upper and Lower California from Their First Discovery to the Present Time.* 1839. Reprint, New York: Arno Press, 1973.

Forbes, Jack D. *Columbus and Other Cannibals: The Weitko Disease of Exploitation, Imperialism, and Terrorism.* New York: Seven Stories Press, 1992.

———. *Warriors of the Colorado: The Yumas of the Quechan Nation and Their Neighbors.* Norman: University of Oklahoma Press, 1965.

Forbes, John, Alexander Tweedie, John Conolly, and Robert Dunglison, eds. *Cyclopaedia of Practical Medicine: Comprising Treatises on the Nature and Treatment of Disease, Materia Medica and Therapeutics, Medical Jurisprudence, Etc., Etc.* Vol. 4. Philadelphia: Lea and Blanchard, 1850.

Ford, Lacy K. *Deliver Us from Evil: The Slavery Question in the Old South.* New York: Oxford University Press, 2009.

Foreman, Grant. *The Five Civilized Tribes: Cherokee, Chickasaw, Choctaw, Creek, Seminole.* Norman: University of Oklahoma Press, 1934.

———. *Indian Removal: The Emigration of the Five Civilized Tribes of Indians.* Norman: University of Oklahoma Press, 1932.

Fowles, Severin. "From Social Type to Social Process: Placing 'Tribe' in a Historical Framework." In *The Archaeology of Tribal Societies*, edited by W. Parkinson, 13–33. Ann Arbor, MI: International Monographs in Prehistory, 2002.

Fox, William A. "Events as Seen from the North: The Iroquois and Colonial Slavery." In *Mapping the Mississippian Shatter Zone: The Colonial Indian Slave Trade and Regional Instability in the American South*, edited by Robbie Ethridge and Sheri M. Shuck-Hall, 63–80. Lincoln: University of Nebraska Press, 2009.

REFERENCES

Freire, Paulo. *Pedagogy of the Oppressed.* New York: Continuum International Publishing Group, 2005.

Gallay, Alan. *The Indian Slave Trade: The Rise of the English Empire in the American South, 1670–1717.* New Haven, CT: Yale University Press, 2002.

———, ed. *Indian Slavery in Colonial America.* Lincoln: University of Nebraska Press, 2010.

———. "Introduction: Indian Slavery in Historical Context." In *Indian Slavery in Colonial America*, edited by Alan Gallay, 1–32. Lincoln: University of Nebraska Press, 2010.

Galloway, Patricia. "Choctaws at the Border of the Shatter Zone: Spheres of Exchange and Spheres of Social Value." In *Mapping the Mississippian Shatter Zone: The Colonial Indian Slave Trade and Regional Instability in the American South*, edited by Robbie Ethridge and Sheri M. Shuck-Hall, 333–364. Lincoln: University of Nebraska Press, 2009.

———. "Henri de Tonti du Village des Chacta, 1702: The Beginning of the French Alliance." In *LaSalle and His Legacy: Frenchmen and Indians in the Lower Mississippi Valley*, edited by Patricia Galloway, 146–175. Jackson: University of Mississippi Press, 1983.

Gammel, H. P. H. *The Laws of Texas, 1822–1897.* 12 vols. Austin, TX: Gammel Book Company, 1898.

Gandert, Miguel A. *Nuevo México Profundo: Rituals of an Indo-Hispano Homeland.* With essays by Enrique R. Lamadrid, Ramón Gutiérrez, Lucy Lippard, and Chris Wilson. Santa Fe: Museum of New Mexico Press, 2000.

García, Peter J. *Decolonizing Enchantment: Echoes of Nuevo Mexicano Popular Musics.* Albuquerque: University of New Mexico Press, 2015.

García, Peter J., and Enrique R. Lamadrid. "Performing Indigeneity in the Nuevomexicano Homeland: Antiguo Mestizo Ritual and New Mestizo Revivals, Antidotes to Enchantment and Alienation." In *Comparative Indigeneities of the Américas: Toward a Hemispheric Approach*, edited by M. Bianet Castellanos, Lourdes Gutiérrez Nájera, and Arturo J. Aldama, 96–112. Tucson: University of Arizona Press, 2012.

Garth, Thomas R. "The Plateau Whipping Complex and Its Relationship to Plateau-Southwest Contacts." *Ethnohistory* 12, no. 2 (Spring 1965): 141–170.

Gatschet, Albert Samuel. *Klamath Indians of Southwestern Oregon.* 2 vols. Washington, DC: US Department of the Interior, 1890.

Genovese, Eugene, and Elizabeth Fox Genovese. *Fatal Self-Deception: Slaveholding Paternalism in the Old South.* New York: Cambridge University Press, 2011.

Gibbons, Richard P., Linda R. Keintz, Sharon K. Lemke, Carol G. Mellom, Diane K. Rochel, Amy M. Silberberg, Henry Ladislaus Sledz, and Georgia A. Smith. "Indian Americans in Southside Minneapolis: Additional Field Notes from the Urban Slum." Center for Urban and Regional Affairs, University of Minnesota, Minneapolis, 1970. http://www.cura.umn.edu/publications/catalog/m1027.

References

Giobbe, Evelina. "An Analysis of Individual, Institutional, and Cultural Pimping." *Michigan Journal of Gender and Law* 1, no. 1 (1993): 33–57.

———. "Juvenile Prostitution: Profile of Recruitment." In *Child Trauma: Issues and Research*, edited by Ann W. Burgess, 117–126. New York: Garland Publishing, 1992.

Goings, Henry. *Rambles of a Runaway from Southern Slavery*. Edited by Calvin Schermerhorn, Michael Plunkett, and Edward Gaynor. Charlottesville: University of Virginia Press, 2012.

Goldberg-Ambrose, Carole. *Planting Tail Feathers: Tribal Survival and Public Law 280*. Berkeley: University of California Press, 1997.

González, Michael J. *This Small City Will Be a Mexican Paradise: Exploring the Origins of Mexican Culture in Los Angeles, 1821–1846*. Albuquerque: University of New Mexico Press, 2005.

Gough, Peter. "Continuity, Convergence, and Conquest: A New History of the Old Spanish Trail." Master's thesis, California State University–Long Beach, 1997.

Goulding, Warren. *Just Another Indian: A Serial Killer and Canada's Indifference*. Ontario: Fifth House Publishers, 2001.

Graham, Dee L. R. *Loving to Survive: Sexual Terror, Men's Violence, and Women's Lives*. New York: New York University Press, 1994.

Graves, Theodore D. "Urban Indian Personality and the Culture of Poverty." *American Ethnologist* 1, no. 1 (1974): 65–86.

Green, George D. *Finance and Economic Development in the Old South: Louisiana Banking, 1804–1861*. Stanford, CA: Stanford University Press, 1972.

Green, Stanley. *The Mexican Republic: The First Decade, 1823–1832*. Pittsburgh: University of Pittsburgh Press, 1987.

Greene, Jody M., Susan T. Ennett, and Christopher L. Ringwalt. "Prevalence and Correlates of Survival Sex among Runaway and Homeless Youth." *American Journal of Public Health* 89, no. 9 (1999): 1406–1409.

Greer, Allan. *The Jesuit Relations: Natives and Missionaries in Seventeenth-Century North America*. Boston: Bedford / St. Martin's, 2000.

Gregg, Josiah. *Commerce of the Prairies: or, the Journal of a Santa Fé Trader, during Eight Expeditions across the Great Western Prairies, and a Residence of Nearly Nine Years in Northern Mexico*. Vol. 2. New York: Henry G. Langley, 1844.

Grobsmith, Elizabeth. "Review of *Inventing the Savage: The Social Construction of Native American Criminality* by Luana Ross." *Great Plains Research* 9 (1999): 175–177.

Gudmestad, Robert H. *Steamboats and the Rise of the Cotton Kingdom*. Baton Rouge: Louisiana State University Press, 2011.

———. *A Troublesome Commerce: The Transformation of the Interstate Slave Trade*. Baton Rouge: Louisiana State University Press, 2003.

Guerrero, Vladimir. "Lost in the Translation: Chief Palma of the Quechan." *Southern California Quarterly* 92, no. 4 (2010): 327–350.

References

Gumbs, Anthony G. "Prostitution: A Return to Slavery." *Jamaica Gleaner*, April 24, 2006. Accessed April 26, 2006. http://www.jamaicagleaner.com/gleaner/20060424/letters/letters1.html.

Gutiérrez, Ramón A. *When Jesus Came, the Corn Mothers Went Away: Marriage, Sexuality, and Power in New Mexico, 1500–1846*. Stanford, CA: Stanford University Press, 1991.

Gutman, Herbert. *The Black Family in Slavery and Freedom, 1750–1925*. New York: Vintage Books, 1977.

Guyatt, Nicholas. "'The Outskirts of Our Happiness': Race and the Lure of Colonization in the Early Republic." *Journal of American History* 95 (2009): 986–1011.

Haas, Lisbeth. "Indigenous Ethnic and Interethnic Relations in the Spanish/Mexican Borderlands: The Chumash Revolt." In *Journey into Otherness: Essays in North American History, Culture, and Literature*, edited by Ada Savin, 135–148. Amsterdam: VU University Press, 2005.

———. "Luiseño Scholar Pablo Tac." In *Alta California: Peoples in Motion, Identities in Formation, 1769–1850*, edited by Steven W. Hackel, 79–110. San Marino: Huntington Library / University of California Press, 2010.

———. *Saints and Citizens: Indigenous Histories of Colonial Missions and Mexican California*. Berkeley: University of California Press, 2013.

Habicht-Mauche, Judith A. "Captive Wives? The Role and Status of Nonlocal Women on the Protohistoric Southern High Plains." In *Invisible Citizens: Captives and Their Consequences*, edited by Catherine M. Cameron, 181–204. Salt Lake City: University of Utah Press, 2008.

Hackel, Steven W. *Children of Coyote, Missionaries of Saint Francis: Indian-Spanish Relations in Colonial California, 1769–1850*. Chapel Hill: University of North Carolina Press, 2005.

———. "Sources of Rebellion: Indian Testimony and the Mission San Gabriel Uprising of 1785." *Ethnohistory* 50 (2003): 643–669.

Hafen, Ann, and LeRoy Hafen. *Old Spanish Trail: Santa Fe to Los Angeles*. Glendale, CA: Arthur H. Clark, 1954.

Hagan, Kenneth J., and Ian J. Bickerton. *Unintended Consequences: The United States at War*. London: Reaktion Books, 2007.

Hague, Harlan. *The Road to California: The Search for a Southern Overland Route, 1540–1848*. Los Angeles: Arthur C. Clark, 1978.

Hahn, Steven C. *The Invention of the Creek Nation, 1670–1763*. Lincoln: University of Nebraska Press, 2004.

Haines, Francis. "The Northward Spread of Horses among the Plains Indians." *American Anthropologist* 40, no. 3 (September 1938): 429–437.

Hall, Joseph M. *Zamumo's Gifts: Indian-European Exchange in the Colonial Southeast*. Philadelphia: University of Pennsylvania Press, 2009.

Halliburton, R., Jr. "Chief Greenwood Leflore and His Malmaison Plantation." In *After

REFERENCES

    Removal: The Choctaw in Mississippi, edited by Samuel J. Wells and Roseanna Tubby, 56–63. Oxford: University Press of Mississippi, 1986.

Hämäläinen, Pekka. *The Comanche Empire*. New Haven, CT: Yale University Press, 2008.

———. "The Politics of Grass: European Expansion, Ecological Change, and Indigenous Power in the Southwest Borderlands." *William and Mary Quarterly* 67, no. 2 (April 2010): 173–208.

Hammond, John Craig. *Slavery, Freedom, and Expansion in the Early American West*. Charlottesville: University of Virginia Press, 2007.

———. "Slavery, Settlement, and Empire: The Expansion and Growth of Slavery in the Interior of the North American Continent, 1770–1820." *Journal of the Early Republic* 32 (Summer 2012): 175–206.

Hardin, Nathan. "Woman Charged with Prostituting for Gas." *Salisbury Post* (NC), July 21, 2011. Accessed January 15, 2012. http://www.salisburypost.com/Crime/072111-WEBcouplechargedwithprostitution-qcdChristopher%20Riddle.

Harley, Bruce. "Did Mission San Gabriel Have Two Asistencias? The Case of Rancho San Bernardino." *San Bernardino County Museum Association Quarterly* 36, no. 4 (1989): 1–69.

Harley, Sharon, ed. *Sister Circle: Black Women and Work*. Piscataway, NJ: Rutgers University Press, 2002.

Harrington, John. *Tobacco among the Karuk Indians of California*. Washington, DC: US Government Printing Office, 1932.

Harris, Charles. *A Mexican Family Empire: The* Latifundio *of the Sánchez Navarros, 1765–1867*. Austin: University of Texas Press, 1975.

Harris, Rachel, and Katharine Gelber. "Defining 'De Facto' Slavery in Australia: Ownership, Consent, and the Defence of Freedom." *International Criminal Law Review* 11, no. 3 (June 2011): 561–578.

Harrod, Ryan P. "Centers of Control: Revealing Elites among the Ancestral Pueblo during the 'Chaco Phenomenon.'" *International Journal of Paleopathology* 2, nos. 2–3 (2012): 123–135.

Hasson, Alexander B. "Medical Topography and Diseases of Post on Clear Fork of Brazos River (Phantom Hill)." In *Statistical Report on the Sickness and Mortality in the Army of the United States, Compiled from the Records of the Surgeon General's Office; Embracing a Period of Sixteen Years, from January, 1839, to January, 1855*, edited by Robert H. Coolidge, 375–378. Washington, DC: A. O. P. Nicholson, 1856.

Hauptman, Laurence M. *Tribes and Tribulations: Misconceptions about American Indians and Their Histories*. Albuquerque: University of New Mexico Press, 1995.

Haynes, Robert. *The Mississippi Territory and the Southwest Frontier, 1795–1817*. Lexington: University Press of Kentucky, 2010.

Hedges, Chris, and Joe Sacco. *Days of Destruction, Days of Revolt*. New York: Nation Books, 2012.

References

Heizer, Robert F. "Walla Walla Indian Expedition to the Sacramento Valley, 1844–47." *California Historical Society Quarterly* 21 (1942): 1–7.

———, ed. *The Destruction of California Indians*. Santa Barbara, CA, and Salt Lake City, UT: Peregrine Smith, 1974.

Henderson, Timothy. *A Glorious Defeat: Mexico and Its War with the United States*. New York: Hill and Wang, 2007.

Herman, Judith. *Trauma and Recovery: The Aftermath of Violence from Domestic Violence to Political Terror*. New York: Basic Books, 1992.

Historical Census Browser, Geospatial and Statistical Data Center, University of Virginia. Accessed October 16, 2012. http://fisher.lib.virginia.edu.

Hochschild, Adam. *Bury the Chains: Prophets and Rebels in the Fight to Free an Empire's Slaves*. New York: Houghton-Mifflin, 2005.

———. *King Leopold's Ghost: A Story of Greed, Terror, and Heroism in Colonial Africa*. Boston: Houghton-Mifflin, 1998.

Hodge, David R. "Sexual Trafficking in the United States: A Domestic Problem with Transnational Dimensions." *Social Work* 53 (2008): 143–153.

Hodson, Christopher. *The Acadian Diaspora: An Eighteenth Century History*. New York: Oxford University Press, 2012.

Hoigard, Ceilie, and Liv Finstad. *Backstreets: Prostitution, Money, and Love*. University Park: Pennsylvania State University Press, 1986.

Horsman, Reginald. *Race and Manifest Destiny: The Origins of American Racial Anglo-Saxonism*. Cambridge, MA: Harvard University Press, 1981.

Howe, Daniel Walker. *What Hath God Wrought: The Transformation of America, 1815–1848*. New York: Oxford University Press, 2007.

Hudson, Charles. *Knights of Spain, Warriors of the Sun: Hernando de Soto and the South's Ancient Chiefdoms*. Athens: University of Georgia Press, 1997.

———. *The Southeastern Indians*. Knoxville: University of Tennessee Press, 1976.

Human Rights Watch. *No Escape: Male Rape in US Prisons*. New York: Human Rights Watch, 2001.

Humphries, Jane. *Childhood and Child Labour in the British Industrial Revolution*. Cambridge: Cambridge University Press, 2010.

Hurtado, Albert L. "Hardly a Farm House—A Kitchen without Them: Indian and White Households on the California Borderland Frontier in 1860." *Western Historical Quarterly* 13, no. 3 (1982): 245–270.

———. *Indian Survival on the California Frontier*. Yale Western Americana Series. New Haven, CT: Yale University Press, 1988.

———. *Intimate Frontiers: Sex, Gender, and Culture in Old California*. Berkeley: University of California Press, 1999.

———. "Sex, Gender, Culture, and a Great Event: The California Gold Rush." *Pacific Historical Review* 68 (1999): 1–19.

References

Hymes, Dell. *"In Vain I Tried to Tell You": Essays in Native American Ethnopoetics.* Philadelphia: University of Pennsylvania Press, 1981.

I. R. R., Dr. "Great Facility of Raising Corn in Texas." In *Texas Almanac for 1859*, 73–74. Galveston, TX: Willard Richardson, 1859.

Igler, David. *The Great Ocean: Pacific Worlds from Captain Hook to the Gold Rush.* Oxford: Oxford University Press, 2013.

———. *Industrial Cowboys: Miller & Lux and the Transformation of the Far West, 1850–1920.* Berkeley: University of California Press, 2005.

Isenberg, Andrew C. *The Destruction of the Bison: An Environmental History, 1750–1920.* Cambridge: Cambridge University Press, 2000.

———. *Mining California: An Ecological History.* New York: Hill and Wang, 2005.

Jackson, Peter. "Turkish Slaves on Islam's Indian Frontier." In *Slavery and South Asian History*, edited by Indrani Chatterjee and Richard M. Eaton, 63–82. Bloomington: Indiana University Press, 2006.

Jackson, Robert H., and Edward Castillo. "The Changing Economic Structure of the Alta California Missions: A Reinterpretation." *Pacific Historical Review* 61 (1992): 387–415.

———. *Indians, Franciscans, and Spanish Colonization: The Impact of the Mission System on California Indians.* Albuquerque: University of New Mexico Press, 1995.

Jacobs, Margaret. "Breaking and Remaking Families: The Fostering and Adoption of Native American Children in Non-Native Families in the American West, 1880–1940." In *On the Borders of Love and Power: Families and Kinship in the Intercultural American Southwest*, edited by David Wallace Adams and Crista DeLuzio, 19–46. Berkeley: University of California Press, 2012.

Jacoby, Karl. *Shadows at Dawn: An Apache Massacre and the Violence of History.* New York: Penguin Books, 2008.

Jaget, Claude. *Prostitutes—Our Life.* Bristol, UK: Falling Wall Press, 1980.

Jagodinsky, Katrina. "Territorial Bonds: Indenture and Affection in Intercultural Arizona, 1864–1896." In *On the Borders of Love and Power: Families and Kinship in the Intercultural American Southwest*, edited by David Wallace Adams and Crista DeLuzio, 255–277. Berkeley: University of California Press, 2012.

Jameson, Frederick. *The Political Unconscious: Narrative as a Socially Symbolic Act.* Ithaca, NY: Cornell University Press, 1981.

Janicek, Ricki S. "The Development of Early Mexican Land Policy: Coahuila and Texas, 1810–1825." PhD diss., Tulane University, 1985.

Jennings, Matthew H. "Violence in a Shattered World." In *Mapping the Mississippian Shatter Zone: The Colonial Indian Slave Trade and Regional Instability in the American South*, edited by Robbie Ethridge and Sheri M. Shuck-Hall, 272–294. Lincoln: University of Nebraska Press, 2009.

Jennings, Thelma. "Us Colored Women Had to Go through a Plenty: Sexual Exploitation of African American Slave Women." *Journal of Women's History* 1 (Winter 1990): 45–74.

References

Jeter, Marvin. "Ripe for Colonial Exploitation: Ancient Traditions of Violence and Enmity as Preludes to the Indian Slave Trade." In *Native American Adoption, Captivity, and Slavery in Changing Contexts*, edited by Max Carocci and Stephanie Pratt, 23–46. New York: Palgrave Macmillan, 2012.

Johnson, Jay K., John W. O'Hear, Robbie Ethridge, Brad R. Lieb, Susan L. Scott, and H. Edwin Jackson. "Measuring Chickasaw Adaptation on the Western Frontier of the Colonial South: A Correlation of Documentary and Archeological Data." *Southeastern Archaeology* 27 (Summer 2008): 1–30.

Johnson, Susan Lee. *Roaring Camp: The Social World of the California Gold Rush*. New York: W. W. Norton, 2000.

Johnson, Walter. "Agency: A Ghost Story." In *Slavery's Ghost: The Problem of Freedom in the Age of Emancipation*, Walter Johnson, Eric Foner, and Richard Follett, 8–30. Baltimore, MD: Johns Hopkins University Press, 2011.

———. *River of Dark Dreams: Slavery and Empire in the Cotton Kingdom*. Cambridge, MA: Harvard University Press, 2013.

———. *Soul by Soul: Life inside the Antebellum Slave Market*. Cambridge, MA: Harvard University Press, 1999.

Jones, Jacqueline. *Labor of Love, Labor of Sorrow: Black Women, Work, and the Family, from Slavery to the Present*. Rev. ed. Philadelphia: Basic Books, 2009.

Jordan, Kurt A. "Incorporation and Colonization: Postcolumbian Iroquois Satellite Communities and Processes of Indigenous Autonomy." *American Anthropologist* 115 (March 2013): 29–43.

Jordan, Winthrop D. *White over Black: American Attitudes toward the Negro*. Chapel Hill: University of North Carolina Press, 1968.

Jung, Moon-Ho. *Coolies and Cane: Race, Labor, and Sugar in the Age of Emancipation*. Baltimore, MD: Johns Hopkins University Press, 2006.

Junker, Laura Lee. "The Impact of Captured Women on Cultural Transmission in Contact-Period Philippine Slave-Raiding Chiefdoms." In *Invisible Citizens: Captives and Their Consequences*, edited by Catherine M. Cameron, 110–137. Salt Lake City: University of Utah Press, 2008.

Kan, Sergi. *Symbolic Immortality: The Tlingit Potlatch of the Nineteenth Century*. Washington, DC: Smithsonian Institution, 1989.

Karmen, Andrew. *Crime Victims: An Introduction to Victimology*. 7th ed. Stamford, CT: Cengage Learning Publishing, 2009.

Kastor, Peter J. "The Many Wests of Thomas Jefferson." In *Seeing Jefferson Anew: In His Time and Ours*, edited by John B. Boles and Randal L. Hall, 66–102. Charlottesville: University of Virginia Press, 2010.

Katyal, Neal K. "Men Who Own Women: A Thirteenth Amendment Critique of Forced Prostitution." *Yale Law Journal* 103 (December 1993): 791–826.

Katznelson, Ira. "Flexible Capacity: The Military and Early American Statebuilding." In *Shaped by War and Trade: International Influences on American Political Development*, edited by Ira Katznelson and Martin Schefter, 82–110. Princeton, NJ: Princeton University Press, 2002.

References

Kavanagh, Thomas W., ed. *Comanche Ethnography*. Lincoln: University of Nebraska Press, 2008.

Kelley, Sean M. *Los Brazos de Dios: A Plantation Society in the Texas Borderlands, 1821–1865*. Baton Rouge: Louisiana State University Press, 2010.

Kelly, Isabel T. "Ethnography of the Surprise Valley Paiute." *University of California Publications in American Archaeology and Ethnology* 31 (1932): 67–210.

Kelton, Paul. *Epidemics and Enslavement: Biological Catastrophe in the Native Southeast, 1492–1715*. Lincoln: University of Nebraska Press, 2007.

Kilbourne, Richard Holcombe, Jr. *Slave Agriculture and Financial Markets: The Bank of the United States in Mississippi, 1831–1852*. London: Pickering and Chatto, 2006.

King, Wilma. *Stolen Childhood: Slave Youth in Nineteenth-Century America*. 2nd ed. Bloomington: Indiana University Press, 2011.

Klein, Herbert S. *The Atlantic Slave Trade*. New York: Cambridge University Press, 2010.

———. *A Population History of the United States*. New York: Cambridge University Press, 2012.

Klein, Herbert S., and Ben Vinson III. *African Slavery in Latin America and the Caribbean*. 2nd ed. New York: Oxford University Press, 2007.

Klein, Martin A., ed. *Breaking the Chains: Slavery, Bondage, and Emancipation in Modern Africa and Asia*. Madison: University of Wisconsin Press, 1993.

Knack, Martha C. *Boundaries Between: The Southern Paiutes, 1775–1995*. Lincoln: University of Nebraska Press, 2001.

Kniffen, Fred B. "Achomawi Geography." *University of California Publications in American Archaeology and Ethnology* 23 (1928): 297–332.

Knight, Alan. "Mexican Peonage: What Was It and Why Was It?" *Journal of Latin American Studies* 18 (May 1986): 41–74.

Koepplinger, Suzanne. "Sex Trafficking of American Indian Women and Girls in Minnesota." *University of St. Thomas Law Journal* 6 (2008): 129–137.

Kohler, Timothy A., and Kathryn K. Turner. "Raiding for Women in the Prehispanic Northern Pueblo Southwest? A Pilot Examination." *Current Anthropology* 47, no. 6 (2006): 1035–1045.

Kolchin, Peter. "The Big Picture: A Comment on David Brion Davis, 'Looking at Slavery in a Broader Perspective.'" *American Historical Review* 105 (2000): 467–468.

Konings, Martijn. *The Development of American Finance*. New York: Cambridge University Press, 2011.

Konstam, Angus. *Renaissance War Galley, 1470–1590*. Oxford: New Vanguard, 2002.

Kopytoff, Igor. "Slavery." *Annual Review of Anthropology* 11 (1982): 207–230.

Kornblith, Gary J. *Slavery and Sectional Strife in the Early American Republic, 1776–1821*. Lanham, MD: Rowman & Littlefield, 2009.

Kowalewski, Stephen. "Coalescent Societies." In *Light on the Path: The Anthropology and History of the Southeastern Indians*, edited by Thomas J. Pluckhahn and Robbie Ethridge, 94–122. Tuscaloosa: University of Alabama Press, 2006.

References

Kroeber, Alfred. *Handbook of the Indians of California.* New York: Dover Publications, 1976.

Kuttner, Robert E., and Albert B. Lorincz. "Promiscuity and Prostitution in Urbanized Indian Communities." *Mental Hygiene* 54, no. 1 (1970): 79–91.

Kyckelhahn, Tracy, Allen J. Beck, and Thomas H. Cohen. *Characteristics of Suspected Human Trafficking Incidents, 2009.* US Department of Justice. Washington, DC: Bureau of Justice Statistics, 2010.

LaLande, Jeffrey M., and Peter Skene Ogden. *First over the Siskiyous: Peter Skene Ogden's 1826–1827 Journey through the Oregon-California Borderlands.* Portland: Oregon Historical Society Press, 1987.

Lamadrid, Enrique R. "Faith and Intercultural Relations in Two New Mexican Inditas: Plácida Romero and San Luis Gonzaga." In *Nuevomexicano Cultural Legacy: Forms, Agencies, and Discourse,* edited by Francisco A. Lomelí, Víctor A. Sorrell, and Genaro M. Padilla, 164–184. Albuquerque: University of New Mexico Press, 2002.

———. *Hermanitos comanchitos: Indo-Hispano Rituals of Captivity and Redemption.* With photographs by Miguel A. Gandert. Albuquerque: University of New Mexico Press, 2003.

———. *Tesoros del espíritu: A Portrait in Sound of Hispanic New Mexico.* With Jack Loeffler, recordist, and Miguel A. Gandert, photographer. Embudo, NM: Academia / El Norte Publications, 1994.

Lambert, Patricia M. "Infectious Disease among Enslaved African Americans at Eaton's Estate, Warren County, North Carolina, ca. 1830–1850." *Memórias do Instituto Oswaldo Cruz, Rio de Janeiro* 101, supplement 2 (2006): 107–117.

Landers, Jane. *Black Society in Spanish Florida.* Urbana: University of Illinois Press, 1999.

Landers, Jane G., and Barry M. Robinson, eds. *Slaves, Subjects, and Subversives: Blacks in Colonial Latin America.* Albuquerque: University of New Mexico Press, 2006.

Lange, Charles H. *Cochití: A New Mexico Pueblo, Past and Present.* Albuquerque: University of New Mexico Press, 1959.

Lawson, John. *A New Voyage to Carolina,* edited by Hugh Talmage Lefler. Chapel Hill: University of North Carolina Press, 1967.

Layton, Thomas N. "Traders and Raiders: Aspects of Trans-Basin and California-Plateau Commerce, 1800–1830." *Journal of California and Great Basin Anthropology* 3, no. 1 (1981): 127–137.

Lecompte, Janet. "Independent Women of Hispanic New Mexico, 1821–1846." *Western Historical Quarterly* 12, no. 1 (January 1981): 17–35.

Lederer, John. *The Discoveries of John Lederer,* edited by William P. Cumming. Charlottesville: University of Virginia Press, 1958.

Lee, Nelson. *Three Years among the Comanches: The Narrative of Nelson Lee, Texas Ranger.* Guilford, CT: Globe Pequot Press, 2004.

Lightner, David L. *Slavery and the Commerce Power: How the Struggle against the Interstate Slave Trade Led to the Civil War.* New Haven, CT: Yale University Press, 2006.

References

Limerick, Patricia Nelson. *Something in the Soil: Legacies and Reckonings in the New West.* New York: W. W. Norton, 2001.

Lindsay, Brendan C. *Murder State: California's Native American Genocide, 1846–1873.* Lincoln: University of Nebraska Press, 2012.

Littlefield, Daniel F., Jr. *Africans and Creeks: From the Colonial Period to the Civil War.* Westport, CT: Greenwood Press, 1979.

———. *Africans and Seminoles: From Removal to Emancipation.* Westport, CT: Greenwood Press, 1977.

Littlefield, Daniel F., Jr., and James W. Parins, eds. *Encyclopedia of American Indian Removal.* 2 vols. Santa Barbara, CA: ABC-CLIO, 2011.

Loeffler, Jack, Katherine Loeffler, and Enrique R. Lamadrid. *La música de los viejitos: Hispano Folk Music of the Río Grande del Norte.* Albuquerque: University of New Mexico Press, 1999.

Lomawaima, K. Tsianina. *They Called It Prairie Light: The Story of Chilocco Indian School.* Lincoln: University of Nebraska Press, 1994.

Lopez, Steve. "The 'Repugnant, Vile Truth' about Sex Trafficking in L.A. County." *Los Angeles Times*, August 31, 2013. Accessed September 10, 2013. http://www.latimes.com/local/la-me-0901-lopez-prostitution-20130901,0,4024210.column51.

Lovejoy, Paul E. *Transformations in Slavery: A History of Slavery in Africa.* Cambridge: Cambridge University Press, 1983.

Loveman, Brian. *No Higher Law: American Foreign Policy and the Western Hemisphere since 1776.* Chapel Hill: University of North Carolina Press, 2010.

Lowe, Richard G., and Randolph B. Campbell. *Planters and Plain Folk: Agriculture in Antebellum Texas.* Dallas: Southern Methodist University Press, 1987.

Lyman, Edward L. *The Overland Journey from Utah to California: Wagon Travels from the City of Saints to the City of Angels.* Reno: University of Nevada Press, 2004.

Lynne, Jackie. "Colonialism and the Sexual Exploitation of Canada's First Nations Women." Paper presented at the American Psychological Association 106th Annual Convention, San Francisco, August 17, 1998. http://www.prostitutionresearch.com/colonialism.html.

———. "Street Prostitution as Sexual Exploitation in First Nations Women's Lives." Master's thesis, University of British Columbia–Vancouver, 1998.

MacKinnon, Catharine A. "Prostitution and Civil Rights." *Michigan Journal of Gender and Law* 1 (1993): 13–31.

———. *Toward a Feminist Theory of the State.* Cambridge, MA: Harvard University Press, 1989.

MacRaild, Donald M., and Avram Taylor. *Social Theory and Social History.* New York: Palgrave Macmillan, 2004.

Madley, Benjamin. "American Genocide: The California Indian Catastrophe, 1846–1873." PhD diss., Yale University, 2009.

References

———. "Reexamining the American Genocide Debate: Meaning, Historiography, and New Methods." *American Historical Review* 120, no. 1 (February 2015): 98–139.

Magliari, Michael. "Free Soil, Unfree Labor." *Pacific Historical Review* 73 (2004): 349–390.

Malone, Patrick M. *The Skulking Way of War: Technology and Tactics among the New England Indians.* Baltimore, MD: Johns Hopkins University Press, 1991.

Maloney, Alice Bay. "The Fur Brigade to the Bonaventura: John Work's California Expedition, 1832–1833, for the Hudson's Bay Company." *California Historical Society Quarterly* 22, no. 3 (September 1943): 193–222.

Malouf, Carling, and A. Arline Malouf. "The Effects of Spanish Slavery on the Indians of the Intermountain West." *Southwestern Journal of Anthropology* 1 (1945): 378–391.

Marcy, R. B. *Thirty Years' of Army Life on the Border.* New York: Harper and Brothers, 1866.

Marr, Stella. "Pimps Will Be Pimps, Part 2." *The Survivor's View Blog*, June 28, 2012. http://prostitutionresearch.com/pre_blog/2012/06/28/pimps_will_be_pimps_part_2_of/.

Martin, Bonnie. "Slavery's Invisible Engine: Mortgaging Human Property." *Journal of Southern History* 76 (November 2010): 817–866.

Martin, Debra L. "Ripped Flesh and Torn Souls: Skeletal Evidence for Captivity and Slavery from the La Plata Valley, New Mexico, AD 1100–1300." In *Invisible Citizens: Captives and Their Consequences*, edited by Catherine M. Cameron, 159–180. Salt Lake City: University of Utah Press, 2008.

Martin, Nick. "Mexican Woman Tells of Ordeal with Cross-Border Child Traffickers." *The Guardian* (UK), January 11, 2010. Accessed December 12, 2013. http://www.theguardian.com/world/2010/jan/11/mexican-woman-border-child-traffic.

Martinez, Michael. "Prostitution Ring in Madrid Tattooed Nineteen-Year-Old Woman with Bar Code." *CNN World*, March 24, 2012. Accessed March 29, 2012. http://articles.cnn.com/2012-03-24/world/world_europe_spain-prostitution-tattoo_1_prostitution-ring-ring-leader-bar-code?_s=PM:EUROPE.

McArthur, Judith N. "Myth, Reality, and Anomaly: The Complex World of Rebecca Hagerty." *East Texas Historical Journal* 24, no. 2 (Fall 1986): 18–32.

McCawley, William. *The First Angelinos: The Gabrielino Indians of Los Angeles.* Banning, CA: Ballena Press, 1996.

McDowell, John H. "Folklore as Commemorative Discourse." *Journal of American Folklore* 105, no. 418 (1992): 403–423.

McElhannon, Joseph Carl. "Imperial Mexico and Texas, 1821–1823." *Southwestern Historical Quarterly* 53 (October 1949): 117–150.

McGinty, Brian. *The Oatman Massacre: A Tale of Desert Captivity and Survival.* Norman: University of Oklahoma Press, 2005.

References

McIntyre, Mike. "Hundreds of Kids in Sex Trade." *Winnipeg Free Press*, February 20, 2007. http://www.cyc-net.org/features/viewpoints/c-sextrade.html.

McKeown, Iris, Sharon Reid, and Pamela Orr. "Experiences of Sexual Violence and Relocation in the Lives of HIV Infected Canadian Women." *International Journal of Circumpolar Health* 63, no. 5 (2003): 399–404.

McLean, Malcolm D., ed. *Papers Concerning Robertson's Colony in Texas*. Vols. 1–3, Fort Worth: Texas Christian University Press, 1974–1976; vols. 4–18, Arlington: University of Texas at Arlington Press, 1977–1993.

Mead, Rebecca. "Letter from Nevada—American Pimp—How to Make an Honest Living from the Oldest Profession." *New Yorker*, April 23, 2001.

Meillassoux, Claude. *The Anthropology of Slavery: The Womb of Iron and Gold*. Chicago: University of Chicago Press, 1991.

Meltzer, Milton. *Slavery: A World History*. Updated ed. Boston: DeCapo Press, 1993[1971–1972].

Mensing, Scott, and Roger Byrne. "Pre-Mission Invasion of *Erodium Cicutarium* in California." *Journal of Biogeography* 25 (1998): 757–762.

Mertl, Steve. "Pickton's Lawyer Wants Top Court Appeal." *CNEWS* (Canada), September 10, 2009. http://cnews.canoe.ca/CNEWS/Canada/2009/09/10/10824936-cp.html.

Metcalf, Ann. "Navajo Women in the City: Lessons from a Quarter-Century of Relocation." *American Indian Quarterly* 6, nos. 1–2 (1982): 71–89.

Michener, Ronald, and Robert E. Wright. "Development of the US Monetary Union." *Financial History Review* 13, no. 1 (April 2006): 19–41.

Miers, Suzanne, and Igor Kopytoff, eds. *Slavery in Africa: Historical and Anthropological Perspectives*. Madison: University of Wisconsin Press, 1977.

Mifflin, Margot. *The Blue Tattoo: The Life of Olive Oatman*. Lincoln: University of Nebraska Press, 2009.

Mihm, Stephen. *A Nation of Counterfeiters: Capitalists, Con Men, and the Making of the United States*. Cambridge, MA: Harvard University Press, 2007.

Milanich, Jerald. *Laboring in the Fields of the Lord: Spanish Missions and Southeastern Indians*. Washington, DC: Smithsonian Institution, 1999.

Miles, Tiya. *The House on Diamond Hill: A Cherokee Plantation Story*. Chapel Hill: University of North Carolina Press, 2010.

———. *Ties That Bind: The Story of an Afro-Cherokee Family in Slavery and Freedom*. Berkeley: University of California Press, 2005.

Miller, Joseph C. *The Problem of Slavery as History: A Global Approach*. New Haven, CT: Yale University Press, 2012.

———. "A Theme in Variations: A Historical Schema of Slaving in the Atlantic and Indian Ocean Regions." *Slavery and Abolition* 24 (2003): 169–194.

Mirabal, Robert. *Running Alone in Photographs*. Taos, NM: Red Willow Press, 2008.

———. *Skeleton of a Bridge*. Taos, NM: Blinking Yellow Press, 1994.

References

Mirabal, Robert, and the Rare Tribal Mob. *Music from a Painted Cave*. Red Feather Music, B00005ARF3, 2001, compact disk.

Mitchell, Donald. "Predatory Warfare, Social Status, and the North Pacific Slave Trade." *Ethnology* 23, no. 1 (1984): 39–48.

Mitchell, Pablo. *Coyote Nation: Sexuality, Race, and Conquest in Modernizing New Mexico, 1880–1920*. Chicago: University of Chicago Press, 2005.

Moorhead, Max L. "Spanish Deportation of Hostile Apaches: The Policy and the Practice." *Arizona and the West* 17, no. 3 (Autumn 1975): 205–220.

Morgan, Jennifer. *Laboring Women: Reproduction and Gender in New World Slavery*. Philadelphia: University of Pennsylvania Press, 2004.

Morgan, Kenneth. *Slavery, Atlantic Trade, and the British Economy, 1660–1800*. Cambridge: Cambridge University Press, 2000.

Morgan, Philip D. *Slave Counterpoint: Black Culture in the Eighteenth-Century Chesapeake and Lowcountry*. Chapel Hill: University of North Carolina Press, 1998.

Most, Stephen. *River of Renewal: Myth and History in the Klamath Basin*. Seattle: University of Washington Press, 2006.

Muñoz, Fray Pedro. "The Gabriel Moraga Expedition of 1806: The Diary of Fray Pedro Muñoz," edited by Robert Glass Cleland and Haydée Nova. *Huntington Library Quarterly* 9, no. 3 (1946): 223–248.

Murdock, George Peter. "Ethnographic Atlas: A Summary." *Ethnology* 6 (April 1967): 109–236.

Murray, Keith A. *The Modocs and Their War*. Norman: University of Oklahoma Press, 1959.

Murrow, Edward R., and Fred W. Friendly, producers. "Harvest of Shame," *CBS News*, November 26, 1960.

Musicar, Jessica. "Blood and Tears." *The World* (Coos Bay, OR), July 20, 2009. http://www.theworldlink.com/articles/2009/07/20/news/doc4a64a52a6b346607966876.txt.

Nairne, Thomas. *Nairne's Muskogean Journals: The 1708 Expedition to the Mississippi River*, edited by Alexander Moore. Jackson: University of Mississippi Press, 1988.

Nash, Gary B. *The Urban Crucible: Social Change, Political Consciousness, and the Origins of the American Revolution*. Cambridge, MA: Harvard University Press, 1979.

Nash, Linda. *Inescapable Ecologies: A History of Environment, Disease, and Knowledge*. Berkeley: University of California Press, 2006.

Nash, Philleo. "The Place of Religious Revivalism in the Formation of the Intercultural Community on Klamath Reservation." In *Social Anthropology of North American Tribes*, edited by Fred Eggan, 375–442. Chicago: University of Chicago Press, 1955.

"National Capital Topics: Slavery in the Navajo Nation Tribe; Agent Riordan Discovers That Slavery Exists among the Savages—His Efforts to Break Up the Evil." *New York Times*, May 15, 1883.

References

Naylor, Celia E. *African Cherokees in Indian Territory: From Chattel to Citizens.* Chapel Hill: University of North Carolina Press, 2008.

Nelson, Scott Reynolds. *A Nation of Deadbeats: An Uncommon History of America's Financial Disasters.* New York: Knopf, 2012.

Nelson, Thomas. "Slavery in Medieval Japan." *Monumenta Nipponica* 59 (Winter 2004): 463–492.

Nelson, Vednita. "Prostitution: Where Racism and Sexism Intersect." *Michigan Journal of Gender and Law* 1 (1993): 81–89.

New Mexico State House and Senate. "A Memorial Recognizing the Role of Genízaros in New Mexico History and Their Legacy." *House Memorial 40, Senate Memorial 59.* Santa Fe: New Mexico State Legislature, 2007.

Newell, Margaret Ellen. "Indian Slavery in Colonial New England." In *Indian Slavery in Colonial America*, edited by Alan Gallay, 33–66. Lincoln: University of Nebraska Press, 2010.

Northup, Solomon. *Twelve Years a Slave: Narrative of Solomon Northup, a Citizen of New York, Kidnapped in Washington City in 1841 and Rescued in 1853, From a Cotton Plantation near the Red River in Louisiana.* Buffalo, NY: Derby, Orton, and Mulligan, 1853.

O'Connell Davidson, Julia. *Prostitution, Power, and Freedom.* Ann Arbor: University of Michigan Press, 1998.

Officer, James. *Hispanic Arizona, 1536–1856.* Tucson: University of Arizona Press, 1987.

Omolade, Barbara. "Hearts of Darkness." In *Powers of Desire: The Politics of Sexuality*, edited by Ann Snitow, Christine Stansell, and Sharon Thompson, 350–367. New York: Monthly Review Press, 1983.

Onuf, Nicholas, and Peter S. Onuf. *Nations, Markets, and War: Modern History and the American Civil War.* Charlottesville: University of Virginia Press, 2006.

Ooms, Herman. *Imperial Politics and Symbolics in Ancient Japan: The Tenmu Dynasty, 650–800.* Honolulu: University of Hawaii Press, 2009.

Operé, Fernando. *Indian Captivity in Spanish America: Frontier Narratives.* Translated by Gustavo Pellón. Charlottesville: University of Virginia Press, 2008.

Opler, Morris. *Apache Lifeway: The Economic, Social, and Religious Institutions of the Chiricahua [Apache] Indians.* New York: Cooper Square Publisher, 1965.

Orsi, Richard J., and Ramón Gutiérrez, eds. *Contested Eden: California Before the Gold Rush.* Berkeley: University of California Press, 1998.

Orsi, Richard J., and Kevin Starr, eds. *Rooted in Barbarous Soil: People, Culture, and Community in Gold Rush California.* Berkeley: University of California Press, 2000.

Ortega, Juliana. "Indita de Juliana Ortega." Folder 2, serial box no. 19831, c. 1860, Albuquerque Museum Collection of Hubbell Family Papers (Collection 2002–049), New Mexico State Records and Archives, Santa Fe.

Ortelli, Sara. *Trama de una guerra conveniente: Nueva Vizcaya y la sombra de los apaches (1748–1790).* Mexico City: Colegio de México, 2005.

References

Ortiz, Alfonso. "Genízaros." In *Handbook of North American Indians*, vol. 9, edited by William C. Sturtevant, 198–200. Washington, DC: Smithsonian Institution, 1979.

Ortiz, Alfonso, and William C. Sturtevant, eds. *Handbook of North American Indians*. Vol. 10, *Southwest*. Washington, DC: Smithsonian Institution, 1978.

Osburn, Katherine M. B. *Choctaw Resurgence in Mississippi: Race, Class, and Nation Building, 1830–1977*. Lincoln: University of Nebraska Press, 2014.

"Out of the House of Bondage: Runaways, Resistance and Marronage in Africa and the New World." Special issue, *Slavery and Abolition* 6, no. 3 (1985): "Part 2: Runaways and Resistance in the New World," 37–128, and "Part 3: Marronage," 131–184.

Palacios, Janelle F., and Carmen J. Portillo. "Understanding Native Women's Health: Historical Legacies." *Journal of Transcultural Nursing* 20, no. 3 (2009): 15–27.

Panich, Lee M. "Missionization and the Persistence of Native Identity on the Colonial Frontier of Baja California." *Ethnohistory* 57, no. 2 (2010): 225–262.

Parsons, Edmund Morris. "The Fredonian Rebellion." *Texana* 5 (Spring 1967): 11–52.

Paton, Diana. "Enslaved Women and Slavery before and after 1807." *History in Focus*, issue 12 (Spring 2007), Institute of Historical Research, University of London. http://www.history.ac.uk/ihr/Focus/Slavery/articles/paton.html.

Patterson, Orlando. *The Ordeal of Integration*. Washington, DC: Counterpoint, 1997.

———. *Slavery and Social Death: A Comparative Study*. Cambridge, MA: Harvard University Press, 1982.

Pavao-Zuckerman, Barnet. "Rendering Economies: Native American Labor and Secondary Animal Products in the Eighteenth-Century Pimería Alta." *American Antiquity* 76 (2011): 3–23.

Peers, Laura. "Trade and Change on the Columbia Plateau, 1750–1840." *Columbia Anthology* 10, no. 4 (Winter 1996–1997): 6–12.

Perdue, Theda. *Slavery and the Evolution of Cherokee Society, 1540–1866*. Knoxville: University of Tennessee Press, 1979.

Perdue, Theda, and Michael Green. *The Cherokee Nation and the Trail of Tears*. New York: Penguin, 2007.

Peregrine, Peter. "Social Death and Resurrection in the Western Great Lakes." In *Invisible Citizens: Captives and Their Consequences*, edited by Catherine M. Cameron, 223–232. Salt Lake City: University of Utah Press, 2008.

Perry, Barbara. "From Ethnocide to Ethnoviolence: Layers of Native American Victimization." *Contemporary Justice Review* 5, no. 3 (2002): 231–247.

Perry, Steven W. *American Indians and Crime: A BJS Statistical Profile, 1992–2002*. US Department of Justice, Bureau of Justice Statistics. Washington, DC: US Government Printing Office, 2004.

Phillips, George Harwood. *Indians and Intruders in Central California, 1769–1849*. Norman: University of Oklahoma Press, 1993.

References

———. *Vineyards and Vaqueros: Indian Labor and the Economic Expansion of Southern California, 1771–1877*. Norman: University of Oklahoma Press, 2010.

Pierce, Alexandra (Sandi). *Shattered Hearts: The Commercial Sexual Exploitation of American Indian Women and Girls in Minnesota*. Minneapolis: Minnesota Indian Women's Resource Center, 2009.

Pike, Ruth. "Penal Servitude in the Spanish Empire: Presidio Labor in the Eighteenth Century." *Hispanic American Historical Review* 58, no. 1 (1978): 21–40.

Piper, Alexander. "Reports and Journal." *Oregon Historical Quarterly* 69, no. 3 (September 1, 1968): 223–268.

Podruchny, Carolyn. *Making the Voyageur World: Travelers and Traders in the North American Fur Trade*. Lincoln: University of Nebraska Press, 2006.

Pomeroy, Earl. *The American Far West in the Twentieth Century*. New Haven, CT: Yale University Press, 2009.

Porter, Kenneth W. *The Black Seminoles: History of a Freedom-Seeking People*, edited by Alcione M. Amos and Thomas P. Senter. Gainesville: University Press of Florida, 2013.

Powers, Stephen. "The California Indians." *Overland Monthly* 10, no. 6 (June 1873): 535–545.

———. *Tribes of California*. Berkeley: University of California Press, 1977.

Preston, William. "Serpent in Eden: Dispersal of Foreign Diseases into Pre-Mission California." *Journal of California and Great Basin Anthropology* 18, no. 1 (1996): 2–37.

Pritchett, Jonathan B., and Herman Freudenberger. "A Peculiar Sample: The Selection of Slaves for the New Orleans Market." *Journal of Economic History* 52 (1992): 109–128.

Proctor, Frank. *Damned Notions of Liberty: Slavery, Culture, and Power in Colonial Mexico, 1640–1769*. Albuquerque: University of New Mexico Press, 2010.

Prucha, Francis Paul. *American Indian Policy in the Formative Years: The Indian Trade and Intercourse Acts, 1790–1834*. Cambridge, MA: Harvard University Press, 1962.

———. *American Indian Treaties: The History of a Political Anomaly*. Berkeley: University of California Press, 1994.

———. *The Great Father: The United States Government and the American Indians*. Vol. 1. Lincoln: University of Nebraska Press, 1984.

———, ed. *Americanizing the American Indians: Writings by the "Friends of the Indian," 1880–1900*. Lincoln: University of Nebraska Press, 1973.

Rael-Gálvez, Estevan. "Identifying Captivity and Capturing Identity: Narratives of American Indian Slavery, Colorado and New Mexico, 1776–1934." PhD diss., University of Michigan, 2002.

———. "Identifying Mestizo Phenomena: Representation and Reclamation of Mestizaje's Foothold." In *The Interpretation and Representation of Latino Cultures: Research and Museums Series*, 8. Washington, DC: Smithsonian Center for Latin Initiatives, 2011.

References

Ramsey, William. *The Yamasee War: A Study of Culture, Economy, and Conflict in the Colonial South.* Lincoln: University of Nebraska Press, 2008.

Rashid, Khalidid. "Slavery of the Mind: Carter G. Woodson and Jacob H. Carruthers, Intergenerational Discourse of African Education and Social Change." *Western Journal of Black Studies* 29, no. 1 (2005): 542–546.

Rawick, George P., ed. *The American Slave: A Composite Autobiography.* Supplement, series 2, vols. 2–10, *Texas Narratives.* Westport, CT: Greenwood Press, 1979.

Rawls, James J. *Indians of California: The Changing Image.* Norman: University of Oklahoma Press, 1986.

Ray, Verne F. *Disease, Depopulation, and Culture Change in Northwestern New Spain, 1518–1764.* Salt Lake City: University of Utah Press, 1991.

———. *Primitive Pragmatists: The Modoc Indians of Northern California.* Seattle: University of Washington Press, 1963.

———. *Proceedings of the 1957 Annual Spring Meeting of the American Ethnological Society.* Seattle: American Ethnological Society, 1957.

Raymond, Janice G. "The New UN Trafficking Protocol." *Women's Studies International Forum* 25, no. 5 (2002): 491–502.

Raymond, Janice G., and Donna M. Hughes. *Sex Trafficking of Women in the United States.* Coalition Against Trafficking in Women, National Institute of Justice, 2001.

Razack, Sherene H. "Gendered Racial Violence and Spatialized Justice: The Murder of Pamela George." *Canadian Journal of Law and Society* 15, no. 2 (2000): 91–130.

Rebolledo, Diana. "Las hijas de la Malinche: Mexicana/India Captivity Narratives in the Southwest, Subverting Voices." In *Nuevomexicano Cultural Legacy: Forms, Agencies, and Discourse,* edited by Francisco A. Lomelí, Víctor A. Sorrell, and Genaro M. Padilla, 129–150. Albuquerque: University of New Mexico Press, 2002.

Reff, Daniel T. *Disease, Depopulation, and Culture Change in Northwestern New Spain, 1518–1764.* Salt Lake City: University of Utah Press.

Reid, John Phillip. "Principles of Vengeance: Fur Trappers, Indians, and Retaliation for Homicide in the Transboundary North American West." *Western Historical Quarterly* 24 (1993): 21–43.

Republic of Texas. Treaty between Texas and the Comanche Indians, May 29, 1838. In *Texas Indian Papers,* vol. 1, *1825–1843,* edited by Dorman H. Winfrey, 50–52. Austin: Texas State Library, 1960.

Research Network on the Legal Parameters of Slavery. "Bellagio-Harvard Guidelines on the Legal Parameters of Slavery." *Global Dialogue* 14, no. 2 (Summer–Autumn 2012). Accessed September 15, 2013. http://www.worlddialogue.org/content.php?id=530.

Reséndez, Andrés. *Changing National Identities at the Frontier: Texas and New Mexico, 1800–1850.* Cambridge: Cambridge University Press, 2005.

Richter, Daniel K. *The Ordeal of the Longhouse: The Peoples of the Iroquois League in the Era of European Colonization.* Chapel Hill: University of North Carolina Press, 1992.

———. "War and Culture: The Iroquois Experience." *William and Mary Quarterly* 40, no. 4 (1983): 528–559.

Rister, Carl Coke, ed. *Comanche Bondage: Dr. John Charles Beale's Settlement of La Villa de Dolores on Las Moras Creek in Southern Texas of the 1830s, with an Annotated Reprint of Sarah Ann Horn's Narrative of Her Captivity among the Comanches, Her Ransom by Traders in New Mexico and Return via the Santa Fé Trail*. Glendale, CA: A. H. Clark, 1955.

Rivaya-Martínez, Joaquín. "Becoming Comanches: Patterns of Captive Incorporation into Comanche Kinship Networks, 1820–1875." In *On the Borders of Love and Power: Families and Kinship in the Intercultural American West*, edited by David Wallace Adams and Crista DeLuzio, 47–70. Berkeley: University of California Press, 2012.

———. "Captivity and Adoption among the Comanche Indians, 1700–1875." PhD diss., University of California–Los Angeles, 2006.

Roberts, Christine. "Victim of Torture Murder in Oklahoma May Have Been Alive When She Was Dismembered." *New York Daily News*, July 25, 2012. Accessed July 30, 2012. http://www.nydailynews.com/news/national/victim-torture-murder-oklahoma-alive-dismembered-article-1.1121416#ixzz254a87p00.

Rockman, Seth. *Scraping By: Wage Labor, Slavery, and Survival in Early Baltimore*. Baltimore, MD: Johns Hopkins University Press, 2011.

Rockwell, Stephen J. *Indian Affairs and the Administrative States in the Nineteenth Century*. New York: Cambridge University Press, 2010.

Rodríguez, Sylvia. *The Matachines Dance: Ritual Symbolism and Interethnic Relations in the Upper Río Grande Valley*. Albuquerque: University of New Mexico Press, 1996.

Roemer, Ferdinand. *Texas*. Translated by Oswald Mueller. San Antonio, TX: Standard Printing Company, 1935.

Rogin, Michael Paul. *Fathers and Children: Andrew Jackson and the Subjugation of the American South*. New York: Alfred A. Knopf, 1975.

Roland, A. E. Bob. "The Ballad of Plácida Romero: History of an Apache Raid, a Captured Woman, and a Song." *New Mexico Historical Review* 86, no. 3 (Summer 2011): 279–324.

Romero, Brenda M. "Cultural Interaction in New Mexico as Illustrated in the Matachines Dance." In *Musics of Multicultural America: A Study of Twelve Musical Communities*, edited by Kip Lornell and Anne K. Rasmussen, 157–186. New York: Schirmer, 1997.

———. "The Indita Genre of New Mexico: Gender and Cultural Identification." In *Chicana Traditions: Continuity and Change*, edited by Olga Nájera-Ramírez and Norma Cantú, 56–80. Chicago: University of Illinois Press, 2002.

Rothman, Adam. *Slave Country: American Expansion and the Origins of the Deep South*. Cambridge, MA: Harvard University Press, 2005.

Rothman, Joshua D. *Flush Times and Fever Dreams: A Story of Capitalism and Slavery in the Age of Jackson*. Athens: University of Georgia Press, 2012.

References

Rotman, Youval. *Byzantine Slavery and the Mediterranean World*. Translated by Jane Marie Todd. Cambridge, MA: Harvard University Press, 2009.

Ruby, Robert H., and John A. Brown. *Indian Slavery in the Pacific Northwest*. Spokane, WA: A. H. Clark, 1993.

Ruíz, José Francisco. *Report on the Indian Tribes of Texas in 1828*. Edited by John C. Ewers, translated by Georgette Dorn. New Haven, CT: Yale University Library, 1972.

Rushforth, Brett. *Bonds of Alliance: Indigenous and Atlantic Slaveries in New France*. Chapel Hill: University of North Carolina Press, 2012.

———. "'A Little Flesh We Offer You': The Origins of Indian Slavery in New France." *William and Mary Quarterly* 60, no. 4 (2003): 777–809.

———. "'A Little Flesh We Offer You': The Origins of Slavery in New France." In *Indian Slavery in Colonial America*, edited by Alan Gallay, 353–389. Lincoln: University of Nebraska Press, 2010.

Sagel, Jim. *Siempre el corazón/Always the Heart*. Santa Fe, NM: Red Crane Books, 1998.

Samels, Mark, and Sharon Grimberg, executive producers. *We Shall Remain*, episode 5, "Wounded Knee." WGBH Boston, May 2009. http://www.pbs.org/wgbh/amex/weshallremain.

Sánchez, José María. "A Trip to Texas in 1828." Translated by Carlos E. Castañeda. *Southwestern Historical Quarterly* 29, no. 4 (April 1926): 249–288.

Sanchez, Joseph P. *Explorers, Traders, and Slavers: Forging the Old Spanish Trail, 1678–1850*. Salt Lake City: University of Utah Press, 1997.

Sandefur, Gary D., Ronald R. Rindfuss, and Barney Cohen, eds. *Changing Numbers, Changing Needs: American Indian Demography and Public Health*. Washington, DC: National Academy Press, 1996.

Sandos, James A. *Converting California: Indians and Franciscans in the Missions*. New Haven, CT: Yale University Press, 2004.

Santiago, Mark. *The Jar of Severed Hands: Spanish Deportation of Apache Prisoners of War, 1770–1810*. Norman: University of Oklahoma Press, 2011.

———. *Massacre at the Yuma Crossing: Spanish Relations with the Quechans, 1779–1782*. Tucson: University of Arizona Press, 1998.

Santos-Granero, Fernando. *Vital Enemies: Slavery, Predation, and the Amerindian Political Economy of Life*. Austin: University of Texas Press, 2009.

Sato, Shigeru. "Forced Labourers and Their Resistance in Java under Japanese Military Rule, 1942–45." In *Resisting Bondage in Indian Ocean Africa and Asia*, edited by Edward Alpers, Gwyn Campbell, and Michael Salman, 82–95. New York: Routledge, 2007.

Saunt, Claudio. *Black, White, and Indian: Race and the Unmaking of an American Family*. New York: Oxford University Press, 2005.

———. "History until 1776." In *Handbook of North American Indians*, vol. 14, *Southeast*, edited by Raymond D. Fogelson, 128–138. Washington, DC: Smithsonian Institution, 2004.

———. *A New Order of Things: Property, Power, and the Transformation of the Creek Indians, 1733–1816*. Cambridge: Cambridge University Press, 1999.

———. "Taking Account of Property: Stratification among the Creek Indians in the Early Nineteenth Century." *William and Mary Quarterly* 57, no. 4 (October 2000): 733–760.

Savitt, Todd L. "Black Health on the Plantation: Owners, the Enslaved, and Physicians." *OAH Magazine of History* 19, no. 5 (September 2005): 14–16.

Scarry, Elaine. *The Body in Pain: The Making and Unmaking of the World*. New York: Oxford University Press, 1985.

Schaafsma, Polly. "Head Trophies and Scalping: Images in Southwest Rock Art." In *The Taking and Displaying of Human Body Parts as Trophies by Amerindians*, edited by Richard J. Chacon and David H. Dye, 90–123. New York: Springer, 2007.

Schermerhorn, Calvin. "The Everyday Life of Enslaved People in the Antebellum South." *OAH Magazine of History* 23, no. 2 (April 2009): 31–36.

Schmidt-Nowara, Christopher. *Slavery, Freedom, and Abolition in Latin America and the Atlantic World*. Albuquerque: University of New Mexico Press, 2011.

Schwartz, Harvey L. *Dialogues with Forgotten Voices: Relational Perspective on Child Abuse Trauma and Treatment of Dissociative Disorders*. New York: Basic Books, 2000.

Schwartz, Harvey, Jody Williams, and Melissa Farley. "Pimp Subjugation of Women by Mind Control." In *Prostitution and Trafficking in Nevada: Making the Connections,* by Melissa Farley, 49–84. San Francisco: Prostitution Research & Education, 2007.

Schwartz, Stuart B., ed. *Tropical Babylons: Sugar and the Making of the Atlantic World, 1450–1680*. Chapel Hill: University of North Carolina Press, 2004.

Schweikart, Larry. *Banking in the American South from the Age of Jackson to Reconstruction*. Baton Rouge: Louisiana State University Press, 1987.

Scott, A. F. *Southern Lady: From Pedestal to Politics, 1830–1930*. Chicago: University of Chicago Press, 1970.

Scott, Rebecca J. "Small-Scale Dynamics of Large-Scale Processes." *American Historical Review* 105 (2000): 472–479.

Serrill, Michael. "Prostitution: Defiling the Children." *Time* 141, no. 25 (June 21, 1993): 52–55.

Shah, Svati. *Street Corner Secrets: Sex, Work, and Migration in the City of Mumbai*. Durham, NC: Duke University Press, 2014.

Sharp, Lesley A. "The Commodification of the Body and Its Parts." *Annual Review of Anthropology* 29, no. 1 (2000): 287–328.

Shoemaker, Nancy. "Race and Indigeneity in the Life of Elisha Apes." *Ethnohistory* 60, no. 1 (Winter 2013): 27–44.

Shuck-Hall, Sheri M. "Alabama and Coushatta Diaspora and Coalescence in the Mississippi Shatter Zone." In *Mapping the Mississippian Shatter Zone: The Colonial Indian Slave Trade and Regional Instability in the American South*, edited by Robbie Ethridge and Sheri M. Shuck-Hall, 250–271. Lincoln: University of Nebraska Press, 2009.

References

Shuman, Amy. "Entitlement and Empathy in Personal Narrative." *Narrative Inquiry* 16, no. 1 (2006): 148–155.

Silko, Leslie Marmon. *The Turquoise Ledge*. New York: Viking, 2010.

Silliman, Stephen. *Lost Laborers in Colonial California: Native Americans and the Archaeology of Rancho Petaluma*. Tucson: University of Arizona Press, 2004.

Skinner, Benjamin. *A Crime So Monstrous*. New York: Free Press, 2009.

Skinner, Claiborne A. *The Upper Country: French Enterprise in the Colonial Great Lakes*. Baltimore, MD: Johns Hopkins University Press, 2008.

Sklar, Deirdre. "All the Dances Have a Meaning to That Apparition: Felt Knowledge and the Danzantes of Tortugas, New Mexico." *Dance Research Journal* 31, no. 2 (1999): 14–33.

Smail, Daniel Lord, and Andrew Shyrock. "History and the 'Pre.'" *American Historical Review* 118 (2013): 709–737.

Smallwood, Stephanie. *Saltwater Slavery: A Middle Passage from Africa to American Diaspora*. Cambridge, MA: Harvard University Press, 2008.

Smit, Pieter C. "Slavery on World Bank Projects Mauritania." November 27, 2002. https://openlibrary.org/works/OL5293036W/Slavery_on_World_Bank_projects_in_Mauritania.

Smith, Andrea. "Sexual Violence and American Indian Genocide. In *Remembering Conquest: Feminist/Womanist Perspectives on Religion, Colonization, and Sexual Violence*, edited by Nantawan Boonprasat Lewis and Marie M. Fortune, 31–49. New York: Routledge, 1999.

Smith, Ashbel. *An Oration Pronounced before the Connecticut Alpha of the Phi Beta Kappa at Yale College, New Haven, August 15, 1849*. New Haven, CT: B. L. Hamlen, 1849.

Smith, Gerald A., and Clifford Walker. *The Indian Slave Trade along the Mojave Trail*. San Bernardino, CA: San Bernardino County Museum, 1965.

Smith, Stacy L. *Freedom's Frontier: California and the Struggle over Unfree Labor, Emancipation, and Reconstruction*. Chapel Hill: University of North Carolina Press, 2013.

Smith, Victoria. *Captive Arizona, 1851–1900*. Lincoln: University of Nebraska Press, 2009.

Snow, Dean, Charles T. Gehring, and William A. Starna, eds. *In Mohawk Country: Early Narratives about a Native People*. Syracuse, NY: Syracuse University Press, 1996.

Snyder, Christina. "Conquered Enemies, Adopted Kin, and Owned People: The Creek Indians and Their Captives." *Journal of Southern History* 73, no. 2 (2007): 255–288.

———. *Slavery in Indian Country: The Changing Face of Captivity in Early America*. Cambridge, MA: Harvard University Press, 2010.

Snyder, Terri L. "Suicide, Slavery, and Memory in North America." *Journal of American History* 97, no.1 (2010): 39–62.

Spier, Leslie. *Klamath Ethnography*. Vol. 30, *University of California Publications in American Archaeology and Ethnology*. Berkeley: University of California Press, 1930.

References

Spier, Leslie, and Edward Sapir. *Wishram Ethnography*. Seattle: University of Washington Press, 1930.

Spinden, Herbert J. "Nez Perce Tales." Part 2. *Journal of Folk-Lore* 21, no. 81 (1908): 13–23.

Sreenivasan, Ramya. "Drudges, Dancing Girls, Concubines, Female Slaves in Rajput Polity." In *Slavery and South Asian History*, edited by Indrani Chatterjee and Richard M. Eaton, 136–161. Bloomington: Indiana University Press, 2006.

Srivastava, Piyush. "Tensions Brew in Meerut as Woman, 20, Is Kidnapped, Gang Raped, and Forced to Change Religion." *Daily Mail India*, August 4, 2014. Accessed September 6, 2014. http://www.dailymail.co.uk/indiahome/indianews/article-2715890/Tensions-brew-Meerut-woman-20-kidnapped-gang-raped-forced-change-religion.html.

St. Jean, Wendy. "Trading Paths: Mapping Chickasaw History in the Eighteenth Century." *American Indian Quarterly* 27 (Summer/Fall 2003): 758–780.

Starna, William A., and Ralph Watkins. "Northern Iroquoian Slavery." *Ethnohistory* 38, no. 1 (1991): 34–57.

Stern, Steve J. *The Secret History of Gender: Women, Men, and Power in Late Colonial Mexico*. Chapel Hill: University of North Carolina Press, 1995.

Stern, Theodore. "Columbia River Trade Network." In *Handbook of North American Indians*, vol. 12, *Plateau*, edited by William C. Sturtevant and Deward E. Walker, 641–652. Washington, DC: Smithsonian Institution, 1998.

———. "Ideal and Expected Behavior as Seen in Klamath Mythology." *Journal of American Folklore* 76, no. 299 (January 1, 1963): 271–30

———. "Klamath and Modoc." In *Handbook of North American Indians*, vol. 12, *Plateau*, edited by William C. Sturtevant and Deward E. Walker, 446–466. Washington, DC: Smithsonian Institution, 1998.

———. "The Klamath Indians and the Treaty of 1864." *Oregon Historical Quarterly* 57 (December 1956): 229–273.

———. *The Klamath Tribe: A People and Their Reservation*. Seattle: University of Washington Press, 1965.

Stiffarm, Lenore A. "The Demography of Native North America: A Question of American Indian Survival." With Phil Lane Jr. In *The State of Native America: Genocide, Colonization, and Resistance*, edited by M. Annette Jaimes, 23–54. Norman: University of Oklahoma Press, 1988.

Stoltenberg, John. "Male Sexuality: Why Ownership Is Sexy." *Michigan Journal of Gender and Law* 1 (1993): 59–64.

Stone, Selden E. "California's Twenty-Second and Twenty-Third Missions: The Colorado Missions." Master's thesis, La Verne College, 1972.

Strachey, William. *The Historie of Travell into Virginia Britania*. Edited by Louis Wright and Virginia Freund. London: Hakluyt Society, 1953.

Strecker, John K. *Chronicles of George Barnard: The Indian Trader of the Tehuacana, and Other Bits of Texas History*. Waco, TX: Baylor University, 1928.

REFERENCES

Suarez-Potts, William. *The Making of Law: The Supreme Court and Labor Legislation in Mexico, 1875–1931.* Stanford, CA: Stanford University Press, 2012.

Sullivan, Mary L. *Making Sex Work: A Failed Experiment with Legalized Prostitution.* North Melbourne: Spinifex Press, 2007.

Sutton, Mark Q. "Warfare and Expansion: An Ethnohistoric Perspective on the Numic Spread." *Journal of California and Great Basin Anthropology* 8, no. 1 (1986): 65–82.

Swanson, Donald A. "Coacoochee [Wild Cat]." *Handbook of Texas Online*, Texas State Historical Association. Accessed September 9, 2013. http://www.tshaonline.org/handbook/online/articles/fcoaz.

Sweet, James H. *Recreating Africa: Culture, Kinship, and Religion in the African-Portuguese World, 1441–1770.* Chapel Hill: University of North Carolina Press, 2006.

Swift, Ebenezer. "Medical Topography and Diseases of Camp J. E. Johnston." In *Statistical Report on the Sickness and Mortality in the Army of the United States, Compiled from the Records of the Surgeon General's Office; Embracing a Period of Sixteen Years, from January, 1839, to January, 1855*, edited by Robert H. Coolidge, 378–386. Washington, DC: A. O. P. Nicholson, 1856.

Tadman, Michael. *Speculators and Slaves: Masters, Traders, and Slaves in the Old South.* Madison: University of Wisconsin Press, 1989.

Takaki, Ronald T. *Iron Cages: Race and Culture in Nineteenth-Century America.* 2nd ed. New York: Oxford University Press, 1990.

Taussig, Michael. *Mimesis and Alterity: A Particular History of the Senses.* New York: Routledge, 1993.

Taylor, Alan. *American Colonies: The Settling of North America.* New York: Penguin Press, 2001.

Taylor, Orville W. *Negro Slavery in Arkansas.* 1958. Reprint, Fayetteville: University of Arkansas Press, 2000.

Taylor, Quintard. *In Search of the Racial Frontier: African Americans in the American West, 1528–1990.* New York: W. W. Norton, 1998.

Taylor, Timothy. "Believing the Ancients: Quantitative and Qualitative Dimensions of Slavery and the Slave Trade in Later Prehistoric Eurasia." *World Archaeology* 33 (June 2001): 27–43.

Taylor, Virginia H., trans. and ed. *The Letters of Antonio Martínez: Last Spanish Governor of Texas, 1817–1822.* Austin: Texas State Library, 1957.

Thompson, E. P. *The Making of the English Working Class.* London: V. Gollancz, 1963.

Thompson, Gerald. *Edward F. Beale and the American West.* Albuquerque: University of New Mexico Press, 1983.

Thornhill, Ted, Jack Doyle, Jason Groves, and Andrew Malone. "Paraded by a Blood-Crazed Fanatic, the Terrified Schoolgirl Captives: Boko Haram Release Chilling Videos of Missing Nigerian Girls as They Reveal They Have All Been Forced to Convert to Islam." *Daily Mail* (UK), May 12, 2014. Accessed

September 6, 2014. http://www.dailymail.co.uk/news/article-2626019/We-know-Nigerian-governor-claims-intelligence-missing-schoolgirls-leader-Anglican-church-says-talks-need-start-Boko-Haram-back.html.

Thornton, John. *Africa and Africans in the Making of the Atlantic World, 1400–1800*. Cambridge: Cambridge University Press, 1992.

Thornton, Russell. *American Indian Holocaust and Survival: A Population History since 1492*. Norman: University of Oklahoma Press, 1987.

Thwaites, Ruben G. *The Jesuit Relations and Allied Documents*. 73 vols. Cleveland: Burrows Brothers, 1896–1901.

Tijerina, Andrés. *Tejanos and Texas under the Mexican Flag, 1821–1836*. College Station: Texas A&M University Press, 1994.

Tinker, George E. *Missionary Conquest: The Gospel and Native American Cultural Genocide*. Minneapolis: Fortress Press, 1993.

Tinling, Marion, ed. *The Correspondence of the Three William Byrds of Westover, Virginia, 1684–1776*. 2 vols. Charlottesville: University of Virginia Press, 1977.

Tomlins, Christopher. *Freedom Bound: Law, Labor, and Civic Identity in Colonizing English America, 1580–1865*. New York: Cambridge University Press, 2010.

Trafzer, Clifford E., and Joel R. Hyer. *Exterminate Them! Written Accounts of the Murder, Rape, and Enslavement of Native Americans during the California Gold Rush*. East Lansing: Michigan State University Press, 1999.

Trennert, Robert A. "Corporal Punishment and the Politics of Indian Reform." *History of Education* 29, no. 4 (1989): 595–617.

———. "Victorian Morality and the Supervision of Indian Women Working in Phoenix, 1906–1930." *Journal of Social History* 20, no. 1 (1986): 113–128.

Trigger, Bruce G. *The Children of Aataentsic I: A History of the Huron People to 1660*. Montreal: McGill-Queen's University Press, 1976.

———. "Early Iroquoian Contacts with Europeans." In *Handbook of North American Indians*, vol. 15, *Northeast*, edited by Bruce G. Trigger, 344–356. Washington, DC: Smithsonian Institution, 1978.

———. "The Mohawk-Mahican War (1624–28): The Establishment of a Pattern." *Canadian Historical Review* 52 (1971): 276–286.

Trudelle Schwarz, Maureen. "Unraveling the Anchoring Cord: Navajo Relocation, 1974 to 1996." *American Anthropologist* 99, no. 1 (1997): 43–55.

Trujillo, Michael L. *Land of Disenchantment: Latina/o Identities and Transformations in Northern New Mexico*. Albuquerque: University of New Mexico Press, 2009.

Tuck, James A. "Northern Iroquoian Prehistory." In *Handbook of North American Indians*, vol. 15, *Northeast*, edited by Bruce G. Trigger, 322–333. Washington, DC: Smithsonian Institution, 1978.

Turner, Sasha. "Home-Grown Slaves: Women, Reproduction, and the Abolition of the Slave Trade, Jamaica, 1788–1807." *Journal of Women's History* 23, no. 3 (2011): 39–62.

References

12 Years a Slave. Directed by Steve McQueen, written by John Ridley. Los Angeles: Fox Searchlight Pictures, 2013.

Tyler, Kimberly. "Risk Factors for Trading Sex among Homeless Young Adults." *Archives of Sexual Behavior* 38, no. 2 (2009): 290–297.

Unger, Jennifer B., Claradina Soto, and Natalie Thomas. "Translation of Health Programs for American Indians in the United States." *Evaluation and the Health Professions* 31, no. 2 (2008): 124–144.

United Nations. Convention against Torture and Other Cruel, Inhuman, or Degrading Treatment or Punishment. 1465 U.N.T.S. 85. December 10, 1984.

———. Convention for the Suppression of the Traffic in Persons and of the Exploitation of the Prostitution of Others. 96 U.N.T.S. 271. December 1949. http://www.ohchr.org/EN/ProfessionalInterest/Pages/TrafficInPersons.aspx.

———. *Report of the Special Rapporteur on the Human Rights Aspects of the Victims of Trafficking in Persons, Especially Women and Children*. Commission on Human Rights. UN Doc. E/CN.4/2006/62. February 20, 2006.

———. Rome Statute of the International Criminal Court. 1998. http://legal.un.org/icc/statute/99_corr/cstatute.htm.

United Sioux Tribes of South Dakota Development Corporation Services. Accessed November 18, 2009. http://unitedsioux.com/services.html.

US Department of Health and Human Services. *Assessment of US Government Efforts to Combat Trafficking in Persons in Fiscal Year 2005*. Washington, DC: US Government Printing Office, 2006.

US Department of the Interior. *Annual Report of the Commissioner of Indian Affairs, 1889*. Office of Indian Affairs. Washington, DC: US Government Printing Office, 1889.

US Department of Justice. "Fact Sheet: Drug-Related Crime." Bureau of Justice Statistics. Washington, DC: US Government Printing Office, 1994.

US Department of State. "The Link between Prostitution and Sex Trafficking." Bureau of Public Affairs. Washington, DC, 2004. http://www.2001-2009.state.gov/r/pa/ei/rls/38790.htm.

———. *Trafficking in Persons Report*. Washington, DC, 2006. http://www.state.gov/documents/organization/66086.pdf.

———. *Trafficking in Persons Report*. Washington, DC, June 2007. http://www.state.gov/documents/organization/82902.pdf.

US House of Representatives. *Investigative Indian Affairs: Hearings before Subcommittee of Committee of Indian Affairs*. Committee of Indian Affairs. 78th Cong., 1944.

———. *Official Copies of Correspondence Relative to the War with the Modoc Indians in 1872–73*. 43rd Cong., 1st Sess., 1874, House Executive Document 122. Washington, DC: Adjutant General's Office, 1874.

US Office of Indian Affairs. *Report of the Commissioner of Indian Affairs*. Washington, DC: A. O. P. Nicholson, 1856.

REFERENCES

US Senate. *Annual Report of the Commissioner of Indian Affairs to the Secretary of the Interior for the Year 1843*. Washington, DC: US Government Printing Office, 1843.

———. *Annual Report of the Commissioner of Indian Affairs to the Secretary of the Interior for the Year 1844–1845*. Washington, DC: US Government Printing Office, 1845.

———. *Annual Report of the Commissioner of Indian Affairs to the Secretary of the Interior for the Year 1900*. Washington, DC: US Government Printing Office, 1900.

———. *Oversight Hearing to Examine the Increase of Gang Activity in Indian Country*. Committee on Indian Affairs. Hearing on SD 628, 111st Cong., 2009.

———. "Statement of Senator Beck." *Congressional Globe*. 41st Cong., 3rd Sess. 733, 1871.

Usner, Daniel H., Jr. *Indians, Settlers, and Slaves in a Frontier Exchange Economy: The Lower Mississippi Valley before 1783*. Chapel Hill: University of North Carolina Press, 1992.

Valdez, Diana Washington. "Families of Victims Received Tips about Possible Killers." *El Paso Times*, February 15, 2014. Accessed February 16, 2014. http://www.elpasotimes.com/news/ci_25155150/families-victims-received-tips-about-possible-killers?IADID=Search-www.elpasotimes.com-www.elpasotimes.com.

———. "Families Offer Clues in Albuquerque's 'Crime of the Century': Tips in Albuquerque Crimes Hint at Drug Gangs, Dirty Cops." *El Paso Times*, February 15, 2014. Accessed February 16, 2014. http://www.elpasotimes.com/news/ci_25146711/families-offer-clues-albuquerques-crime-century?source=JBarTicker.

Valdez, Facundo. "Vergüenza." In *The Survival of Spanish American Villages*, edited by Paul Kutsche, 99–106. Colorado College Research Committee Publication no. 15. Colorado Springs: Colorado College, 1979.

Van Cleve, George William. *A Slaveholders' Union: Slavery, Politics, and the Constitution in the Early American Republic*. Chicago: University of Chicago Press, 2010.

Van Deusen, Nancy. "Diasporas, Bondage, and Intimacy in Lima, 1535 to 1555." *Colonial Latin American Review* 19, no. 2 (August 2010): 247–277.

———. "Seeing Indios in Sixteenth-Century Castile." *William and Mary Quarterly* 69, no. 2 (April 2012): 205–235.

Van Hoak, Stephen P. "Waccara's Utes: Native American Equestrian Adaptations in the Eastern Great Basin, 1776–1876." *Utah Historical Quarterly* 67 (1999): 309–330.

Vanwesenbeeck, Ine. *Prostitutes' Well-Being and Risk*. Amsterdam: VU University Press, 1994.

Varney, James. "Child Prostitution Is a Flourishing Business in Costa Rica, a Business Some Activists Are Trying to Stamp Out." *New Orleans Times-Picayune*, May 7, 2000, A1.

Vatuk, Sylvia. "Bharattee's Death: Domestic Slave-Women in Nineteenth-Century Madras." In *Slavery and South Asian History*, edited by Indrani Chatterjee and Richard M. Eaton, 210–233. Bloomington: Indiana University Press, 2006.

References

Vázques Cienfuegos, Sigfrido, and Antonio Santamaria Garcia. "Indio foráneos en Cuba a principios del siglo XIX: Historia de un suceso en el contexto de la movilidad poblacional y la geoestrategia del imperio español." *Colonial Latin American Historical Review*, 2nd series, vol. 1, no. 1 (2013): 1–34.

Victor, Frances. *The River of the West: Life and Adventure in the Rocky Mountains and Oregon*. Hartford, CT: Columbian Book Company, 1870.

Vinson, Ben, and Matthew Restall, eds. *Black Mexico: Race and Society from Colonial to Modern Times*. Albuquerque: University of New Mexico Press, 2009.

Virginia General Assembly. Division of Legislative Services. S.J. Resolution 332, by Henry L. Marsh. Richmond, 2007.

Wald, Elijah. *Narcocorrido: A Journey into the Music of Drugs, Guns, and Guerrillas*. New York: Rayo, 2002.

Walker, Ronald W. "Walkara Meets the Mormons, 1848–52: A Case Study in Native American Accommodation." *Utah Historical Quarterly* 70 (2002): 215–237.

Wallace, Anthony F. C. *Jefferson and the Indians: The Tragic Fate of the First Americans*. Cambridge, MA: Harvard University Press, 1999.

———. *The Long, Bitter Trail: Andrew Jackson and the Indians*. New York: Hill and Wang, 1993.

Wallace, Edward S. Introduction to *Thirty Years' of Army Life on the Border*, by R. B. Marcy. New York: Harper and Brothers, 1866.

Wallace, Ernest, and E. Adam Hoebel. *The Comanches: Lords of the South Plains*. Norman: University of Oklahoma Press, 1987.

Wallerstein, Immanuel. *The Modern World-System IV: Centrist Liberalism Triumphant, 1789–1914*. Berkeley and Los Angeles: University of California Press, 2011.

Waltman, Max. "Prohibiting Sex Purchasing and Ending Trafficking: The Swedish Prostitution Law." *Michigan Journal of International Law* 33 (2011): 133–157.

———. "Sweden's Prohibition of Purchase of Sex: The Law's Reasons, Impact, and Potential." *Women's Studies International Forum* 5 (2011): 449–474.

Ward, Kathleen. "Before and after the White Man: Indian Women, Property, Progress, and Power." *Connecticut Public Interest Law Journal* 6 (2007): 245–267.

Warner, Ted J., ed. *The Dominguez-Escalante Journal: Their Expedition through Colorado, Utah, Arizona, and New Mexico in 1776*. Provo: University of Utah Press, 1976.

Warren, James Francis. "The Balangingi Samal: The Global Economy, Maritime Raiding, and Diasporic Identities in the Nineteenth-Century Philippines." *Asian Ethnicity* 4 (March 2003): 7–29.

———. *Iranun and Balangingi: Globalization, Maritime Raiding, and the Birth of Ethnicity*. Honolulu: University of Hawaii Press, 2003.

———. *The Sulu Zone, 1768–1898: The Dynamics of External Trade, Slavery, and Ethnicity in the Transformation of a Southeast Asian Marine State*. Singapore: Singapore University Press, 1981.

Warren, Stephen, and Randolph Noe. "'The Greatest Travelers in America': Shawnee

Survival in the Shatter Zone." In *Mapping the Mississippian Shatter Zone: The Colonial Indian Slave Trade and Regional Instability in the American South*, edited by Robbie Ethridge and Sheri M. Shuck-Hall, 163–187. Lincoln: University of Nebraska Press, 2009.

Waselkov, Gregory. "The Macon Trading House and Early European-Indian Contact in the Colonial Southeast." In *Ocmulgee Archaeology, 1936–1986*, edited by David J. Hally, 190–195. Athens: University of Georgia Press, 1994.

———. "Seventeenth Century Trade in the Colonial Southeast." *Southeastern Archaeology* 8, no. 2 (1989): 117–133.

Waselkov, Gregory A., and Kathryn E. Holland Braund, eds. *William Bartram on the Southeastern Indians*. Lincoln: University of Nebraska Press, 1995.

Watson, Alan. *Roman Slave Law*. Baltimore, MD: Johns Hopkins University Press, 1987.

Watson, James L. "Slavery as an Institution: Open and Closed Systems." In *Asian and African Systems of Slavery*, edited by James L. Watson, 1–15. Berkeley: University of California Press, 1980.

Weaver, Hilary N. "The Colonial Context of Violence: Reflections on Violence in the Lives of Native American Women." *Journal of Interpersonal Violence* 1 (2008): 1–12.

Webb, Walter Prescott. "The Last Treaty of the Republic of Texas." *Southwestern Historical Quarterly* 25, no. 3 (January 1922): 151–173.

Weber, David J. *Bárbaros: Spaniards and Their Savages in the Age of Enlightenment*. New Haven, CT: Yale University Press, 2005.

———. *The Mexican Frontier, 1821–1846: The American Southwest under Mexico*. Albuquerque: University of New Mexico Press, 1982.

———. *The Spanish Frontier in North America*. New Haven, CT: Yale University Press, 1992.

West, Elliott. *The Last Indian War: The Nez Perce Story*. New York: Oxford University Press, 2009.

Weston, Rose. "Facing the Past, Facing the Future: Applying the Truth Commission Model to the Historical Treatment of Native Americans in the United States." *Arizona Journal of International and Comparative Law* 18 (2001): 1017–1058.

Whalen, Brett E. "A Vermonter on the Trail of Tears." *Proceedings of the Vermont Historical Society* 66, nos. 1–2 (Spring 1998): 31–38.

Whaley, Gray. *Oregon and the Collapse of Illahee: US Empire and the Transformation of an Indigenous World, 1792–1859*. Chapel Hill: University of North Carolina Press, 2010.

Wheeler-Voegelin, Erminie. "The Northern Pauite of Central Oregon: A Chapter in Treaty-Making, Part 1." *Ethnohistory* 2, no. 2 (Spring 1955): 95–132.

———. "The Northern Paiute of Central Oregon: A Chapter in Treaty-Making, Part 2." *Ethnohistory* 2, no. 3 (Summer 1955): 241–272.

———. "The Northern Paiute of Central Oregon: A Chapter in Treaty-Making, Part 3, Conclusions." *Ethnohistory* 3, no. 1 (Winter 1956): 1–10.

References

———. *Pitt River Indians of California.* New York: Garland, 1974.

White, Deborah Gray. *Ar'n't I a Woman? Female Slaves in the Plantation South.* Rev. ed. New York: W. W. Norton, 1999.

White, Richard. *The Middle Ground: Indians, Empires, and Republics in the Great Lakes Region, 1650–1815.* Cambridge: Cambridge University Press, 1991.

Wichterich, Christa. *The Globalized Woman.* London and New York: Zed Books, 2000; North Melbourne: Spinifex Press, 2002.

Widom, Cathy Spatz. "Victims of Childhood Sexual Abuse: Later Criminal Consequences." *National Institute of Justice Research in Brief.* Washington, DC: US Department of Justice, 1995. http://www.ncjrs.gov/pdffiles/abuse.pdf.

Widom, Cathy Spatz, and Joseph B. Kuhns. "Childhood Victimization and Subsequent Risk for Promiscuity, Prostitution, and Teenage Pregnancy: A Prospective Study." *American Journal of Public Health* 86, no. 11 (1996): 1607–1612.

Wilentz, Sean. *Chants Democratic: New York City and the Rise of the American Working Class, 1788–1850.* New York: Oxford University Press, 1984.

Wilke, Philip J. *The Expedition of Capt. J. W. Davidson from Fort Tejon to the Owens Valley in 1859.* Socorro, NM: Ballena Press, 1976.

Wilkinson, Boyden, Cragun and Barker, and United States, eds. *Klamath, Modoc, and Yahooskin Documents in Connection with Litigation before the Indian Claims Commission Dkt. no. 100.* University of Oregon Special Collections & University Archives, Eugene. Originally from National Archives and Record Administration, Washington, DC, n.d.

Williams, Allison. "Canadian Urban Aboriginals: A Focus on Aboriginal Women in Toronto." *Canadian Journal of Native Studies* 1 (1997): 179–215.

Williams, Kristian. *American Methods: Torture and the Logic of Domination.* Cambridge: South End Press, 2006.

Williams, Raymond. *Marxism and Literature.* Oxford: Oxford University Press, 1977.

Willingham, John. "George Barnard: Trader and Merchant on the Texas Frontier." *Texana* 12, no. 4 (1974): 306–334.

Wilson, Jane Adeline. *A Thrilling Narrative of the Sufferings of Mrs. Jane Adeline Wilson during Her Captivity among the Comanche Indians.* Fairfield, WA: Ye Galleon Press, 1971.

Winfrey, Dorman H., ed. *Texas Indian Papers*, vol. 1, *1825–1843*, vol. 2, *1844–1845.* Austin: Texas State Library, 1960.

Winkler, Ernest William, ed. *Journal of the Secession Convention of Texas, 1861.* Austin, TX: Austin Printing Company, 1912.

Wood, Peter. "The Changing Population of the Colonial South: An Overview by Race and Region, 1685–1790." In *Powhatan's Mantle: Indians in the Colonial Southeast,* edited by Peter Wood, Gregory Waselkov, and Thomas Hatley, 35–103. Lincoln: University of Nebraska Press, 1989.

Woodard, Stephanie. "South Dakota Boarding School Survivors Detail Sexual Abuse." *Indian Country Today,* July 28, 2011.

References

Worcester, Donald E., and Thomas F. Schilz. "The Spread of Firearms among the Indians on the Anglo-French Frontiers." *American Indian Quarterly* 8, no. 2 (Spring 1984): 103–115.

Worth, John E. "Razing Florida: The Indian Slave Trade and the Devastation of Spanish Florida, 1659–1715." In *Mapping the Mississippian Shatter Zone: The Colonial Indian Slave Trade and Regional Instability in the American South*, edited by Robbie Ethridge and Sheri M. Shuck-Hall, 295–311. Lincoln: University of Nebraska Press, 2009.

———. "Spanish Missions and the Persistence of Chiefly Power." In *The Transformation of the Southeastern Indians, 1540–1760*, edited by Robbie Ethridge and Charles Hudson, 39–64. Jackson: University of Mississippi Press, 2002.

Wright, J. Leitch, Jr. *Creeks and Seminoles: The Destruction and Regeneration of the Muscogulge People*. Lincoln: University of Nebraska Press, 1987.

Wright, Robert E. *The Wealth of Nations Rediscovered: Integration and Expansion of American Financial Markets, 1780–1850*. Cambridge: Cambridge University Press, 2002.

Wypijewski, JoAnn. "Reproductive Rights and the Long Hand of Slave Breeding." *The Nation*, March 21, 2012. Accessed April 8, 2012. http://www.thenation.com/article/166961/reproductive-rights-and-long-hand-slave-breeding.

Yarbrough, Fay A. *Race and the Cherokee Nation: Sovereignty in the Nineteenth Century*. Philadelphia: University of Pennsylvania Press, 2008.

Yaremko, Jason M. "Colonial Wars and Indigenous Geopolitics: Aboriginal Agency, the Cuba-Florida-Mexico Nexus, and the Other Diaspora." *Canadian Journal of Latin American and Caribbean Studies* 35, no. 70 (2010): 165–196.

Yellow Horse Brave Heart, Maria, and Pemyra M. DeBruyn. "The American Indian Holocaust: Healing Historical Unresolved Grief." *Journal of National Center for American Indian and Alaska Native Mental Health Research* 8, no. 2 (1998): 56–78.

Young, Mary Elizabeth. *Redskins, Ruffleshirts, and Rednecks: Indian Allotments in Alabama and Mississippi, 1830–1860*. Norman: University of Oklahoma Press, 1961.

Zakoji, Hiroto. "Klamath Culture Change." Master's thesis, University of Oregon, 1953.

Zappia, Natale A. *Traders and Raiders: The Indigenous World of the Colorado Basin, 1540–1859*. Chapel Hill: University of North Carolina Press, 2014.

Zellar, Gary. *African Creeks: Estelvste and the Creek Nation*. Norman: University of Oklahoma Press, 2007.

Zimmerman, Cathy, Mazeda Hossain, Kate Yun, Brenda Roche, Linda Morison, and Charlotte Watts. *Stolen Smiles: A Summary Report on the Physical and Psychological Health Consequences of Women and Adolescents Trafficked in Europe*. London: London School of Hygiene & Tropical Medicine, 2006. http://www.lshtm.ac.uk/php/ghd/docs/stolensmiles.pdf.

Index

Abiquiu, New Mexico, 240–241, 248–249, 261
abolitionist movements, 175, 179–181, 186, 188–189, 283–285, 299–305
Abu Ghraib, 295
abuse, 3, 99, 237, 300; of captives, 14–15, 20, 106, 204, 241–242, 245–248; of Native slaves, 81; physical, xxii, 3, 190, 225, 245, 262, 278n80, 283, 288–289, 291, 294–295, 297–298; psychological, xxii, 245, 259, 262, 278n80; of slave trade, 230; of slaves, xviii, 286, 298; verbal, 289, 294, 303; of women, 15, 245–248, 301. *See also* sexual abuse
acculturation, 72, 109, 265
Achomawis, 97, 101–102, 105, 107, 120n41
Act for the Government and Protection of Indians, 113, 138
adaptation, 64, 69, 87, 265
adoption, 250, 285; of Native captives, 4, 13–14, 16–19, 24–25, 38, 42, 49–50, 54, 87, 99, 106, 127–128, 203–204; of Native children, xxi, 14, 16, 71–72, 128, 205, 241, 261; of Native women, xxi, 14, 16, 24, 205
Africa, xviii–xix, xxxivn38, 156, 283, 303, 314n120
African Americans, xxiv, xxvn1, 4, 115, 216n1, 267, 277n73; Anglo-Americans' notions of, 210–211, 214; capture of, 65, 197, 200–203, 207; as farming labor, xvi–xvii, xix, xxi, 152, 198, 201–203, 207, 210, 213–216, 304; "fit" for enslavement, 214, 216; forced relocation of, xx, 64, 151–153; owned by Anglo-Americans, 198, 201–203, 207, 210, 213–216; owned by Indians, 213–214; price of, 164, 203; as slaves, 64–65, 66n5, 206, 260, 278n80; torture of, 288–289; trading of, xix, xxiv, 200–203, 207. *See also* chattel slavery; emancipation
Africans, enslaved, xxii, 4, 83–84, 302–303; and British slave trade, 314n120; in Cuba, 68–70, 77–79, 81–82, 85–86;

dehumanization of, 284, 285–287; escape of, 69, 82; expanding market for, 53–54; freedom of, 188; harsh treatment of, 189, 286; importations of, 39, 156–157; in Mexico, 175, 188, 191; trading of, 46, 202; and women, 304
Age of Revolutions, 64
agriculturalists, 152, 161, 163–164
agriculture, xx, 20, 130, 151, 165, 173–174, 187, 200, 209, 211–213, 298. *See also* cotton; farming
Alabama, xx, 64, 152–160, 172, 174, 177, 192
Alabama Emigrating Company (AEC), 158, 160
Alaska, 13, 142n5, 258, 270, 280n108
Alcalde, New Mexico, 249
alcaldes (village leaders), 128, 131–132, 141
alcohol, 37, 115, 128, 200, 234, 265–266, 268, 275n43, 289, 296
Algonquians, xxii, 11, 51
alliance building, 20–21, 26, 39, 44, 51, 99, 108, 110, 116
Almodovar, Norma Jean, 314n130
Alta California, 54, 126–134, 139, 142n7, 143n12, 143n14, 147n38
Always the Heart (Sagel), 249
American Land Company, 159
Ames, Kenneth M., 7n6
Amnesty International, 270
Anglo-Americans, 204, 249; captured by Indians, 197, 202, 205–206, 209; in Mexican Texas, xxiv, 171–174, 176–192, 184; and Native diplomacy, 197–200; in New Mexico, 231, 250; racial ideologies of, 198, 210–216; and slave labor, 64, 173–192, 213–214; in Texas, 200–203, 206, 209–216; uprising among, 184–186
antislavery: conference, 302; laws, 140, 179–182, 189; movements, 65, 174–175, 179–181, 185–186, 188–189, 301; proposals, 177–185

365

Index

Antonito, Colorado, 232
Anzaldúa, Gloria, 226n3
Apache Wars, 128–129
Apachería, 71, 126, 129–130, 133
Apaches, 12, 48, 50, 143n12, 236–237; baptism of, 75–76; campaigns against, 242; as captives/slaves, xvii, xxii, 18, 44, 67–82, 88n2, 129, 230; capture Hispanos, 239–240, 245, 249; confined in Mexico, 72–74; in Cuba, xx, xxiii, 75–87; diaspora of, 68, 70, 73, 82, 87; forced migration of, 63, 69–75, 84–85; homelands of, 70–71, 75, 86; raiding of, 133, 172, 176; and religious instruction, 67–68, 77–78; and the Spanish, 69–72, 79–80, 85–86. *See also* Chiricahua Apaches; Gileño Apaches; Plains Apaches
Apalachicolas, 157–158
Applegate, Lindsay, 115
Archuleta, Benjamín, 240–242
Arciniega, José Miguel, 190
Arizona, 127, 135, 142n2, 142n5, 263
Arkansas, 44, 50, 154–155, 157–158, 160, 172, 179, 213
Arkansas Gazette, 179–180
Armfield, John, 161. *See also* Franklin and Armfield
Arthur, Gabriel, 42
Asia, xvii–xix, xxxivn38
assimilation, 72, 229–230, 242, 262–264, 273n21
Athapaskans, 12
Atlantic Coast, xxiii, 37–41, 179–180, 284
Atsugewis, 97, 107
Austin, James "Brown," 180–181, 183
Austin, Stephen F., 174, 176–177, 178–181, 184–191
Australia, xxxiiin38, 300–301
Ávila, Lorenzo de, 77
Aztecs, 37, 231

Ballard, Rice C., 161–165
banking, 152, 154, 158, 161–165
Bannocks, 103
baptism, 75–76, 81, 130, 142n7, 146n28, 230, 232, 245
Baptist, Edward, 286
Barbados, xx, 39
Barnard, George, 203
Barr, Juliana, 98
Bartram, William, 16, 21
baskets, 100, 138, 140
Bastrop, Baron de, 177, 180–181, 188

beads, 37, 97, 138
Beale, Edward, 139
Bean, J. H., 137
Beattie, William, 152–160, 165
Beaver Wars, 36, 46
Ben Wright massacre, 113
Bentham, Jeremy, 182, 189
Bernalillo, New Mexico, 235
Big Dreams and Dark Secrets in Chimayó (Córdova), 249
Big Wolf, Chief, 206
Black Belt lands, 154, 156
black market, 48
black slaves, xv–xix. *See also* African Americans; Africans, enslaved; chattel slavery
Blackfeet Confederacy, 103
Blackhawk, Ned, 65n2, 98
blankets, 97, 134, 197, 199
boarding school education, 5, 224, 260–263, 273n21, 273n23, 273n27, 274n31–32, 274n35, 275n36–37, 275n42–43, 278n80
bondage, xvii, xxi–xxii, 5, xxxivn38, 69, 72, 86–87, 87n2, 127, 130, 225, 230–232, 245, 248, 297–298
bonds people, 152, 156, 159, 161, 163
Booker, Richard L., 165
Borica, Don Diego de, 132
Bosque Redondo concentration camp, 231
Boston and Mississippi Cotton Land Company, 159
Boston and New York Chickasaw Land Company, 159
Bourke, Joanna, 295
Bourne, Edward G., 21
Bowne, Eric E., xxiii, 4–5, 99
bows and arrows, 42, 97, 100, 241
Brazos River (Texas), 199, 202, 213
British: abolitionists, 175, 182–183, 189, 283, 301–302; banks/bankers, 161, 165; capital, 152; capture of, 205; colonies/colonists, xx, xxii, 47–48, 54, 70, 260, 285, 304; and cotton industry, 172; firearms, 52; imperialism, 102; and Indian captives/slaves, xx, 4, 53, 84, 260; and Native allies, 43, 52; sailors, 134; slave trade, xxii, 162, 285, 302, 314n120; traders, 43, 46, 84
Brooks, James F., 248, 285
brothels, 225, 287–288, 293, 296, 300, 303, 314n130
Brown, Jacob, 160
Brujula, 67–68, 70–71, 75, 79–80, 82

366

INDEX

buffalo, 15, 100, 103, 139, 197, 199–200, 203, 207–209, 211, 215
Bulin, Amabel, 266, 277n73
Bureau of American Ethnology, 109, 120n41
Bureau of Indian Affairs (BIA), 262, 264, 274n31, 275n42, 276n51, 276n60–61, 278n80
Byrd, William, 45

Caddos, 40, 44, 202
Cahuillas, 126, 133, 137, 143n12
California, 13, 64, 101–102, 142n5, 145n17; economy of, 129, 134; governor of, 126–127; Indian deaths in, 122n71; Indian slaves in, 134, 138, 140, 143n14, 148n53, 149n58, 260; Mojave attacks/raids in, 135–137; Native rights in, 130–131; population influx in, 140–141; prostitution in, 283, 294; slave raiding in, 126–127, 129, 131–132, 134, 138–141; slave trade in, 98, 113–114, 126–129, 134, 138–141; Spanish colonies in, 130, 132–135; and statehood, 130, 137, 141. *See also* Alta California; gold rush; Klamaths; missions: in California; Southern California; Upper Klamath Basin
Call, Anson, 139
Cameron, Catherine M., xxiii, 3–5, 98, 100, 106, 225, 296
Camp J. E. Johnston, 212
Campbell, Randolph, 200
Canada, 12, 51, 101, 224, 260, 262, 267, 270–271, 278n82–83, 280n105, 282n119. *See also* French Canadians
capitalism, 4, 64, 165–166, 258
captive taking, 9, 226n3, 296; celebration of, 12, 15, 20; cultural practices of, 99; and male honor/status, 20–22, 206; networks of, 127–129, 131; reasons for, 11–13; and replacing dead, 4, 14, 18, 38, 138
captor societies, xxi; and children, 17–19; and enhanced status, 17–23, 25–26; ideology of, 13, 16–19, 25; incorporation into, 10, 13–19; and kinship, 13–19; and male honor/status, 20–22; and social boundaries, 23–26
Caribbean, xx–xxiii, xxviiin6, 17, 39, 53, 63, 67–70, 73–75, 79, 84, 87
Carolina, 36, 39, 42–48, 51, 53. *See also* Goose Creeks
Carrillo, Manuel, 177–178, 180–181, 185
Cass, Lewis, 159
caste, xvii, 86, 111
Castro, Josefa de, 78

Catholic Church, 70, 73, 81, 239, 263
cautivo criado (family-raised captive), xxii; description of, 229–230; literature about, 248–250; narratives of, 236–248; photographs of, 232–233; sexual abuse of, 245–248; songs of, 236–238
Cavello, Manuel, 78–80
Cayuse, 104, 113
ceremonies, xvii, 11–12, 16, 18, 20–24, 39, 71, 106
chattel slavery, xxi, 64, 68, 87n2, 297, 313n118; abolition of, 301; and Comanches, xviii, xx, 200–203, 207, 215; in Indian country, xvii, 127; in Mexico, 174–178, 190–191; opposition to, 191; in the South, 65, 127, 231; in Texas, 65, 198, 200–203, 207, 210, 215; and trafficking/pimping, 285, 300
Chávez, Alex, 247
Cherokees, 17, 21, 23–24, 53, 152, 154–155, 159, 197
Chesapeake Bay, 38, 160, 162–164
Chickasaws, 4, xxxin19, 21, 42, 44, 46–48, 152, 154, 159
chiefdoms, 10–12, 47
chiefs, xix, 12–13, 20–21, 37, 97, 109–110, 112, 115–116, 116n1, 206, 213, 224, 232
Chihuahua, Mexico, xx, 69, 71–72, 205
children, xviii, 81, 278n78, 285; of captives/slaves, 17–19, 24, 180–181, 183–184, 186–189, 293–294; capture/enslavement of, xv–xvi, xviii–xix, 4, 13–15, 18, 71, 97, 120n38, 127–128, 134–135, 138–140, 149n58, 205, 224, 230–231; captured by Navajos, 241–242; captured in New Mexico, 233–234, 241, 249; exploited for labor, 263, 274n35, 275n36–37; fates of, 14–15, 128; and prostitution, 264, 267–269, 280n105, 301, 303–304; removal of, 261–263, 266; sale/trading of, xx, 113, 114, 137, 139, 250, 264, 290; and sexual relations, 246–248; targeting of, xvii, xxii, 4, 10, 65, 72, 224, 262–264. *See also* adoption: of Native children; boarding school education; sex trafficking; slave labor: children as
Chiloquin (Klamath *laláki*), 107, 111, 116, 121n54
Chinooks, 109, 112, 285
Chinuk Wawa, 98
Chiricahua Apaches, 70
Choctaws, xx, 4–5, 53, 152–153, 155
Christianity, xvii, 37, 70, 72–78, 81–82, 131, 231
Chumash, 131–132
Ciudad Juárez, Mexico, 5
Civil War, 198, 207, 216, 224, 231, 241–242, 304

367

Index

clans, 16–18, 20, 23–24, 130
Clarke, Samuel A., 108
Clatsop Indians, 285
Clear Fork reservations (Texas), 213, 216
clothing, xxi, 16, 125, 200, 204, 209, 213, 287, 292
Coahuila-Texas, xxvn1, 64, 171, 173, 176–178, 181–190
Coahuiltecan bands, 70
coalescence, 41, 46–47, 52, 55
Coalition Against Trafficking in Women (CATW), 303
Cochiti Pueblo, 246–248
Cole, Harrison, 197, 201–202
Collier, John, 232, 252n9, 275n42
colonialism, xxiv–xxv, 49, 86, 98–100, 105–108, 111–116, 141, 171–172, 224, 234, 259, 261, 272n10
colonization: American, 176–180, 191–192, 198, 258, 297; and antislavery activists, 179; by British, 304; by Euro-Americans, 100, 126; by Europeans, 258; in Mexico, 173–174, 180, 191–192; and Native children, 261–262; and sex trafficking, 258, 269, 297; in Upper Klamath Basin, 100; in United States, 261–262, 269
Colorado, 232–233, 252n14
Colorado River, 125–129, 133–135, 137, 139, 141, 141n1, 147n35
Columbia River, 108; slave markets on, 64, 97–99, 104–107, 111, 114, 116; trade network of, 98, 100–101; tribes of, 98, 100, 106, 109, 117n5
Columbus Land Company, 157
Comanchería, 130, 207–209, 215, 219n47
Comanches, xix, 4–5, 48, 69, 130, 237; abuse captives, 15, 205–207, 219n39; adopt captives, 203–204; and black slaves, xv–xvi, xviii, xx, xxiv, 200–203, 207; and captives/slaves, xx, xxiv, 12, 18, 21–22, 24, 41, 65, 65n2, 198, 200–209, 215, 230, 249; capture/enslavement of, 18, 230; customs of, 210–213, 215–216; and gender roles, 207–209, 211–212; and horses, xvi, xx, 15, 21, 50, 54, 203–204, 207–209, 212, 215; incest taboo of, 205–206; and male honor/status, 21–22, 24; migration of, 43, 50, 54–55; in New Mexico, 230, 236; portrayals of, 231–236; raiding of, xx, 12, 21–22, 55, 172, 176, 202–204, 206–208, 212, 215–216; removal of, 209–210, 213–216; trade in captives, 55, 65n2, 197–198, 200–209, 219n47; trade in goods, 65n2, 197–203, 209, 216; and warfare, 22, 236. *See also* "Los Comanches";

Hispano-Comanche: celebrations/plays; Nuhmuhnuh (tribal Comanches)
Comanches de la Serna, 249
commerce, 4, 36–37, 45, 87, 108, 137, 230, 236, 286
commercial slavers: and coalescence, 41, 46–47, 52, 55; decline in, 51–55; effects of, 46–55; and forced migration, 49–51; and geo-economics, 42–46, 54–55; introduction to, 35–41; and market access, 44–46; and military advantage, 41–43, 46, 54–55; narratives about, xv–xvi; power/influence of, 41–46, 53–55; and vulnerable Natives, 40, 43–44
commodities: children as, xviii; Indian slaves/captives as, 4–5, 99, 106, 138, 305; Native women as, 138, 206, 259, 285–287, 310n66; slave-produced, xxi, 132, 162
Company of New France, 38
Confederate States of America, 191–192
Congo, 302
Conrad, Paul, xxiii, 63, 175
convicts, 68, 70, 75–76, 79–81, 84, 88n2
cooking, xxi, 209, 212, 243
Coos women, 296–297
copper, 197, 200
Córdova, Gilberto Benito, 248–249
Coronado, Francisco Vásquez de, 12
Correa, Domingo, 78
cosmologies, 224
Cothran, Boyd, xxiii, 63
cotton, xix, 165–166, 193n15; grown in Mexican Texas, 172–174, 176–177, 180; grown in Texas, 192, 200–201; lands for, 154–156, 163–164, 174; profits from, 5, 173, 180; rising price of, 172–174; sale/export of, 152–153, 162, 164, 172–173; and slave labor, xvi–xvii, xxiv, 64–65, 127, 151–152, 160–162, 173–174, 177, 180, 198
courts, 68, 245, 255n53
crafts, xxi, 4, 22, 138, 140
Crawford, S. Wylie, 211–212
credit, 151, 161–165. *See also* banking
Creek Indians, 16, 18, 21, 36, 54, 152–160, 213–214, 221n70, 224
Creek War, 160
crimes, 68, 75, 80, 85, 111–112, 250, 257–258, 260, 269, 295, 299, 305
Cuba, xvi, 129; Apache captives in, xx, xxiii, 63, 67–72, 74–81; Apache runaways in, 82–87; governors of, 67, 69, 75–86; as slave society, 68, 77, 85. *See also* Havanna, Cuba

368

INDEX

Cubero, New Mexico, 238–239

Cuerno Verde (Comanche chief), 232–234

cultural: accommodation, 47; adaptation, 64; consequences, 223, 225; diversity, 54; estrangement, 263; geographies, 130; heritage, 237; hybridity, 231, 250, 251n8; memories, xxii, xxiv, 229, 242, 250–251; norms, xvii, xxi–xxii; power, 130; practices, 25, 111, 131, 207–208, 231, 236, 251; prejudice, 306n10; recovery, 251; replication, 23, 25–26; revitalization, 267; survival, 46

Dalles, 100–101, 104–108, 112

dance traditions, xxiv, 16, 231, 233–236, 242, 244, 249–251

Davis, David Brion, 3

Davis, James, 190

death: Apache rituals for, 74; and buffalo meat, 208; and burials, 164, 245; and burning property, 111; of captives, 86; and forced migration, 158; and forced removal, 70; high rates of, 288; of male warriors, 97; and mourning wars, 11; and prostitution, 298; recording of, 81; by violence, 122n71, 288. *See also* diseases: epidemics; murder

debt peonage, 190, 225, 229, 232, 296, 298, 304, 315n139

Deer, Sarah, xxiv–xxv, 5, 224–225, 282n123, 297

democracy, 64, 173, 175, 177–178, 187, 258

demographics, xviii, 4, 48–49, 53–55, 64, 102, 112–113, 140–141

diet, 3, 132, 207, 211, 216, 289

diseases, 74, 164; in California, 130–131; and captive taking, 49, 52, 55, 138; and coalescence, 46–47; Comanches susceptible to, 203, 211–212; devastation of, 36, 39, 113, 138; epidemics, 37–38, 40–41, 49, 98, 102, 113, 127, 203; in mining camps, 127; and "mission Indians," 37, 49; in Pacific Northwest, 98, 102, 113; and prostitution, 225, 266, 289; and trade networks, xxviiin6, 38, 40–41, 48–49, 53, 55. *See also* smallpox

domestics: African women as, 78–79; children as, 138, 275n37; in Cuba, 63, 78–81; Indian slaves as, 5, 18, 22, 67, 69, 127; Native women as, xvii, 18–19, 63, 73, 78–81, 128, 204–205, 209, 212, 230, 243, 263; in New Mexico, 230, 243

Domínguez, Fray Francisco Atanasio, 229–230, 236

Donald, Leland, 106

Doogan, Maxine, 314n130

drought, 130, 140

drug abuse/trafficking, 224, 260, 268–269, 279n93, 280n100, 283, 289

Dutch. *See* Netherlands

Dutch West India Company, 38

DuVal, Kathleen, 98

Eagle Pass, Texas, 205

East, xxiii, 38, 40, 42, 44, 47, 49, 52–55, 65, 159, 201, 210

East Coast, 162, 179–180

Eastern Woodlands, 35, 41, 46

eating, 198, 207–208, 216

economic: alliances, 111; competition, 38, 178; consequences, 223, 225; development, 55; growth, 36, 151; hierarchy, 213; inequality, 305; influence, 127; injustices, 301; landscape, 98–100; links, 215; mobility, xix; policies, 53; power, 130; pressures, 224–225; relations, 103, 199; relationships, 99, 176; success, 4; transformation, 113; value, xviii

education, 76, 78, 258, 264, 267, 278n79, 283, 296, 305. *See also* boarding school education

Edwards, Haden, 184

elderly captives, 72, 161

elites, 13, 16, 22, 78, 165, 178, 207–209, 216, 302

Elizondo, Dionisio, 178, 181–183, 187–188

emancipation, xviii, 66n4, 177–184, 187–189, 191, 222n73, 284, 301. *See also* freedom

Emancipation Proclamation, 231

Embudo, New Mexico, 229

empresarios (colonization agents), 173–174, 180, 184, 188–189

Enemy Way Ceremonies, 24

England, 36–40, 42, 153. *See also* British; Great Britain

Enlightenment, 175, 189

epidemics. *See* diseases: epidemics

equestrianism, xvi, 132, 203–204. *See also* horses

Erie Indians, xx, 4–5

Escalante, Silvestre Vélez de, 138–139

escape. *See* runaways

Eufaula, Alabama, 155–157

Eufaula Indians, 155, 157

Euro-American: colonialism, 99–100, 102, 141; control of borderlands, 126, 129; fur trappers/traders, 103–104; imperialism, 65n2, 98; Indian removal policies, 151–160; labor system, 128; land grab, 155, 159, 165;

369

INDEX

marriage to Indians, 115; migration, 64, 134, 139–140; and property protection, 111–112; racism, 16; ruling class, 130; settler colonies, 64, 99–100, 106–108, 111–116, 140; slave systems, 3–5; slave trade, xvii, xxi, xxiii, 106, 113–114, 285; soldiers, xx. *See also* trade goods: Euro-American

Europeans, 21, 26, 129, 161, 189, 285; arms/ammunition of, 46–48, 54; colonizing of, 37–41, 45–46, 55, 258; commerce of, 36–37, 49; contact with, 11, 13, 19; demand for captives/slaves, 19, 35–36, 53–54; enter into North America, xx, 4, 10, 26, 36–39; explorers, 20, 42, 48; and illegal gun trade, 38, 43; military of, 45–46, 52–53; and Native allies, 37–38, 40, 43–44, 46–47, 50–53; and slaves/slave trade, xviii, 4, 21, 63, 302; traders, 42, 45, 48, 51–52

exchange, xx, 216, 226n3; of captives/slaves, xx, 21, 36, 43, 54–55, 197, 200–204, 206; economy of, 203–206; networks of, 40–41, 198, 202; politics of, 52; of prisoners, 39, 51; systems of, 4–5, 50, 55, 200, 206; women's role in, 138

exclusion, ideologies of, 10

export trade: of captives/slaves, 35, 39, 47, 53, 106, 152, 189; of cotton, 172–173; of hides, 5, 135; of tobacco, 39

Family separation, xxiv, 65, 71, 289–291
Far West, 127–129, 135–136, 140, 142n5
Farley, Melissa, xxiv–xxv, 5, 224–225, 268, 282n123
farming, 164; of Anglo-Americans, 64, 152, 198, 200–202, 210, 212–216; and clearing land, 198, 201; in Mexico, 131, 189; at missions, 128, 131; of Native peoples, 40, 131, 140–141; and rise in prices, 161; and slave labor, xxi, 39, 132, 141, 156, 201–202, 206–207, 213; in Texas, 176–178, 198, 200–202, 206, 210. *See also* agriculture; cotton
Farnham, Thomas J., 126, 139
Federal Bureau of Investigation (FBI), 270
festivals, 108, 231–236, 247–249, 251n8, 252n9
Few, Robyn, 314n130
Fiesta de Santo Tomás Apóstol, 248–249
finance: development of, 151–152, 160–162; international system of, 152; and slave trade, 64, 162–166. *See also* banking; money
firearms, 37, 63, 69, 99; and arms race, 38, 46; and Comanches, 197; competition over, xxviiin6; illegal trade in, 38, 42, 48; illegal use of, 111–112; increased availability of,

52, 55; Native access to, 41–44, 46, 49–50, 52, 54, 103; and slave raids, 50–53, 107; and slave trade, 38–43, 47–48, 54, 116; trade in, 36–42, 46, 48, 52, 54, 103–104, 114–115, 132, 197

fishing, 11, 16, 38, 102, 296
Fitch, H. D., 137
Florida, xvi, xx, 17, 21, 36–38, 42–44, 46, 51, 157, 298, 304
food, 197, 211, 296; deprivation, 3, 296, 298, 300; of Native peoples, 131, 133, 135, 215; preparation, 4, 79, 207, 209, 243; production, 13, 22; and slave labor, xxi, 13, 128; trade in, 100–101
foodways, 207–208, 223, 225, 242–243
forts, 68–69, 71–72, 106, 114, 139, 158, 160, 210–211
Franciscans, 15, 131–133, 145n22, 229–230
Franklin and Armfield, 160–165
Franklin, Isaac, 161–165
Franklin, James, 161, 164
Fredonian Rebellion, 184–186
freedom, 115, 159, 171, 230, 298; of Africans/African Americans, 179, 260; of children, 17–18, 180–181, 183–184, 186–189, 241; of Indian captives/slaves, 16, 19, 81–82, 115, 120n38, 149n61; lack of, 247, 259, 295–296, 305; of Mormon captives, 149n61; petitions for, 81–82. *See also* abolitionist movements; antislavery; emancipation
Freire, Paolo, 229, 251n2
French: arms, 40–41, 52; colonies, 260; diplomacy, 51; explorers, 11, 37, 40, 44–45, 49, 50; and Indian captives/slaves, 260; influence, 37, 39; markets, 44, 50, 54; in Mexico, 184; missions, 38–39; Native allies of, 51–53; outposts, 50–51, 53–54, 70; traders, 38–40, 44–46, 48, 52
French Canadians, 104–105
Frierson farm, 202
Fugitive Slave Law, 309n55
fur trappers/traders, 103–105, 126, 136, 139, 285
furs, 23, 48, 100, 103–104, 130, 134

Gallegos de Valdés, Gertrudis, 232–233
Gallegos, Domingo, 238–239
Gálvez, José de, 147n38
Gamonales, Ana María, 77
Gandert, Miguel, 232, 248, 252n12
García, Pacífica, 242–245
Gatlin, James, 201–202
Gatschet, Albert, 109, 116n1, 120n41

Gavilán, José, 82–86
Gelber, Katharine, 299–300
gender, 231, 259, 265; captives divided by, 80–81; and captives' fates, 13, 73, 79–80, 204–206; captivity networks of, 130, 137–140; and Comanches, 207–209, 211–212; and mobility, 207; and slavery, xviii, 299
General Gálvez, 76
genízaros, xvi–xvii, xxiv, 230, 240–241, 243–244, 248–250, 255n53
genocide, 113, 130, 140, 160, 259
George, Vincent, 293
Georgia, 43, 52, 153–155, 157–159
gifts, xxi, 3, 20, 69, 115, 208
Gila River, 126–127
Gila River tribes, 129
Gilbert, Fabiola Cabeza de Baca, 243–244
Gileño Apaches, 70–71, 75
Glasker, George, 201
Global Alliance Against Trafficking in Women (GAATW), 303
gold rush, 63, 130, 140, 144n16. *See also* mining
Goldberg, Mark Allan, xxiv, 65, 192
Gómez, Cynthia, 250
Good Life, The (Gilbert), 243
Goose Creeks, 45, 50
Gover, Kevin, 278n80
grasslands, 132–133, 147n40, 203, 215
Great Basin, xx, 54, 65n2, 103–104, 106, 108, 114, 129, 149n57, 204
Great Britain, 4, 45, 79, 152–153, 179–180. *See also* British; England
Great Depression, 243
Great Lakes, xxii, 4, 11, 14, 17, 37, 39, 41, 51
Great Peace of Montreal, 51, 53
Great Plains, xvi–xvii, xxviiin6, 40, 142n7, 198, 207, 233
Great Southeastern Smallpox Epidemic, 49
Gregg, Josiah, 204–206
Guardian, The, 5
Guerra, José de la, 133
Gulf Coast, 40, 44, 47, 49, 73–74, 172–174
Gulf of Mexico, 37, 70, 177
Gumbs, Anthony, 305
Gunn, Marcus, 97–98, 116
Gustin, Samuel, 164

Hagerty, Spire, 213–214
Hämäläinen, Pekka, 15, 65n2, 98, 219n39
Handbook of North American Indians (Smithsonian), 248

Hanson, George, 113
Hardage, Siah, 155
Harrington, John Peabody, 101
Harris, Ladonna, 250
Harris, Rachel, 299–300
Harrison, James E., 197, 201–202
Harwell, Alice, 202
Haskins family, 205
Hasson, Alexander B., 211–212
Havana, Cuba, 63; African slaves in, 77–79, 81–82; Native prisoners in, 67–73, 75–80, 86; Native runaways in, 63, 82–83; residents of, 75–80
Hawaii, 115, 134, 142n5
Hawkins, Benjamin, 213, 221n70
Hawkins, Louisa, 213–214
Hawkins, Rebecca McIntosh, 213, 221n70
health issues, 210–213, 216, 225, 288–289, 301. *See also* diseases
herding, xx, xxi, 15, 18–19, 241
Hermanitos comanchitos: Indo-Hispano Rituals of Captivity and Redemption (Lamadrid), 232
Hidalgo y Costilla, Miguel, 174–175
hides/hide trade, xvii, xx, 5, 15, 40, 48, 100, 135, 138, 197–200, 204, 206–209, 212, 216
Hill County, Texas, 201–202
Hill, David, 107, 120n41
Hispano-Comanche: captivity songs, 223–224, 236–238; celebrations/plays, 232–236, 249–251
Hispanos, 72, 75, 81, 223, 240–249
HIV, 267, 289
Hopi mesas, 12
Horn, Sarah Ann, 209
horses, 37, 69, 72, 119n28, 145n22; in California, 130–131, 147n38; introduction of, 40–41, 54, 103, 116, 203; and military advantage, 42, 54; and raiding, 97, 99, 103, 105, 107, 132–133, 138; raiding of, 141, 147n42, 202; sale of, 108, 132; and slave labor, 15, 201; and slave trade, 41, 99, 114, 116, 137, 140; and social status, 21; theft of, 104, 135–137; and trade, 40–41, 103, 107, 112, 197; trading of, 100, 114, 134, 141, 201, 203, 206. *See also* Comanches: and horses; herding
horticulturalists, xx, 11
houses, 11, 22, 103–104, 106, 211–213, 302
Houston, Sam, 199
Hudson's Bay Company, 97, 103, 105
human rights, 64, 175, 178, 187, 270, 286, 297, 299, 303, 305

INDEX

Human Rights Watch, 295
hunters/hunting, 11–12, 40, 47, 70, 103, 139, 205–207, 209, 211–212, 215–216
Huntington, J. W. P., 110, 114
Hurons, 38–39, 42, 52

Identity, xxiv, 4, 23–24, 74, 231, 287, 290, 295
Illinois Indians, 42
India, xvii–xviii, 173, 315n139
Indian agents, 114–115, 202–203, 213, 221n70, 261
Indian captives: and black chattel slavery, 198; captured by Indians, xx, xxiii, 36, 39–40, 42, 47–48, 53, 64, 71, 97–98; decline in, 51–54; demand for, 52–54; as diplomatic tool, 39; as economic assets, 5, 7n6, 19, 23, 26, 36, 116; enhance owners' status, 17–23, 285; exile of, 69–71, 73, 82; fates of, 13–17, 20, 70, 73, 127, 224; given as gifts, 19–23, 26; importance of, 99; incorporation of, 242–245; narratives of, 236–248; networks of, 142n7; as "others," 25; portrayals of, 233–236; sacrifice of, 18–21; sale of, 4–5, 15, 18–19, xxxin19, 22, 44, 69, 72, 97–98, 126, 128, 138–139; and social identity, 14–16, 25; social location of, 13–16, 25; social value of, 18–23
Indian Civil Rights Act, 281n116
"Indian negro," 214, 222n73
"Indian New Deal," 232, 252n9
Indian removal, 64, 151–161, 165, 174, 198, 209–210, 213–216, 259–266, 273n26. *See also* urban relocation
Indian Removal Act, 153–154
Indian Self-Determination and Education Assistance Act, 278n79
Indian slaves: and black chattel slavery, 198; classed as animals, 16–17; competition over, 50; as degraded social class, 10, 20, 23, 25–26, 106; demand for, xx, 4, 12, 19, 39–40, 106–107, 132, 138, 149n58; as economic assets, xx; enhance owners' status, 25–26; forced migration of, 63–64; harsh treatment of, xix, xxiii, 18–20, 110–111, 141; integration of, 115–116; marketing of, 64; mutilation of, 14; owned by Indians, 155, 159; ownership of, 22, 64; past vs. present, 4–5; as personal servants, 20–22; as property, 17, 19, 111; sacrifice of, 19–20, 23; sale of, 77, 114–115, 149n58, 159; social value of, 19–23, 25–26; strategies of, 69; symbolic value of, 19–20, 22, 25–26; systems of, xxiii; theft of, 135–136; value of, 10, 106

Indian societies, early, 5
"Indita de Cochiti," 246–248
"Indita de Juliana Ortega," 246–247, 254n47
Indo-Hispano culture, 216, 229, 236, 243–244, 248–251
inequality, 229, 267, 284, 294, 296, 305
infant mortality, 211, 230
intellectual property, 16, 25
intermarriage, 111, 115–116, 120n38
International African Association, 302
International Criminal Court (ICC), 295, 299
Internet, 287, 303–304
Iraq, xviii
Iroquois, xix–xx, 4, 14, 17, 25, 38–39, 42–44, 48–52, 54
Islam, xviii
Iturbide, Agustín, 175

Jackson administration, 152–154, 157, 161
Jackson, Andrew, 152–154, 159
Jackson, Henry, 116
Jacobs, Harriet, 287, 289, 297
Jaget, Claude, 288
Jamaica, xx, 305
Janos, Nueva Vizcaya, 71, 90n14
Jesuits, 11, 20
jewelry, 37, 97, 138, 200
John W. A. Sanford Company, 158–159
Johnson, Andrew, 231
Johnson, Jim, 202
Jones, Anderson, 202
Jumanos, 40

Kansas, 159
Karoks, 101, 102
Kearney, S. W., 137
kidnapping, 149n58, 292; of African Americans, 65; of children, 5, 15, 137–139, 223, 235, 261–262, 274n27; of Indians, 3–5, 15, 21, 64, 113, 128, 131–135, 137–139, 223; of Mexicans, 205–206; in New Mexico, xxiv, 223, 235, 238–239, 250; of women, xviii, 5, 65, 223, 261, 291
Kimberling, Benjamin, 214
kinship, 11; of Apaches, 71; and Indian captives, 13–19, 24–25, 69, 71–72, 99, 106, 116, 127–128, 244; networks of, 130; and slaves, xviii, 10; systems of, 4, 16–18; and trade, 108
Kiowas, 12, 236–237, 240

372

Index

kíuks (shamans), 99, 109–110, 112, 116, 118n13
Klallams, 109, 112
Klamath Lake, 97, 101, 108
Klamaths, 119n28; and commercial slavery, 99; description of, 102; and Indian captives/slaves, 97–99; *laláki* (entrepreneurs) of, 63–64, 97–99, 108–116, 116n1; *lúgsh* (slaves) of, xxii, 97–98, 106, 109–111, 113–116, 117n2, 120n37; marriage of, 120n38; slave raiding of, xvii, xxiii, 105–107, 120n41; and slave trade, 63–64, 104–109, 116; trade of, 97–98, 104–105. See also *kíuks* (shamans); Upper Klamath Basin
Knack, Martha, 139
Ku Klux Klan, 288–289
Kumeyaays, 126, 131, 137, 140, 143n12
kwoxots, 130, 141n1

"La cautiva Marcellina," 224, 234–235, 237–238
La Florida. *See* Florida
La Purísma Mission, 125, 133
labor, 3–4, 46, 299; exploitation of, 98, 130, 263–264, 274n35, 275n36; forced, xvii, xxii, 65, 68, 75, 78, 81, 86, 87n2, 127–130, 133, 261, 264, 298; gender divisions in, 207–208, 211–212; harsh conditions of, 128, 141; productive/reproductive, 72; relationships, 133–134; systems of, 65, 128, 141. *See also* slave labor
Laguna Pueblo, 248, 255n57
Lake Erie, 43, 50
Lamadrid, Enrique, xxiv, 216, 223–225, 226n3
land, 141, 164, 174, 260; Indians removed from, 151–161, 165, 224, 259; inheritance of, 116; private ownership of, 152–153, 155, 160; speculation in, 64, 151, 153–159, 165–166, 184; in Texas, 172–173, 215; theft of, 261; and treaties, 115–116, 153–155. *See also* cotton; farming; plantations
Las Californias, 125
Law for the Protection of the Indian, 260
laws, xxii, 111–113, 131–132, 138, 140, 156, 173–174, 179, 187–191, 260, 267, 298–301, 305. *See also* antislavery: laws; Nez Perce Laws
Layton, Thomas, 104, 119n28
Lee, Nelson, 205–207
Leopold, Belgian King, 302
liberalism, 64, 171, 173, 175, 177–178, 187, 189
Lileks (Klamath *laláki*), 111–112, 114–115
Lincoln, Abraham, 231
Link River Jack (Klamath *laláki*), 108, 111

livestock, xx, xxiii, 15, 22, 64, 125, 127–133, 135, 137–141, 147n38, 147n40, 198, 200–201, 208–209, 215, 296
Long Walk, 231, 241, 243
Lorenzana, Apolinaria, 137
Los Angeles, 126–128, 134–139, 148n53, 149n58
"Los Comanches," 232–234, 249
Los Lunas, New Mexico, 248
Louisiana, 40, 44, 51, 54, 64, 66n5, 158, 161–165, 172, 177
Louisiana Advertiser, 185
Louisville Public Advertiser, 179
Lowe, Richard, 200
Lower Colorado River, xxi, 125, 130–131, 134
Lower Creek peoples, 43, 52
Lower Klamath River, 101–102
Lower Mississippi River, 44, 51, 160
Luiseños, 131
Lynne, Jackie, 263

Madero, José Francisco, 189
Madrid, Nicolás, 71–72
male captives: arduous work of, 63, 161; as commodities, xviii; and construction projects, 132; duties of, 204–205; fates of, 16, 129; forced migration of, 129; preference for, xviii, xxii; in the South, 161
male status striving, 10, 12, 19–20, 22
Marcy, Randolph B., xvi–xx, xxiv–xxv, 65
marginality, 24, 26, 282n125, 285–286, 300, 305
Maricopas, 143n12, 149n57
markets, 51, 126, 149n57, 204; access to, 42, 44–46, 50, 54; in California, 127, 135; for captives/slaves, 12, 26, 53, 107, 113, 206; on Columbia River, 107; development of, 47–48, 53, 152; European, 36, 40, 44–46, 48, 50, 54; expansion of, 45, 48, 55; federally protected, 161–162; geopolitics of, 45; global, 12, 26; international, 105–106; local, 215; and migration, 49; national, 215; in New Mexico, 135; system of, 39–41, 43. *See also* Columbia River: slave markets on
Marr, Stella, 300, 303–304
marriage, 4, 13, 15–19, 22, 24, 102, 106, 120n38, 128, 205–206, 208–209, 213, 223, 230, 232, 245, 247, 255n53, 285, 303. *See also* intermarriage
Martely, María Josefa, 78
Martin, Nick, 5
Martínez, Pedro, 146n28
Maryland, 38, 42, 161, 163

373

INDEX

masculinity, 21, 24, 286
Massachusetts, 179, 186
Massachusetts Bay Company, 38
Matachines dance, 249, 251
maternal mortality, 212
Mauritania, xxxivn38, 297
McDougal, John, 126–127, 148n49
McDowell, John, 240
McEvers, Bache, 162–163
McIntosh, Rebecca, 213, 221n70
McIntosh, William, 155
McIntosh, William (Creek chief), 213
McLennan County, Texas, 199, 200
mecos/mecas, 75–82, 84
Mediterranean biota, 130–131, 133, 141
menial tasks, 14–15, 21–22, 26, 98, 106, 156, 204–205, 239
mestizos/mestizas, xvii, 223, 230–231, 248, 250
Mexican-American War, 136–137, 140
Mexicans, 209; Anglo-Americans' notions of, 210, 216; captives, 15, 18, 197, 205–206; gender/sexual norms of, 206; independence of, 86, 134–135, 171–175, 204; in New Mexico, 230, 250; settlements of, 130, 133–134, 140; as slaves, xx, 204; and trade, 134–135, 198, 200, 204
Mexico, xxviiin6, 37, 84, 126, 128, 134, 229, 237, 239; African slaves in, 175; Anglo-Americans in, xxiv, 171–174, 176–192; antislavery forces in, 189; and Apaches, xxiii, 69, 72–75, 85–86, 129; and Article 13, 177–181, 183–184, 186–190; colonization laws of, 173–174; Comanches in, 197, 200, 207; constitution of, 65, 171–173, 176–191; cotton farming in, 173–174, 177, 180; debt peonage in, 190; and Decree 56, 189–191; festival traditions of, 231; Indian captives/slaves in, 69, 72–75, 85–86, 129, 175; Indian raiding in, 4, 140, 202; liberal democracy in, 64, 173, 175, 177–178, 187; poverty in, 173–174; slavery in, xvi, 64–65, 171–192; uprising in, 184–186. *See also* Coahuila-Texas; Sonora, Mexico; Texas: Mexicans in
Mexico City, Mexico, 69, 72–75, 85, 130, 172–174
Mexico, Viceroy of, 76
mid-Atlantic region, 43–44, 49, 53, 288
migration, xvi; to Arkansas, 213; to California, 140–141; in cross-cultural trading networks, xix–xx; forced, xix–xx, 63, 69–76, 260, 264; to Great Plains, xvi; to Gulf Coast, 172–174; to hunt buffalo, 207; increase in, 63; to Mexico, 63–64, 171–174, 178, 186, 190–191; of Native peoples, 41–43, 46–47, 49–50, 54–55, 131; overland, 140, 159, 161; reasons for, 4; and slave trade, xix–xx, xxiii; to southern US, xix, 172–173; to Texas, 64, 200–201, 206, 213–214; to US-Mexico border, 172–173; to the West, 64. *See also* Indian removal

military, 125; advantage, 41–43, 54–55; alliances, 4, 111; campaigns, 41–42, 69–71, 74, 113, 130, 136–137, 242, 248, 260; conflicts, 231; incompetence, 45–46, 55; interference, 52–53; medical reports, 210–213, 216; of Mexico, 172; and Native allies, 53, 71; power, 130, 133; and prostitution, 285; prowess, 208; records, 245; service, 70, 230; in Texas, 209. *See also* forts
militias, 46, 70, 113, 137
mining, 113, 115, 127–131, 141, 230, 296
Minnesota, 259, 266, 268–269, 277n73, 280n107, 297
Minnesota Indian Women's Sexual Assault Coalition, 268, 282n123
Mirabal, Robert, 226n3
Mission San Buenaventura, 133
missionaries, 11, 125, 127–128, 130, 205
missions, 125, 142n7, 146n28, 147n40; attacks on, 132–133; in California, 104, 127–133, 145n22; economy of, 128, 131–132, 143n14; goods produced at, 128; horses of, 104; Indians at, 36–37, 43, 46, 49, 132–133; in New Mexico, 229; in Oregon City, 97; Presbyterian, 113; secularization of, 134; and slave labor, 128–133; system of, 36–39, 43, 51, 69, 130
Mississippi, xx, 37, 44, 64, 153–154, 158, 163–165, 172, 174, 177, 184, 192, 294
Mississippi River, xvi, 157–158, 160, 164
Mississippi River valley, 40, 42–45, 49, 54
Missouri, 40, 44, 103, 179
Missouri Compromise, 159
Mobile, Alabama, 152, 156–157
Modoc Expedition, 113
Modoc War, 116
Modocs, 97, 99, 102, 105, 107, 109, 111, 114–116, 120n38
Mohawk-Mahican War, 44
Mohawks, 38, 42–44
Mojave Desert, 133, 136, 139
Mojaves, 125–126, 128, 132–136, 138–140, 143n12
Molalas, 97, 112
money, 160, 162–164, 225, 259, 298–299. *See also* banking

374

Montesquieu, Charles-Louis, 189
Moraga Expedition, 146n28
Morgan, Thomas J., 274n31
Mormons, 139–140, 149n61, 205
mourning wars, 11, 38–39
mulattos, 81, 286
Mullin, Tom, 201
Muñoz, Don José, 80
murder, 5, 75, 149n58, 302; of black slaves, 65, 82–86; of captives/slaves, xvii, 13–17, 21, 25–26, 47, 205, 238, 304; of missionaries, 113; of Native peoples, 113; in New Mexico, xxiv, 223–224, 238–239; of prostitutes, 269–270, 282n119, 304; of traders, 45, 53
music, 223–224, 236–238, 242, 249–251. *See also* songs
Muskogee-speakers, 154

Nambé, New Mexico, 242
natal alienation, 15, 25
Natchez, Louisiana, 162–165
nation building, 151, 171–177, 207, 210
Native peoples: Anglo-Americans' notions of, 210–216; "civilizing" of, 210–214, 216, 258, 261; competition between, 44–45; conflicts between, 50–51, 55; conversion of, 37, 70, 72–78, 81–82, 131, 149n61, 231; customs of, 45, 210–213; devastation of, 140, 144n16; and diplomacy, 197–200; economies of, 130–133; and European allies, 37–38, 40, 43–44, 46–47, 50–53; exploitation of, xxiv, 278n80; face disparities, 267; fear enslavement, 53; leaders of, 47; as military auxiliaries, 53; musical traditions of, 236, 252n19; and Native allies, 116, 133; own black slaves, 213–214; polities of, 35–36, 41, 47, 52, 55; protect Europeans, 45; protection of, 43, 48, 50–51, 131; relocation of, 259–267, 276n51, 297; and slave trade, xxi, 63; vulnerable to capture, 40, 42–44, 47, 49, 52–55, 128
Nava, Pedro de, 71–72
Navajos, xix, xx, 12, 54, 69, 148n53, 236; campaigns against, 242; and captive children, 232, 238; captive taking by, 12, 15, 18–19, 24, 237, 240–242; and captive women, xvii, 15, 24; captured by Hispanos, 231, 242–245, 248–249; and Indian slaves, 15, 18–19; and the Long Walk, 231, 241, 243; matrilineal clan of, 18, 22; in New Mexico, 240–245; raiding of, 12, 15, 18, 22
Navarro, Diego José, 76
Navarro, José Antonio, 176, 190

Neighbors, Robert, 213
Netherlands, 38, 42–43, 46, 50, 296, 300–301
Nevada, 135, 142n5, 225, 286, 296, 301
New England, 38, 42, 154, 186, 225
New France, xxii, 38–40, 42, 44
New Mexico, xxiv, 63–64, 81, 136, 142n5; American settlers in, 231, 250; and captivity narratives/songs, 236–250; *cautivo criados* in, xxii, 90n14, 229–232, 236–240, 242–250; Comanches in, 43, 219n47, 230, 236; cultural history of, 237, 239, 250; festival traditions of, 231–236, 249–251; genízaros in, xvi–xvii, xxiv, 240–241, 243–244, 248–250, 255n53; Hispano children captured in, 240–242; and histories of captivity, 242–245; Indian captives/slaves in, 142n7, 230–232, 242–245; legacy of slavery in, 230–232, 248, 285; mestizos in, xvii, 223, 230–231, 248, 250; Nativity plays in, 234–236, 249; sexual relations law of, 246; slave raiding in, xxiv, 139; slave trade in, xxii, 44, 54, 106, 126, 129–130, 134–135, 138, 250; Spanish in, 37, 54, 130, 134, 223, 230; trade in, 203, 219n39; US invasion of, 231, 242; warfare in, 223, 231
New Netherland, 38, 42–43, 50
New Orleans, 158, 161–163, 165, 176, 179, 185, 189, 191, 286, 290
New Spain, 63, 67–74, 79, 81, 84–85, 127, 147n38, 172, 203
New York, xx, 162–165, 185, 198, 300, 303
New York Daily Advertiser, 185
New York, Mississippi, and Arkansas Land Company, 159
New York Observer, 185–186
Nez Perce Laws, 111–112
Nez Percés, 103–104
nijoras (Indian captives), 127–129, 142n7
Niles' Weekly Register, 185
nomadism, 12, 75, 203, 211–213, 216
North Carolina, 289
Northeast, xxviiin6; antislavery activism in, 179; arms race in, 46; Beaver Wars in, 36, 46; captive taking in, 9–11, 14–20, 24–25, 43; and cultural replication, 23, 25–26; diseases in, 49, 51; French traders in, 38; Indian slaves in, 17–18, 23, 25–26; and land speculation, 159; and male honor, 20; raiding in, 10, 49, 51; warfare in, 9–11, 20, 25
Northern Paiutes, 102, 104, 107–108
Northern Shoshonis, 103
Northup, Solomon, xvi–xvii, xxviin3

375

INDEX

Northwest Coast, 6n6, 112, 116; captive taking in, 9–10, 16, 19; Indian captives/slaves in, xxviiin6, 13, 16, 19, 22–25, 98, 106–107; Native peoples of, 12–13, 106; prostitution in, 285; raiding in, 10, 13, 16; and salmon, 16; and social differentiation, 13, 24; warfare in, 9–10, 13, 19

Nueva Vizcaya, 230

Nuevas Leyes de Indias, 230

Nuevo México Profundo: Rituals of an Indo-Hispano Homeland (Gandert), 248

Nuhmuhnuh (tribal Comanches), 230, 236, 250

Oatman, Olive, 140

obsidian, 23, 100–101, 106

Ogden, Peter Skene, 103–105, 119n28

Ohio River, 51

Ohio Valley, 39, 43–44, 49–50, 52

Oklahoma, xix–xx, 158, 275n43

Old Spanish Trail, 126, 134–138, 140

Oliba-blanca, 76

Oliver, Joe, 201–202

Oliver, Rod, 201

Olleyquotequiebe, 125–128, 130, 141

Oneidas, 25

oppression, 131, 141, 224, 229, 248, 261, 267, 278n82, 300

oral histories/traditions, 207–208, 236–237, 240, 242–245, 248

Oregon, xix, 63, 97–98, 102, 111–114, 142n5, 275n43, 278n78, 296. *See also* Klamaths; Lower Klamath River; Upper Klamath Basin

Oregon City, Oregon, 97, 116

orphans, xvii, 71–72, 87, 90n14, 113, 188, 235

Ortega, Juliana, 246–247

Osages, 40, 44–45, 48, 52

Ottawas, 39, 52

ownership, 64, 111, 152, 155, 160, 225, 286, 290, 299–300, 312n106

Pacific Coast, 69, 129

Pacific Northwest, xvii, xxii–xxiii, 64, 98, 100–101, 109, 113, 134

Pacific Rim, 134, 143n14

Page, John, 155, 158

Paiutes, 15, 18, 99, 104, 137. *See also* Northern Paiutes; Southern Paiutes; Yahooskin Paiutes

palenque, 83–86

Palermo Protocol, 299

Palma, Salvador, 127–128. *See also* Olleyquotequiebe

Panic of 1819, 174

pantomimes, 233–235, 250–251

Papel periódico de la Habana, 76

parades/pageantry, 223, 231

Patterson, Orlando, 302

Pattie, James, 136

Pawnees, 237, 240, 278n80

Pays d'en Haut (Great Lakes region), 11, 39, 43–44, 50, 53–54

peace negotiations, 20–21, 51–53, 69, 71, 103, 114, 125, 200, 206, 241. *See also* treaties

Pease, E. M., 213

Pecos Pueblo, 233–234

Pecos River, 231

pelts, xxviiin6, 46, 48, 134, 136

Pequot War, 38

Perrault, J. B., 165

Philadelphia, 162, 164

Philip, Nancy, 112

Philippines, 68

Phoenix Indian School, 275n42–43

photography, documentary, 232–233, 248, 252n9

Pickett, William, 111

Picurís Pueblo, 252n9

Piedmont, 38–39

Pilar, Juan Manuel del, 81

pimps, 283–287, 289–296, 298–300, 302–304, 306n3, 309n55, 314n130

Piper, Alexander, 114

Pit River tribes, 97, 101–102, 105, 107, 111, 114–115, 120n41

plains, xv, xix–xx, 12, 40, 43–44, 47, 50, 54–55, 65n2, 224. *See also* Great Plains

Plains Apaches, 40–41, 43, 55

plantations, xxi, 304; and breeding slaves, 293–294; in Cuba, 82–84, 87; economies of, 46, 53; and Native lands, 152, 156, 159, 163–164; and prostitution, 286–287, 290–293, 302; and slave labor, xvi, xxi, 3–5, 35, 46, 63–65, 156, 164, 190–191, 197, 302; in South, xvi, xxiii, 46, 65, 231; in Texas, 64–65, 197, 198, 201–202, 206. *See also* cotton

Plateau, 100–101, 103, 112

plays, 224, 231–236, 247, 249

Pocahontas, 285

poetry, 223–224, 226n3, 236–240, 242, 244, 247

political: alliances, 102, 111, 114; coalescence, 55; development, 55; diversity, 36; economy, 41,

151; formations, 12; hierarchy, 213; identity, 99; independence, 146n25; influence, 127–128; instability, 133–134; institutions, 41; landscape, 98, 100, 105, 110, 116; leadership, 99, 116; philosophies, 64; power, 208; relations, 103; relationships, 21, 99; strategies, 47; will, 152
politics, 21, 152, 154, 165, 177–180, 236
Polonia, 67–68, 70–71, 75, 79, 82
polygyny, 205, 209
poorhouses, 73
Porras, Jacinto de, 81
pottery, 4, 138, 140, 243
poverty, 66n5, 173–174, 224, 259, 264–265, 267–269, 285, 289, 296, 298, 304–305
power, xix, xxi–xxii, 112, 130, 215, 232, 284–285, 290, 295
Powers, Stephen, 111
Powhatan, 285
prehistoric societies, 9
presidios, 69, 71–72, 86, 90n14, 125, 127, 232. See also forts
prestige, 11, 99, 106, 116, 117n1, 204, 208–209, 285
prestige goods, xxi, 5, 19, 21–22
Preston, Charlie, 108
prisons, 72–74, 79, 268–269, 280n108, 295
proslavery advocates, 157, 186, 188, 191–192, 214, 302
prostitution, xvii, xxiv, 73, 279n88, 280n100, 281n112, 281n115; abolition of, 284–285, 300, 303, 305; of African American women, 315n138; definition of, 299, 302; and degradation of women, 287–289, 294–295; electronic market for, 287, 303–304; erotic core of, 286; escape from, 283, 290–292, 295–296, 301, 304, 309n55, 313n116, 315n138; as form of slavery, 304–305; and harm reduction programs, 313n116; laws regarding, 298–300, 305; legalization of, 296, 299, 301, 305, 314n130; of Native women, 5, 115, 224, 282n119, 285, 296–297, 304, 306n10, 315n138; and organized crime, 284–285, 300, 303; and pregnancy/children, 294; psychological/physical harm of, 225, 287–295, 312n106; and slaves, 285–287, 292–293; and survivor's narratives, 303–304; and torture, 288–289, 294–295; women coerced into, 224, 295–300, 304–305. See also pimps; sex buyers; sex trafficking
Pueblo Revolt, 230, 252n9

Puebloans, 12, 37, 40, 54, 223, 230, 232–234, 236, 246, 248–249, 251, 252n9
punishment, 110–112, 138, 225, 250, 263, 275n42–43, 294, 304. See also abuse; torture; whippings

Quapaws, 40, 44, 50, 52
Quechans, xxi, 125–127, 135, 141, 141n1, 143n12

Race, 79, 86–87, 179, 189, 198, 207, 210–216, 285–286, 305
racism, 66n5, 224, 260, 265, 277n63, 277n73, 283, 285, 296, 300, 305
Rael-Gálvez, Estevan, 248, 252n12
raiding, 4, 10, 12, 65, 103–104, 130, 133, 135–137, 203–204, 208. See also slave raiding; violence: and raiding
ranches/ranchers, xxxiiin38, 82, 85, 116, 127, 129–138, 140–141, 190, 202, 204–208, 212, 238–239, 255n57
Ranchos de Taos, New Mexico, 233–234, 249
ransom/ransoming, 230, 233–234
rape, 204–205, 219n39, 259, 261, 268, 281n115, 286, 291–300, 304
Recopilación, 230
Red River valley, 40, 44
redemption, 128, 230, 234, 237, 247
religious: customs/songs, 242; institutions, 245; instruction, 77–78, 84, 108, 132; leaders, 110; practices, 132, 291; redemption, 230; services, 109. See also Christianity; missions; Native peoples: conversion of
reservations, xix, 115–116, 130–131, 141, 209–210, 213–216, 224, 241, 260–262, 264–269, 271, 273n26
resistance, xxxivn38, 63, 69–70, 74–75, 82, 87, 229, 231, 241, 255n53, 291, 304
resolanas, 249, 256n60
Richmond, Virginia, 161–163, 179
Rio Chama valley, 240, 249
Rio Grande valley, xv, xix, 12, 40, 54, 202, 204, 231
Rio Puerco valley, 235
rituals, xx–xxi, 14, 16, 19–20, 45, 111, 132, 206, 211, 231–233, 236, 250–251, 290
Rivera y Moncada, Fernando, 125
Rocky Mountains, 37, 207
Rogers, Emos, 114–115
Romero, Plácida, 238–240, 245, 255n57
Ruíz, José Francisco, 176, 204, 207–208
runaways, xxxivn38, 47, 63, 69–70, 72–73, 75–77,

Index

82–87, 128, 132–133, 141, 203, 214, 239, 247, 291, 309n55
Russia, 102, 134

Sagel, Jim, 249
Saint Louis, Missouri, xx, 179
Salishes, 103
salmon, 16, 100, 109
Saltillo, Mexico, xxiv, 177–192
Sampson, Samuel, 202
San Antonio, Texas, 172, 176–178, 181, 184, 189–190, 199
San Bernardino settlement, 135–136
San Diego, 136–137, 145n22
San Gabriel Mission, 127–128, 131, 133, 145n22
San Gabriel Valley settlement, 135–136
San Joaquin Valley, 129, 132, 146n25
San Juan de Ulúa castle (Cuba), 74–75, 86
San Luis Obispo Mission, 133
Sánchez, José María, 209
Sanford, John, 158–159. *See also* John W. A. Sanford Company
Santa Barbara, California, 131, 136, 145n22
Santa Fe, New Mexico, 126, 134–135, 232–233, 246, 248
Santa Ynez Mission, 133
Santo Niño de Atocha, 224, 234–236
Saucedo, José, 178
Savanna Indians, 50–51
scalps, 20–21, 120n41, 205
Scarry, Elaine, 297
Schermerhorn, Calvin, xxiii–xxiv, 64, 174, 215
School for Advanced Research (SAR), xvi, xxiv
Scott, John, 157
sedentary lifestyle, 12, 204, 211–213
Seminole Wars, 154
Seminoles, xv, xviii–xx, xxvn1, 16, 21, 152, 154
Serranos, 132–133
servitude: indentured, 39, 53, 190–191, 285; involuntary, xxv, 87n2, 203, 278n80, 297–298; marks of, 290
Seven Years' War, 79
sex buyers, 225, 284–295, 298–301, 303, 305
sex trafficking, 279n90, 279n95, 280n107, 281n112; abolition of, 300, 305; across US-Mexico border, 226n6; definition of, 299; laws regarding, 281n115, 298–300; opposition to, 298–300, 303, 312n106; in United Kingdom, 291; in United States, 257–261, 271, 272n5, 272n7, 272n9, 293; of

women, 264, 266–271, 272n8, 305. *See also* prostitution
sexism, 285, 296, 300, 305, 306n10
sexual abuse, 5, 15, 205–207, 219n39, 224, 226n6, 245–248, 258–263, 268, 270, 279n96, 281n115, 283, 288, 294, 296–298
sexual exploitation, xviii, 277n72, 283–284, 286; of Native children, xxiv, 260, 262–263, 278n83, 281n115; of Native women, 224–225, 257–263, 265–266, 270
shamans, 99, 109–110. See also *kíuks* (shamans)
Shastas, 102, 107, 116, 120n41
Shawnees, 43
sheep, xix, 37, 134
shells, 97, 100–101, 138
Shorter, Eli S., 157
Shoshones, 12
Silko, Leslie Marmon, 248, 255n57
Simpson, Burke, 201
Sioux, 11, 52
Sisneros, Samuel, 250, 254n47
skeletal remains, 3
Skinner, Benjamin, 300
slave labor, 3–4, 12–13, 20, 25, 204; children as, xx, 15, 18, 71–72, 241; competition over, 214; and construction projects, 70, 79–80; harsh treatment of, 131; high demand for, 19, 70, 72, 127, 160–161, 165; "ideal" type of, 214; importance of, 13, 19; and life expectancy, 161; purchase of, 156, 162–165. *See also* Africans, enslaved; farming: and slave labor; missions: and slave labor
slave owner–slave relationship, 284–298, 304
slave raiding, xvii, 4, 15–16, 22–23, 38, 40, 42, 44, 46–52, 54–55, 107, 126, 132–133, 135, 138–140, 147n35, 227n6
slave ships, 175, 189, 283, 301–303
slave trade, xv–xix, xxviiin6, 116n1; abuses of, 230; cessation of, 138, 181; control of, 36, 108, 112; decline in, 51–55; definition of, 312n106; demographic effects of, 48–49; and diseases, 51, 55; economic impact of, 5; enhance owners' status, 285; expansion of, 36, 38–39, 47, 98, 134; fetishization of, 286–287; financing of, 162–166; and horses, 141; illegal, 35, 48, 68, 184, 188; importance of, 35, 41, 114; increase in, 63, 161; of Indian captives, 3–5; indigenous, 5, 19, 125–127, 130; international, 175, 184; interstate, 151, 157, 160–162, 165; lucrative, 106, 165; networks of, xxiii–xxiv, 65, 127–129, 131, 134; and prostitution, 285–287, 292–293;

378

INDEX

regulation of, 48; routes of, 4, 23, 44–45; and slave narratives, 303–304; transatlantic, xviii

slavery: abolition of, 115–116, 174–180, 258, 260, 283–286, 298, 300–304, 313n116; and breeding slaves, xviii; coercion into, 295–298; collective memory of, 231–232, 235; debates over, 171–192; definitions of, xxii, xxiv, 225, 297–301, 305, 312n106, 313n118; and degradation of women, 287–289, 294–295, 304; as diplomatic tool, 20; global dynamics of, xx; and harm reduction, 300–301, 313n116; history of, xvii–xix, 9–11; illegal, xxiv; justifications for, 141; legacies of, xvii, 66n5, 266, 270; literature about, 243–244; opposition to, 173–184; precontact systems of, xix, xxi, 3–5; and prostitution, 224–225, 283–286; psychological/physical harm of, 287–295; as socioeconomic practice, 98; systems of, xvi–xxv, 3–5, xxxiiin38, 302, 310n66, 315n139; today, xviii, 225, 257, 268, 270, 298–300, 304

Slavery in Indian Country (Snyder), 99

small-scale societies, 9–10, 16–17, 23–24, 26, xxxivn38

smallpox, 49, 74, 102, 113

Smith, Jedediah, 134, 136

Smithsonian Institution, 248

Snyder, Christina, 99

social: boundaries, 10, 23–26; categories, xviii, 23–24, 26, 68–69; class, 10, 109; coalescence, 55; codes, 263; death, 287; destruction, 153; diversity, 36, 54; equality, 175; hierarchy, 11–13, 20–21, 106; identity, 14–16; inequality, 209; injustices, 284, 300–301, 305; institutions, 41; isolation, 291–292; liberation, 230; mobility, xix, 110; movements, 298; norms, 224; order, 267; organization, xx, 26; relations, 103; relationships, 16–17, 127; roles, 207; stratification, 109; taboos, 99; transformation, 113; value, xviii, 21; vulnerabilities, 268–269, 298

Someruelos, Marqués de, 67, 79, 81–86, 95n57

songs, xxiv, 16, 232, 242; of captivity, 12, 223–224, 236–238, 245–248, 254n47; *corridos*, 237, 239; *cuándos*, 237; of Hispano-Comanche celebrations, 233–236; *inditas*, 224, 226n3, 235–239, 245–249, 251; of Klamaths, 108–110; lullabies, 236–237, 247–249; *narcocorridos*, 224

Sonora, Mexico, 125–131, 134–135, 137–138, 142n5, 142n7, 143n12, 149n57

Soto, Hernando de, 12, 21

South, 7n6, 38, 51, 186, 192; African Americans in, xix, xxiv, 4, 46, 64–65, 260; chattel slavery in, 215, 231; cotton grown in, xix, xxiv, 172–173, 176–177; migration from, 64, 213; migration to, 172; plantations in, xvi, xix, xxiii, 46, 53, 65, 231; slave trade in, xxiv, 36, 53, 63, 151–165, 284. *See also* plantations; Southeast; Southwest Borderlands

South Carolina, 52, 156, 293

South Dakota, 263

Southeast, xxviiin6, 14, 25, 37, 47, 52, 63; captive taking in, 9–12, 15–16, 19–21; Indian removal in, 151–161, 165; Indian slaves in, 16–18, 20–21, 23, 53; and male social status, 20–21; Old World diseases in, 48–49; rulers of, 11–12; warfare in, 9–12, 15, 20–21

Southern California, 135–136, 138, 150n64, 202

Southern Methodist University, xvi

Southern Paiutes, 126, 134–135, 138–139, 143n12, 149n58, 149n61

Southwest, xxviiin6, 68, 129; enslavement in, 72; exchange networks in, 202; mestizo traditions in, 250; Native peoples in, xix, 37, 40; profitable cotton growing in, 173; slave trade in, xxiii, 47, 54, 112, 285; Spanish colonies in, xxiii, 37, 40; sparse population of, 70; whipping in, 112

Southwest Borderlands, xviii, 4–5, 25, 37, 42, 224; and Apache captives, 72, 75, 84, 86; captive taking in, 9–10, 12, 15, 17–19, 21, 90n14; Indian slaves in, 17–19, 23–24, 35, 80–81; Indo-Hispano culture in, 229; and male honor/status, 21–22; raiding in, 10, 12, 15, 18; warfare in, 9–10, 21

Spain, 37, 68, 130, 134, 171, 174–175, 204

Spanish, 36, 44, 184; captives, 18, 21, 125–127; colonialism, 171–172, 203–204; colonies/colonists, 15, 37, 40, 54, 63, 70, 128, 130, 132–135, 172, 260; economies, 130–131; explorers, 11–12, 21, 37, 48, 138–139, 146n28; imperialism, 69–70, 79–80, 82, 86–87, 102; and Indian captives/slaves, 15, 22, 67–73, 87, 223–224, 260; markets, 50, 54; military/military campaigns, 69–71, 74; Native allies of, 37, 40, 43, 46–47, 51–53, 69, 71, 125; in New Mexico, 223, 230, 250; officials, 69–72, 132, 147n35; resistance to, 75, 82; and slave trade, xx, 141; soldiers, 129, 132–133; in the South, 46, 49, 53; traders, 48, 203–204. *See also* Florida; missions

Spier, Edward, 104–105

379

Index

Spier, Leslie, 109, 112
spiritual practices, xxi, 81, 106, 236
St. James, Margo, 314n130
Starna, William A., 14
starvation, 3, 104, 203, 246, 261–262, 291–292, 296
Statistical Report on the Sickness and Mortality in the Army of the United States (US Congress), 210–211
status, xix, xxi–xxii, 11–26, 68, 78, 81, 285
Stern, Theodore, 109
Stockholm syndrome, 292
Stoltenberg, John, 286
sugar, 66n4, 66n5, 160–162, 302
suicide, 291
Susquehannas, 38
Sweden, 38, 299, 305
Swift, Ebenezer, 212

Taensas, 47
tallow, 135
tamemes (captives/slaves), 21
Taos, 12, 226n3
Tarabal, Sebastián, 127–128
tattoos, 20, 206, 283–284, 290, 293
Taussig, Michael, 234
Tejanos, 175–178, 181, 184–185, 187–192
Texas, 54, 183–184, 213, 242; African American slaves in, 64–65, 66n5, 197–198, 200–203, 206, 213–216; Anglo-Americans in, xxiv, 64–65, 172–173, 176–192, 198, 206, 209–216; cotton growing in, 173–174, 176–177, 198, 200–201; economy of, 64; Indians in, 197–216, 219n47; Mexicans in, 171–173, 175–176, 206, 215–216; military physicians in, 210–213, 221n65; multiracial makeup of, 214; proslavery forces in, 186–188, 191–192; as republic, 191–192, 199–200, 202–203, 207, 215; slavery in, xxiv, 64–65, 66n4, 171–192, 197–203, 210, 213–216; Spanish settlers in, 37, 63, 171–172, 206; trade in, 44, 197–203. *See also* Coahuila-Texas
textiles, 138, 140
Third Treaty of Washington, 154–157
Thirteenth Amendment, 231, 260, 296–298, 301
timber, 39
Tlingits, 19, 24, 106
tobacco, 5, 39, 109, 200, 211
Tomahitans, 42
Tongva, 131, 133
tools, xxi, 37, 101, 125, 200–201, 204, 210

Torget, Andrew, xxiv, 64, 215
Torrey, John, 197
Torrey's Trading Post No. 2, 65, 197–203, 207, 209–210, 213, 215
torture, xv–xviii, 14, 16, 65, 288–289, 294–295, 298, 302, 304, 313n118
trade, 155, 209; alliances for, 20; of Anglo-Americans, 65; in California, 132, 135, 140; in captives, 54–55, 206, 215; centers of, 108; by Comanches, 197–203, 206–207, 209–210, 214–215; competition over, 42, 44–46, 51; and diplomacy, 197–198; of Euro-Americans, 98, 114, 176; of Europeans, 37–46; federal policies of, 152; and the horse, 103–104; illegal, 42, 48; and Indian diplomacy, 197–203; international, 134; liberalized, 152–153, 161, 165; and Mexico, 176, 200; by Native peoples, xx, 37–46, 54, 65, 113, 114, 126, 133, 197–199; in southern plains, 43; in Upper Klamath Basin, 97, 97–101, 104–108; wars, 45; women's role in, 138. *See also* firearms: trade in; horses: trading of; markets
trade goods, xxviiin6, 38, 160; British, 4, 39; in California, 135; and captives, 23, 206; of Comanches, 197–198; competition over, xxviiin6, 99; Euro-American, 102–103, 105–108; European, xvii, xxviiin6, 36–37, 40, 98, 101; foodstuffs, 101; indigenous, 23, 54, 97, 100–101, 108, 131, 199–200, 206–207, 215; of Mexico, 200; of Pacific Northwest, 64, 101; Spanish, 131; of Upper Klamath Basin, 97–101; various types of, 39, 100–101, 200
trade networks/routes, xvi, xix–xx, xxviiin6, 19, 23, 48–49, 51, 53, 98–101, 103, 107, 113, 131, 136, 202, 207, 209, 216, 219n47, 233. *See also* Old Spanish Trail
trading posts, 48, 197–203, 207, 215. *See also* Torrey's Trading Post No. 2
trafficking, xxiii, 4, 224; of black slaves, xx, 200; and breeding programs, 294; of children, 5, 71–72, 225, 262–264, 270–271, 299; by Comanches, 200, 204; consequences of, 225; definition of, 298–299; laws regarding, 298–300; of Native peoples, 64, 261–263; opposition to, 175, 187; in United States, xix, 257–258, 297–298; of women, 5, 225, 284–285. *See also* sex trafficking
Trafficking Victims Protection Act, 257, 264
Trail of Tears, 159, 165
trans-Mississippi West, 35, 40, 42, 47, 54
treaties, 69, 200; enforcement of, 155, 157;

380

establish reservations, 130–131; with Klamaths, 108, 111, 114–115; and land allotments, 153–154, 157, 159, 161; and stolen property, 202–203; violations of, 154, 156
Treaty of 1864, 115
Treaty of Dancing Rabbit Creek, 153–154
Treaty of Fort Jackson, 154
Treaty of Guadalupe Hidalgo, 231
tribal communities: criminal authority of, 269, 281n114–116; and gangs, 269, 281n111; governments of, 269, 271, 278n79; self-determination of, 267, 278n79; targeted by criminals, 268–269, 279n93
tribute, 12, 20
Turquoise Ledge, The (Silko), 248

United Kingdom, 291, 300. *See also* British; England; Great Britain
United Nations, 312n106
United Nations Special Rapporteur on the Human Rights Aspects of the Victims of Trafficking in Persons, Especially Women and Children, 299
United States, xvi, 5; bans importing slaves, 293; colonizing strategies of, 260–263; conquests of, 198, 216, 259; early republic of, 151; imperialism of, 102, 198, 210, 213–215; invades New Mexico, 231, 242; legal system of, 111–112, 269, 271; military of, 126, 153–154, 210–213, 221n65, 295; national economy of, 209, 213; press of, 185–186, 191; slave economy of, 192; slave system of, 310n66; and westward expansion, xxiv, 198, 209–210, 212, 214, 216. *See also* sex trafficking: in United States
Unzaga y Amezaga, Luis de, 76
Upper Klamath Basin: and captive taking, 105–106; cultural practices of, 111; description of, 101–104; economy of, 98–100, 106–107, 114, 116; and epidemics, 113; Euro-American colonization of, 99–100, 102; Indian life in, 100–104; slave raiding in, 97, 99, 105–107, 114, 120n41; and slave trade, 97–100, 104–108, 111–116; violence in, 104, 113, 116; warfare in, 97–99, 105–107, 114, 116, 120n41. *See also* Klamaths
urban relocation, 260–262, 264–267, 276n60–62, 277n63, 277n72, 278n82
Uribe, Joseph Antonio, 72–73
US Army, xvi, 210–212, 216, 221n65, 231, 241
US Congress, 153–154, 159, 165, 210, 257, 264, 266, 273n26

US Department of Justice, 298
US federal government, 64, 130, 151–154, 156–160, 165, 200, 213, 215–216, 257–262, 265–268, 271, 275n36, 280n100, 297
US-Mexico border region, 69–70, 140, 171–173, 184, 191, 226n6
US State Department, 268, 272n9, 298
US Supreme Court, 269
US War Department, 154, 165
Utah, xvi, 64, 135, 139, 142n5, 205
Utes, 12, 143n12; attack settlers, 140; capture/enslavement of, 18, 149n58; and New Mexicans, 134–135, 203, 230, 236–237, 240; and Old Spanish Trail, 134–136, 138, 140; and peace treaties, 69; raiding of, 132, 134–136, 138–140, 147n42, 203–204; and slave trade, 15, 106, 134–135, 138–140, 149n61, 204; territory of, 126, 129

Vagrancy laws, 113, 131, 260
Valle, Santiago de, 183
Valverde War, 242
Varela, Mariano, 71–72
Veracruz, Mexico, 72, 75–76, 78, 80–81, 86
Vermont, 151–152, 154, 158, 186
Victoria, Guadalupe, 184
Viesca, José María, 181, 183, 188
vigía (defensive watchtower), 133
violence, 42, 47, 51, 69, 265; against British, 53; and captives/slaves, xxii, 10, 12–16, 20, 286, 305; of colonialism, 98, 234; and Comanches, xviii, 212; domestic, 260, 281n114; against Native peoples, 113, 122n71, 224; physical, 223, 225, 259; political economy of, 99, 109, 116; and prostitution, 225, 283, 291–292, 295, 304–305; psychological, 223, 225; racial, 216; and raiding, 12, 22, 203–204, 207; sexual, 219n39, 224, 258–259, 292; by slave owners, 291–292, 295, 304; and slave raiding, 49, 105, 134–135, 137, 139–140; and slave trade, xviii, xxiv, 55, 106, 116; and trade, 45, 103, 209, 272n9; against women, xxiv, 224–225, 282n119, 304. *See also* murder; rape; torture
Violence Against Women Act, 271, 281n114
Virginia, xx, 38–39, 42–44, 46, 49, 52–53, 156, 161–163, 165, 278n80
Voluntary Relocation Program, The, 264

Waco Indians, 197, 200
Waco, Texas, 65, 197, 199, 201–202
Wakara (Ute raider), 139

INDEX

Wallawalla, 104

warfare, xix, 50–51, 53, 126, 133, 252n14, 259, 262, 273n26; and Apaches, 71; and captive taking, 9–15, 17, 25, 99, 105–106, 230, 250, 285; celebration of, 208; and Comanches, 22, 208, 230; geo-economic, 44–45; and *guerra justa*, 230; and horse raiding, 103; increases in, xvii, 10, 26; and Indian captives, 12, 127, 129; Indian prisoners of, 67–82, 86–87, 87n2; and male prestige, 19–20, 22; portrayals of, 232–235; prisoners of, 67–75, 78–79; prizes of, 12; profit-making, 107; against settlements, 137; and slave trade, 26, 230; and women, 138, 247, 261. *See also* mourning wars

Warm Springs Indians, 111

Wascos, 101, 109

Washington, xix, 142n5

Washington, DC, 165, 179

Watkins, Ralph, 14

wealth, 16, 151, 173; accumulation of, 207–209; displays of, 101; and horses, 208–209; and Indian captives/slaves, 12–13, 21–23, 99, 106, 116; and Klamath *laláki*, 97, 99, 112; and land ownership, 116; and raiding, 204; and slave labor, 16, 22, 25–26, 209; and slave trade, xx–xxii, 109–110, 116, 285; and trade, 103, 117n1

weaving, 15, 24

Webster, Dolly, 202, 205

Webster, Patsy, 202

West, xix, xxiv, 39, 40, 42–43, 51, 54, 70–72, 87, 130, 159, 204, 210, 214, 216, 219n47

West India Committee, 302

West Indies, 302

West War of 1680, 45

Western, Thomas, 202–203

Westo Indians, 36–37, 39, 42–44, 48, 50–53, 55

whale oil, 100

Whaley, Gray, 296–297

whippings, 111–112, 138, 190, 205, 289

White, Elijah, 111–112

White Wolf, Howard, 205, 207

Whitman, Marcus and Narcissa, 113

Wichitas, 197, 200

Willamette Valley, 108, 112–113

William P. Clements Center for Southwest Studies, xvi, xxiv

Williamston, Alabama, 152

Wilson, Benjamin D., 136

Wilson, Jane Adeline, 205

Winberg, Margareta, 305

Wisconsin, 39

Wishrams, 101, 109

Wolfskill, William, 136

women, xvii–xviii, 229, 310n66; and breeding slaves, 293–294; and captivity networks, 137–140; capture/enslavement of, xviii, xx, 4–5, 13–15, 18–19, 21–22, 24, 70–71, 97, 127, 134–135, 202, 216, 271; as *criadas*, 73, 230; decide captives' fates, 15–16; degradation of, 287–289, 304; fates of, 14–15, 128; objectification of, 285–287; power of, 137–138; in prisons, 268–269, 280n108; protection of, 205, 261; sale/trading of, xx, 114, 139, 202, 292; sexual relations of, 115, 246–248, 306n10; targeting of, xvii, xxii, 4, 6n3, 10, 209, 264, 266, 270, 282n119, 285; torture of, 288–289, 294–295; trafficking of, 304; vital roles of, 138–140, 150n64, 204–205, 207, 212; as wife-laborers, 15–16, 18–19, 26, 204–206. *See also* adoption: of Native women; domestics: Native women as; prostitution; sex trafficking; sexual abuse; sexual exploitation: of Native women; violence: against women

Woodward, Henry, 43, 52

wool, 134

Work, John, 105

Wuornos, Aileen, 304

Yahooskin Paiutes, 115

Yainax Butte (trade center), 108

Yamasee people, 36, 43, 52–53

Yamasee War, 53

Yokuts, 126, 132–133, 140, 143n12, 146n25, 146n28

Young, Ewing, 136

Yount, George C., 136

Yuroks, 102

Zappia, Natale, xxiii, 64, 99, 202

School for Advanced Research Advanced Seminar Series

PUBLISHED BY SAR PRESS

CHACO & HOHOKAM: PREHISTORIC
REGIONAL SYSTEMS IN THE AMERICAN
SOUTHWEST
Patricia L. Crown & W. James Judge, eds.

RECAPTURING ANTHROPOLOGY: WORKING
IN THE PRESENT
Richard G. Fox, ed.

WAR IN THE TRIBAL ZONE: EXPANDING
STATES AND INDIGENOUS WARFARE
*R. Brian Ferguson &
Neil L. Whitehead, eds.*

IDEOLOGY AND PRE-COLUMBIAN
CIVILIZATIONS
*Arthur A. Demarest &
Geoffrey W. Conrad, eds.*

DREAMING: ANTHROPOLOGICAL AND
PSYCHOLOGICAL INTERPRETATIONS
Barbara Tedlock, ed.

HISTORICAL ECOLOGY: CULTURAL
KNOWLEDGE AND CHANGING LANDSCAPES
Carole L. Crumley, ed.

THEMES IN SOUTHWEST PREHISTORY
George J. Gumerman, ed.

MEMORY, HISTORY, AND OPPOSITION
UNDER STATE SOCIALISM
Rubie S. Watson, ed.

OTHER INTENTIONS: CULTURAL
CONTEXTS AND THE ATTRIBUTION OF
INNER STATES
Lawrence Rosen, ed.

LAST HUNTERS–FIRST FARMERS: NEW
PERSPECTIVES ON THE PREHISTORIC
TRANSITION TO AGRICULTURE
*T. Douglas Price &
Anne Birgitte Gebauer, eds.*

MAKING ALTERNATIVE HISTORIES:
THE PRACTICE OF ARCHAEOLOGY AND
HISTORY IN NON-WESTERN SETTINGS
Peter R. Schmidt & Thomas C. Patterson, eds.

CYBORGS & CITADELS: ANTHROPOLOGICAL
INTERVENTIONS IN EMERGING SCIENCES
AND TECHNOLOGIES
Gary Lee Downey & Joseph Dumit, eds.

SENSES OF PLACE
Steven Feld & Keith H. Basso, eds.

THE ORIGINS OF LANGUAGE: WHAT
NONHUMAN PRIMATES CAN TELL US
Barbara J. King, ed.

CRITICAL ANTHROPOLOGY NOW:
UNEXPECTED CONTEXTS, SHIFTING
CONSTITUENCIES, CHANGING AGENDAS
George E. Marcus, ed.

ARCHAIC STATES
Gary M. Feinman & Joyce Marcus, eds.

REGIMES OF LANGUAGE: IDEOLOGIES,
POLITIES, AND IDENTITIES
Paul V. Kroskrity, ed.

BIOLOGY, BRAINS, AND BEHAVIOR: THE
EVOLUTION OF HUMAN DEVELOPMENT
*Sue Taylor Parker, Jonas Langer, &
Michael L. McKinney, eds.*

WOMEN & MEN IN THE PREHISPANIC
SOUTHWEST: LABOR, POWER, & PRESTIGE
Patricia L. Crown, ed.

HISTORY IN PERSON: ENDURING
STRUGGLES, CONTENTIOUS PRACTICE,
INTIMATE IDENTITIES
Dorothy Holland & Jean Lave, eds.

THE EMPIRE OF THINGS: REGIMES OF
VALUE AND MATERIAL CULTURE
Fred R. Myers, ed.

CATASTROPHE & CULTURE: THE
ANTHROPOLOGY OF DISASTER
*Susanna M. Hoffman &
Anthony Oliver-Smith, eds.*

URUK MESOPOTAMIA & ITS NEIGHBORS:
CROSS-CULTURAL INTERACTIONS IN THE
ERA OF STATE FORMATION
Mitchell S. Rothman, ed.

REMAKING LIFE & DEATH: TOWARD AN
ANTHROPOLOGY OF THE BIOSCIENCES
Sarah Franklin & Margaret Lock, eds.

TIKAL: DYNASTIES, FOREIGNERS,
& AFFAIRS OF STATE: ADVANCING
MAYA ARCHAEOLOGY
Jeremy A. Sabloff, ed.

Published by SAR Press

Gray Areas: Ethnographic
Encounters with Nursing Home
Culture
Philip B. Stafford, ed.

Pluralizing Ethnography: Comparison
and Representation in Maya Cultures,
Histories, and Identities
John M. Watanabe & Edward F. Fischer, eds.

American Arrivals: Anthropology
Engages the New Immigration
Nancy Foner, ed.

Violence
Neil L. Whitehead, ed.

Law & Empire in the Pacific:
Fiji and Hawai'i
Sally Engle Merry & Donald Brenneis, eds.

Anthropology in the Margins
of the State
Veena Das & Deborah Poole, eds.

The Archaeology of Colonial
Encounters: Comparative
Perspectives
Gil J. Stein, ed.

Globalization, Water, & Health:
Resource Management in Times of
Scarcity
Linda Whiteford & Scott Whiteford, eds.

A Catalyst for Ideas: Anthropological
Archaeology and the Legacy of
Douglas W. Schwartz
Vernon L. Scarborough, ed.

The Archaeology of Chaco Canyon:
An Eleventh-Century Pueblo
Regional Center
Stephen H. Lekson, ed.

Community Building in the Twenty-
First Century
Stanley E. Hyland, ed.

Afro-Atlantic Dialogues:
Anthropology in the Diaspora
Kevin A. Yelvington, ed.

Copán: The History of an Ancient
Maya Kingdom
E. Wyllys Andrews & William L. Fash, eds.

The Evolution of Human Life History
Kristen Hawkes & Richard R. Paine, eds.

The Seductions of Community:
Emancipations, Oppressions,
Quandaries
Gerald W. Creed, ed.

The Gender of Globalization: Women
Navigating Cultural and Economic
Marginalities
*Nandini Gunewardena &
Ann Kingsolver, eds.*

New Landscapes of Inequality:
Neoliberalism and the Erosion of
Democracy in America
*Jane L. Collins, Micaela di Leonardo,
& Brett Williams, eds.*

Imperial Formations
*Ann Laura Stoler, Carole McGranahan,
& Peter C. Perdue, eds.*

Opening Archaeology: Repatriation's
Impact on Contemporary Research
and Practice
Thomas W. Killion, ed.

Small Worlds: Method, Meaning,
& Narrative in Microhistory
*James F. Brooks, Christopher R. N. DeCorse,
& John Walton, eds.*

Memory Work: Archaeologies of
Material Practices
Barbara J. Mills & William H. Walker, eds.

Figuring the Future: Globalization
and the Temporalities of Children
and Youth
Jennifer Cole & Deborah Durham, eds.

Timely Assets: The Politics of
Resources and Their Temporalities
*Elizabeth Emma Ferry &
Mandana E. Limbert, eds.*

Democracy: Anthropological
Approaches
Julia Paley, ed.

Confronting Cancer: Metaphors,
Inequality, and Advocacy
Juliet McMullin & Diane Weiner, eds.

Published by SAR Press

Development & Dispossession: The Crisis of Forced Displacement and Resettlement
Anthony Oliver-Smith, ed.

Global Health in Times of Violence
Barbara Rylko-Bauer, Linda Whiteford, & Paul Farmer, eds.

The Evolution of Leadership: Transitions in Decision Making from Small-Scale to Middle-Range Societies
Kevin J. Vaughn, Jelmer W. Eerkins, & John Kantner, eds.

Archaeology & Cultural Resource Management: Visions for the Future
Lynne Sebastian & William D. Lipe, eds.

Archaic State Interaction: The Eastern Mediterranean in the Bronze Age
William A. Parkinson & Michael L. Galaty, eds.

Indians & Energy: Exploitation and Opportunity in the American Southwest
Sherry L. Smith & Brian Frehner, eds.

Roots of Conflict: Soils, Agriculture, and Sociopolitical Complexity in Ancient Hawai'i
Patrick V. Kirch, ed.

Pharmaceutical Self: The Global Shaping of Experience in an Age of Psychopharmacology
Janis Jenkins, ed.

Forces of Compassion: Humanitarianism between Ethics and Politics
Erica Bornstein & Peter Redfield, eds.

The Shape of Script: How and Why Writing Systems Change
Stephen D. Houston, ed.

Enduring Conquests: Rethinking the Archaeology of Resistance to Spanish Colonialism in the Americas
Matthew Liebmann & Melissa S. Murphy, eds.

Dangerous Liaisons: Anthropologists and the National Security State
Laura A. McNamara & Robert A. Rubinstein, eds.

Breathing New Life into the Evidence of Death: Contemporary Approaches to Bioarchaeology
Aubrey Baadsgaard, Alexis T. Boutin, & Jane E. Buikstra, eds.

Nature, Science, and Religion: Intersections Shaping Society and the Environment
Catherine M. Tucker, ed.

The Global Middle Classes: Theorizing Through Ethnography
Rachel Heiman, Carla Freeman, & Mark Liechty, eds.

Keystone Nations: Indigenous Peoples and Salmon across the North Pacific
Benedict J. Colombi & James F. Brooks, eds.

Big Histories, Human Lives: Tackling Problems of Scale in Archaeology
John Robb & Timothy R. Pauketat, eds.

Reassembling the Collection: Ethnographic Museums and Indigenous Agency
Rodney Harrison, Sarah Byrne, & Anne Clarke, eds.

Images That Move
Patricia Spyer & Mary Margaret Steedly, eds.

Vital Relations: Modernity and the Persistent Life of Kinship
Susan McKinnon & Fenella Cannell, eds.

Anthropology of Race: Genes, Biology, and Culture
John Hartigan, ed.

Street Economies in the Urban Global South
Karen Tranberg Hansen, Walter E. Little, & B. Lynne Milgram, eds.

Cash on the Table: Markets, Values, and Moral Economies
Edward F. Fischer, ed.

Published by SAR Press

(Mis)Managing Migration: Guestworkers' Experiences with North American Labor Markets
David Griffith, ed.

Katherine Dunham: Recovering an Anthropological Legacy, Choreographing Ethnographic Futures
Elizabeth Chin, ed.

Bioinsecurity and Vulnerability
Nancy N. Chen & Lesley A. Sharp, eds.

Things in Motion: Object Itineraries in Anthropological Practice
Rosemary A. Joyce & Susan D. Gillespie, eds.

Artisans and Advocacy in the Global Market: Walking the Heart Path
Jeanne Simonelli, Katherine O'Donnell, & June Nash, eds.

Disturbing Bodies: Perspectives on Forensic Anthropology
Zoë Crossland & Rosemary A. Joyce, eds.

Timeless Classics from SAR Press

Ancient Civilization and Trade
Jeremy A. Sabloff & C. C. Lamberg-Karlovsky, eds.

The Archaeology of Lower Central America
Frederick W. Lange & Doris Z. Stone, eds.

Chan Chan: Andean Desert City
Michael E. Moseley & Kent C. Day, eds.

The Classic Maya Collapse
T. Patrick Culbert, ed.

Demographic Anthropology: Quantitative Approaches
Ezra B. W. Zubrow, ed.

The Dying Community
Art Gallaher Jr. & Harlan Padfield, eds.

Elites: Ethnographic Issues
George E. Marcus, ed.

Entrepreneurs in Cultural Context
Sidney M. Greenfield, Arnold Strickon, & Robert T. Aubey, eds.

Explanation of Prehistoric Change
James N. Hill, ed.

Explorations in Ethnoarchaeology
Richard A. Gould, ed.

Late Lowland Maya Civilization: Classic to Postclassic
Jeremy A. Sabloff & E. Wyllys Andrews V, eds.

Lowland Maya Settlement Patterns
Wendy Ashmore, ed.

Methods and Theories of Anthropological Genetics
M. H. Crawford & P. L. Workman, eds.

Morleyana: A Collection of Writings in Memoriam, Sylvanus Griswold Morley—1883–1948

New Perspectives on the Pueblos
Alfonso Ortiz, ed.

The Origins of Maya Civilization
Richard E. W. Adams, ed.

Photography in Archaeological Research
Elmer Harp Jr., ed.

Reconstructing Prehistoric Pueblo Societies
William A. Longacre, ed.

Shipwreck Anthropology
Richard A. Gould, ed.

Simulations in Archaeology
Jeremy A. Sabloff, ed.

Structure and Process in Latin America
Arnold Strickon & Sidney M. Greenfield, eds.

The Valley of Mexico: Studies in Pre-Hispanic Ecology and Society
Eric R. Wolf, ed.

Published by Cambridge University Press

The Anasazi in a Changing Environment
George J. Gumerman, ed.

Regional Perspectives on the Olmec
Robert J. Sharer & David C. Grove, eds.

The Chemistry of Prehistoric Human Bone
T. Douglas Price, ed.

The Emergence of Modern Humans: Biocultural Adaptations in the Later Pleistocene
Erik Trinkaus, ed.

The Anthropology of War
Jonathan Haas, ed.

The Evolution of Political Systems
Steadman Upham, ed.

Classic Maya Political History: Hieroglyphic and Archaeological Evidence
T. Patrick Culbert, ed.

Turko-Persia in Historical Perspective
Robert L. Canfield, ed.

Chiefdoms: Power, Economy, and Ideology
Timothy Earle, ed.

Published by University of California Press

Writing Culture: The Poetics and Politics of Ethnography
James Clifford & George E. Marcus, eds.

Published by University of Arizona Press

The Collapse of Ancient States and Civilizations
Norman Yoffee & George L. Cowgill, eds.

Published by University of New Mexico Press

Sixteenth-Century Mexico: The Work of Sahagun
Munro S. Edmonson, ed.

Meaning in Anthropology
Keith H. Basso & Henry A. Selby, eds.

Southwestern Indian Ritual Drama
Charlotte J. Frisbie, ed.

Participants in the School for Advanced Research advanced seminar "Uniting the Histories of Slavery in North America" chaired by James F. Brooks and Bonnie Martin, October 12–13, 2012. *Standing, from left:* Andrew J. Torget, Mark Allan Goldberg, Melissa Farley, Natale Zappia, Eric E. Bowne, Calvin Schermerhorn, Paul Conrad, Catherine M. Cameron; *seated, from left:* Enrique R. Lamadrid, Bonnie Martin, James F. Brooks. Not pictured, Boyd Cothran, Sarah Deer.